'OTHER' SPANISH THEATRES

Lluís Pasqual and Nuria Espert in *La oscura raíz* (1998)

'OTHER' SPANISH THEATRES
Erasure and inscription
on the twentieth-century Spanish stage

Maria M. Delgado

Manchester University Press
Manchester and New York

distributed exclusively in the USA by Palgrave

Published by Manchester University Press
Oxford Road, Manchester M13 9NR, UK
and Room 400, 175 Fifth Avenue, New York, NY 10010, USA
www.manchesteruniversitypress.co.uk

Distributed exclusively in the USA by
Palgrave, 175 Fifth Avenue, New York, NY 10010, USA

Distributed exclusively in Canada by
UBC Press, University of British Columbia, 2029 West Mall, Vancouver, BC, Canada V6T 1Z2

British Library Cataloguing-in-Publication Data
A catalogue record for this book is available from the British Library

Library of Congress Cataloging-in-Publication Data applied for

ISBN 0 7190 5975 5 *hardback*
    0 7190 5976 3 *paperback*

First published 2003

11 10 09 08 07 06 05 04 03   10 9 8 7 6 5 4 3 2 1

Typset in Simoncini Garamond
by Northern Phototypesetting Co. Ltd, Bolton
Printed in Great Britain
by Biddles Ltd, Guildford and King's Lynn

For Henry B. Little and Thomas Louis Delgado-Little

and in memory of my father
Alfonso Delgado Álava (1925–2003)

Contents

List of illustrations

Lluís Pasqual and Nuria Espert in *La oscura raíz* (The Dark Root), 1998, directed, conceived and adapted from the writings of García Lorca, by Pasqual. Photographer: Ros Ribas. Source: Lluís Pasqual   *frontispiece*

While every effort has been made to contact copyright holders, the author apologises in advance
for any omissions and welcomes corrections which will be incorporated into any future editions
of the book.

Acknowledgements

The genesis of the book owes much to conversations over the years with Guillem Balagué, Len Berkman, Peter Byrne, Olga Celda, Daniel and Irene Delgado-Byrne, Maria Irene Fornes, Sandra Hebron, Pamela Howard, Peter Lichtenfels, Martin Lowe, Mark Ravenhill, Jacqueline Roy, Maria-Isabelle San-Ginés and Caridad Svich. I would like to acknowledge a debt of thanks to those who shared with me copies of their own work, facilitated access to their own archival material, or answered my queries on their specialist areas: Fernando Arrabal, Maria Antònia Babí i Vila, Julia Butrón, Michel Dumoulin, Monique Dureville, Gwynne Edwards, Peter W. Evans, David Fancy, Trader Faulkner, Josep-Anton Fernàndez, Enric Gallén, Luciano García Lorenzo, Nigel Glendenning, John Hall, François Koltès, John London, Felicia Hardison Londré, Frédéric Maurin, Jim McCarthy, Marcos Ordóñez, Chris Perriam, Gonzague Phélip, Annabel Poincheval, Juan Carlos Pérez de la Fuente, Emilio Sanz de Soto, Rodolf Sirera, Paul Julian Smith, Eric Southworth and Phyllis Zatlin. I am grateful to Silvia Davini who looked up information on Xirgu and Casares for me at Buenos Aires' Instituto Nacional de Estudios de Teatro, Sally Donohue, Kelly Wetherille and Nanci Young who retrieved archival papers on Xirgu's time at Smith College, and especially Fernando Villar who located key material in Barcelona and shared with me his own specialist knowledge of Catalan performance groups. David Bradby and Óscar Cornago Bernal have had a very direct impact on the writing of this book. My collaborations over the past three years with the former have allowed me to radically rethink the interrelations between French and Spanish theatre. The latter introduced me to many of his own ideas (and references) around the role of the director in twentieth-century Spanish theatre.

A number of the productions dealt with in this book I was able to review for *Plays International*. I would like to extend my thanks to the magazine's editor Peter Roberts for publishing my regular reports on the contemporary Spanish theatre scene. Parts of Chapters 2 and 5 have been published in *Contemporary Theatre Review* (Delgado 1998a, 1998b), an anthology of criticism on García Lorca (Delgado 1999), the journal *European Studies* (Delgado 2001a), and Queen Mary, University of London's 'Papers in Spanish and Latin American Theatre History' (Delgado 2001b). I am grateful for permission to use the reworked material here.

I owe special debts of gratitude to the School of English and Drama, Queen Mary, University of London which funded both a semester's leave and numerous valuable research visits to Spain. I am especially grateful to colleagues in the School of English and Drama whose intellectual support, friendship and guidance marks the book in many complex ways: David Colclough, Michael Edwards, Annie Janowitz, Morag

Shiach, and especially Paul Heritage. Susan Cook, Patricia Hamilton, Andrew Penman, Richard Schoch, and Gregor Turbyne provided practical support when I most needed it. The students at Queen Mary, University of London who have taken my 'Contemporary Spanish Performance' course provided the forum for the debate of many ideas juggled in the book. I am grateful also for funding received from the Spanish Embassy's Cultural Office in London, the Cañada Blanch Foundation and the Instituto Cervantes in London to cover the costs of photographs which appear in the book. The friendship, advice and support of the latter's director, Enrique Wulff Alonso, also deserves a special mention. The AHRB (Arts and Humanities Research Board) granted me a semester's leave under the Research Leave Scheme without which I would have been unable to complete this book.

Special thanks are due to the staff at the institutions and archives where my research was carried out: Ana Vázquez Estévez and Isidre Bravo at the Institut del Teatre (Barcelona), the Arxiu Històric de la Ciutat (Barcelona), the Biblioteca Juan March (Madrid), the Bibliothèque Nationale (Paris), Brian McMaster and the Edinburgh International Festival, Carme Puig Martín at Catalan Films (Barcelona), the Fundación Federico García Lorca (Madrid), the Hemeroteca Nacional (Madrid), Javier Herrero at the Filmoteca Nacional (Madrid), the London International Festival of Theatre [LIFT], Lorna Black at the National Library of Scotland, Carles Cano and Marc Gall at the Teatre Lliure (Barcelona), Marie-Claude Billard at the Maison Jean Vilar (Avignon), Maryse Badiou at the Teatre Nacional de Catalunya (Barcelona), Núria Ferrer at the Biblioteca de la Filmoteca de la Generalitat de Catalunya (Barcelona), Pascal Senatore at the Odéon-Théâtre de l'Europe (Paris), Queen Mary Library (London), the Royal National Theatre (London), the Royal Opera House at Covent Garden (London), Scottish Opera (Glasgow), the Théâtre des Amandiers at Nanterre, Florence Thomas and the Théâtre National de la Colline (Paris), the University of London Library, and Victòria Sanz and Àgia Luna at La Cubana. The support of Andrés Amorós, Víctor Aranda, Eduardo Galán, and Cristina Santolaria Solana at the Ministerio de Educación, Cultura y Deporte is appreciated. Lola Puebla at the Centro de Documentación Teatral (Madrid) has become a valued friend and collaborator. The CDT's director Julio Huélamo Kosma generously passed on valuable in-house publications. Finally, Joan Matabosch facilitated access both to the archives at the Teatre del Liceu (Barcelona) and to his own extensive collection of materials relating to opera and theatre. His specialist knowledge of opera has proved invaluable to me.

I am indebted to the photographers who have provided copies of their work. Ros Ribas especially has been a generous friend and his coverage of Pasqual's work has proved a valuable research tool. I am grateful for the hospitality received from Yann Houbre, Evaldo Medeiros and Deborah Richmond in Paris, Mario Arnaiz, Elena Martín, and José Ocaña in Madrid and Alfonso Delgado Álava, Ángela Delgado, Severina González Pérez, Xavi Labarias Vicente, Ventura Pons and Mercè Saumell in Barcelona. The intellectual generosity of Saumell and Pons deserves a special mention. Their opinions, assistance and knowledge have been woven into this book in a series of ways. Both have shared with me material from their own archives, both have generously located key information for me and I am fortunate to have accessed their expertise.

I would like to thank those who spoke to me about their work: Gabi Álvarez, Frederic Amat, Calixto Bieito, Rafael Borque, Josep Maria Flotats, Jorge Lavelli, Jordi Milán, Lluís Pasqual, Josep Pons and Carlos Saura. I benefited greatly from the comments of the readers who assessed this proposal for Manchester University Press: Viv Gardner and David George. David George has gone on to read every word of the manuscript and his incisive comments have greatly helped shape the final form of this book. Joel Anderson was an imaginative and diligent research assistant and deserves my special thanks. My final debt of thanks is to Matthew Frost at Manchester University Press, an astute editor and valued friend, to my parents for their unwavering support and to my partner Henry Little to whom this book and I owe so very much.

Cañada Blanch
FUNDACIÓN

Instituto Cervantes
Londres

Author's note

I have used the author/date referencing system.[1] In the main text I have, on the whole, included page numbers for newspaper articles. Page numbers for journal articles are only provided when quoting from an article which spreads over more than a page or when the reference would be unclear without them. Full page references are provided in the bibliography. Everybody in Spain has two surnames; some use both, some use the first, some use the second. I have respected the convention for each individual. I always feature the date in the text as well as the author when citing, and this has allowed me not to use initials to differentiate authors who share the same surname. Instead the date will facilitate any search for the reference in the bibliography. Only exceptionally, when authors sharing the same surname share a reference in the same year, have I used initials. I am responsible for the translation of all quotations from the Castilian-Spanish, Catalan or French unless otherwise stated.

All Castilian, Catalan or French play or production titles are accompanied by an English translation. Where an English-language translation exists, the translation is quoted in italics. Where, to the best of my knowledge, no translation exists, I have translated the title and given it in roman. The primary source for references of Spanish-language works are Rudder 1975 and O'Connor 1988b, and for Catalan-language works George and London (eds) 1996. To differentiate plays and productions and probe the implications of particular stage readings, when I discuss the play the original title is given where possible, and when the production is being considered I give the title used for the staging.

For the collective/co-operative theatre groups (Els Joglars, La Cubana, La Fura dels Baus, Els Comediants, etc.) I have used the plural when referring to them although, strictly speaking, it may be grammatically correct to use the singular.

I have consulted a range of newspapers during the course of this study. A number of the most important newspapers in Spain have a long tradition of publishing different editions for different cities with special supplements and these are referred to where appropriate. During the Franco era, the Catalan daily *La Vanguardia* appeared as *La Vanguardia Española*.

---

1 For the benefit of those readers not familiar with the system, where I refer to publications, within the text, these are cited by the author's surname, the year of publication, and, if appropriate, the relevant page number(s). Full details of cited publications are listed in alphabetical order, according to the author's surname, in the bibliography. Where the same author has published two or more works in the same year, these are distinguished through the use of additional letters after the year of publication (e.g. 1946a, 1946b etc.).

This study tends to use the word Castilian to refer to Spain's most widely spoken language, although references to Spanish and Castilian-Spanish also appear. While I refer to the Catalan nation as Catalonia, the Catalan version Catalunya and the Spanish Cataluña also feature. The chapters also juggle both the Castilian-Spanish and Catalan spellings of a number of the practitioners dealt with. Xirgu is known most habitually by the Castilianised spelling of her name, Margarita. It is not uncommon, however, to come across occasional references to the Catalan spelling of her name (Margarida or Marguerida). Pasqual, however is referred to by the Catalan spelling of his name (Lluís) rather than the Castilianised Luis, although references are made to his Castilianised spelling by other critics. Nuria Espert, like Xirgu, is known by the Castilianised spelling of her name although quotes from Catalan critics refer to the Catalan Núria.

As this is, in part, a reference work, birth and death dates are provided for a significant number of dramatists, directors, playwrights and performers to whom I refer.

exile in Paris and his decision to write in French secured recognition only within the realms of that band of playwrights classified as 'the theatre of the absurd' and appropriated by the French theatre establishment because of their Parisian base.[4]

What is in many ways most interesting about this list is that it echoes the approaches of numerous authors who have published English-language studies of twentieth-century Spanish theatre. These have tended to revolve around the figure of the playwright with dramatists like Buero Vallejo and Sastre eulogised,[5] while scant attention has been paid to the work of practitioners who have employed the physical and material (as opposed to the literary) resources of the stage. The ephemeral nature of the theatrical event necessarily renders documentation an elusive proposition, and perhaps goes some way towards explaining the construction of a theatrical hierarchy that places the playwright at its pinnacle. Nevertheless, theatre history in the age of historicism where the past can only ever remain unknowable and 'other' has begun to move away from an assumption that performance can be reconstructed and written down, towards an understanding that all histories have sought to obliterate certain figures, events, and occurrences whilst privileging others. Performers, directors, designers, and producers have too often been decisively marginalised in chronicles of the period, relegated to secondary roles in narratives where theatre remains primarily a literary pursuit, the power of the playtext growing as the performance recedes from cultural memory.

This study will seek to present alternative readings of Spanish theatre in the twentieth century mapping out a terrain which differs from that presented by Hispanists like Gwynne Edwards, Martha Halsey, Victor Dixon, Patricia O'Connor, Francisco Ruiz Ramón and George Wellwarth.[6] While I acknowledge the importance of these readings, the interest invested in Spanish playwrights by foreign academics is not matched by the presence of their plays on European stages. Although Federico García Lorca and increasingly Ramón del Valle-Inclán occupy significant roles within the European repertory, their successors working within the difficult climate of the Franco era have failed to occupy a similar position. Claims have been made that Buero Vallejo is a 'constant experimenter' (Edwards 1985: 173) on a par with García Lorca and Valle-Inclán but such views are simply unsubstantiated by the derivative nature of Buero Vallejo's theatre.

In a provocative unpublished paper C. H. Cobb writes of the cultural policy of the Franco regime as 'an attempt to persuade international opinion that they were the civilised inheritors of a cultural tradition rather than the authors of the savage post-war repression of their enemies' (n.d.: 3). It is often erroneously assumed that this process took place simply through a rather heavy-handed manipulation of the media that involved the promotion of zealous xenophobia, prudish conservatism and strict gender roles, and a celebration of the Catholic values which formed the

4 London (1997: 17–18, 205–29) provides a valuable Spanish reappropriation of Arrabal.
5 See, for example, Edwards 1985 and Halsey and Zatlin (eds) 1988. For Spanish-language examples of this approach, see Bonnín Valls 1998 and Ruiz Ramón 1984.
6 See, especially, Edwards 1985, Halsey and Zatlin (eds) 1999, Holt 1975, O'Connor 1988a, Ruiz Ramón 1984, and Wellwarth 1970.

backbone of this supposedly homogenous nation. Although the crippling effects of the censorship in operation in the aftermath of the Civil War have been well documented,[7] it is misleading to construe that somehow Hispanists working abroad were able to rise above such constrictions in determining their own teaching and research agenda which opposed that legitimised by the regime. The subject of legitimisation, however, is a slippery one for, as Cobb points out, collaboration, albeit unwitting, with the regime's objectives took place on a whole series of levels with the curriculum's reduction to a series of 'endorsed' texts (11–12). The regime's lasting achievement lies in the obliteration of the margins, margins which were not necessarily appropriated by those working within Hispanism abroad. Although Cobb does not really concentrate on playtexts or theatre productions to illustrate his thesis – with the exception of using García Lorca's theatre as an 'endorsed' subject area – his argument does provide some indication as to why certain areas of Spanish theatre studies have remained painfully ignored. The regime permitted the promotion of certain dramatists, perhaps most conspicuously Buero Vallejo, Alfonso Sastre (b. 1926) and Lauro Olmo (1925–94), as radical dissident figures but their plays are often highly conservative in form, adhering to a linear formula that undermines claims to the contrary. Additionally, certainly in Buero Vallejo's case, the works were staged in both commercial and state-nationalised theatres. What is perhaps most interesting is that there is a consensus of opinion as to what the plays mean, i.e. they are about individuals struggling against an oppressive regime, that is 'readerly' as opposed to 'writerly' texts where meaning is ever-elusive (Barthes 1975). Ironically, in their emphasis on enouncement, they may therefore have more in common with the officially endorsed playtexts of the regime than may at first be apparent. This is not to equivocally deny the achievements of such playwrights, merely to posit that their claims and those of their champions to be forging an alternative discourse of theatre is perhaps not as valid as they may wish.

My own point of departure for this monograph came from my sense of disillusionment as a student reviewing the work of twentieth-century dramatists. Whilst admiring the creative imagination and technique of Valle-Inclán and García Lorca's plays, I was always perplexed by the scant attention accorded to their work as theatre artists rather than playwrights. In addition, when considering the dramatic landscape of the post-Civil War era, I was always disappointed by the dramaturgical work of the playwrights who emerged in the aftermath of these two pioneers. The work of their European contemporaries – Beckett, Brecht, Genet, Ionesco, Heiner Müller – always seemed so much more satisfying and provocative and I was always somewhat perplexed that the dramatist who seemed to be working most imaginatively with plot and genre, Arrabal, had been appropriated by the French and forgotten by the Spanish.

This is not, however, to denigrate the important work undertaken by English-language scholars documenting and assessing the work of Spanish dramatists. Dramatists play an important role in shaping the theatrical landscape of a country.

---

7 See for example, O'Connor 1966, O'Connor 1984 and Gubern 1981.

The work of Hazel Cazorla, John Dowling, John P. Gabriele, Martha Halsey and Peter Podol in the US and Victor Dixon, Gwynne Edwards, Derek Gagen and David Johnstone in the UK and Ireland has played a significant role in alerting both Hispanists and theatre scholars to the varied texts of the past century's dramatic literature. Nevertheless, for many G. G. Brown's opinions, articulated in his 1972 study, *A Literary History of Spain: The Twentieth Century*, hold sway: 'In the twentieth century, drama is unquestioningly the branch of the arts in which Spain has least to offer to the common store of European culture' (1972: 110). That which has failed to adhere to the criteria for literary worth has failed to be judged as good theatre. It is for this reason that Brown can boldly go on to assert that 'the last thirty years have been among the dreariest in the history of the Spanish stage' (157). Using only plays to illustrate his argument, he blurs the lines between theatre and dramatic literature to a degree where the latter is the only indicator of the former. Indeed for too many critics the only trace of a theatrical culture has been dramatic literature. This study differs in that it builds on the recent work of Dru Dougherty, Sharon Feldman, David George, Marion Peter Holt, John London, Paul Julian Smith, and Phyllis Zatlin in the UK and US and Óscar Cornago Bernal, Luciano García Lorenzo, Víctor García Ruiz, Jesús Rubio Jiménez, María-José Ragué-Arias, Ricard Salvat, José Sánchez, Mercè Saumell, and María Vilches de Frutos (among others) in Spain who have been mapping out performative histories which recognise that the playtext is just one of many tools relied on by the theatre historian.

If radical theatre practice is at least partly determined by the denial of the playwright, or at least the authority invested in the playwright by liberal humanist criticism, practitioners who move away from the written word towards what Artaud termed a 'theatre of deviation from the groundwork of a pre-established text' (cited in Derrida 1978: 185), offer some challenge to dominant traditions. A theatrical hierarchy that positions the playwright at its apex is fundamentally challenged by practitioners who employ the physical and material (as opposed to the literary) resources of the stage. In addition, the ephemeral nature of the theatrical and its gilded artifice renders it harder to fix and read. It is thus not surprising that directors, designers, performers and producers who have left no written traces of their work should have slipped through the 'official' documentation of Spanish theatre in the first seven decades of the last century.

'Other' Spanish theatres

This study will consider the role of a series of figures and companies who have exercised a notable impact in their time on both the practice and the public perception of theatre. Rather than attempt an exhaustive or inclusive chronological account which would be perfunctory in its listing of names, production titles and dates, the book investigates, through six case studies, the ways in which Spanish theatre history throughout the century has been documented and assessed. As such it examines how theatre has provided indicators as to the social, political and cultural struggles of the time and interrogates the ideological agendas of both theatre makers and theatre historians. The focus will be on constructing production and performance histories that investigate how each of these figures or companies has worked within a (social, political, economic and cultural, regional, national and international) context where they have had a radical impact on repertoire and audience culture. Current theories are used to dissect the ways in which individual narratives are tested against wider, more general histories.[8] Drawing on a range of different pictorial, literary and oral sources, *'Other' Spanish Theatres* presents six case studies which map out an alternative reading of Spanish theatre throughout the twentieth century.

Crucially none of the practitioners I have chosen to concentrate on is a playwright. Rather, I draw on a range of critical material to construct a series of interconnecting narratives which argue that the impact of Spanish artists on European and American theatres is perhaps more pervasive than previously acknowledged. Playwrights, part-authors of perhaps the most resonant trace of the transactions between artists and audiences, will here be allocated a secondary role. Moving away from the totalising tendencies or a historical overview, I shift the focus to establishing how these practitioners have expanded the parameters of theatrical practice both in their own nation and beyond, positing a theatrical history which moves away from dramatic intentionalism towards a wider understanding of the 'doing' of theatre. This book does not set out to offer a historical coverage of the period; rather it offers a detailed analysis of a number of practitioners whose work has hitherto received limited critical attention, looking at the possibilities for reading their work in different ways. Theoretical insights inform the construction of the argument. Links are drawn between the chapters in the hope of indicating how successive generations of practitioners acknowledged and commented on each other's work both on the Spanish mainland and beyond. Although the focus is on developments in Madrid and Barcelona, the study will look beyond theatrical production in these cities to encompass a framework of references that acknowledge tensions around the nation-state and the regional autonomies. The cultural policies of both the central and regional governments are discussed in order to appropriately assess their shaping of past and present theatrical landscapes.

'Other' Spanish Theatres recognises the impossibility of locating what is understood by 'Spanish theatre'. Too often this has been seen as the work of the Madrid stage and while the developments on the Catalan stage are now rightly accorded a significant role in assessing what has customarily been referred to as Spanish theatre, this study moves beyond the Iberian mainland to assess the impact of the diaspora of exile which followed the outbreak of the Civil War in 1936. Around 100,000 Spaniards are thought to have emigrated to Argentina in the period between 1930 to 1946 (Lewis 1983: 236). Almost half a million fled Spain for France during the Civil War, although subsequent emigration to Latin America and death in concentration camps was to see the number fall to around 250,000 by the end of 1939

8 A point made in Williams 1981: 86. See also Preston 1999 where a similar approach is used to 'provide a different perspective on the complexity of the Spanish Civil War [. . .] studying the lives of nine of its most prominent protagonists' (4).

(Zatlin 1994: 15–16). The significant number of Spanish theatre practitioners who left for foreign shores during this period poses significant questions about how theatre histories are constructed. My approach views intersections with France and Latin America as crucial to an understanding of Spain's theatrical culture. Two of the practitioners that I concentrate on, Margarita Xirgu and María Casares, lived in exile for significant periods of their lives. In Xirgu's case this has seen her work conveniently divided into her Spanish and her Latin American eras. My own argument avoids such divisions in charting trends that can be traced across her entire career. With all the practitioners I have sought to move away from opinions formulated solely from a consideration of their work in Madrid or Barcelona. Rather I have consulted reviews from across Spain and beyond in appraising their impact. A discussion of how touring has impacted on each practitioner or company is crucial to an understanding of how reputations are constructed.

All of these practitioners have juggled theatrical work alongside cinematic and/or operatic ventures. Again here I have drawn on these projects when constructing my arguments. As such I argue for a construction of theatrical histories that recognises intersections with film and opera, often a resonant reference point for audiences. Furthermore, *'Other' Spanish Theatres* does not merely concentrate on work in traditional spaces but rather encompasses ventures beyond the proscenium-arch stage. In addition, a select number of key dramatic works feature across chapters. The different stage treatments of García Lorca's *Yerma, La casa de Bernarda Alba (The House of Bernarda Alba)*, and *Doña Rosita la soltera (Doña Rosita the Spinster),* Oscar Wilde's *Salomé,* Valle-Inclán's *Divinas palabras (Divine Words),* Shakespeare's *The Tempest* and Seneca's *Medea* considered in the book allow for a discussion of the appropriation and reinvention of texts by successive generations of practitioners for the demands of the age in which they have worked.

The chapters do not follow a prescribed format. Some, like Chapters 1 and 6, provide largely chronological assessments of a body of work. Others, like 3 and 5, are organised around thematic concerns that allow for the detailed exploration of a select number of key productions. While there is a recognition that these stagings need to be presented in a context that recognises their position within the artist's wider body of work, I have sought to avoid reducing each chapter to a year-by-year summary of productions. Rather the emphasis is on constructing an argument that encompasses stagings produced outside Madrid and work that has offered a representational space for marginalised subject positions. *'Other' Spanish Theatres* documents a theatrical culture where balance has shifted from a centralised landscape 'exporting' productions to the provinces to the Catalan capital. It is in Barcelona where innovative theatrical forms have taken root before shifting along to the rest of the nation. In John Hooper's words:

most of the ideas that have shaped Spain's modern history – republicanism, federalism, anarchism, syndicalism and communism – have found their way into Spain by way of Catalonia. Fashions – whether in clothing, philosophy or art – have tended to take hold in Barcelona several years before they gained acceptance in Madrid. (Hooper 1995: 405)

Theatre generally fits the pattern outlined by Hooper.

Chapter 1 offers an English-language overview of the actress-manager Margarita Xirgu (1888–1969), analysing her contribution to Spanish theatre in the early decades of the twentieth century. Whilst Xirgu's importance has been recognised within Spain and Latin America, outside the Spanish-speaking world she has never been acknowledged alongside her European contemporaries, Sarah Bernhardt, Eleonora Duse and Réjane. The Argentine director Jorge Lavelli (b. 1931) has judged her as 'muy por encima del nivel medio de su época' (cited in Molinero 1985: 25) (far above the mediocre level of her time) and yet there has been no real English-language evaluation of her body of work. Even the numerous Spanish-language appreciations of her career sometimes fail to evaluate just what made her so unique as a performer. As such my explication concentrates on locating the characteristics of her work as an actress and director both in Spain in the period between 1906 and 1936 and in exile in Latin America in the aftermath of the Civil War.

Chapter 2 examines the work of the actor-manager Enrique Rambal (1889–1956). With Rambal I move away from the stages of Madrid and Barcelona, for he was to premiere much of his work in Valencia, a metropolis recognised by critics in the 1930s as standing alongside Madrid and Barcelona as one of the country's three most theatrically active cities (London 1997: 25). In dissecting the importance of Rambal's populist work in both the pre- and post-Civil War years, I argue that Rambal's trajectory has too often been relegated to the margins of twentieth-century Spanish theatre history. This may in part be due to the breadth of his work – an actor, director, impresario, dramatist, adaptor and translator, he was a veritable theatrical polymath. Certainly the fact that only a selection of his adaptations were published have seen him categorised as a figure who lacked 'literary merit', and yet, his impact on generations of future practitioners has been considerable.

Chapter 3 provides an introduction to the work of a Spanish-born actress, María Casares (1922–96), who is best known as one of the most significant *tragédiennes* of the French stage in the second half of the century. Rather than concentrate exclusively on the French-language work for the Théâtre National Populaire (TNP) in the 1950s for which she is perhaps best known, in 're-appropriating' her for the Spanish stage I focus on certain Spanish-language productions undertaken in Argentina in the 1960s and Spain in 1976, her work with Lavelli on *Médéa* (1967), *La Nuit de Madame Lucienne* (The Night of Madame Lucienne) (1985), *Comédies barbares* (Savage Plays) (1991) and the reception of her 1950 film *Orphée*, released in Spain in 1953. Casares' career is contextualised within the experience of exile with thematic patterns picked out through a career spanning over fifty-two years.

Chapter 4 interrogates the position of Nuria Espert (b. 1935) as the premier actress of the second half of the century within a framework that acknowledges her intersecting identities (a Catalan who has worked primarily in Castilian), her directorial choices and the role played by her producer-husband Armando Moreno (1919?-94). Considerable space is given to her early work promoting Brecht and O'Neill in Spain as well as her seminal collaborations with Argentine director Víctor García (1934–82) who, Moreno was to recognise, occupies a unique place in the post-War theatrical pantheon for his genius in interpreting the metaphorical resonance of texts, circumventing the possibility of being accused of staging texts 'about' contemporary Spain (cited in Cruz 1982: 32). While the critic María-José Ragué-Arias argues that until 1975 feminism was primarily articulated as an element of clandestine political organisations, the power of Espert's company during the Franco era suggests that its influence was more pervasive in theatre than has otherwise been accepted (1993: 203).

Chapter 5 concentrates on the trajectory of Lluís Pasqual (b. 1951), a director who was at the forefront of a generation that helped shape Barcelona's theatrical milieu during the transition from dictatorship to democracy. In exploring his long-standing working relationship with scenographer Fabià Puigserver (1938–91), firstly at the Teatre Lliure in Barcelona in the late 1970s and then at Madrid's Centro Dramático Nacional (CDN), the Spanish National Theatre Centre, in the 1980s, the chapter documents how their artistic ventures established new parameters for international collaborations which were to have wide repercussions in both cities. While the scope and scale of Pasqual's work render it impossible to provide comments on all his stagings, by exploring his association with certain key dramatists I indicate how he consolidated the idea of 'director's theatre' within Spain.

The final chapter turns again to more populist theatrical forms in assessing the phenomenon of La Cubana, who have produced one of Spain's most commercially successful theatrical productions, *Cegada de amor* (*Blinded by Love*). Appraising the company's production history within the wider context of Catalan performance, I argue that, unlike their contemporaries, La Fura dels Baus, their metatheatrical work does not translate easily to the demands of the international festival circuit and as such it has limited the exposure of the company beyond the Spanish-speaking world. This may, in part, account for the fact that they have never attracted the international academic attention of La Fura dels Baus despite resonant box-office success in the domestic market. The exuberant theatricality of La Cubana's devised work, their subversion of plot and the established dramatic canon, and their irreverent onstage antics have boldly demonstrated a multitextured exploration of the ephemerality of performance whose grammar is intrinsically dependent on challenging discursive, visual and aural systems. Examining their interdisciplinary ventures, the chapter will conclude by indicating how their inversionist strategy has offered a paradigm which, similarly embraced by La Fura dels Baus, Els Comediants and Carles Santos, has shifted public conception of theatre firmly from the page to the stage.

Patterns of association emerge between the practitioners considered in the book. Xirgu directed Casares in *Yerma* in Buenos Aires in 1963. Espert sought to lure Casares back to Spain with *Las criadas*, a Castilian-language production of Genet's *Les Bonnes* (*The Maids*) presented in 1969. Jorge Lavelli has proved a preferred director of both Espert and Casares. Indeed he had originally intended to direct *La Nuit de Madame Lucienne* with Espert in the role eventually taken by Casares in 1985. Another of Lavelli's key projects with Casares, Valle-Inclán's *Comedias bárbaras*, had been planned for what would have been Espert's third season as artistic director of the CDN (Espert and Ordóñez 2002: 200, 204). Espert has been directed by Pasqual, a figure who had also planned to produce *Comedias bárbaras* at the CDN, on numerous occasions. Jordi Milán (b. 1951), director of La Cubana, acknowledges his own roots within a tradition of popular theatre and delicious stage trickery promoted by Rambal. La Cubana were involved in the celebrations of the centenary of Xirgu's birth at Molins del Rei (Badiou 1988: 35). Performers like Walter Vidarte and Alfredo Alcón who collaborated with Xirgu in Argentina have gone on to work with Espert and/or Pasqual. The practice of Xirgu has proved a potent model for successive generations of performers and directors, as Espert and Pasqual both acknowledge.

The rise of the director, the place of the actor

In the prologue to Antonina Rodrigo's biographical study of Xirgu, the director and theatre historian Ricard Salvat wonders what remains of the performer and director when time has buried their work: some photographs, critical commentaries and reviews, perhaps a recording or a film (Salvat 1974: 11). Writers and musicians, as Xirgu herself articulated to a class of students at the University of Montevideo, 'dejan sus obras, quedan en ellas. El triunfo del actor, en cambio, debe ser inmediato, constante, hoy mismo' (cited in Salvat 1974: 12) (leave their works, they remain in them. The triumph of the actor, on the other hand, has to be immediate, constant, absolutely today). Whereas my study of Espert and Casares has been facilitated by the recordings of their work preserved on video, with Xirgu the traces of performance remain more obscure: a few recordings of her voice from radio broadcasts made in Buenos Aires and Montevideo during her long period of self-imposed exile, filmed productions of *La casa de Bernarda Alba* and *La dama del alba* (*Lady of the Dawn*) for Argentine television and crucially, the memories of those who saw her, worked with her and wrote about her work.

It is these memories, annotated, documented in some cases, preserved only in the minds of those who recall meeting Xirgu or seeing the work that I have drawn on in crafting this book. Rambal too, while often relegated to a footnote or a short paragraph in studies of Spanish theatre, has exerted a powerful influence on those who saw his work from the early 1920s until his death in 1956. Certainly, the fact that performers like Xirgu, Casares, Espert, and Rambal have left few remnants of their work, may, in part, account for the fact that their contributions have often come second to those of the dramatists they championed or the directors with whom they collaborated. In addition, theatre histories are often structured around male dramatists, directors and performers. *'Other' Spanish Theatres* announces its feminist credentials both in viewing the work of female theatre practitioners at the very centre of key developments in Spanish theatre throughout the century and in constructing alternative prisms through which to view a theatrical culture. Indeed while the influence of women dramatists like Ana Diosdado (b. 1938), Concha Romero (b. 1945), Paloma Pedrero (b. 1957), and María Manuela Reina (b. 1958) has been well documented by academics like María-José Ragué-Arias and Patricia

O'Connor as an indication of the emergence of a feminist theatre in the post-Franco era, a feminist prototype can clearly be located in both Xirgu and later Espert's work. All too often, however, actresses are not featured in the equation of a feminist theatre, as their influence is negated in a culture which views dramatic writing as the major qualification for theatre.

A study of this nature must, necessarily, be selective. The choice of Xirgu comes from my own indignation at her repeated omission from English-language encyclopedias of theatre or studies of seminal European performers. Theatre of the pre-Civil War era has all too often been viewed through the prisms of male drama-tists like García Lorca and Valle-Inclán, and, to a lesser extent, burgeoning direc-tors like Cipriano de Rivas Cherif (1891–1967) and Adrià Gual (1872–1943) where she is allocated a supporting role. It is Xirgu, nevertheless, who can be seen as a link between all these innovators. Here she emerges from their shadows and takes centre stage, positioned as the seminal theatre figure of the pre-War era. The actress-manager María Guerrero (1868–1928), who traversed both the nineteenth and twentieth centuries, could have been an alternative choice here. If I opted ulti-mately for Xirgu, it is because in her understanding of theatre's social and political functions she proved such a role model for future theatre makers. In addition, her work across two continents asks seminal questions about how national theatre cul-tures are documented and assessed. Beginning her professional career in 1906, her work effectively traverses much of the century. Her training within the alternative theatre societies that sprung up in middle of the nineteenth century points to the importance of an 'amateur' theatre scene in Barcelona which has had considerable impact throughout the century, later nurturing Espert, Pasqual and a generation of alternative theatre practitioners including Els Joglars, Els Comediants, La Fura dels Baus and La Cubana.

Xirgu's career was also forged within a context still dominated by the actor-manager. Gies quotes from Manuel de la Revilla's 'La decadencia de la escena española y el deber del gobierno' (The decadence of the Spanish stage and the gov-ernment's duty), first published in *El Globo* in 1876, which draws attention to the problems manifest when actors served as directors of companies and impresarios, advancing a system with few controls where repertory was selected according to the roles which promoted the main actor's talent or placed few demands on them (1994: 28). Certainly some actors may have been ill-prepared to determine the repertoire, but in the period after the mid-1870s which saw the demise of the cen-sors, others brilliantly executed the challenge of programming a season which sought to bring variety and innovation to the Spanish stage. Companies were then organised around clear hierarchical structures with grand applause greeting the diva's first appearance, the repetition of certain key scenes, and intervals used to host parties in dressing rooms (Joya 1999: 222–3). Xirgu entered into a profession which still viewed actresses as women of ill repute.[9]

---

9 Gies notes how in moral *alta comedias* the women leading husbands astray were habitually actresses or singers; see Gies 1994: 275.

The beginning of the twentieth century is sometimes seen to be dominated by the memory of two actors – Rafael Calvo (1842–88) and Antonio Vico (1840–1902) – who had gone against the tendencies of the day in their more low-key, 'realistic' registers.[10] Nevertheless, theatre companies were generally in the hands of women as is clear from the substantial number of companies named after leading actresses: Carmen Díaz, Irene López Heredia, Josefina Díaz de Artigas, and Irene Alba. During these years actresses enjoyed substantial prowess (Rodrigo 1974: 124). Whereas María Guerrero is often touted as the most significant actress of her generation, her contemporary María Tubau (1854–1914) also generated consequential plaudits. Guerrero, a celebrated champion of Àngel Guimerà (1845–1924) and Benito Pérez Galdós (1843–1920), was also José de Echegaray's premier actress, articulating the new language of the upper middle classes and the spirit of the age put forward in differing forms by Ibsen, Strindberg and later Pirandello and Shaw. Would José de Echegaray's plays have enjoyed such a conspicuous public success or would he have won the Nobel Prize for literature were it not for her presence? The fact that critics like Ruiz Ramón are so scathing about his dramatic output may indeed substantiate assertions that the appeal of the works lay primarily in their productions rather than in the scripts themselves (1984: 350–1). Benavente too benefited both from Guerrero's astute eye and ear and from the decision of her actor husband Fernando Díaz de Mendoza (1862–1930) to turn increasingly to directing, taking overall responsibility for the shape of the Guerrero-Díaz de Mendoza company productions.

Xirgu too was to emerge as a director by default, turning to direction in an attempt to introduce more professional production standards to the Spanish stage. Her own work as a director really singles her out from two of her most significant contemporaries, Catalina Bárcena (1896–1977) and Rosario Pino (1870–1933). In addition, her collaborations with two of the earliest recognised directors in Spain, Gual and Rivas Cherif, served to distance her from the practices of actor-managers who failed to recognise the need for an intermediary who would prise apart the actor–spectator relationship in their guidance of the theatrical staging.

The rise of the director in Spain, however, as I indicate in Chapter 1, came much later than in the rest of Europe. While the work of European pioneers such as André Antoine, Gordon Craig, Max Reinhardt and George Pitoëff was known and debated in Spain,[11] the director was not really to emerge as a significant force in Spanish theatre until the 1950s. While Rambal was clearly an imaginative and technically adventurous director, his position within his company as actor-manager and his work within populist genres may have served rather inappropriately to classify him within a nineteenth-century model of theatre organisation. In 1943, the critic José María Carretero (writing under the pseudonym 'El Caballero Audaz') was to bemoan the devaluation of the performer in favour of the writer, lamenting the progressive shrinking of the stage from the arena of large anguished issues to

10 For further details, see Joya 1999: 223–4.
11 For further details, see Dougherty and Vilches de Frutos 1990, Vilches de Frutos and Dougherty 1997 and Vilches de Frutos 1998.

petty domestic discussions (1943: 523–4). Carretero's views may well have been shaped by the turgid dramaturgy of these years. Phyllis Zatlin has documented elsewhere the predominance of a rather limited repertoire of revivals: mediocre comedies by Pedro Muñoz Seca and Joaquín Álvarez Quintero (1893–1944), and grandiose historical dramas by Eduardo Marquina (1879–1946) and José María Pemán (1897–1981) were especially popular (1999: 223). But even the domestic dramas of Nobel Prize-winning dramatist Benavente and the torrid melodramas of Adolfo Torrado (1904–58) in the 1940s or the metatheatrical and far more dramatically accomplished comedies of Enrique Jardiel Poncela (1901–52) and Miguel Mihura failed to engage with the difficult socio-political conditions, economic recession and systematic repression which followed the end of the Civil War in 1939. The period between 1939 and 1943 was to see the execution of around 193,000 Republicans and the imprisonment of a further 400,000, the obstruction of social progress and a climate of profound disenchantment (Carr 1980: 155–8; Preston 1996: 217–22; Thomas 1990: 919–29, 947–57).

It was the nationalisation of the María Guerrero and Español theatres in the aftermath of the Civil War that was to begin the consolidation of the *metteur en scène* within Spain. Under the directorship of Felipe Lluch (1906–41), an assistant of Rivas Cherif, and then Cayetano Luca de Tena (1917–97) between 1942 and 1952, and José Tamayo (1928–2003) between 1954 and 1962, the Español was to be dedicated to classical work while the María Guerrero, under the stewardship of Luis Escobar (1908–91) and his deputy Huberto Pérez de la Ossa (1897–1983) between 1940 and 1952, was to concern itself with modern drama. Despite the scant rehearsal time allocated to each production, these directors were able to use the funding allocated by the state to raise production standards (Oliva 1989: 70–9; Higuera 1993: 81; García Ruiz 1999: 133–46; Cornago Bernal 2001: 76–84). Escobar and Pérez de la Ossa were French and English speakers. Both shared an interest in international works, adapting plays from both languages and inviting to the María Guerrero the companies of Eve Francis in 1941, Jean Venier the following year and Louis Jouvet in 1950 (Cañizares Bundorf 2000: 203–4).

During these years the director was to question the primacy of the playwright. Initially Escobar and Pérez de la Ossa were responsible for practically all the productions, but as their own directing commitments took them away from Madrid they engaged guest directors to stage programmed works. Perhaps the most significant of these was José Luis Alonso (1924–90), arguably the most important director of the Francoist years. Alonso was to succeed Claudio de la Torre (1895–1973) as director of the María Guerrero in 1960. Óscar Cornago Bernal argues that these national theatres were islands in a sea of desolation during the early post-Civil War years, introducing challenging international dramas that were to prove a point of reference for a generation of future practitioners (2001: 76). The creation of the Teatro Nacional de Cámara y Ensayo (National Chamber and Rehearsal Theatre) by the Government in 1954, directed by a colleague of García Lorca's at La Barraca, Modesto Higueras (1910–85), further broadened opportunities for introducing unconventional plays to Spain. And while the figure of the director was not

really consolidated in the commercial theatre until the 1960s, the institutes for theatre training that sprung up in the late 1950s and 1960s offered a further fertile
preparatory base for a later generation of directors including Ricard Salvat (b.
1934) and Miguel Narros (b. 1932) (Cornago Bernal 2001: 79, 186–206).[12] The
international perspective gained by Alonso, who had attended Jean-Louis Barrault's rehearsals, Salvat and Narros who had spent time in West Germany and
France respectively, and the Polish-trained designer-director Fabià Puigserver
(1938–91) was to see the introduction of more pliant forms of stage practice to a
theatre culture dominated by the parameters of pseudo-realism (Cornago Bernal
2001: 82). Alonso and Adolfo Marsillach (1928–2002) too countered the insularity
of the regime by travelling regularly to see theatre outside Spain, introducing a
wider repertoire of international works to Madrid.[13]

While director Juan Germán Schroeder (1918–97) was to view the figure of
the director as marginalised within the Spanish commercial theatre during this time
(1971: 23), José Tamayo was to recognise the fact that during the 1950s and 1960s
the director gradually came to displace the lead actor or actress, impresario or
dramatist as the figure with overall responsibility for the artistic shape of the production (1953: 33–4). Perhaps, as Pasqual indicates in his opening epigraph, the
Franco era curtailed the conditions that might have allowed playwrights to evolve
their craft within a receptive creative environment. Indeed Cornago Bernal argues
that, by the 1960s, significant developments within Spanish theatre have not been
linked to the dramatists but rather to the work on dramaturgy undertaken by 'hombres de teatro' (2001: 91) (men of theatre) like Alonso. To these 'hombres de
teatro' I would add Nuria Espert. In both her collaborations with Alonso and Salvat
and her invitation to García to work in Spain, Espert was to recognise the possibilities offered by a director who saw the job as going beyond the coaching of performers to an orchestration of scenic resources which recognised that decor was not
simply a passive backdrop to the action.

The restrictive censorship apparatus put into operation by Franco was to radically shape the work of all the directors of this era. The Press Law introduced in
1938 by Ramón Serrano Suñer, and only replaced in 1966, introduced prior censorship on all dramatic works, films and *revistas* (musical revues). A further piece
of legislation put in force in 1939 introduced readers who would monitor and
police, on behalf of the Ministry of Information and Tourism, all public shows
(London 1997: 11). While guidelines were not properly laid out until the 1963, the
censoring bodies were keen to ensure that negative references to the regime, the

12 While it is beyond the remit of this introduction to deal with the structures for actor and
director training in Spain, a professional training structure really sprung up in the late
1950s. For details of these initiatives, see Cornago Bernal 2001: 180–220. For details on
the training offered by the Real Conservatorio de Música y Declamación established by
Queen María Cristina in 1831, see Joya 1999: 220–33. While this institution was to train
performers like Emilio Thuiller, the route of amateur theatre was employed by successive
generations from lower-class backgrounds, like Xirgu, Enric Borràs and Espert, who have
attributed to it a more 'immediate' training on the job.
13 For further details, see Alonso 1991 and Marsillach 1998.

Roman Catholic Church and the army were erased while any allusions to the Civil War referred to it as a 'Crusade' rather than a fratricidal conflict.[14] Inspectores de espectáculos (theatre censors) attended rehearsals to monitor the implementation of any 'authorised' cuts, ensuring that nothing contentious slip through. Nevertheless, as John London has indicated, a system

concerned with live performance was complicated further and made more random in its application to theatrical productions. These complications resulted from the transitory nature of the theatrical act and the inevitable gaps between text, rehearsal, and production, not to mention differences from performance to performance. The illogicality and disorganization of the system seem to have been born from a ludicrous all-fearing severity. (1997: 12)

Practitioners soon developed strategies for evading the censor's watchful glance. Double versions of scripts existed with one presented at rehearsals where the censor was present and another saved for performances where friends assured the performers that there was no government representative in the house. Cultural meanings were formed and exchanged through the use of shared conventions and sign systems. While successive generations (Xirgu, Arrabal, Josep Maria Flotats [b. 1939], Francisco Nieva [b. 1927]) chose to leave Spain to train and/or find work in less politically compromised societies, other practitioners who remained worked within the censorship regulations producing defiant, ambitious work. Whilst the social protest dramatists who emerged in the wake of Buero Vallejo's *Historia de una escalera* in 1949, Sastre, Olmo, José Martín Recuerda and José María Rodríguez Mendez (b. 1925) are perhaps the best known 'rebels', other practitioners were, arguably, to have a more significant impact on *stage practice* during these years. Perhaps the most internationally recognised of these is Espert, who, with her own company, redefined the role of the actor-manager for the demands of the post-Civil War era. While she is primarily known internationally for her collaborations with García, the breadth of her work during the 1960s and early 1970s served to open up foreign interest in more textual forms of theatre at a time when international programmers were viewing Spanish theatre through the 'unwritten' theatrical languages of companies like Els Joglars and La Cuadra de Sevilla.

Liminality: the margins and the centre

Theatre, Sarah Wright reminds us, is 'the "safe" arena for the playing out of dangerous pursuits. It provides the safe distance from which to explore fears surrounding loss of control in the face of disorder, while the playful combinations of categories presents the thrill of risking new possibilities and suggestive freedoms' (2000: 6). In a century marked by industrial disputes, a bloody fratricidal conflict and a thirty-six year dictatorship, theatre in Spain has functioned, often to the despair of the authorities, as a marginal space, a place for questioning boundaries

14 For further details of these guidelines and the operation of the censors, see O'Connor 1966 and Abellán 1989.

that might have once been sacred. Both the Primo de Rivera dictatorship (1923–30) and the Franco years (1939–75) may have sought to marginalise and confine certain forms of theatre, but the spillage of theatre from contained 'authorised' spaces to the streets in the later years of *El Caudillo*'s dictatorship and the more recent appropriation of non-theatre spaces like the old flower market in Barcelona (the Mercat de les Flors) and the former church which is now the Teatro de la Abadía in Madrid, the home of José Luis Gómez's company and theatre school, is testimony to a theatrical culture which has defiantly refused to take second place to the literary text. While theatre is often marginalised as a liminal space, it is this very liminality which, as La Cubana's work so brilliantly indicates, has allowed it to remain in the public domain.

It is beyond the remit of this book to provide a detailed historical contextualisation of the century under consideration. Each chapter, nevertheless, attempts to frame the work of the practitioner within the wider socio-political context in which they were working. Xirgu was to make her professional debut in 1906 against the backdrop of Catalan industrialisation and demands for autonomy from the Spanish state. Indeed the marked presence of Catalan practitioners in the book necessitates not just an acknowledgement of centralised politics but also a recognition of Catalonia's political and social history. Catalonia's economic power in the later half of the nineteenth century was to generate a strong Catalan nationalist movement cultivated by both cultural figures (through the *Renaixença*) and politicians who sought to celebrate their own language, history and national identity (Castells 1997: 45).[15] In 1913 the formation of the Mancomunitat, a form of self-government made up of a 'commonwealth' of the four Catalan provinces, offered a model for autonomous administration which was to finance Adrià Gual's Escola Catalana d'Art Dramàtic (ECAD), a Catalan theatre school which was to suffer a name change to 'Instituto del Teatro Nacional' under the 'Spanishification' imposed by Primo de Rivera's dictatorship (Villar de Queiroz 2000: 125–6). While home rule status was promised to the Catalans in 1931 and the Generalitat, an autonomous government, established in 1932, tensions with Alejandro Lerroux's Madrid government led to the proclamation of Catalan State of the Spanish Federal Republic in 1934 and a retaliation by Lerroux through Barcelona's Civil Governor, General Batet. The subsequent surrender and imprisonment of Catalan president Lluís Companys and the suspension of the Catalan government was followed in 1936 by an amnesty granted by the Popular Front government which had been elected to central government in February of that year (Hooper 1995: 405–18). The gains made in 1936 with the restoration of autonomy were short-lived. The end of the Civil War saw Companys flee Barcelona for France where the Gestapo were to capture and hand him over to Franco who ordered his execution in 1940. Chapter 6 delineates some of the measures introduced by Franco to curb nationalist aspirations (225). Catalan book burnings, the banning of religious services and newspapers in Catalan, the imposition of teaching solely in Castilian and the prohibitions

---

15 For further details on the *Renaixença*, see George 2002: 4–8 and Terry 1972: 3.

of dialects made law in 1941 was to ensure that 'full-scale theatrical productions in Catalan recommenced only in 1946' (London 1997: 13).

There is no doubt that the need to attract economic assistance from Western Europe and the USA in the 1950s – the UN boycott was lifted in 1950; Spain was permitted to join the UN in 1955 and the International Monetary Fund in 1958; and land for the construction of US bases was matched by substantial American aid in the period following 1953 – was to see a gradual softening of the regime's discrimination against Catalonia with regard to state investments (Keating 1996: 150–2). The transition to democracy that followed Franco's death has seen legislative measures put in place which have allowed for a reconstruction of Catalonia's national identity that has been conspicuously played out in the cultural sphere. The reinstatement of the Catalan Statute of Autonomy by Adolfo Suárez, Spain's Prime Minister between 1976 and 1981, and the subsequent restoration of the Generalitat – and return of its president in exile, Josep Tarradellas – allowed the issue of illiteracy in Catalan to be addressed and a policy of cultural *normalitat* (normality) was promoted in the hope of remedying the situation. Josep-Anton Fernàndez views the creation of the Generalitat's Departament de Cultura as both 'the first major step to implementing this programme' and 'central to the dramatic growth of the Catalan cultural market since then' (1995: 343). Both Chapters 4 and 5, however, point to the tensions between the Departament de Cultura and Barcelona City Council, the Ajuntament, whose cultural division has also played a significant part in the funding of theatre in the metropolis. Significantly, in Barcelona's Plaça de Sant Jaume the two institutional power bases of the Generalitat (Palau de la Generalitat) and Ajuntament (the Casa de la Ciutat where the Spanish Republic was proclaimed in 1931) face each other. While the Generalitat has been under the control of the centre-right Catalan nationalist CiU (Convergència i Unió) formation led by Jordi Pujol since 1980, the Ajuntament, under their deadly socialist rivals, have held onto power in municipal elections under the guidance of socialist mayors. Their ideological struggles have often been played out in the cultural sphere as the Generalitat's funding of the Teatre Nacional de Catalunya and the Ajuntament's funding of the Ciutat del Teatre delineated in Chapters 4 and 5 indicates (166–72; 182–4).

Ideological, political and cultural tensions between Madrid and Barcelona also inform much of the book. The alternating democracies and dictatorship of the pre-Civil War years were to impact on the burgeoning nationalist movement in Catalonia.[16] A rapid succession of governments in the years following the declaration of the Second Republic and departure of King Alfonso XIII in 1931 generated a climate of political instability and polarisation that was to lead to the outbreak of civil war in 1936. The victory of the Nationalist forces was to see the 'other' republican Spain persecuted in an attempt to obliterate any political challenges it might mount. The aftermath of the war, *los años de hambre* (the hunger years), was bleak

---

16 For further details on how this was manifested in the relations between theatre practitioners in the two cities, see George 2002: 27–81, 108–73.

with 'real income *per capita* [. . .] cut [. . .] to nineteenth century levels' (Hooper 1995: 15). However, *los años de desarrollo* (years of development) between 1961 and 1973 which followed the foreign investment, easing of trade restrictions and the encouragement of private enterprise of the 1950s was to witness an impressive economic growth that lifted Spain out of the UN category of 'developing nations' (Hooper 1995: 17–20). By the time Franco died in 1975 tourism, immigration from rural areas to the major cities, and the 'economic miracle' were 'responsible for redistributing the country's wealth and creating a "new middle class". Together these [. . .] factors helped to remove, or rather to bridge, the gulf which had existed up until then between the "two Spains", and which had been responsible for the civil war' (Hooper 1995: 26).

Under Suárez's prime ministership the seeds of parliamentary democracy were laid with the formation of a two-chamber parliament and the introduction of wide legislation which initiated political reform, the introduction of democratic elections, and the approval of a new Constitution which granted autonomy to the different nationalities and regions while affirming 'the indissoluble unity of the Spanish nation' (cited in Elorza 1995: 333).[17] The implications of greater autonomy saw a significant proportion of arts funding move to the regional governments and, as such, the concentration of cultural assets in Madrid and Barcelona was challenged by a policy of decentralisation which was to see the restoration and refurbishment of local theatres, the funding of new cultural institutions and the support of regional companies (Hooper 1995: 324). The establishment of a Ministry of Culture in 1977 based on the French model also paved the way for further cultural expansion. Its foundation of a Centro Dramático Nacional (CDN or Spanish National Theatre Centre) in 1978, under the initial directorship of Marsillach, has allowed for the cultivation of both radical stagings of new or experimental plays at the Sala Olimpia and more mainstream twentieth-century works at the María Guerrero theatre. The election of the PSOE (Partido Socialista Obrero Español) or Socialist Worker's Party in 1982 saw a high-profile promotion of the arts 'both through state support and by encouraging private sponsorship' (Coad 1995: 373). The election of Pasqual to the artistic directorship of the CDN was to witness a veritable augmentation of the CDN's profile. In 1985 a classical company, the CNTC (Compañía Nacional de Teatro Clásico), was set up along the lines of the Royal Shakespeare Company and the Comédie Française with the precise mandate of promoting Spain's Golden Age repertory. The company, first under Marsillach's direction (1986–89, 1992–97), and subsequently under the stewardship of Rafael Pérez Sierra (1989–91, 1997–99), Andrés Amorós (1999–2000) and José Luis Alonso de Santos (from 2000), has, however, on the whole, failed to revitalise or revise the classical canon for the contemporary age.[18]

---

17 For further details, see Hooper 1995: 29–38 and Chapter 6, 225.
18 Calixto Bieito's 2000 staging of *La vida es sueño,* first presented at the Edinburgh International Festival as *Life is a Dream* in 1998, is a notable exception. Bieito (b. 1963) and Sergi Belbel (b. 1963), both associate directors of the company, are unusual in that they attempt to interrogate the performative expectations around the Golden Age

With the shrinkage of the Ministry's budget in the 1990s, the euphoria of the previous decade was replaced by a more subdued mood. In 1984 Madrid had thirty-nine theatres which had fallen to thirteen by 1993 (Hooper 1995: 326). As property prices soared, a number of theatres in both Madrid and Barcelona were refurbished as cinemas. The waning of the traditional proscenium-arch venue, however, has also brought with it the inhabitation and re-appropriation of non-purpose-built spaces, *salas alternativas* (alternative spaces) which have sprung up across both cities. José Sanchis Sinisterra's work with new writing at Barcelona's Sala Beckett and the richly interdisciplinary ventures of Madrid's Cuarta Pared provide some indication of the diverse works inhabiting the 'fringes' of these *salas alternativas*.

The centre-right PP (Partido Popular) that came to power in 1996 has subsequently amalgamated the Ministry of Culture with that of Education, effectively pointing to a devaluation of Culture which no longer merits its own ministry. The high-profile reopening of Madrid's opera house, the Teatro Real, in October 1997 was clouded by the plethora of scandals around its renovation costs, its opening season and the resignation of its artistic director Stephane Lissner in February of that year, leading to accusations of political machinations as the PP were seen to oust an administrative and artistic regime brought in by the previous socialist government.[19] The replacement of artistic directors of subsidised national theatres with each power change at governmental level has served to arouse suspicions of 'political' appointments at the helm of cultural organisations seeking to forge international collaborations. While production standards at national theatres with their extensive resident technical staff are on the whole good, certainly, as Marion Peter Holt has noted, 'some commercial offerings present a scenic shabbiness that goes beyond cost-saving' (2001: 146).

Beyond the limitations of such commercial theatre, the success of such companies as La Cubana, who have moved from the fringes to occupy a position at the very centre of both Catalonia and, more recently, Spain's theatrical landscape, points to the fact that the 'alternative' and 'mainstream' labels are no longer as fixed as they were once thought to be. Indeed, all the practitioners discussed in this book have moved from positions on the margins (amateur, regional and/or Catalan-language theatre), redefining those margins in theatrical endeavours that have questioned established artistic approaches, Madrid's dominance as the country's theatrical power base, and stimulated debate around the purpose and practice of performance. Indeed Catalan performance, having played a significant role in transforming the region's physical, social and economic landscape, has now become a desirable export and thus firmly placed Catalonia at the forefront of European theatrical innovation.

repertoire. Nevertheless, it is unfortunate that the CNTC's rather stolid stagings visited the Edinburgh Festival in 1989 and London's Spanish Arts Festival in 1994, drawing unfavourable comparisons with the Royal Shakespeare Company.

19 For further details, see Beckmesser 1997, Hermoso 1997, Santero 1997, Ruiz Mantilla 2000, and Wonenburger 2000.

It is this theatrical innovation that *'Other' Spanish Theatres* celebrates. For a discipline that finds its most persuasive definition in an eternal present tense, the challenges lie in documenting *the thing done*,[20] that residue that is most easily reduced to the component that is the playtext. Theatre resists reproduction. In asking what remains of the theatrical performance this book asks pertinent questions about how performances are tested against the texts that remain. If performance is an action towards disappearance, writing is a step to preservation. It is not the performances of Xirgu, Rambal, Casares, Espert, Pasqual and La Cubana that are preserved in this study but rather the unknowable 'other' of live theatre and the ways in which its performance moments have been constructed, documented and experienced.

20 A term used by Diamond (1996: 1) who defines performance as 'the doing and the thing done'.

1
An author of authors: Margarita Xirgu

The memory of the actors really only lasts as long as the recollection of their contemporaries. Once our voice is silenced in time, our memory fades. We are not a statue, a painting, a poem, a melody. (Xirgu, cited in Kelley 1967: 32)

Rising from the estuaries of the Rivers Besós and Llobregat, the sloping hill of Montjuïc provides one of Barcelona's most intriguing cultural industries. Its imposing castle, where Lluís Companys, President of the Generalitat, was shot on Franco's orders in 1940, points towards the area's geographical defensive position as both fortress and barrier. Its name is testament to the city's Jewish community that had settled centuries earlier along the hillside. During the 1929 Universal Exhibition Montjuïc was landscaped according to the plans of Jean Forestier and Nicolau Maria Rubió i Tudurí. The palaces, pavilions, fountains, gardens and Grec theatre constructed for the exhibition do not resemble the *modernista* landmarks of the Parc de la Cuitadella, walkable from the Barri Gòtic and site of the 1888 International Exhibition. The gateway to Montjuïc lies in the aptly named Plaça d'Espanya, bordering the Avinguda del Paral.lel where until recently the now closed El Molino and the refurbished Arnau Music Hall remained testament to the area's less salubrious roots as the home of Barcelona's raucous vaudeville theatres. Taking the steep walk along to the Palau Nacional, home of the Museu d'Art de Catalunya, towards Poble Sec, El Mercat de les Flors, one of the city's more adventurous performance spaces, comes into view. Housed in one of the 1929 Exhibition pavilions whose 'residual styling [. . .] now looks like a Hollywood version of Spanish architecture' (Woodward 1992: 103), its facade faces onto a yard which is now, under the city's Ciutat del Teatre regeneration programme, also home to Barcelona's Institut del Teatre and two auditoria of the Fundació Teatre Lliure. Entering a stucco arch marked with ornate terracotta decorations, accessed via the Plaça Margarida Xirgu, the square is named after the Catalan actress who dominated the early twentieth century Spanish stage. Finding herself on tour in Latin America during the outbreak of the Civil War, the death of a number of her collaborators during the early stages of the conflict convinced her that she should remain in the Americas and here she was to exert a definitive influence on the theatrical infrastructures of Uruguay, Chile and Argentina before her death in 1969. A potent symbol of the Republic in exile, it was in Latin America that she staged the Castilian-language premiere of a series of works that could not be seen in the censorious climate of post-Civil War Francoism.

Despite the fact that Xirgu is widely acknowledged as a definitive figure within twentieth-century Spanish theatre,[1] she has never really permeated the consciousness of the English-speaking world in the way that the Italian *grande dames* Adelaide Ristori and Eleonora Duse or her French contemporary, Sarah Bernhardt, have.[2] This may certainly have been due, in part, to the fact that she never toured outside the Spanish-speaking world. A planned tour to Italy, accompanied by García Lorca, in 1935, organised as part of celebrations of the tricentenary of Lope de Vega's death, which Luigi Pirandello had been involved in arranging, was indefinitely postponed following Mussolini's invasion of Abyssinia.[3] She visited Paris for the first time in early 1912 when the city was in the throes of spectacular modernisation and home to a community of international artists including her fellow Spaniards Juan Gris and Pablo Picasso. The actress Réjane introduced Xirgu to Parisian society and she met a number of the vaudeville dramatists whose work she had been staging at the Nou theatre on Barcelona's Avinguda Paral.lel. She is known to have returned to Paris at least once a year as a way of keeping abreast of the latest dramaturgical and scenographic developments (Burgos n.d.: 38). Photographs from the summer of 1933 show her in Stratford-upon-Avon at a Shakespeare Festival with the Nobel Prize-winning dramatist Jacinto Benavente. She never performed, however, in either Britain, France or Italy. Nevertheless, her own pioneering work, alongside and with the directors Adrià Gual and Cipriano de Rivas Cherif, in introducing contemporary international plays into first Catalan and then Castilian was to win her a select band of European admirers. These included Pirandello, whose work she premiered in Spain and who thought her performance in *Como tú me quieres* (*As You Desire Me*) vastly superior to Greta Garbo's film rendition of the role, and Henri-René Lenormand who judged her a superb interpreter of his work (cited in Rodrigo 1974: 10).[4]

It was, however, her work in nurturing and promoting Castilian-language drama where perhaps her most lasting influence lies. Collaborating with living writers from both the generations of 1898 and 1927 she helped cultivate a theatrical

1 Both academic critics and theatre professionals acknowledge Xirgu's contribution. For Espinosa Domínguez (1988: 67), for example, she is the greatest Spanish actress of the twentieth century. For further opinions, see Delgado 1998b: 105, Rubio Jiménez 1999a: 119 and Amestoy 1999. For two English-language articles on theatre in the period 1898–1936 which briefly mention Xirgu's contribution, see Sánchez 1998 and Dougherty 1999. The most detailed English-language treatment of Xirgu can be found in George 2002.

2 For Ristori, see Bassnett 1996. For Duse, see Le Galliene 1966 and Pontiero 1982. For Bernhardt, see Baring 1934, Skinner 1966 and Agate 1969. Xirgu is absent from both significant English-language encyclopedias of theatre which feature entries on the above named actresses: *The Cambridge Companion to Theatre* (Banham [ed.] 1988) and *The Oxford Companion to the Theatre* (Hartnoll [ed.] 1967).

3 For further details, see Rodrigo 1974: 225 and Gibson 1989: 411, 416.

4 The production of *Como tú me quieres* which had been translated from the Italian by Rivas Cherif was one of the productions proposed for the 1935 tour of Italy. Xirgu produced Lenormand's *Les Ratés* (*The Failures*) as *Los fracasados* in the 1928–29 season and again in 1932.

renaissance in the 1920s and 1930s not seen since the Golden Age of Calderón, Tirso de Molina and Lope de Vega. Working within the commercial sector, rather than the fringe, she played a key role in radicalising the conservative private theatres of Madrid and Barcelona during this period. As such it is perhaps not surprising that Valle-Inclán referred to her as unique: 'haber visto trabajar a Margarita Xirgu será un orgullo para los públicos' (cited in Rodrigo 1974: 10) (having seen Margarita Xirgu at work is an honour for audiences). Alejandro Casona (1903–65) was to recognise the fact that Xirgu had guided onto the stage the early works of Rafael Alberti (1902–99) and García Lorca as well as his own (cited in Rodrigo 1974: 10).[5] His articulation of Xirgu's role as both performer and director equates her with the *doing* of performance. Her stagings were to be instrumental in the dissemination of these dramatists and makes it redundant to try and prise the plays' 'literary' status from their cultural performance histories. Detailing her performances and performance choices across the various stages of her long career, this chapter will present a series of 'transpositions, transcriptions and transfigurations' (Phelan 1998: 9) which narrate a trajectory that has, at least in the English-speaking world, too often been unacknowledged by those celebrating and/or interrogating the textual remnants of those icons whose dramatic writings she helped shape.[6]

A Catalan actress

Born in Molins del Rei (Barcelona) on 18 July 1888 to a working-class family, Xirgu made her debut at an early age in the amateur working-class theatres of Barcelona which she had frequented with her father as a child.[7] Recognition came with a production of Zola's *Thérèse Raquin* which opened on 4 October 1906 at the Teatre dels Proprietaris de Gràcia when she replaced a better known actress, Laia Guitart, who had pulled out at the last minute, uncomfortable at being seen by the audience in her petticoat.[8] Her performance was distinctive enough to attract the attention of *El Noticiero Universal*'s critic Bernat y Durán, who suggested to the impresario Ramon Franqueza that Xirgu join the resident Catalan-language company at the

5 For appreciations of Xirgu by both García Lorca and Alberti, see Rodrigo 1974: 9–10.
6 This is not the case in Spain where a series of detailed volumes on twentieth-century Spanish theatre have delineated Xirgu's contribution to the Spanish stage; see, for example, Fàbregas 1978, Dougherty and Vilches de Frutos 1990, Vilches de Frutos and Dougherty 1997, and Aguilera Sastre and Aznar Soler 1999.
7 See López Pinillos 1920: 143–4 for Xirgu's version of making her stage debut at the age of thirteen as the servant Curra in *Don Álvaro o la fuerza del sino*. Guansé, who covers her debut in some detail (1988: 31–2), also deals with the repertoire of these theatres which relied on popular works like Zorrilla's *Don Juan Tenorio,* as well as plays by Catalan dramatists like Rusiñol and Ignasi Iglesias and even perhaps more unexpectedly adventurous foreign pieces like translations of Ibsen and Strindberg. Xirgu's family planned for her to train as a haberdasher but when her father lost his job because of a strike, she was able to turn to the theatre full-time, supporting her family by taking on as much work as possible with these amateur companies.
8 See López Pinillos 1920: 143–4. Montero Alonso (1969: 5) claims that Guitart had to withdraw because she had coughed up blood.

Romea theatre (Rodrigo 1974: 42; Guansé 1988: 33). Invited to join the Companyia Catalana del Teatre Romea, she made her debut with Àngel Guimerà's *Mar i cel* (Sea and Sky) that same year. The choice of play is not insignificant for it was to indicate an early interest in the promotion of Catalan dramaturgy which was to determine her production choices throughout the period leading up to her first departure for Latin America in 1912.

Enric Gallén indicates that it was, a few days later, the opportunity to replace Emilia Baró in the role of Ernestina in *Els pobres menestrals* (The Poor Labourers) by Adrià Gual which led to her meeting the dramatist-director who was then one of the most powerful figures in the Catalan theatre scene (1988: 7). Gual had founded the Teatre Íntim in Barcelona in 1898 in the hope of providing Catalonia with a 'progressive' laboratory theatre along the lines of Aurélien Lugné-Poe's Théâtre de l'Œuvre, Paul Fort's Théâtre d'Art or the Moscow Art Theatre. Here, introducing radical innovations including the dimming of lights during performances,[9] he collaborated with innovative stage designers like Oleguer Junyent and Salvador Alarma in pursuing a theatrical aesthetic which sought to simultaneously promote symbolist practices and the corporeal presence of the performer which had grounded naturalism's materialist rationalism. Staging not only his own work but that of international, national and Catalan contemporaries, Gual's productions oscillated between André Antoine's naturalistic explorations of the relationship between environment and character and the mannered abstract styling of Lugné-Poe both of whose work he had seen on a visit to Paris in 1901.[10] Taking responsibility for the selection of new European works to be translated into and presented in Catalan for the Teatre Íntim at the Romea, Gual cast Xirgu in a series of international plays including D'Annunzio's *The Torch Under the Bushel* (*La llàntia de l'odi*) (1908), Henry Arthur Jones's *The Triumph of the Philistines* (*La victòria dels filisteus*) (1908) and Gerhart Hauptmann's *The Sunken Bell* (*La campana submergida*) (1908). Not only did this awaken an interest in contemporary dramaturgy, it also allowed her to learn French and Italian in the hope of better acquainting herself with the latest developments in European writing.[11]

At the Romea Xirgu was to come into contact with the most established dramatists of the Catalan modernist movement: Santiago Rusiñol, Àngel Guimerà and Ignasi Iglesias. She was to get to know all three of them personally. Iglesias was already firmly established as a dramatist, working within an Ibsenesque naturalistic formula of questioning conventional assumptions, before Xirgu performed in *La*

9 George (2002: 23) posits that Gual introduced this innovation to Barcelona years earlier than its adoption in Madrid.

10 See London 1998: 32. For further information on Gual, see Bravo 1986: 191–7 and García Plata 1996. García Plata (1996: 308) mentions that in his memoirs Gual (1960: 141–2) explains his admiration for productions seen at the Odéon by the Comédie Française, especially a staging of *Oedipus Rex* with the actor Jean Mounet-Sully. Gual mispells his name as Monet Souli.

11 See Burgos n.d: 38 where Xirgu talks of learning both languages. For a full chronology of Xirgu productions, see Rodrigo 1988: 65–71.

barca nova (The New Boat) (1907). The production, however, was not a success.[12] She went on to perform in a number of his other works during these years at the Romea, including *L'alegria del sol* (The Happiness of the Sun) (1908) and *Joan dels miracles* (John of the Miracles) (1908).[13] Rusiñol was already recognised as a major theatrical innovator in both Madrid and Barcelona by the time Xirgu became familiar with his work.[14] Although a desire to appear in Wilhelm Meyer Föster's *Old Heidelberg* (*Joventut de príncep*) is often cited as the reason for her signing to Enrique Giménez's company at the Principal theatre in 1908,[15] Rusiñol was to feature, alongside the veteran Guimerà, in her repertoire, with productions of *El redemptor* (The Redeemer) in 1909 and *El pintor de miracles* (The Painter of Miracles) in 1912. Guimerà had been appropriated by the Madrid stage during the 1890s with high profile productions of *Maria Rosa* at the Princesa theatre in 1894, *Terra baixa* (*Marta of the Lowlands*) at the Español theatre in November 1896 and *La filla del mar* (The Daughter of the Sea) in 1899.[16] Guimerà's *Andrònica* was staged for the first time in Catalan by Xirgu in 1911, having been seen in 1905 at the Novetats theatre in Luis López Ballesteros Castilian version staged by the María Guerrero-Díaz de Mendoza company. Guimerà's increasing involvement in Catalan politics was to place a strain on his relationship with the Guerrero-Díaz de Mendoza company. Admiring Xirgu's performance in *Andrònica*, Guimerà stated a wish to write for her. In 1911, she was to perform at the Principal in *Maria Rosa* with Enrique Borràs – the only one of the cast not from 1894 premiere at Novetats theatre (Rodrigo 1974: 71). In 1911, directed by Enrique Giménez, then one of the most accomplished actor-directors working in Barcelona, she performed in the only Guimerà play she was to premiere, *La reyna jove* (The Young Queen). Although often viewed as one of Guimerà's lesser works, the political machinations suffered by the popular young queen Alexia may well have struck an emotional chord with an audience who had lived through the 'tragic week' anti-militarist protests in 1909 and were now pressing for greater autonomy from the country's centralised government.

These years witnessed the manifestations of a political consciousness in Xirgu which was to be progressively displayed in her socially cognisant choice of plays. Iglesias's *Joan dels Miracles* revolves around the faith placed by the masses in tricksters whose sceptical cures renounce the progressive path of scientific disclosures. Juli's Vallmitjana's *Els Zin-calós* (The Gypsies) (1911) took the fate of nomadic gypsies as its subject. Rusiñol's writings archly articulate modernist dilemmas around

12 For further details, see Guansé 1988: 33–4.
13 For a full list of the repertoire of plays at the Romea during the 1907–8 season which included works by Iglesias, Rusiñol, and Apel.les Mestres as well as Jules Renard, Gabriele D'Annunzio and W. Jacobs, see Vàzquez 1989: 134–5.
14 See George 2002: 27–9, 40–3 for a discussion of Rusiñol's influence in the early years of the twentieth century.
15 Rodrigo (1974: 50) claims that she was offered a greater salary at the Novetats but chose to go to the Principal because she wished to see *Old Heidelberg* performed in Barcelona.
16 For further details on these productions, see George 2002: 37, 108–17, Martori 1995 and Martori 1996.

the role of art in an increasingly bourgeois society. Even Guimerà, often dismissed within the parameters of late-Romanticism, articulates valuable questions about the conflicts between individual and collective identities.[17] Xirgu's departure to Latin America in 1913 coincided, as Enric Gallén notes, with the crisis suffered by Catalan theatre between 1911 and 1917, following the loss of the Romea theatre to Castilian-language plays and the increasing unwillingness of the Principal theatre to stage Catalan work (1988: 9). There was a certain resentment of Xirgu's decision to perform 'abroad' in Castilian-language theatre with angry critiques, referred to by Gallén (1988: 9,11), appearing in *El Teatre Català* both in 1914 and 1916 (Vilaró i Guillemí 1914: 358; Carrion 1916: 54). Nevertheless while Xirgu may have chosen, like María Morera and Enric Borràs before her, to work primarily in Castilian, her knowledge of and affection for Catalan dramaturgy was to play a part in determining her repertoire in Madrid during the period between 1915 and 1936,[18] and she was to return to the city both during the Primo de Rivera dictatorship (1923–30) to premiere key works like *Mariana Pineda* (1927) and during the Second Republic (1931–6) to further promote García Lorca's work with productions of *Yerma, Bodas de sangre (Blood Wedding)* and *Doña Rosita la soltera o El lenguaje de las flores (Doña Rosita the Spinster or The Language of Flowers)* (1935). Even during her thirty-three years of exile in Latin America, she is known to have maintained contacts with the precarious situation of Catalan dramaturgy through Domènec Guansé who was able put her in contact with writers like the poet and translator Josep Carner (Rodrigo 1974: 307–8; Guansé 1988: 57). Home for her was always Barcelona (Guansé 1988: 57), and despite her many years of exile, it was always her wish to be buried in Molins del Rei.

Salomé (1910)

As mentioned earlier in the chapter, it is often speculated that one of the reasons that Xirgu joined Enrique Giménez's company at the Principal theatre in 1908 was to premiere *Old Heidelberg* which opened on 10 October in a Catalan translation by Carles Costa and Josep Maria Jordà. The 1908–09 season saw Catalan-language versions of a number of foreign works including Hauptmann's *Henry of Auë (El pobre Enric)*, Conan Doyle's *The Hound of the Baskervilles (El gos dels Baskerville)* and Henry Arthur Jones's 1897 play *The Liars (Els mentiders)*. It was to be the Catalan-language premiere of Oscar Wilde's *Salomé*, written in French by the dramatist in 1891 and first published in French in 1893, which was to prove Xirgu's most con-

---

17 For further information on Rusiñol, see Casacuberta 1997; on Guimerà, see Fàbregas 1971.

18 One of the two pieces she chose to open with at Madrid's Princesa theatre in 1914 was Rusiñol's *El patio azul* (The Blue Patio). She was to tour her 'Compañía Dramática Española de Margarita Xirgu' with Guimerà's *La chica y la pecadora* (The Girl and the Sinner) in 1919. In 1919, 1927, 1931 and 1932 she was to perform in Marquina's *La alimaña* (The Vermin) at the Centro theatre, *La ermita, la fuente y el río* (The Hermitage, the Spring and the River) at the Fontalba, *La fuente escondida* (The Hidden Fountain) at the Español, and *Los Julianes* (The Julians) at the Español theatre respectively.

tentious early production, articulating contemporary fears about control, illness and the body which were being vehemently debated in the intellectual crisis which followed the loss of the remains of the Spanish Empire in 1898.[19] Wilde's single-act play, fashioned in a baroque, overwrought language displays a telling fascination with the pursuits and (non-) limits of sexual gratification. Its excessively rhetorical style, bold lyricism and intensely sensual language, may have displayed echoes of Flaubert, but the straddling of different generic registers and insolent verbal and visual symbolism firmly anchor it within *fin de siècle* decadent modernism. Inside early twentieth-century Spain, where, as Susan Kirkpatrick has persuasively argued, 'the rhetorical association' of the country with 'decadence, impotence, and implicit feminisation was particularly powerful in that it served as an explanation for the disaster of 1898' (2000: 147), the overt aestheticism and eroticism of Wilde's play was to strike a telling emotional and political chord.

Set in the first century AD, the play revolves around the Jewish princess Salomé, the stepdaughter of Herod Antipas, tetrarch of Galilee. Lusting after Salomé, Herod rashly agrees to reward any demand she may have if she agrees to dance for him. Her dance of the seven veils produces an agreement on Herod's part to bring her the head of John the Baptist (Iokkanaan), imprisoned by the tetrarch for reproaching his marriage to his half brother Philip's ex-wife, Herodias. First staged in 1896 at the Théâtre de l'Œuvre in a production by Lugné-Poe, further European productions followed – including Max Reinhardt's 1902 and 1903 stagings and the premiere of Richard Strauss's operatic version in 1905 at the Dresden Opera House. Sarah Bernhardt's plans to stage the play in London, however, were abandoned when a licence was refused by the British Lord Chamberlain's Examiner of Plays, thus creating an aura of notoriety around the piece.[20] Viewed as an example of the 'total theatre' which Wilde had once referred to as 'the meeting place of all the arts' (cited in Tydeman and Price 1996: 3), its symbolist credentials were, as Delfina P. Rodríguez has exhaustively detailed, to attract a range of Spanish and Spanish-American writers including Rubén Darío, Francisco Villaespesa, Goy de Silva, Ramón Gómez de la Serna and Ramón del Valle-Inclán (1997). The latter was, of course, to render his own dramatic version of the myth in *La cabeza del Bautista* (The Baptist's Head), tellingly subtitled 'melodrama para marionetas' (a melodrama for marionettes) which negotiates similarly brusque transitions of tone.[21]

The play was translated into Castilian as early as 1902,[22] but Joaquim Pena's Catalan translation that Xirgu was to use in her 1910 production was published in

19   For further details on the 1898 crisis, see Harrison and Hoyle (eds) 2000. Ferran y
      Mayoral's review of the production hinges around the staging's graphic sexual iconography
      and its presentation of the sick and dismembered body (1910: 257–8).
20   For further details on these early productions, see Tydeman and Price 1996: 12–77. Their
      study purports to survey the play's 'principal realisations in the European theatre' (i) but
      fails to make any mention of either the 1910 or 1914 production.
21   See Valle-Inclán 1961b: 153–84. For details on the Madrid premiere of the play performed
      by a company including Xirgu's contemporary Mimí Aguglia, see Dougherty and Vilches de
      Frutos 1993.
22   For a discussion of the early translations, see George 2000: 114–15.

1908. Guansé claims that on reading Pena's version she articulated grave doubts about interpreting the role (1988: 37), and it was only on seeing Gemma Bellincioni perform in Strauss's operatic reworking at the Gran Teatro del Liceu in January 1910 that she appears to have understood both the piece's linguistic texture of excess and its portrayal of psychological states in purely physical ways. The difficulties she encountered in preparing the role tell us much about her groundwork as a performer. In later years she was to articulate both the antipathy the character held for her (cited in Rodrigo 1984a: 12) and the fact that she considered it a favourite role (cited in Carretero n.d.: 31),[23] but what Xirgu terms the lack of *situación,* the play's failure to provide a measured, rational psychological build-up and its brooding verbalisation of emotion (cited in Burgos n.d.: 39), evidently necessitated a different approach to theatrical representation. In order to execute the dance of the seven veils, Xirgu is known to have taken a week of intense classes with Pauleta Pamiès who was teacher of the *corps de ballet* at the Liceu[24] and the licentious nature of her gyratory moves visibly whipped Jaume Borràs's Herod into an erotic frenzy (Jordà 1910: 5).

The Catalan-language production, with sets by Brunet y Pous and staging by Jaume Borràs, premiered on 5 February 1910 at Barcelona's Principal theatre, polarising the Catalan press. Antonina Rodrigo collects a series of responses in her biography of Xirgu (1974: 56–8). These include *La Tribuna*'s outraged view of Salomé as a figure too dangerous to be seen on the Catalan stage, and *La Escena Catalana*'s observation that the piece was appropriate for all different sectors of the audience from the most vulgar to the most refined, recording, in addition, the enthusiastic audience reception. Although progressive critics like *La Publicidad*'s J. M. Jordà recognised the play's groundbreaking qualities in pushing the boundaries of what is understood as appropriate stage material (1910: 5), the staging was denounced as pornographic. Such accusations eventually resulted in the production being pulled from the Principal, with Xirgu moving 'downmarket' to the rather more raucous Teatre Nou, part of the Paral.lel group of music-hall and vaudeville venues which enjoyed a different audience base to the more bourgeois Principal and Romea.[25]

Certainly, as David George notes:

the fact that 1910 was a year of relative radicalism in Barcelona and Spain, as in the rest of Europe – it marked the formation of the government of the radical anti-clerical Canalejas, and the Setmana Tràgica in Barcelona had taken place during the preceding year – did not alter the city's underlying conservatism, reflected in the *Diario de*

---

23 In an interview given around 1917 (Uriarte n.d.: 195), however, Xirgu denies that Salomé is a favourite role.

24 For further details, see Guansé 1988: 37. Wilde is known to have wanted an actress who could dance for the role; see Tydeman and Price 1996: 19.

25 For details of the scandal provoked by the play, see Guansé 1988: 38. The Principal is still located at the bottom of Las Ramblas. The Romea on the Carrer Hospital in the *Barri Xinès* is now run by Calixto Bieito.

1 Margarita Xirgu in *Salomé* (1910)

Barcelona's description of *Salomé* as 'una obra detestable por más de un concepto' (a detestable work in more than one way). (2000: 118)

Responses to the production indicate that this conservatism was especially played out through the prisms of gender politics. The hysterical female, unbound and unrestrained, chaotic and seductive – photographs of the production show Xirgu in a beaded dress which revealed her shoulders (see Figure 1) and accounts also verify that in one of her costumes her midriff was exposed (Rodrigo 1984a: 12) – may have proved too overt an indication of what can befall a society when traditional gender hierarchies are overturned and feminine wiles are allowed to triumph. Even the death of Salomé, pointing to the re-establishment of an order momentarily disturbed, failed to quell anxieties around the feminisation of Spain, which the defeat of 1898 and the implications of social change on women's positions within late industrialisation had awakened. Reinforcing the body as the site of the story, Xirgu's Salomé articulated an urge not to be desired as an object but to sexually desire – carnal activity as opposed to passivity. The latent sexuality of Xirgu's costume, the graphic immediacy of Xirgu's lips touching the bloodied mouth of the dismembered head of the Baptist, the amorous tensions played out in Xirgu's voluptuous dealings with Borràs's Herod clearly generated conspicuous critical disapprobation. The fact that the supposedly decadent aestheticism represented by Wilde had been denounced as early as 1899 by such 'enlightened' writers as Pío Baroja and Miguel de Unamuno (Davies 1973: 140–3) indicates the unease provoked during this volatile time by Wilde's allegorical parable on the perils of obsession. The play was to form part of Xirgu's touring repertoire to Málaga, Santa Cruz de Tenerife and Latin America in 1913 and opened in Madrid at the Princesa theatre on 20 May 1914. The press response in Madrid appears to have been far less provocative than in Barcelona (Miquís 1914: 1; Tristán 1914: 3; García de Candamo 1914: 1). This may have been due, in part, to the fact that the Italian actress Lydia Borelli had already presented the piece in the city in April 1912, or to the changing mood of the country as *fin-de-siècle* soul-searching was replaced by the pragmatics of sup-plying the allies with raw materials during the Great War.

'Conquering' Madrid

The street on which the María Guerrero theatre now stands, Tamayo y Baús, is named after the prominent playwright of the 1850s. The building itself, however, bearing the name of the actress, is far more imposing and majestic than the small street that it dominates. It was here that Xirgu made her Madrid debut in May 1914 while the theatre, which was still called the Princesa, was loaned to her company by the then owners, the actress María Guerrero and her husband Fernando Díaz de Mendoza.[26] She chose to open with Hofmannsthal's *Elektra* and Rusiñol's *El patio azul* (from the Catalan *El pati blau*) (The Blue Patio).[27] The choice is not insignifi-cant. As well as lending themselves to different playing styles, the works herald a commitment to presenting both the Catalan and foreign 'other' within the estab-lished stages of the capital city. Already in Barcelona, at the Paral.lel's Nou theatre in 1910, Xirgu had pursued an unconventional path, gaining critical attention for a rather denigrated repertoire consisting of the Parisian vaudevilles of Maurice Hen-nequin and Paul Bilhaud and Robert de Flers and G. A. de Caillavet – she appeared in adaptations of *Pastille Hércules* (*Pastillas Hércules*) and *L'Âne de Buridan* (The Ass of Buridan) translated as *El asno de Buridán* – which were presented alongside *Salomé*.[28] Xirgu's presence in a programme that often featured popular singers and dancers like Carmelita Ferrer and Paquita Egea, may well have helped shape a celebrity status which transcended habitual class boundaries.

By the time she opened in Madrid, Xirgu was already a significant player within the Catalan theatre scene, having set up her own company, at the suggestion of the

---

26 For further details, see Rodrigo 1974: 87. The theatre was renamed after Guerrero in 1928. For further details on the history of the theatre, see Cañizares Bundorf 2000.
27 Xirgu was to return to *Elektra* regularly. During the Second Republic she chose the play for an outdoor performance in Madrid's major park, El Retiro.
28 For further details, see Guansé 1988: 41 and Rodrigo 1974: 59–63. For an introduction to El Paral.lel, see Salaün 1996.

Aragonese actor Miguel Ortín (who was to become her second husband), with the actors Enrique Giménez and Alejandro Nolla, which had toured around Catalonia. In addition she had performed with Enrique Giménez at the Principal where, after a performance of Henri Meilhac and Ludovic Helévy's *Froufrou*, she had come into contact with the impresario Faustino da Rosa. Rosa, having organised successful tours of Latin America for both Guerrero and Duse, encouraged her to leave the comfort of the Catalan stage for the 'unknown' shores of another continent. Both the Latin American tour in 1913–14 and her debut in Málaga in 1913 had well prepared her for the challenges of performing in Castilian, but the arrival in Madrid had, for Xirgu, an element of entering a foreign land (Amestoy 1999: 242).[29] David George's key study of Madrid and Barcelona theatre during the period 1898–1936 valuably charts the reception of Catalan actors who left Catalonia for the attraction of larger audiences and more lucrative touring contracts in Madrid (2002: 55–81). As with Enric Borràs before her, who had viewed himself as an emissary for Catalonia and its theatre in choosing to perform with companies like that of Rosario Pino which he joined for the 1905–6 season (cited in Bonavía 1913: 317–18), Xirgu faced antagonism from sections of the Catalan press who resented her eschewal of Barcelona for what they saw as a vain search for glories far from home.[30] This may have been in part, as George also notes, due to the 'growing nationalist sentiments within Catalonia' at this time (2002: 75). The Mancomunitat, a partially autonomous administrative body created in 1913, nailed its cultural colours to the mast by choosing to fund Gual's Escola Catalana d'Art Dramàtic (ECAD) that same year. Within a climate of emergent Catalanism, seeking to articulate the complex social, economic and political circuits of cultural production, Xirgu's decision to 'defect' to Madrid may well have been read as irresponsibly compromised.

Certainly, the period after 1914 was to see Xirgu performing predominantly Castilian-language works. For she was never to follow Enric Borràs's example during this time of relying on an increasingly staid repertoire of familiar early roles like those of *Terra baixa* and *El místic* (The Mystic).[31] The difficulty in placing her accent, which featured what Guansé terms 'un deje indefinible que no era patrimonio de ninguna de las regiones de la lengua española' (1988: 43) (an undefinable inflection which was not associated with any of the Spanish-language regions), and the praise heaped on her by Madrid-based critics who admired her supposedly conscious erasure of Catalan intonation (Yorick 1914: 370–1) seem to imply an easy transition to Madrid's stages. But the move to Castilian-language theatre appears

---

29 For a charting of the problems Xirgu encountered during this period in performing in Castilian, see Guansé 1988: 42–3.

30 See, for example, Amich i Bert 1914 and Vilaró i Guillemí 1914. These comments are made around reviews of Dario Niccodemi's *L'Aigrette* which Xirgu performed at the Novetats in May and June 1914.

31 Although an interview with her published in 1935 (Artis 1935a) does draw attention to the fact that, when she does occasionally perform in Catalan in Barcelona, her repertoire seems curiously outdated: a veritable contrast to her pioneering Castilian-language theatre.

to have involved Xirgu having to learn the language from scratch.[32] Xirgu's response to Carmen de Burgos who observes that the actress no longer has a Catalan accent, '¿Cree usted que lo he perdido?' (cited in Burgos n.d.: 38) (Do you think I've lost it?), however, belies a resistance to unquestioning assimilation. This was to manifest itself in the risks she took working both with performers whose styles did not necessarily complement her own, such as Emilio Thuillier, who accompanied her on the 1913 Latin American tour,[33] and a range of writers who were sometimes openly hostile to each other's work.[34]

Promoting internationalism

Any consideration of Xirgu's Madrid seasons reveals a marked emphasis on foreign works. As with Guerrero before her who was to be associated both with nurturing Spanish dramaturgy – the Álvarez Quintero brothers, Echegaray, Benavente, Martínez Sierra – and with widening the dramatic repertoire to include international works like those of Gaston Leroux, Oscar Wilde and Tagore Rabindranath, Xirgu was to play a significant role in modernising Madrid's theatrical landscape.[35] D'Annunzio was a favourite author, with a production of *The Daughter of Jorio* (*La hija de Yorio*) opening the 1916–17 season at the Princesa on 5 October in a Castilian version by Felipe Sassone. In involving a wide range of Spanish writers in the translation of the international works she brought to the stage, Xirgu actively encouraged poet-dramatists like Eduardo Marquina and Joaquín Montaner to remain in touch with key dramaturgical trends, substantiating Jesús Rubio Jiménez's view that Spain was far more receptive to European work than critics may have previously argued (1999b: 18–26).

Xirgu's presence in Madrid coincided with a number of experiments in forging an 'art' theatre which would pioneer alternative staging techniques based on the practices of vanguard practitioners like Edward Gordon Craig, Adolphe Appia and Fritz Erler. At the Teatro Eslava, home to Martínez Sierra's Teatro de Arte company (1917–20), the presence of a set-building workshop enabled scenographers like Siegfried Burmann, Rafael Pérez Barradas and Manuel Fontanals to experiment with alternatives to the painted backdrop. Cipriano de Rivas Cherif (1891–1967) was to be involved in numerous ventures – including the Escuela Nueva (New School), Teatro de los Amigos de Valle-Inclán (Theatre of the Friends of Valle-Inclán), El Mirlo Blanco (The White Blackbird) and El Caracol (The Snail) – that sought to promote the idea of the stage director as orchestrator of the production. Rivas Cherif had spent time in Italy (between 1911 and 1914) where he became

32 In Carretero (n.d.: 54) Xirgu states that she knew 'ni una palabra' (not a word) of Castilian when she was contracted by Rosa.
33 For Thuillier's sceptical views on Xirgu as a 'believable' performer, see Uriarte n.d.: 166.
34 A production of Joaquín Montaner's *El hijo del diablo* at the Fontalba in 1927, for example, was interrupted by Valle-Inclán, openly voicing his disapproval; see Guansé 1988: 56.
35 For a discussion of Guerrero's work in this area, see Cañizares Bundorf 1999.

highly influenced by Craig's ideas, and in Paris (during 1919–20) where he was introduced to the practices of Diaghilev, Georges Pitoëff and Jacques Copeau. His return to Spain prompted more adventurous stagings that drew their inspiration from popular Soviet drama, Craig's *übermarionette* and Copeau's reformist actor-centred theatre.[36] Rivas Cherif saw much of Xirgu's work at the Princesa and the Fontalba during the 1920s, and is known to have commented on the impact made by the international flavour of her repertoire (Rodrigo 1974: 126; Aguilera Sastre and Aznar Soler 1999: 167–73). Rodrigo comments that in 1923, prior to Xirgu's departure for her third Latin American tour, four of the seven productions she premiered before Barcelona audiences at El Dorado were of foreign works: François de Curel's *L'Ivresse du sage* (The Blind Drunkenness of the Wise) (*Los sabios no ven*, translated by Eduardo Marquina), L. de Azertis' *The Magic of the Desert* (*La magia del desierto* translated by Martínez Sierra), Georges Rivollet's *Jérusalem* (*Jerusalén*), and Henry Kistemaeckers's *The Princess Masha* (*La princesa Mascha*), both translated by Alejandro P. Martistany (1974: 126).

During these years, Xirgu was to premiere Bernard Shaw's *Saint Joan* (*Santa Juana* in a translation by Julio Broutá), first in Barcelona and subsequently in 1924 at Madrid's Eslava theatre. In 1926, at the Fontalba, Massimo Bontempelli's *Our Goddess* (*Nuestra diosa*) which had been premiered in Rome by Pirandello's company, was presented in a translation by Salvador Vilaregut. The Fontalba also witnessed Lenormand's *Les Ratés (The Failures),* adapted by Montaner as *Los fracasados* in 1928. The opening was attended by Lenormand who spoke prior to the performance about new French writing and the radical revolutionary work being carried out by Pitoëff, Gaston Baty, Jouvet, Copeau, Firmin Gémier and other directors in France. In his memoirs, *Les Confessions d'un Auteur Dramatique,* Lenormond wrote of the emotive violence of the Madrid audience and of the burning intensity of Xirgu's performance as Ella/Her (cited in Rodrigo 1974: 157).

In 1930, Xirgu was to join forces with Rivas Cherif at the Español that was, alongside the Princesa (now renamed the María Guerrero), to function as a *de facto* national theatre. Xirgu's company, having merged with that of Enric Borràs, was granted use of the theatre from Madrid's City Council and it was here that they remained until 1935.[37] Here Rivas Cherif was to play a wider role, as a literary advisor with responsibility for production staging, building on his previous work with the companies of Mimí Aguglia, Irene López Heredia and Isabel Barrón. While Rivas Cherif may have functioned, in effect, as a stage director, the term was still not accepted as part of the theatrical vocabulary within Spain (Sánchez 1998: 10; Aguilera Sastre and Aznar Soler 1999: 173). Rivas Cherif was to recognise that, despite Xirgu's significant merits as a performer and her innovative choice of texts, the production quality of stagings for which she often assumed directorial respon-

36 For further details, see Aguilera Sastre and Aznar Soler 1999: 85–164. For an English-language introduction to alternative theatre at this time, see Sánchez 1998.

37 Rodrigo (1974: 220–1) cites the increasingly conservative climate in 1935 as one of the reasons for the non-renewal of Xirgu's contract, providing details on the procedures initiated to review the Español's future.

sibility was not as professional as it might be (1922: 222–4). While, as Aguilera Sastre and Aznar Soler observe, Rivas Cherif's presence was not to affect the structure of Xirgu's company, which revolved, like all other companies of the same period, around a generic pool of actors, he was to take a clear responsibility in coordinating the selection of the repertoire, casting, press relations and the annotation of stage movement (1999: 172). His guidance and enthusiasm was to see the premiere of Elmer L. Rice's Pulitzer Prize-winning *Street Life* (*La calle,* adapted by Juan Chabás) in 1930 and Goethe's *Clavigo* (*Clavijo*) in 1932, staged to mark the centenary of the dramatist's death. Cultural initiatives like La Barraca and Teatro del Pueblo were also to reverberate on the programming of the theatre with a diversification in 1932 that saw dramatic works presented alongside concerts by Madrid's Philharmonic Orchestra, lectures, and recitals, and plans for reduced-price performances for students and blue-collar workers, together with performances in prisons.[38]

The internationalism of these years was visible not merely in the choice of repertoire. Just as Guerrero had brought a range of international companies to the city,[39] so Xirgu invited the Moscow Arts Theatre who presented twelve performances between 28 February and 14 March 1932 (Rey Faraldos 1986: 273–8). Exchange visits were also planned with Charles Dullin's Atelier in Paris and the National Theatre of Lisbon but these were blocked by the increasingly conservative city council (Aguilera Sastre and Aznar Soler 1999: 185–7). It is perhaps not surprising that the critic Enrique Díez-Canedo was to refer to Xirgu's years at the Español as one of the two great periods in the theatre's history (cited in Rodrigo 1974: 163). It was in Xirgu's attempt to shape the theatre into a venue for Spanish dramaturgy where possibly her most pervasive influence remains.

Fostering Spanish dramaturgy

While Xirgu's promotion of Spanish dramaturgy is frequently located in the period beginning with her premiere of García Lorca's *Mariana Pineda* in 1927, Benavente, the Álvarez Quintero brothers, and Martínez Sierra had all featured heavily in Xirgu's touring repertoire to Latin America in 1913. Benito Pérez Galdós's 1877 novel *Marianela,* adapted by the Álvarez Quintero brothers, provided Xirgu with an early Castilian-language success at the Princesa theatre in 1916 (George 2002: 160–6). Xirgu went on to perform Pérez Galdós's *Santa Juana de Castilla,* which was written especially for her, at the Princesa in 1918. Benavente first wrote a play for her to premiere, *El mal que nos hacen* (The Evil that is Done to Us) in 1917. She was to go on to open *Una señora* (*A Lady*) in 1920, and *La mariposa que voló sobre el mar* (The Butterfly that Flew Over the Sea), an investigation of the suicide of

---

38 For further details on this programming, see Aguilera Sastre and Aznar Soler 1999: 180–2 and Rodrigo 1974: 183, 186–7.

39 Including those of Dario Niccodemi, Ermete Zacconi and Marie Thérèse Pierat/Aurélien Lugné-Poe. For further details, see Cañizares Bundorf 1999: 168–70.

French actress Geneviève Lantelme, in 1926.[40] Between 1916 and 1927 Xirgu was to appear in a wide range of Benavente's works including *Gente conocida* (Known People) (1916), *Rosas de Otoño* (*Autumnal Roses*) (1918), *La noche del sábado* (*The Witches' Sabbath*) (1922), *La comida de las fieras* (*The Banquet of the Wild Beasts*) (1922), and *La noche iluminada* (The Illuminated Night) (1927). Despite the fact that J. López Pinillos views *El mal que nos hacen* as the production which rendered Xirgu 'la actriz del día' (1920: 143) (the actress of the day), Guansé is of the opinion that Xirgu's production style was not suited to Benavente's work. The naturalistic decor his stage directions specified constricted Xirgu within the trappings of realism. As such she tended to favour Benavente's more fantastical works like *El dragón de fuego* (The Dragon of Fire) (1918), which reflected a taste for exoticism that was also to be played out on the Spanish stage in Manolita Chen's vaudeville shows. Guansé attributes Xirgu's serious consideration of Spanish drama to her gaining concession of the Español in 1920 where it would have been considered irreverent to stage foreign works in translation (1988: 49).

These years were to see a 're-theatricalisation' of the Spanish stage visible in the ideas around cinematic influence, visual performance and the 'non-reality' of the stage debated by thinkers like Ortega y Gasset, as well as the plasticity of the theatrical models put forward by such dramatists as Ramón Gómez de la Serna and Ramón del Valle-Inclán.[41] Although Xirgu had staged Valle-Inclán's *El yermo de las almas* (The Wilderness of Souls) in 1915, helping him negotiate the transition from novelist-poet to dramatist, he was to resent having the work performed, claiming he wrote it under the ill-fated influences of Henri Bataille and Henri Bernstein (cited in Guansé 1988: 47–8). Relations were to be further strained by his vocal protests at a performance of Joaquín Montaner's *El hijo del diablo* (The Devil's Son) at the Fontalba in 1927 in which Xirgu appeared. They were not to collaborate again until Rivas Cherif directed *Divinas palabras* (*Divine Words*) in 1933.

Certainly the association with Rivas Cherif in the period following 1930 was to see Xirgu's espousal of a more imagistic theatre, but any examination of her repertoire at the Español during the period between 1930 and 1935 displays an eclectic programme of writers from Benavente to Joaquín Dicenta – both part of the 1933–34 season – Calderón to Marquina, Antonio and Manuel Machado to Unamuno. The Machados's *La duquesa de Benamejí* (The Duchess of Benameji), an epic Hugoesque work set during the Napoleonic invasion at beginning of the nineteenth century, was presented in early 1932, while Unamuno's reworking of the Cain and Abel legend, *El otro* (The Other), came in December of the same year.[42] In 1934, at the Español, Xirgu was also to premiere the Lope de Vega Prize-win-

40 The latter play was dedicated to Xirgu: 'A Margarita Xirgu, con la promesa que ella estrenará mi última obra' (cited in Rodrigo 1974: 137) (To Margarita Xirgu, with the promise that she will premiere my latest play).

41 For examples of Ortega y Gasset's writings on the theatre, see Ortega y Gasset 1963 and 1982.

42 For further information on these productions, see Aguilera Sastre and Aznar Soler 1999: 181, 219–23.

ning play, *La sirena varada* (The Stranded Mermaid), written by the director of the Teatro del Pueblo de Misiones Pedagógicas, Alejandro Casona.[43] Casona dedicated the play to Xirgu and the production was to initiate a collaboration which was to see *Otra vez el diablo* (The Devil Again) staged at the Español in 1935 in a production designed again by Siegfried Burmann with music by Enrique Casals of the Teatro Escuela de Arte. At the outbreak of the Civil War the fate suffered by fellow dramatist García Lorca precipitated Casona's flight from Spain. He settled in Argentina where he continued to work as a dramatist, collaborating with the Díaz-Collado touring company who premiered many of his new works in the 1940s and early 1950s. *La dama del alba (Lady of the Dawn),* however, was premiered by Xirgu, opening on 3 November 1944 at Buenos Aires' Avenida theatre with Xirgu in the title role.[44] Casona's tale of a grief-stricken family separated from a beloved daughter may well have struck resonant chords with Xirgu and her company, made up, in part, of fellow exiles. Unlike Xirgu, Casona was to return to Spain in the 1960s. Writing to Xirgu in 1965 following the Madrid restaging of *La sirena varada,* he observed how the press, commenting on the fact that Burmann had also been responsible for the decor, recalled the memorable premiere with Xirgu and Enric Borràs in 1934 (cited in Rodrigo 1974: 316–17). Even in exile Xirgu was evoked as a key interpreter of cutting-edge writing, a phantom presence haunting the regime with past dramatisations enshrined in frozen images and the memories of those who had witnessed her performances.

Rafael Alberti was to prove a more controversial choice of dramatist. The premiere of *Fermín Galán* (directed by Rivas Cherif and designed by Burmann) on 1 June 1931 at the Español attracted veritable controversy in the sensitive political climate which followed the proclamation of the Second Republic in 1931. The theatre's metal emergency curtain, for use only in case of fire, had to come down. Centring on the 1930 insurrection at Jaca by rebel Republican officers, the historical proximity of the incident clearly incensed the more conservative elements of the Spanish press who were unable to reconcile themselves to Xirgu appearing as the icon Virgin descending from her altar with rifle and bayonet in hand.[45] Enrique Díez-Canedo may have praised the ensemble acting (1931: 1), but José de la Cueva was to launch a bitter diatribe in *Informaciones* arguing that Xirgu's poor choice of play – an attempt on Alberti's part to rework the ballad form of the *romance de ciego* towards a politically engaged theatre – indicated that her repertoire should be examined before she be allowed to present another season at the Español (1931: 6). In his autobiography, Alberti notes that Xirgu suffered physical abuse for her

---

43 For further information on this production, see Aguilera Sastre and Aznar Soler 1999: 223–30.
44 For further details, see Rodrigo 1974: 266–7. The production was televised in 1958 following an extensive tour encompassing Uruguay, Chile and Peru.
45 For critical responses to the production, see Monleón 1990: 110–21 and Aguilera Sastre and Aznar Soler 1999: 194–7.

decision to produce the play, slapped in Madrid's Retiro Park by an outraged con-servative *señora* (1987: 14).

In Latin America, her association with Alberti continued. In 1943, as General Director of the SODRE (Servicio Oficial de la Difusión Radioeléctrica) theatre, of the Instituto de Montevideo, then under the patronage of the Uruguay's Ministry of Education, Xirgu surrounded herself with figures who had worked with her in Spain, like the actors Amelia de la Torre and Enrique Diosdado, as well as fellow exiles Isabel and Teresa Pradas and Aurora and Loyda Molina, daughters of the politician Manuel Molina Conejero, who had been shot at the end of the Civil War (Rodrigo 1974: 260–1). Here she was to stage Alberti's *versión libre* of Cervantes' *Numancia* designed by Santiago Ontañón, who had been responsible for the decor of the 1937 production at the Teatro de Arte y Propaganda del Estado (Theatre of Art and Propaganda of the State) at the Zarzuela theatre in Madrid, directed by Alberti's wife, María Teresa León. The casting of Xirgu in the symbolic role of Spain was not lost on the critics who reviewed the production, with one referring to her as 'símbolo de la España desterrada y la más pura tradición de su teatro' (cited in Rodrigo 1974: 262) (symbol of an exiled Spain and the purest tradition of its the-atre) and another commenting on Xirgu's 'recitando, con dolorida voz, las estrofas en que se lloran las amarguras de España' (cited in Rodrigo 1974: 262) (reciting, with a pained voice, the verses in which the grief of Spain is wept over).

In 1944 Xirgu was to premiere Alberti's *El adefesio* (The Absurdity) at Buenos Aires' Avenida theatre. Alberti's grotesque vision of Spain's insularity saw Xirgu disguised in a mask and long beard in the role of Gorgo.[46] The sour, resentful crone of Alberti's play was to have much in common with García Lorca's Bernarda Alba, a role Xirgu was to take on the following year, demonstrating the commitment of the actress to representing works where, as a performer, she could move beyond the limits of a social world where the female is cast in markedly constricted ways. Writ-ten in exile, Alberti's work constructs a deformed image of a country whose motifs and iconography he was to draw upon in crafting his piece. The dismembered hos-tile landscape of the play may stand as a binary opposite to Casona's romanticisa-tion of his Asturian homeland but, through the stagings of both *El adefesio* and *La dama del alba*, Xirgu, as both actress and director, was to re-create a mythical Spain where the female body, as subject rather than object, embodies both the vulnera-bility of the flesh and the corruptibility of the spirit, the site of death and the hope for resurrection. The defiant look back of the female performer from the stage functioned both as a critique of the fetishisation of the female body and as a stark reminder of the nomadism of both playwright and performer/director, unable to stage such depictions of rural seclusion within Spain.

With the premieres of three works during the Second Republic, Valle-Inclán too benefited from the more liberal political climate that followed Primo de

---

46 For a synopsis of *El adefesio,* see Chapter 3, 123. Reviews of the production heaped superlative praise on Xirgu's performance; see, for example, Eichelbaum 1946.

Rivera's dictatorship.[47] Xirgu's corrosive performance as Mari-Gaila, the lustful antiheroine of *Divinas palabras* in 1933 at the Español, however, did not convince the more conservative elements of the press who were soon celebrating the defeat of the centre-left government in the general election held three days after the production opened. Luis Araujo-Costa, writing in *La Época*, expressed alarm at the presentation of 'lo más abyecto, sucio y repugnante de la naturaleza caída. En sus escenas y sus monstruosidades sólo pueden tener satisfacción escatófagos y coprónimos' (1933: 1) (the most degraded, dirty and loathsome aspects of our fallen nature. Only shit-eaters and those who admire excrement can take pleasure in its scenes and monstrosities). While expressing disdain that an actor of Borràs's calibre be obliged to enact as unpleasant a character as the sexton Pedro Gailo, Xirgu is conspicuously absent from Araujo-Costa's review – a reflection perhaps of the unease around Xirgu's sexually licentious role and her marked association with the cultural politics of the centre-left government. Jorge de la Cueva in *El Debate* (1933: 6) and José de la Cueva in *Informaciones* (1933: 7) also voiced unease at the choice of play which they regarded as old-fashioned, poorly structured and bereft of credible characterisation. Juan Chabás, writing in *Luz*, applauded Xirgu, whose 'esfuerzo siempre vigilante e innovador' (vigilant and innovative efforts) have brought this theatrically dynamic work to the stage (1933: 6). Admiration for the play was articulated by M. Fernández Almagro (1933: 8), Manuel Machado (1933: 4) and Félix Paredes (1933: 2), among others, with Alfonso Castelao, Piti Bartolozzi and Pedro Lozano's sets singled out for bringing a touch of the colour and textures of Galicia to the stage of the Español (Chabás 1933: 6). Chabás also expressed dismay at the poor commercial response to the play, which closed after just a two week run.

Xirgu's interpretation of the wayward Mari-Gaila was singled out for praise by a marked percentage of the critics including *ABC*'s C. (1933: 37), *Ahora*'s Alberto Marín Alcalde (1933: 22) and *El Liberal*'s Arturo Mori (1933: 6). The contrasting of Xirgu's less rhetorical performance style with Borràs's more mannered affectivity by Jorge de la Cueva (1933: 6) and Buenaventura L. Vidal (1933: 9) aptly indicates how Xirgu had pursued coherent interpretations of character that moved away from the legacy of eighteenth-century gestural theatrics. Borràs/Pedro Gailo was associated with outdated rituals and decay, something perhaps doubly significant in view of Borràs's association with Francoism post 1939, while Xirgu/Mari-Gaila was equated with vitality and reinvention: a point that no doubt engendered Valle-Inclán's observation that 'nunca ha existido una actriz como ésta' (cited in García Pintado 1988: 16) (there has never been an actress like her). Marín Alcalde may have unwittingly articulated some of the unease of the age around female

47 *Farsa y licencia de la reina castiza* (The Licentious Farce of the Chaste Queen) was premiered by the López Heredia company at the Muñoz Seca theatre on 3 June 1931, *El embrujado* (The Bewitched) by the same company at the same theatre on 11 November 1931. *Divinas palabras* was the last work to be premiered during the author's lifetime opening at the Español on 16 November 1933. For a synopsis of the play, see Chapter 4, 151–2.

power and political redemption when he bemoaned the fact that *La Celestina*, Fernando de Rojas's tale of female sorcery, is never seen on the contemporary Spanish stage (1933: 22). The public staging of female insurrection, articulating the desires of the female subject within the proscenium frame, was in some ways as contentious in 1933 as it had been in 1910 when Xirgu first performed in *Salomé*. Even in her artistic ventures with García Lorca, Xirgu's personification of the *nerveuse* may have struck a chord in an audience with a strong female component, but it continued to dismay those who perceived gender in strict binary ways.

Intersections with García Lorca

He de manifestarle mi agradecimiento y expresarle de manera fría y razonada la profunda admiración que siento por su labor en el teatro de nuestro país; porque ella es la actriz que rompe la monotonía de las candilejas con aires renovadores y arroja puñados de fuego y jarros de agua fría a los públicos dormidos sobre normas apolilladas.

Margarita Xirgu tiene la inquietud del teatro, la fiebre de los temperamentos múltiples. Yo la veo siempre en una encrucijada, en la encrucijada de todas las heroínas, meta barrida por un viento oscuro donde la vena aorta canta como si fuera un ruiseñor. (García Lorca 1996c: 194)

(I have to show her my gratitude and indicate to her in a cool and rational way the profound admiration that I feel for her work in our country's theatre; because she is the actress who breaks the monotony of the footlights with the spirit of renovation. She throws handfuls of fire and jars of cold water at the audiences sleeping through moth-eaten conventions.

Margarita Xirgu has the restlessness of the theatre, the fever of multiple temperaments. I always see her at a crossroads, at the crossroads of all heroines, an objective swept by a dark wind where the aorta sings as if it were a nightingale.)

Ángel García Pintado sees Xirgu's trajectory as marked by two key features: boldness and generosity. For him, the latter was probably visible most clearly in her promotion of and faith in the dramaturgy of Federico García Lorca (1988: 15). Too often, Xirgu is viewed as a supporting player in García Lorca's evolution from poet to dramatist. A tendency to see her as his muse ultimately denigrates her own achievements, viewing them as subservient to his literary endeavours. His own comments on their relationship, his dedication of a poem to her – 'Prendimiento de Antoñito el Camborio en el camino de Sevilla' (Arrest of Antoñito el Camborio on the road to Seville) – as well as interviews given by both practitioners during the period between 1927 and 1936 indicate that Xirgu may have shaped the Granadine's theatrical vision in ways which are too rarely acknowledged.

The dramatist and critic José R. Morales recalls Xirgu telling him that García Lorca cried as his first play, *El maleficio de la mariposa* (*The Butterfly's Evil Spell*) was shouted down by the audience when first produced by Martínez Sierra at the Eslava theatre in 1920 (cited in Joven 1982: 109). Despite a bold design by Fernando Mignoni and costumes by Rafael Pérez Barradas, the production was perceived as an embarrassing failure (Vilches de Frutos and Dougherty 1992a: 13–14, 23–32).

There was little doubt of García Lorca's poetic abilities, but, as Manuel Machado (1920: 2) and F. Aznar Navarro (1920: 4) noted in their reviews of the production, these had yet to show themselves on the stage which demands an intricate tension between the verbal and the visual. According to Morales, García Lorca appeared to have reached the decision, at that moment, not to do any more theatre (cited in Joven 1982: 109).[48]

During the difficult years of the Primo de Rivera dictatorship (1923–30) it is hardly surprising that García Lorca struggled to find a producer for his 1924 play *Mariana Pineda,* a romantic treatment of the nineteenth-century Granadine martyr. As Dru Dougherty has observed, an extensive number of theatrical figures were to play a part in trying to get the work staged (2000: 17, 22). After Martínez Sierra refused to stage it, probably in fear of recriminations from the regime but also perhaps because his mistress, the actress Catalina Bárcena, was then pregnant, García Lorca is known to have approached the actresses Carmen Moragas and Josefina Díaz de Artigas. When García Lorca first met Xirgu in the summer of 1926, through the Cuban writer Lydia Cabreras, he voiced concerns that Xirgu might not stage the work when she realised how many others had turned it down, but Xirgu remained firm that if she liked the work she would (Rodrigo 2000: 33–4). There can be little doubt that Xirgu's decision to stage a work which dealt with an icon of the nineteenth-century struggle for republican independence would be viewed with suspicion at a time when Primo de Rivera's tight control appeared to be under question with military officers 'in open rebellion against his projected reform of the promotion system' (Álvarez Juno 1999: 81).[49] The uncertain political situation may well have motivated Xirgu's hesitation for she did not agree to produce the play until 1927 and its position in the season after Marquina's *La ermita, la fuente y el río* may well have been due to its political resonances as much as to Xirgu's recognition of its dramatic flaws: flaws identified by García Lorca who distanced it from his current theatrical interests, calling it 'the frail work of a beginner' (cited in Stainton 1999: 211).[50]

The play was premiered in Barcelona by Xirgu's company at the Goya theatre on 24 June 1927, later opening at Madrid's Fontalba theatre on 12 October. As Dougherty indicates, it was not a commercial success with only six performances in Barcelona and a further twenty-six in Madrid (2000: 26). The production is now perhaps best remembered for Salvador Dalí's stylised, curvacious set – it was the only staging on which García Lorca and his friend from the Residencia de Estudiantes were to collaborate. Critical opinion was on the whole positive with a few dissenting views lamenting the outdated artificiality of the play and Dalí's ill-suited

---

48 García Lorca's biographer, Leslie Stainton, however, makes reference to the various production projects he was involved with between 1920 and the writing of *Mariana Pineda* in 1924; see Stainton 1999: 102–6, 112.

49 The fact that Primo de Rivera was an admirer of Xirgu may also have held some sway in allowing the play to be presented. Rodrigo (1974: 127) refers to an interview with Xirgu which mentions that Primo de Rivera may have assisted her company in 1923 in getting sets and costumes transported to Argentina.

50 For further details, see Dougherty 2000: 24–5 and García Lorca 1996c: 194–6.

decor.[51] The identification between Xirgu – a friend of the future president Manuel Azaña who had attended the reading of the play in March 1927 – and the emblematic heroine was to shape an increasing perception of Xirgu as a markedly politicised figure. As both performer and producer her freedom to choose roles rendered her a powerful figure, which Rodrigo implicitly recognises when she refers to her as 'la piedra del teatro lorquiano' (2000: 39) (the rock of Lorcan theatre). As the film critic Thomas Harris expounds, 'the star system is based on the premise that a star is accepted by the public in terms of a certain set of personality traits' which permeate his or her roles (1991: 40). Xirgu's decision to perform García Lorca's protracted prelude to Mariana's death served to establish her as a powerful social icon, carrying the ideological values of artists censored by the regime.[52] In depicting a situation of insurrection, the production allowed an outlet for emotions that were severely controlled by the dictatorship. Guansé's categorisation of the production as the revelation 'de un poeta lírico con temperamento dramático' (1988: 60) (of a lyric poet with a dramatic temperament) echoes Díez-Canedo's review of the production, which thanked Xirgu for opening her doors to García Lorca, tacitly acknowledging the risk she had taken. In drawing a parallel between Dalí's design and Picasso's ground-breaking aesthetic, Díez-Canedo positioned this venture at the vanguard of theatrical practice in Spain (1968: 131–4). Even such dissenting reviewers as *La Vanguardia*'s R. C. recognised the innovative nature of Dalí's set (1927: 15). As the epigraph to this section makes clear, García Lorca was quick to recognise his debt to Xirgu and visibly displaced praise to the actress when *Mariana Pineda* was lauded by Ruiz Carnero, the editor of *El Defensor de Granada*, during a run in the city in 1929.[53]

In his statement that 'un teatro es, ante todo, un buen director' (cited in Vilches de Frutos and Dougherty 1992b: 241) (a theatre is, above all, a good director), García Lorca was to recognise that performance can never be replaced by what remains of the text. García Lorca's revision of his work in rehearsal – he was credited as director for *Mariana Pineda* and assisted Rivas Cherif on *La zapatera prodigiosa* (*The Shoemaker's Prodigious Wife*) that opened at the Español on 24 December 1930 – points to the importance the rehearsal process was to occupy in shaping his dramaturgy. The remains of a play like *El público* (*The Public*), which was unstaged in his lifetime, can only ever remain a partial document of what might have been. With *La zapatera prodigiosa*, García Lorca added the prologue to the play during rehearsals and he was to perform it himself for the Rivas Cherif production. He is also known to have worked with Salvador Bartolozzi on the garish set and costume design. For García Lorca, the production's success had much to do with

51 For further details, see Vilches de Frutos and Dougherty 1992a: 39–42. For photographs of the production which indicate the decorative characteristics of Dalí's set, see Comisión Nacional del Centenario García Lorca 1998: 268.
52 García Lorca's *El amor de don Perlimplín con Belisa en el jardín*, rehearsed at Rivas Cherif's El Caracol, was to be closed down by the authorities in February 1929. For further details, see Stainton 1999: 200–5.
53 The play was also subsequently dedicated to her (García Lorca 1996b: 82).

Xirgu's performance as the animated wife: 'dio al personaje un ritmo y un color que le valió un triunfo' (cited in Rodrigo 1974: 163) (she gave the character a rhythm and colour which served to make it a triumph). Xirgu's articulated awareness of García Lorca's musical and visual sense – 'Veía la escena como pintor, y el desarrollo de la acción como músico'[54] (cited in Rodrigo 2000: 38) (He saw the scene like a painter and the development of the action like a musician) – and support of his involvement in rehearsals may have well been a factor, according to García Lorca's biographer Ian Gibson, in encouraging 'the poet to continue writing for the theatre' (1989: 307).

García Lorca's association with La Barraca, the student theatre company funded by the Republic, between 1931 and 1935, served as an apprenticeship for the aspiring dramatist, allowing him to remove the Golden Age dramatic canon from the libraries where it had languished and take it to the streets where it could be revised, restaged and reformulated for the demands of the age. Indeed García Lorca was to rework *La dama boba* (*The Stupid Lady*) which was presented by Xirgu's company as part of the Lope de Vega tricentenary celebrations in 1935. For Stainton, the experience of producing theatre was to teach García Lorca, as it had Shakespeare and Molière before him, how to write plays, for he drafted *Bodas de sangre* in less than four weeks (1999: 298).[55] Gibson views *Bodas de sangre* as written 'almost certainly' for Xirgu (1989: 314–15), but it was to be Josefina Díaz de Artigas and Manuel Collado's company which premiered the play in 1933 at the Beatriz theatre. Xirgu's company staged the play, with Rivas Cherif directing, in November 1935 at Barcelona's Principal theatre on an angular set designed by José Caballero. Xirgu's performance as the Mother was singled out by María Luz Morales in *La Vanguardia* – 'una maravilla de composición: sobria de aliento trágico [. . .] Esa figura hierática, silenciosa, amargada, de dramatismo contenido, interno, profundo tiene escaso contacto con las figuras de las otras heroínas del teatro' (1935b: 11)[56] (a wondrous composition: sober with a tragic pulse [. . .] That severe figure, silent, bitter, with a contained drama, internalised, deep, has scant contact with other theatrical heroines) – and was much admired by García Lorca who told journalists that this production constituted the play's real premiere (1996c: 617).[57]

With *Yerma* too he appears to have written the play with Xirgu in mind, although the actress was aware of the fact that once in Montevideo in October 1933 he might feel pressurised to allow Lola Membrives to premiere it (cited in Stainton

54 For a discussion of the production and its critical reception, see Vilches de Frutos and Dougherty 1992a: 47–8, 52, 65.

55 In an interview with Nicolás González Deleito in 1935, however, García Lorca (1996c: 565) claimed that the work was conceived over a five-year period.

56 Bernat y Durán's review (1935) recognises the importance of Xirgu's contribution in its very title: 'En el Principal Palace. *Bodas de sangre*. De Federico García Lorca, interpretada por Margarita Xirgu' (At the Principal Palace. *Blood Wedding*. By Federico García Lorca, performed by Margarita Xirgu). Artis (1935b) is similarly impressed with Xirgu, categorising her as indispensable to the success of the staging.

57 For a selection of eleven production photographs which provide a strong indication of the production's aesthetic, see Comisión Nacional del Centenario García Lorca 1998: 276–8.

1999: 328). While Stainton suggests that this does appear to have been the case, the fact that García Lorca appears to have been unable to finish the play before leaving Latin America led him to inform Membrives that the play had been written for Xirgu. He then offered Membrives *Así que pasen cinco años* (*When Five Years Pass*) which Xirgu had been uncomfortable about staging in 1930 when she opted instead for *La zapatera prodigiosa* (Stainton 1999: 346–51, 377; Hernández 1979: 292–5). Rivas Cherif is known not to have shared Xirgu's faith in the play (Aguilera Sastre and Aznar Soler 1999: 263), and this may be partly recognised in Díez-Canedo's review of the production which, while commending Rivas Cherif, who was to go on to direct the premiere of *Doña Rosita*, cites Xirgu as García Lorca's most loyal actress (1934: 3). Indeed, after the first-night curtain call, García Lorca remarked to the actress that 'Tu mano me sacó a escena por primera vez [. . .] Tú me diste la mano entonces y sigues dándomela' (cited in Rodrigo 1974: 208) (Your hand led me to the stage for the first time [. . .] You gave me your hand then and you continue to give it).

Reviews of the opening night of *Yerma* on 24 December 1934 were split along predictably polarised lines, testifying to the political tensions that were soon to erupt in civil war. Certainly numerous conservative elements had not forgiven Xirgu for presenting Alberti's controversial *Fermín Galán* in 1931. In addition, the fact that Manuel Azaña, playwright, Minister of War from 1931 to 1933, and later President of the Republic between 1936 and 1939 had been released from prison in Barcelona, where he had been held since 10 October, incensed right-wing ideologues. Azaña, a friend of Xirgu who was married to Rivas Cherif's sister Lola, had been arrested on 8 October for supposedly aligning himself with the establishment of a Republican government in Catalonia. On his release Xirgu had offered him and his wife access to her home in Badalona. In December 1931 Xirgu had produced Azaña's *La corona* (The Crown) at Barcelona's Goya theatre, later opening at the Español in Madrid on 12 April 1932. Clearly such affiliations were to mark Xirgu as a Republican sympathiser and she was increasingly to be seen as a subversive figure. As José Luis Salado, the critic of *La Voz,* indicates: 'Para mucha gente, nombrar a Lorca es nombrar al diablo [. . .] Como la última obra de Lorca que ha estrenado Margarita Xirgu [. . .] y como Margarita Xirgu ofreció su casa en Barcelona al señor Azaña [. . .], consecuencia: que *Yerma* está muy mal' (cited in Hernández 1979: 309) (For many people, to name Lorca is to name the devil [. . .] As with the latest Lorca play which Margarita Xirgu has premiered [. . .] and as Margarita Xirgu offered her house in Barcelona to Mr. Azaña [. . .], the result: *Yerma* is very bad). Right-wing diatribes against the play included those of *ABC*'s C. who found the 'sensualidad franca y descarada' (cited in Hernández 1979: 309) (open and brazen sensuality) distasteful. *La Nación* and *El Siglo Futuro* also responded with predictable degrees of outrage to the play's arresting treatment of desire and infertility (cited in Hernández 1979: 301–2). Throughout, Xirgu seemed healthily aware of the fact that those who attacked the production so vehemently in print were responding publicly to her Republican associations (cited in Rodrigo 1974: 205).

The premiere itself was disrupted by insults hurled at the actress, García Lorca and the absent Azaña. The hecklers were soon cleared from the auditorium and the remainder of the performance continued undisturbed (Morla Lynch 1958: 432–6; Gibson 1984). The more progressive critics endorsed the production unequivocally, commenting on Manuel Fontanal's suggestive evocation of a whitewashed village and the admirable choral work undertaken by Rivas Cherif.[58] Running to 20 April 1935, the production was to clock up one hundred and fifty performances in its run – including a 2.00 a.m. performance for fellow actors who recognised that the venture 'destaca muy indiscutiblemente en nuestra contemporánea producción' (cited in Hernández 1979: 308) (undoubtedly stands out amongst contemporary stagings). The production and play both came to be identified with Xirgu whose personification of the barren Yerma enacted an increasingly rebellious female sexuality, which moved the plot forward. Díez-Canedo's recognition of the presence of a different kind of audience, which heralded a break with the old and the ushering in of the new (1934: 3), points to the production's expression of cultural dissent, denaturalising and subverting dominant gender roles and overtly indicating the ideological struggles of the time (see Figure 2).

The attendance of liberal dignitaries like Unamuno and Ortega y Gasset at the premiere, as well as Valle-Inclán and Azaña's presence at a homage to Xirgu and García Lorca at the Español in February 1935 where she was publicly thanked for her support of the ex-prime minister, served to further consolidate the credentials of the actress as a purveyor of socially committed theatre which recognises performance's role in conditioning and shaping what we see rather than simply reproducing it. For the Barcelona run at the Barcelona theatre (from 17 September to 20 October), Xirgu's recognition of the volatile responses which the play was capable of generating led to a note being added to the programme, verifying the Catholic credentials of the work (Vilches de Frutos and Dougherty 1992a: 103). The Barcelona opening, however, was marked only by a clamouring for tickets and animated clapping after every scene (Stainton 1999: 404; Anon. 1935b: 27).[59] García Lorca was once again to acknowledge Xirgu's contribution to the work (Morales 1935a: 10; Palau Fabre 1935: 2), and the Catalan critics were to echo the playwright's view in solidly identifying the actress with the play. Again it was Xirgu who was the focus of their admiring comments. *La Veu de Catalunya*'s critic, S., proudly stressed that it was the company of Catalonia's premier actress' that presented the play, commending Xirgu's 'eminent' performance (1935: 9), while *La Vanguardia*'s María Luz Morales went as far as to state that '*Yerma* es Margarita Xirgu' (1935a: 10) (*Yerma* is Margarita Xirgu). The Barcelona run could not be extended because of touring commitments to Tarragona and Valencia where the play was enthusiastically received, and this may well have prompted Guansé's remark that 'La Xirgu y

---

58   See Fernández Almagro 1934. See Hernández 1979: 301–5 for a collection of reviews including Antonio de Obregón's for *Diario de Madrid* and Eduardo Haro's for *La Libertad*. Edwards (1999: 435–7) also provides a further compilation of reviews.

59   It was not uncommon at the time for audiences to express their pleasure at a work by applauding after each scene.

2 Yerma (Margarita Xirgu) kills her husband Juan (Pedro López Lagar) in the final scene of *Yerma* (1934)

García Lorca mantenían en expectación al país. Representasen donde represen-tasen, había cola en las puertas de los teatros' (1988: 60) (Xirgu and García Lorca had the whole country in a state of expectation. Wherever they appeared, there was a queue at the theatre door).[60]

Dona Rosita la soltera, the last of García Lorca's works to be premiered during his lifetime, was produced by Xirgu's company, opening at Barcelona's Principal Palace theatre on 12 December 1935, following *Bodas de sangre* which had opened on 12 November, and running until 6 January 1936. Again the production was directed by Rivas Cherif with Fontanals taking responsibility for the design. Vilches de Frutos and Dougherty recognise that the success of *Yerma* and the prestige of Xirgu served to generate substantial critical and audience interest and the premiere attracted a dozen Madrid critics who travelled into Barcelona especially for the occasion (1992a: 105–7). Questions might have been raised as to whether to posi-tion García Lorca's bittersweet Chekhovian elegy to lost love as a comedy or a tragedy, but reviews were glowingly positive with Xirgu once more being singled out for her performance, skilfully negotiating the transition from a love-struck teenager in a jovial pink dress to an elderly spinster clad in sterile white.[61] No longer were the critics articulating doubts about the tensions between the dramatist and the poet

60 For details of critical and audience responses on the tour, see Stainton 1999: 408.
61 The one dissonant review was by Agustí (1935). Reviews which praise the production and performances include Cruz Salido 1935, Obregón 1935 and Sánchez Boxa 1935.

(Vilches de Frutos and Dougherty 1992a: 107). Now the dramatist prevailed and it was a dramatist with an agenda to address the social and the sexual (García Lorca 1996c: 612–14). As with his previous collaborations with Xirgu, the piece reinscribed the absence of women as subjects by placing on stage female cultures. *Mariana Pineda* had explored allegorical uses of the female as an emblematic image of liberty. *Bodas de sangre* had foregrounded the isolation faced by rural women drawn into arranged marriages. *La zapatera prodigiosa* and *Yerma* had explored marital incompatibility and the problems of childlessness in a society where women are defined by their ability to procreate. Now *Doña Rosita la soltera* mapped out the emotional geography of middle-class women who are unable, or choose not to, marry. Xirgu's performance intricately negotiated the play's comic and tragic registers, leading Eduardo Haro to conclude that Xirgu had provided a 'jalón indestructible para la edificación del nuevo teatro castellano' (1935: 1–2) (an indestructible plank for the construction of a new Castilian theatre), while Lluís Capdevilla referred to her as one of the three or four best actresses currently working in Europe (1935: 2). For Xirgu, as the programme notes to *Doña Rosita* make clear: 'Ninguna ocasión más grata para mí que estrenar una comedia de García Lorca, en el Principal Palace, levantado en el solar del antiguo Principal, donde di mis primeros pasos de actriz' (cited in Rodrigo 1974: 229) (There is no more pleasurable occasion for me than staging a García Lorca play at the Principal Palace, situated at the spot of the old Principal where I took my first steps as an actress).

In January 1936 Xirgu left for Latin America for a planned six months' tour. García Lorca was due to join her there in February but postponed his visit to April to be able to finish *La casa de Bernarda Alba* so Xirgu could stage it in Argentina before returning to Spain. Political events were to intervene and García Lorca was shot soon after the outbreak of the Civil War in Granada in the early hours of 18 or 19 August 1936 (Gibson 1989: 464). Prior to her departure she had told the Catalan daily, *El Día Gráfico*, that the hopes of the Spanish theatre lay with García Lorca (cited in Rodrigo 1974: 233). She last saw him in Bilbao where they gave a joint recital on 26 January and García Lorca watched her perform in *Bodas de sangre* two days later (Gibson 1989: 427). Although there is evidence suggesting that García Lorca had purchased the tickets to join Xirgu in Mexico when the war began (Gibson 1989: 440), he remained in Spain where his cruel death rendered him an early martyr of the Civil War. His name has consequently stood as a potent symbol of a liberal era brutally brought down by an illegitimate alliance of repressive elements keen to curb the path of change on which the elected left-wing Popular Front government was decisively embarking.

With García Lorca in exile

Xirgu's involvement with García Lorca's work did not cease after his death. Her association both with García Lorca with the Popular Front government, which had narrowly won the 16 February elections and whose legitimacy was questioned by the nationalist insurrection of 18 July led by General Franco, were clear obstacles blocking a return to Spain. On 6 October 1935 she had accompanied García Lorca when he gave a public reading at Barcelona's Atheneum to commemorate the first anniversary of the Asturian miners' revolt that had been brutally suppressed by Franco, who had been placed in charge of military operations. On 14 October, García Lorca accompanied her to a performance of *Fuenteovejuna* organised in her honour at the Olimpia Circo theatre where the proceeds gained from the 8,000-strong crowd were targeted to assist the political prisoners still languishing in Spanish prisons. The imprisoned President of the Catalan Government Lluís Companys, Azaña, and the cellist Pau Casals all sent messages of support (Gibson 1989: 417; Stainton 1999: 406–7). Earlier humanitarian gestures including benefits for the Red Cross at Barcelona's Principal theatre in 1909 where she performed alongside Enric Borràs, a benefit in 1931 at the Casa del Pueblo for victims of a labour accident the previous year at Plaza de Cánovas, and another in 1932 at Montjuïc's Grec theatre for the Hospital de la Esperanza, as well as her support of La Barraca and the Teatro del Pueblo, firmly cemented her liberal credentials (Rodrigo 1974: 174).

In addition, her initiation of perhaps the most significant cultural event of the Second Republic, the reopening of the excavated Roman theatre at Mérida in June 1933, with a production of Seneca's *Medea*, pointed to a partisan alliance that the right were unable to condone. Xirgu had procured subsidies for the renovation of the theatre from the Consejo Superior de Cultura and secured the financial involvement of major public bodies. Attended by an audience of 3,000, which included the President of the Republic, Azaña, the Mayor of Madrid, the Italian Ambassador and other political dignitaries, broadcast on the radio and filmed by Gaumont, the outdoor event acquired the notoriety of a political rally (Pérez Coterillo 1983: 18). Guerrero had aspired to stage *Medea* at the theatre, excavated in 1910 by José Ramón Mélida and Maximiliano Macías, but the painted backdrops she had hoped to employ were resolutely opposed by the curators and it wasn't until Xirgu conceived of presenting Seneca's *Medea*, until then unperformed in Spain, in a version by Miguel de Unamuno, using the physical landscape of the theatre, that permission was granted. Dispensing with the sanitised nineteenth-century readings personified in Ernest Legouvé's romantic version, Xirgu presented a resonant spectacle, which envisaged the myth of the abandoned woman as an arresting mother ferociously protecting what remains of her family. Here was a public ceremony of cultural excavation and a daring treatment of infanticide – to be distortedly replayed in the bloody fratricidal conflict that was to erupt in 1936. Resonances of the event must have lingered within the explosive early months of the Civil War.

Even in Latin America she was unable to escape political tainting. Her arrival in Buenos Aires especially, in May 1937, was marked by controversy regarding her political associations and there were vitriolic attempts to stain her as a subversive figure who posed a danger to respectable society (Rodrigo 1974: 246–9). García Pintado collects a selection of these comments:

En Colombia un diario les tilda de 'milicianos y descamisados'; en Perú, es Felipe Sassone el encargado de orquestrar la compañía [*sic*] de la infamia, logrando que la 'buena' sociedad limeña no asista al estreno; en Buenos Aires, la actriz Irene López Heredia[62] pide que se le aplique a la Xirgu la ley de Represión del Comunismo, y Margarita es acosada por algún periodista para que aclare la orientación política de su repertorio. (1988: 19)

(In Colombia, one paper brands them 'militias and down-and-outs'; in Peru, Felipe Sassone is in charge of orchestrating the hate campaign, ensuring that 'respectable' Lima society did not attend the premiere: in Buenos Aires, the actress Irene López Heredia asks that the Repression of Communism law be applied to Xirgu, and Margarita is pestered by a journalist to clarify the political alignment of her repertory.)

The years between 1936 and 1949 were nomadic ones for Xirgu, viewed by María Esther Burgueño and Roger Mirza as dominated by extensive touring across a continent where certain countries were, ironically, as politically volatile as Spain (1988: 21–2). The decision to remain in Latin America may partly have been due to the warm reception she had received on her previous three visits in 1913, 1921 and 1923–24. On her arrival in Buenos Aires on 4 May 1937, Xirgu herself admitted that the city had opened its arms to her before Madrid and that she owed it her consecration as a Castilian actress (cited in Rodrigo 1974: 249–50).

She arrived in Havana in February 1936, where her first husband, Josep Arnall, was to die. In April she left for Mexico where she remained for five months. It was here that Rivas Cherif left her in July 1936 and here where she learnt of the death of García Lorca. Periods at the Colón theatre in Bogotá and the Municipal theatre in Lima were to follow before she ended up in Buenos Aires in May 1937. The repertory during these years was dominated by works by Lenormand, Kayser, Pirandello, Giraudoux, Mauriac, and, of course, García Lorca. Perhaps more so than Membrives, who had premiered a number of García Lorca's works in Argentina in the early 1930s, Xirgu was seen as the faithful cultivator and promoter of García Lorca's legacy in the Americas. The institutionalisation of the dramatist was undertaken not merely through the programming of the García Lorca repertory that she had premiered in Spain, but also through numerous reformulations of the dramatist's work that she was to become involved with. Hers was not a folkloric appropriation of the dramatist and his plays: 'yo creo que en arte no existen exclusivas' (cited in Rodrigo 1974: 305–6) (I don't think there are exclusives in art) was her response to Álvaro Custodio's request to the Spanish Society of Authors for exclusive performance rights for *Bodas de sangre* in Mexico in 1957. On the contrary, she seems to have been willing to associate herself with projects which sought to re-envisage the works within different media. In 1939 at Montevideo's Teatro SODRE she directed a musical reworking of *Bodas de sangre* by Juan José Castro. In 1949 she staged an opera of *La zapatera prodigiosa* by the same composer in Buenos Aires. At the beginning of 1938 she was involved in a film version of *Bodas de sangre* with which she was disappointed, stating to the actor Alfredo Alcón that

62 Burgueño and Mirza (1988: 21–2) erroneously refer to her as Inés López Heredia when they describe the same incident.

the director Guibourg was a fine critic but a poor film director (cited in Burgueño and Mirza 1988: 22).

While Xirgu certainly helped to cultivate a portrait of the dramatist which recognised his constant negotiation of the boundary between truth and lies and the way this was played out in seductive games,[63] she was also instrumental in establishing the beginnings of the García Lorca cult by ensuring that his death was marked with a minute's silence during the performances of his work in 1936 (Rodrigo 1974: 244–5). She was also ferociously active in ensuring that the work moved beyond established proscenium-arch theatres to reach wider audiences. In 1937, while in Buenos Aires, she regularly performed extracts of *Yerma* and *Doña Rosita* on Radio Ridavera.[64] While performing *Yerma* in December 1937 at the city's Smart theatre, she was also involved in a homage to the dramatist entitled 'Cantata en la tumba de Federico García Lorca' (Cantata at the tomb of Federico García Lorca), a stage poem by Alfonso Reyes with music by Jaime Pahissa, another Catalan in exile. In 1952, while touring with the Comedia Nacional de Uruguay, Xirgu was present at the inauguration of a simple stone wall, erected in honour of the dramatist at the Harriague Park in Salto, Uruguay (Rodrigo 1974: 253–4, 291–2).

During the post-Civil War years, García Lorca's work was decisively absent from the Spanish stage. As John London specifies, *Yerma* was staged by the Teatro Experimental in 1947, and a non-commercial staging of *Bodas de sangre* was produced in 1946, but these years witnessed a marked erasure of García Lorca from the major theatres of Madrid and Barcelona (1997: 35). Across Spanish America, however, Xirgu was to forge his institutionalisation, and was greatly in demand to render productions of *Bodas de sangre*, *Yerma*, *Doña Rosita* and *Mariana Pineda*. These works were to feature regularly during her seasons at the SODRE theatre in Montevideo between 1943 and 1945 and later in the 1950s at the Solís theatre, but she also directed *Bodas de sangre* and *La casa de Bernarda Alba* at the Teatro del Bosque in Mexico in 1957 (Rodrigo 1974: 261–306). As an associate of the dramatist, she was consulted in 1956 by a fellow exile, the Paris-based actress María Casares, over a tribute to García Lorca which was to be held in the French capital and which Picasso, yet another Spanish exile based in the city, had pledged to support:

Habíamos pensado organizar un acto conmemorativo; pero a mí me parece que después de todo lo que aquí se ha hecho, tendría interés verdadero organizar un doble homenaje al poeta y a la actriz que *nos lo reveló* [my italics], y representar algunas veces una obra de Lorca en español, dirigida e interpretada por Margarita Xirgu. (cited in Rodrigo 1974: 296)

(We had thought of organising a commemorative act; but it seems to me that, after everything that has been done here, it would be really interesting to organise a double

---

63 For details of these characteristics in the dramatist, see Fernández Cifuentes 1988: 92; see also Stainton 1999: 290, 328, 343–6.

64 This also served to advertise these productions which were then playing at the Odeón theatre; see Rodrigo 1974: 253–4.

homage to the poet and to the actress who *revealed him to us*, presenting a number of performances of a production of Lorca's work directed and performed by Margarita Xirgu.)

She was later to direct Casares in *Yerma*, her first Spanish language production in 1963 at Buenos Aires' San Martín theatre.[65]

While these productions can on one level be seen as gradual displacements of the plays into a romantic context of authorial commemoration, Xirgu's distinctive archival role in promoting an 'unknown' García Lorca should also be acknowledged. García Lorca is known to have read the first act of *Comedia sin título* to Xirgu twice in 1935 and she is thought to have been 'fascinated' by what she heard (cited in Gibson 1989: 409–10). We know from Xirgu that the second act was to occur in a mortuary and the final act in a heavenly sphere populated by Andalusian angels. García Lorca also had plans for the Autor/Author to perish on the streets during the revolution (Rodrigo 1984b: 291–2; Stainton 1999: 420–1). Xirgu's testimony on the 'unknown' García Lorcas has played a role in piecing together some sort of chronology for incomplete works that lay dormant for decades. When García Lorca first read *Así que pasen cinco años* to Xirgu in Madrid's El Pardo in 1930, she viewed it as unstageable. Years later she was to state her desire to see it staged with designs by Salvador Dalí (cited in Rodrigo 1974: 168). But the imaginary pairing of one of García Lorca's most ambitious plays with surrealism's most flamboyant exponent by Spain's most influential performer of the first half of the twentieth century indicates her own recognition of the need for stage practice to re-imagine perceptions of time and space as well as the relationship between representation and the real.

Although García Lorca completed *La casa de Bernarda Alba* in 1936, the sensitive climate of Francoist Spain rendered a high profile premiere problematic. It received a rehearsed reading in Barcelona in 1948 and a minor production by La Carátula in 1950 but its commercial opening in Spain was not to be until 1964 in a production by Juan Antonio Bardem (Cornago Bernal 2001: 311–14; Marqueríe 1950: 21). Indeed for John London

the drastic displacement in the international significance of post-Civil War Spanish drama is marked, and subsequently typified, by the premiere of Lorca's *La casa de Bernarda Alba* in Buenos Aires [. . .] forced abroad, not because it had been acknowledged as being of 'foreign' stature, but simply because of the adverse reaction which greeted (or would have greeted it) in Spain. (1997: 17)

Although Xirgu was not present at the reading of the play which García Lorca undertook for friends in Madrid on 24 June 1936, there is evidence from both García Lorca's and Xirgu's biographers to deduce that the play was written with Xirgu in mind, and indeed her comments to the theatre critic of Uruguay's *La Nación*, Octavio Hornos Paz, on 9 March 1945, indicate that the actress asked García Lorca to write the play for her, wanting the chance to play a hard character who stood in

---

65 For further details, see Chapter 3, 112–13.

opposition to the tenderness of Rosita (cited in Rodrigo 1974: 268). The play reached her in January 1945 via Julio Fuensalida, a friend of the García Lorca family. We know from a letter written to her friend Isabel Pradas, who was to play Adela in Xirgu's staging, that she saw the play as 'tan preciosa o más que las otras de Federico' (cited in Rodrigo 1974: 269) (as beautiful or even more so than Federico's other works). The production premiered on 8 March 1945 at Buenos Aires' Avenida theatre with a cast that included several performers who had appeared in earlier stagings of the dramatist's work (Edwards 2000: 672). An interview given by Xirgu shortly after the work opened indicates her preoccupation as both performer – she was to take the role of Bernarda – and director, with a psychological approach to character which would highlight the humanity of each role (cited in Rodrigo 1974: 269–70). The view of stage director Pedro Álvarez Ossorio that the first initials of the daughters' names spell out a dedication 'a mamá' (cited in Delgado 2000: xiii–iv) (to mother) suggests the ambiguity of a play that may function as both a study of dictatorial oppression and intimidation and an interrogation of familial dysfunction.

The design by Santiago Ontañón, who had worked on the Madrid premiere of *Bodas de sangre* in 1933, proffered an austere penal environment of thick claustrophobic walls. Recognising the power base of her house, to which the title attests, Ontañon provided three different spaces, all distinguished by a harsh coldness: the white room of Act One with curtains adorned with red tassels, the arched passageway of Act Two with the five rooms marked by heavy wooden doors running off it and the large moonlit enclosed *corral* of Act Three.[66] Here Xirgu's Bernarda established her boundaries and limits as Carlos H. Faig's review in *El Hogar* notes: 'adquiere significación de bronce sostenida en la rotundidad de los gestos, en la plenitud de las actitudes, en la seguridad de los tonos dramáticos hasta llegar a las afirmaciones trágicas que son el móvil determinante del asunto' (cited in Rodrigo 1974: 272) (she acquires the signification of bronze sustained through the expressiveness of gesture, though the abundance of body postures, finally reaching the certainty of the dramatic tones and on to the tragic affirmations which are the determining motive of the subject). *La Nación*'s critique, published on 9 March 1945, points to the severity of Xirgu's embodiment of authoritarianism conveyed though her voice and bodily stance (cited in Rodrigo 1974: 272). Both reviews were also to comment on Xirgu's directorial work in fostering an ensemble cast where, when gesture was used selectively, it appeared to gain in significance. Clearly the interplay between silence and malicious accusations which Xirgu's staging was to delineate revealed a microcosm of the larger conflicts played out on Spain's political stages at the time García Lorca wrote the piece. Performed towards the end of the Second World War, as the spectres of fascism were being laid to rest elsewhere in Europe, Bernarda's opening and closing words in the play – 'silencio' (silence) – were to resonate as a defiant comment on the silencing of the dramatist's works which was observed in Spain. In a telegram to Xirgu after the opening of *La casa de Bernarda Alba* García Lorca's father was to praise the role of the actress in keeping alive the dramatist's memory (cited in Rodrigo 1974: 272).

66   For Ontañón's description of the set, see Vilches de Frutos and Dougherty 1992a: 114.

While acknowledging that García Lorca's plays, correspondence, poems and lectures revolve around the presentation of a series of complex coexisting identities which endanger any attempt to determine what the 'truth' of his position might have been, there are enough comments made by García Lorca during the period between the premiere of *Mariana Pineda* in 1927 and his death in 1936 to affirm Xirgu's importance in shaping his theatrical trajectory. At a banquet in 1935 he was to state that 'debo a Margarita Xirgu cuanto he logrado en el teatro' (cited in Rodrigo 1974: 232) (I owe to Margarita Xirgu everything I have achieved in the theatre). Certainly as Vilches de Frutos and Dougherty observe, at the time of his death, García Lorca had published only two dramatic works, *Mariana Pineda* in 1928 and *Bodas de sangre* in 1936 (1992a: 113). As such his reputation lay in the stage works not in the printed word which has now reclaimed him. Writing is often seen as an act of preservation, performance can only ever be a movement towards disappearance. The presence of the García Lorca playtext, in many cases the residue of his collaborative work with Xirgu, may have served to gradually lessen the memory of her impact, but the plethora of roles written by García Lorca for women may remain as the most permanent attestation for even the most entrenched literary critic that the theatrical climate in which the dramatist worked, dominated by companies run by actresses, shaped his dramatic output.[67]

Pedagogy and exile

As early as 1914 in an interview with José María Carretero 'El Caballero Audaz', Xirgu made it clear that, although she may have been associated with the work of Echegaray, Benavente and the Álvarez Quintero brothers, their work was written with other actresses in mind, namely Rosario Pino and María Guerrero: 'veremos el día que yo estrene obras al corte y a medida de mi temperamento' (n.d.: 32) (let's wait for the day that I premiere works tailored to the measurements of my personality), she concluded. The longevity of her association with the dramatist's work and the close nature of their collaboration certainly points to García Lorca as her favoured dramatist. Xirgu, however, also cites the death of García Lorca as one of the reasons she began teaching and he was to remain a palpable presence in the repertory to which students were introduced in the various theatre schools with which she was involved (cited in Rodrigo 1974: 244).

Xirgu was aware of Rivas Cherif's pedagogical incentives in the 1930s, including the Estudio de Arte Dramático (Dramatic Art Studio) that had plans for the students to then pass on into the Xirgu-Borràs company based at the Español theatre.[68] But it was to be in 1942 in Santiago de Chile, where she lived for prolonged periods between 1937 and 1943, that she was to put into operation a venture she

---

67 For an assessment of the importance of these companies run by women on García Lorca, see García-Posada 1982: 86.

68 For further details, see Aguilera Sastre and Aznar Soler 1999: 300–42. García Pintado (1988: 18) also discusses this venture although he refers to it as an Escuela Elemental de Artes y Oficios de Teatro.

originally hoped to undertake in Barcelona: the creation of a theatre school (Rodrigo 1974: 259). Her introduction of García Lorca's work to Chile in the late 1930s is seen by Catherine Boyle as crucial in 'exposing the underdevelopment of Chilean theatre, the unadventurous use of the stage, and the dated treatment of themes' (1992: 26). For Boyle there is a direct link to be traced from Xirgu's presence in the city to the founding of the Teatro Experimental de la Universidad de Chile by a selection of students from the Instituto Pedagógico in 1941. Xirgu's own pedagogical endeavour, a private Drama Academy in Santiago with staff including fellow exiles like the actor Edmundo Barbero, the designer Santiago Ontañón, and the writer and journalist Antonio de Lezama, was initially housed in a space belonging to the Municipal theatre, although it was to eventually become tied to the Ministry of Culture and affiliated to the University of Chile (Rodrigo 1974: 258–64).[69] Here Alberto Closas (1921–94), then in exile, first came into contact with Xirgu, articulating to her his wish to become an actor. 'A ella le debo todo lo que sé' (cited in Rodrigo 1974: 260) (I owe her everything I know), he was to state in 1970. Closas was to remain in Latin America working with Xirgu in her company until the mid-1940s,[70] when he then set up his own touring company before returning to Spain to play the brooding lover Juan (ironically in view of his own exile), an ex-nationalist soldier, in Bardem's seminal 1955 film *Muerte de un ciclista/Death of a Cyclist*. Xirgu was to see something of Enric Borràs in Closas's individualistic virility and alluring physique (cited in Guansé 1988: 63).

In 1943 Xirgu left Chile for Uruguay where at the SODRE theatre she was to forge a programming policy which brought together works by Uruguayan dramatists like Justino Zavala Muñiz as well as Molière, Gogol and Calderón. If Xirgu's first visits to Spanish America had been part of a general Spanish exportation of theatrical and filmic works which sought to compensate for the loss of empire by seeking to exert cultural hegemony, her work within Uruguay and Argentina in the 1940s was to recognise the need to move beyond the 'importation' of foreign work. Touring in towns and cities within the interior of the country and collaborating with Morales and the Cruz del Sur publishing house, Xirgu was to produce performance editions of the works performed by the SODRE company. Handing these out to spectators alongside the programme, Xirgu was to recognise the possibilities for lasting modifications to theatrical infrastructures (cited in Rodrigo 1974: 264).

Although Xirgu had initially been invited to Montevideo to direct *La Celestina* at the Solís theatre in 1949, she was to make Uruguay her base for the remaining

69 Rodrigo (1974: 259–60) associates José Ricardo Morales with Xirgu's venture. Morales was the former director of the student theatre company, El Búho (The Owl). He had fought for the Republicans during the Civil War and then in 1939 left for Chile where he was to work at both the state and Catholic universities in Santiago. In an interview published in the early 1980s, Morales states that he only met the actress in 1944 when she staged his play *El embustero en su enredo* (The Imposter in his Maze), and that his involvement was with the Teatro Experimental de la Universidad de Chile; see Joven 1982: 108.

70 Closas's roles included Cástor in the premiere of Alberti's *El adefesio* in 1944 and Martín de Narcés in *La dama del alba* that same year, both at the Avenida theatre.

twenty years of her life.[71] In Montevideo she was to be appointed director of the Escuela Municipal de Arte Dramático del Uruguay (EMAD), the Municipal Theatre School of Uruguay, officially inaugurated on 12 November 1949 and based at the Solís theatre where she was also to serve as co-director of the Comedia Nacional, the first resident company in Montevideo, established by the City Council in 1947. EMAD today bears her name, and this may be one reason why, in 1982, the journal *Primer Acto* speculated that she might be 'más recordada por los uruguayos que por los españoles' (Anon 1982a: 106) (remembered more by the Uruguayans than by the Spanish). As with fellow Catalan Antonio Cunill Cabanellas, who was to play a key role in formalising actor training in Argentina, Xirgu was to devise a curriculum which recognised the importance of physical education, history of theatre and visual scenography, running across a preparatory course and three years of intensive training (Burgueño and Mirza 1988: 24; Rodrigo 1974: 281–5). In addition to a staff base that included the Russian Vladimir Irmann, and the translator Carlos M. Princivalle, Xirgu was able to draw on eminent performers and directors like Jean-Louis Barrault, Madeleine Renaud and Paolo Grassi, who were visiting the Solís theatre with touring productions. Indeed the building was much admired by Louis Jouvet and itself played host to a range of international performers including Sarah Bernhardt (Rodrigo 1974: 296).[72]

Sharing responsibility for the artistic direction of the Comedia Nacional company based at the Solís with Armando Discépolo and Orestes Caviglia, Xirgu was also able to pursue a policy of cultural expansionism directing pieces by local dramatists like Juan León Bengoa's *La patria en armas* (The Fatherland in Arms), a patriotic exploration of the hero of Uruguayan independence, José Gervasio Artigas, alongside Florencio Sánchez's *Cédulas de San Juan* (The Decrees of St. John), performed by ENAD students. She was also to introduce Jean Giraudoux's poetic dramas to the Uruguayan stage, presenting his final play *La Folle de Chaillot* (*The Madwoman of Chaillot*) as *La loca del Chaillot* in 1951 and, as such, bringing something of the renovative spirit of Giraudoux's partnership with actor/director Jouvet to Uruguayan theatre. Although never seen as a Shakespearean actress, one of her

---

71 Segments of an interview with Xirgu, published in Rodrigo (1974: 279) suggest that it was the offer to direct *La Celestina* which first brought her to Uruguay in 1949. Burgueño and Mirza (1988: 23) state that it was Justino Zavala Muñiz, president of the first Comisión de Teatros Municipales, who initially pursued Xirgu to assume the directorship of the EMAD which the commission were hoping to set up. The difficult political climate in Argentina following the military coup of 1943, which was to see Uruguay receive a significant proportion of political refugees, may also have played a significant part in convincing Xirgu that she was safer within the more receptive climate of Montevideo. Montevideo's rich theatrical culture, which included a consequential number of alternative groups, was to be alarmingly curtailed by the absolutist regime which followed the 1973 military coup. For further details, see Rela 1980.

72 Rodrigo (1974: 296) claims that Bernhardt inaugurated the theatre's electricals on 25 August 1857, a year after the theatre opened with a production of Verdi's *Ernani*. This is not possible as the actress was only thirteen at the time and had not yet commenced her professional career.

rare forays into the canon was embarked on at this time when, in 1954, she was to both direct and perform in *Macbeth*.

Former ENAD students were increasingly to form part of the Solís company. Walter Vidarte (b. 1931), who went on to forge an influential career in Spain as well as Uruguay, appeared in *Macbeth* and as Sosia in the 1956 production of *La Celestina* which toured to Argentina where it was to impress the future Nobel Prize-winning novelist Miguel Ángel Asturias (Rodrigo 1974: 299).[73] Between 1954 and her resignation from ENAD and the Solís in 1957, her touring schedule ensured that the Comedia Nacional de Uruguay become one of the most acclaimed companies in Latin America, visiting Chile with Goldoni's *The Fan* (*El abanico*) in April 1955 and Argentina at what is now the Nacional Cervantes theatre following the fall of Juan Domingo Perón in 1956 with six plays including Thornton Wilder's *Our Town* (*Nuestro Pueblo*) and *La Celestina* (Burgueño and Mirza 1988: 25).[74]

She was to return to direct at the Solís in 1962. Between 1957 and 1962 she was associated with the Summer theatre at Montevideo's Rivera Park where she staged *A Midsummer Night's Dream* (*Sueño de una noche de verano*) and *Don Gil de las calzas verdes* (*Don Gil of the Green Breeches*) in 1957 and helped establish La Casa del Actor for the benefit of elderly actors near her home in Punta Ballena, on the outskirts of Montevideo. While increasingly frail, she was to continue touring with a five-month visit to Mexico beginning in April 1957, and television recordings of *La casa de Bernarda Alba* and *La dama del alba* in Argentina in 1958. At the Solís, in association with Miguel Ortín, she was to stage *Peribáñez y el Comendador de Ocaña* (*Peribañez*) for the Comedia Nacional 1962 in celebration of the four-hundredth centenary of Lope de Vega's birth as well as Cervantes' *Pedro de Urdemalas* in 1966.[75]

In 1967 Xirgu travelled to Smith College, Massachusetts as the first in a series of visiting artists who were to include Eugenie Leontovich and Curt Dempster. Here she was to direct a Spanish-language *Yerma* that was presented between 12 and 14 May following an English translation directed by John G. Fisher, then Chair of the Department of Theatre and Speech, seen from 3–6 May.[76] Xirgu appears to have been hospitalised while in Northampton and Ortín is known to have taken over rehearsals of the piece for a number of days. On her return to Montevideo, in an interview given to *El Día*'s Ángel Curotto, Xirgu mentioned how impressed she had been with the enthusiasm and dedication of the student cast (cited in Rodrigo 1974: 318). Photographs from the production indicate that the costumes clearly followed the line of Fontanals's 1934 designs and Xirgu is known to have worked

73 For details on *Macbeth*, see Burgueño and Mirza 1988: 25.

74 Xirgu's resignation in 1957 appears to have been prompted by the political machinations of Montevideo's Council wishing to assume control of the Comisión de Teatros Municipales. For further details, see Rodrigo 1974: 301–2.

75 For further details of this period, see Rodrigo 1974: 301–20.

76 Rodrigo (1974: 318) claims that she was invited to direct both the English- and Spanish-language versions of the play, but press reports of the production make it clear that Fisher directed the English version; see Anon. 1967a and Anon. 1967b.

closely with the performers, acting out the roles to indicate how they might be done, sharing her knowledge of the play and answering questions and queries 'in a simple, direct, energetic and frank manner' (Kelley 1967: 32).[77]

Sixty years of theatre

Margarita Xirgu died on 25 April 1969 in Montevideo and was buried at the city's Buceo cemetery with a Catalan flag draped over her coffin (Rodrigo 1974: 321–2). Although she was to request that she be buried in Molins del Rei, it was not until 1988, on the centenary of her birth, that the Generalitat, seeking to 'normalise' the use of Catalan through the promotion of culture, was able to oversee the return of her remains to the town where she was born (Badiou 1988: 35). A limited formal tribute was hosted by Mario Cabré at the Romea theatre at the end of January 1970, and Nuria Espert's company had marked the death of the actress with a photograph of Xirgu placed in the foyer of the Poliorama theatre in Barcelona where they were presenting, perhaps appropriately, a groundbreaking production of Genet's *Les Bonnes (The Maids),* presented as *Las criadas,* at the time of Xirgu's death.[78] It was not until the centenary of her birth, however, that her contribution to the Spanish stage was fittingly celebrated with a series of events at the Centro Dramático Nacional and the Español theatre which brought together different generations of critics, directors and performers, including Alberto Closas, Susana Canales, Sancho García, Chicho Ibáñez Serrador and Walter Vidarte, all of whom had worked with her in Latin America (Anon. 1988: 149). Both Felipe González's PSOE government and Pujol's Generalitat were involved in ventures to 're-appropriate' Xirgu as a Socialist artist and a Catalan icon whose association with the cultural initiatives of the Second Republic and status during the Franco era as a symbol of the Republic in exile promoted her as a powerful symbol of democratic aspirations.

Xirgu's political affiliations may have been in part determined by her class background or the industrial unrest she witnessed as a child (Guansé 1988: 31). But they appear to have been played out in more complex ways than a mere association with Azaña whom it is thought she first met when he was president of Madrid's Ateneo where *Mariana Pineda* was first read in March 1927. Xirgu's trajectory is marked by a choice of works that overtly tackled the corrupt political body, social discontent and government injustice. Pérez Galdós's *Santa Juana de Castilla*, presented at Madrid's Princesa theatre in 1918, Alberti's *Fermín Galán* at the Español in 1931, and *Doña María de Castilla*, written by Marcelino Domingo,

---

77 Kelley's report provides a description of Xirgu's activities at Smith which also included her reading of the play, a lecture by Francisco García Lorca who was then based at Columbia, a lecture on García Lorca by a member of staff in the Hispanic Studies Department and the critique sessions which followed the performance of the plays.

78 For details of the Cabré tribute, see Gallén 1988: 13. For the Nuria Espert company's homage, see Primer Acto 1969a: 9. For further information on this production of *Les Bonnes,* see Chapter 4, 140–6.

Azaña's Minister of Agriculture, while imprisoned during Primo de Rivera's dictatorship, and performed by Xirgu in 1933 at the Español, all debated political and social topics around the role of the monarchy, oppositional political formations, and the possibility of promoting radical socio-cultural ideologies in relatively conservative contexts.[79] The staging of Leo Ferrero's anti-fascist drama *Angélica* in 1937 and Alberti's adaptation of *Numancia* in 1943 saw Xirgu's continued investigation into theatre's role as an agent for political change while in exile. *Numancia*, like the 1935 production of *Fuenteovejuna* and García Lorca's reworking of *La dama boba*, again produced by Xirgu in 1935, offered a transformative dismemberment of works which had lain too comfortably within the Spanish repertory and as such posed pertinent questions about the ideological role of the canon in a society seeking to embark on the route to modernisation. While conservative critics may have expressed trepidation at Xirgu's revisionist approach, these productions, following on from the work of La Barraca, renewed audience interest in texts that had been primarily presented through a nineteenth-century theatrical vocabulary.

Xirgu had hoped to return to Barcelona in 1949 with her second husband Miguel Ortín, but, despite the support of Guillermo Díaz Plaja, then director of the Institut del Teatre, it became increasingly clear to Xirgu that the hostile climate of Francoist Spain had not thawed sufficiently to allow her to remain untainted by the political polarities upheld by the regime. Reports of her supposedly imminent arrival and possible plans for a stage production as early as October at the Calderón theatre were accompanied by journalistic tirades from the pens of José Maria Junyent and César González Ruano, who drew attention respectively to the Marxist inclinations of her stage work and her promotion of inappropriate plays like *Salomé* (González Ruano 1949: 2). Gallén holds sway with Ángel Zuñiga's opinion that it was the threatening tone of González Ruano's article which convinced her that she would not be safe in Spain and, therefore, she chose to remain in Montevideo preparing a production of *La Celestina* which premiered at the Solís theatre on 28 October (1988: 12–13). A 1972 article by Xavier Regás in *Tele/eXpres* certainly upholds this view, arguing that González Ruano's resentment of the possible return of the actress to Spain was motivated less by worries of her supposedly 'staining' the patriotic homeland with her unsavoury political affiliations and more by a financial loan he received from Xirgu which he might be forced to pay back with interest should she return (1972: 8). As late as 1966, plans for a Madrid theatre to be renamed in her honour were thwarted by the authorities for whom Xirgu remained a political pariah (Rodrigo 1988: 71).

Franco's centralist regime may also have seen the return of a Catalan icon as problematic at a time when Catalan resistance to the dictatorship was being consolidated within the cultural field. In 1957, the Spanish socialist leader Indalecio Prieto was to equate her with the cellist Pau Casals when he stated that 'corresponde a Cataluña la gloria de haber proporcionado a la emigración republicana española las dos figuras egregias con que ésta cuenta' (cited in Rodrigo 1974: 304)

79 For details on Domingo and other political dramatists of the era, see Castellón 1975: 7–8.

(the glory of having given Spanish Republican emigration its two most eminent fig-ures falls to Catalonia). Although she became equated with the Castilian stage post 1913, her elegant, sonorous voice was never able to totally eliminate traces of the Catalan accent which remained as a constant reminder of her 'otherness' within the national and international stages on which she performed.[80] Certainly on her death, the Catalan press, while not going into the reasons for her exile, was to lament that she had been 'alejada de nosotros durante muchos años' (Anon. 1969a: 4) (distant from us for many years). *Diario de Barcelona* was one of a number of newspapers which guardedly acknowledged her contribution to the Hispanic stage – 'Con Mar-garita Xirgu ha perdido el teatro hispánico una de sus actrices mas importantes' (With Margarita Xirgu Hispanic theatre has lost one of its most important actresses) – while stressing her Catalan credentials – 'catalana de nacimiento y cata-lana siempre en su añoranza de América' (Anon. 1969a: 4) (Catalan by birth and Catalan always in her longing from America). Its photomontage of the actress the following day was accompanied by a headline 'Muere Margarita Xirgu, una cata-lana universal' (Margarita Xirgu has died, a universal Catalan), which was then qualified by a statement which observes that 'llevó el nombre de España por todos los países de habla hispana' (Anon. 1969d: 2) (she took the name of Spain to all Spanish-speaking countries). *El Correo Catalán*'s short report on her death was positioned alongside accounts of civil strife in Belfast and De Gaulle in crisis, as such perhaps allowing readers to draw parallels between the conditions that had led to Xirgu's self-imposed exile (Anon. 1969b: 3). In its subsequent edition, the paper was to echo *Diario de Barcelona*'s line in describing Xirgu as 'una catalana de talla universal' (Anon. 1969e: 36) (a Catalan of universal dimensions) who represented sixty years of theatrical practice. A similar approach was visible in *El Noticiero Uni-versal* where Julio Manegat's appreciation of the actress opens with 'murió una de las máximas figuras de la escena española: la actriz catalana Margarita Xirgu' (1969: 24) (one of the most important figures of the Spanish stage has died: the Catalan actress Margarita Xirgu). The fact that the weekly *Destino* dismissed its theatre critic Federico Roca – interestingly a veritable champion of *teatro independiente* – , following his submission of a tribute to Xirgu which the magazine had commis-sioned, indicates the volatile climate in which the *teatro independiente*'s re-imagin-ing of theatrical discourse was being forged as well as the links between Xirgu and this later generation of practitioners.[81]

In an obituary of Xirgu published in *Primer Acto* in May 1969, the editors ask what lessons can be learnt from Xirgu by those who were not able to see her per-form (Primer Acto 1969a: 8). Their answer refers to the coherence of a body of work that was never safe or commercially inclined. As *La Vanguardia* was also to observe in its assessment of the extensive career of the actress, she was always attracted to dramatists who sought to re-envisage the conceptual possibilities of the

---

80   For observations on her Catalan accent, see Carretero n.d.: 26 and Uriarte n.d.: 194.
81   See Cruz Hernández 1969. For further details of *teatro independiente*, see Chapter 6, 225–8.

stage, analysing rather than describing a particular milieu, and conjuring experiments with narration and character. Néstor Luján's view that Xirgu represented 'todo el teatro de las tres primeras décadas de nuestro siglo en Barcelona' (1969: 66) (all the theatre of the first three decades of our century in Barcelona) is in many ways a comment on her working relationship with the major practitioners of the time: Guimerà, Rusiñol, Benavente, Gual, Rivas Cherif, Casona, Alberti, Valle-Inclán and García Lorca as well as the international leanings of her repertory – a contribution recognised as early as 1935 by *L'Esquella de la Torratxa* (Anon. 1935a: 1481). *El Correo Catalán*'s valuation of Xirgu's contribution to the Spanish stage, published on her death, indicates that the commitment of the actress to Benavente's work during her Madrid years played a vital part in consolidating the dramatist's reputation (Anon. 1969e: 36). In viewing *Yerma* as a metaphor for Xirgu's trajectory – the demanding and unapologetic scream of a woman on a journey – , the author further suggests associations with García Lorca. For *La Vanguardia Española* Xirgu was no less than 'la impulsora y creadora práctica del teatro de García Lorca, cuyas obras, merced a ella, han conquistado posteriormente todos los escenarios del mundo' (Anon 1969c: 5) (the driving and practical creator of García Lorca's theatre, whose works, thanks to her, subsequently conquered all the stages of the world).

The scope of her *oeuvre* may certainly account for Guansé's belief that 'ninguna actriz española había representado en las repúblicas hispanoamericanas un repertorio tan importante como el suyo' (1988: 61) (no Spanish actress had presented such an important repertoire within the Spanish-American republics). This opinion is posited not only on the basis of her introduction of the more avant-garde dramatists like Alberti and García Lorca but also through, during the post-War exile years, the premiering of works which were only seen later in Spain with another generation of performers. These pieces include Alberti's *El adefesio* and Camus's *Le Malentendu* (*Cross Purpose*), which she staged and performed as *El malentendido* in May 1949 at Buenos Aires' Argentino theatre. In the latter case, the production, staged during the Perón dictatorship, was closed down after the third performance by the City Council who deemed the distressing bleakness of the theme unsuitable for the stage. Distress from the country's intellectual community, as Camus's visit to Buenos Aires was imminent, led to the waging of a high profile polemic in the press. Camus cancelled his visit to Argentina in protest and Xirgu refused to return there until after Perón's fall in 1956.[82] *Diario de Barcelona*'s assessment of Xirgu as 'la primera actriz de América Latina' (Anon. 1969a: 4) (the premier actress of Latin America) may have as much to do with her political credentials as her pedagogic practice and theatrical endeavours.

For the Spanish critic Díez-Canedo, Xirgu's merits lie in her pursuit of complex theatrical works: 'los buenos comediantes parecen aún mejores en lo difícil' (1968: 23) (good performers appear even better in difficult works), he remarked of

---

82   For further details, including a letter from Camus to Xirgu in appreciation of her efforts, see Rodrigo 1974: 273–9.

her performance in Unamuno's *El otro* in 1932. Because she was such a strong and able performer, dramatists seemed willing to craft works for her that decisively displaced the male from centre stage. If Spanish dramatists like Benavente, Valle-Inclán and García Lorca are often credited with having composed plays around the dichotomies of female subjectivity, then Xirgu's characterisation of these roles served to widen the debate of what constitutes a female subject with multiple and at times seemingly contradictory identities rather than the simplistic angel/whore binarism reverberating across to the audience. With women's individuality too often ignored on stage and regimentally controlled in society, Xirgu broke the mould. The variety of the roles she enacted transcended the immediate relationship of empathy. Although Xirgu herself preferred to work within the tragic or dramatic register – 'siempre he notado que lo dramático llega más al corazón del público' (I have always noticed that the dramatic reaches further into the audience's heart) she remarked to Carmen de Burgos (n.d.: 38) around 1920 – she was able to move between the *coquette*, *nerveuse*, *tragédienne* and comic with veritable ease. In this respect she differed from her contemporaries like Catalina Bárcena and Lola Membrives. Bárcena, who had trained with Guerrero, lacked Xirgu's penchant for tragedy and Membrives seemed a more volatile performer constantly at the mercy of a passionate pressure that rose uncontrollably to the surface. While certain critics may have sought to orchestrate a myth that positioned these performers competitively across each other in the quest to gain male approval, Xirgu was always generous in acknowledging the contribution of her female contemporaries to the renovation of the Spanish stage (Higuera Rojas 1980: 113). Guerrero was perhaps her most conspicuous Spanish role model but, as Jesús Rubio Jiménez has indicated, both could be seen as indicative of facets of the two Spains that were to implode in 1936 (2000: 189). Despite her popularity Guerrero relied on the patronage of the aristocracy and they were her most robust fans. Xirgu's appeal lay within the emergent middle classes from which the intelligentsia came and her political allegiances differed from those of the more conservative Guerrero.

Xirgu's own frame of performative reference was decisively shaped by international performers. On numerous occasions she expressed admiration for Eleonora Duse who was performing in Havana in *La Città Morta* (The Dead City) when Xirgu was also on tour there in 1923–24. She had not seen Duse when she played at Barcelona's Novetats theatre in D'Annunzio's *La Gioconda* in 1900, but her remarks to Carmen de Burgos in around 1920 about a love of Italian actresses (n.d.: 38) seem to indicate that the exhaustive preparation and expressive countenance of Italian *tragediénnes* like Adelaide Ristori – who had toured South America in 1869 and 1874 – were to prove a significant influence for her.[83] Borràs's comment that Xirgu 'se cree una Duse' (Carretero 1943: 271) (she thinks she's a Duse), while

---

83 For information on Ristori in South America, see Bassnett 1996: 158–9. We know that Xirgu cherished a signed portrait Duse gave her when they met in 1923 as Duse was on the way to North America where she was to die the following year; see Burgueño and Mirza 1988: 21.

acknowledging Xirgu's debt to the Italian actress, is often interpreted as a reprimand of what he perceived as her divaesque tendencies, but it may perhaps also indicate Borràs's provincialism and increasing discomfort at playing a secondary role to Xirgu within the panorama of the contemporary theatre scene. Emilio Thuillier too appears to have been disparaging of Xirgu's dramatic persona, 'a mi entender, el "Champagne Codorniú" de las actrices' (cited in Uriarte n.d.: 166) (to my understanding, like the Codorniú cava to champagne). Xirgu and Thuillier appear to have fallen out during their 1913 tour to Latin America where, like Borràs, he seems to have resented playing second fiddle to the much younger performer within a rigidly hierarchical company system (Carretero n.d.: 29–30).

While it is possible to see parallels with the 'simple and understated' (Whitton 1987: 98) acting of the Paris-based Russian Ludmilla Pitoëff, who Xirgu saw in Shaw's *Saint Joan* in Madrid in 1926 while she too was performing Shaw's rebellious martyr, it is perhaps with Bernhardt that she is most often compared. Ricard Salvat (1988: 19) echoes *El Correo Catalán*'s view (Anon 1969e: 36) that Xirgu was to repeat many of the successes of the French actress. One of these was her appropriation in 1938 of Hamlet, the eponymous protagonist of Shakespeare's tragedy. The gender recasting permitted a disarming of the audience, in allowing the angry rivalry with his dead father to acquire an Oedipal dimension. The ambiguously sexual nature of the Hamlet/Ophelia encounter and the repositioning of the Gertrude/Hamlet relationship away from a simplistic male reverence and fear of the maternal body also served to render this just as radical a reading as Bernhardt's. It is worth considering that, while Xirgu's Shakespearean ventures were few, the choice of plays was significant: *Macbeth*, staged while in exile, as a study of the execution of dictatorial power, the fear of the erotic feminine and the frayed ties of the family unit; *A Midsummer Night's Dream*, García Lorca's favourite Shakespearean work, whose intertextual traces linger in *Comedia sin título*; and *Hamlet*, a mercurial feminisation of the agonised prince.

Xirgu certainly distinguished herself through her portraits of rebellious, defiant (anti)heroines. Her resolution and strength of character were to see her increasingly turn to directing. She appears to have been an adventurous presence in the rehearsal room, urging performers to try something different, even when the first easy option appeared to work (Guansé 1988: 52). As with the French nineteenth-century actress Rachel Felix, 'the Romantic aura of an untutored "genius" continued to surround her, all her life' (Stokes 1996: 69), but Xirgu was a voracious reader who read in Italian and French as well as Catalan and Castilian. An admirer of the writings of the medic Gregorio Marañón, whom she tried to persuade to write for the stage (Guansé 1988: 49–50), she was to bring something of the scientific investigation of behaviour to the psychological crafting of her roles. Discipline appears to have been crucial to her work both in rehearsal and in actor training, as she made clear to a critic following a performance of *La Celestina* in Buenos Aires in 1956: 'el actor debe estudiar duramente, hasta convertir su cuerpo en una máquina perfecta y sensible' (cited in Rodrigo 1974: 298) (the actor needs to study harshly to convert his body into a perfect and sensitive machine).

Despite the mechanistic approach suggested by this remark, what appears to have distinguished Xirgu's work was the meticulous study that marked out each play she chose to appear in and/or direct. Narcís Oller, who had provided the version of Guiseppe Giacosa's *Sad Loves* (*Tristos amors*) which Xirgu performed in 1908, states in his memoirs that from the first day of rehearsals she differed from the rest of the cast in having memorised her role, an unusual occurrence in that most performers of the time tended to learn the role from a prompter (cited in Gallén 1988: 7). Adrià Gual in his memoirs writes of her willingness to listen and to make physical the comments given in rehearsal (1960: 208). Guansé also draws attention to her detailed preparation and her unwillingness to improvise (1988: 40). He also posits the possibility of Xirgu possessing a photographic memory when he states that 'le bastaba leer una página para sabérsela al dedillo, de cabo a rabo, sin un error, sin inventar ni una palabra' (1988: 31) (she only had to read a page to know it by heart, word for word, without an error, without inventing a single word). Xirgu herself refers to studying prospective works after evening performances, reading the play three or four times, then reading it quietly and then more loudly until she had memorised it, which is when she began the psychological preparation and musical tuning (cited in Rodrigo 1974: 228; Uriarte n.d.: 196). Tough in rehearsals and intolerant of lateness or absences, she was, like Rivas Cherif, to see the preparatory process as an intrinsic component of the production. Indeed, the actor Enrique Guitart mentions that she refused to allow performers to read or smoke during rehearsals, expecting them to be present in the room even when their own scene was not being rehearsed (cited in Montero Alonso 1969: 5).

While Xirgu may have identified with some of the roles she was to enact, she came across as a performer always consciously in control of her identification. Her protagonists like Yerma might lose control, but Xirgu's performance was dominated by a restraint that prevented that marked identification of actress with character which is such a trait of realistic acting. The disruptive power of her performance in *Yerma* may explain why Díez-Canedo chose to provide such an extensive review of the production in 1934 (1934: 3). Despite the fact that from 1910 she was a major celebrity, feted in the streets, monitored for her response to any major theatrical event and accompanied by daily press reports when she was in rehearsal, her performances were all rooted in a personality that never swamped the role. Her theatrical representation appeared grounded in the delicate interplay between personality and role, and it was this that allowed her to stretch her repertoire beyond the boundaries of convention.[84]

In this she was aided by a number of key advisers whose counsel she was to prudently solicit. In the early days these included the translator Salvador Vilaregut

---

84 Rodrigo (1974: 121) cites an article by Valentín de Pedro which records the feverish crowd response to 'La Xirgu's' presence at a balcony of the Hotel París by Madrid's Puerta del Sol as Pérez Galdós's funeral cortege passed by. Xirgu's association with bullfighters like José Gómez Ortega 'Gallito', the grand celebrities of the day, also served to widen her iconic status. For Xirgu's love of bullfighting and other outdoor spectacles, see Uriarte n.d.: 196–7.

who advised her to team up with the powerful impresario Faustino da Rosa – the figure behind her transition to Castilian-language theatre – as well as Adrià Gual, whose pioneering work at the Íntim was to help consolidate Barcelona's status in the early decades of the century as the more radical city for theatrical innovation.[85] Rivas Cherif, an admirer of Gual, was to prove an indispensable associate during her years at the Español in the 1930s.[86] Moving away from autocratic actor-director model she was to encourage more collaborative working relationships, as her involvement of García Lorca in the rehearsal process makes clear. The dramatist José R. Morales recalls her actively courting his opinion about the company's work on *El embustero en su enredo* in rehearsal (cited in Joven 1982: 110). He was further to acknowledge her deft dramaturgical eye in ensuring a lean adaptation of *La Celestina* for the Comedia Nacional de Uruguay in 1949. Her remarks to him that 'lo que se borra no lo silban' (cited in Joven 1982: 109) (that which is erased cannot be booed) demonstrates Xirgu's understanding of the stage as a transfigurative and kinesic space, where the unfolding action is witnessed by, rather than explained to, the audience.

Xirgu's view that 'toda interpretación es la ilustración de un texto, una explicación' (cited in Guansé 1988: 38) (all interpretation is the illustration of a text, an explanation) serves as further indication of the importance of visual vocabularies to her work. For Guansé, Xirgu's visual and spatial orientation allowed her to think pictorially about stage images, and indeed she often used colour and texture as a way into the psychological construction of a character (1988: 50).[87] Even Benavente was to acknowledge that 'Margarita Xirgu pone al descubierto bellezas de las obras que sus propios autores no sospechábamos' (cited in Rodrigo 1974: 9) (Margarita Xirgu discovers beauty in the works that we, their authors, never suspected). As a director she was to pay close attention to stagecraft, ridding the stage of the cumbersome prompt box and ensuring that productions did not open until all the performers were familiar with their roles. She was also to collaborate largely with designers who were pursuing iconically diverse and conceptually driven scenic environments. Simplifying stage machinery, she moved away from the painted backdrop and freed the stage of naturalistic paraphernalia that might impede or distract from the centrality of the performer. Extravagant staging was replaced by a scenario that was tailored to the demands of each individual work (Guansé 1988: 50–2; Díez-Canedo 1935: 5). With costume too she was to move towards a less constraining and simpler cut of attire that did not restrain or trap the female performer within a limited range of gestures. She was the first Catalan actress to appear on

85 Hormigón (1999: 117–26) suggests that Barcelona had a more interesting non-commercial circuit. For a discussion of the impact of Gual, see George 2002: 23–5, 29–30, 44–7.
86 For further information on Gual's influence on Rivas Cherif, see Aguilera Sastre and Aznar Soler 1999: 41, 48, 50–51, 104, 106, 108, 118, 158.
87 Xirgu mentions the importance of colour in allowing her to craft a role in Burgos n.d.: 38. As such she differed from a number of the actresses of her generation who often, allegedly, used the stage as a catwalk; see Rodrigo 1974: 94.

stage in a bathing costume because, she claimed, the role demanded it (cited in Rodrigo 1974: 61). Moving away from the trend towards excessive make-up that she felt impeded the subtlety of facial expressions, Xirgu was to forge a less codified performance style manoeuvring the malleability of her facial features to potent effect. Her technical skills were to ensure that she could move across a range of moods with subtlety, for, as with Ristori, acting was for her 'a public demonstration of a range of skills and professional expertise, not an expression of her own inner feelings and certainly not a neurosis' (Bassnett 1996: 120). As such she was able to embark on a plethora of different roles asserting the primacy of the physical body beyond the norms of the 'speaking body'. She was to mould the latter practices, inherited from melodrama, with the more pervasive techniques of the new realism articulated by figures like Stanislavsky whose work she was to defend and draw on in her own pedagogic training (Rodrigo 1974: 286–7).

Writing in *Mundo Gráfico* in 1914, José Alsina was to refer to her as 'una gran actriz moderna, distinta de la corriente, personalísima, sensible y cerebral' (cited in Rodrigo 1974: 95) (a great actress, different from the norm, highly individualistic, sensitive, cerebral). Reviews often mention her play with silence and pace and the importance of gradations in crafting her roles. In an interview with López Pinillos, Xirgu credits Gual with teaching her the importance of measuring pauses (1920: 144–5). Her ability to work within silence was to be admired by the actor Ignacio López Tarso who saw her work in the late 1950s (cited in Rodrigo 1974: 304). Silence offered her a unique bond with her audiences which she described in 1958 as the 'silencio tan peculiar del público del teatro, que establece la comunión espiritual entre intérpretes y espectadores' (cited in Rodrigo 1974: 309) (special silence of the theatre audience, which establishes the spiritual communion between performers and spectators). Although the use of silence by García Lorca in works like *La casa de Bernarda Alba* has been well documented by critics like C. Brian Morris (1989), there has been no real attempt to draw links between the dramatist's textual strategies and the performative strengths of his favourite actress. With clear melodious enunciation bereft of the excessive vibrato which had often characterised the work of her predecessors, she was consistently, as *El Debate*'s critic was to note in her first Madrid season, 'dueña de la voz' (cited in Rodrigo 1974: 94) (mistress of her voice) in a country which was progressively losing control of its political and social body. While not viewing her voice as robust, Guansé did hold it to be inspiring in that the audience always expected it to break at moments of tension, yet it held almost against the odds (1988: 58). In Hauptmann's *The Sunken Bell* (1908), playing the role of a fairy, Guansé recalls the fascination she was able to exert over the audience with her fragile, small voice and ephemeral presence (1988: 35). For Eduardo Blanco-Amor, cited in *La Vanguardia Española*'s obituary coverage of Xirgu, her voice was more that of 'el más noble metal, batida de armónicos a todo lo largo y lo grueso de las sílabas, encastrando unas en otras como "motu perpetuo"' (Anon. 1969f: 24) (the most illustrious metal, beaten with harmonies across and along the syllables, linking one to another in 'expressivity'). Her dark, sharp features, emotive eyebrows, strong nose and thin lips, while not classically beautiful, offered a striking profile which was often unrecognisable in its chameleonic pliability from role to role.

Xirgu's revealing use of her hands seemed to impress itself on Ortega y Gasset and the Álvarez Quintero brothers (cited in Rodrigo 1974: 10, 229). The actor Alberto Closas too comments on Xirgu painting in the air as she moved her hands (cited in Rodrigo 1974: 260). She appears to have consciously sculpted her performances using referents from El Greco and Velázquez. Like Duse, she spent long periods studying art works in the Prado and other cultural institutions (Guansé 1988: 47; Stainton 1999: 400–1). Any examination of the photographic images that provide frozen poses from a range of her roles indicate, at least when the camera was before her, a statuesque persona. While an interview with Carmen de Burgos, conducted soon after her Madrid debut, appears to eschew the false faces and expansive gestures of melodrama, in search of 'la naturaleza más absoluta' (cited in Rodrigo 1974: 136) (purest nature), Xirgu was to recognise the impossibility of realism in the theatre as early as 1935 when she articulated a view of theatre as essentially larger than life, where the proportions of the human and its environment embark on a process of constant metamorphosis.

Xirgu was also to have her detractors who remained unimpressed by her attempts, like Duse before her, to forge her own mannerisms within a largely modernist body of work. Antonin Artaud seems to have been irritated by her performative idiom (cited in Salvat 1974: 14). The Catalan critic and poet Sebastià Gasch, reporting in *Mirador* on Xirgu's 1934 season, lamented her monotone diction, a marked pronunciation of syllables, and declamatory tone punctuated by faint sighs and fastidious pauses (1934: 5). Such a diatribe might have been in part an articulation of Gasch's unease at Xirgu's affiliation with Castilian-language theatre at a time when he felt that Catalan theatre was in dire need of a new lease of life. During the time of Xirgu's proposed return to Spain in 1949, *Arriba's* César González Ruano, following the paper's right-wing agenda, was to bemoan her acting style as 'el teatro amanerado, pretencioso, insufrible, y monocorde elevado a mito por mil circunstancias insinceras y por el papanatismo que no se atreve a discrepar del tópico formado' (1949: 2) (mannered, pretentious, insufferable and monotonous, elevated to mythical status because of a thousand insincere circumstances and because of a gullibility which does not dare to differ from widely-held clichés). The carved intensity that is often seen as a hallmark of her stage work may indeed have proved cumbersome within the motion pictures. She was to make a range of films between her debut in 1909 in *Guzmán el Bueno/Guzmán the Good* – which marked a conscious move away from theatrical sets – and 1917; from 1918, however, she was only to commit sporadically to film projects.[88] The absence of a significant body of films or a collated theoretical output laying out her teaching, performative or directing techniques may also account for the scant attention she has attracted in the English-speaking world.

---

88 For further details on these projects, see Rodrigo 1974: 113–15.

It is in her vision of theatre as a living breathing organum responding to the mood of the times that her real importance lies. A polymath who resisted categorisation, she was to pursue a theatrical aesthetic where excavation – as with the incorporation of dances and popular ballads from the seventeenth century and a methodical research of costumes of the time for the 1935 production of *Fuenteovejuna* – ran alongside innovation. *Mundo Uruguayo* was to testify to this in 1949 as it positioned her alongside Jouvet and Pitoëff for the disciplined beauty of her staging of Camus's *Le Malentendu* (cited in Rodrigo 1974: 274). As early as 1917 she was seen by *La Publicidad*'s critic Manuel Sarmiento as both the embodiment and the muse of the new Spanish theatre (1917: 3). Her promotion of a theatrical revolution in Spain is visible not merely in the dramaturgy, where her traces remain, or in the practices she promoted but also through the cultural regeneration programme of the Second Republic. Her *Medea* in 1933 at the Roman theatre in Mérida was to inaugurate both an annual theatre festival and a strategy of state intervention in cultural funding which was to be built on in the post-Franco period by the PSOE through their own artistic policy. Despite being plagued by lung problems from an early age, which periodically necessitated a rest from the stage, Xirgu was to dominate the Spanish theatre during the period up to 1936 and even in her absence when she continued to haunt the country's theatrical psyche with memories of her most provocative roles. Had her exile been in France or Italy Xirgu might well have secured recognition within the English-speaking world. For Adolfo Marsillach, the former artistic director of the Compañía Nacional de Teatro Clásico, himself responsible for premiering Weiss's controversial *Marat/Sade* in October 1968 at the Español theatre, her collaboration with García Lorca remains unmatched in twentieth-century Spanish theatre (1999: 237). A Catalan play premiered in 2000 by Xavier Alberti, *Okupes al Museu del Prado* (Squatters at the Prado Museum), presented Xirgu alongside Alberti, Picasso, Ortega y Gasset, García Lorca and Luis Buñuel as emblematic Hispanic twentieth-century cultural icons defending the Prado against a possible sale to the Guggenheim. Xirgu's waving of the Republican flag during the performance locates her as a Spanish Marianne, a mythical symbol of cultural determination and (Spanish) national identity. It also consolidates an institutionalisation of this 'autora de autores' (Rodrigo 2000: 39) (author of authors) who re-envisaged theatre's purpose across sixty years and two continents.

2
The popular and the intertheatrical: Enrique Rambal

Desde niño yo he estado muy influenciado por un director de teatro llamado Rambal.
Este hombre debía de haber sido muy importante no sólo en España, porque recuerdo
que Orson Welles en una entrevista muy antigua decía que uno de los grandes
hombres de teatro mundial era un español que se llamaba Rambal. Rambal escenificaba
grandes novelones – *Miguel Strogoff* de Jules Verne, por ejemplo, *20.000 leguas de viaje
submarino* – en el teatro y lo hacía con un ingenio fantástico. (Carlos Saura, cited in
Castro 1979: 48)

(Since childhood I have been very influenced by a theatre director called Rambal. This
man must have been very important not only in Spain, for I remember Orson Welles in
a really old interview stated that one of the great men in world theatre was a Spaniard
called Rambal. Rambal designed grand, long novels – Jules Verne's *Michael Strogoff* and
20,000 Leagues Under the Sea, for example – for the theatre and he realised them with
fantastic ingenuity.)

The invisibility of Rambal

In an essay entitled 'Reading the intertheatrical; or, The mysterious disappearance
of Susanna Centlivre', the theatre historian Jacky Bratton writes of how the British
eighteenth-century dramatist Susanna Centlivre's plays have been condemned as
'inferior' because they fail to conform to bourgeois society's prerequisite that art be
the 'unique product of the autonomous artist, the individual "genius" at work
alone, challenging and expanding the horizons of human experience' (2000: 8–9).
After arguing that all dramatists are reliant on the collaboration of other artists
(scene painters, actors, etc.) who 'transform' the work through the production
process, she moves on to expand her argument in explaining how 'the aesthetic of
autonomy [. . .] first articulated in western literary and philosophical thought
around 1800' was accompanied by what she terms 'a strong move to free the dramatic writer from what was perceived as the impediment of theatrical realisation'.
As such the dominant imperative became the production of work 'best appreciated
as literature, by the solitary reader' (9). In nineteenth-century Spain the usurping
of Romanticism first by the bourgeois *alta comedia* and then by Benito Pérez
Galdós's particular brand of naturalism pointed to a model of dramatic writing
which facilitated the expansion of the play-publishing industry providing a legacy of

works which in the words of David T. Gies are 'better read than performed' (Gies 1994: 350).[1]

Those who have demonstrated themselves unable to create 'literature' have, as Bratton argues, been denigrated as second-rate artists. For those composing theatre histories 'literary' playwrights have therefore provided the measure against which all other theatre workers have had to compete. The absence of a figure like Enrique Rambal from published histories of Spanish theatre may have much to do with the fact that his collaboratively written plays, extricated from their theatrical context, have been read, to appropriate Bratton's term, as 'incomplete', partial documents (9). Collaborative work is therefore read as 'not literature [. . .] compromised by the populist and commercial creative processes of the theatre [. . .] morally and aesthetically suspect because it provokes and includes rather than suppresses bodily response from an audience' (12).[2] Bratton allocates the term 'intertheatrical' to encompass particular kinds of dramatic writing that refuse to be understood on the page as 'Drama' or 'Literature'. Such texts, Bratton posits, have frequently met with dismissal or disregard because they do not fit readily within socially endorsed discourses:

their capacity to please must therefore be challenged or obscured, lest the autonomy of art be undermined by it. Their excellence is not in spite of, but because of their multiple strands of connection, their place within their milieu, meshed to writing past and present, to actors and their strengths and needs, to music, dancing the audience's pleasures. (15)

Until very recently dismissal or disregard have also marked the theatre of Enrique Rambal, an actor-writer-director who chose largely to work within the realms of popular theatre. Touring the regions rather than simply frequenting the capital city's stages, he has effectively slipped through the 'official' documentation of Spanish theatre in the first five decades of the twentieth century. Rambal enjoyed significant success in the period between 1920 and his death in 1956 but has remained conspicuously absent from existing studies of Spanish theatre during this period. Drawing on critical material located in theatre archives in Madrid and Barcelona as well as oral testimonies obtained from collaborators and individuals who recall seeing Rambal's work, this chapter will seek to detail why he has been subject to such neglect and confirm his position as a key director of the era whose productions of adventure yarns, religious epics and classical dramas redefined pleasure and morality during the turbulent pre- and post-Civil War years.

Academic interest in Rambal's work has certainly been aroused by recent comments by prominent Spanish performers and directors like Carlos Saura and Fernando Fernán-Gómez concerning the influence that this actor-manager-dramatist

---

1 For information on the rise of the *alta comedia* and the lucrative play-publishing industry, see Gies 1994: 174–90. For further information on Pérez Galdós, see Gies 1994: 336–48.
2 Earlier in the article Bratton (2000: 10–11) argues how this kind of work undermines 'the fundamental binary, the distinction between mind and body, upon which western patriarchal culture rests'.

exerted on their own aesthetic, through his magnificent special effects and his fusion of a variety of techniques appropriated from the early cinema. He still remains a figure conspicuously absent from many significant published studies of the twenti-eth-century Spanish stage.[3] Perhaps this is partly to do with the fact that histories of Spanish theatre tend, as with historical, political or sociological studies, to be organised around the key date of the Civil War. Rambal's career was effectively established before the Civil War and continued largely unperturbed in the post-War years, much like that of his friend, the Nobel Prize-winning playwright, Jacinto Benavente. One could argue, however, that, unlike Benavente, he did not achieve the unequivocal critical success necessary to warrant inclusion in studies of the period 1898–1936. In the politically charged climate of the Franco era his populist work – largely within the much maligned genre of melodrama – may have been regarded as unworthy of seri-ous study by scholars of both the right and the left. The low critical regard in which some popular actors have traditionally been held may also have caused him to be considered undeserving of historiographers' attention. The fact that he had a long association with the major theatres of Valencia – Princesa, Principal, Ruzafa, Apolo and Olimpia – and often chose to spend long seasons there rather than in Madrid may also have served to position him as a local rather than a national figure. Addi-tionally, Rambal left no great body of playtexts or theoretical writings behind him. In a society where such authority is vested in the written word, the absence of such material has served to render him a figure of negligible importance. Whatever the reasons, there can be little doubt that his spectacular repertory of 1,789 productions[4] made him a legend amongst audiences in his time, and that the last five years have witnessed the beginning of a re-appropriation of a figure whose contribution to twen-tieth-century Spanish theatre has been warmly acknowledged by a range of fellow professionals, including Andrés Amorós (1999a; 1999b), Rodolf Sirera (1989) and most recently Marcos Ordóñez. Ordóñez's novel, *Comedia con fantasmas* centres around the company of a thinly veiled Rambal-figure, Ernesto Pombal (2002).

Enrique Rambal García[5] was born on 21 September 1889[6] in the town of Utiel in the province of Valencia into a relatively poor family. Receiving little formal edu-

3 See, for example, García Templado 1980, Torrente Ballester 1957 and Ruiz Ramón 1984. Oliva (1989) mentions his successful tours (24), the influence of cinema on his work (27, 101), and his status as one of a number of Spanish artists who chose to work for extensive periods in the Americas (138). Rodríguez Méndez (1974: 89) also features a brief reference to him. See Amorós 1999b: 135–45 for other minor references to Rambal's work within an overview of Spanish popular theatre. More recently Rubio Jiménez (1999a: 120) has also acknowledged the paucity of information published on Rambal.

4 A figure given by Vizcaíno Casas (1981: 196).

5 *Quién es quién en el teatro y el cine español e hispanoamericano* (Centro de Investigaciones Literarias Españolas y Hispanoamericanas 1990: 744–5) lists him as Enrique Rambal Sacia but this was actually the name of his son, an actor who settled in Mexico in the mid-1940s and went on to work with Buñuel. Rambal Sacia's daughter is the New York-based actress Virginia Rambal; see Falquez-Certain 2000.

6 This is the date given on the baptism certificate reproduced in Martínez Ortiz 1989: 17. 21 November is the date given by Álvarez Barrientos 1991: 92. *Quién es quién en el teatro y el cine español e hispanoamericano* (Centro de Investigaciones Literarias Españolas y Hispanoamericanas 1990: 744) claims he was born in 1890.

cation, he was sent out to work in early adolescence where, employed in a printing press, he claimed to have learnt to read, gradually taking on the responsibility of putting together the serialised novels that were a significant bulk of the press's business. His first visit to the theatre came in 1904 when he saw a staging of Victorien Sardou's *Fédora* at Valencia's Principal theatre with the well-known actress Julia Cibera. At the Principal he was also able to see María Guerrero and the work of other major companies on tour in the city. Joining up with a group of five other *aficionados* he then formed a theatre company that rehearsed at his home, improvising with an array of household items. His early performances in Joaquín Dicenta's *Juan José*, at a small venue of one of the city's then numerous theatre societies, were seen by the renowned Valencian comic actor Manuel Lloréns, who then invited Rambal to work with him. He remained with Lloréns until the latter's death in 1910 when he appears to have formed his own company.[7]

The company's debut is listed by Martínez Ortiz as *El perro fantasma* (The Phantom Dog), a version of Arthur Conan Doyle's *Hound of the Baskervilles* premiering at Valencia's Princesa theatre on 20 April 1912 (1989: 27).[8] It was followed by a production of *La Dame aux Camélias* (*La dama de las camelias*)and later Rafael María Liern's *La almoneda del diablo* (The Devil's Auction) that opened at the larger Principal theatre in December of that same year with Rambal as lead actor, director and producer. With a staging of *La pata de cabra* (The Goat's Hoof), Juan de Grimaldi's 1829 comic drama, Rambal decisively occupied the terrain of the spectacular *comedia de magia* that had entertained audiences throughout the eighteenth and early nineteenth centuries.[9] During these years (1912–20) he built up a repertory of works that included Zorrilla's *Don Juan Tenorio*, the Duque de Rivas's *Don Álvaro o la fuerza del sino* (Don Álvaro or the Force of Destiny) and Ventura de la Vega's 1845 drawing room drama *El hombre de mundo* (The Man of the World). Although the latter dramatist's work marks a fierce rejection of romanticism in its articulation of domestic stability as the desirable model for the new bourgeois society, these other plays, like *La pata de cabra* and *Don Álvaro o la fuerza del sino* challenged the parameters of what was possible on a stage through their dependence on innovative visual effects, rapid changes of location and an elastic repertory of performers. Often denounced by critics as 'escapist' and 'frivolous', Gies points to the social criticism that can be traced in these works (1994: 83). He goes on to argue that these magical comedies 'died a slow but sweet death in the nineteenth century' (87), but an examination of Rambal's repertoire suggests that they were a central hallmark of his company's work and that their dramatic techniques were to resonate in the spectacular productions he was to create in the years following

---

7 Although Álvarez Barrientos (1991: 92) and Ureña (1942: 19) cite Manuel Llorente as the actor-manager whose company Rambal joined, Martínez Ortiz (1989: 24) refers to him as Manuel Lloréns. Press reviews from the 1910 season at the Principal certainly confirm the name as Lloréns and a street in Valencia now bears the actor's name.

8 The piece received a poor review in *Las Provincias* on 21 April 1912 although Rambal and the *primera actriz* Justa Revert were seen as deserving of the audience's applause.

9 For further details of the *comedia de magia* see Álvarez Barrientos 1987, Caro Baroja 1974, Gies 1994: 70–87, and Gies 1988: 1–134.

1920, when popular novels were adapted to provide theatrical extravaganzas not dissimilar to the *refundiciones* or reworkings of Golden Age plays which had dominated Madrid's mid-nineteenth-century commercial theatres.[10]

Rambal's early season at the Principal theatre in 1912–13 where his production was wedged between an orchestral overture and cinematic projections may also have alerted him to the advantages of incorporating both music and film into his work. Martínez Ortiz, lists a substantial number of composers and musicians who worked with Rambal on crafting scores for each production (1989: 116–17).

An extensive company tour of Andalusia and North Africa, punctuated by Rambal's own travels across Europe, saw a widening of the company's pool of productions. His staging of Sardou's last play *L'Affaire des poisons* (*La corte de los venenos*) premiered at Valencia's Princesa theatre in 1913, marked a commitment to the staging of French plays which had begun with the 1912 production of Alexandre Dumas's *La Dame aux Camélias*.

The prominence of nineteenth-century works and conspicuous classics from Spain's Golden Age like Calderón's *La vida es sueño* (*Life is a Dream*) was, however, mixed with more contemporary pieces – most discernibly the plays of Jacinto Benavente. Quickly realising, however, that his production of *Cyrano de Bergerac* could not pull in the numbers that gathered to see his adaptations of intriguing adventure tales like Jules Verne's *Michael Strogoff: A Courier of the Czar,* presented as *Miguel Strogoff* in 1928 (see Figure 3), he modified his repertoire accordingly, creating the lavish, colourful productions which were to make him the most celebrated actor-manager of the early decades of the twentieth century.

During these years, in association with the impresario and author Álvarez Angulo,[11] Rambal also ventured into crime dramas, exploiting a genre which, although popular in Paris in the latter decades of the nineteenth century, had never really enjoyed a similar degree of success in Spain. Although these dramas largely featured characters from popular late-century crime fiction, like Sherlock Holmes, Raffles, Arsène Lupin, and Nick Carter, they appropriated the conventions of the melodramatic form in their action-filled story lines, excessive situations, formulaic character types and moralistic endings. Rambal, attuned to the impact the new cinematic medium was enjoying, however, incorporated into his adaptations a series of magical special effects – thought, in part, to be developed from tricks he had been taught from experienced stage hands. It was these effects that were to become his hallmark. Machinery purchased in North America in 1930 allowed him to create a storm at sea, a sunrise, a rainbow, rain, snow, the effect of an aeroplane flying through the clouds, 'todo lo que pueda hacer el cine' (Rambal, cited in Martínez Ortiz 1989: 32) (everything that cinema can do). In the 1929 production of *Las mil y una noches* (A Thousand and One Nights), adapted with Valencian dramatist

---

10 For further details on these *refundiciones*, see Gies 1994: 10.
11 Fernando Fernán-Gómez (1990: 133–4) argues that it was only after his rupture with Álvarez Angulo that Rambal went in for the *gran espectáculo* (grand spectacle) that became his definitive hallmark. Until then he was largely concerned with small-scale melodramas and crime dramas.

Fausto Hernández Casajuana, footlights, fireworks and industrial fans served to create the impression of a desert sirocco. In the 1929 version of *Miguel Strogoff,* adapted by Rambal and Emilio Gómez de Miguel, the effect of a burning forest was created through some hollow iron trees which camouflaged burning torches.[12]

For a number of years in the 1920s, beginning with an adaptation of Feuillade's 1913–14 film serial *Fantômas,* he delighted audiences across Spain, North Africa and Latin America (and made a veritable fortune) with a series of animated and fiercely paced crime dramas, whose technical effects included walls which swallowed individuals, carnivorous snakes, invisible men and chairs which appeared to move of their own accord. When the success of this formula began to wane, he turned to a more methodical adaptation of established novels that offered the possibility of transformative visual images and effects. Shrewdly choosing as his co-adaptors journalists (amongst them Tomás Borrás Bermejo and José María Arráiz Eguía), popular dramatists like Hernández Casajuana and José Peris Celda, and screen writers like Jesús Vasallo, who were aware of the necessity of providing pacy intriguing episodic dramas, he produced lavish spectacles which merged high action with musical interludes.[13] Fernán-Gómez recalls the chorus girls who would double as extras playing everything from monks to French revolutionaries (1990: 134–5). Indeed, shifts of mood, expansive casts, heightened hyperbole, multiple locations, musical underscoring and appropriate sound effects all allowed for a spectacular celebration of aesthetic artifice. At a time when critics were doggedly predicting the imminent death of theatre, Rambal astutely reworked the conventions that were generating appealing moving pictures for the stage. He was to exploit the parallels between nineteenth-century theatre and twentieth-century cinema – both effortlessly nurturing stars and appropriating popular literature – in creating the theatre/film fusion that was to distinguish his theatrical extravaganzas.

Never travelling with a company of less than sixty and a minimum of twenty tons of luggage, his grandiose spectacles were eagerly awaited, attracting phenomenal audiences. Rambal was an idol of the pre-Civil War theatre, enjoying the star status habitually reserved for film celebrities.[14] The technical virtuosity of his productions was not lost on the major film studios and he appears to have been solicited by Paramount in 1930 to make two 'talkies' (cited in Martínez Ortiz 1989:

12 These examples are all given by Amorós (1999a: 4). Amorós also mentions the conjuring of an erupting volcano in another production. This effect may also have been generated by the machinery obtained in North America. *Miguel Strogoff o El correo del Zar,* to cite its full title, premeried at the Principal theatre Valencia on 17 October 1929. It was one of Rambal's most tantalising productions and remained within the repertoire well into the 1940s. For a review testifying to the production's Madrid success, see T. 1928.

13 Tomás Borrás Bermejo was to work with Rambal on a version of Pirandello's *Henry IV* and to collaborate with Valentín de Pedro on adapting Cardenal Wiseman's novel *Fabiola.* José María Arráiz and Jesús Vasallo were to adapt various films for and with Rambal, including Korda's *The Four Feathers* (1939). For further details of collaborations with all the figures mentioned, see Martínez Ortiz 1989: 109–11.

14 Ureña (1942: 128, 133) writes of assaults in the queues for tickets and of a storming of the stage by an audience in Caracas in 1935 demanding a further performance of their two favourite productions *La dama de las camelias* and *Felipe Derbley.*

32). He declined, preferring to remain in Spain where he was to work as an actor in two features: the first *El crimen del bosque azul/The Crime of the Blue Forest* made in 1920 and the second *El desaparecido/The Missing Man* in 1934. *El desparecido* was produced by Meyler Films and directed by Antonio Graciani. Reviews were poor but Antonio Guzmán's critique of the film in *Cinegramas* does draw attention to the pull of Rambal's presence in the film, recognising him as a more resonant figure with Spanish audiences than Boris Karloff (1934: n.pag.).

Amongst his most prominent stage successes with his Compañía de Grandes Espectáculos (Company of Grand Shows) were three adaptations of Jules Verne's novels, *La vuelta al mundo en ochenta días* (Around the World in Eighty Days) (1934), *Veinte mil leguas de viaje submarino* (20,000 Leagues Under the Sea) (1928), and *Miguel Strogoff*. *Veinte mil leguas de viaje submarino* offered a musical re-writing of Verne's novel through the employment of a prima ballerina and twelve chorus girls who emerged from the giant shells resting in the sea. Here film merged with

3 A chorus finale from *Miguel Strogoff* directed by Enrique Rambal and presented at Madrid's Novedades theatre in 1930

4 Matinee idol of the stage Enrique Rambal, *c.* 1930

theatre as the Nautilus's sinking was accompanied by a cinematic projection of animal life at the bottom of the sea especially prepared by Rambal at the Universum Film Aktiengesellschaft (UFA) Studios in Naples. Such a mergence of the conventions of operetta with technological innovation and intriguing plot lines (anticipating the blockbuster musicals of the 1980s) was also a characteristic of *La vuelta al mundo en ochenta días*, first performed in 1934 with twenty rotating backdrops designed by Amadeo Asensi and Joan Morales showing different sights around the world. This latter production involved a procession through the central aisle including three constructed elephants and the shifting of the action from the proscenium stage to other parts of the auditorium.[15]

15 For further details, see Fernán-Gómez 1990: 135–6.

Although Rambal is primarily remembered for his lavish swashbuckling adventure yarns-cum-romances, his extensive repertory, often having up to fifty productions in each season, incorporated horror – *El hombre invisible* (The Invisible Man) (1918), *La carta del terror* (The Letter of Terror) (1918), *El crimen de nadie* (Nobody's Crime) (1919) – classical drama – Shakespeare's *King Lear* (1942), Lope de Vega's *Fuenteovejuna* (1954) – historical drama – *Isabel la Católica. Madre de España* (Isabel the Catholic. Mother of Spain) (1942) and Alejandro Casona's little known play *El misterio del María Celeste* (The Mystery of the Marie Celeste) (1934) – together with religious epics – *Fray Luis de Sousa* (1943), *Calasanz* (1945) and *El Mártir del Calvario* (The Martyr of Calvary).[16] The *mise en scène* of this latter production was inspired by recognisable religious paintings and prints, and conceived as an attempt to provide a Spanish equivalent of the famous dramatisation of the events at Golgotha performed (every ten years) at Oberammergau (Germany) since 1633. First staged in Madrid at the Cervantes theatre in 1921, Rambal's arrangement of scenes from the life of Christ was presented over 5,000 times in the period up to 1942, allegedly earning him over six million pesetas (Ureña 1942: 83). In the late 1940s during a Central and South American tour, contracted to play in Mexico for a week as part of the Easter Week celebrations, it ran for five months. Eye-witness accounts by members of Rambal's company testify to audiences breaking down in tears and screaming in fear as Rambal, in an emotive performance as Christ – a role later taken on by his son – was hammered to the cross.[17] The production's visually opulent set had been painted by three artists, Vicente Sanchis, Paula and Díaz Peris, and the two hundred costumes were designed and made up by Insa, the tailoring house run by Juan Ferrés Insa and his cousin Miguel Insa, which was to take responsibility for most of Rambal's costume requirements. Special effects included Rambal (as Christ) walking across Lake Tiberias, a trick achieved through a sheet of painted canvas stretched and moved to simulate waves by members of the company.

During the Civil War Rambal was crippled by a shortage of money and materials that restricted his activities to seasons at Valencia's theatres. These included various benefit performances for the Republican effort.[18] Although he spent time at the Eslava and Princesa – renamed Libertad – theatres in the Autumn of 1936, in May 1937 Rambal based his company at the Principal remaining there until 22

16 Amorós (1999a: 2–3) places Rambal's work into seven categories: melodramas and *folletines* (serialised novels), adventure yarns, biographical works, crime dramas, religious works, Spanish classics and universal classics. These categories obviously blend into one another as *La dama de las camelias* can be viewed as both a melodrama and a 'universal' classic.

17 Gabi Álvarez in a private, unpublished interview with the author, July 1994. All further comments from Gabi Álvarez are from this interview. There are known to have been two different versions of the script. The earlier version was put together by Emilio Gómez de Miguel and Luis Grajales in 1921. Another later version by Grajales, Pacheco and Rambal was first produced in 1940.

18 For further details, see Martínez Ortiz 1989: 43, 45 and Bellveser 1987: 29–30, 75.

March 1938.[19] His repertory, although limited by pre-War standards, included a series of more socially compromised works including *Los miserables* (Les Misérables), Benavente's *Santa Rusia* (Holy Russia), a treatment of the Dreyfus affair *El proceso de Dreyfus*, and *Las dos huérfanas de París* (The Two Orphan Girls of Paris) – the latter possibly drawing on Juan de Grimaldi's 1825 reworking of the French melodrama *El abate L'Epée y el asesino o La huérfana de Bruselas* (The Abbot from Epée and the Assassin or The Orphan Girl from Brussels).[20]

In the period immediately following the War Rambal is thought to have enjoyed a number of successful years touring in Mexico. He returned in the early 1940s and revised his repertoire to include a greater number of stage adaptations of popular films. These included *Guerreras rojas,* a stage handling of Cecil B. de Mille's 1940 film, *North West Mounted Police*, which, in turn, had been based on R. C. Fetherstonhaugh's novel, *Royal Canadian Mounted Police* which premiered at Valencia's Ruzafa theatre on 21 May 1947 and *¡Arsénico!* (Arsenic!) (1953), commonly known by the title of the 1945 film it was based on – John M. Stahl's *Leave Her to Heaven* (dubbed into Spanish as *Que el cielo la juzgue*).[21] *¡Arsénico!*, a volatile courtroom melodrama centring on the suicide of a woman who has calculated that her sister will be condemned for the deed that will be read as murder, conjured an interface of tricks – including the simulated drowning of a child in a lake. Adapted by Rambal with Rafael Martí Orbera from Ben Ames Williams's novel, and featuring a specially composed score by José García Bernalt, the piece was premiered in Madrid at a time when the Madrid critics were tiring of Rambal's stage trickery and reviews lamented the actor's decision not to appear in the production (A. 1953: 31; P. 1953: 2) (see Figure 5).

Nevertheless, adaptations like *¡Arsénico!* and *Las cuatro plumas* (The Four Feathers) – again adapted by Vasallo and Arráiz and based on Zoltan Korda's 1939 film – ensured Rambal remained a popular box-office draw in Latin America and the regional theatres of Spain throughout the late 1940s and early 1950s, allowing him to assimilate into his company the eighteen members of the Lope de Rueda company previously based at the Español theatre. Roberto Pérez Carpio, known professionally as Roberto Carpio, the company's director, married Rambal's daughter and went on to become a key associate working with Rambal on choreography and textual adaptation.

It was during these years that he married for a second time – he had been widowed in 1929 (Martínez Ortiz 1989: 112). His bride was the company's premier dancer, Cecilia Martínez Cifuentes. During the early 1950s, however, he risked an

19 There also appears to have been a short season at the Ruzafa theatre in May 1939. For further details of Rambal's work during the Civil War see Bellveser 1987: 11, 29–33, 65–6, 75.

20 This play, reworked from the French by Grimaldi and frequently shortened to *La huérfana de Bruselas* (The Orphan Girl of Brussels) was a spectacular success playing in Madrid six years after its first production. For further details, see Gies 1994: 92.

21 The first production, which opened in Madrid on 18 January 1953, seems to have gone by the title *¡Arsénico!* Martínez Ortiz (1989: 121) states that when the production opened in Valencia at the Principal on 24 February 1954, it was given the title *Que el cielo la juzgue.* It returned to Madrid's Fuencarral theatre in July 1954 with this latter title.

5 An attempt to capture the 1940s film look. A still from *¡Arsénico!* with Rambal in the left of the photo (1954)

expensive musical at Madrid's Lope de Vega theatre where he contracted a costly team, including the costume designer Pepito Zamora (best known for his work with the Folies Bergère in Paris). The spectacular box-office failure of this project brought him to the point of bankruptcy and he was obliged to disband his Compañía de Grandes Espectáculos. Although Rambal planned to re-form the company, soliciting government funds to tour the religious drama *El Soldado de la Fe* (The Soldier of Faith) across Spain, he was never able to realise it. He died in Valencia on 10 May 1956 from injuries sustained after being knocked down by a motorcycle.[22]

Rambalesco

The numerous entertaining anecdotes regarding Rambal's tumultuous life which litter both Luis Ureña's romanticised biography and Martínez Ortiz's more recent study render him as breathtaking and irresistible a hero as the protagonists of his high-action productions and threaten to obliterate his considerable theatrical achievements. These receive scant attention in Ureña's appreciative study. Although Rambal refused to divulge the secrets of his stage effects, which led to the

22 See Martínez Ortiz 1989: 76–80 for details of Rambal's final plans. *El Soldado de la Fe* (The Soldier of Faith), a biographical study of the Franciscan friar Francisco Gálvez Iranzo, had premiered at Utiel's Rambal theatre on 16 December 1955. The theatre had been renamed after Rambal in 1933. A square in Valencia also bears Rambal's name (Martínez Ortiz 1989: 66).

collapse of his company on his death, it is thought he picked some of them up during his early travels in Europe and Russia. The few play scripts published by La Farsa and Talía in the 1930s and 1940s offer little indication as to how the effects were achieved. They do, however, provide a taste of the style that was to generate the adjective *rambalesco*.

¡Jonathan! El monstruo invisible (Jonathan! The Invisible Monster), first staged in June 1940 at Madrid's Fontalba theatre and published by Talía in 1944, is a late example of the crime dramas which had made his reputation in the 1920s. Described as 'intriga de miedo y de misterio en cuatro actos' (Moreno Monzón and Baerlam 1944: 1) (an intriguing story of fear and mystery in four acts), it is set largely in interior locations with a smaller cast than his historical adaptations. Written by Rambal – under the pseudonym Baerlam he adopted in 1933 on gaining entry to the Sociedad de Autores (Society of Authors) – and Eduardo Moreno Monzón, it tells the tale of an invisible monster terrorising London with Scotland Yard's finest on his trail. Mystery surrounds his identity as it becomes clear that he is the dangerous Jonathan Maddon, a criminal supposedly sent to his death in 1923 but able, through malevolent means, to ensure that an innocent man takes his place. Even the romantic interest of the dedicated policeman, Rex Walton, is brought into the drama as it is revealed that Alicia (his sweetheart) is the daughter of the executed man. Her mother, disguised as her nanny, finally executes revenge by killing the villain, thus allowing the couple to enjoy a blissful reunion.

As with his later adaptation of Daphne du Maurier's *Rebecca (Rebeca),* this is a romantic portrait of the English as a fundamentally decent, law-abiding people – the threat is seen to come from without, i.e. a lone criminal element presented as a subhuman power who joins up with another 'external' force, the Jewish money-lender, Isaac Brolsky, an offensively stereotypical portrait which seems to owe a great deal to Dickens's Fagin. The foreign is an undesirable and threatening element that must be eradicated and it is the job of the rational, male policemen – the elite of Scotland Yard – to achieve this perilous task. Sinister atmospherics allowed the audience to experience a 'world' markedly different from the Spain of the time – dangerous, glamorous and synonymous with that of the popular Hollywood products enjoying success with the Spanish public of the 1940s.

First performed in August 1945 at Madrid's Coliseum theatre, *Venganza oriental* (Oriental Vengeance) provides an analogous vision of the British. Written by Rambal in collaboration with Manuel Soriano Torres, it was to exploit the fascination with the exotic which was also to be played out in the later police drama *Chu-Chin-Chow*. Here a vengeful Chinese husband, Yuan-Sing (played by Rambal), takes revenge on his English wife Clara and her lover Eduardo Priestley by poisoning the latter. Lusting after her sister Carlota, he devises a plot to rid himself of Carlota's fiancée, Ricardo, brother to the deceased Eduardo Priestley. Things, however, do not go according to plan, for Sing takes the poisoned chalice destined for Ricardo, dying as his wife apologises for her misdemeanour. Descriptions of Yang-Sing provided by the stage directions (Soriano Torres and Rambal 1945: 13, 23–7, 29) clearly seek to place him within the realms of the unknown 'other'. Here an

'Orientalisation' of the Orient, to use Said's term (1995: 202–3), presents a ludicrously fictional image of the 'native' as a cruel and vengeful figure who betrays any trust mistakenly placed in him.

Nevertheless, the image of the British, all safari suits and pristine uniforms, is equally ridiculous and shown through such discursive excess to exist as another construct: the meaning of both dependent on the dialectical relationship existing between them. As with so many of the female protagonists of the Spanish *españoladas* (folkloric musicals of the 1940s and 1950s), which would prove a potent referent for the audiences, the wayward, transgressive woman suffers substantial inner torment which she shares with the audience, repenting before punishment – here the death of her 'true' love and the public disclosure of her infidelity – is executed.

Fabiola o Los mártires cristianos (Fabiola or The Christian Martyrs), adapted by Tomás Borrás and Valentín de Pedro from the novel by Cardenal Wiseman and premiered on 11 April 1930 at the Gran Metropolitano theatre in the heavily populated working-class district around Madrid's Cuatro Caminos, gives a highly dramatic rendition of the martyrdom of Saint Inés and Saint Sebastián for a cast of twenty-five. Divided into fourteen scenes (a conspicuously small number compared to later shorter adaptations like *Drácula* and *Rebeca*), *Fabiola* is a moralistic but highly enjoyable account of the perils of decadence and the worship of false gods (as personified by an array of misled and wicked Romans), and the salvation and inner strength offered by adherence to the one 'true' deity – the Christian God for whom all good Christians go willingly to their death. Excessive dogmatism is avoided through a plot that depends on suspense, intrigue and a range of melodramatic devices (including a dastardly villain, disguise, a lost handkerchief and a case of mistaken identity), and the scattering of the action across multiple 'exotic' locations including elegant gardens, dark catacombs, a Roman court and an amphitheatre. Consecutive scenes (always summarised by a brief title pointing to the action that is to ensue) never take place in the same location, thus attempting to ensure the audience remain attentive. The martyrs suffer a range of horrific punishments – sensationally enacted on stage for the 'moral' benefit of the Christian audience – including decapitation (for Saint Inés), and the launching of arrows against the tied Saint Sebastián. The final tableau provides a cathartic experience for an audience subjected, much like the troubled and noble heroine Fabiola, to a torment from which respite comes only through Christianity. Visited by the ghost of Saint Sebastián, who promises vengeance on all those who have thwarted the Christians, Fabiola's conversion provides the emphatic climax of the piece:

El fantasma de Sebastián se desvanece. Fabiola avanza hacia él algunos pasos y cae en rodillas; las manos juntas, los ojos al cielo. Donde estaba el fantasma de Sebastián empieza a diseñarse una cruz luminosa, que va creciendo, como si lo llenara todo; cada vez mayor, cada vez más resplandeciente. Y así queda Fabiola, arrodillada al pie de aquella cruz immensa, transfigurada al transformarse su amor humano en amor divino. (Borrás and Pedro 1930: 79)

(The ghost of Sebastián disappears. Fabiola takes a few steps towards him and falls on her knees; her hands clasped together, her eyes looking up towards heaven. At the place where Sebastián's ghost was a luminous cross begins to appear, as if filling the whole space; growing larger and with each moment more brilliant. And there Fabiola remains, kneeling at the foot of that immense cross, transfigured by the transformation of her human love into divine love.)

Gender politics are, interestingly, not as predictable as might be expected. With the exception of Saint Sebastián, men are generally portrayed in a less than favourable light as flippant hedonists excessively concerned with material wealth, political power and the gratification of the flesh. It is the men who are seen as the abhorrent 'other' – excessively pure and righteous in Sebastián's case, and arrogant, manipulative and dangerous in Fulvio's. Women (through the characterisation of Fabiola, Inés and the disguised Syra/María) are representative of order, stability and reason. Interestingly, the only character who articulates 'desire' (apart from the lascivious Fulvio who arduously pursues the adolescent Inés) is Fabiola. Desire, however, remains unconsummated, always exceeding the means by which it can be satisfied.

Desire – as well as its allure and its satisfaction – is also a key motif of the 1943 adaptation of Bram Stoker's *Dracula* undertaken by Rambal in association with Manuel Soriano Torres and José Javier Pérez Bultó which premiered at Madrid's Fontalba theatre on 6 July 1943. Both *Drácula* and *Rebeca* – the adaptation of the Daphne du Maurier novel undertaken by the same team the following year and premiered at Madrid's Calderón theatre on 10 June 1944 – are significantly narratives of transformation where identity is provisional and constantly subject to redefinition. In *Drácula* the environment in which the action evolves is an idealised space where character is markedly performed – the English are prim, polite and drink tea in a civilised manner at delightful town residences that would have proved alluringly 'exotic' to a post-War audience suffering economic hardship. And yet, incongruously, names are, as with all his productions set in England, Hispanicised – thus Lucy becomes Lucía, Arthur Arturo, Mina Guillermina. The play is shorter and swifter in pace than *Fabiola*. Its twenty-five scenes move from darkest Transylvania (as represented by various quarters of Drácula's castle) to genteel London (personified by Lucía Westenra's elegant residence) and incorporate a variety of locations including an East European train station and inn, Kingstead cemetery and London docks, Renfield's cell in the sanatorium and the ruins of Carfax Abbey. All twenty-five scenes are brief and episodic and rely substantially on the characters explaining the lapses in time and place. The play begins with what is presumably a projection onto a back wall or curtain (although it could also be a backdrop with the material already written onto it) of information on vampires (Rambal *et al*. 1944a: 3). This device, probably appropriated from Hollywood films, which flashed onto the screen a newspaper headline to contextualise or explain subsequent events, recurs in Scene Thirteen when Drácula's rampage through London is announced by a headline that mentions the disappearance of children who are subsequently found with strange wounds on the throat (Rambal *et al*. 1944a: 27). It is a technique used also in *Rebeca,* where a picturesque postcard of Manderley Castle serves to indicate its awe-inspiring 'splendour' to the audience (Rambal *et al*. 1944b: 6). It is highly possible that projected film clips (obtained from the Kielg

Bross Studios in New York) were used in both *Drácula* and *Rebeca* to provide some of the more elaborate locations. The critic Joaquín Álvarez Barrientos posits that in Scene Five of *Rebeca*, as Max drives Carolina out in Montecarlo (Rambal *et al*. 1944b: 11), a short film of a road in motion would be projected, against which Max's still car would appear to be in motion (1991: 99). This technique was also probably used in Scene Three of *Drácula* as Jonatán is driven in a carriage to the haunted castle (Rambal *et al*. 1944a: 5). It is possible that film was also used again in Scene Eighteen of *Rebeca* to show the diver swimming though the remains of the boat where Rebeca allegedly met her death, and encountering her skeleton (Rambal *et al*. 1944b: 43).

Rebeca, like *Drácula,* is characterised by multiple locations – a high-class hotel in Montecarlo, different rooms in Manderley Castle, valley views, rugged coastlines, a courtroom and, perhaps most spectacularly, the burning remains of the Castle which constitute the play's final scene: the curtain falling on 'la demoníaca figura de la señora Danvers [. . .] en medio del espantoso infierno de llamas' (Rambal *et al*. 1944b: 59) (the demonic figure of Mrs Danvers [. . .] in the midst of the horrific inferno of flames). There are indications from reviews of the production that the effect of flames was achieved, as with the forest set alight by the Tartars in *Miguel Strogoff,* through the cinematic projection of flames against the back wall, fireworks, and red bulbs which were inserted into the simulated beams (Marqueríe 1944: 34). Back lighting may have been used to provide the illusion of Mrs Danvers being on fire. Although Alfredo Marqueríe, who reviewed the production for *ABC*, was scathing about some of the tricks, denouncing the outdated painted backdrops and the backstage noise of the stagehands over which the performers had to make themselves heard, he is also generous in his praise for a production which had audiences leaving the auditorium claiming they had never seen anything like it in their lives (1944: 34).

Drácula too occupies a narrative space of transformative sensationalism. The script is scattered with references to wolves, bats, a brig battling at sea to avoid sinking and Drácula climbing the walls of his castle like a lizard. There are also two grand crashes – one involving the derailment of a train in the mountains in Scene Twenty-One (Rambal *et al*. 1944a: 42), the other a ship catching fire in Scene Twenty-Three after hitting some rocks (45). Álvarez Barrientos maintains that the former was achieved in the following manner:

el telón representaba la salida de un túnel, en negro, ésta se iluminaba en el fondo o en el centro con una luz que cada vez se hacía más grande mediante una diafragma, dando la sensación de que el tren avanzaba. Al tiempo se oía el sonido de un tren acercándose. En su momento, el ruido del choque, oscuro, confusión, gritos de angustia, etc. (1991: 98–9)

(the backdrop presenting the opening of a tunnel, in black and white; this was lit at the bottom or the centre with a light that gradually became larger through a diaphragm, giving the impression that the train was getting closer. At the same time the sound of an approaching train could be heard. At that moment the sound of the crash, dark, confusion, anguished screams, etc.)

These surviving texts provide some indication of the scope of his theatrical tricks, but spectators who saw his productions speak of even more spectacular effects. Fernando Fernán-Gómez recalls seeing *El signo de Zorro* (The Mark of Zorro) in 1928, dazzled by the intrepid hero's ability to escape a group of soldiers avidly pursuing him by piercing bags of flour with his sword. The white dust filled the stage, confusing the soldiers and allowing the resourceful Zorro to escape (1990: 135). Fernán-Gómez also writes of a production entitled *Volga, Volga*, based on episodes from the life of the Russian revolutionary Stenka Racine, which took place on a pirate ship travelling along the Volga river. His mother, Carola Fernán-Gómez, then an actress with Rambal's company, played a maiden kidnapped by pirates who was delivered wrapped in a carpet, and unrolled before an astonished audience (1990: 135). Rafael Borque, an actor who worked with Rambal in the 1940s, recalls a scene from *El Conde de Montecristo* (The Count of Montecristo) (1942) where the hero changes places with the dead abbot and is cast in a sack into the sea.[23] Against a backdrop of projected images of the sea, the Count was seen fighting his way out of the sack and then rising up to the surface – an effect achieved through the use of a double and the technical recourse to a pulley system.

It is assumed that these effects were devised and developed in Rambal's studios in Valencia. Here he had a permanent staff of designers, carpenters, tailors and hairdressers with whom he worked intensely for at least two weeks a year over the summer. Some would remain there while the majority of the company went on tour. In an arrangement with the Spanish rail company RENFE, he had two reserved wagons – one for actors, the other for sets, props and costumes – which would be attached to the end of trains for domestic travel. He was also known to have three warehouses in Madrid where a selection of the 15,000 sets, 19,000 costumes and props for 3,000 different stage tricks were stored (Vizcaíno Casas 1984: 230). Despite the fact that we know from posters that his company was divided into departments (electrical affairs, stage machinery, costumes, prompts, scenery, hairdressing and make-up, and music) each with a designated head, Rambal oversaw all aspects of the theatrical process, supervising the design and construction of sets and costumes, and organising and attending all rehearsals. He rehearsed daily (usually for a three-hour period), the time of rehearsals depending on the time of the first performance. Although he is known to have performed less in later years, his own reputation as an actor proved one of the company's most alluring attractions. This may have been, certainly in the early part of his career, due to his matinee idol looks and swashbuckling antics (both on- and offstage). The actress Gabi Álvarez recalls him as a confident, jocular and energetic performer who enjoyed a sharp sense of comic timing and a talent for improvisation that helped remedy the accidents that occasionally occurred onstage. He boasted of having been courted by the largest Madrid theatres where he was offered both comic and romantic leads, but reviews tend to suggest that his most conspicuous talents lay in his skills as a master

---

23 Rafael Borque, in a private, unpublished interview with the author, July 1994. All further anecdotes from Rafael Borque are from this interview.

of disguise able to conjure a theatrical space of physical metamorphoses where sets and characters are transformed within a convergent aesthetic of excess. The postures struck in the surviving photographs suggest Rambal modelled a number of his romantic and villainous roles on the early silent American films he so enjoyed.[24] Ureña certainly suggests as much when he calls him the Rudolph Valentino of Spanish theatre (1942: 143). Álvarez Barrientos believes him to have been a 'grand' and emphatic actor in the nineteenth-century tradition (1991: 101). Ureña tentatively admits as much when he makes a brief reference to an affected performance style and a slight tendency to over-enunciate (1942: 137). Marquerie records a voice defect that necessitated a clear delivery of each syllable (1969: 204). Gabi Álvarez substantiates this argument, as does Luis Maté, who observes that 'garganta' was always pronounced as 'ga-ra-gan-ta' (1978: 27). Maté may have situated Rambal as one of the great underrated Spanish actors of the twentieth century (1978: 26, 28) but judging Rambal's achievements on the basis of his abilities as an actor, however, is misleading. For as Fernán-Gómez indicates: 'Rambal fue sobre todo, además de un actor eficaz para el género que cultivaba, un extraordinario director, excepcional en el panorama español y que no tuvo continuadores' (1990: 133) (Rambal was an effective actor for the genre within which he worked but an extraordinary director, unique on the Spanish stage who had no successor). Rambal's importance lies in his promotion of theatre as a visual rather than a primarily verbal activity, with 'a dynamic use of spatial and musical categories as opposed to intellectual or literary ones' (Elsaesser 1985: 176). As such, he did not spend great amounts of time working in detail with actors on characterisation as his primary concern lay with the pictorial and physical orchestration of the *mise en scène*. Within the spectacles that Rambal created, the actor was merely another graphic component, working in conjunction with a series of other scenic elements in the rendering of stage spectacle. As such the few remaining scripts should serve not as comprehensive documents but as 'pretexts' in the sense that they provided only a point of origin for the production rather than the measure against which the production could be judged. Rambal's use of different systems of representation sought to privilege the visual, thereby questioning what Jacques Derrida refers to 'a theological stage [. . .] dominated by speech' (1978: 235). In the early years of the twentieth century, Antonin Artaud sought, in the words of Derrida, 'to reconstitute the stage [. . .] and overthrow the tyranny of the text' (1978: 236). Rambal may not have used the same strategies to achieve 'the triumph of pure mise-en-scène' (1978: 236) which proved Artaud's determining factor but his analogous achievements in positing a theatrical practice which refused to revolve around the centrality of the playtext is unquestionable.

Collaborating with a wide range of associates on the rehearsal texts, Rambal failed to adhere to the autonomous expectations of the dramatist. Eschewing the single author as the font of theatrical creation, Rambal enjoyed productive working relationships with a number of dramatists and journalists. The fact that some were

24 His summer home at Burjasot, holding a library of over 35,000 books, is known to have also had a private cinema; see Martínez Ortiz 1989: 100.

Valencian-based figures within the highly centralised culture of post-Civil War Spain may also have served to denigrate these artistic encounters within the literary establishment. The Valencian dramatist Fausto Hernández Casajuana (1888–1972), primarily known as an author of the populist *sainetes,* worked with Rambal regularly between 1929 and 1934 on projects including *Las mil y una noches* (A Thousand and One Nights) (1929) and *Al Capone* (1934), and between 1948 and 1954 on *La mujer adúltera* (The Adulterous Woman) (1948) and *Los cuarenta ladrones y Ali Babá* (Ali Baba and the Forty Thieves) (1954). Rafael Martí Orbera (1881–1963), who had also worked with Lloréns' company, provided a version of *Isabel la Católica* that premiered in 1942 (see Figure 6). The work was known under a series of titles including *La gran reina (Isabel la Católica y el descubrimiento de América)* (The Great Queen [Isabel the Catholic and the Discovery of America]), another strategy that would have made the plays harder to pin down and fix in an artistic culture which prizes a literary text which remains fixed in publication.[25] As I mentioned earlier in this chapter, Rambal's textual associates were drawn from a pool of journalists, dramatists and screenwriters including Aurelio Varela and Javier de Burgos who worked on *Volga, Volga* in the late 1920s, Pascual Guillén and Miguel Carballeda who adapted *Veinte mil leguas de viaje submarino* for its premiere at Madrid's Principal theatre in 1928 and Antonio Pérez de Olaguer who worked with Rambal on *Otra vez Pimpinela* (Pimpinela Again), an adaptation of Baroness Emmuska Orczy's novel, *Adventures of the Scarlet Pimpernel,* which premiered at Seville's Cervantes theatre on 26 November 1953. The Spanish Society of Authors holds details of 115 adaptations which Rambal worked on. The fact that so few of these were consecrated in print may partly account for the fact that he is all too often seen as a footnote in Spanish twentieth-century theatre history.[26]

Rambal and his team of collaborators, I would argue, crafted productions 'within, instead of at odds with, the context in which the theatre artist works' (Bratton 2000: 16). Drawing on a range of genres and memories rooted in both past and contemporary cultures, his company sought to provide performative utterances which engaged with popular referents and which were adapted in response to audience feedback. The work may have been dubbed commercial, inferior entertain-

25 All these collaborations are explored in much greater detail by Martínez Ortiz (1989: 109–12).

26 As well as the texts published by Talía, a number of works where Rambal was not directly involved in the adaptation, were published in magazine journals. A children's play, *El gato con botas* (Puss in Boots), adapted by Tomás Bórras and Valentín de Pedro from a tale by Charles N. Perrault, premiered in Madrid at the Novedades theatre on 5 January 1928, was published in *La Farsa,* 18 (1 January 1928); *Veinte mil leguas de viaje submarino,* adapted by Pascual Guillén and Miguel Carballeda from the novel by Jules Verne, premiered in 1928 at Madrid's Principal theatre, was published in *Comedias,* 100 (14 January 1928); *Los cuatro jinetes del Apocalipsis* (The Four Horsemen of the Apocalypse), adapted by Luis Linares Becerra from the Valencian writer Vicente Blasco Ibáñez's novel, premiered at Valencia's Principal theatre on 15 September 1923, was published in *Comedias,* 104 (11 February 1928); *Miguel Strogoff,* premiered at Valencia's Principal theatre on 17 October 1928, was published in the 110 issue of *Comedias* published later that year (Martínez Ortiz 1989: 120–34).

6 A 1952 production of *Isabel la Católica* directed by Rambal

ment but the emphasis on 'non-verbal systems of spectacle and sound' (Bratton 2000: 21) served to articulate an alternative theatrical tradition to that of the single-authored play.

Actor-impresario-director

Despite the fact that my assessment of Rambal's work with his Compañía de Grandes Espectáculos has largely concentrated on his scenic practice, the duration of his company through several decades points to him as an astute impresario who was able to exploit the fact that the films of the 1920s were silent and in black and white, thereby offering 'live' colour cinematic theatre to the motion picture hungry audiences of the time. Rodolf Sirera views him as an impresario first and an actor second, who was able to exploit the devastation suffered by the home film industry in providing alternative cinematic-driven entertainment (1989: 11–12). In the 1930s, as cinema changed, so did his repertoire and stage effects. Taking his cue from films of the time, more and more action took place against the backdrop of screen projections. To audiences accustomed to the pace of cinematic pictures and the spatial and geographical cuts which cinema facilitated, Rambal introduced an analogous practice within theatre. Indeed, his 1934 production of *Al Capone* was described as 'superproducción filmada en tres épocas y catorce fonogramas . . . con ilustraciones sonoras radiadas' (cited in Martínez Ortiz 1989: 120) (superproduction filmed in three periods and fourteen phonograms [. . .] with broadcast sound effects). For Fernando Vizcaíno Casas, Rambal's swashbuckling production of *Don Quijote* staged at Valencia's Principal theatre during the Civil War put Cecil B. de Mille to shame (1984: 232). César Oliva credits him with inventing theatrical cinemascope before the Americans and for revolutionising stage effects (1989: 101).

Vizcaíno Casas refers to him as 'el auténtico percursor de los grandes montajes escénicos' (1981: 196) (the authentic forerunner of the grand stage productions) and Álvarez Barrientos as 'un mago del teatro' (1991: 105) (a magician of the theatre). An unnamed critic went as far as to claim that, 'si Rambal hubiera nacido en otro país, su obra sería hoy célebre en todo el mundo' (A. 1946: n.pag.) (had Rambal been born in another country, he would now be a figure celebrated across the world), and A. Rodríguez de León praises him as the only modern Spanish director to achieve popular success for Lope de Vega, Pirandello and Shakespeare (1956: n.pag.). For the Venezuelan theatre critic Silvio Santiago, Rambal offered 'acaso el mejor espectáculo teatral en Europa' (cited in Martínez Ortiz 1989: 108) (perhaps the best theatrical show in Europe). Although no biographical or critical study of Orson Welles recalls his debt to Rambal, he is known to have mentioned to a number of Spanish film critics a fascination with the range of theatrical effects Rambal was capable of generating.[27] Carlos Saura features a direct homage to Rambal's production style during three episodes of his 1978 film *Mamá cumple cien años/Mamá Turns One Hundred*. The first, as the eponymous Mamá is grandly flown down into the expansive living room from the unseen heavens to the sound of popular *sevillanas*; the second a sham 'miracle' sequence, and the third Mamá's extraordinary rise from the dead accompanied by excessive theatrical effects.

Saura is not the only filmmaker to feature references to Rambal in his work. José Luis Borau's 1986 feature *Tata mía/My Nanny* has a remark about his superlative acting skills when the aged Tata, played not insignificantly by the great music hall star Imperio Argentina, refers to the timid Teo's improvised performance as 'divino, mejor que Rambal' (divine, better than Rambal). Although there is some evidence that Rambal's popularity waned in the early 1950s when his scenic effects no longer seemed as magnificent as they had done in earlier decades, actors and technicians who worked with him at this time recalled his professional designs, the intricate and demanding nature of his stage trickery, and the box-office 'pull' his name still enjoyed in the provinces (Oliva 1989: 27–8).

For Sirera, Rambal's achievements lie in the conjuring of great possibilities from antiquated theatrical machinery in the early decades of the twentieth century. Had Rambal chosen to work with more 'innovative' plays, rather than with a more populist repertoire, Sirera goes onto to argue, he might well have attracted greater attention from theatre historians (1989: 12–13). Álvarez Barrientos associates Rambal with Ramón Caralt and Doroteo Maté who also used cinematic projections as backdrops to the action. The latter, Álvarez Barrientos notes, is referred to by Mario Vargas Llosa in *La tía Julia y el escribidor* (*Aunt Julia and the Scriptwriter*) (1991: 96–7). For Vizcaíno Casas, however, his legacy spills over into a further generation of directors, anticipating José Tamayo, Luis Escobar and Cayetano Luca de Tena in dispensing with simplistic painted backdrops in favour of more adventur-

---

27 Emilio Sanz de Soto told me in June 1990 that he once heard Orson Welles say as much to a group of critics in the 1960s. Carlos Saura mentioned to me in 1990 that he remembered reading a published interview with Welles in which he recalls that Welles mentioned Rambal. I have not, to date, been able to trace this interview.

ous scenic manoeuvres (1984: 230). Indeed Luca de Tena was among a group of Spanish theatre professionals (including Benavente, Irene López Heredia and Claudio de la Torre) who proposed Rambal for the Medalla al Mérito en el Trabajo (Professional Medal of Merit) in 1947 (Martínez Ortiz 1989: 56). Vizcaíno Casas also traces an influence through Rambal's son-in-law Roberto Carpio who was to work with Samuel Bronston on the production design for a number of the large-budget films he was to make in Spain between 1959 and 1964 (1984: 232). Carpio was also to work as assistant art director on Michael Powell's *Luna de miel/Honeymoon* in 1959.

Although it could not be claimed that Rambal's was an actors' theatre, it is known that a number of renowned actors including Carmen Bernardos, Ismael Merlo, Carlos Lemos, Nati Mistral, Alberto Lorca and José Luis Lespe passed through his company. Gabi Álvarez recalls him as a demanding choreographer of stage action, who expected great physical precision from his performers. Critics may have denounced the shallow characterisation that ran through his dramas (Álvarez Barrientos 1991: 99), but a marked interest in 'character' as psychological construct never seemed a motivating factor in his work. Character was effectively of secondary importance. Through his orchestration of the characters and action like a puppet-master – or 'maestro de cuentos'[28] (master storyteller) as Saura refers to him – Rambal aspired to a different type of theatre where the visual does not merely serve to illustrate or support the verbal. He drew on characteristics which the Spanish theatre in its striving for naturalistic idioms of performance had lost. Rambal showed the possibilities that theatre still offered as spectacle, a means of bringing together an entire community to participate in the type of theatrical pageants visible before theatre moved into indoor spaces at the end of the sixteenth century. Rambal's spectacles did not attempt to hide their status as dramatic artefacts. On the contrary, they glorified in a recognition of their existence as 'theatre' as opposed to 'life', in many cases depending on, or at least exploiting as a marketing tool, the audience's prior knowledge of a referent – as with the theatrical adaptations of American cinematic successes. There was no attempt to exclude the spectator on the part of the actor, no attempt to pretend, as in the work of classic realist writers, that the audience is an invisible witness. In the 1940s and 1950s when the Franco dictatorship advocated conformism and conservatism, Rambal's theatre actively encouraged vociferous audience participation. Gabi Álvarez has spoken of audience members screaming out directions and advice in the hope of reuniting the two orphan girls in his 1955 production of *Las dos huérfanas de París*. The directions displayed an awareness on the audience's part of the theatrical space as 'other', where intervention – strongly discouraged in the public arena by the Franco regime – was encouraged. Audiences were agitated and aroused, stimulated and provoked. In contrast to the celebration and promotion of the Hispanic in endorsed films and songs of the time, Rambal used a significant number of foreign texts as the basis of his productions providing audiences with the thrill of a taste of

28 Carlos Saura, in a private, unpublished interview with the author, June 1990.

'the foreign' without ever leaving their seat. The local extras – often up to a hundred – employed during the tours ensured 'participation' on a series of levels in a systematic manner unseen for centuries.

In the difficult years of the post-Civil War period the pleasure offered to a significant proportion of the population by Rambal's dramas should not be underestimated. Emotionally-charged productions staging family loss and separation, amorous intrigue and anguish, and gruesomely enacted crucifixions offered catharsis for those who had suffered upheavals, bereavement and injury during the fratricidal Civil War. In the Franco years especially, the baroque *mise en scène* and open episodic non linear nature of Rambal's productions offered both a commentary on the gulf between a theatrical aesthetic of excess and a social environment of material poverty and deprivation, and a positing of alternative co-existing narratives which strongly contrasted with the singular and unified version of 'truth' and 'self' promoted by the dictatorship. The gaps of narrative ellipsis allowed a voice for the silence that permeated a society and whose political infrastructure disallowed the articulation of its causes. Errant heroes and heroines may have suffered for their non-conformity but the swift punishments enacted at the close could not eradicate the vicarious pleasures enjoyed (by both cast and audience) during the course of the performance. Identification with the 'other' served, as Jo Labanyi notes with regard to spectators who identified with the seductive females of the folkloric musical films of the 1940s and 1950s, to construct the audiences of both sexes as female: 'in the process, they are also constructed as belonging to a social outgroup – one represented as infinitely more attractive than the stiff, repressed dominant classes' (1997: 225). The emphasis in Rambal's repertory on texts like Joaquín Dicenta's 1895 'proletarian' play *Juan José* with its emphasis on contentious class polemics, Lope de Vega's *Fuenteovejuna,* Hugo's *Los miserables* and Benavente's first play premiered in 1894, *El nido ajeno* (The Distant Nest), an audacious interrogation of marital infidelities and stultifying social conventions, indicate a commitment towards narratives of social marginalisation and domestic discontents which may perhaps have provided moments of what Labanyi refers to as 'carnivalesque reversal', offering those habitually classified as inferior in terms of class and gender moments of 'cathartic release' (1997: 226).[29] In the variety of a repertoire which embraced over a thousand works and eschewed easy categorisation, Rambal pointed to a hybridity which defies attempts to locate him solely within the sphere of popular adaptations of *folletines* or populist texts of the time as critics have tended to do.[30]

Rambal's diverse body of work served to indicate a strategy that Melveena McKendrick observes at work among the seventeenth-century dramatists whose metatheatrical spectacles of self-conscious reflexivity and illusionist interplay she deconstructs in a study of stage portraits in the theatre of the Golden Age:

---

29 For further information on the polemics engendered by *Juan José,* see Gies 1994: 325–30 and Mas Ferrer 1978: 108–38.
30 See, for example, Vilches de Frutos 1998: 8 and Rodríguez Méndez 1974: 89.

If the theatre, in its procedures and in its very consideration of its own task, its own identity, called on images of representation which echoed an entire nation's concern with its own appearance, it reflected back at that nation a world of illusion and make-believe which served as a paradigm for its own attempts at self-construction. If the theatre was life, then the life of the nation [. . .] was pure theatre. (1994: 3)

Staging dissonance, distress and disorder, Rambal's Compañía de Grandes Espectáculos presented self-conscious performance as the definitive idiom. Voicing pain and pleasure in terms of visible enactment, their staginess served to remind audiences of the constructed nature of all representation. The political, social and cultural controls of the state were robustly delineated in Rambal's narratives of a dissolving social order curtailed and corrected by the forces of state represented by the patriarchal characters who imposed discipline and direction on the seductively wayward protagonists.

Apparently pro-Republic during the Civil War, he reinvented himself in the post-War era. Attuned to the precarious demands of the Francoist censor, Rambal astutely tailored his exotic spectacles to the demands of the time. Scripts submitted for scrutiny had few stage directions. Polemical issues and sexual innuendo were conspicuously avoided with a firm emphasis placed on anti-naturalism in both set and performance design. Material which might have been judged 'realist' was re-presented within an aesthetic of playful and decorative excess. As such, intervention by the censors was rare and seems to have been limited to the proportion of cleavage costumes were permitted to display. In addition, the staging of *Calasanz*, a grandiose treatment of the Aragonese saint San José de Calasanz written by the poet and cleric Liborio Portolés Piquer, which opened in Madrid in 1945, may have proved an astute choice in keeping the censors at bay. Although the piece was not to play a prominent role in the company's repertory, its presence in the 1945 season at Valencia's Principal theatre conveniently served to articulate publicly the company's Catholic and nationalist credentials.

Rambal's accommodation of the renowned (pre-Civil War) Catalan husband and wife actors Maria Vila and Pius Daví during his 1944–45 season in Barcelona certainly points to a willingness to incorporate into his company performers judged contentious by the Franco regime. Vila and Daví who were to take the roles of Guillermina and the professor in the Barcelona performances of *Drácula*, here enjoyed an onstage visibility which was denied to them while Catalan remained an unendorsed stage language in the years before the *represa* or relaunch of theatre in Catalan post-1946. While research remains to be done on how long the couple remained with the company, Enric Gallén's *El teatre a la ciutat de Barcelona durant el règim franquista (1939–1954)* indicates how Rambal was to offer professional sanctuary to Vila and Daví at a time when their stage presence alone constituted a political act (1985: 108–10).

As the ideology promoted purity and the return to fifteenth-century values, Rambal forged ahead in his hybridisation, anticipating current mixed media theatre practice with his appropriation and utilisation of film. He took risks when other companies preached frugality and economy – risks which Álvarez Barrientos states sometimes necessitated a splitting of the company in two to fulfil all contractual obligations (1991: 104).[31] The absence of legislation regarding the number of permitted daily performances allowed Rambal to provide three or even four performances a day. He was therefore able to accommodate huge audience numbers. Additionally, he appealed not simply to the middle classes that populated the fashionable theatres of Madrid and Barcelona but also to the workers and peasants who travelled from distant towns and villages to catch sight of his productions. Through his popular adaptations of successful films and novels of the time he won over an audience who were then willing to watch the company perform classic pieces like Rostand's *Cyrano de Bergerac* and Calderón's *El príncipe constante* (*The Constant Prince*).[32] It is hard to think of another Spanish theatre practitioner of this era, excluding García Lorca, who aspired to such a radical agenda or made such a profound impact across the class divide.

31 Rafael Borque mentions that Rambal had two different designs for *Don Juan Tenorio*: one for larger theatres and another for smaller venues. As such, when asked by a theatre in Murcia to return with *Don Juan Tenorio,* he remained with the production in Alicante, sending half the company with a new production that he blocked in two days.

32 Marquerie (1969: 205) writes of him 'moving the masses' with his classical productions.

3
A Spanish actress on the French stage: María Casares

L'art de Maria Casarès possède le pouvoir capital de la tragédie: fonder le spectacle sur l'évidence de la passion. Si elle crie, si elle pleure, si elle attend, c'est jusqu'au bout, c'est jusqu'au seuil de l'intolérable, qui est aussi celui d'une intelligence débarrassée de ses doutes. L'intonation, le geste, la marche, l'attitude, sont à chaque fois risqués dans leur totalité, poussés si loin qu'il n'y a plus de place pour les fuir: le spectateur est lié par ce sacrifice de l'ombre, qui a lieu devant lui, sur une scène incendiée, où toutes les petites raisons du spectacle (coquetterie, cabotinage, belles voix, beaux costumes, nobles sentiments) sont jetées au bûcher, dissipées par un art qui est véritablement tragique parce qu'il inonde de clarté. (Barthes 1993: 410)

(The art of Maria Casarès possesses the capital power of tragedy: the spectacle is founded on the conspicuousness of passion. If she shouts, if she cries, if she waits, it is taken to its limits, to the threshold of the unbearable, which is also that of an intelligence with all doubt removed. The intonation, the gestures, the walk, the attitude are always risked in their entirety, pushed so far that there is nowhere left to run from them: the spectator is bound by this shadow sacrifice, which takes place before him, on a burned-out stage where all the little reasons of the play (coquetry, ham acting, beautiful voices, pretty costumes, noble sentiments) are tossed on to the fire, dispersed by an art that is truly tragic because it floods them in sunlight.) (trans. Joel Anderson)

All great performers articulate the conflicts of their time. (Stokes 1996: 116)

The cover of Colin Crisp's 1993 survey of French film during the mid-decades of the twentieth century, *The Classic French Cinema, 1930–1960*, features a poster of *Les Enfants du paradis*, Marcel Carné's emblematic 1945 film, produced during the German occupation (see Figure 7). The film's importance in celebrating a cultural tradition that recognises both the popular and the elite posits the nineteenth-century theatrical world created by Carné and his performance and production team as a milieu of transformation and artistic invention. Revolving around the prisms of freedom and imprisonment, it has often been read as a political allegory in which Arletty's enigmatic Garance personifies the French 'spirit of resistance' and María Casares' Nathalie 'compliance with the values of the Vichy regime' (Forbes 1997: 29, 11). As Arletty's Garance stares alluringly at the viewer from the poster in a seductive revealing dress, Casares' face rests among the other facades from the ensemble cast (Jean-Louis Barrault's Baptiste Debureau, Pierre Brasseur's dashing Frédérick Lemaître, Marcel Herrand's dastardly Pierre-François Lacenaire, Louis

7 A poster for Marcel Carné's 1945 film *Les Enfants du paradis*

Salou's discerning Count Edouard de Montray and Pierre Renoir's worldly wanderer Jericho). The pictorial composition of the poster positions Arletty's Garance as the individualist and it is Casares – in her first film role – who is placed alongside the other protagonists staring out past Garance. While critics have tended to view Casares' lovelorn Nathalie, pining for Barrault's Baptiste, whose affections lie with the elusive, unknowable Garance, as a conservative being, Garance herself demonstrates a remarkable capacity to adapt to the demands of any situation, functioning as a symbol of versatile self-sufficiency as she takes on the varied roles allocated to her. It is Casares' Nathalie who breaks the rules of the game in crying out Baptiste's name as he observes the flirting of Garance and Frédérick backstage. And it is Nathalie in the film's second part, 'L'Homme blanc', who stands by Baptiste as he falls into a desperate depression fearing once more the loss of Garance. While Jill Forbes may argue that the performers in the film 'enact what they are in more ways than one', in her assessment of Casares' 'conformity to offscreen type' she is only able to cite a supposed infatuation with the homosexual Herrand, unable to return her affections, as one of the complex ways in which the 'real-life habits and tastes' of the performers are 'knowingly, if obliquely, referred to in the film narrative' (1997: 56). The bulk of the *Les Enfants du paradis* was shot between February and December 1944. By May of that year Casares was already romantically involved with the writer Albert Camus (1913–60) in whose play *Le Malentendu* (*Cross Purpose*) she was to appear in June.

The 'interpenetration of life and art', which Forbes views as one of the key motifs of *Les Enfants du paradis*, does indeed spill over into Casares, although not in the way that Forbes suggests. Nathalie's loyalty and protectiveness of Baptiste are echoed in Casares' strong political affiliations with Spain's Second Republic in whose government her father, Santiago Casares Quiroga, had served through a number of prominent political positions including Minister of War and Prime Minister. As a Republican exile in German-occupied Paris, Casares' own precarious position is delineated in her autobiography, *Résidente privilégiée,* first published in France in 1980 and published by Barcelona's Editorial Argos Vergara in a Spanish edition the following year. Her assistance in concealing Jewish friends, her association with Camus's Resistance activities, her father's escape to Britain to avoid the Germans, and her contact with the Spanish émigré community in Paris all rendered her a dubious figure within the suspicious culture of occupied France.[1] Occupying an uneasy position between French and Spanish, theatre and film, resident and foreigner, Casares' association with a film now exuberantly acknowledged as a subversive study of imaginative creativity and cultural resurgence was to initiate a screen career whose ascendancy was marked by dazzling performances in *Les Dames du Bois de Boulogne/The Ladies of the Bois de Boulogne* (1945), *La Chartreuse de Parme/The Charterhouse of Parme* (1947) and *Orphée* (1950). If Arletty's cinematic work was to be largely curtailed by her wartime liaison with a German soldier, Casares' was to ascend in spectacular fashion. If I have chosen to open this chapter with a discussion of Casares' links to *Les Enfants du paradis,* it is because it serves not only to throw up some key issues around Casares' dual Spanish/French identities which this study seeks to pursue, but also because it distinguishes Casares (alongside Herrand and Barrault especially) as a theatrical performer who was to forge a distinctive trajectory within Occupied and post-War France. Now cited one of the great *tragédiennes* of the twentieth century, her 'difference' was to be played out across the French stage and screen in a network of intricate ways. Casares' extraordinary voice: deep, resonant, hoarse, tinged with a Galician musical lilt, and the rich rolling r's which she was never entirely to banish from her French inflection, together with her distinctive appearance: the slanted almond-shaped eyes, pronounced chin, and angular chiselled features were to mark her as 'other' – an actress who went against the grain of increasing naturalism in theatrical work during the post-War era. Casares may be absent from such reference volumes as the *Encyclopedia of European Cinema* (ed. Vincendeau 1995), ironic in view of her screen work in both Spanish and French, but her presence in such encyclopedic works as Aguilar and Genover's *Las estrellas de nuestro cine* (1996: 140–1) and the *International Directory of Theatre* (Thody 1996: 154–5) recognises the extraordinary scope of her theatre and filmic work. This included collaborations with Artaud, Cocteau, and Vilar in the 1940s and 1950s, the premiere of Genet's controversial study of the Algerian war, *Les Paravents* (*The Screens*) in 1966, a long association with Argentine director Jorge Lavelli beginning with *Divinas palabras* (*Divine Words*) in 1964 and a productive relationship with Bernard Sobel at Gennevilliers in the 1990s. Rather than provide a chronological exploration of her work on the Paris stage, this chapter serves to trace out the tensions between Casares' Spanish

---

1 For further details, see Casarès 1980: 213–16, 246–9, 163, 140–50.

identity and French training – embodied in the dual spellings of her name[2] – by focusing on particular productions that indicate this dialectic at work.

The condition of exile and the Spanish Civil War

Exiled figures are rarely featured as objects of study within studies of their native theatrical traditions. If, as Hans-Bernhard Moeller states, the motif of exile itself occurs explicitly or implicitly in the work of exiled writers (1983a: 9), it may be productive to examine how traces of Casares' status as a political refugee are played out in her choice of repertoire. Spanish cultural identity is irrevocably bound up with the identities of the figures who were forced into exile by the circumstances of the Civil War and its aftermath. Luis Cernuda, Max Aub, Alejandro Casona, José R. Morales and Rafael Alberti all produced works of poetry and drama in exile which may have first been produced before a non-target audience. These figures were isolated from their native processes of production and obliged to work within non-familiar editorial presses or theatrical venues. As such it is possible to argue that there was both a domestic theatrical culture during the Franco regime and an 'alternative' culture in exile which incorporates the theatrical ventures of Margarita Xirgu in Argentina, Chile and Uruguay, the dramatic output of Rafael Alberti and Alejandro Casona in Argentina, the work of José R. Morales in Chile, Max Aub and León Felipe in Mexico, and Pedro Salinas in the US, among others.[3] The role of publishing houses like the Argentine based Losada (formed in 1938), in diffusing works through the Spanish-speaking world should not be underestimated for between 1938 and 1977 they were responsible for the publication of over 2,000 titles of which a significant proportion were dramatic works (Moeller 1983b: 60). The Franco-Argentine director Jorge Lavelli has articulated the importance of the generation of Spanish theatrical performers who sought refuge in Argentina in consolidating both a theatrical training infrastructure and a rich performative culture (cited in Delgado 2002a: 225). The performers, directors and writers who arrived in France either in the first wave of exile during the Civil War, like the teenage Casares, Jorge Semprún and Carlos Semprún-Maura, or Arrabal (and to a lesser extent José Martín Elizondo and Agustín Gómez Arcos), who went into self-imposed exile in Paris during the post-War period, have slipped through categorisation or been classified as French because they chose to perform or write in the language of their new adopted state.[4] The fact that, as John London has outlined, Arrabal tends to write his plays in Spanish and then work with his wife Luce on the French version has not prevented an identification of Arrabal as French (1997:

2 This chapter will use the Spanish María Casares rather than the French Maria Casarès, although French bibliographical references will feature the French spelling of her name.
3 Mexico, the most active supporter of the Spanish Republic, which refused to recognise the Franco regime, accepted the greatest proportion of Republican refugees. For details on Mexico, Chile and Argentina's response to the Civil War and its refugees, see Szuchman 1983: 33–8.
4 For further details on the work of these figures in Paris, see Bradby and Delgado 2002: 17–19.

211). Casares too has tended to be displaced onto histories of French theatre, positioned as a key collaborator of Jean Vilar at the Théâtre National Populaire (TNP) between 1954 and 1959, an important Shakespearean actress with a clinical Lady Macbeth in 1954, a delicately mannered Titania in *Le Songe d'une nuit d'été* (*A Midsummer Night's Dream*) in 1959 and a seminal Cleopatra in 1975, and as an eclectic champion of more controversial writing as witnessed by her involvement in *Les Paravents* in 1966 and 1983 and Koltès's *Quai Ouest* (*Quay West*) in 1986.[5]

Phyllis Zatlin has meticulously chronicled the intercultural relationship between the Spanish and French stages during the twentieth century, but she is the first to acknowledge that this symbiosis can be seen much earlier in 'Spanish sources for seventeenth-century French plays', as with Molière's debt to Spanish dramatists, and Beaumarchais's absorption of 'Spanish plot construction' (1994: 1–2). In nineteenth-century Spain Mariano José de Larra, who was to provide translations for a range of French plays, located in France that which he most admired in contemporary society (Gies 1994: 107–8). The allure of France, and more specifically Paris, as a training ground for performers is not a recent phenomenon. David Thatcher Gies explains that during the 1800–1 theatrical season Madrid's most eminent actor, Isidoro Máiquez, had ventured to Paris to study the techniques of much-admired French actor François Joseph Talma who was seen as the purveyor of a more natural performance style (1994: 6). Xirgu was to be a regular visitor to Paris in the pre-Civil War era, ordering costumes there and collecting works for tentative translation into Castilian.[6] The directors Adrià Gual and Cipriano de Rivas Cherif had spent formative periods in Paris in 1901 and 1919–20 respectively, and bohemian *fin-de-siècle* Paris was to prove a prominent model for Barcelona's artists and architects in the early twentieth century.

It was the Spanish Civil War, 'sometimes labelled the last great "romantic" war' (Zatlin 1994: 3), which, as well as providing controversial subject matter for politically committed writers like Albert Camus and Armand Gatti, brought into France an influx of exiles – over 400,000 during the closing months of the war alone (Zatlin 1994: 15) – who were to decisively shape the cultural environments of the areas in which they settled. Zatlin documents the Spanish theatre groups that were to emerge in Toulouse (1994: 25), the TIEIT university-theatre of Bordeaux (22–4) and the theatrical trajectories of Jorge Semprún (Socialist Minister of Culture from 1988 to 1991) and his brother Carlos Semprún-Maura, who both left Spain in 1936, settling in France following a brief period in Holland where their father was the Republican Government's Ambassador (75–7, 191–206). While the performers Albert Boadella, Anna Lizaran, Joan Font, José Luis Gómez and Josep Maria Flotats all trained in France during the Franco regime, only Flotats was to carve out a career in French theatre before returning to Barcelona in the mid-1980s.[7]

5 For examples of such an approach, see Kirkup 1996 and Ortega 1997: 112–15.
6 For further details, see Chapter 1, 22.
7 For further details, see Bradby and Delgado 2002: 27–8. The dramatist-designer Francisco Nieva was based in Paris for a twelve-year period beginning in 1952 where he worked with such figures as Georges Wilson.

It was María Casares, however, who was to forge the way for these performers in pursuing her training in Paris and then cultivating a career on the Parisian stage. Unlike Flotats, who attended the French Lycée in Barcelona and was therefore fluent in French by the time he arrived at the Strasbourg Theatre School in 1959, Casares was to learn French only on her arrival in Paris in November 1936. She was to remain in France for the remainder of her life, working in Argentina and Spain only for brief periods in the mid-1960s and 1976–77 respectively. While she proved not particularly attached to the promotion of Spanish theatre in Paris in the way that Franco-Spanish actress Germaine Montero (1909–2000) was to be, the body of her production work does indicate certain motifs which clarify how her 'difference' was played out on the French stage and screen.

Casares in Paris

María Victoria Casares Pérez was born on 21 November 1922 in Galicia, the Celtic corner of north-west Spain. In her autobiography she writes of how Maria Casarès was in many ways her pseudonym, acquired in France to protect her name (1980: 142). The difference between Spanish and French accentuation was to render the final 'es' of her name silent in French. As such she was to add a grave accent to the final e to preserve the Spanish pronunciation of her name. Known as a child as Vitoliña or Vitola, it is perhaps not surprising that she should refer to the birth of Maria Casarès at the Mathurins theatre where she was to debut in John Millington Synge's *Deirdre of the Sorrows* (*Deirdre des douleurs*) in November 1942 (1980: 344).

The novelist Manuel Rivas describes Galicia as 'a land of emigration', claiming that the largest *gallego* cemetery in the world was to be found in Havana and that the biggest Galician city in the world was Buenos Aires (cited in Eaude 2001: 11). Emigration for Casares involved an initial move to Madrid due to her father's political career. Casares Quiroga was so strongly identified with the Republic that any decision to remain in Spain after the Civil War would have resulted in imprisonment for the family and possible death for Casares Quiroga. Already in the early 1930s, Casares Quiroga had spent time in Madrid's Modelo prison after his death sentence for involvement in the Jaca rebellion had been commuted to life imprisonment.[8] Casares' elder half-sister Esther, married to her father's associate Enrique Varela, remained in Spain following the outbreak of the Civil War, and was to be imprisoned for three years when Franco came to power for simply being the daughter of Casares Quiroga.[9]

---

8 For details on the Jaca rebellion and its place in the climate of political dissent that predated the Civil War, see Thomas 1990: 30–1. The Jaca insurrection was to provide the genesis for Alberti's 1931 play *Fermín Galán*. Casares was later to appear in a seminal 1976 staging of Alberti's *El adefesio* (The Absurdity); see 122–7.
9 Esther was only allowed to leave Spain for Mexico in 1955 where she joined her husband who had gone to Central America at the end of the Civil War; see Casarès 1980: 50–1, 258.

During the early months of the War, Casares had worked with her mother as a volunteer at Madrid's ophthalmic hospital where she came into contact with some of the early casualties (Casarès 1980: 114–27). As nationalist forces approached Madrid, Casares and her mother, Gloria Pérez, left for Paris. Their father joined them at the end of the War. When the Germans invaded Paris, the family aimed to leave France for Britain but only Casares Quiroga could be accommodated on the boat from Bordeaux and Casares and her mother returned to Paris (Casarès 1980: 158–63) where the daughter prepared to enter the Conservatoire.

The decision to train as an actress appears to have its roots in numerous sources. While Casares states that the profession was chosen for her by her mother who had a great love of theatre (1980: 42–3), she writes of reciting Valle-Inclán from a young age (1980: 36), and of an awareness of the theatrical renovation being undertaken by Rivas Cherif, García Lorca and Xirgu among others in the period 1931–36 (1980: 85). Indeed Casares was taught by García Lorca's sister Isabel at the liberal educational establishment, El Instituto Escuela, where she studied during her time in Madrid (Casarès 1980: 85–6). At school she was to appear in numerous productions, including Benavente's *El príncipe que todo lo aprendió en los libros* (*The Prince Who Learned Everything out of Books*) where she was to play a witch (1980: 91) and a project directed by Rafael Alberti with whom she was to later collaborate on *El adefesio* (The Absurdity) (1980: 105–6). At the home of the Palencia family she was to perform in two of Isabel de Palencia's pieces to an audience formed of friends and intellectuals including García Lorca and Valle-Inclán (1980: 105–6).

On her arrival in France early friends included the Spanish actor Pierre Alcover and his wife Colonna Romano, who was with the Comédie Française (Casarès 1980: 140). Romano especially was to encourage Casares – then studying at the Lycée Victor-Duruy – introducing her to the elderly André Antoine in Brittany for whom she recited a Verlaine poem in the summer of 1937 (Casarès 1980: 154–5). The encounter, recalled by Casares in her autobiography, was greeted with a single chastising remark by Antoine, which was to teach her the value of a better economy of gesture, especially the need to avoid undertaking unnecessary or clumsy hand movements. Although Casares first auditioned for Le Conservatoire in 1939, it was not until her third attempt, in 1940, that she was to be accepted (1980: 155–75). She attributes this failure to her poor French that was at the time marked by Spanish inflections (of pronunciation). As a visitor to Louis Jouvet's workshops and René Simon's diction classes at Le Conservatoire and working regularly with a diction coach between 1939 and 1940, she laboured to open her As, smooth out her guttural tones and her southern nasality, and efface her Spanish accent (Casarès 1980: 158).

In 1942 Casares joined the Mathurins theatre, which was run by Herrand and Jean Marchat. Herrand and Marchat had succeeded the Russian émigrés George and Ludmilla Pitoëff who had re-styled the boulevard theatre into an adventurous venue balancing both lesser-known classics and new works. Appearing in *Deirdre des douleurs* in November, she failed to attend classes regularly and was unceremoniously dismissed from Le Conservatoire (Casarès 1980: 211). Although critics were generally unimpressed with the play, Casares' performance was singled out for superlative praise with *Cahiers du Sud* referring to her as 'a surprising conductor of dramatic energy' (cited in Lottman 1981: 275). Key roles in *Les Enfants de paradis* and *Les Dames du Bois du Boulogne* followed, opening up the option of pursuing a film career. Her role as the defiant Deirdre in Synge's play, a Helen of Troy refusing her designated bridegroom for a younger lover, and then returning seven years later to her death, which triggers the demise of a city, was to initiate a theatrical career defined by the enactment of bold, resistant characters on the margins of social convention. The damaged outsiders she was to personify were marked by temperamental contrasts and dismantled existing hierarchies. Her low, husky, resonating voice, contrasting with her seductive, darkly wistful feminine features, incorporated signs of both genders. It is perhaps not surprising that the terms that littered the obituaries of her death on 22 November 1996 were the masculine *mito* (myth) and *monstruo sagrado* (*monstre sacré*) rather than the feminine *estrella* (star).[10] This may have been, in part, both recognition of the tough-spirited resilience which was to infuse her roles, interrogating what it means to be a woman at a time of gender insecurity, and her personification of two key male roles at Gennevilliers' Centre Dramatique National: a twitching, elderly Lear in Bernard Sobel's production of *King Lear, Threepenny Lear*, in 1993, and the Pope in Genet's posthumous play *Elle* (1990) directed by Bruno Bayen.

Existentialism and exile

John Spalek is one of numerous critics who have drawn attention to the links between 'the existentialist and the exile experiences' highlighting the prototypes – the prisoner, the rebel, the political refugee – that feature in the work of both (1983: 80). While little was made of Albert Camus's theatrical output in the Spanish obituaries of his death – interestingly, it was observed that *La Peste* (*The Plague*) was to reach Spain a good ten years later than the rest of Europe (Manegat 1960: 11) – the plays have enjoyed a prolific history south of the Pyrenees with productions of *Le Malentendu* (*Cross Purpose*), translated as *El malentendido*, in 1955, 1969 and 1970.[11] This may in part be due to a debt to García Lorca's *La casa de Bernarda Alba* (*The House of Bernarda Alba*), recognised by critic André Camp (1985: 51), or what Zatlin terms Camus's 'strong moralistic bent' (1994: 118). It may also have to do with Camus's affiliations with Republican Spain or with the disturbing thematics of absence and belonging that define his work, populated by outsiders who struggle to make sense of the suspended state they are obliged to negotiate. It may be for this reason that, when Herrand first handed Casares a copy of Camus's *Le Malentendu* while she was shooting *Les Dames du Bois de Boulogne*, she was immediately taken with it. Her association with Camus's work – as well as *Le Malentendu*

---

10 See, for example, Kirkup 1996 and Caballero 1996.
11 For further details, see London 1997: 120 and Zatlin 1994: 118–19.

in June 1944, she went on to premiere *L'État de siège* (The State of Siege) and *Les Justes* (*The Just*) in October 1948 and December 1949 respectively – was to see her labelled as Camus's muse, a classification she resolutely denied, affirming a fraternity based on shared interests and Hispanic origins (cited in Oltra 1988: 94). Camus's maternal grandmother had been born in San Luis, a village near Mahon (Todd 1998: 255). At the publishers Gallimard Camus had worked with translators on an edition of García Lorca's works and had staged the Spanish dramatist's plays while in Algiers (Todd 1998: 290).

According to Camus, *Le Malentendu,* written far from Algiers during the Vichy regime, 'wears the colors of exile' (cited in Todd 1998: 186). Indeed at one point he toyed with calling it *L'Exilé.* The play was premiered in a climate of uncertainty on 24 June 1944 with the Battle of Cherbourg raging. Earlier performances had been postponed because of electricity restrictions. The play was performed on 25 June and then 2–23 July, returning again after the liberation of Paris in October.[12] Casares took the role of the austere Martha, running an isolated inn in inhospitable Czechoslovakia with her elderly mother, who longs to escape to the warm south. When visited by their long-disappeared brother Jan (played by Herrand), they fail to recognise him and murder him for his money as they have done with all previous guests. The revelation of his identity by his wife Maria comes too late and both mother and daughter kill themselves in horror. Despite the play's poor reception, Simone de Beauvoir writes in her autobiography of the impact of Casares' performance (1965: 587). The press's hostility has been partly attributed by Lottman to Camus's presence in the resistance, Casares' father's status in England and the fact that Jan's wife Maria was played by Hélène Vercors, whose husband Pierre Bourdan worked for Free French radio (1981: 320–1). Casares' embittered Martha, characterised by a harshly clamped-back hairstyle, secured praise even from the collaborative press like *Le Gerbe* where the writer André Castelot, dismissing the play as *Grand Guignol,* singled out Casares' performance as superb (cited in Todd 1998: 186). Béatrice Dussane, Casares' former acting teacher, has described the booing and sneering that accompanied the production, outlining the resilience of the actress in dominating the commotion breaking out in the stalls, as 'la révélation d'une Casarès guerrière' (1953: 40) (the revelation of a warrior Casares).

Camus's *Caligula* (1945) was to launch the career of twenty-three year old Gérard Philipe who had appeared earlier that year with Casares in René Laporte's *Federigo* at the Mathurins and who was, alongside Casares, to go on to form part of the TNP company during the 1950s. Casares' next collaboration with Camus was to be *L'État de siège* (almost called *L'Inquisition à Cadix*) written specifically for Casares and Philipe.[13]

Opening at the Marigny theatre on 27 October 1948, it proved a high-profile production by the Madeleine Renaud-Jean-Louis Barrault company, directed by

12 For further details about the conditions in which the production was staged, see Lottman 1981: 318–20.
13 For further details, see Todd 1998: 244.

Barrault with scenery and costumes by the painter Balthus and a cast including Pierre Brasseur – another member of *Les Enfants du paradis* cast – as the villain Nada. Like his earlier *Révolté dans les Asturies* (Revolt in Asturias), the play, set in Cadiz, revolves around the politics of rebellion. Written at a time when Camus was very involved with the Republican exile community in Paris, not merely through Casares, with whom he had resumed an affair in June 1948, but through his involvement with the Federación Española de Deportados e Internados Políticos (FEDIP) and Confederación Nacional de Trabajo (CNT), French-based émigré organisations, the plague which engulfs the characters clearly stands as a symbol for totalitarianism and has echoes of both Franco's occupation of Republican Spain and the German rampage through France.[14] Casares' character, the fiancée of rebel Diego (Barrault), is given the name Victoria – Casares' own middle name. The production, however, failed to convince the critics who lambasted both the poor characterisation and Camus's decision to set the play in Spain, rather than Eastern Europe (Marcel 1948: 8; Barjaval 1948: 11). They were also unimpressed by the uneasy coalition between Barrault's mannered staging that visualised the plague in an Artaudian sense, and the allegorical tone of the play which recalls Calderón's *autos sacramentales*, a debt Camus was to acknowledge (Todd 1998: 263). Casares may have felt a strong affiliation with the play, but according to Dussane, she was emphatically miscast in a dull romantic pairing with Barrault (1953: 48–9).

Casares classifies her third collaboration with Camus, *Les Justes*, which opened at the Hébertot theatre on 15 December 1949 in a production by Paul Oettly, as the role where she gave the greatest of herself (cited in Soriano 1988: 62). Cast as the young terrorist, Dora Doulebov, part of a team seeking to assassinate Grand Duke Sergei Alexandrovitch, the uncle of Tsar Nicholas II, in 1905, Casares was again to elicit adulation from sections of the press who proved much harsher on the play itself. Certainly critical opinion was split along partisan lines with ideological debates raging on the play's merits in the right- and left-wing press.[15] There can be little doubt that *Les Justes'* exploration of the boundaries of terrorist action recalled, perhaps to an uncomfortable degree, the activities of the Resistance, with its echoes in very recent French history. The fact that the play was still running after six months with only two performances cancelled following the death of Casares' father on 17 February 1950, suggests that its conflicting arguments around the limits of political terrorism struck a potent chord with post-War audiences.

Casares' impact on Camus's writing goes far beyond her roles in these three works. Indeed much of what we know about the chronology of certain Camus pieces, like *L'Homme révolté (The Rebel)*, written in Cabris in 1950, comes from Casares. Even works like his adaptation of Faulkner's *Requiem for a Nun (Requiem*

14 Casares and Camus had embarked on an initial affair in 1944 during the production of *Le Malentendu*. The affair had ended with Camus's announcement of impending fatherhood – his wife Francine had been based in Algiers during the War. For further details, see Casarès 1980: 325 and Todd 1998: 210–11. For further details on Camus's involvement with FEDIP and CNT, see Lottman 1981: 455.

15 For a summary of the reviews, see Lottman 1981: 475.

pour une nonne), which was premiered by Catherine Sellers at the Mathurins on 22 September 1956, was written with Casares in mind (Lottman 1981: 589). Casares was to have been part of the company Camus planned to form with Micheline Rozan – the agent who was to go on to become Peter Brook's producer – at the Nouveau theatre in September 1960. As early as 1952 Casares had also been an associate in Camus's plans for a company at the Récamier. She had introduced Camus to Rozan who was to work with him on the production side of *Les Possédés*, the adaptation of Dostoevsky's *The Possessed*, which opened on 30 January 1959 (Todd 1998: 396–8).

Spain is a recognisable presence in Camus's theatrical *oeuvre*, present in his early play *Révolte dans les Asturies* (1936), co-written with three university friends and banned by the Algerian authorities because of its contentious treatment of the 1934 miners' revolt,[16] and visible in his production of Fernando de Rojas's *La Celestina* with Le Théâtre de l'Équipe in 1937 and plans to stage Cervantes' *Los baños de Argel* (The Bagnios of Algiers) as *Comédie des Bagnes d'Alger* in 1939. Whilst it is erroneous to suggest that Casares was responsible for Camus's promotion of the Spanish Republican cause and Spanish theatre in France, as Camus's biographer Herbert Lottman indicates: 'She represented Camus' Spanish blood, later his concern not only for Spain's political plight but for its literature, its stage; she was his private way to remain in touch with the Mediterranean' (1981: 317–18). During the early 1950s she was to collaborate with Camus on translations of Calderón's *La devoción de la cruz* (The Devotion to the Cross) and Lope de Vega's *El caballero de Olmedo* (The Knight of Olmedo), which were presented at the Angers Festival d'Art Dramatique in 1953 and 1957 respectively. Although Casares appears uncredited as a co-translator, we know from Camus's biographers that he meticulously worked through the translation of both plays with her (Lottman 1981: 595; Todd 1998: 315). Casares' association with Camus, who once referred to her as 'the genius of my life' (cited in Todd: 300), has served to render her 'la musa teatral del existencialismo' (Benach 1996: 43) (the theatrical muse of existentialism) and fuelled speculation that she is the autobiographical source for the actress Josette in the philosophical essay *L'Homme révolté* (1951) (with whom the protagonist Henri has an affair). Certainly, Casares herself recognised that Camus anchored her to Spain (1980: 244). It was through him that she became involved in certain Resistance activities (1980: 246–8), acting as a courier for *Combat*, the clandestine Resistance newspaper Camus edited and assisting Camus in evacuating a printing press at a difficult moment in 1944.[17] While she was to appear as Hilda in Sartre's *Le Diable et le Bon Dieu* (The Devil and the Good Lord) at the Antoine theatre in 1951 – a piece which incorporates material from St. John of the Cross – she was never to articulate the affinity with Sartre's writing which permeated her relationship with Camus's theatrical work (Casarès 1980: 376; Burguet i Ardiaca 1985: 21).

16 For further details, see Freeman 1971: 20–34.
17 For further details of Casares' Resistance activities, see Lottman 1981: 323 and Todd 1998: 182.

A Franco-Spanish actress

España está en mi. Pero hay algo que sucede con el exilio y es que llega un momento en que no se es de ninguna parte. Cuando estoy en España tengo ganas de defender a Francia [. . .] Cuando estoy en Francia, me ocurre lo contrario. (Casares, cited in Oltra 1988: 94)

(Spain is in me. But there's something that happens with exile. There comes a moment where you aren't from anywhere. When I'm in Spain I feel like defending France [. . .] When I'm in France, the opposite happens.)

The significance of exile permeated Casares' existence. In her autobiography she writes of her country of origin as 'Espagne Réfugiée' (1980: 353) (Refugeed Spain), articulating a concept of exiles as an alternative nation:

Toda esta gente, que son hoy muchos y que yo pienso que forman como una nueva nación, y que en el fondo, ya no saben de dónde son porque han perdido la noción de las fronteras [. . .] Yo he tenido que hacer un esfuerzo enorme para 'entrar' en el espíritu francés. (cited in Soriano 1988: 62)

(All these people, a great number today, who I think form almost a new nation, and who deep down no longer know where they are from because they have lost the notion of frontiers [. . .] I have had to make a great effort to 'enter' into the French spirit).

Numerous interviews granted by Casares during her lifetime, as well as her autobiography, reflect on her Franco-Spanish identity. While she refers to herself as a French actress, modelled entirely by French criteria, she is aware of the paradox of also representing 'l'Espagne errante en France' (1980: 354) (the wandering Spain in France).

The debt to her Spanish education, however, appears far-reaching. Casares attributes her recognition of the importance of team work as a governing principle in her life and profession to her experiences at the liberal Escuela Instituto in the early 1930s (1980: 102, 387). Her association with Vilar's TNP in the 1950s sought to make theatre more accessible to working-class audiences while also broadening the range of theatre available in Paris to include significantly more international work. Promoting a vision of culture as public service, it offered a powerful model for companies (such as Barcelona's Teatre Lliure and Companyia Flotats) that were to flourish in post-Franco Spain. While committed to the concept of *création collective*, she was never to remain with companies for more than five years, recognising the need for renovation to come through new performers and a constant renewal of personnel and ideas (cited in Monleón 1990: 426–7).

Certainly the perception of Casares on her death was of a politicised actress. As the daughter of a prominent Republican, she was aware of the need to perform 'une certaine Espagne' (1980: 77) (a certain Spain). On 18 October 1944 she was involved in a benefit for families of Spaniards killed during the liberation of France (Lottman 1981: 341). *Combat* was to publish an unsigned article on her on 4 October 1944, associating her with Republican Spain and testifying to her unique theatrical magic (cited in Lottman 1981: 341). In July 1945 she took part in a Spanish festival, reciting the work of Machado and García Lorca (Dussane 1953: 48–9). Through her father and his links, she was to keep in touch with significant sectors of the Republican émigré community in Paris. Overtones were made by the Spanish ambassador Lequerica in 1943 to enquire as to whether she would return to Spain to perform in Madrid. She refused the request, making it clear she would not see Lequerica again (Casarès 1980: 214). Her refusal to take a French passport while Franco remained in power – she was unable to become a *Sociétaire* (affiliated artist) of the Comédie Française because she would not renounce her Spanish nationality – served to ensure she would remain, like Xirgu, a powerful symbol of the liberal Republic in exile (Martí 1996: 27). As late as 1989, on being awarded the Molière prize for her performance as Hecuba (in *Hécube* directed by Bernard Sobel at Gennevilliers in 1988), she made an impassioned speech to Jack Lang to improve French theatre subsidy on his reinstatement as Minister of Culture (Quiñonero 1989: 89).

Casares stated in an 1988 interview while shooting the only film she was to make in Spanish, *Monte bajo/The Hills* (1989), that she had never consciously wished to work on Spanish theatre in French (cited in Bayón 1988: 45). Any examination, however, of the work she was to undertake demonstrates a strong Spanish slant, from the subject matter of Molière's *Don Juan* at the Comédie Française in 1952, to her presence in an adaptation of Blasco Ibáñez's *Sangre y arena* (*Blood and Sand*) made for cinema in the late 1980s (*De Sable et de sang*, directed by Jeanne Labrune, 1987). Although Casares was to be involved in tributes to García Lorca's work in Paris, including a recital of *Romancero gitano* (*Gypsy Ballads*) at the Pleyel Hall in 1944, it was with Valle-Inclán that she was to have a firmer affiliation, performing in Lavelli's staging of *Comedias bárbaras* (Savage Plays), presented as *Comédies barbares* in 1991. She was to perform twice in Fernando de Rojas's *La Celestina* (*La Célestine*), taking a secondary role in 1942 and the title role in Jean Gillibert's 1972 production at the Festival de Châteauvallon. A number of her projects with the choreographer Maurice Béjart revolved around Spanish texts or subjects including *À la recherche de Don Juan* in 1968. Latin American collaborators too were to feature in a number of her projects. Henri Pichette's *Épiphanies* (1947), which paired Casares with Gérard Philipe, featured backdrops by the Chilean surrealist Roberto Matta. Casares was later to perform in Frank Hoffman's production of Chilean Marco Antonio de la Parra's *Dostoïevski va à la plage* (Dostoevsky goes to the Beach), adapted by fellow Spaniard Armando Llamas and premiered at Paris' Théâtre National de la Colline in 1994.

Casares writes of the allure of arriving in Paris in late 1936, comparing it to entering the twentieth century (1980: 110). The need to learn French and make it her own necessitated a distancing from the Spanish language. This involved both avoiding contact with Spaniards (1980: 138) and Spanish literature, which threatened her newly cultivated French accent. Casares refers to it as 'un esfuerzo continuo para separarme de España' (cited in Monleón 1990: 444) (a continuous effort to separate myself from Spain). The dilemma of trying to keep loyal to her language while learning to dominate another (Casarès 1980: 144) was articulated through the choice of a lexicon of works which veered between the rigidity of the French canon – Racine and Marivaux were her telling choices on first attempting to enter the Conservatoire in 1939 (Casarès 1980: 156) – , projects with Spanish thematics or links like Alain Resnais's short film *Guernica* (co-directed with Robert Hessens) (1950), where her impassioned reciting of Paul Eluard's texts resonates across the devastating on-screen images, and collaborations with Hispanic émigrés like Copi and Lavelli. As *ABC*'s Juan Pedro Quiñonero was to observe in his obituary of Casares, 'Ella sirvió de puente entre las culturas de España, Francia y América, en momentos muy difíciles para toda España' (1996: 103) (She served as a bridge between the cultures of Spain, France and the Americas during difficult moments for all of Spain).

Casares cites her involvement as one of the select audience members in Picasso's *Le Désir attrapé par la queue* (*Desire Caught by the Tail*) as a chance to present 'auprès de Picasso un peu de son Espagne' (1980: 225) (side by side with Picasso a little of her Spain). The text, dispensing with the rules of the well-made play, pursues a surrealist vein in its plotless juxtaposition of seemingly unrelated events. A public reading of the piece was held in the expansive living room of Louise and Michel Leiris' flat on the Quai des Grands-Augustins in the sixth *arrondissement* on 19 March 1944. Camus acted as *compère*, reading out the stage directions, and the cast included Sartre, the Leirises, Simone de Beauvoir and Dora Maar. Casares was one of a prominent group of spectators, among whom were Georges Braque, Georges Bataille, Paul Eluard, Barrault, the dramatist Armand Salacrou, Jacques Lacan, and the photographer Brassaï, whose images of the production served to preserve it as a unique testament to avant-garde theatrics during the Occupation.[18] It was here that Casares first saw Camus, initiating both a professional and a personal association that was to last until his death on 4 January 1960 (Casarès 1980: 224–5).

It may also have been a shared émigré culture that attracted her to the Argentine director Jorge Lavelli, based in Paris since the early 1960s. With him she was to forge one of her most lasting creative relationships. Meeting in Paris in 1963, they hatched plans to collaborate on a project. They were first to work together on an Argentine production of Valle-Inclán's *Divinas palabras* (*Divine Words*) in 1964 – to be examined later in the chapter. A stark production of O'Neill's *Welded* (produced as *Enchaînés*) at the Récamier theatre was to follow in 1965. Casares credits Lavelli with having introduced her to a different form of theatre, that which she terms 'acuático [. . .] entre dos aguas, muy musical' (cited in Burguet i Ardiaca 1985: 21) (aquatic [. . .] between two waters, very musical). Collaborating on *Medea* (*Médéa*) in 1967, they were both to turn to Seneca's version of the myth (adapted by Jean Vauthier), which Casares, stressing an affinity with the Spanish Seneca, perceived as rawer, crueller and more immediate than the better known treatment by Euripides.[19] Although, as with most intellectuals of the age, Seneca

18 For further details on the production, see Cohn 1998: 25–36.
19 These opinions are articulated in *Maria Casarès, Médéa: La vie d'un rôle*, directed by Michel Dumoulin and broadcast on Radio Télévision Française 15 January 1968.

had spent most of his adult life in Rome, he had actually been born in Córdoba, southern Spain, around 1 BC. For Lavelli, Seneca's reading allowed for a clear opposition between passion and reason – the latter embodied by the Chorus who remain partisan to Jason throughout (cited in Saintova 1967: 8). Lavelli and Casares were to approach the piece musically 'negotiating the different registers, the different tonalities, the tempo'. According to Lavelli Casares 'would write down all these things in a notebook and take such pleasure in working them through' (cited in Delgado 2002a: 229). Attempting this icon of female transgression, Casares, like Margarita Xirgu before her, gave an electrifying performance of emotional unpredictability and controlled contempt. Stalking the stage like a wounded warrior queen, she crafted a seductive Médéa of raw, unyielding passions. This was not Médéa as victim, but a study in controlled duplicity and scorn where ferocious vehemence was unleashed to brutal effect. Casares' wronged wife, an alien in Corinth, embodied the plight of the exile, suspended between kingdoms which each wish her elsewhere. Her Médéa oscillated between humane understanding for the plight of those embroiled in the situation and horrifying vengeance. Clad in majestic gilded robes, armour against her assault from Jason and his new wife, Casares' androgynous Médéa lamented her status as a refugee with nowhere to call home, an exile ordered into an undefined territorial landscape which Jason perceived as a reward and she could only view as unjustified punishment.

The production opened at the Festival d'Avignon's Cour d'Honneur in July 1967, before going on to the Odéon-Théâtre de France in October of that year and undertaking a select tour of certain French cities. In both Avignon and Paris Casares' realisation of Médéa, part-priestess, part-warrior, enveloped in the trappings of ritual, provoked extreme reactions. The melodic incantations and trances which grounded Casares' performance (both underscored and counterpointed in Xénakis's music) were, as *Candide*'s critic Pierre Marcabru observed, not to everyone's taste (1967: 43). This was 'une créature droit sortie du chaos' (Galey 1967: 13) (a creature straight out of chaos) who left her unsuspecting audience, comfortably seated in the Odéon's plush red velvet seating, unprepared for the horrors she was to unleash. While Casares' visceral performance might have been excessively mannered for some (Anon. 1967d: 19; Gautier 1967: 24), others admired the laser-like, darting quality of her eyes, her workings within the annals of madness, and her frenetic histrionics (Anon. 1967c: 10; Poirot-Delpech 1967: 14). Lavelli's heavily choreographed performance codes were related to the exquisite mannerism of Japanese No theatre and the writings of Artaud, who had expressed admiration for Seneca's rendition of the myth (Paget 1967: 12; Anon. 1967d: 19). Casares' 'foreignness' was further denoted by her dark, heavily made-up eyes and tousled boyish hairstyle, and by an invasive, violent performance style which transgressed boundaries of taste. Pierre Roumel of *Le Provençal* viewed the tremendous pitch of Casares' intensity (described in animalistic terms by Marcabru [1967: 43]) as 'comme le symbole nucléaire de la destruction qui nous menace chaque jour. Ses cris sont les échos d'une Apocalypse qui nous paralyse [. . .] Maria Casarès cesse d'EXISTER DU moment qu'elle paraît' (1967: 5) (like a nuclear symbol of the destruction that threatens us each day. Her cries are the echoes of an Apocalypse that paralyses us [. . .] Maria Casarès ceases to EXIST FROM the moment she appears). Embracing a performance register that self-consciously contravenes the parameters endorsed by realism, Casares, to appropriate Margaret Reynolds' term, acted 'specifically against what is "natural"' (2000: 132). If Casares' decoding of the journey to murder is now viewed as an emblematic Medea, it is because she embodied the anxieties of an age – as the events of 1968 were to indicate – where established ideological gender demarcations were breaking down and hierarchical infrastructures were being threatened from without and within.[20] If the playwright Bernard-Marie Koltès, who saw the production in 1968 when it played at the Théâtre National de Strasbourg, was to cite it as his reason for entering theatre, initiating a correspondence with Casares which was to lead to numerous collaborations, it is precisely because both Casares and the production challenged the authority of established rules, allowing any possibility within the 'other' spaces of theatre.

In an article significantly entitled 'Una actriz española: María Casares' (a Spanish actress: María Casares), the dramatist Luis Maté was to classify Casares alongside the great actresses of the early twentieth-century Spanish stage: María Guerrero, Rosario Pino, and Xirgu. Maté writes of how she was to remain informed and interested in the state of Spanish theatre, admiring the comedies of Miguel Mihura and the directing of Luis Escobar, having seen his *Celestina* at the Théâtre des Nations in Paris with Irene López Heredia in April 1958 (1978: 152–3). While neither *Les Enfants du paradis* nor *Les Dames du Bois de Boulogne* – both films with sexually wayward protagonists – secured a cinematic release in the censorious climate of Francoist Spain, *La Chartreuse de Parme* (directed by Christian Jacques) and Cocteau's *Orphée* were both distributed in Spain. In her autobiography Casares writes of how Stendhal's works were prohibited under Franco (1980: 85). It is perhaps deliciously ironic that her first filmic release in Spain was *La Chartreuse de Parme*, an adaptation of Stendhal's 1839 novel, first seen at the Calatravas and Gran Vía cinemas in Madrid on 7 August 1953 under the title *El prisionero de Parma*.[21] *Orphée* opened at the Palacio de la Música de Madrid on 10 November 1953 to superlative reviews which recognised the importance of a film already hailed as a classic across Europe (Donald 1953: 39; Anon. 1953b: 6). Both *Orphée* and *La Chartreuse de Parme* were subject to the obligatory dubbing that was imposed on all films shown in Spain after April 1941. Although a select number of special late-night screenings of *Orphée* were allowed in the French language

20 Interestingly Georges Pompidou and his wife attended the opening performance at the Odéon; see Anon. 1967e.
21 For information on the film's critical reception in Spain, see Anon. 1953a and Gómez Tello 1953. Interestingly a poster advertising the film published in *Primer Plano* 13/669 (August 1953) n.pag. mispells Casares as Cazares. While these were the only two Casares films distributed in Spain during the Franco regime information about her cinematic work did filter through the film journals; see, for example, Charensol 1947.

version,[22] Casares' on-screen presence was largely deprived of her distinctive voice: 'rota' (broken) and 'desgarrada' (torn) were the terms which dominated the Spanish obituaries of her death.[23] The voice may have been silenced by the regime – the reviews of *Orphée* avoided any mention of Casares as a Spanish actress forced into exile – but her oppositional appeal lingered in the defiant non-conformity and sexual charge which marks her subversive roles in both these films.

Occupying the margins

la représentation de l'exil m'a orientée vers la meilleure part de moi-même'. (Casarès 1980: 196)

(the representation of exile has orientated me to the best part of myself.)

The vectors of exile clearly exerted a profound influence on both Casares' life and work (Casarès 1980: 136). The Spanish novelist Francisco Ayala views the exile as inhabiting the space of parenthesis – hovering between an often idealised past and the possibility of an imaginable return, suspended within the idea of an endless present (cited in Spalek 1983: 82). For Casares the theatre functioned as the home of exiles, accommodating and offering an 'endless present' to those who did not fit elsewhere (1980: 210). As she was to state in her autobiography, 'ma patrie est le théâtre' (1980: 344) (my country is the theatre). While emigration may have been a theme in some of the work in which she chose to appear – such as *Le Malentendu* – it is the astonishing proportion of work which revolves around issues of banishment, expulsion and marginalisation that the prisms of Casares' status as an exile are most conspicuously played out. Her autobiography, tellingly dedicated to 'personnes déplacées (1980: 7) (displaced persons), articulates the concept of exile, with its attendant sensations of dislocation and confrontation.

In *Orphée*, Cocteau's urban reworking of the celebrated myth, Casares' apotheosis of Death initiates Jean Marais's Orphée's encounter with the unknown. (Interestingly another émigré, Ludmilla Pitoëff had taken the role of Eurydice in the first performance of Cocteau's stage version of the myth in June 1926.) Both Orphée and Death inhabit the realms of the otherworldly in the film. Both are stung by the climate of fear and denunciation which pervades the world – not dissimilar to Occupied France – and which Cocteau creates through optical tricks, multiple mirrors and eerie framing. Hovering in a dismemembered space between the land of the living and a surreal underworld of the dead to which she transports her victims, Casares' Princess of Death is Orphée's forbidden death wish. Envisaged as an alluring vision in starkly contrasted black and white, Casares' Princess of Death is the enigmatic object of desire that Orphée follows through the labyrinthine contours of both worlds. Her almost unnaturally slender waist and fiercely combed-back hair, together with her chilling demeanour and deviant

---

22 See the adverts for the film in *Ya* (13 November 1953): 6, *El Alcázar* (12 November 1953): 4 and *El Alcázar* (19 November 1953): 4.

23 See, for example, Quiñonero 1996 and Gil 1996.

actions, placing her outside the social order, rendered her an archetypal *femme fatale*. Cocteau (1889–1963), who had provided Bresson with the dialogue for *Les Dames du Bois de Boulogne*, the latter's adaptation of Diderot's eighteenth-century novel *Jacques le fataliste*, had remembered Casares' 'grim, businesslike beauty in the picture, and her skill at portraying quiet, total ruthlessness' (Steegmuller 1970: 479). Cocteau may have initially envisaged Marlene Dietrich in the role of Death (Casarès 1997: 13), but Casares was to make the role her own, a portrait of light and shadow which the novelist Nicole Ward Jouve cites as 'what black and white films are made of' (1994: 29).

Casares was to classify Cocteau alongside Genet (1910–86) and Koltès (1948–89) as 'poets', marginalised writers whose psycho-political dramatic canvases juggle epic tales of loss and displacement (Casarès 1997: 13). Writing on the peripheries of realism, all conceived theatre as both sacred and profane, part church, part brothel, an erotic space where mystery prevails and much remains unanswered.[24] Collaboration with Genet on the 1966 production of *Les Paravents* ensured for Casares what she terms a return to 'ma terre' (my land), the terrain of Sancho Panza and Lazarillo de Tormes, 'celle où je me reconnaissais' (1980: 393) (that where I recognised myself). Her meeting with Genet's wild and wonderful world was an encounter with the playful picaresque for the first time in her theatrical trajectory, a picaresque she was to return to in the 1970s with *La Célestine* (1980: 12). Interestingly, Zatlin notes that Genet 'touched a particularly responsive chord in Spain [. . .] Genet's iconoclastic unmasking of decadence from the vantage point of the Other spoke directly to another essential, if contradictory, aspect of both Spanish tradition and of contemporary Hispanic reality' (1994: 127). She goes on to trace the influence of Genet in Nieva, Arrabal and Luis Riaza (127–8). The extraordinary impact of Víctor García's 1969 production of *Les Bonnes* (*The Maids*) (presented as *Las criadas*) will be discussed in Chapter 4, but suffice it to say that Genet was a frequent visitor to Spain throughout his lifetime. The Teatre Lliure's Lluís Pasqual was to enjoy a significant friendship with him, presenting *Le Balcon* (*The Balcony*) first in Catalan in 1981 (*El balcó*) and later in French at the Odéon-Théâtre de l'Europe in 1991. Pasqual too locates in Genet, who had worked as a prostitute in Barcelona's red-light district *Barri Xinès* in 1933–34, a direct affinity with Spain. Indeed, as Genet's biographer Edmund White has astutely noted, 'Genet closes *The Thief's Journal*, his last novel, with the words, "the region of myself which I have called Spain". In a sombre footnote, he [Genet] remarks that, when Cocteau later called him '"his Spanish *genêt*", "he did not know what this country had done to me"' (1993: 118). With Spanish-named characters and references to Franco's mausoleum *El Valle de los Caídos* (The Valley of the Fallen) in *Le Balcon*, Pasqual views Genet's fascination with Spain as a bridge between the Western and Arabic worlds.[25] Indeed in preparing her role as the Mother in *Les Paravents*, Genet was to advise Casares to look inside her 'Hispanic heritage' (cited in Zatlin

24 For Casares' views on theatre as an erotic space where mystery must remain, see Monleón 1990: 422–4.
25 In a private, unpublished interview with the author, July 2000.

1994: 128).[26] In her autobiography Casares herself recalls that the Algerian war, which forms the backdrop to Les Paravents, was for her to recall the horrors of the Civil War she had escaped in 1936 (1980: 113).

Les Paravents was written by Genet in 1958 during the Algerian War. The politically volatile climate of the late 1950s – the war which delivered 100,000 casualties – did not end until 1962 and the necessary rehousing of a million pieds-noirs ('people of French ethnicity, but born and brought up in North Africa') (Bradby 1994: 226) effectively prohibited any possibility of a French production and the play was first premiered in Berlin on 18 June 1961. It was only in 1966 that Roger Blin was finally able to secure a production at the state-subsidised Odéon theatre, then run by Barrault. Opening on 16 April, the piece is now mythologised as a significant landmark in contemporary French theatre, heralding a fragmented poetic theatre that merges a multitude of different narratives in its bold interrogation of the social construction and reflection of imagistic networks. The crude, occasionally obscene language, the far-off fires which serve as a constant reminder of the conflict raging in the distance, the rotting, decomposing society controlled by colonialist infrastructures which the three protagonists, the petty thief Saïd, his unnamed mother (played by Casares) and his ostracised wife Leila inhabit, all served to provoke ire and re-open wounds in an establishment keen to disassociate itself from its imperial past. Blin's production featured an array of mobile screens wheeled in laterally – masks which conceal social hypocrisies, dividing the world of the living from that of the dead. The play was also pruned to fit within four hours, drawing on a cast of 65 actors to take on the 110 roles conceived by Genet.[27]

The 'battle' of Les Paravents was conducted on two fronts. Potent photographic images remain of the police presence outside the Odéon with violence escalating following the whistling and angry shouts which accompanied the scene of the burial of the French lieutenant on the 20 and 21 April. With the right-wing Occident Group mobilising spectators to throw vegetables and bottles onto the stage, Casares was violently insulted during the performance of 30 April. The performance was temporarily stopped while the protesters were forcibly removed from the auditorium (Aslan 1988: 102). The daily press coverage of the controversy (Le Figaro, whose critic Jean-Jacques Gautier had been outraged by the production, was especially concerned to report all details of the violent outbursts) also served to ensure that this was a struggle conducted under the glare of the media spotlight – pre-empting the events of 1968. The production polarised critics with a significant contingent denouncing it as insensitive, irresponsible and toxic (Marcel 1966; Gautier 1966: 18; Audouard 1966: 7) while the remainder acknowledged its seminal importance in forging alternative theatrical paths which gave an indication of where the future of the French stage might lie (Sandier 1966: 57; Paget 1966: 8; Marcabru 1966: 38; Dumur 1966: 38; Poirot-Delpech 1966: 14).

26 Significantly, American director Peter Sellars's recent staging of Les Paravents resituates the action in East Los Angeles' Latino community.
27 For further details, see Aslan 1988: 68–104.

The awkward performance style demanded by Genet's plays, 'based on under-lining and demonstrating the contradictions of the actor's activity on stage' (Bradby 1984: 175), has always presented problems to actors caught between the demands of classicism's grand rhetoric and naturalism's supposed invisibility. Genet's theatre requires the display of performativity or *décalage* as Genet referred to it – 'finding gestures that contradicted the words' (Bradby 1984: 176). If Casares was to become one of Genet's preferred performers it is precisely because she was able to give shape to these contradictions. Her Mother was both pragmatic and supersti-tious, wily and stubborn. For *Le Nouvel Observateur*'s Guy Dumur, she was the pivot of the production, the means to liberate all the other actors – interestingly Genet had first called the play *Les Mères*. Dumur situates her as unique among per-formers in 'jouer avec tout son corps, avec toute sa voix. Elle s'accroupit comme une Arabe, se désarticule comme une Gitane, hurle comme une chienne' (playing with her whole body, with her whole voice. She squats like an Arab woman, con-torts like a gypsy woman, barks like a dog). Her characterisation provided a bridge between classical tragedy and avant-garde performance: 'Qui n'a entendu hurler Maria Casarès comme une louve ne sait pas ce que peut être la tragédie antique' (1966: 38–9) (Whoever hasn't heard Maria Casarès shout like a she-wolf doesn't know what classical tragedy can be). Casares, clad in rags of purple with a scarf tied around her neck, and defined visually by the production's Japanese make-up iconography, was to provide, in the view of *Candide*'s Marcabru, the staging's unfor-gettable moments. 'D'une cruauté tendre et chaude, belle diablesse de la mort. Comme hors d'elle-même et hors du monde' (1966: 38) (Of a tender and hot cru-elty, beautiful she-devil of death. As if outside of herself and outside of the world). Casares' dishevelled and riotous performance style, much admired by André Rivo-llet of *Aux Écoutes* as 'l'originalité d'une présentation stylisée' (1966: 40) (the essence of stylised performance), was viewed by *Arts*' Gilles Sandier as 'digne désormais de l'Opéra de Pékin' (worthy henceforward of the Peking Opera). Indeed her remarkable raspish laughter, precise corporeal expression, haunting singing and uncanny animal noises – vocally it was as if her performance was musi-cally scored – were to lead him to conclude that Casares provided an enigmatic presence which he had never seen in French actors (1966: 57).

It is partly possible that Casares' kinship with Genet may have come from his ideal of a single performance for a production, an ideal which she shared, prefer-ring the experimentational climate of the rehearsal situation to the demands of a conceived performance repeated daily (cited in Soriano 1988: 61). Seventeen years later Patrice Chéreau, with whom she had already worked on *Peer Gynt* (1981), the director's final production as co-artistic director of the TNP at Villeurbanne, asked her to appear in his restaging of *Les Paravents* at the Théâtre Amandiers in the north-eastern Paris suburb of Nanterre. Although she wished to take the role of the old woman who appears at the end of the play, it was Genet who insisted that she reprise the role of the mother (Casarès 1997: 12). Second time around the play failed to ignite the same degree of controversy which had obliged Minister of Cul-ture André Malraux to defend the piece to the National Assembly in 1966, evoking

Goya in his pleas for freedom of cultural expression. Jack Lang, Minister of Culture, was present at the opening night of 4 June 1983 to 'endorse' the production. Richard Peduzzi's set, evoking a disused 1950s cinema with past glories faded into tawdry neglect, spilled over into an audience amongst whom much of the action took place. North African immigration to France over the decades since the Algerian War allowed for new resonances and implications to surface, but it was Casares once more who dominated the production, thrusting the action forward with what one critic referred to as her 'electrifying, sensual, flamboyant presence' (Wehle 1984: 74).[28]

During the 1990s Casares was to work increasingly in theatres based in the outskirts of Paris. At Gennevilliers she was to appear under Bernard Sobel's direction in Gorky/Brecht's *The Mother* (*La Mère*) in 1991, *Threepenny Lear* in 1993, and Pirandello's *The Giants of the Mountains* (*Les Géants de la montagne*) in 1994. She was to return to the 'margins' of Amandiers in 1986, working once more with Chéreau. The play was a new work by a playwright cultivated by Chéreau as a significant dramaturgical innovator, Bernard-Marie Koltès. Koltès, had worked briefly as a *dramaturge* on Chéreau's production of *Les Paravents* and was a great admirer of Casares' work, having first seen her perform in *Médéa* in 1968. She was to take a significant role in his 1972 radio play, *L'Héritage* (*The Inheritance*) and he often spoke of her as his 'grand amour de théâtre' (1999: 120) (great love of theatre). In one of the final interviews before his death on 15 April 1989 at the age of forty-one, Koltès was to state that he always thought of Casares when crafting his plays, because it had been her *Médéa* which pushed him towards theatre (1999: 153). He was to die before being able to fulfil plans to write a play for her based on the Book of Job.

Quai Ouest (*Quay West*) is one of Koltès's most emblematic works, a brutal interrogation of outsiders entrapped in a hostile urban wasteland, an abandoned warehouse, vestige of a once bustling dock in an unnamed city which we presume to be New York. Chéreau's regular design collaborator, Richard Peduzzi, rendered an expansive stage environment of giant metallic walls, opening up particular areas of a stage littered with giant storage crates. The play, rejecting clear plot lines, exposition, narrative development and psychological reasoning, revolves around a series of encounters – all governed by commercial motives – which bring the various displaced persons together. All the characters are compromised and enmeshed in a climate of deals and transactions that bind them in a series of complex and unexpected ways. As the mother of a family who we presume are illegal immigrants, Casares' Cécile, unable to steer her children in the direction she would like, played out her displacement through her vocal recourse to Spanish and Quechua.

While working on the unfinished *Quai Ouest* in 1983, Koltès articulated that French isn't a mother tongue for any of the characters in the play, as such this 'apporte une modification profonde de la langue' (1999: 27) (brings about a deep

---

28 For other reviews which mention Casares' dominance, see Godard 1983, Laubreaux and Marquet 1983 and Dumur 1983.

change in the language they use) with speech and thought patterns altered. While Koltès never explicitly articulated a fascination with Casares based on her 'foreignness', he was to maintain that both the characters and language in his plays are transformed through an infusion of 'otherness'.

La langue française, comme la culture française en général, ne m'intéresse, que lorsqu'elle est altérée. Une langue française qui serait revue et corrigée, colonisée par une culture étrangère, aurait une dimension nouvelle et gagnerait en richesses expressives, à la manière d'une statue antique à laquelle manquent la tête et les bras et qui tire sa beauté précisément de cette absence-là. (1999: 26–7)

(The French language – and in fact French culture in general – interests me only when it is altered somehow. A French language which has been re-written and corrected – colonised – by a foreign culture would gain a new dimension and richness of expression, in the same way that a classical statue without a head or limbs is made beautiful by their very absence). (trans. David Fancy and Delgado)

This process of linguistic and cultural 'colonisation' was to find its emblematic player in Casares. Koltès's fractured narrative of marginalised persons all suspended in a moment of transition was, according to Le Quotidien's Armelle Heliot, grounded in Casares' Cécile (1986: 26). Le Monde's Colette Godard too was to locate the action of the play in a physical and metaphorical 'no-man's land' where Casares' family, mutilated by a lost war, have lost their centre of gravity. Fumbling in the darkness that engulfs them – a darkness rendered onstage through the atmospheric obscurity of Daniel Delannoy's shadowy lighting – Casares was, with Jean-Marc Thibault (in the role of her husband Rodolfe), singled out for a forceful performance where anguish, betrayal and madness brutally thrust the action forward (1986: 18). While Koltès's text, with its hermetic circularity and basis in the monologue, may not have been to the taste of all the critics (Nerson 1986: 22; Coppermann 1986: 30), a significant number were to acknowledge the power of a production which interrogated Western culture's long-standing subscription to foundational and structurally hierarchical binaries such as foreigner/native, civilised/primitive, black/white as paradigms for comprehension and representation (Heliot 1986: 26; Godard 1986: 18; Nussac 1990: 149, 152).

Casares was to recognise Koltès as a visionary who 'raconte des choses qui sont absolument de nos jours, mais qui se passent peut-être à la périphérie du centre où nous sommes' (1990b: 15) (says things which are absolutely of our time, but which take place, perhaps, at the periphery of the centre where we are). Koltès avoids passing judgement on the dispossessed at a time when immigrants are increasingly maligned. For Casares Koltès was a writer ahead of his time in placing the marginal at the centre of his works (1990a: 25–8). Interestingly, Chéreau's staging, a co-production with the Comédie Française, used the two 'establishment' actors, Jean Rousillon and Catherine Hiegel, in the roles of the two bankrupt capitalists trying desperately to find an escape from their financial predicament. The casting of Casares as the ambiguous Cécile, unfixed, undefined, unknowable, was reinforced by her offstage identity as a somewhat anarchic figure: neither French nor Spanish, unmarried until 1978 when she wed TNP actor André Schlesser, outspoken, unpredictably honest and combative in interviews, inquisitive in rehearsals. If Casares was to be drawn to outsiders – both in her life and in her work – it seems precisely because, in a world of increasing classification, they defy the norm. Casares may never have relied on easy spectatorial identification – Cécile, like the unnamed Mother in *Les Paravents*, is not a conventionally 'likeable' character – but this is one of the ways in which she can be seen to have ushered in a broader range of female roles on to the French stage.

Spanish language performances: *Yerma* (1963) and *Divinas palabras* (1964)

As the critic José Monleón's obituary of Casares explains, information about her work reached Spain through various diverse sources in the 1940s, 1950s and 1960s (1997: 103). News of her activities at the TNP filtered through reviews of productions published in specialist journals like *Primer Acto* (founded in 1957) and her flickering presence on the cinema screen of specialist Cine Clubs. Her Spanish name and identity as Casares Quiroga's daughter, despite the assimilation her French-language work suggested, was a constant reminder of her displacement from a Spain then under the grip of Franco's dictatorship. It was only in the early 1960s, following the death of Camus, that Casares chose to work in Spanish. She had travelled to Spanish America with the TNP in the 1950s and established links with various practitioners including Margarita Xirgu, with whom she had corresponded as early as 1956 over a García Lorca tribute to be held in Paris.[29] It was with Xirgu that she was to make her Spanish-language debut in Argentina in 1963 in a production of *Yerma* directed by the veteran Spanish actress. The production came at what Casares cites as 'un momento clave en mi vida personal. Yo había llegado a una especie de esclerosis y no sabía ya muy bien por dónde renovarme' (cited in Soriano 1988: 60) (a key moment in my personal life. I had arrived at a point of sclerosis and really didn't know how to renovate myself). Casares had seen Rivas Cherif's 1934 groundbreaking production of *Yerma* at the age of twelve at Madrid's Español theatre and had met Xirgu when the latter visited Casares Quiroga at the family home during that period. Invited to perform in Buenos Aires – Casares refused to return to Spain until democracy was restored – she had suggested a venture with Xirgu on *Yerma* (cited in Monleón 1990: 441–2). The collaboration at the San Martín theatre, however, was not judged productive by Casares, despite some superlative reviews (Rodrigo 1974: 311). Other reviewers, like *Historium*'s Roberto Medina, seem to have located rather lax direction, which resulted in 'una deficiente pronunciación' (1963) (a deficient pronunciation), rendering a rather forced performance. While the Spanish dramatist Luis Maté writes that Casares 'con ritmo y con dulzura galaicos – conmovió a Buenos Aires [. . .] en una impresionante versión de *Yerma*' (1978: 152) (with a Galician rhythm and sweetness, moved Buenos Aires [. . .] in an impressive version of *Yerma*), Casares never

29 For further details, see Chapter 1, 49–50.

really felt that she had got to grips with the play or her character. This she attributes, in part, to the fact that Xirgu, in her mid-seventies at the time, was in the process of retiring from theatre and no longer possessed the urgency needed to bring together a focused and intellectually relevant production. She also speculates on the fact that it may have been possible that Xirgu 'era una mujer hecha para actuar y no para dirigir' (cited in Monleón 1990: 442) (was a woman made for acting and not directing), although other responses to Xirgu's directorial work in Argentina and Uruguay, delineated in Chapter 1, suggest otherwise. Production photographs certainly point to a visible affinity with the aesthetic of Rivas Cherif's 1934 production, a strategy that may have rendered a visual style acclaimed decades earlier as radical and provocative, dull and outdated.

The following year Casares was to perform at the Coliseo theatre in a production of *Divinas palabras* directed by Lavelli. Casares had first met Lavelli a year earlier in Paris after seeing his acclaimed baroque production of Polish author Witold Gombrowicz's *Le Mariage* (*The Marriage*) – significantly another exiled writer based in Argentina. The piece, gravitating around issues of national dislocation and historical distortion, social identities and the fabrication of mythical landscapes, struck a chord with Casares and a collaboration was proposed. Blin had staged *Divinas palabras* (as *Divines Paroles*) at the Odéon in 1963, but Robert Marrast's translation, like that of Jeanine Worms used by Herrand for his production of the play at the Mathurins in 1946, failed to convince either Casares or Lavelli. This may have, in part, persuaded both that their first outing of Valle-Inclán should be in Castilian. Casares had known Valle-Inclán as a child. He had been amongst the audience at

8, 9 María Casares as Mari-Gaila in *Divinas palabras* and backstage preparing for her role, at Buenos Aires' Coliseo theatre (1964)

the Palencia's home in Madrid in one of her earliest performances and she cites that performance as perhaps the reason she went into theatre. As her mother informed her after the performance, both Valle-Inclán and García Lorca had commented on the fact that the young Casares should devote herself to theatre (cited in Monleón 1990: 441). Valle-Inclán had been a visitor to her Madrid home in the 1930s, an enigmatic being spinning glamorous fabricated tales pertaining to the loss of his arm (Casares 1991: 1–2).

There had been plans for Casares to appear in *Divinas palabras* at the San Martín as they had taken out an option on the play, but new personnel at this municipal theatre no longer valued the venture and Casares was able to secure Lavelli's participation as director and the project's transfer to a commercial theatre.[30] From Paris Lavelli bought with him the Polish-born designer Kristina Zachwatowicz who had worked on *Le Mariage* and who was in time to return to Poland to enjoy a productive career with Andrzej Wajda. The Argentine press were to report this as a more appropriate vehicle for Casares, admiring the playful vivacity and insolent wit of her performance as the wayward housewife who swaps the dull security of domestic duties for a life on the road with her nephew, a hydrocephalic dwarf exhibited for financial gain.[31] Here too Casares was to enact the outsider, an adulterer whose vocal displacement – a Galician accent against the Argentine inflections of the rest of the cast – provided a link between performance and character. Indeed, the early sections of Casares' autobiography reflect on the begging feudal culture of Galicia that she knew as a child and this world, later recalled and reformulated for *Résidente privilégiée* (1980: 26), served as a preparatory register for *Divinas palabras*.

While the project is often just referred to as a footnote in the career trajectories of both Lavelli and Casares, its importance lies in laying the foundations for a working relationship that was to continue across thirty years. As Lavelli was to detail in a homage to Casares published just after her death:

Si j'ai pu construire et faire aboutir tant de projets avec Maria, c'est que notre amitié sans failles était scellée comme par un serment à la vie à la mort depuis notre rencontre. Je crois qu'elle tenait aussi à cette expérience du déracinement et quelque part à ce sentiment de l'exil qui relie parfois les êtres sans attaches. (1997: 5)

(If I was able to construct and accomplish so many projects with María, it is because our friendship was sealed like an oath from the moment we met. I think that she attached a lot of importance to the experience of being uprooted and somehow to the sense of exile, which can sometimes link beings without ties.) (trans. Joel Anderson)

In her own autobiography Casares situates Lavelli as an outsider, who, like the choreographer Maurice Béjart, with whom she was to collaborate on *La Nuit obscure* (The Dark Night) at Avignon in 1968 and 1969, reciting the poems of St. John of the Cross, was to play a part in ensuring Casares 'retrouvait une part d'elle, sa

---

30 For details of the controversy surrounding this decision, see Anon. 1964b.
31 See Anon. 1964a. Doubts were still raised about Casares' inflection, which was judged to be overly French (rather than Galician) by Staif (1965: 61).

langue – sa langue – et un nom – María (1980: 395) (find a part of herself, her language, – her language – and a name – María). On her return to Paris 'María-Maria-Marie sont devenues *unes* réunies' (1980: 395) (María-Maria-Marie were reunited in *one*).

La Nuit de Madame Lucienne (1985)

While it is beyond the scope of this chapter to delineate all her collaborations with Lavelli, which embraced Shakespeare – *The Winter's Tale* (*Le Conte d'Hiver*) (Avignon, 1980) – , contemporary writing – Tabori's *Mein Kampf (Farce)* (1993) – , and an extraordinary proportion of Hispanic writers, those productions seen in Spain merit some consideration. Casares' professional appearances on the Spanish stage were limited to a run in a high-profile production of Alberti's *El adefesio* in 1976, directed by José Luis Alonso, to be dealt with later in the chapter, a single performance of Nathalie Sarraute's *Elle est là* (*It is There*) and *L'Usage de la parole* (The Use of the Word), directed by Michel Dumoulin and presented at Barcelona's Institut del Teatre in 1987, and two pieces directed by Lavelli: Copi's *La Nuit de Madame Lucienne* (The Night of Madame Lucienne), presented at the Grec in 1985, and Valle-Inclán's *Comédies barbares* at the Mercat de les Flors in October 1991. Significantly, perhaps, the three French-language productions were only presented in Barcelona, further serving to position Casares away from the centre (Madrid), whose theatre profession the Argentine director Víctor García had believed stood against her in 1976 (cited in Mariñas 1976: 25).

The Argentine dramatist and cartoonist Copi (1939–87) (pseudonym of Raúl Damonte Taborda) was, like Lavelli, a fellow émigré in Paris, who had also studied in the early 1960s at L'Université du Théâtre des Nations in Paris. He and Lavelli had enjoyed a productive theatrical collaboration beginning in 1967 with *La Journée d'une rêveuse* (The Day of a Dreamer). *La Nuit de Madame Lucienne* was premiered at the Avignon Festival in July 1985 and then played at the Grec from 6–10 August. Copi was relatively well known in alternative Barcelona circles as a number of his works, including his novel *El baile de las locas* (The Dance of the Mad Women) and his volume of short stories *La guerra de las mariquitas* (The War of the Ladybirds), had already been published in Spain. In the early 1970s he had spent time in Barcelona performing his monologue *Loretta Strong* at the Diana Salon and his play *Eva Perón* had been staged at the Regina theatre in 1980. He was also to provide a regular cartoon strip for the weekly magazine *Triunfo*.[32] Lavelli too had an affiliation with the Spanish stage having directed Nuria Espert in two productions: the Castilian-language *Doña Rosita la soltera o El lenguaje de las flores* (*Doña Rosita the Spinster or The Language of Flowers*) in a production for the Centro Dramático Nacional in 1980 and the Castilian and Catalan-language *Tempests* for Espert's

---

32 For further details, see Pérez de Olaguer 1985a. Lavelli was to go on to stage a Catalan version of *Une Visite opportune* for Flotats' company at the Poliorama theatre premiering on 30 December 1989.

10 María Casares as Vicky
Fantomas in *La Nuit de Madame
Lucienne* at the Avignon Festival
(1985)

company in 1983.[33] The Casares-Copi-Lavelli combination ensured widespread press
coverage for the production with the opinions of the French critics at Avignon duti-
fully reported in anticipation of the Barcelona performances (Sagarra 1985a: 21).

Preview articles especially revolved around the symbolic return of Casares to
Spain as the title of *El Periódico*'s feature by Gonzalo Pérez de Olaguer indicates:
'María Casares actúa en España por segunda vez en su carrera' (1985b: 22) (María
Casares performs in Spain for the second time in her career). Reviews of Copi's
metatheatrical exploration of dramatic invention set in a rehearsal room centred
around Casares, who *El País*' Joan de Sagarra recognised as the major selling point
of the production (1985a: 21).[34] Casares played Vicky Fantomas, an ex-striptease
artist from the Crazy Horse with artificial limbs and a face cruelly disfigured by a
bomb attack in a drugstore (see Figure 10). Her first appearance in darkness from
the midst of the audience, with a hat like Garbo, 'como un fantasma arrancado de
un Sunset Boulevard imposible' (Sagarra 1985a: 21) (like a ghost wrenched from
an impossible Sunset Boulevard), accompanied by wild clapping from the audience
acknowledging the significance of Casares' presence on the Catalan stage, drew on

33 See Chapter 4, 156–60 for further details of these productions.
34 Lavelli was also to see Casares as the pivot of the production; see Pérez de Olaguer 1985b.

her mythical persona. In associating her with such icons as Garbo and Dietrich – whose vocal register was not dissimilar to Casares' – there is a recognition of an iconoclastic and singularly unusual presence. The mutilation she had suffered could not fail to recall a civil war that had dismembered her own family body and obliged her to reinvent herself anew. Private and public identities resolved into a character that grounds a play where the boundaries between fiction and the real are constantly subject to re-negotiation.

If the importance of 'la inquietante presencia del personaje que interpreta la Casares' (Pérez de Olaguer 1985c: 27) (the disturbing presence of the character that Casares plays) was not in doubt, not all the Catalan critics were in accord as to the merits of her performance. While *El Periódico*'s Pérez de Olaguer (1985c: 27) and *La Vanguardia*'s Xavier Fàbregas (1985a: 23), both praised her intelligent ability to exert precise control over a performance that always teetered on the precipice of menacing histrionics, *El País'* Sagarra expressed doubts as to whether this was vintage Casares, although he willingly acknowledged that his own reservations may in part have been due to the outdoor Grec theatre which he failed to see as the most appropriate venue for the production. A piece which revolves around the dynamics of theatrical creation, he concluded, would have been better suited to a more conventional and lush proscenium-arch venue like the Romea (1985b: 21). Casares performing a Franco-Argentine play in French in Barcelona's oldest theatre, nevertheless, served both as a means of re-appropriating the actress and simultaneously as an indication of an 'otherness' which defiantly resisted appropriation.

Comédies barbares (1991)

El teatro es un gran reflejo cultural de un país. (Casares, in Martínez 1977: 21)

(Theatre is a country's great cultural reflection.)

Long before 1991 Casares had been associated with Valle-Inclán's *Comedias bárbaras*. Following their 1964 collaboration on *Divinas palabras*, Lavelli and Casares had hoped to present the trilogy at Avignon in the late 1960s or early 1970s when Casares was to have taken the role of Don Juan Manuel Montenegro's goddaughter Sabelita. Problems around an appropriate translation delayed proceedings – at one point Casares was to undertake the French adaptation – and the production, dependent on a huge cast, was eventually shelved. It was not until the early 1990s when the Spanish dramatist then based in Paris, Armando Llamas, who had seen Casares perform in 1964 in *Divinas palabras*, was commissioned to undertake a new translation of the trilogy and Casares agreed to take the role of Montenegro's long-suffering wife Doña María who appears in the trilogy's second play *Águila de blasón* (*Eagle Rampant*).

The three plays which make up *Comedias bárbaras* were written at different stages in the dramatist's career. *Cara de plata* (*Silver Face*), the first play of the trilogy, although the last play to be written, is often grouped alongside the grotesque tragicomedies (or *esperpentos* as Valle-Inclán termed them) published in the early

1920s. *Águila de blasón* and *Romance de lobos* (*Wolves! Wolves!*) both belong to 1907 and are generally perceived to be more nostalgic in tone than the crueller, less romantic *Cara de plata*. The plays, subverting established norms through their vast array of characters and settings, weave together a rich tapestry where sound, taste and smell are as important as the visual in conjuring an epic rural world on the cusp of seminal change. *Cara de plata, Águila de blasón* and *Romance de lobos* remained unstaged during the dramatist's lifetime, and only premiered as late as 1967, 1966 and 1970 respectively. The triptych was staged in its entirety for the first time in 1974 at the Stadt Schauspielhaus Frankfurt in a production by Augusto Fernándes. Lavelli's 1991 production for the Avignon Festival was the second outing for the trilogy, produced the same year as José Carlos Plaza, then director of the Centro Dramático Nacional, gave the trilogy its Spanish-language premiere at the María Guerrero theatre.

Valle-Inclán's work has never enjoyed the same easy point of contact with a foreign readership that García Lorca's has. The Avignon Festival offered Lavelli a remarkable opportunity to secure a new audience for the Galician dramatist who had always languished far behind his younger contemporary in the international theatre stakes. For Casares, Valle-Inclán was the greatest of all Spanish dramatists whose bold moulding of the Castilian language presents veritable linguistic challenges for translators: 'Lui-même disait qu'il fallait presque le traduire en espagnol, qu'il parlait un language wisigothique. Il utilise des mots français, mexicains, irlandais hispanisés' (1990b: 15) (He himself said that he needed to be translated into Spanish, that he spoke a semi-gothic language. He uses French, Mexican, Hispanicised Irish terms). *Comedias bárbaras* defies easy categorisation occupying an ever-shifting space between cinema, theatre and painting. This is, for Casares, part of the triptych's allure (cited in Monleón 1990: 441). Llamas's adaptation – rendering the three plays as *Gueule d'argent, L'Aigle emblématique* and *Romance de loups* – pared down the action. Llamas dispensed with one of Montenegro's rapacious sons, Don Rosendo, and omitted scenes which he and Lavelli felt held up the main narrative (including the opening of *Cara de plata* where shepherds argue about access to the Lantaño bridge and Act Three, Scene Three of the same play when the sexton, Blas de Míguez, attempts to die in the company of his disinterested family). The Argentine designer Graciela Galán, perhaps best known for her film work with María Luisa Bemberg and her designs of Eduardo Pavlovsky and Griselda Gambaro's plays for Laura Yusem, provided Lavelli with an expansive rough ocre landscape bereft of superficial decor. While Plaza's production attempted a literal re-creation of the playwright's effects, resulting in cumbersome scene changes, Lavelli allowed the action and minimal props – often entering through camouflaged trap doors – to create a precise sense of place and thrust the narrative forward. Actors waiting to make their entry at the sides of the set ensured that scenes flowed effortlessly into one another blurring the scenic distinctions laid out by the dramatist.

Premiered in the fourteenth-century courtyard of the Palais des Papes, with a cast of twenty-eight, Valle-Inclán's epic tale of Montenegro's warring relations with his rapaciously materialistic sons failed to convince the French press of the merits of the trilogy. As Lavelli himself had anticipated, French critics found it difficult to accept the conventions of a dramaturgy that disarms the spectator with its harsh episodic structure and melodramatic excess. Casares was, perhaps because of her Galician roots and her long-term affiliation with Lavelli, associated with the venture in a very direct way. Numerous interviews published before the production's Avignon opening revolved around her championing of the texts and her Spanish/Galician ancestry (Lafargue 1991: 34; Josselin 1991: 74–5). While the narrative revolves around Montenegro's predicament, Casares was in many ways able to displace Michel Aumont's Montenegro from centre stage in *L'Aigle emblématique*. While the patriarchy embodied by Montenegro inflicts its most ugly terrors on the women in the trilogy, Casares, like Isabel Karajan's exquisite Sabelita, offered an audacious antidote to her fiery husband. Her coolly defiant expulsion of her husband and his whore from the ancestral home at the end of the play indicated a refusal to play the passive victim – the role in which Doña María is so often cast – and signified the effective waning of this proprietorial Don Juan and the feudal order he once stood at the head of.

Casares' performance, like the production, split both the French and Spanish press at Avignon. *Libération*'s Mathilde La Bardonnie expressed doubts about the translation and the frenetic pace of Lavelli's production but named Casares and a wizened Denise Gence as the loyal servant Micaela – a role reworked by Llamas and Lavelli into a chorus-type figure who opens the trilogy – as the veritable stars of the production (1991: 25–7), a view echoed by Gilles Costaz in *Les Échos* (1991: 26). Marcabru in *Le Figaro* bemoaned the exposition-heavy first half of the trilogy, judging Casares, Aumont and Gence as the only performers able to give the text appropriate weight (1991b: 22). While he was able to see the second part of the trilogy with its macabre scenes of cemeteries being ransacked, chapels ravaged, shipwrecks and ghostly souls haunting the protagonist as infinitely more theatrical, he here viewed Casares as 'curieusement assez effacée' (1991c: 21) (curiously rather unobtrusive), failing to see her more intimate performance style as an intentional decision designed to rest uneasily with the robust acrobatic performances of the servants and sons. For *Le Monde*'s Michel Cournot, the beautiful simplicity of Casares' scene as Doña María with the baby Jesus, which opened the second half of the trilogy (Act Four, Scene Three of *Águila de blasón*), was one of the high points of the production (1991: 11).

For *La Vanguardia*'s Joan-Anton Benach, Casares was disappointing as Doña María and no match for Aumont's majestic Montenegro or the exquisitely choreographed choral work which governed the fairground scenes, processions and other multi-character encounters (1991a: 37). *El Periódico*'s Pérez de Olaguer, however, saw her carry off with precision and 'la fuerza de su mirada' (the force of her gaze) the more problematic intimate scenes which often seemed dwarfed by Galán's curvacious plateau-like set (1991d: 51). Casares herself saw Doña María as a figure who recalled certain Dostoevskian creations. A participant in *Águila de blasón*'s most shrouded and confidential scenes, she recognised the need to re-conceive the character within a more subdued register (cited in Pérez de Olaguer 1991b: 53). While Casares had praised Llamas's translation (cited in Josselin 1991: 74), numerous French critics, including *L'Humanité*'s Jean-Pierre Léonardini, were to label the adaptation dry and stolid (1991: 20). The Spanish critics too probed Llamas version, quibbling over the accuracy in the translation of particular phrases (Sagarra 1991c: 33).

The issues thrown up around the translation and transposition of the works point to key fears articulated by both the Spanish and the French press around issues pertaining to the 'new' Europe of 'super-productions' funded by various partner states. The production merged a fresh interest in Spain, which had entered the European community in 1986, with the reality of a cultural framework that could bring together performers and a production team from across Europe. *Comédies barbares,* a co-production between the Avignon Festival, Le Théâtre National de la Colline and the Olimpiada Cultural de Barcelona, also received significant funding from the Spanish Ministry of Culture and was to count on the Spanish presence of Casares and the composer Carmelo Alonso Bernaola who was responsible for the production's musical score. The Spanish press, however, reporting daily on the critical fate of the production, were quick to pick up 'anti-foreign' remarks in *Le Figaro*'s coverage of the festival. The French newspaper appeared to bemoan opening the festival with a 'foreign' product, which it felt 'questioned' the French focus of Avignon (Benach 1991b: 37). The paradox that Casares should be simultaneously acclaimed as 'Reine incontestée du Festival d'Avignon' (Thébaud 1991: 22) (undisputed Queen of the Avignon Festival), indicates the problematic nationalism of a French press which was to exalt Valle-Inclán as a dramatist of unclassifiable genius while positing that the *Comedias bárbaras* are the most unstageable works in world theatre (Sagarra 1991d: 29). Pérez de Olaguer's belief that Lavelli's production chose to accentuate the more provocative components of Valle-Inclán's text may also have served to alienate an opening night audience expecting more sanitised entertainment (1991d: 51). Lavelli had hoped that the Don Juan myth would offer a way in for a Francophone audience but what he terms a French 'recelo hacia lo hispánico' (cited in Sagarra 1991b: 29) (suspicion of the Hispanic) may well have proved more destructive than he initially suspected. The first hour of the three-hour section was to see a steady stream of spectators leaving the Cour d'Honneur and *El Mundo*'s Borja Hermoso was one of a number of Spanish critics who observed that Valle-Inclán had failed to carve a niche in Avignon (1991: 1).

This may, in part, have been due to the conditions in which the trilogy was presented. *El Diari de Barcelona*'s Francesc Burguet i Ardiaca observed that the invited opening night 2,500-member audience consisted of 400 baseball players who left after half an hour and a number of busloads of Japanese tourists who seemed – clichés notwithstanding – to be interested only in taking photographs (1991: 37). The three hour instalments in which the trilogy was presented – parts one and two each performed on alternate nights beginning at 10.00 p.m. with the whole triptych performed on the 13th and 17th – also seems to have presented problems for what Lavelli terms the 'artificial' first-night audience (cited in Sesé 1991: 46).

Already at Avignon Lavelli had spoken of the need to re-conceive the staging for the indoor spaces of La Colline and El Mercat de les Flors where the production was to travel following the Avignon performances (cited in Pérez de Olaguer 1991c: 51). At Avignon both Léonardini (1991: 20) and Pérez de Olaguer (1991d: 51) drew attention to the problems of an overly horizontal set which proved unable to suggest a bridge between the realms of heaven and hell, the sacred and the profane, the epic and the intimate which the trilogy occupies. The set was subsequently cut from a width of twenty-seven to nineteen metres. Lavelli acknowledged problems of perception from spectators in the cavernous Cour d'Honneur who may have found themselves forty metres away from the performers, but he was also conscious of the fact that the Spanish members of the audience may have felt uncomfortable with a Valle-Inclán reworked in French (cited in Sesé 1991: 44–7) – a point which Sagarra's review of the production during its Barcelona run slyly betrays (1991e: 26). At Barcelona's Mercat de les Flors, despite the fact that the spectacle began at 9.00 p.m. and did not finish until 3.30 a.m., with the audience of 500 dwindling to half that at the interval, the Catalan press approved of the changes wrought in the staging in a reduced stage space. Benach, writing in *La Vanguardia*, thought it a splendid example of epic theatre contorted within the deforming aesthetic of the *esperpento*. Casares' performance, he went on to state, 'muy difuminado en Aviñon' (all over the place in Avignon), was here aided by atmospheric lighting. This delineated her features and grounded the performance (1991c: 79). Pérez de Olaguer saw Casares reach her most powerful moments during the final scenes of *L'Aigle emblématique* as she confronted her estranged husband over the fate of their goddaughter (1991e: 62).

It is perhaps significant that the most ebullient praise for Casares' performance came from the Catalan-language *El Diari de Barcelona* where Burguet i Ardiaca stated in no uncertain terms that each time she appeared on stage the production visibly lifted, stirring both the audience and her fellow performers (1991: 37). Perhaps the Catalan-language press did not share the Castilian-language press's vested interest in seeing the plays in the 'original' language. For *El País'* Sagarra, the expectations awaiting Plaza's production due to visit Barcelona later that year cast an ominous shadow over Lavelli's staging (1991e: 26). Plaza's production may have lacked the imaginative flair and scenic pliancy of Lavelli's reading, but it was perhaps better acclaimed precisely because it delivered the text in the 'original' language. Plaza's conceptual decision to present the three plays individually with a weekly performance of the triptych in its entirety was also perhaps rewarded in that *Comedias bárbaras* were delivered in a more 'palatable' form than Lavelli's division of the trilogy into two parts. The significance of Plaza's rehabilitation of Valle-Inclán following the denigration he had suffered under the Franco regime was not lost on reviewers like *Le Figaro*'s Valérie Duponchelle who recognised the seminal importance of the trilogy's Spanish-language premiere (1991). Lavelli may have viewed the production's Barcelona opening as its true premiere but it was Plaza's staging with heartthrob actor José Luis Pellicena as Montenegro and Berta Riaza as Doña María which the critics saw as the victor. Perhaps the French hostility towards a Spanish dramatist opening at the Cour d'Honneur was equally matched by the Spanish press's reservations towards a 'foreign' staging which reflected the absurdities of Valle-Inclán's world through the rationalism of the French language and where Casares, occupying an ambiguous position between the Spanish and the French, failed to provide the required stamp of authentication.

El adefesio (1976)

José Monleón's introduction to the 1977 published text of *El adefesio* recognises the polemical reception Alberti's theatre has elicited on the Spanish stage through the twentieth century (1977a: 6–10). The response to the 1931 production of *Fermín Galán* has already been delineated in Chapter 1. Alberti had written *El adefesio* with Xirgu in mind while in exile in Argentina. The premiere at Buenos Aires' Avenida theatre saw Xirgu appear with a candlestick in one hand and a club in the other, wearing a dishevelled beard which contrived an alternative physical identity that subverted the audience's expectations.[35] The production is listed by Ricardo Doménech as one of five key stagings in the post-Civil War theatre – the others being the more predictable choices of Antonio Buero Vallejo's *Historia de una escalera* (Story of a Staircase) in 1949, Alfonso Sastre's *Escuadra hacia la muerte* (*Death Squad*) in 1953, Fernando Arrabal's *Los hombres del tricicle* (*Tricycle*) in 1958 and Lauro Olmo's *La camisa* (*The Shirt*) in 1962 (1968: 18–22).

The Madrid premiere of *El adefesio* in 1976 was to prove a distinctive date in the post-Franco theatre, initiating a theatrical appropriation of denigrated or exiled dramatists which was to see key productions of García Lorca and Valle-Inclán's forgotten works, which will be discussed further in Chapter 5. The production's director was José Luis Alonso, one of the most significant directors, alongside Cayetano Luca de Tena and Luis Escobar, of the Franco era. All three had played a significant role in introducing 'alternative' works to Spain. Alonso had taken over the directorship of the María Guerrero national theatre in 1961 and subverted the limited mandate by staging seminal works by Giraudoux, Unamuno, Turgenev, Ionesco and O'Neill. His role in promoting contemporary dramaturgy – most visible in his staging of numerous of Antonio Gala's plays – , his productions of 'forgotten' classics like *Romance de lobos* (premiered in 1970 at the María Guerrero) and Calderón's *La dama duende* (*The Goblin Lady*) at the Español in 1966, as well as his championing of important trends in the international drama – Cocteau, Claudel, Ionesco, Williams – served to accord him a unique role in the modernisation of the Spanish stage. Collaborating with a range of designers including Siegfried Burmann and Francisco Nieva, he had a long-standing interest in the international stage, cultivated during the late 1950s and early 1960s when he filed a range of reports on theatre events in London, Paris, New York, Avignon and other North American and European destinations for *Primer Acto*. Alonso had seen a number of Casares' productions including *Six Personnages en quête d'Auteur* (*Six Characters in Search of an*

---

35 For Alberti's description of Xirgu's first appearance, see Monleón 1977b: 32.

Author) (1952), *Platonov* (1956), and her seminal *Macbeth* with Vilar in 1954. Casares had been looking for a project to bring her to Spain since the death of Franco. Nuria Espert had made her an offer to perform with her in Genet's *Les Bonnes* (*Las criadas*) in 1969 but Casares had refused (Monleón 1997: 104). The proposal to perform in *El adefesio*, coming during the country's transition from dictatorship to democracy, also marked the return to Spain of Alberti, the final living émigré from the Generation of 27 to remain in exile. Xirgu's premiere of the work had, as with *La casa de Bernarda Alba,* associated the play with a theatre in exile and it appeared fitting that Casares, who had carved out a career in exile, should follow in Xirgu's footsteps by performing the central role of Gorgo. The play had already been staged in Italy in April 1966 by the Catalàn director Ricard Salvat and another production by Salvat was seen later that year in Paris at the Gérard Philipe theatre in Saint-Denis, followed by a number of clandestine performances at the Cúpula of Barcelona's Coliseum. The writer and performer Maria Aurèlia Capmany was to take the role of Gorgo for the Paris production.[36] Given that the role of Gorgo had been written for Xirgu (then living in exile in Uruguay) who had premiered the play in Buenos Aires, as well as the fact that Alberti was still living in exile in Rome, the productions served not to indicate the *apertura* (opening) of the censorious climate but rather as a reminder of a bleak and backward Spain where draconian vigilance and all pervasive control functioned as the order of the day.

El adefesio, based on the true story of a female suicide in Andalusia, renders a defiant antidote to the sanitised portrait of southern Spain provided by the dramas of the Álvarez Quintero brothers. Set in a mountainous town in Andalusia, it tells the tale of three dour, resentful women eaten up by unrequited desire who hold prisoner a young girl, Altea, who is the bastard child of the now dead head of the family, Don Dino. Gorgo believes that she is honouring the memory of the dead man by keeping her locked away, avoiding all contact with the outside world. Despite the harsh conditions in which she is held, Altea manages to fall in love with a young man called Castor. Gorgo forbids their union, informing Altea that he has hanged himself. Distraught, she throws herself from a tower in the house. Gorgo then reveals the secret that Altea and Castor are half-siblings.

It is not difficult to see how character of the tyrannical Gorgo trying to keep the lovers apart could be equated with Franco. Clear parallels can also be seen with García Lorca's despotic matriarch Bernarda Alba, who also appropriates a masculine value system which is used to batter the heterosexual desires of a younger member of the household (Adela/Altea). Casares was to view the play as ceremonial, 'la historia en sí no es nada [. . .] son las ceremonias [. . .] que evocan finalmente a España' (cited in Pereda 1976: 31) (history in itself is nothing [. . .] it is ceremonies [. . .] which finally evoke Spain).

Casares was to prepare for some ten days before rehearsals officially began with Alonso in Paris. As well as dissecting the play, Casares was to probe him on the

36 For further details, see Salvat 1975: 14–15. Other pre-democracy productions of the play included a staging by Mario Gas designed by Fabià Puigserver at the Capsa in 1969 and another by Seville's Crótalo company in 1974. All were 'unofficial' small-scale productions.

working methods in Spain as groundwork for the process of rehearsing in a 'new' country whose theatrical infrastructure she was familiar with only indirectly (Alonso 1991: 531). The production marked the coming together of different generations of theatrical practitioners: Alberti from the pre-Civil War era, Alonso, Laly Soldevila (Uva), José María Prada (Bión) and Julia Martínez (Aulaga), all formed during the Franco era, and Victoria Vera and Daniel Alcor as the star-crossed lovers Altea and Cástor, representing the younger generation of performers who now looked forward to working outside the censorious climate of the Franco regime. Manuel Rivera, contracted for the set design, was a painter making his theatrical debut, having recently enjoyed a high profile exhibition at the Musée d'Art Moderne in Paris. Another painter, Antonio Saura, brother of the dissonant filmmaker Carlos Saura, designed the poster.

Applause greeted Casares' first stage appearance at the Reina Victoria theatre on the opening night of 24 September 1976, a gesture of appreciation for the actress and Alberti as two victims of Francoism. The poignancy of the occasion was also heightened by Alberti's absence. (A specially written poem by Alberti ['Nuevas coplas de Juan Panadero] [New verses of Juan Panadero] was read by Casares at the end of the performance.) Alberti had refused to return to Spain while there was no recognition or amnesty for the Communist Party of which he was a member. The opening of a play which Alberti termed both 'muy terrible y muy española' (cited in Monleón 1990: 339) (very terrible and very Spanish), was doubly symbolic, as the critic José Monleón opines, because it functioned as a high profile celebration of the new democratic era (1990: 340). Indeed *ABC*'s Lorenzo López Sancho was to see it as a significant moment in which two Spains, cruelly separated by Civil War, found themselves through art without victors or vanquished (1976: 62). For Carlos Gortari of the theatre monthly *Pipirijaina,* the production marked Casares' return to a society she had been forced to abandon as a child and the Spanish audience's opportunity to 'discover' one of the grand myths of the European stage (1976: 49–50).

Casares rendered a harsh, competitive, hard-drinking Gorgo. Her close-cropped hair and deep, rasping voice suggested a certain androgyny. Appropriating her brother's beard as an outward symbol of her status and a malicious masquerade, Casares' delicious declamation, feverish energy and musicality was, perhaps unpredictably, lauded by *ABC*'s López Sancho, who contrasted her fervent performance with the pervasiveness of naturalism's underplaying in the contemporary theatre (1976: 62). *Arriba*'s Julio Trenas too recognised that Casares appeared grounded in a more rhetorical performative mode although she had sought to adjust her tone to the registers of her fellow performers (1976: 26). Interestingly, Casares was associated with the Comédie Française – that bastion of the French theatre establishment – by *Pueblo*'s Eduardo García Rico (1976: 13) and *ABC*'s López Sancho (1976: 62), despite the fact that her time with the company had been short-lived and she was primarily known in France for her more experimental work with the TNP, Genet and Lavelli. García Rico was to judge Casares' characterisation of the confrontational Gorgo, who masks deception under a veil of piety, as a

performance on a level unseen in contemporary Spanish theatre. Mentally tortur-
ing Altea with an oscillation between tender flattery and inexorable insults, Casares'
Gorgo enacted her transactions with the pawns around her like a master director,
preparing the stage for the final *dénouement* where control eludes her. Only
J. A. Gabriel y Galán, writing in *Fotogramas* – and to a lesser extent *Pipirijaina*'s
Gortari (1976: 49) – were to question Casares' performance. Gabriel y Galán considered it uncontrolled, histrionic and tainted by Alonso's lapse direction of the
actors (1976: 35).

Alonso viewed *El adefesio* as an emblematic work in its recognition of 'el horror
constante de nuestro país al sexo y a las relaciones sexuales' (1991: 334) (the constant horror of our country towards sex and sexual relations). Certainly the reviews
that greeted the Madrid opening were largely focused on the political resonances
of the event with a who's who of the audience made up of the great and good of
the Madrid cultural establishment. The characteristics of the production were
securely relegated to a secondary place. The conceptual set rendered by Rivera both
evoked a giant bat – a potent symbol of blindness and a mammal mentioned repeatedly during the course of the play – and female genitalia which pose such a threat
to the regime that Gorgo wishes to maintain. Cobweb-like skins of black tulle hid,
shaded and concealed, functioning both to evoke a prison and the tomb in which
Altea is trapped. In avoiding pictorial realism, a space was created which, echoing
the texture of the play, was both boldly mythical and mercurially real.

García Rico was to laud the staging as the pinnacle of Alonso's career as a
director and other reviews published in *Cuadernos para el diálogo* and *Blanco y
Negro* were similarly approving (1976: 13). Only Enrique Llovet in the recently
launched *El País* – ironically the voice of the 'new' liberal Spain – was to articulate
grave doubts about the production which it judged misconceived: 'lentísima,
aparatosa, abrumadora [. . .] desequilibrada' (very slow, showy, tiresome [. . .]
unbalanced). For Llovet, Rivera's magnificent design was ruined by poor lighting.
Recognising the brilliance of Casares' mendacity, he nevertheless judged her performance curiously unengaged with that of her fellow actors, whilst simultaneously
recognising her presence as 'la maravillosa trágica que nunca hemos tendido' (cited
in Monleón 1990: 350) (the marvellous *tragédienne* we have never had). If Casares
was not the pivot of the production for *Hoja del Lunes*' Antonio Valencia or *La
Estafeta*'s Juan Emilio Aragonés, the remainder of Madrid's critics were to see in her
performance her habitual tragic register given an esperpentic twist (cited in Álvaro
1977: 91–3).

Casares was to struggle with the demands of two daily performances during the
Madrid run and the early excitement of the opening performances was not sustained with a substantial drop in audience numbers during the final stages of the
run (Alonso 1991: 530–3; Monléon 1990: 356). A brief break was followed by a
Barcelona run in March 1977 at the Barcelona theatre where the permissiveness of
the new era was visible in a production of the *Rocky Horror Show* directed by Ventura Pons, playing at the same time at the Romea. For the Barcelona run Espert's
daughter, Nuria Moreno Espert, replaced Vera as Altea and Nicolás Dueñas

replaced Prada as the beggar Bión. The Catalan press followed Madrid's example in considering the production a landmark of the contemporary Spanish stage. Casares' musical rendition of the text, rich repertoire of gestures, and sonorous intonation was singled out by *La Vanguardia Española*'s A. Martínez Tomás (1977: 51) who, like *El Noticiero Universal*'s Julio Manegat (1977: 33), saw echoes of Valle-Inclán's grotesque world in the landscape conjured by Alberti and Alonso. Benach, writing in *El Correo Catalán*, was the sole voice of dissent, wondering if the production might not be too 'monumental' for its own good in its stressing the mythical at the expense of the domestic (1977: 31). As with the Madrid critics, it was Casares' technique and stage presence rather than the mechanics of her characterisation that was to obsess the Catalan press.

The production's importance lies also, in retrospect, in initiating a process of reflection which was to lead to the penning of Casares' memoirs, *Résidente privilégiée*, in the late 1970s. Her return to Spain in 1976 opens the book, beginning with the contemplation of a childhood in Galicia, displacement to Madrid and her forced move to Paris. The death of Franco in November 1975 was to unleash a flood of tears (1980: 16) and the possibility of a return that remained off-limits while *el caudillo* remained in power and democracy a distant dream. As Casares herself was to state in 1988, 'Nunca hubiera escrito ese libro sin mi vuelta a España' (cited in Soriano 1988: 61) (I would never have written this book without my return to Spain).

The Barcelona dates were to have inaugurated a Spanish tour of the production which was to last until 29 August. Casares, however, was forced to withdraw from the production on contracting suspected hepatitis and the tour was cancelled. It was Casares' final stage performance in Spanish, although offers, including the title role in a Castilian-language production of *La Celestina*, were forthcoming. Her only further Castilian-language roles were on film, in Julián Esteban Rivera's debut film *Monte bajo*, a tale of rural isolation and in Croatian director Goran Paskaljevic's *Someone Else's America* (1996), a British, French, German and Greek co-production set in Brooklyn. The latter, an exploration of social and cultural displacement in a seething urban metropolis, proved to be Casares' final film performance. Juggling both English and Spanish, she appears as a blind seer, clad in black scarf and dark glasses – a filmic nod to her role in *Les Paravents* – longing to return to the Spain of her birth. Dying on-screen following a plaintive request to her son Alonso (Tom Conti) that 'Quiero morir en mi tierra' (I want to die in my own country), Casares' Victoria – coincidentally sharing her own middle name – articulates the pain of defining yourself in an environment bereft of the material landmarks of home. If Casares herself was to define her own *patrie* as the theatre, it is perhaps fitting that she should be rehearsing Spanish dramatist José Sanchis Sinisterra's *El cerco de Leningrado* (*The Leningrad Siege*), a homage to trouping actresses reflecting on a lifetime in the theatre, at Paris' Théâtre National de la Colline, at the time of her death. Perhaps, as Monleón notes, her final project involved casting a glance to a country which could not or did not want to recover her (1997: 105), or perhaps it was simply the indication of the determination of a prolific actress to keep working on quirky projects well into her seventies. Conceivably *El adefesio*, like *Comédies barbares*, and her other projects with Lavelli, all allowed for a degree of recovery of an actress who, in the words of Lluís Pasqual and Lavelli, continued practising 'until the end of her days, the belief that the theatre should always be an act of transgression' (cited in Delgado 2002b: 213) and 'un espace de défoulement' (1997: 5) (a space of release).

La Casares

Siempre me he considerado española. Yo quiero mucho a Francia porque me acogieron muy bien, pero siempre me consideré española. Esto es algo muy difícil de razonar. (Casares, cited in Maso 1977: 37)

(I've always considered myself Spanish. I love France very much because I was received very well there, but I'll always consider myself Spanish. It's very difficult to rationalise this.)

Casares' autobiography touches frequently on her encounters with Spain during her time in Paris: the excitement of passing a Banco de Bilbao building (1980: 110), the contacts with Republican émigrés dealt with earlier in the chapter, the Spanish-language projects realised with Béjart and Lavelli (395–400). Indeed the cover of *Résidente privilégiée* reproduces Goya's 1791 painting *El pelele* (The Puppet), an image Casares was to associate with her father (1980: 22). For Pasqual, she remains a uniquely Spanish figure who was able to liberate French acting from the rhetoric that 'the French actor, a prisoner of his own language, is too often confined by'. Her 'unique way of breathing' gave her 'a kind of personal musicality' and this rendered the

dissonant effect that María Casares generated when she spoke on stage, which made her unmistakable and electrifying even without considering the colour of her voice, due to the magic of the music of her most intimate and personal Galician identity, or her Spanish spoken with a Galician accent and musicality brought to a language as structured and as logical as French. In the Galician language and above all because of its accents, everything is open and ambiguous, susceptible to be interpreted in one way but also in many others. French, however, is a language that always tends towards the most pertinacious precision. The combination of both, in such a pure and uncontrolled way, passed of course through the 'talent sieve' of Casares, produced a third breath, a third 'music' where the effect is of hearing the words as if for the first time: full of new meaning and without becoming inane through familiarity. Genet, as much as Cocteau, and many more, like Bernard-Marie Koltès, for example, thought that in María Casares they had the perfect performer for many of their characters because, I think, they noticed that she embodied and breathed the texts with the same pounding pulse and tranquillity with which they were written. (cited in Delgado 2002b: 214)

Casares believed that French audiences saw the musicality of her voice as 'una musicalidad española o mediterránea, pero en España tengo miedo que pueda ser un problema' (cited in Soriano 1988: 61) (a Spanish or Mediterranean musicality, but in Spain I am afraid that it could be a problem). Indeed her Galician lilt did attract some dissonant comments in her performances in *Yerma* and *Divinas palabras* but it did not serve as an impediment to further work in Castilian. If she chose not to perform more often in Spain or Latin America, Monleón believes that this is due to the greater possibilities offered to her by the French theatre (1997: 105). Her importance to the Spanish theatre, however, should not be underestimated. In the mid 1940s, when she was beginning to achieve international success on both stage and screen, she was a reminder of a dissipated theatrical culture that had suffered exile (Xirgu, Aub, Alberti, Luis Araquistain, Ramón J. Sender), imprisonment (Cipriano de Rivas Cherif was in Francoist prisons until 1946), or murder (García Lorca). The model that she was to be associated with at the TNP served, according to Monleón, to awaken interest in Spain around the articulation of theatre as a profoundly social entity (1997: 103) – an ideal later taken up by a younger generation of practitioners like Flotats and Pasqual.

Despite the fact that Casares is often celebrated as a key member of the TNP, she was to admit in 1985 she was never entirely in accord with Vilar's promotion of public debates after performances: 'a mí me parece que el teatro es todo lo contrario a un debate' (cited in Burguet i Ardiaca 1985: 21) (theatre seems to me to be the opposite of a debate). It was at Amandiers in the 1980s with Chéreau and Koltès that she seems to have located a creative collective model that she found more compatible. Casares was always to stress an affiliation with poetic dramatists like Genet, Cocteau and Koltès: 'escritores quienes me propusieron obras y, sin saber cómo, me dirigí hacia el teatro que yo quería' (cited in Soriano 1988: 61) (writers who proposed works to me and, without knowing how, I gravitated towards the theatre that I loved). For Quiñonero, writing in *ABC* at the time of her death, the scope of Casares' roles from the contemporary European repertoire rendered her a unique figure within modern theatre (1996: 103). The Théâtre National de la Colline's main auditorium, where she enjoyed some of her most resonant successes with twentieth-century international drama in the 1990s under Lavelli's artistic directorship, now bears her name. One of the two auditoria at Gennevilliers (where she regularly collaborated with Bernard Sobel) was also named after her in 1997 and the Cour Maria Casarès now stands in Avignon close to the Palais des Papes, where she performed on numerous occasions. Following her death, Galicia's municipal government council created the María Casares prizes to encourage the promotion of stage work in Galician (Oro 1997: 585). Her Normandy home, La Vergne, left to Alloué's town council, now functions as a theatrical retreat where actors and directors can prepare, rehearse, and develop artistic ventures for the twenty-first century, facilitating the internationalism she did much to promote (Caballero 2000: 61).

Both Vilar (1991: 174) and Lavelli (cited in Delgado 2002a: 229–30) were to see Casares' work as a journey and a search. She herself was to define it as such: a search for the world of the text. This goes some way towards explaining her love for the process rather than the product (cited in Soriano 1988: 61). Rehearsing always took precedence over performances. As such she often wondered if she was 'una verdadera actriz' (cited in Soriano 1988: 62) (a true actress), for she never really enjoyed performing before an audience. Her dream, as with Genet, was always to prepare for a year a work that would receive only a single performance (cited in Pérez de Olaguer 1991b: 53). She would never read reviews until after a production's run was over for fear that their comments might impact on her performance (cited in Martínez 1977: 21). She was to repeatedly refuse offers to return to Spain with a recital of her most 'famous' speeches, waiting for a project, like *El adefesio*, that would stimulate and push her, putting into practice her hopes that theatre could play a role in exorcising taboos within the newly democratic Spain (cited in Martínez 1977: 21).

Octavi Martí's obituary of Casares for *El País* argued that Casares occupies some place between Ludmilla Pitoëff and Sarah Bernhardt in the pantheon of *monstres sacrés* of the French stage (1996: 27). Like Pitoëff she was a foreigner who excelled at the tragic repertory. For Casares' teacher and biographer Dussane, parallels with Bernhardt are also evident in their avid pursuit of less docile female roles (1953: 102–3). As with Bernhardt, hers was a non-conformist femininity that merged the sensual and the cerebral. Her unconventional beauty was to come into its own as she embraced the liminal androgyny that middle age bestowed on her. The film critic Ginette Vincendeau has written of the 'unconventional' looking film stars that France has produced, celebrating difference that the Hollywood industry will try and mould into acceptable images of beauty (2000: 21–2). Casares' pronounced nose and angular features never rendered her conventionally attractive. Her heavy smoking – press conferences and informal photographs often featured her with a cigarette dangling from her fingers – , raucous laugh and discerningly cracked voice signalled an anti-conformist persona. And it was precisely her non-conformity (both offstage/-screen and onstage/-screen) that rendered her such an alluring figure. She was to confess to Alonso that she never liked to play maidens, preferring strong defiant women to angelic females (Alonso 1991: 531). Her roles were those of outsiders, as in Vilar's production of *Marie Tudor* in 1955, Lavelli's staging of *Médéa* in 1967, and Genet's *Les Paravents* (1966 and 1983). While she was never to court cinematic projects, stating that film 'n'est pas mon aventure' (cited in Josselin 1991: 75) (is not my adventure) and preferring the unpredictable ephemerality of performance, which did not allow for repeated takes and the comfort of hiding behind the anonymity of the camera, film was to provide her with a number of her most resonant roles. While Casares was to resent Robert Bresson's autocratic control over all elements of the production process, few can forget the beguiling smile dancing on lips as the vengeful, calculating *femme fatale* Hélène in *Les Dames du Bois de Boulogne* or her passionate enactment of the Princess of Death, at once coolly sensual and passionately fiery in *Orphée*.

In a 1954 article significantly entitled 'Une tragédienne sans public' (a *tragédienne* without an audience) Roland Barthes articulates some of the qualities that made Casares so unique as a performer. Casares, Barthes argues, forced an audience to join her in exploring the entire duration of the dramatic gesture:

si elle pleure, il ne vous suffit pas de comprendre qu'elle souffre, il vous faut aussi éprouver la matérialité de ses larmes, supporter cette souffrance bien après que vous l'avez comprise. Si elle attend, il vous faut aussi attendre, non de la pensée, ce qui vous est facile dans votre fauteuil, mais des yeux, des muscles, des nerfs, subir l'affreux supplice d'une scène vide où l'on ne parle pas et où l'on regarde une porte qui va s'ouvrir (1993: 410).

(if she cries, it is not enough that you understand she is suffering, you have to feel the substance of her tears, bear this suffering long after you have understood it. If she waits, she makes you wait too, not in thoughts, which would be easy from your seat, but in your eyes, your muscles, your nerves, to undergo the horrible torture of an empty stage where nobody speaks and where you watch a door that is to open.) (trans. Joel Anderson)

Good theatre, Barthes goes on to state, can never be that where the spectator constructs the play on his own. Casares was, for Barthes, one of two performers – with Vilar – capable of making an audience participate in a play, taking it with her (411). Casares never protects her face in the way most actresses do. Rather her face contorts and deforms itself, employed like a mask, her whole face used to find 'la beauté d'un mouvement total' (411) (the beauty of a total movement). 'Donnez au larynx du grand tragédien un langage vide, il en sortira tout de même du théâtre' (411) (put empty language into the language of a tragic actor and theatre will still come out). Casares was a great actor not because she saved bad texts but because she unmasked them (411). In stating that Casares acts for nobody, Barthes celebrates a performer who never aimed to please but rather to disturb an audience through *excès* and *distance* (412) (Barthes' italics).

If she was so admired by Edward Gordon Craig and Claudel, Genet and Koltès, Cocteau and Lavelli, Barthes and Vilar, it was precisely because she was able to combine the grand performance style of ancient tragedy with the flexibility demanded by new trends in dramatic composition.[37] She held Artaud and Genet responsible for liberating 'muchas cosas en mí y en el teatro' (cited in Pereda 1976: 31) (many things in me and in my theatre), recognising their pioneering work in freeing theatrical practice from the demands of naturalistic performance and a diction-dominated performance mode. Although she was only to collaborate with Artaud on his radio play *Pour en finir avec le Jugement de Dieu* (*To Have Done with the Judgement of God*), completed shortly before his death in 1948, the fact that the work was banned by the head of the French national radio station Wladimir Porché as 'inflammatory, obscene and blasphemous' (Barber 1993: 157) brought the piece and all those associated with it immediate notoriety. Casares' attraction to Artaud's work may have been due to a shared non-psychological approach to character and a great love of the semantics and musicality of language, which led her to the conclusion that 'parler, parfois, c'est chanter' (1990b: 16) (to talk, at times, is to sing). Her savouring of words, seducing, cajouling, spitting and firing them out was, in the opinion of Lavelli, 'extraordinary, it was almost as if she were singing onstage' (cited in Delgado 2002a: 230). Indeed for Lavelli she remains one of the most significant

---

37 For details of her correspondence with Craig, see Casarès 1980: 221–4. For details of Claudel's admiration of her work, see Ortega 1997: 108.

figures of twentieth-century French theatre. Stimulating those around her with her remarkable energy and vitality, she was valued by Vilar for this very reason (Molinero 1985: 25). Collaborating with Camus, Vilar, Barrault, Chéreau, and Lavelli, her view of theatre as public service links her to the great social directors of the era but the trajectory of this refugee who wanted to train as a doctor but subsequently became an actress, indicates the ways in which the French cultural landscape has facilitated the presence of bodies habitually inscribed as 'other' within its cultural discourses of power.

4
Spain's international actress: Nuria Espert

Antonio Buero Vallejo is often viewed as the defining theatrical figure within Franco's Spain. A prolific dramatist and critic, his body of work is frequently cited as the benchmark against which Spanish theatre of the period is measured, but, as Marion Peter Holt has recently pointed out, 'his plays and distinctive scenic concepts are rarely acknowledged in general discourse on the theater of the twentieth century, and of his twenty-nine plays only one, *El sueño de la razón* (*The Sleep of Reason*), can be said to have achieved a footing in the international repertory with widespread and repeated stagings' (1999: 42).[1] While Holt attributes the 'unfamiliarity with Buero's theater' to 'the long indifference to post-Lorcan Spanish theatre and Spanish culture in general that followed the Spanish Civil War and World War II', such an argument simply does not tally with the exuberant response which greeted the work of such practitioners as Nuria Espert, Els Joglars, and La Cuadra de Sevilla when it was seen outside the Iberian Peninsula from the late 1960s onwards. Perhaps an international theatrical climate which increasingly encouraged an expansion of the parameters of stage language, promoting a dynamic interaction of theatrical vocabularies, recognised the limitations of a philosophical theatre like that of Buero Vallejo which prioritised character, plot and ideas. It was image-based theatre which therefore appealed to the international theatre circuit. As such it is perhaps Nuria Espert who has functioned as the emblematic opposition artist of the Franco era for the international theatre community, opening up festival interest in Spanish work that went beyond the performance practices pursued by companies like La Cuadra de Sevilla and Els Joglars. Her tours of the USA and Paris and London visits were covered by the most important broadsheets of the day. Indeed she cites the extraordinary reception granted to her work in the United Kingdom as the reason for her making her directing debut in London rather than Madrid (cited in Matabosch 1989: 77). An outspoken critic of the theatrical infrastructure and the tame direction of much Spanish theatre, she was to remain a dissonant voice both during and after the Franco regime.

A polymath who has refused easy categorisation, hers is one of the least documented trajectories of the last fifty years. While Buero Vallejo's work has spawned

---

1 For a selection of evaluations of Buero Vallejo that stress his seminal importance, see Nicholas 1972, Halsey 1973 and O'Connor 1996.

numerous English-language monographs, chapters and articles, Espert has usually featured as a secondary figure to studies of the dramatists and directors she has worked with. And yet her influence on contemporary Spanish theatre as performer, director and programmer has been pervasive. Part of the artistic triumvirate (with José Luis Gómez and Rámon Tamayo) which ran the Centro Dramático Nacional (CDN) between 1979 and 1981, she showed herself to be a major cultural strategist. Bringing Barcelona's hugely influential Teatre Lliure to the CDN, and commissioning its artistic director Lluís Pasqual to direct a much admired staging of Calderón's *La hija del aire* (*The Daughter of the Air*) (1981), she effectively promoted a decentralised theatrical culture on the stages of a centralised national theatre. The fulsome praise bestowed on the productions by the Madrid press served to pave the way for Pasqual to be appointed director of the CDN in 1983. A speaker at the 1985 Congrés International de Teatre a Catalunya, her influence escalated in the 1980s as she moved from actress-manager to international director, making a conspicuous debut with García Lorca's *La casa de Bernarda Alba* (*The House of Bernarda Alba*) at the Lyric Hammersmith in London in 1986 before moving into opera with a series of high-profile productions at Scottish Opera, the Royal Opera House and Brussels' La Monnaie in the late 1980s and early 1990s. The decision that Espert should stage the new Liceu's opening production of *Turandot* in the Autumn of 1999 marked a return to opera following a five-year absence generated by the death of her husband Armando Moreno in 1994. The resonance of Espert inaugurating this iconic symbol of Catalan culture further served to consolidate her visibility as a representative of both the operatic traditions embodied by the Liceu and the adventurous new directions the opera house hoped to follow.

Espert's presence at the major 'Cultures i territoris' event at Barcelona's Centre de Cultura Contemporània (CCCB) in September 1999 (alongside fellow actress Mercedes Sampietro, director Lluís Pasqual, architect Richard Rogers and former French cultural minister Jack Lang) served to firmly position her among the prime movers and shakers of European culture, gathered to facilitate an exchange of different cultural policies on the eve of a new millennium.[2] The fact that she was a signatory to a letter to the Catalan newspaper *La Vanguardia* about La Fura dels Baus's performance installation *L'Home del Mil.lenni* (Millennium Man) on New Year's Eve 1999 (Rossell *et al.* 1999: 24), criticising the show's masculine title as anachronistic in a century marked by the protagonism of women, indicates her feminist affiliations in a supposedly post-feminist era. Espert is the mother of a powerful theatrical dynasty. One of her daughters, Alicia Moreno, now Cultural Counsellor of the Community of Madrid, was previously at Madrid's Autumn Festival and an administrative collaborator of Espert's at the CDN in the late 1970s.

---

2 Other participants included writers Miquel de Palol, Antoni Puigverd, Michel Tournier, Javier Tomeo, painter Joan-Pere Viladecans, musicians Oriol Pi de la Serra and José María Cano, architect Oriol Bohigas and a range of politicians and writers from Italy, Chile and Puerto Rico including Francesco Rutelli, Isabel Allende and Rafael Hernández Colón. For further details, see Ayén 1999.

Her second daughter is an actress who has appeared alongside her mother in *Divinas palabras* (*Divine Words*) (1975) and *Doña Rosita la soltera o El lenguaje de las flores* (*Doña Rosita the Spinster or The Language of Flowers*) (1980). An outspoken critic, Espert has used her high profile media presence to publicly voice sometimes contentious views on the state of theatre in Spain.[3] She has been critical of all Spain's post-Franco prime ministers for failing to prioritise culture within their political agendas (cited in Hermoso 1998: 59). While alienating components of the Madrid theatre community by emphasising the superiority of Barcelona's theatrical culture (cited in Hermoso 1998: 59), her decision to perform largely in Castilian has served to cultivate a distance from Barcelona's theatrical networks (Espert and Ordóñez 2002: 328).

Firmly associated with progressive politics, she was affiliated with the Spanish socialist party (the PSOE), and toured Spain and beyond with Communist poet-playwright Rafael Alberti throughout the 1980s in public recitals of twentieth-century Spanish poems, *Aire y canto de la poesía a dos voces* (Air and Song in Poetry for Two Voices); the inclusion of Alberti's own writings a defiant act of re-appropriation for a playwright who only returned to Spain in the late 1970s when democracy had been reinstated.[4] During the Burgos trials of ETA (Euskadi Ta Askatasuna) members in December 1970, she was one of a number of cultural figures to lock themselves in a monastery in protest at their treatment. An ardent monarchist, quick to credit King Juan Carlos for the country's stable transition to democracy, she was a guest at the wedding of his daughter Cristina to Iñaki Urdangarín at Barcelona Cathedral on 4 October 1997. Queen Sofia was present at the opening night of Espert's production of *The House of Bernarda Alba* at the Lyric theatre London on 8 September 1986. Certainly Espert recognises that, during the Franco era, theatre provided her with a freedom which was not enjoyed by many women of her generation trapped by the conventions of bourgeois respectability or the working-class demands of earning a living through exhausting manual work (cited in Sánchez Mellado 2000: 58).

Her distinctive physical features have rendered her an attractive actress even now that she is well into her sixties. With her almond-shaped eyes, often adorned with the darkest of kohl, and a pale angular face contrasting with her jet black hair, suggesting an intellectual femininity, she has something of Maria Callas's dramatic features. It is perhaps no coincidence that Espert played Callas in the Spanish premiere of Terrence McNally's *Master Class* (1998). Her well-modulated, low-centred, resonant, melodic voice, with its deep throaty tones, negotiates the tragic register with veritable ease, rising as if to breaking point as the dramatic situation requires it. Hers has been an emphatic, mournful vocal register suited to the demands of the grand tragic roles. Nevertheless, while recognising that it is not her forte, Espert turned to comedy in the 1990s in the hope of expanding her repertoire (cited in Anon. 1983a: 5). Able to bring together the naturalistic performance

---

3 See, for example, Gómez 2000.
4 For Espert on her political affiliations, see Marks 1986. For further information on her collaboration with Alberti, see Espert and Ordóñez 2002: 207–19.

discourse that gained ground in the Francoist theatre with more epic acting techniques, she has appeared to exert a detached observatory quality over her acting. While judged an intuitive actress, a steely intelligence has infused all her roles. She has boldly embraced alternative cultural performance registers as her collaboration with Japanese director Koichi Kimura on Hisashi Imoue's play *Make-up* (1990) testifies.

Despite having a strong character, she views herself as a mouldable, malleable performer, resiliently surviving the demands of different eras (1990: 88). Hers has been a career marked by meticulous professionalism where detailed study of the work precedes the preparation of her own role, learnt, as a rule, before rehearsals begin. She has never favoured a process of identification with her roles and has consciously avoided bringing her own experiences to bear on any preparatory work (cited in Torre *et al.* 1965: 20–1). She has also avoided comparison with other actresses by shunning the study of the work of other performers in her preparation for a role (cited in Hermoso 1998: 59). Certainly hers have been characters existing on the peripheries of society: child killers (Medea, Abbie in *Desire Under the Elms*), victims of rape (Laurencia in *Fuenteovejuna*) and prostitutes (Anna Christie). She has always excelled at larger than life characters and admits to being 'una actriz extrema' (an extreme actress) who has never felt comfortable with overly feminine or easy comic roles using 'las aristas más fuertes de mi carácter sobre el escenario, y eso puede resultar fatigante para el espectador' (cited in Santa-Cruz 1989: 38) (the strongest edges of my character on the stage, which may prove tiring for a spectator).

While perceived as a forceful character, she has described herself as 'una persona muy dócil a la dirección porque nunca he aceptado que me dirija ningún tonto' (cited in Anon. 1967f: 19–20) (a very docile person when it comes to being directed because I've never accepted being directed by a fool). Indeed she has brought to Spain a range of prominent international directors to collaborate with her, despite the hostility generated by such decisions. She had also hoped to collaborate with such well-known exiles as María Casares and Luis Buñuel. She invited the latter to direct *Macbeth* for her company, an offer he did not eventually take up (Roberts 1969: 56; Espert and Ordóñez 2002: 122). The international success which her collaborations with Argentine director Víctor García generated were suspiciously greeted in Spain, as Espert herself testifies:

He tenido mucho tiempo la impresión de trabajar contra corriente en España. Como de que cada estreno mío era mirado con desconfianza por la profesión, por la crítica, por los estudiosos [. . .] No por el público, afortunadamente [. . .] Toda mi vida de actriz en este país ha sido polémica. (cited in Santa-Cruz 1989: 38)

(For a long time I've had the impression of working against the tide in Spain. As if each opening were regarded with suspicion by the profession, by the critics, by scholars [. . .] Not by the public, luckily [. . .] My whole life as an actress in this country has been polemical.)

Nevertheless, able to count on influential friends, like Peter Brook in France and Arnold Wesker in Britain, throughout the 1970s she mobilised international support whenever threatened by the censors. With the Fuenlabrada municipal theatre, inaugurated in October 1999, bearing her name, she now stands as a powerful symbol within the contemporary Spanish theatre. Over four decades the most puissant facets of her acting have proved 'the moments of transition that reveal the workings of change itself, the process of coming into being' (Stokes 1996: 77) that has proved a potent metaphor for the changes that have marked the Spanish nation during this time.

La Compañía Nuria Espert

Nuria Espert was born in Santa Eulàlia, L'Hospitalet de Llobregat (Barcelona) to working-class parents on 11 June 1935. Her father was a carpenter, her mother worked in a textile factory, but both were involved in amateur theatre and as a child she was taken to *nius d'art* (art nests), bars with a raised stage where she was encouraged to recite verses. Here she was seen by pedagogue Sandro Carreras who invited her to join his school, where she remained for three years. After a successful audition for the Romea's Compañía Titular Infantil de Teatro, she made her theatrical debut in a children's show at the age of eleven, then passing on to the adult company at the age of fifteen. At seventeen she joined director Esteve Polls's company at the Orfeó Gracienc, broadening her scope and technique. Collaborations with the new generation of Catalan directors, Juan German Schroeder, Antonio de Cabo and Rafael Richart, led to the opportunity of replacing an indisposed Elvira Noriega in *Medea* at the Grec in 1954, and, as with Xirgu before her, gained renown overnight – a factor obliquely commented on in Ventura Pons's astute film *Actrius/Actresses* (1996) an adaptation of Josep Benet i Jornet's *ER,* where Espert was to play a theatrical diva whose career appears to find points of contact with Espert's own.[5]

She married the actor-writer-director Armando Moreno at the age of nineteen in 1955. The couple then formed their own theatre company opening with *Gigi,* directed by Cayetano Luca de Tena, at the Recoletos theatre in Madrid on 8 April 1959. This production initiated a theatrical journey that was to see Espert work largely within the private sector, collaborating with the most significant Spanish directors of the day, on both classical texts with particular resonance within the enclosed climate of Francoism and on contemporary writing that was redefining western dramaturgical practice. Her playing of Hamlet at the Grec theatre in 1960 was conceived as a stubborn adolescent wilfully annoyed by his mother's impending nuptials, sullenly seeking amusement by teasing those around him. In this conservative, pre-feminist era, her cross-dressing revealed gender as a socially constructed position rather than an immutable fact. While Espert's performance, in which she juggled romantic antecedents and a scheming control, may have been admired, critics were harsh on a production that appeared to anachronistically

---

5 For further details on these early years, see Rodrigo and Romà 1989: 4–10 and Espert and Ordóñez 2002: 7–58. Despite the critical success of *Medea*, Espert documents that the production failed to generate further opportunities in Barcelona and she left for Madrid in search of theatrical work; see Espert and Ordóñez 2002: 44–55.

merge different historical periods in its costumes (Cantieri Mora 1960: 60; Espert and Ordóñez 2002: 66).

Moreno's productions of *Anna Christie*, which opened at the Infanta Isabel theatre in Madrid on 29 October 1959, and *Desire under the Elms* (*El deseo bajo los olmos*), which opened at the now defunct Talía theatre Barcelona on 5 May 1962 (later moving into Madrid's Reina Victoria theatre on 14 September of the same year) sought, alongside Alberto González Vergel's staging of *Long Day's Journey into Night* (as *Largo viaje hacia la noche*) in 1960, to bring O'Neill to a wider audience. *Anna Christie* was judged by dramatist Alfonso Sastre a welcome break with a tame boulevard-comedy dominated theatre season and its protagonist a Hedda Gabler for the modern era with echoes of Lady Macbeth and Medea (1959: 7–9). The 200 performances of *El deseo bajo los olmos* in Barcelona awakened interest in an author who until then had been seen as 'rigorosamente minotoritario' (Monleón 1962b: 39) (strictly minority taste), and relegated to individual performances in the *teatro de cámara*.

José Monleón's review of *El deseo bajo los olmos* at the Reina Victoria recognised Espert as superior to the theatrical milieu in which she was obliged to work and speculated whether the run would have been possible without the extraordinary Barcelona spell at the Talía theatre (Monleón 1962b: 39). Espert's rhetorical performance style appeared well suited to O'Neill's characters who personify psychological extremes. While Enrique Alarcón's set may have been conceived in naturalistic terms, the performances, under Moreno's direction, were emphatic with Espert singled out by Monleón during the earlier Barcelona outing for persuasively personifying the contradictory traits of Abbie – sweet and violent, generous and calculating (1962a: 50). *La Vanguardia Española*'s A. Martínez Tomás (1962: 27), *El Correo Catalán*'s José María Junyent (1962: 11) and *Diario de Barcelona*'s María Luz Morales (1962: 40) also proved fulsome in their praise of Espert's dynamic performance. Terenci Moix cites her Abbie as a definitive performance which he saw ten or twelve times and which provided the embryo for the character of Amelia in his novel *El día que va morir Marilyn* (1998: 31). Nevertheless, the choice of play, featuring the heinous crime of infanticide, polarised a substantial element of Madrid's theatre critics who proffered moral judgements on Abbie's killing of her child and expressed outrage at the tone of the work, appearing to justify its 4 classification as 'gravemente peligrosa' (cited in London 1997: 107) (very dangerous). Espert was surprised that the play was approved by the censor (Espert and Ordóñez 2002: 70), and indeed *ABC*'s Alfredo Marquerie offered a good example of the tone of the more conservative Madrid reviews when he stressed that Spanish theatre had already provided a superior treatment of the subject in Benavente's *La malquerida* (*The Passion Flower*) (1962: 73).[6]

Espert's third O'Neill venture was a collaboration with director José Luis Alonso on *Mourning Becomes Electra* (*A Electra le sienta bien el luto*) premiering at the María Guerrero theatre on 28 October 1965. Alonso was then director of the

---

6 For a detailed analysis of the Spanish press reviews, see London 1997: 103–7.

María Guerrero, a position he held between 1961 and 1975, working within the difficult limitations of the official theatre system to promote a more adventurous repertoire and a professionalism which was frequently lacking in the tawdry government-monitored conditions in which he was obliged to work. Espert's admiration for Alonso's efforts as both director and translator within Madrid's theatrical panorama are well documented (Anon. 1967f: 18), and, while they were only to collaborate on *A Electra le sienta bien el luto*, the production served to consolidate Alonso's reputation as the foremost exponent of Stanislavskian practice in Spain (Llovet 1965: 17; Doménech 1965: 27). While the play failed to convince the more conservative elements of the press corps like *ABC*'s Enrique Llovet (1965: 17), Alonso's intimate, condensed production, reworking León Mirlas's translation and juggling classical architectural iconography within the aesthetic of mid-1860s New England, received appreciative reviews in *La Gaceta Ilustrada* and *Informaciones* (cited in Álvaro 1966: 277–8). Indeed Espert composed a Lavinia Mannon who appeared poised between the melodramatic and tragic, at once a participant in the action and spectator of her own demise. Alonso was to recall the experience of working with Espert as unforgettable, classifying her as 'una actriz ejemplar' (1965: 24) (an exemplary actress) in her preparatory work, her methodical approach to character and her rehearsal-room discipline. Indeed O'Neill's welding of classicism within the vocabulary of urban vernacular was to find in the gamine Espert its most resonant Spanish performer.

The Nuria Espert company succeeded in presenting a radical repertoire despite the censorship regulations within which they were obliged to exist and no government funding. All plays were submitted to the censors and Espert estimates that somewhere in the region of fifty of them were turned down between 1959 and 1975. Seasons at the Valle-Inclán theatre in Madrid and the Principal theatre in Valencia in 1962–63 allowed for productions of Strindberg's *Creditors* (*Los acreedores*) and *The Seagull* (*La gaviota*) in idiomatic new translations by Alfonso Sastre and Alberto González Vergel respectively. Her selection of plays demonstrates significant political choices. Despite her reservations about Alejandro Casona's theatrical merits, she was to champion his works when he returned to Spain following years spent in exile in Argentina, staging *La sirena varada* (The Stranded Mermaid) in 1963 and *Nuestra Natacha* (Our Natacha) in 1966. Indeed Casona was to refer to her as 'la heredera de Margarita Xirgu' (Espert and Ordóñez 2002: 76) (Margarita Xirgu's heir). Like Xirgu, Espert was to associate herself with contentious European works. Sartre's *Huis clos* (*No Exit*), presented as *A puerta cerrada*, and *La Putain Respectueuse* (*The Respectful Prostitute*), presented as *La puta respetuosa* in translations by the dramatist Alfonso Sastre at the Poliorama theatre Barcelona in 1967, reintroduced the French existentialist to the official Spanish stage after a twenty-year absence. The Barcelona run was followed by an extended period at Madrid's Reina Victoria theatre in 1968 where the production clocked up over 200 performances (Zatlin 1994: 123–4; Espert and Ordóñez 2002: 91–5).

Espert also played a key role in introducing Brecht to Spain. As John London (1997: 137–8) and Phyllis Zatlin (1990: 58, 61) have delineated, reports of French visits by the Berliner Ensemble and French premieres of Brecht's plays played a fundamental role in disseminating information about the German playwright in Spain. The monthly theatre magazine *Primer Acto* was to feature regular commentaries on Brecht's writings throughout the 1960s and both Alfonso Sastre and Buero Vallejo, who translated a number of his works, were to publicly acknowledge his influence on their dramaturgy (London 1997: 137–8; Zatlin 1990: 57–8). Espert and Moreno had purchased Castilian-language rights to *The Good Person of Setzuan* in the late 1950s but had waited for a more receptive climate which allowed a full commercial production before introducing the play to Spanish audiences (cited in Anon 1967f: 19). Although, as Zatlin notes, until the early 1960s the censors forbade professional stagings of Brecht, permission was given for individual *teatro de cámara* performances or staged readings which played to invited non-paying audiences (1990: 58). London lists the first significant 'large-scale public performance' of Brecht as the Agrupació Dramàtica de Barcelona's Catalan production of *The Threepenny Opera* in 1963 (1997: 137). *Mother Courage and Her Children* had been seen at Madrid's Bellas Artes theatre in a version by Buero Vallejo (*Madre Coraje y sus hijos*) opening on 6 October 1966, and the Teatro National Universitario had premiered *The Caucasian Chalk Circle* at the María Guerrero theatre on 29 March 1965 (as *El círculo de tiza caucasiano*).

The Good Person of Setzuan presented by Espert's company built on the growing interest in Brecht, contracting the West German-trained director Ricard Salvat, who was pioneering epic playing styles and gestic modes of performance within Spain. Salvat had already presented a critically well-received Catalan version of the piece with Espert, *La bona persona de Sezuan,* for the Adrià Gual company opening at the Romea theatre on 21 December 1966.[7] His staging for Espert's company, opening at Madrid's Reina Victoria theatre on 1 February 1967, dispensed with the tokens of oriental exoticism and psychological approaches to character construction in favour of a more demonstrative performance style and a costume design which harked back to pre-Second World War Europe.[8] Moreno and José Monleón prepared a Castilian-language version which condensed the action into a viable two-hour spectacle which could be presented twice daily. Although coolly greeted by the more conservative critics, Zatlin locates a positive television review by *ABC*'s Llovet as responsible for turning the production's fortunes, attracting an audience of university students recently returned from a spring break and more progressive spectators who were to ensure the production counted among that season's most lucrative box-office successes (1990: 61). Espert, however, was the subject of practically unanimous praise from the Madrid critics who were of the opinion that her expert juggling of the dual roles of Shen-Te and Shui-Ta was a significant landmark both in her career trajectory and in the contemporary Spanish theatre (Álvaro 1968: 233–42).

---

7 For reviews of the production, see Pedret Muntañola 1966 and Sagarra 1966. The latter review located some faults in the actors' performances but considered the production 'extraordinariamente inteligente' (extraordinarily intelligent) and the veritable premiere of Brecht in Spain.

8 For details on Salvat's approach, see Salvat 1967.

Re-envisaging *Les Bonnes* (*The Maids*) as *Las criadas* (1969)

Pienso que el éxito de *Las criadas*, tanto en Belgrado como en Madrid, se debe a que es un espectáculo profundamente español. (Espert, cited in Primer Acto 1969b: 40)

(I think that the success of *The Maids*, both in Belgrade and in Madrid, is due to the fact that it is a profoundly Spanish show.)

Espert has spoken of *La persona buena de Sezuan* as 'el final de una étapa que ha terminado' (cited in Anon. 1967f: 18) (the end of an era that has finished). The collaboration with Paris-based Argentine director Víctor García, which was to commence in 1969 with Genet's *Les Bonnes*, is cited by Espert as one of four or five definitive moments in her career – the others being her *Medea* at eighteen, the formation of her own company with Moreno and her directing debut with *The House of Bernarda Alba* (cited in Santa-Cruz 1989: 38). Born in Tucaman, North-West Argentina of Spanish-born parents, on 16 December 1934, García had studied medicine and architecture before coming to Paris at the age of twenty-nine to work at the French Radio Station, then enrolling alongside fellow Argentine Jorge Lavelli at l'Université du Théâtre des Nations in the early 1960s. Although he had been involved in a number of theatrical productions in Argentina, it was in Paris where he was to forge his reputation as a bold theatrical innovator. Like Lavelli, he was to fashion alternative directions in French theatre during the mid-1960s, pursuing a vision of theatre as a baroque space of arresting images where the sensory and the visceral displaced the rational in a ritualistic ceremonial pageant where naturalism was resolutely banished from the stage. As early as 1964, staging *Le Cimetière des voitures* (*Automobile Graveyard*) at a hangar in Dijon, García's conception of space as an environmental, architectural arena of breathtaking audacity demonstrated an imagistic performance idiom where the text was subsumed and re-envisaged within a spectacle of haunting excess. García's interest in psychiatry, his medical specialisation, was to prove a strong influence on his work with actors and may, in part, explain his attraction to dramatic works that interrogate the construction of the psyche. His architectural training was also to shape his conception of scenic space, played out, as David Whitton has expertly articulated, 'not merely in a command of line but the much rarer ability to conceptualise complex constructions and movements in three dimensions' (1987: 164).

By 1967 Espert was already aware of García's adventurous work on the Parisian stage and admired the 'aggressive lack of restraint he displayed'. Sensing that her own company 'had reached the ceiling of what could be done in Spanish theatre at the time', the need to 'expand further' involved contracting someone from 'outside Spain' although Espert and Moreno felt that the company's own history, irrevocably 'bound up with the contemporary history of Spain', necessitated they remain in Spain with 'Spain imprinted' on all future work (cited in Londré: 1985: 4). The venture with García was originally conceived as a double bill. Genet's *Les Bonnes* was scheduled to open as *Las criadas,* presented in Spanish along with Fernando Arrabal's one-act play *Los dos verdugos* (*The Two Executioners*), on 7 February 1969, but Arrabal's play was banned by the censors following the final dress rehearsal.[9] The censors, however, leaving Madrid's Reina Victoria theatre before *Las criadas* had begun, failed to prohibit Genet's play, but Francisco Muñoz Lusarreta, then director of the Reina Victoria, dismissed the company who, unable to open on 7 February as planned, were obliged to find an alternative venue at desperately short notice. They transferred to Barcelona's Poliorama theatre for 21 February, which had been freed up by the closure of Adolfo Marsillach's staging of Peter Weiss's *Marat/Sade*.[10]

The censorship suffered by Espert's company may have inadvertently served to promote the production, for it played in Barcelona for three months despite some rather tepid critical reviews from the Catalan press who resented its fiercely aggressive tone. Initially the piece was accompanied by a series of Yiddish songs translated into Catalan, which were presented by Espert 'attempting to free herself from a confining net' (Londré: 1985: 6), but these were gradually dropped from the programme as it became clear that the audiences needed no 'supporting' programme.

Based on the 1933 case of the Papin sisters, Léa and Christine, who murdered their mistress and her daughter, Genet's play focuses on two sisters Claire and Solange who are servants to a capricious Madame (renamed 'La Señora' in García's production) who furnishes them with her cast-offs. Both indulge in a series of role-play games where they replay their relationship with Madame, planning her murder, but Madame's disappearance to join her lover who has just been released from prison, disables their plans. They decide, however, despite this setback, to carry though their charade whatever the consequences. The Catalan press dedicated much space to contemplations of the thematics of the play and of Genet's chequered personal life before offering rather bemused commentaries on a production which they claimed defied easy understanding (Martín 1969: 30; Martínez Tomás 1969: 44). Only veteran critic María Luz Morales was to judge the production a remarkable success in rendering in scenic terms the dynamics of Genet's ceremonial study of domestic oppression and social discontent (1969: 25). García's concept of an enclosed performance space made up of a raked plane surrounded by fourteen matt and shiny aluminium sheets, made it difficult for an audience to locate mimetic referents. Genet's stage directions situate the play within Madame's bedroom, an opulent space filled with Louis XV furniture (a bed, a chest of draws), abundant flowers, and an upstage window that looks out onto the facade of the building opposite. García, collaborating on the design with Enrique Alarcón, provided a circular, non-decorative, chapel-like space. The high-mirrored pivoting panels allowed for a constant interplay between the real and its imaginary, under-

---

9 Espert's memoirs mention that it was Arrabal who first suggested García as a possible director for the double bill when she and Moreno visited Paris to discuss a possible staging of *Los dos verdugos*; see Espert and Ordóñez 2002: 99.

10 The events around the opening of the production are narrated by Espert in Monleón 1982: 44–5 and Espert and Ordóñez 2002: 99–109. The interview with Monleón also has information on the set for *Los dos verdugos*, which consisted of a tank which would rise up from the floor of the space used for Madame/La Señora's suite in *Las criadas*.

lining a fascination with the reflection of social and political hierarchies which is present in all Genet's work. For, as David Bradby has astutely noted, Genet's plays operate primarily at the level of metaphor, 'the figures of [. . .] the maids [. . .] do not represent the reality of power or slavery, but its image [. . .] they become figures onto which the audience projects its own image of social roles and power relations' (1984: 174). García's production eschewed naturalistic detail in favour of emphatic stylisation. These maids first appeared as plaintive cries from the darkness. Espert's Claire emerged from a pool of light in the centre of the space, rising up like a peacock with a grand ceremonial headdress to begin her impersonation of La Señora. This was theatre as ceremony, with the cathedral-like stage functioning as a conscious mirror where images of the self were constantly viewed through images of the other.

The sharply raked stage was marked by a central circular, hollowed enclosure covered with a black cloth evocative of a bedspread. This functioned as altar, bed and tomb: a throne where La Señora lies pontificating on her goodness to the maids and Claire's sacrificial place of slaughter where she falls dead having drunk from the poisoned chalice that contains the laced camomile tea. Espert has spoken of how the space initially terrified the performers but they learnt to appropriate it (cited in Monleón 1982: 45). This involved dispensing with psychological reasoning as the motivating impetus of behaviour, instead opting to explore the relationship between dominator and dominated, love and hate, as a means of positioning the two maids within the parameters of saintliness/sanctity and criminality around which much of Genet's work revolves. As such Espert's Claire and Julieta Serrano's Solange appeared almost as facets of the same being rather than individual entities, enacting a series of rituals endlessly reflected in the wall of mirrors which never allowed the audience to forget that the characters were, above all, their social roles: life as performance.

I have commented in Chapter 3 on the particular acting style that Genet's plays necessitate, with all interaction ceasing to be natural or essential but rather becoming conscious imitation or performance with an emphasis on gestures that do not necessarily complement or suit the word (109). García's rehearsal work with Espert (Claire), Julieta Serrano (Solange) and Mayreta O'Wisiedo (La Señora) sought to construct an anti-realistic acting aesthetic where appearance was both form and subject, an intriguing game of mirrors providing layers of endless artifice where 'truth' and 'reality' remained elusive concepts that defied revelation. All three characters were defiantly exposed as actors, enacting roles within a circular holy arena where imprisonment and surveillance are the order of the day. While the giant metallic panels slid open vertically, each exit was marked by a barrage of noise, reinforcing the culture of surveillance. When Claire sought to open the windows she found only hard panels which she knocked into and which hurled her back into the constrained space. Light streaming through the cracks in the panels in tiny narrow paths reminded the audience and performers of a world beyond.

For *Le Balcon (The Balcony)* Genet had set particular demands for actors contracted to perform the play, envisaging them wearing shoes with twenty-inch soles, shoes that would demand the actors perfect a new sense of balance to avoid top-pling over (cited in Aslan 1988: 87). García was to appropriate this ideal in *Las criadas*, as Espert's Claire clambered up from the floor in high platform shoes (recalling the stilts used by ancient Greek actors) in her first impersonation of La Señora (see Figure 11). These shoes were also worn by La Señora who similarly tottered across the stage, looking down both figuratively and literally on her maids. Solange and Claire were dressed in simple black tunic dresses and black stockings, their straight black hair further emphasising the mirror motif. While the maids occupied the horizontal plane, crawling across the floor like beasts preparing for the kill, an effect described by *Diario de Barcelona*'s Morales as rather like observing repulsive reptiles (1969: 25), La Señora was emphatically associated with the vertical, flying down through an opened vertical panel like an ephemeral blonde being, an exaggeratedly regal image in pale, flowing, translucent fabric, whose elevated feet never come close to touching the ground. The roles were emphasised both visually and verbally as Solange spoke to La Señora in a marked declamatory tone, as if reciting particular learned responses and Claire adopted a more overt whining voice. All were enveloped in the trappings of performance, appearing to say one thing while their tone exposed their devotion as jealous contempt. As outside factors intruded – the alarm clock warning of La Señora's imminent return, flaws which Solange located in Claire's performance as La Señora and Claire pinpointed in Solange's performance as Claire – anger and frustration enveloped the sisters and they tore at each other like wild panthers. Bodies thrust around the room at a frenzied pace, Solange's bitter thumps against the echoing panels and Claire's self-flagellation all served to delineate the unholy ritual enacted before the audience. The robes in which Claire was clad by Solange in the opening scene of the play and the spectral white cassock and nun-like headpiece in which Claire made her final appearance as La Señora, as well as the goblets which replaced the cup and saucer china of Genet's text, all sought to underline the ritualistic, mass-like associations of the production which reinforced Genet's own views on the high theatrics of the Catholic mass.[11]

Whatever the Catalan critics' reservations about a staging that was denounced as cold, dehumanised and more audacious than imaginative (Martínez Tomás 1969: 44), Espert, Serrano and O'Wisiedo were commended for rendering remarkable performances of rigorous discipline on the awkwardly steep rake of the stage (Benach 1969: 26). This aggressive intensity was achieved through what Espert terms 'sensaciones utilizadas en el momento justo, un momento que no podía ser otro' (feelings used at the exact moment, a moment that could not be any other). Rehearsals depended on García knowing the state the performers were in at the start of the session. After a technical warm up, then came

la conquista de una tensión espiritual; y a partir de ahí, los estímulos podían llegar a través de agresiones, siempre llenas de amor, o de sugerencias, a veces difíciles de com-

---

11 These associations have been explored in greater detail by Whitton (1987: 174–7) and Cornago Bernal (1999: 91–8).

11 Nuria Espert (standing) as Claire and Julieta Serrano (kneeling) as Solange in *Las criadas* (1969)

prender, y que deberíamos traducir a un lenguaje orgánico y perceptible para los demás. Con ningún director de los que conozco, el término intérprete adquiere una justificación más precisa. (cited in Monleón 1982: 44)

(the conquest of a spiritual tension; and from there, stimulation could come from acts of aggression, always filled with love, or suggestions, sometimes difficult to understand, which we had to translate into an organic and detectable language for others. With no other director that I know has the term performer acquired a more precise justification.)

Espert has acknowledged how the dialogue of Genet's play was the last element to be incorporated into the rehearsal process, fixed only days before the opening (cited in Primer Acto 1968: 20). It was indeed around the very eschewing of the play's literary allusions and connotations that the production's aesthetic pivoted, rendering the audience silent, participating witnesses to the slaughter enacted before them.

The use of the highly formalist Sarabande from Bach's Cello Suite 2 in D Minor interpreted by Pau Casals (1876–1973), the Catalan cellist still living in exile in Puerto Rico, in the final instances of the play as Claire drinks from the poisoned chalice, further served to underline the baroque rigidity and ritualistic form of the world in which the maids are trapped. Interestingly the radical musician, who was not to return to Spain until his remains were interred in his home town of El Vendrell in 1979, was perceived as one of Franco's most vociferous critics. The use of his recording of Bach's Second Cello Suite, advertised on the poster and publicity for the production, further emphasised the anti-authoritarian associations of a production that was to serve as the veritable introduction of Genet's corrosive work to Spain.

With this production, which García came to acknowledge as his finest piece of work (cited in Pérez Coterillo 1984b: 10), Espert consolidated her company's reputation as both an exponent of alternative modes of performance and innovator of a repertoire that moved marginal playwrights to the very centre of theatrical debate and culture in Spain. *Primer Acto*'s José Monleón was to recognise the importance of the staging in opening up new possibilities for a less literal theatre culture in Spain (1970: 10–11). The production finally premiered at the Madrid's Fígaro theatre on 9 October 1969 where it clocked up 190 performances in its now legendary five-month run (Cornago Bernal 1999: 97). Madrid's critics too were, barring a few predictable exceptions, fulsome in their praise for a production which broadened the parameters of theatrical representation within Spain's censorious cultural climate. *Hoja del Lunes*' theatre critic Gabriel García Espina was one of those who claimed not to understand the work (cited in Álvaro 1970: 230) and *Insula*'s Ángel Fernández Santos (1969: 30) lamented the limiting self-referential nature of the production. The critics of *Ya, Dígame, Pueblo* and *Informaciones*, however, all recognised its significance as well as the radical nature of Espert and Serrano's characterisations (cited in Álvaro 1970: 227–9). Indeed *Informaciones*' Llovet was to judge Espert's avant-garde performance as indicative of her theatrical adventurousness and curiosity (cited in Álvaro 1970: 229).

Abroad too the production's delirious critical response served to indicate that Spanish theatre did provide 'exportable' products within the selective arts festival circuit. Invited by Mira Trailovic to the Belgrade Theatre Festival, the staging won a number of significant prizes. Indeed Espert has subsequently recognised the importance of the Belgrade Festival in promoting *Las criadas,* creating international interest in the work and ensuring a more receptive climate greet the play on its return to Spain for the Madrid run (cited in Monleón 1983a: viii).[12] The production was then seen in 1970 at Paris' Théâtre de la Cité Universitaire where it was much admired by Genet (Olivier 1970: 52). A French staging was planned with a different cast, but when produced at the Espace Pierre Cardin in 1971, it never generated the same critical accolades as the original production (Aslan 1975; Bablet 1975; Whitton 1987: 177–8). The attention devoted to García's production by the

---

12 In her memoirs, Espert articulates the view that it was press reports of the company's impending visit to the Belgrade Festival which led to an invitation to bring the staging to the Fígaro which was then functioning as a cinema; see Espert and Ordóñez 2002: 112.

French critical establishment (including a collected dossier of commissioned articles published by Éditions du Centre National de la Recherche Scientifique in 1975) served to further highlight the acclaim the production, which effectively launched Espert's international career, had gained abroad – it played at the Aldwych Theatre's World Theatre Season of 1971 and was also seen in Florence, Vienna and Shiraz-Persepolis.[13]

Revived in 1983 following García's death, it opened at the Principal theatre Valencia with Espert and Serrano reprising their earlier roles.[14] The major change involved a new Castilian adaptation by Armando Moreno replacing Manuel Herrero's earlier translation. Thirteen years after its first outing, the production, acknowledged by Espert as the finest of her three collaborations with García, the most significant production of her career and probably García's strongest *mise en scène* (Millas 1982: 7; Espert and Ordóñez 2002: 110), was now discernibly recognised as a classic by Spanish critics who benefited from the hindsight of fourteen years of theatrical innovations. A two-year tour involving international dates in Argentina, Italy and Switzerland as well as an extensive Spanish tour (which had been prohibited when it was first produced in 1969) served to introduce the play to a new generation of spectators and, while the production may not have had the monumental force of its first outing in the repressed socio-political climate of the late Franco years, its impact, as *El País*' theatre critic Eduardo Haro Tecglen rightly indicated, remains profound (1984: 39).

Revolutionising the stage: *Yerma* (1971)

Me parece que Víctor [García] llegó a España en el momento más oportuno y que marcó mucho nuestro teatro. Es algo que ha dicho con otras palabras el *New York Times* cuando murió, que la *Yerma* había abierto en aquel país un camino distinto por donde transitaba el nuevo teatro norteamericano (Espert, cited in Pérez Coterillo 1984b: 10).

(I think that Víctor [García] arrived in Spain at the most opportune moment and that he really made a mark on our theatre. It's something that was said, in other ways, by the *New York Times* when he died, that *Yerma* had opened up in the USA a different path which the new North American theatre was following.)

ABC's Santiago Trancón was to recognise in 1988 the importance of *Las criadas* as a production which 'revolucionó nuestros escenarios' (revolutionised our stage). *Yerma* too he cites as 'una referencia fundamental en la reciente historia teatral española' (1988: 113) (a fundamental reference point in recent Spanish theatre history). *Yerma* may have been Espert's first García Lorca venture but Víctor García had already worked on *El maleficio de la mariposa* (*The Butterfly's Evil Spell*) in Argentina in 1956 and the prize-winning production of *Retablillo de don Cristóbal* (*The Puppet Play of Don Cristóbal*) at l'Université du Théâtre des Nations in 1963.

13 The production's success was eagerly reported on by the Spanish press; see, for example, Soria 1971.
14 Marisa Paredes was initially cast as La Señora and took the role in the play's Valencian run at the Principal theatre in January 1983. She was later replaced by O'Wisiedo.

It was Espert who persuaded García to turn his hand to another García Lorca work at a time when he was working in Brazil on Genet's *Le Balcon* and had little interest in returning to Spain (cited in Monleón 1971b: 18). As with *Las criadas* and the later *Divinas palabras,* the production was to dispense with naturalistic parameters of characterisation and *mise en scène* in favour of a poetic logic which re-envisaged the stage as a pliant membrane. García Lorca's play revolves around the protagonist from which the play takes its title, Yerma (signifying barren) whose marriage produces no children. In a society where female identity is constructed almost exclusively through motherhood, Yerma is increasingly isolated from the women and children. Unable to achieve the conformity which motherhood bestows, her marriage to Juan suffers but she is unwilling to incur the wrath of the community by seeking alternative satisfaction with the shepherd Víctor who shares her views on the necessity of children. Her frustration leads her to strangle her husband in the play's closing moments.

Espert recalls that the set was conceived by García while sitting in a Madrid restaurant playing with a napkin (Espert and Ordóñez 2002: 139–40).[15] Finding a visual analogy for the play's references to the female body, crops, and fertility, García and designer Fabià Puigserver created a diamond-shaped olive-grey canvas membrane at a vast height of eighteen metres operated through pulleys which raised and lowered the main fabric tarpaulin.[16] Resembling a trampoline, its undulating surface moved with the actors scrambling up its sides to create a landscape that evoked the crests and valleys of a barren rural landscape (see Figure 12). Hoisted up to give the impression of claustrophobic caves and other interior spaces, it proved as difficult to navigate as a moist marsh. With its frame hovering ominously over the stalls, the stretchable membrane, suggestive of a womb, served as a constant reminder of childlessness and the constraints it produces. García described the set as both a lunar landscape and a desert (cited in Monleón 1971b: 16), while Pedro Laín Entralgo writing in *La Gaceta Ilustrada* referred to it as an elastic floor, sunken earth, a tent in which life is lodged and a sail stretched out by the wind (1972a: 3). García and Puigserver's allegorical set, conceived alongside the tunic-like costumes in tones of black and white, proved pivotal to a production which broke with established trends in the staging of García Lorca's rural trilogy. There were no attempts at mimetic or symbolic realism, and all of the recognisable symbols of García Lorca's Andalusia-located work – women dressed in black and whitewashed houses – were banished from the stage.

15 José Monleón has a slightly different take, mentioning that the set was conceived by García in a Parisian restaurant (cited in Martínez Roger 1997: 41).

16 Puigserver was credited as set designer with García but a dispute seems to have emerged over Puigserver's role which García viewed as that of executing his stage directions. Puigserver's name was removed from the production's programmes for almost two years, returning only for the Barcelona run; see Corberó 1973 and Cornago Bernal 1999: 99. Espert claims that Puigserver's annoyance over García receiving primary credit for the design was to result in Puigserver claiming sole credit for the design which she argues was conceived by the former and realised by the latter; see Espert and Ordóñez 2002: 145.

The design was originally conceived to work in the open air as a giant canvas sheet stretched out along a metallic hexagon that was then reworked as a pentagon for reasons of space (Cornago Bernal 1999: 99; Eder 1971: 36). The García Lorca family opposed the production's staging at Granada's Corral del Carbón, an Arabic coal yard, and a government injunction then prevented its proposed opening at Barcelona's Grec theatre in Montjuïc. Planned premieres at indoor theatres in Tarragona and Madrid also met with police intervention and only when the company mobilised the theatre profession to bombard the government with a threat to strike that would effectively have closed all the capital's theatres was the production finally allowed to open (Eder 1971: 36). Specific reasons for the government's intransigence over the production were never given but speculation abounded that it had to do with Espert's affiliation with Arrabal, the Spanish playwright then living in exile in Paris.[17] Her appearance in his subversive 1971 film *Viva la muerte* as a mother – loosely based on Arrabal's own – who betrays her husband to the Nation-

12 Fabià Puigserver's pliant canvas set for García's 1971 staging of *Yerma*

17 For further details, see Monleón 1971a: 11, Monleón 1971b: 19 and Londré 1985: 9–11. In her memoirs, Espert mentions that she chose the play following the censors' rejection of Alberti's *La lozana andaluza* (The Voluptuous Andalusian) because, knowing it had been approved by the censors for Escobar's production eleven years earlier, she didn't think she'd have problems securing permission for performance. Unable therefore to ban the play, the authorities' strategy was then to ban the individual performances; for further details see Espert and Ordóñez 2002: 143.

alists during the Civil War suggested an anti-Franco affiliation which evidently rested uneasily in the authorities' minds.

The production, finally premiering at Madrid's Comedia theatre on 29 November 1971, opened up a veritable debate both in Spain and abroad around the concept of director's theatre and the extent to which the visual could legitimately subsume the verbal (Mortimer 1972: 31). In *Pueblo*, Alfredo Marqueríe, describing a stunned audience, lamented the negligent treatment of language in the production which was subsumed under the dominant aesthetic of the giant membrane and marked by a costume design which seemed more rooted in the Orient than Andalusia (1971: 48). *Hoja del Lunes'* García Espina shared the view that the machinery strangled the music of the language (cited in Álvaro 1972: 131). Enrique Romero, writing in the liberal *Triunfo*, was similarly appalled by the set's dominance of the stage and by a performance on Espert's part which he denounced as excessively individualistic (1972: 42). *ABC's* Adolfo Prego too saw the text as frighteningly divorced from the production, and characterised it not as a re-creation but an adulteration of García Lorca's text (1971: 81). As with Xirgu's performance thirty-seven years earlier, much of the unease about the production seemed to pivot around the representation of female sexuality, with references made to a semi-naked woman in the fertility fresco (Marqueríe 1971: 48), the set tellingly described as a 'cama elástica' (Prego 1971: 81) (elastic bed). Ironically Xirgu's performance – similarly lambasted at the time for its radical approach – was held up as 'inolvidable' (Díez Crespo 1971: 16) (unforgettable), its admirers likely to feel cheated by Espert's vision of the role. *El Noticiero Universal's* Pablo Corbalán (1971: 7) and *Triunfo's* Emilio Menéndez Ayuso (1973: 32–5) were among the few critics to rise above the scandal concerning the alleged adulteration of the text, situating the production within the dramatist's radical aesthetic and applauding its attempts to free his work from the clichés around which stagings often gravitated. Laín Entralgo's dissection of the polemic around the staging divided the response into the nostalgics who valued the textual 'purity' of the play and resented any attempt to distort or deform their concept of it and the innovators who believed that any scenic approach can be justified by the needs of the moment in which the piece is staged (1972a: 3). In a companion piece published a week later he expressed admiration for Espert's performance which he saw as supported by García's staging (1972b: 3). While appreciating the physical discipline of the performers, *El Alcázar's* M. Díez Crespo articulated doubts around the clarity of the principal actors (1971: 16). For *Ya's* José María Claver, however, Espert's performance was incomparable, and further confirmation of her status as a *grande tragédienne* (1971: 43).

The production was finally seen in Barcelona at the former Coliseum cinema for a twenty-six day run beginning 14 February 1973 following its nineteen-week run in Madrid and international dates in New York, Washington, Los Angeles, San Francisco, Venice, Belgrade and Berlin. The Barcelona critics may have been more welcoming of the production but their reviews were strongly grounded in the impact that the staging was already generating worldwide. *La Vanguardia Española* quoted Peter Brook's view that this production was 'uno de los mejores trabajos que he visto en mi vida' (one of the best pieces of work I have ever seen) and relayed its significance as standing alongside Brook's own playfully irreverent *Midsummer Night's Dream* of 1970 (Anon. 1973: 53). This was a staging whose international repercussions were still being felt and which had no precedent in this respect in the contemporary Spanish theatre. The poster campaign, showing Espert fondling her naked breasts, delineated the radical nature of the production and *La Vanguardia Española*'s A. Martínez Tomás was quick to point out that neither of the play's previous Barcelona outings – Xirgu's 1935 performance or Luis Escobar's 1960 production with Aurelia Bautista in the title role – had been so eagerly anticipated (1973: 56). Nevertheless, the critics were largely in accord with their Madrid counterparts that the production sacrificed the literary at the expense of the visual (Martínez Tomás 1973: 56; Oliva 1973: 15). *Yorick*'s Gonzalo Pérez de Olaguer had no doubt, however, of the production's importance within the country's 'decaído y pobre panorama teatral' (1973: 103) (poor and decayed theatrical panorama). Joan-Anton Benach, writing in *El Correo Catalán*, also articulated the futility of trying to provide a reading in 1973 concordant with what might have been Rivas Cherif's aesthetic almost forty years earlier, although he voiced concerns about Espert's performance which 'alterna la dicción escolar con el desgañitamiento, sirviéndose de matices a menudo incómodos y falsos' (1973: 34) (alternates scholastic diction with screeching, embellishing itself with hues which frequently sound uncomfortable and false). Pérez de Olaguer too had certain misgivings about García's direction of the actors that failed to provide a single interpretative aesthetic for the production, singling out Espert as particularly problematic in this respect (1973: 104). Both these responses indicate how even the most progressive elements of the Catalan critical establishment still largely adhered to a 'desirable' model of mimetic parameters of character and diction.

García's production, however, failed to prioritise such concerns. The cast was choreographed as a chorus, echoed in the costume design, and the play's animal imagery often found an echo in the performers' movements which seemed to resemble those of beasts moving in packs. The writhing males in the fertility ritual of Act Three who fight to reach a young woman up high – a vision which greets Espert's Yerma on her visit to the Chapel of the Infertile – , positioned on the canvas hoisted up into a forbiddingly vertical position, offered a Dantesque vision of tormented souls which owed as much to Bosch and Goya as to García Lorca's text.

These visual homages seemed to be picked up more systematically by international critics who, as Felicia Hardison Londré has also suggested, located the production's success significantly in Espert's enactment of the title role (1985: 11–12). Of the Spanish critics only A. Martínez Tomás (1973: 56) and Salvador Corberó (1973: 19) really felt that Espert's performance was able to rise to the challenges of the space, providing the key to its multipurpose use in her gestural conveyance of the frustration of infertility. But for the international critics – *Yerma*'s international tour lasted three years – Espert was able to negotiate the binarisms of strength and fragility in articulating the dilemma of a woman caught between personal and social desires (Dumur 1973: 62; Eder 1971: 36). Hers was indeed a performance, as Robert Brunstein observed in his review of the production at the Aldwych theatre's World Theatre Season of 1973, rooted in the physical language of the desperation of childlessness: raising her legs up as if to give birth, gently touching the leg of a pregnant woman, caressing her breasts as if to stimulate the production of milk (1973: 34).

Espert revived the production to commemorate the fiftieth anniversary of the dramatist's death in 1986. She was frank in interviews about the difficult personal and political context in which the work was first staged – the climate of fear, García's increasing mental instability, the initial four bannings of the piece – which led to her first performing the role as if in a trance (cited in Anon. 1986: 36–7). Recognition of the importance of the production came during both its Madrid run at the Comedia theatre in February of that year and the international performances which followed. Michael Ratcliffe reviewing it for the *Observer* on the company's visit to the Edinburgh Festival in August 1986 was to assess the staging as 'the kind of choreographic dance play for actors whose influence has been felt in European theatre' ever since it was first seen in the early 1970s (1986a: 17). The artist Joan Miró felt that the set ought to be preserved in the contemporary art museum that is now the Reina Sofía in Madrid (cited in Anon. 1987c: 132). While doubts might have crept in from the *Daily Telegraph*'s John Barber (1986: 8) and the *Guardian*'s Nicholas de Jongh (1986: 9) as to Espert's appearing rather old for the role, her decision to restage García's production fifteen years after it was first seen may have been dismissed by *ABC*'s conservative Lorenzo López Sancho, who still failed to appreciate the staging's innovations (1986b: 78), but it was generally recognised as a production embedded in the memory of the country's theatrical psyche (Alonso de Santos 1986: 105).

Divinas palabras (1975)

Divinas palabras was the third of Espert's collaborations with García. He had already staged *La rosa de papel* (*The Paper Rose*) in 1964 for the Serreau-Perinetti company at the Marsan Pavilion and he and Espert had frequently discussed the possibility of staging the Galician dramatist's work in such a way that did not ignore the extraordinary, allusive stage directions with which Valle-Inclán paints his rural landscapes. The corrosive vision of rural life conjured by Valle-Inclán in *Divinas palabras* had secured only one significant production during the Franco era: José Tamayo's 1961 staging at Madrid's Bellas Artes theatre, seen a couple of months later at Barcelona's now closed Calderón theatre with Nati Mistral in the title role. The play juggles an expansive cast in its portrait of Mari-Gaila's breakaway from conservative family life when she gains partial custody over her nephew, Laureano, a hydrocephalic dwarf whom she plans to drag around local fairs displaying his genitalia in the hope of securing a regular income from begging. This brings her into contact with a picaresque world of wily beggars, repentant pilgrims and shrewd tinkers who include the roguish Séptimo Miau, a mysterious nomad with whom she embarks on a passionate affair. The community's discovery of their adultery leads to Mari-Gaila being dragged back to the village in a Bacchae-like procession through the fields. She is saved from death by her husband's utterance of certain divine words ('Let him who is without sin cast the first stone') in Latin outside the church that he serves as sexton.

The play's anticlerical tone, Biblical parodies, irreverent language, and unmitigated exposition of hypocrisy and avarice made it an interesting directorial choice in the politically charged atmosphere of the mid-1970s. Rehearsed for eight months, it opened in October 1975, a month before Franco's death but two years before the final repeal of the country's draconian censorship regulations.[18] As with *Yerma*, García and Espert – working as his directorial assistant – had planned to premiere the piece in an unconventional location: volcanic caves in the Canary Islands (Cornago Bernal 1999: 102), but the premiere actually took place in Palma de Mallorca's Auditorium theatre. The scenography, designed by García in collaboration with Enrique Alarcón, proved as audacious as that of *Yerma*. Dispensing with any attempt to fix the action to a particular local milieu, García and Alarcón invented a mobile set consisting of portable trucks each filled with organ pipes of different lengths and jutting trumpets, and a twenty-metre battered harmonium on which Laureano was dragged along. These trunks could be easily pushed into different shapes and configurations to suggest the multiple settings of Valle-Inclán's play. An aggressive physical performance style by the cast of fourteen, at times almost sensually balletic, complementing the baroque connotations of the organ pipes, served to delineate the rapacious avarice of the community. A complex soundtrack of animal and bird sounds was devised by García and Espert, embellished by the gasping monotone sound of the harmonium, the animal noises made by the actors and the emblematic organ music heard at two key moments – the death of Laureano in Act Two, Scene Seven and the ascension of Mari-Gaila at the end of the play. Séptimo Miau (Antonio Canal) incorporated the movements of the dog into his own performance to further delineate the animalistic overtones of the characters' actions. Textual modifications included the culmination of the incest scene (Act Two, Scene Six) where the drunken Pedro Gailo (Walter Vidarte, then replaced later in the run by Argentine actor Héctor Alterio) attempts to rape his daughter Simoniña (Maite Brik), the goat-goblin of Act Two, Scene Eight re-conceived as two men astride an organ pipe, and Mari-Gaila (Espert's) fleeing from the baying crowds who move the trucks to barricade her in. Her reappearance, moments later, naked, perched up high on a phallic beam, catapulted her high into the upper recesses of the stage, to receive salvation from the Latin words the community cannot understand as the organ pipes moved into the shape of a vast church organ trapping the villagers behind. Pedro Gailo did not throw himself off the top of the church roof as the stage directions specify.

18 While the programme and Cornago Bernal (1999: 102) list October as the premiere month, in her memoirs Espert delineates that the production was due to open on 20 November, the night of Franco's death and that the opening was postponed for three days because of the mourning guidelines laid down by the state; see Espert and Ordóñez 2002: 158.

For Londré, Espert's decision to open the production away from Madrid marked a commitment to the decentralisation of Spanish theatre which continued with the premiering of later stagings like *Doña Rosita la soltera* and *La tempestat* at the Guimerá theatre of Santa Cruz de Tenerife on 29 February 1980 and Barcelona's Romea theatre on 20 May 1983 respectively (1985: 13–14). *Divinas palabras* embarked on a Spanish tour which encompassed a performance at Barcelona's Grec theatre on 24 August 1976 and a month's run at the Tívoli theatre beginning 5 October of the same year – similarly transformed, as with the Coliseum for *Yerma,* from a cinema to a theatre for the event. The remarkable nature of the performance was commented on by *Pipirijaina*'s Ángel Alonso who recognised that Barcelona audiences were not used to such theatrical endeavours (1976: 51). He was, however, alongside *Mundo Diario*'s Joan de Sagarra (1976: 21) and *El Noticiero Universal*'s Julio Manegat (1976: 30), critical of the production's manipulation of Valle-Inclán's play, bemoaning the triumphalism that the international profile of the production had generated in Espert's company, asking for Espert (as company impresario) to deal with the pay disputes that were then affecting the cast, and asking for the actress to stop using the term 'recuperation' when discussing the treatment of Valle-Inclán's text when what seemed to be taking place was a much more overt form of exploitation towards clear commercial objectives.[19]

Tele/eXpres's Jaume Melendres commented on the gulf between the international press's praise of the spectacle and the rather tepid reception the piece had received at the hands of the Catalan theatre establishment, speculating as to whether it might be jealousy or fear of the unknown that provoked such a response (1976: 20). Ferrán Monegal inferred that the bemused responses the production had received might have to do with the fact that in Spain, where 'el teatro se murió hace años' (theatre died years ago), Valle-Inclán remains a largely unknown entity and the obligation remains to present the dramatist's work in the clearest way possible, and only in future years will the climate be able to accept the 'magníficos saltos mortales' (magnificent somersaults) which the staging presented (1976: 20). Manegat, however, chastising every aspect of the production (including Espert's performance) as misconceived, located the staging's international success in foreign audiences's ignorance of the richness of Valle-Inclán's language which struggled to be heard against the mechanical din of the scenery (1976: 30). Ángel Cuevas perhaps unwittingly revealed another reason for the staging's poor reception in Spain when he stressed the imperative need for all aspects of the *mise en scène* to play second fiddle to the text (1976: 25). But staging a text, as director's theatre was to consistently show throughout the 1970s, 1980s and 1990s, involved transforming texts into living, breathing architectural structures which display the complex and sometimes contradictory meanings that dramatic works articulate when staged at particular moments in history. If *Divinas palabras* failed to convince, it may have been precisely because its reinvention and revision within the larger context

---

19 For further information on the pay disputes and proposed resolutions, see Rodrigo and Romà 1989: 20 and Espert and Ordóñez 2002: 167–8.

of the country's uneasy transition from dictatorship to democracy defied established bounds of directorial practice, dispensing with such woolly concepts as 'fidelity', 'authorial intentions' and 'authenticity' in favour of a re-imagining of the text in ways that the press corps clearly found unsettling

Melendres failed to see any relation between the visual aesthetic of the production and the text, judging the organ pipes to function only as a sexual and religious metaphor (1976: 20). *La Vanguardia Española*'s Martínez Tomás too, while qualifying it a 'singular espectáculo' (unique spectacle), thought it inferior to Tamayo's more conventional staging fifteen years earlier (1976: 62). *El Noticiero Universal*'s Carmelo Ochoa had doubts as to whether the spectacular ending actually impeded understanding of the play's final moments when the angry crowd back away from stoning Mari-Gaila to death through the Latin of the divine words. By having the villagers imprisoned in a jail-like church where organ tubes functioned as railings, Ochoa wondered whether the action was being unnecessarily obscured. Nevertheless, he commended the production's ability to render the climate of avarice, lechery and death which permeates Valle-Inclán's play (1976: 23). *La Vanguardia Española*'s P. also praised the production's magical qualities delivered through the decisive break with naturalistic trappings and the monumental nature of the set capable of creating endless unusual configurations which fitted the wily demands of the dramatist's quirky stage directions (1976: 32).

Espert was targeted by a significant proportion of the Catalan press – *La Vanguardia Española*'s Martínez Tomás was a prominent exception – for delivering a performance that failed to meet their expectations. Alonso voiced unease at Espert's protagonism which he located as evolving on both the horizontal and, in the final moments of the play, vertical planes, elevating her above the level of the other performers (1976: 52). For Sagarra, Espert was overreliant on a repertoire of gestures and vocal intonations already seen in her earlier collaborations with García (1976: 21). Ochoa too felt that the performance of the Catalan actress was overly concerned with inviting identification as Espert the star rather than Mari-Gaila the character (1976: 23), as if the meanings of Espert as star celebrity could somehow be conveniently effaced. Espert's body movements were often set against the spoken text, making visible the conflicts being played out in the narrative. Even when she was silent, her body articulated that which could not be spoken, presenting an image of female dissent and resistance. Espert was the transgressive orator and voice of a silenced generation, and her belligerent histrionics offered an outpouring of repressed desire in the production. Espert's hippie image – wild hair, crumpled cheesecloth skirts and tight skimpy tops with which she often appeared in publicity shots – may also have played a part in categorising her as a product of the sexual revolution sweeping Western Europe. Her presence in *Las criadas, Yerma* and *Divinas palabras* evoked a displaced female sexuality which returns to haunt the centre. The pleasure in her eroticism and sexuality in *Divinas palabras* may have shocked the critics but it provided a refreshing image of female emancipation for a younger generation of audiences. A number of the critics chronicling the Grec performance in August 1976 wrote of stampeding audiences, long queues and an atmosphere of frenzied excitement which seems to be more suggestive of the dynamics of a pop concert than a theatrical event (Sagarra 1976: 21; Castells 1976: 24). It may be no coincidence that *La Vanguardia Española*'s review of the Grec performance appears on the same page as an article on whether Just Jaeckin's controversial film *Emmanuelle* (1974) would be approved for screening in Spain.

The Madrid opening on 28 January 1977 at the Monumental theatre was similarly greeted by a bemused and largely hostile press response. While there was some recognition of the tensions between text and *mise en scène* which the production articulated and the cinematic pace of the action by *Arriba*'s Julio Trenas and *Informaciones*' Corbalán respectively (cited in Álvaro 1978: 9), *ABC*'s López Sancho viewed it a performance of 'títeres hipertrofiados' (grotesque, disproportionate puppets) which had nothing to do with *Divinas palabras* (cited in Álvaro 1978: 8). *Hoja del Lunes*' Antonio Valencia, *Blanco y Negro*'s C. Luis Álvarez, and *Gaceta Ilustrada*'s F. Lazaro Carreter were in general agreement that the production was a travesty of Valle-Inclán's text (cited in Álvaro 1978: 8–10). The production received fifty performances in Madrid. It was left, however, to the international critics who saw the play either at Paris' Chaillot theatre where it played for a month in February-March 1976, London's National Theatre where it was performed sixteen times in June 1977, or a host of other arts gatherings in Europe and North America including the Venice Biennale and the Belgrade International Festival, to provide a more measured commentary on the production's conceptual aesthetic. The organ pipes were thus viewed as a metaphor for the Church's controlling watch encapsulating 'a whole society in one image: detached they become outsize phalluses, grouped into a circle they form the bars of a prison, swinging outward they become cannons trained on the audience' (Wardle 1977: 11); 'the bell-like trumpets [. . .] visually representing the divine words of the title' (Elsom 1977: 828). While much was made by the Spanish critics of the rapturous reception the production received abroad, the British press appear to have been baffled by aspects of the production (Barber 1977: 15): questioning García's concentration on 'the histrionic elements in the text' and the abandonment of all 'social delineation of the villagers [. . .] in favour of a sustained group image' (Coveney 1977: 3). While the brilliance of García's effects was applauded and Espert's 'open and revealing performance' (Chaillet 1977: 27) singled out for praise, the reception of a piece cryptically referred to as 'an international showpiece for the Nuria Espert company' (Elsom 1977: 828) may not have been as unequivocally unanimous as the Spanish critics appear to have indicated. The French critics certainly appear to have been more enthusiastic, applauding García's scenic mechanism and its capacity to create different areas within the cavernous space of the newly opened Chaillot theatre and the musicality of the language (Galey 1976: 11; Godard 1976: 20). The production was applauded as a choreographic opera where burlesque and grandeur go hand in hand (Nourry 1976: 21), and a comet lighting up the French theatrical landscape (Gousseland 1976: 98–9). Espert was singled out as the star dancer in a troupe of performers whose magical evocation of Valle's world shone out in an auditorium that was perhaps not best suited to the work (Dumur 1976: 85; Marcabru 1976: 13).

García and Espert were not to collaborate again. Espert has spoken of the fact that three productions are the most that an artistic relationship can sustain (cited in Pérez Coterillo 1984b: 11), and their working relationship ended in 1977 in what Espert termed 'una forma violenta y terrible' (1982: 20) (a violent and terrible way). García returned to Paris, where he died on 28 August 1982 at the age of forty-seven after a number of years suffering from depression and cirrhosis. Despite the polemical responses that his works had received in Spain – his production of Arrabal's *El cementerio de automóviles* was bought to Madrid's Barceló theatre by Antonio Redondo in 1977 – he was recognised on his death as a seminal figure whose demise, as Espert noted, left a veritable hole in Spanish theatre and whose legacy could be seen in many of the works that were being produced in Madrid and Barcelona in the post-Franco era (Espert 1982: 20). The fact that García's death made the front page of *El País*, Spain's best known post-dictatorship newspaper, indicates the importance his 1970s collaborations with Espert were now recognised to have enjoyed. His classification by theatre critic Haro Tecglen, as 'un héroe roto en la batalla para conseguir que el teatro fuera otra cosa' (1982: 32) (a hero broken in the battle to ensure that theatre may become something else) serves as further recognition of Cornago Bernal's view that the series of works initiated by *Las criadas* constituted one of the international pinnacles of ritual theatre and its consolidation in Spain (1999: 91). Espert herself, in categorising García as the architect to her and Moreno's 'albañiles' (1990: 87) (bricklayers), has acknowledged his contribution in preparing her for her own future work as a director, opening to her 'las puertas del mundo' (the doors of the world): 'su entrada en mi vida fue, junto con la decisión de Armando y mía de formar compañía, lo más importante' (cited in Anon. 1983a: 5) (his entrance in my life was, alongside the decision Armando and I took to form our own company, the most important thing).

Doña Rosita la soltera (1981) and *La tempestat/La tempestad* (*The Tempest*) (1983)

The late 1970s and 1980s proved a fertile period for Espert. The break-up with García initiated a new partnership with Lluís Pasqual, then based at the dynamic Teatre Lliure in Barcelona. Their collaboration on the Catalan poet Salvador Espriu's reworking of the Phaedra myth, *Una altra Fedra, si us plau* (Another Phaedra, Please), which was especially written for Espert, opened on 3 March 1978 at the Barcelona theatre, and served to consolidate the Catalan credentials of the actress at a time when the new Spanish Constitution establishing the autonomies of the nationalities was being drawn up.[20] The success of this collaboration was to initiate further collaborative ventures with Pasqual, including another outing for *Medea* in 1981 – Espert has gone on to direct Irene Papas in the role opening on 28 July 1992 at the Grec theatre Barcelona as part of the Olympic Arts Festival and

---

20 For further details on the production, originally conceived for Andrei Serban to direct, see Gisbert 1978 and Espert and Ordóñez 2002: 175–88.

made her final appearance as the calculating antiheroine in August 2001, again at the Grec under the direction of Michael Cacoyannis.[21] At the Centro Dramático Nacional between 1979 and 1981 Espert further consolidated a policy of decentralisation and cemented the international profile of the venue through a high profile collaboration with Jorge Lavelli on García Lorca's *Doña Rosita la soltera*, which was seen by 86,674 spectators in Tenerife, Las Palmas, Valencia, Zaragoza, Reus, Girona, Murcia, Alicante, Valladolid, Granada and Seville before opening at Madrid's María Guerrero theatre on 10 September 1980 (García Osuna 1980: 23). The production was subsequently seen in Israel, Mexico, Venezuela, France, Russia and Scotland.

Espert had sought to collaborate with Lavelli in the late 1960s but at the time he had been adamant that he would not work in Spain while Franco remained in power (cited in Molinero 1985: 25). She had proposed ways around this that would allow all rehearsals to take place in Paris but Lavelli felt uneasy about staging a work which he would not be able to guide through to opening night. He had seen and much admired *Yerma* when it had been at the Théâtre de la Ville in Paris in 1973, but when Espert proposed they collaborate on another García Lorca play, Lavelli felt that the playwright had perhaps been overdone in Spain and it might be more productive to turn to a lesser-known dramatist. When Espert pointed out to him that García Lorca's 1935 play, *Doña Rosita la soltera*, had never seen in Madrid, Lavelli looked at it again and a production was planned under the auspices of the Centro Dramático Nacional.[22] For Lavelli, known for a rawer, crueller, more baroque theatre, the delicately Chekhovian slant with which he staged the work confounded critical expectations. Without obliterating the political edge of the play with its damning indictment of marriage as a financial transaction, Lavelli crafted a meticulous rendition of the norms, conventions and expectations of a particular cross section of society over three periods around turn-of-the-century Granada.

The action evolved in a semicircular space by Max Bignens, a parlour backing onto a botanical garden masked by the finest gauze which separated the blooming flowers from the stolid, heavy wooden cupboards which hold Rosita's white trousseau. Punctuated by a series of doors which served as a constant reminder of the world outside the house with which Rosita gradually loses touch, the gauze suggested a fragile ephemeral landscape wearing the passage of time. In the final act, the parlour, a potent symbol of bourgeois respectability and security/isolation disintegrated (both physically and emotionally) into an empty wasteland, where the doors which led out to the garden, now bereft of plant life, stood out starkly against the empty room. Espert's Rosita remained alone as her uncle's house was to be sold, crying uncontrollably over her wedding dress before abandoning the home with her aunt and housekeeper in the production's final moments.

Espert recognised the benefits of working with such a meticulous director of actors as Lavelli, who was able to guide her into crafting a performance where the

21 For further details of these productions, see Sagarra 1992b, Ley 2001 and Delgado 2001c.
22 Information narrated by Jorge Lavelli in a private, unpublished interview with the author, Paris, May 2001.

feminine exuberance of Act One was gradually eroded into the weary exhaustion of the final act (cited in Anon. 1983a: 5). *El País*' Haro Tecglen (1980: 28) and *El Imparcial*'s Carlos García Osuna (1980: 23), however, failed to be convinced by Espert's performance. The former felt that she was unable to adequately negotiate the shift from the charming adolescent of the first act to the wounded middle-aged woman of the final act but similarly recognised that, despite this, the production far surpassed the majority of the theatrical fare habitually on offer in Madrid. The latter thought Espert's mannerisms converted Rosita into the limited characterisation of a spoilt provincial woman. Both shared M. Díez Crespo's view that she was outclassed by Encarna Paso's Ama (1980: 35). Their international counterparts, however, did not express such reservations, echoing *La Vanguardia*'s Baltasar Porcel's opinion that this was Espert at her finest, showing a veritable and, until then, unknown panache for comedy in the first act (1980: 5).

At the Edinburgh International Festival in 1983 superlative press responses commented, almost without exception, on the grace of her young girl skipping on stage with her straw boater, parasol and bright red dress at the beginning of the play (see Figure 13) and the carefully drawn transition into the more reticent woman of Act Two and the bowed, ageing spinster of Act Three (Craig 1983: 36): hair scraped away from her face, plainly dressed, dragging her feet and 'pacing the perimeter of the stage in frustration and finally clinging to her aunt and nurse in desperate companionship' (Billington 1983: 9). Hope had wrought desperate changes in Espert's Rosita, converting the open playful woman into a hollow reflection of her former

13 Nuria Espert as the young Rosita in Act One of *Doña Rosita la soltera o El lenguaje de las flores* (1980)

self, now hovering on the peripheries of madness as she wandered as if in a daze. Espert was able to provide a living breathing image of the *rosa mutabile* nurtured by her uncle which fades from scarlet red to pale white during the course of a day, shedding its petals as day blends into night. She was for the *Guardian*'s Michael Billington 'a great actress [. . .] unafraid of the grand gesture: when her lover abandons her, she crumples to the ground and rolls helplessly down stage as if the vitality has been drained out of her' (1983: 9). 'She has the ability to make every external action seem a spontaneous expression of an inner state', commented Mary Brennan of the *Glasgow Herald* (1983: 4). *The Stage*'s David F. Cowan also applauded Espert's ability to use 'her whole self, voice and body, to convey every twist of her character's tortured imagination' (1983: 23). The Spanish press may not have been as impressed but the compilation of Edinburgh reviews that appeared in *El País* indicates the importance that such success signified for both the company and the country's young Centro Dramático Nacional aspiring to compete in the international festival circuit (Anon. 1983b: 19).

Although Espert and Lavelli had planned a subsequent collaboration on a contemporary Spanish play, they turned to Shakespeare's *The Tempest* when they failed to find anything that sufficiently intrigued them within the modern Spanish repertory. Subsidised by the Generalitat de Catalunya and presented as a co-production between Espert's own company and the recently formed Centre Dramàtic de la Generalitat, the play opened as *La tempestat* in mid-May at Barcelona's Romea theatre, traditionally the home of Catalan drama, using Josep Maria de Sagarra's Catalan translation. It was then presented as *La tempestad* in a new Castilian version prepared by novelist Terenci Moix, opening in Madrid on 5 October. The production cast Espert as both Prospero and Ariel, with Ariel functioning as the part of Prospero's personality that seeks release from the island. The femininity of Espert in *Doña Rosita* was here counterpointed by a masculinity which played on Espert's androgyny in the way *La persona buena de Sezuan* had seventeen years earlier. This was not Espert playing Prospero as a man but rather as a cryptic exiled being, operating within an aesthetic of disruption, dislocation and dispossession. Appropriating Shakespeare's cultural authority to engage with issues around exclusion and stigmatisation, the production was staged in two languages (Catalan and Castilian) by an Argentine director now possessing French nationality and living in Paris working in his first language (Castilian) and an unfamiliar language (Catalan). Designed by the German Bignens, it was performed by a Catalan cast at a time when the Generalitat was attempting to promote a Catalan-language theatre which would work towards the promotion of Catalan culture both at home and abroad. *The Tempest,* a study of colonialism and its discontents, was to prove the enabling tool which the temporary collaboration between the Compañía Nuria Espert and Centre Dramàtic de la Generalitat used to articulate what may have been conflicting political desires, crafting a production that centred around diverse and multiple identities that may not necessarily coexist in easy harmony.

Espert was to refer to the role as the most difficult she had ever embarked on and came close to cancelling the production after the initial rehearsal period with

Lavelli – the two spent several weeks rehearsing without the rest of the cast – because she felt she could not find a register with which to interpret Prospero-Ariel. The role necessitated a rethinking of what Espert has termed her '*tics* femininos sin tratar de adoptar los masculinos' (cited in Anon. 1983a: 5) (feminine tics without adopting masculine ones). As such she was obliged to rework her repertory of tragic gestures and habitual vocal register in favour of something much starker and cleaner. Espert found a visual analogy for this vocal modification in the chopping of her mane of hair which was replaced by a neat trimmed bob.

The production, situated on Bignens' magical set crafted entirely of wood, conceived the island as a magic box of tricks. Characters flew down on giant ropes which were also used by Miranda and Ferdinand so that they could reach each other from the windows located stage left and stage right. The audience were consistently surprised by the tiny windows and multiple panels opening and closing to show the different pockets of characters brought together on the island. Espert's Prospero, a master director, controlled the proceedings with sedate ease. Espert's performance, however, failed to convince all the Catalan critics. While *El Periódico*'s Gonzalo Pérez de Olaguer (1983: 35) and *El País*' Martí Farreras (1983: 35) applauded her characterisation as revelatory, *El Noticiero Universal*'s Patricia Gabancho viewed her Ariel as a forced creation dependent on high-pitched unconvincing tones and risible laughter (1983: 30). *La Vanguardia*'s Xavier Fàbregas was in agreement with Gabancho that Espert failed to resolve the dual characterisation of Ariel and Prospero convincingly (1983: 63). The Madrid critics voiced doubts around the coldness of Bignens' set, the inferior quality of Moix's Castilian translation and Espert's decision to perform the piece in a commercial theatre in Madrid (Álvaro 1984: 165–70). Following the production's Madrid run, Espert was to acknowledge that it had proved polemical; nevertheless, she felt, irrespective of the critics' responses, both Barcelona and Madrid audiences responded positively to it (cited in Monleón 1983b: 87). As with her earlier collaboration with Lavelli, *The Tempest* proved, both in its Catalan and Castilian manifestations, a desirable export, seen in Rome, Pisa, Milan and Paris during 1983 and 1984.

An iconic presence: playing performers

Espert's roles have always tended to gravitate around self-conscious performativity. She has returned to certain roles that have intrigued her on a regular basis. These have included Salomé in a Catalan-language version by Terenci Moix filmed for television in 1977 and a later 1985 staging by Mario Gas seen at Mérida's Roman theatre and Barcelona's Grec theatre, in Castilian but again in a translation by Moix. The latter staging, choreographed by Cesc Gelabert, proved contentious in its plasticity. Ezio Frigerio's decorative swimming pool dominated the set, providing the location for the dance of the seven veils. Luis Paniagua's languid music evoked the Orient as did Franca Squarciapino's jewel-laden costumes which, while eschewing historical realism, similarly provided an iconic representation of affluent courtly excess. The production style seemed to revolve around self-consciously cinematic references – *La Vanguardia*'s Fàbregas wrote of the initial fight scene looking like a scene from *Quo Vadis?* (1951) while Salomé's dance recalled Esther Williams in *Bathing Beauty* (1944) (1985b: 19). The extras (soldiers and slaves) lolling around helped conjure an aura of lethargic decadence that evoked Charles Bryant's 1923 film adaptation of Wilde's play. Espert's characterisation of Wilde's erotic anti-heroine, viewed by *El País'* Sagarra as a caricature of Theda Bara or Nita Naldi (1985c: 21), revolved around *femme fatale* performative excess. As such she could be seen flamboyantly frolicking in the pool with Carlos Lucena's Herod in a display of lascivious sexual provocation which culminated in her stepfather performing *cunnilingus*. Like Xirgu before her, Espert's association with Wilde's rebellious protagonist further served to delineate her own 'feminist' credentials.

Since *Salomé*, part of Espert's process of turning herself into an iconic presence within the Spanish theatrical establishment has come through a choice of roles which have commented on her own offstage identity. In productions such as *Maquillaje (Make-up)* (1990), *El cerco de Leningrado (The Leningrad Siege)* (1994), *Master Class* (1998), and *La gavina* (Chekhov's *The Seagull*) (1997), as well as the film adaptation of Benet i Jornet's *E.R.*, *Actrius,* Espert's visualisation of a performer has offered both a commentary on the theatrical climate of democratic Spain and a recuperative appropriation of women's theatrical histories. The plays may all have been written by men but their focus on the female served to provide potent models which moved beyond the angel/whore binarism and refused to endorse motherhood and marriage as key female necessities.

Spectator identification with Espert as a performer has certainly been facilitated by such roles, which have progressively blurred the space between actor and role. Moving beyond a characterisation of women as decorative prizes hanging off the arm of a male protagonist, such parts have validated identities that do not represent the mainstream. In *Make-up*, a monologue by Inoue Hisashi adapted from the French version by Moreno and directed by Japanese Koichi Kimura, Espert made her debut on the 'alternative' stage of the Lliure following five years in which she had been concentrating primarily on directing. Trapped in a squalid dressing room, Espert personified an ageing actress of limited talent, Yoko Satsuki, head of an itinerant company performing *shingeki* (kabuki for the masses), who had been acting since the age of six. The parallels between performer and role were not lost on *El País'* Sagarra who saw in the versatile Yoko Satsuki running her own company as writer, director, make-up artist, wardrobe mistress, technical director, head of public relations and a performer who takes both male and female roles an echo of Espert (1990c: 49). Indeed Espert produced the show under the auspices of her own company (in a co-production with the Centre Dramàtic de la Generalitat Valenciana), opening at Valencia's Rialto theatre on 23 May. Espert's Satsuki was a willing raconteur, sharing with the audience the highs and lows of a life treading the boards. In the sanctuary of her dressing room, Espert/Satsuki enacted backstage rituals, evoking emotions associated with high theatrics for the audience's consumption. The private/public dynamic that infuses the play was implicitly recognised by Espert, who openly acknowledged the points of contacts between herself and the character: both personalities who had spent their lives on a stage and never ceased performing (cited in Anon. 1990: 103). The key difference between them lay in the fact that Espert had enjoyed success and Satsuki had not. While *La Vanguardia*'s Benach observed that there were clear cultural differences between the trajectories of Espert and Satsuki, he felt that the boundaries between performer and role did blur and that they threw into further relief the international success that Espert was currently enjoying as an opera and stage director (1990b: 45). On seeing the piece for a second time at the Lliure on 14 November, Sagarra felt that Espert effaced Satsuki on the stage. For Sagarra hers was a performance marked by the high rhetoric which often characterises metatheatricality: 'teatro para un monstruo del teatro: para una Glenda Jackson, una Valentine Cortese, una Anne Girardot o una Nuria Espert' (1990c: 49) (theatre for a monster of the theatre: for a Glenda Jackson, a Valentine Cortese, an Anne Girardot or a Nuria Espert). As such the performance embodied the very best and the very worst of Espert:

Es la Nuria de siempre: genial, alternando la mirada y la voz de trágica – por la gracia de Dios – con ese mohín de niña mimada, de eterno primer premio del conservatorio, del viejo conservatorio. Hay momentos en que te la comerías, en los que le aplaudirías esa payasada que sólo ella puede permitirse, y otros en los que te levantarías de la butaca y abandonarías la sala. Pero Nuria Espert es una actriz de todo o nada, y ése es su mérito. (Sagarra 1990a: 48)

(It is the same old Nuria: inspired, alternating the tragic countenance and voice – by the grace of God – with that air of a spoilt girl, of endlessly winning first prize at the conservatoire, the old conservatoire. There are moments when you could eat her, when you could applaud that tomfoolery that only she can permit herself, and other moments when you'd get up from your seat and walk out of the auditorium. Yet Nuria Espert is an actress of all or nothing, and that's her *forté*.

In *El cerco de Leningrado* too the metaphor of a ruined theatre was again used to reflect an increasingly dismembered society. Espert, performing alongside María Jesús Valdés, played Natalia to Valdés' Priscila, the mistress and widow respectively of a now deceased theatre director, Néstor. Néstor died in mysterious circumstances while rehearsing 'El cerco de Leningrado', a manuscript about the heroic, patriotic defence in World War II of the besieged Russian city by its communist inhabitants against the impending danger of Nazi control which both actresses now search for relentlessly. Both defend his political and cultural legacy in a climate marked by the fall of the Berlin Wall, the demise of the Soviet Union and the rise of a fast-food instant-gratification culture. As such they espouse an unfailing belief in communist principles and occupy a ramshackle old theatre, significantly named Teatro del Fantasma (Theatre of the Ghost), threatened with demolition so a giant underground car park can be built in its place. Dramatist José Sanchis Sinisterra reproduced here the metatheatrical formula which had served him so well in *¡Ay, Carmela!*, his groundbreaking 1987 drama of two music-hall artistes caught behind nationalist lines during the Spanish Civil War, to comment on the demise of a particular ideology which fuelled idealists of a certain generation at a time when corruption scandals were rocking the PSOE's powerbase. The PSOE was to fall from power in 1996 when José María Aznar of the Partido Popular was elected Prime Minister. Espert viewed the piece as delineating some of the measures theatre professionals like herself were obliged to take during the censorious climate of the Franco era as well as articulating the crisis affecting Spanish theatre in the mid-1990s when it seemed to lose its direction, capable only of voicing discontent around the political and social dilemmas of the time through a disassembling of the classics (cited in Monleón 1994: 87–90).

The play premiered in the Basque country, at the Barakaldo theatre, on 10 March 1994, going on a Spanish tour which incorporated dates at Madrid's María Guerrero theatre from 12 October 1994 and Barcelona's Goya theatre from 3 May 1995. For *El Periódico*'s Pérez de Olaguer *El cerco de Leningrado* was a political study of those working within ideologies of the left who opportunistically moulded their politics to the demands of the moment (1995b: 58). The convenience culture of car parks was situated against a dying theatrical culture, personified by the utopian visions of both protagonists.

The critics appeared largely in agreement that Espert and Valdés' performances were forced into a laboured comic register by the heavy-handed direction of Argentine Omar Grasso (Benach 1995: 44; Pérez de Olaguer 1995b: 58). *El País'* Haro Tecglen (1994: 8), *Ya*'s Alberto de la Hera (1994: 35) and *ABC*'s López Sancho (1994: 100) judged the play a rather limp formulaic work invigorated only by Espert and Valdés' virtuoso performances as the forgetful thespians, anachronisms in a society that can no longer accommodate them. *El Mundo*'s Javier Villan may have berated Espert's tendency to overact (1994: 91), but the fact that she was playing an actress who, in turn, performs a series of roles, justified such an approach to the part. The implications of casting Valdés, who had married Franco's doctor Vicente Gil and effectively retired from the stage for a significant number of years, alongside the progressive Espert were not lost on Haro Tecglen, who applauded the casting dynamic (1994: 8). Indeed, references to Doña Rosita and Mari-Gaila in the play's early moments served as intertextual references to two of Espert's most famous earlier roles. A photo of Natalia in *Antigone* functioning as a symbol of resistance to the despotic Creon, recalled Espert's numerous incarnations of Medea, another symbol of female resistance and transgression. Theatre in *El cerco de Leningrado* was portrayed as a space of resistance at a time when theatres were being reoccupied and re-envisaged. Perhaps the most prominent examples of this restoration process were the fate of Teatriz, the former Beatriz theatre, opening in 1990 as a Philippe Starck designed restaurant on Madrid's Hermosilla Street, and the renovation controversies around the Real theatre which finally opened in 1997. As with *Make-up,* the destruction of a theatrical building was used to delineate the obliteration of a particular form of theatre and the audience (functioning as a mirror) had the performers seated before them negotiating a series of crises around identity and representation.

In both *Actrius* (1996) and *Master Class* (1998), Espert, now recognised as the *grande dame* of the Spanish stage, took the role of a teacher/mentor to a pupil/protégé. Both texts demonstrate a fascination with the process of creation and the cult of celebrity. The latter, a Castilian version of Terrence McNally's play by Fernando Masllorens and Federico González del Pino, reunited Espert with *Salomé* director Mario Gas. Assuming the role of the opera icon Maria Callas – the first time she had played a non-fictive role – marked a new departure for Espert. Using accumulated references to Callas, she crafted a performance which observed the diva's mannerisms and gestures, citing Gas's role as that of curbing and placing clear boundaries around her interpretation. Having worked from Callas's recordings of *Carmen, La Traviata, Madama Butterfly* and *Rigoletto* when staging these operas, Espert attributed much of her love of opera to the Greek soprano (cited in Bravo 1998: 104–5).

The play, a fictional re-creation of a set of master classes Callas gave at New York's Julliard School in October–November 1971 and February–March 1972, presents Callas as a tortured being for whom artistic discipline is paramount. Premiered at the newly renovated Marquina theatre in Madrid on 17 March 1998, Espert's Callas, clad in Purificación García (sometimes referred to as the Spanish Armani for her classical fitted tailoring), was conceived as a disruptive force in the master class. Identifying with Callas (both Mediterranean, both from poor families), Espert's visualisation of the soprano was governed by a conscious sense of role-play, a disguise which presented Callas at her most naked and where performance is identity. Her master class, staged with exhibitionist artifice, delineated the links between gender and performance that marked both *Maquillaje* and *El cerco de Leningrado*. Performance for Callas facilitated social mobility and advancement. It may have been used in the past as a means of promoting the stereotype of woman as duplicitous being, forever performing, but Espert's personification of subversive stage figures has served to suggest the ways in which, as references to Onassis and Callas's husband, Battista Meneghini, in *Master Class* make clear, patriarchy shapes gender roles.

In *Actrius,* too, Espert's character Gloria, a successful *tragédienne*, finds self-determination outside the constricting politics of the nuclear family. The film centres around the audition preparations of a young theatre student (Mercè Pons) who hopes to be cast as Empar Ribera, a legendary actress who later became a celebrated, if contentious, acting teacher. Interviewing three of Ribera's former students, Glòria Marc (Espert), Asumpta Roca (Rosa Maria Sardà) and Maria Caminal (Anna Lizaran), she gains conflicting views of the now mythical Ribera. *All About Eve* (1950) meets *Rashomon* (1951), as the ambitious student meanders her way through the different narratives woven by the competitive professionals. As with Satsuki and Callas, Glòria Marc is a socially mobile woman, meandering across Europe from one grand role to another. Her capacity to 'act' quickly secures her the role of Iphigenia, and Sardà's Asumpta (who has found fame as a popular television star) and Lizaran's Maria, the least assuming of the three who now works, not insignificantly, in dubbing, languish behind her in terms of celebrity.

The film's success in Spain was no doubt due, in part, to the identification between performer and role of all three actresses. Glòria's echoes of Espert's international career, the parallels between Asumpta's acerbic persona and the comic

14 Rosa Maria Sardà (as Asumpta Roca), Anna Lizaran (as Maria Caminal) standing, and Nuria Espert (as Glòria Marc), in *Actrius/Actresses* (1996)

roles which have become Sardà's forte, and Lizaran's invisibility as one of the Teatre Lliure's stalwart performers placing the company's commitment to co-oper-ative ensemble work before individual success, were not lost on reviewers (Cendrós 1997: 8; Cominges 1997: 10; Costa 1997: 37).

This may have had much to do with the film's poor critical reception on its British release. The specific cultural references thrown up by the casting were largely lost on the English reviewers who failed to situate the performers within the self-referential context in which the film works. The intertextual references that the film juggles – *Iphigenia* is the most conspicuous dramatic presence but the final sequence sees Glòria and Asumpta descending the central stairway of Reus's ele-gant Fortuny theatre reciting Ibsen, Shakespeare, Euripides and Espriu – situates both performers as well as the now dead Maria within a network of female protag-onists: those like Iphigenia who are sacrificed to maintain the dominant order and others like the defiant Nora from *A Doll's House*, Juliet from *Romeo and Juliet* and Esther from *Primera història d'Esther* (*The Story of Esther*) who resist and challenge the shackles of male oppression. These are not actresses as malleable objects in the hands of a writer or director (the conspicuous absence of male figures in the film should be noted) but rather opinionated beings who celebrate and promote the subjective nature of memory and the shifting nature of meanings which represen-tation engenders. Duplicity in *Actrius* is shown to be a social construct with all three women's enactments evidently constructed around social expectations. This was a film whose performance register was conceived beyond the realms of mimesis within a self-conscious theatricality that clearly left some (male) critics ill at ease.[23]

23   See, for example, Bradshaw 1999, Gilbey 1999 and Andrews 1999.

Indeed, Espert's protagonists frequently perform out of turn, defying established rules as mistresses (Natalia, Glòria, Callas) and nomads (Satsuki) within a male dominated profession – the ghost of Néstor hangs over both women in *El cerco de Leningrado* and Callas's husband and manager, Meneghini, is an evoked presence in *Master Class*. These are characters who, like herself, have constructed non-domestic roles for themselves. The very title of the film, *Actrius*, functions as an implicit criticism of the absence of female work in the canons of theatre and the derogatory associations of the female actor. As the toy theatre possessed by the student burns in the film's final moments, we are reminded that theatre needs none of the paraphernalia that the ornate miniature represents; theatre is performers, here specifically actresses. In *Actrius* the women talk incessantly – the film negotiates long monologues and a focus on wordy dialogue that is unusual in cinema. *Actrius* offers no coherent single image of either the theatrical profession or of women. These women resist commodification and value solely in the sexual marketplace. Exhibitionism may be explicitly acknowledged through the self-conscious presentational style as an identifying characteristic of theatre, but the different points of view articulated ensure that the subject field remains anything but fixed. *Actrius's* persuasive thesis seems to be that re-conceptualising representation in the symbolic order of theatre may provide the initial means of shifting the social order's outdated preconceptions of gender.

Metatheatricality and the aesthetic of excess in a Catalan-language *Seagull*: *La gavina* (1997)

It is perhaps her performance as Arkadina in Chekhov's *The Seagull* in the tumultuous context of the storm that followed Josep Maria Flotats's public dismissal as artistic director of the Teatre Nacional de Catalunya (TNC) that indicates most pertinently how Espert's iconic status has functioned through metatheatrical means as both social and cultural commentary. The production was a telling response to critics who accused her of rarely performing in Catalan: her most prominent Catalan ventures to this point included the music-hall *Amics i coneguts* (Friends and Acquaintances) at the Poliorama theatre in 1969, the television *Salomé* in 1977 and her collaboration with Pasqual on *Una altra Fedra, si us plau* in 1978 but she had not, unlike Lizaran, chosen to affiliate herself with demands for or endeavours towards a Catalan-language theatre. The TNC had been inaugurated on 11 September 1997 with Santiago Rusiñol's *L'auca del senyor Esteve* (Mr Stephen's Collection of Drawings), in a production by Adolfo Marsillach. Standing like a grand mausoleum by the Parc des Glòries, the TNC, the Catalan National Theatre, presents an imposing sight. Grounded on an island circled by traffic, surprisingly inhospitable and austere, it stares out like an unreachable white stone temple. Indeed, Albert Boadella of the performance group Els Joglars was one of a number of theatre practitioners in Barcelona who distanced himself from the venture, calling it a Catalan Valley of the Fallen and expressing disapproval at the fact that the Generalitat had paid Flotats in the region of 265 million pesetas for his association with the TNC (cited in Sagarra 1997b: 31).

Designed by Ricardo Bofill, the theatre featured three auditoria; the Sala Gran with a stage 32 metres deep, 50 metres wide, and an 18-metre proscenium arch seating 894, the Sala Petita seating 500, and the Sala Tallers seating 228. Appointed director of the TNC project in 1992, Flotats was unexpectedly sacked by the Generalitat's Cultural *Conseller* Joan Maria Pujals in October 1997 just a month after the theatre's official opening, for supposedly being a bad manager (Amestoy 1997: 4). Despite vociferous protests from renowned figures in Catalonia's theatre community, including Lluís Pasqual, Rosa Maria Sardà, Carles Santos and Sílvia Munt, who called for Pujal's dismissal, Flotats's contract would expire on 30 June 1998. Rehearsals for *La gavina* were thus carried out in a politically charged climate. Marking Espert's return to the Catalan-speaking theatre, as well as her first collaboration with Catalonia's most renowned actor-director, press interest in the production was understandably significant. With the announcement of Flotats's dismissal, the subsequent press conference to announce the production's opening night saw Espert positioned strategically at Flotats's side. Flotats refused to talk directly of his unceremonious sacking, insisting merely that Chekhov's play may have been written almost one hundred years earlier but that its resonances made it particularly appropriate today (cited in Aranda 1997: 4).

The Seagull, presented as *La gavina,* was conceived on a large scale matching Flotats, a Francophone who had trained in Strasbourg and enjoyed a prolific career in Paris, with Espert: a high-profile stage meeting for two of the Catalan stage's most international figures. Bringing together an illustrious Catalan cast including Josep Maria Pou, Mercè Pons, and Ariadna Gil – then enjoying a degree of cinematic success with a succession of films including Fernando Trueba's Oscar-winning *Belle Époque* (1992) and Emilio Martínez Lázaro's *Los peores años de nuestra vida/The Worst Years of Our Life* (1994) – with a new translation from the Russian by Raquel Ribó, the production was envisaged as a testament to Catalan performers.

Opening on a stage bathed in melancholy blue light, an impressionist-painted gauze allowed for a ghostly three-piece band to be made out. Playing a wistful melancholy tune framed against the picturesque lake surrounded by profuse rushes, the musicians set the scene for a narrative of nostalgic contemplation. From Mercè Pons's first appearance as the resigned Masha in solemn black, curly hair, harshly clamped back, heavily treading the whitewashed wooden floorboards as preparations for Trepliov's play were finalised, signals were given that this dissection of domestic angst was located within the parameters of the performative. The makeshift stage curtain supported by two parallel poles, the chairs positioned around the raised platform, the spectacular lakeside location, all served to fix the action around the self-consciously theatrical. Roles were demarcated as soon as the characters appeared on the TNC's vast proscenium stage. Pere Arquillué's Trepliov was heavily infantilised in knee-length trousers, ankle boots and boyish socks. Joan Borràs's Sorin appeared excessively detached with his wispy grey hair, ephemeral summer beige suit and languished gait. Ariadna Gil's Nina was all girly grin and ruffled white cotton. Flotats's Trigorin was marked by a stubble length beard, bohemian length hair and a casually cultivated artistic pose. Espert's Arkadina entered as the master player onto a picturesque Ezio Frigerio set dominated by a 36-metre lake holding 50,000 litres of water which, whilst paying homage to the language of naturalism in its attention to detail, was sufficiently pictorial to prevent any kind of 'lived in' feel. In a delicate dress, glistening in the dusk light, she created an alternative stage – one of many conjured by the furniture and props laid out in the play's four acts – where an adoring band of devotees gathered around her to witness her flirtatiousness, itself an indication of her penchant for playing younger roles on stage. Her grandiloquent rendition of the quotation from Act Three, Scene Four of *Hamlet* while her son hurries to ensure all is in place for Nina's performance, was met with an especially rapturous applause.[24] The moment also ensured that parallels between the *Hamlet/Seagull* narrative were stressed from the very start – (Arkadina/Gertrude, Trepliov/Hamlet, Trigorin/Claudius, Nina/Ophelia). Even while Nina attempted to emulate the theatrics of Arkadina, standing rigid on the makeshift stage formally reciting Trepliov's lines, Arkadina continued to hold court, fabricating another performance in her fidgety gossiping to Sorin and her consciously bored distraction. Espert's was a performance of restless impatience abruptly halted by Arquillué's increasingly frustrated Trepliov as he attempted to close the stage curtain which resolutely defied him. Arkadina's congratulatory words to the stage-struck Nina as she playfully caressed her face served to remind us of her accomplished sense of timing, diffusing Trepliov's outrage. The latter nevertheless ended the act weeping before Josep Maria Pou's resigned and sympathetic Dorn.

Pou's Dorn functioned in many ways as a surrogate audience, offering comfort to the distraught Masha and Trepliov in Act One and laughing in all the right places as he lounged on a wooden sun chair with Arkadina in Act Two. Sombrely dressed, he was repeatedly placed by Flotats unobtrusively on the peripheries of the action where he could be both witness and spectator. As Arkadina in summer sailor's dress and wide-brimmed straw hat read out from Dorn's book, pointing with deliberate care at lines on the page, Dorn observed her detachedly. Her hardening tone as Nina enthuses about Trigorin was shrewdly registered through the most minimal of eye movements. From his outlying position he watched as Nina took over Arkadina's chair as the latter rose anxiously: the pretender seeking to occupy the throne of the actress she hopes to be, draping herself over the chair in emphatically tragic poses.

Arkadina's intensifying restlessness at Trigorin's absence from her side, echoing her son's in Act One, served to set in place the mother/son parallels which were played out with increasing Oedipal overtones. As Trepliov sought solace in the lake – a return to the womb he may wish he'd never left – fished out by an alarmed Nina, firing his gun in desperation as he stumbled offstage, Trigorin's carefully stage-man-

---

24 Oh Hamlet, speak no more!   Hamlet, no parlis més!
    Thou turn'st mine eyes into my very soul;   Obligues els meus ulls a veure'm l'ànima
    And there I see such black and grained spots   i m'hi veig unes taques tan negres i encastades
    As will not leave their tinct.   que ja no marxaran mai més (Chekhov 1997: 1

aged entrance, with fishing-rod slung carelessly over his shoulders, initiated the courtship of Nina. Punctuated by Arkadina's calls for him from offstage, Flotats knowingly enacted the role of tormented artist. Handing Gil's Nina a handkerchief in a gesture of chivalric assistance, he began a performance that served to entice her. Performing with the handkerchief and removing his small-rimmed glasses when the narrative emphasis called for it, he wove a woeful tale of his distaste of himself as a writer which unsurprisingly pulled Nina towards him. Arkadina haunted the scene, however, for her disembodied voice calling his name reminded all of the fact that Trigorin was still her lover and companion. This mythical space remained contaminated by her presence and a kiss was never consummated.

Act Three may have moved indoors to a dining-room in Sorin's house but the games continued. Masha's description of Trigorin as a genuine and sincere man just as he is about to continue his avid seduction of Nina further consolidated the play element. Duplicity and deception permeated all the relationships depicted in the production for as Arkadina entered asking who had just left, she too avoided Trigorin's glance. Evasion was the order of the game. Now wearing glasses – perhaps indicating a greater willingness to see what was going on around her – Espert's Arkadina appeared in a delicate lace-trimmed gown with matching bolero jacket. The jacket, redolent of that worn by bullfighters, may perhaps have provided a visual indication of the role she was now preparing to play. Feigning penury to Sorin, who continues to flatter her mercilessly, her organisation of the departure pointed to a clinical recognition of the need to get Trigorin away from Nina. Having played the dismissive mother in Acts One and Two, she here lovingly changed her son's bandage, gently wiping the wound while whispering softly and telling him off like a naughty child. Oedipal conflicts within the family were exposed as, in the absence of the father and with the ineffective surrogate Sorin dispatched from the stage, Trepliov's patricidal impulses were displaced onto Trigorin. Standing in for the missing father, Espert's Arkadina functioned as an obstacle to the erotic desires of her son. Her entreating plea to him to not say horrible things about Trigorin was met with rage as he ran away to face her from the other side of the room, casting down with disdain the bandage she had wrapped round his head. Both wept as she came to him and held his head against her breast, his rapid exit precipitated by Trigorin's entry.

Espert's Arkadina here proved an erotic rival to the more pliant Nina for both Trepliov and Trigorin: the latter enacted a not dissimilar scenario of desperate clinging and pulling back as he begged her to release him. Fortifying herself with wine, she alleged that she was the one person to tell him the truth while spinning a rhetorical yarn claiming him as the best of all modern writers and hope of Russia, and stressing his simplicity, sincerity and humour. Denying that it was hero worship, she appealed to his flattery in soliciting him not to leave her. As sexual subject dynamically pursuing her own desire, she seduced Trigorin as she had earlier failed with Trepliov, into satisfying her request. Against Gil's monotone virginal Nina, Espert's profane performer reduced the presumably eloquent Trigorin to silence as he slumped into a chair. Her triumph was emphatically marked by the putting on of her mustard-coloured double-breasted garment, suggestive of a military trench coat and a powdering of her face restoring its composure and unblemished facade. Having dispensed with her competing object of desire, or so she thinks, Espert's Arkadina prepared for a decisive exit from the house. This orchestrated departure, however, was blotted by Trigorin's having to return for his cane. Here, reunited with Nina once more, they plotted their Moscow meeting like excited adolescents – suggesting another association with the agitated Trepliov.

Act Four continued the incestuous associations with Arkadina sitting in the flickering light close to Trigorin, bored with the game of lotto and unwilling to play the maternal role imposed on her by Trepliov. As the sounds of the storm – deafening thunder and rain – penetrated the inner recesses of the house, danger was clearly signalled. The entry of a dishevelled Nina, once all the others have left for supper, allowed Trepliov to transfer the incestuous desire he felt for his mother onto the younger actress. His seeking of consolation on her breast recalled an earlier gesture towards his mother and indeed the scene deliberately echoed the volatile Act Three encounter between mother and son. Nina, however, although rejected by Trigorin, refused to remain with Trepliov. Her infantilisation of him drew attention to his impotence at a time when he had gained increasing recognition as a writer. Destroying pages of what we assume is his newest work, he shot himself offstage as his mother sat at the card table alongside Trigorin. Once more it was Dorn who alerted the audience to Trepliov's suicide as he pulled Trigorin away from the table, requesting him to take the shaken Arkadina away from the vicinity.

Flotats's theatrically driven production did not meet with critical endorsement and it was, significantly, Espert's performance that was particularly targeted as aesthetically misguided. Juan Carlos Olivares, writing in the Madrid-based *ABC*, commented on 'el fracaso de convertir a Nuria Espert en una actriz para Chejov' (the failure in converting Espert into a Chekhovian actress), emphasising her overacting in the first half, and an inability to locate the intimate dimension of the character. Referring to her as 'perdida en un inclasificable tono histérico de vodevil' (lost in an unclassifiable and hysterical tone of vaudeville), he saw this as the antithesis of Chekhov (1997: 95). Joaquim Noguero, too, wrote derogatively in *Avui* of the auto-parody of Espert and Flotats (1997: 42) and in *La Vanguardia* Benach singled out Espert and Gil for the incongruities displayed by their character construction (1997: 53). All these critics failed to pick up on the proximity of vaudeville to Chekhov's world.

If I have chosen to provide such a detailed analysis of the staging, it is precisely because so few critics recognised that the production's positing of theatre as a central discursive idiom was central to Espert's performance. Sagarra, recognising that the production stressed affinities with *Hamlet,* saw Espert as 'la triunfadora indiscutible' (1997c: 43) (the undeniable winner) but he, like Pérez de Olaguer, writing in *El Periódico* (1997c: 60), was uneasy about the production's oscillation between different genres ('¿Comedia, farsa, vodevil, drama?') (Comedy, farce, vaudeville, drama?) which failed, in his view, to provide any kind of homogeneous spectacle. It seems, however, misguided to acknowledge the production's gravitation around interpretative idioms whilst simultaneously castigating it for refusing to position itself firmly within a particular 'style'. Theatricality acknowledges play as its central register, highlighting the manufactured nature of the event. Only Marcos Ordóñez in *Avui* was able to recognise the production's skill in allowing the different character registers to coexist and indeed noted that Espert's Arkadina, both maternal and manipulative, contained and powerful, oscillating between bitchy ferocity marked by touches of vulgarity and a moving hysterical desperation, was one of the finest performances of her long career in theatre (1997: 39), a view echoed by *El Mundo*'s María-José Ragué-Arias (1997: 55).

The idea of numerous playing areas was indeed central to a reading of the production in that the first night critics framed the production within the larger events being played out around Flotats's dismissal as director of the TNC which Espert had so vociferously opposed. Commenting on the failure of the Generalitat's cultural voice, Pujals, to greet Flotats, Pérez de Olaguer argued that the public areas of the theatre were as closely watched as the stage in the pre- and post-performance gatherings (1997c: 60). Aranda's review noted the resonances of Trigorin's speech towards the end of Act Two where the writer talks of himself as more than a landscape painter, rather a citizen of his country, duty-bound to chronicle the adventures of the people while being hurried and prodded from all sides like a fox hunted by hounds (1997: 4). Benach opened his review with a reference to the 'caso Flotats' (Flotats's case) which he summarised as a 'tragicomedia sociopolítica de amplísimo reparto' (socio-political tragicomedy with a very large cast) graced by its large component of extras on *La gavina*'s opening night and in veritable danger of degenerating into a stupid history of heroes and villains.[25] Acknowledging Flotats as an 'actor de gran gestos' (an actor of grand gestures) he described a curtain call where Flotats knelt to kiss Espert's hand in a public gesture of adoration towards a figure who had remained supportive throughout the difficult period of Flotats's sacking (1997: 53).

During its two-month run at the TNC over 44,000 spectators saw the production which played to almost 100 per cent capacity audiences. It is not the place of this study to discuss whether Espert's observation that 'sense Flotats, el TNC serà un museu' (cited in Antón and Fancelli 1997: 1) (without Flotats, the TNC will be a museum) has proved astute, but Espert has only performed in a visiting production of *La oscura raíz* (The Dark Root) on 1–2 February 1998 at the TNC while Flotats's successor Domènec Reixach has remained at the helm.[26] At a time when the socialist party's deadly rivals the nationalist CiU (Convergència i Unió) controlled the Catalan government which had funded the TNC, Espert's perceived

---

25 Benach (1997: 53) names the 'extras' of the 'caso Flotats': Marta Ferrusola, Pujol's wife, the ex-*consellers* Rigol and Cahner, Vicenç Villatioro, General Director of Cultural Promotion, the actress Aitana Sánchez Gijon and the writer Vicente Molina Foix. Attention is also drawn to those who were absent including the Lliure's artistic team, and Eduard Carbonell.

26 For details of *La oscura raíz*, see Chapter 5, 218. For Espert's views on the controversy, see Espert and Ordóñez 2002: 327–31.

links with the PSOE may perhaps have resulted in the Generalitat distancing itself from a figure who refused to affiliate herself with its brand of nationalism. Just prior to the production's opening, Flotats's described *The Seagull* as 'el grito del censurado' (cited in Amestoy 1997: 4) (the scream of the censored). Whether he was referring to himself, Espert or Chekhov in this remark remains unclear but the resonance of this production within the compromised political situation that generated Flotats's dismissal is unquestionable.

Espert as director

El problema de Víctor [García] era seleccionar entre sus ideas geniales; el mío es tener una idea'. (Espert 1990: 87)

(Víctor [García's] problem was choosing between his great ideas; my problem is having an idea.)

It is beyond the scope of this chapter to deal in detail with Espert's operatic ventures but some attention does need to be given to Espert's work as a director that began in 1986 with an English-language production of *La casa de Bernarda Alba* (*The House of Bernarda Alba*) at the Lyric theatre Hammersmith in London. Espert has attributed part of her own success as a director in London to the circumstances of the mid-1980s with a renewed interest in all things Spanish following the country's transition to democracy (cited in Matabosch 1988: ix). When an offer was made by the Lyric's artistic director Peter James to direct a García Lorca play for the fiftieth anniversary of the dramatist's death, Espert declined. A letter from Arnold Wesker, encouragement from Moreno and dinner with Glenda Jackson, however, helped her change her mind and Espert returned to notes made in 1973 when she had been invited to direct *La casa de Bernarda Alba* in San Francisco (cited in Sola 1986: 6). While Espert felt that Jackson had initially been attracted to *Yerma,* Espert could not envisage working on a play that was so marked by the associations of García's production. Espert regarded Jackson as too old for the role of the Bride and too young for the role of the mother in *Bodas de sangre* and thus settled for *La casa de Bernarda Alba,* which offered both a feasible role for Jackson and fewer problems for a translator who would not be obliged to negotiate the poetic registers of the other rural tragedies (Espert 1986: 9). An extensive seven-week rehearsal period saw Espert steer clear of exoticism in crafting a production in which Andalusian referents were largely absent. Interestingly this proved contentious with the *Daily Telegraph*'s Eric Shorter who thought the production effaced the Spanish context of García Lorca's play with the 'nice' English accents locating the play too firmly within 'an English theatrical drawing-room' (1987: 9).

Ezio Frigerio's austere setting, a courtyard of high, weather-worn, white-washed walls where small, barred windows protrude offering only a tiny view of the outside world, was reinforced by the sound of monotonous tolling bells which opened the piece. Part nunnery, part prison, here the daughters, clad in Squarciapino's black costumes, redolent of the mid-1930s, enacted their daily rituals, interrupted only by the jealousies generated by the preparations of eldest daughter

Angustias's contentious wedding to Pepe el Romano. Against the harsh blackness, Bernarda's octogenarian mother, played by Patricia Hayes, stumbled in 'wearing muslin rags over white flesh like a feverish and ecstatic moth' (Ratcliffe 1986b: 23) and the sisters scurried like black beetles staggering around a stone well (Espert 1986: 9). The three settings specified by the dramatist were replaced with a single space of claustrophobic oppression that seemed to progressively close in on the sisters as the action developed across the three acts.

Opening on 8 September 1986, it then transferred to the West End's Globe theatre in January of the following year. Jeremy Kingston in *The Times* was a dissonant voice in judging the production disappointing (1987: 16), for the majority of the London critics argued that it served to open up García Lorca's work for the English speaking world (Billington 1986: 9; Ratcliffe 1986b: 23; Wardle 1986: 11). Indeed the staging was followed by the opening of a number of García Lorca productions in venues across the country, including *Yerma* at the National Theatre directed by Di Trevis in 1987, *Doña Rosita the Spinster* at the Theatre Royal Bristol in 1989 directed by Phyllida Lloyd, *The Public* at the Theatre Royal Stratford East in 1998 directed by David Ultz and *Blood Wedding* at Manchester's Contact theatre, The National Theatre Studio, the Leicester Haymarket theatre and by a range of touring companies including Communicado and the Asian Theatre Co-operative in the late 1980s and early 1990s.

Dramatist Arnold Wesker holds Espert responsible for finding a stage register for García Lorca's work in Britain. While Billington may have attributed the production's success to Robert David McDonald's translation, Wesker disagreed, finding the staging a revelation in the contemporariness of García Lorca's text. Against the showiness of much director's theatre this was rather than 'el espectáculo de Espert [. . .] la obra de Lorca', (1986: 3) (Espert's show [. . .] Lorca's work). For Wesker, Espert's self-effacing direction proved the production's great strength, heralding the arrival of a brilliant new director. Espert herself may have judged it a flaw that she lacks a distinctive style (1990: 86–8), but the realistic register of the play may have resisted a more conceptual agenda. The Spanish press followed Espert's foray into direction with great interest, documenting her work in rehearsal and later commenting on the positive British press response.[27]

Espert has always envisaged clear demarcations between her acting and directing. While rehearsing *Master Class* she mentioned that she had never experienced any tension between her performing and directing selves (cited in Hermoso 1998: 59). As a director, she has always seen her role as over after the dress rehearsal in opera or the opening night in theatre. In the mid-1980s directing offered Espert a way of renewing her interest in theatre at a time when she feared repeating herself excessively. As a performer she recognises that she learned a great deal from the cerebral approach of the English actresses she worked with on *The House of Bernarda Alba,* questioning established assumptions about the director and/or writer as 'author' of a production (cited in Sola 1986: 7). Whilst recognising that

27 See, for example, García-Garzón 1986, M. P. 1986 and Torres 1986.

she is not a director-*auteur* in the mould of García, whom she recognises as the greatest director she has worked with and a huge influence on her own aesthetic, she has gone on to stage *La casa de Bernarda Alba* in both Hebrew and in Japanese. Plans to direct Joan Plowright (who took the role of La Poncia in the London staging of the play) in Fernando de Rojas's bawdy *La Celestina* and Jackson in Calderón's *La hija del aire (The Daughter of the Air)* may never have materialised but Espert has subsequently forged a prolific career in opera direction.

Not one to spend large chunks of time in rehearsal discussing a work as the actresses in *The House of Bernarda Alba* did, rather Espert prefers to work with the performers as a fellow performer allowing them to respond to her characterisation of a particular role: 'No hago lo que quiero que hagan, sino que explico haciendo lo que quiero transmitirles' (1990: 89) (I don't do what I want them to do, rather I explain by doing what I want to convey to them). Her approach, fundamentally emotional – 'siempre comienzo a dirigir desde un punto de vista emocional no intelectual' (cited in A. Monleón 1988: 44) (I always begin from an emotional rather than intellectual viewpoint) – has shown itself well suited to a certain operatic repertoire (Puccini, Verdi, Strauss, Bizet). 'When you direct opera, a large part of it is already done for you by the composer – I must just finish his ideas', Espert stated in 1988 when explaining how her approach to operatic direction where 'the music tells you how you must move, much more than words' (cited in Werson 1988: 12). Her first operatic venture, for Scottish Opera, a revelatory, anti-romantic *Madama Butterfly*, re-envisaged the action away from a romantic hilltop villa in 1912 in a squalid tenement building circa 1937, an imposing corrugated, crowded labyrinth designed by Frigerio, marked by a culture of oppressive surveillance and devastating poverty. Greeted on the whole both in Scotland in 1987 and later at Covent Garden in 1988 by superlative reviews,[28] it paved the way for an intimate *La Traviata,* again for Scottish Opera in a co-production with Madrid's Teatro Lírico de la Zarzuela, opening in April 1989. The staging demonstrated Espert's 'familiar attention to period detail and the confident filling of the full proscenium space' (Clements 1989: 27), 'effective chorus groupings, unobtrusive placing and shifting during the long arias' (Monelle 1989: 18), and defied critics who expected a feminist re-reading of the piece with Violetta envisaged in sordid surroundings exploited by men in the fashion of *Madama Butterfly*.

Frigerio's towering architectural sets, applauded in *La Traviata* for providing a sense of contrast between 'the frenetic city scenes and the cool beauty of the second act in the country' (Kenyon 1989: 45) had been regarded with more suspicion in Espert's earlier staging of *Rigoletto*. Opening at the Royal Opera Covent Garden on 8 December 1988, the staging re-situated the opera in a nineteenth-century world where censorship had prevented Verdi placing it. Frigerio's picturesque 'massive, gaunt and handsome images of classical Mantua' set behind a hazy gauze were judged by certain critics to have 'overawed' Espert (Northcott 1988: 31). The

28 For a selection of the excellent reviews, see Finch 1987, Hayes 1987, Higgins 1988, and Blyth 1989.

Spanish critics who reported on the staging may have admired Espert's approach but British critics were far more subdued in their response.[29]

Carmen, too, was largely denounced in its Covent Garden run in 1991 as a lacklustre, picture-board rendition of the tale, parading flamenco choreography, a vast array of unconvincing period models, a pair of horses and a pristine sanitised tobacco factory which may have been intended to provide '"authentic" local colour', but instead resulted a 'clichéd touristic view of Spain' (Canning 1991: 5).[30] Only the *Independent*'s Robert Maycock appeared in agreement with those Spanish critics who, reviewing the production on its later Seville and Barcelona performances, judged the characters to be composed 'as carefully as a painting' (1991: 14).[31]

While Espert's international directing career was enthusiastically documented by the Spanish press, it was not until 27 January 1990 that she made her operatic debut in Spain when her staging of Strauss's *Elektra,* realised for Brussels' La Monnaie two years earlier, was seen at Barcelona's Liceu theatre. Re-situating the action within Mussolini's Italy during World War II, Espert sought to ground the staging in a climate of savage fear, violence and betrayal. This was a domestic tragedy with Elektra portrayed as a hounded, frightened animal in a Frigerio-designed environment of grand imposing columns, towering wooden doors and ornate balustrades. The production was enthusiastically received by both press and audience and was broadcast on Spain's TVE 1 channel on 11 March of that same year.[32]

More recently Espert inaugurated Barcelona's Liceu opera house rebuilt in record time at a cost of 18,000 million pesetas (around £70.3 million), five and a half years after it was reduced to ashes in a fire that stripped the city of Spain's premier operatic venue. *Turandot* had been scheduled for the Liceu's programme at the time but the fire which ravaged the building put a premature end to Andrei Serban's production. The decision to invite Espert to direct the inaugural production on 7 October 1999 served both to validate the Catalan credentials of the institution and to herald a bold new programming policy by general director Josep Caminal and his new artistic director, fellow Catalan Joan Matabosch, both locals who know their audience and are keen to integrate the venue within the city's performance landscape.

This was visible in the choice of Espert as the director of *Turandot*. A woman working in the male-dominated environment of lyric opera production delivering Caminal's dictum that the venue be re-situated as 'El Liceu de tots' (everybody's Liceu) and a local figure who embodied in her own reputation the Liceu's aspira-

29 For the admiring Spanish critics, see Radigales 1988 and Haro Tecglen 1988b. For the more dismissive British critics, see Loppert 1988 and Milne 1989.

30 For other disappointed reviews, see Milne 1991 and Kennedy 1991.

31 The production opened at Seville's Teatro de la Maestranza on 24 April 1992 and at the Liceu Barcelona on 17 March 1993. For a selection of the positive Spanish reviews, see, for example, Fancelli 1992 and Matabosch 1993. The production, however, also left a substantial contingent of the Spanish press unimpressed; see, for example, Alier 1993 and Pujol 1993.

32 For a selection of the positive reviews, see Alier 1990, Fancelli 1990 and Matabosch 1990.

tion to be a premier international opera house, the decision clearly fulfilled many criteria. Prior to this, however, during the company's enforced relocation to the Teatre Victòria on the Avinguda del Paral.lel, Matabosch had firmly established both his and the opera house's Catalan credentials by engaging Els Comediants's director Joan Font for a new production of *Die Zauberflöte*, conducted by Catalan maestro and former director of the Teatre Lliure's chamber orchestra, Josep Pons. The production has now been seen at the new Liceu in the 2000–2001 season alongside La Fura dels Baus's staging of a new opera by José Luis Turina, *D.Q*, based on the Don Quixote myth (2000), and a production of Verdi's *Un ballo in maschera* directed by Calixto Bieito (2000).

While Espert may have tampered with score of *Turandot*, using segments of the longer original ending by Franco Alfano (who completed the opera on the death of Puccini in 1924) to endorse the suicide of Turandot, the production was a technically undemanding and largely unchallenging interpretation designed in a luxurious traditional 'Chinese' setting signed by Frigerio. As such, the new building, boasting improved sight lines ensured by a slanted orchestra pit and a larger stage area three times the area of its pre-fire dimensions, remained the unquestioned protagonist of the opening night. Tradition merged with hypermodernity: the former visible in the design of the auditorium, retaining its established horseshoe design characteristic of other European houses of the same epoch and the latter seen in the cupola's *medaillons* produced by one of Catalonia's foremost artists, Perejaume, featuring a surreal design which both comments on the paintings that were there prior to the fire and mirrors the stalls of the theatre, relocating the seats in a futuristic exterior landscape. The production too delivered such a combination: the sumptuous set and impressive choral deployment evoked celebrated past productions by John Copley and Pierre Luigi Pizzi, but in its ultimate scene Espert departed from the norm by staging the final duet between Turandot and Calaf (immediately prior to the former's suicide) against a glittering star backcloth suggesting the heavenly firmament and the larger universe in which they exist. This was a production that satisfied the royalty, politicians and business impresarios who had funded the rebuilding programme and who made up the invited audience for the opening two performances. It was in this spirit that it was reviewed by the Spanish critics who, whilst recognising its safe approach, praised the grandness of the show as an appropriate complement to the political spectacle of the occasion.[33]

From the margins to the centre

Whilst the early years of the twenty-first century have seen Espert cut down on her performing and directing engagements, recent stagings of *Who's Afraid of Virginia Woolf?* and *Medea* – the former premiering at Pamplona's Gayarre theatre on 9 May 1999 before undertaking a nine-month tour of commercial theatres in major Spanish cities concluding in Madrid in February 2000, the latter opening at the

33 See, for example, Cester 1999, Fancelli 1999 and García del Busto 1999.

Grec Festival Barcelona in August 2001 – have served to further consolidate Espert's reputation as Spain's premier *tragédienne*. *Who's Afraid of Virginia Woolf?* presented as *¿Quién teme a Virginia Woolf?*, reunited Espert with actor-director Adolfo Marsillach: two 'grandes mitos del teatro español' (Sandoval 1999: 62) (great myths of the Spanish theatre) who had not acted together since 1967.[34] For Marsillach, now primarily recognised as a director, it marked a return to the stage following a seventeen-year absence and a recent recovery from cancer.[35] The production served as a commentary on Espert's entire trajectory in that it decisively revolved around the ludic with play seen as the only constant in Martha/Marta and George/Jorge's relationship, defining their every interaction and motivating all their exchanges. Marta and Jorge as conceived by Espert and Marsillach were dark, playful and cruel pranksters. The final line of the production '¿Tú juegas?' (Are you playing?), was added by Marsillach as a way of insisting on this element of the play as the definitive impulse of the characters' conduct both towards each other and their unsuspecting guests (cited in Torres 1999: 44).

Alfonso Barajas' cold, cavernous set served almost as an oblique comment on that of *Las criadas* thirty years earlier, a space tailored for the protagonists' constant battle, with light seeming to paint a kind of boxing ring or bullring in the centre of the room. A wide bar dominating the stage served to remind the audience of the lubricant that fuels the volatile disputes which form the backbone of the play. The robust sofas that cluttered the central stage area offered obstacles and fences around which the boundaries were drawn. Marta and Jorge created by Espert and Marsillach appeared older than the age specified by Albee.[36] Marsillach's Jorge veered away from Richard Burton's prickly, physically dextrous bruiser in presenting a tired intellectual for whom verbal venom served as a primary weapon. His wife's baiting met with ironic deflation and a tone of almost humorously sceptical resignation. Oscillating between haughty indifference and pointed retorts, Espert's lithe Marta provided an image of bitter apathy and vicious social snobbery. Visibly enacting the love/hate ambivalence she now feels towards a husband for whom she has little respect, Marta is seen to have succumbed to an existence of social rituals that no longer hold any allure. Espert's view of Marta as a professional performer proved significant in indicating how she made the most of the presence of Toni and Linda – the names allocated here to Albee's Nick and Honey – to provide an audience for the interpretation of hate behind which she veils her destructive love for Jorge (cited in Belasko 1999). Hers was a perfectly groomed pristine Marta unlike Elizabeth Taylor's progressively dishevelled figure. As Jorge opened the door to Linda and Toni, Espert touched up her make-up before a compact mirror. The mask must be in place. The stage must be prepared for the performance the couple

---

34 They last appeared together in two short Sartre plays at Barcelona's Poliorama theatre in 1967. For further details, see 138.
35 For further details, see Torres 1999. The cancer was to return and Marsillach died on 21 January 2002.
36 The text (Albee 1965: 9) states that Martha is 'a large, boisterous woman, 52, looking somewhat younger. Ample but not fleshy' while George is '46. Thin; hair going grey'.

will enact for an unsuspecting audience. These were the cruel games of a couple of senile soaks refuelling between the argumentative bouts. Without play, human beings cannot exist and here the liminal dimensions of those games took on a deadly dimension.

It is worth noting that Espert referred to the game in which Jorge and Marta find themselves embroiled as a vampirical way of relating to each other (cited in Fernández 1999). The critic Elisabeth Bronfen understands vampires as

doubles that were not successfully delivered from the corpse, as animated corpses preserved in the dangerous liminal realm, as moments of failed decomposition that consequently also meant an arrestation of decathexis on the part of the mourners [. . .] A rational explanation for the image of the vampire in folklore is that it was merely an exhumed dead body, monstrously threatening because still undergoing a process of decomposition. (1992: 295)

Here it was the marriage that was seen to be decomposing, a destabilised body falling apart before a startled audience who gazed in horror at the figures mutating before them. The vampirical analogy is also pertinent here with regard to the threat posed by Marta's sexuality. When Jorge referred to the question of his wife's hips, his comments seemed not lewd but rather the erratic ramblings of a haggard old man wanting to find some terrain of understanding with Toni, a younger counterpart at the University and possible double. Espert's red jersey dress with a matching plume wrap, however, provided a pointer to the sexuality that drives Marta towards Toni and visibly located her within the realm of duplicitous females who have animated cultural discourses with their questioning of established hierarchies. The sacrifice of Espert's Marta may not be necessary in Marsillach's reading but her denigration and punishment was still seen as indispensable to the preservation of the social values to which all four characters initially pay lip service. This performance of emotional cruelty enacted through a series of vicious games witnessed by two reluctant spectators who are gradually converted into unwitting participants proved shocking in its clinical orchestration. Pitted against Marsillach's Jorge and Espert's Marta, Pep Munné's earnest Toni and Marta Fernández-Muro's giggly Linda became bland toys cast aside by a fickle couple for whom nothing alleviates the numbing pain of boredom.

If the production proved emblematic of much of Espert's work, it is precisely because it transcended the register of controlled naturalism, placing both performance itself and female subjectivities at the centre of the staging. Her female characters have never been bland male projections but rather aggressive agents with far reaching implications on the social order. In this respect they have commented on her own position within the cultural infrastructure of Spain. Espert has refused to be pinned down as a passive actress. She has, in her own words, 'hecho de todo [. . .] ser empresaria en los sesenta-setenta, ayudante de direccíon de todos mis directores, he tocado textos, he hecho traducciones que no he firmado ni he cobrado; he hecho de todo' (1990: 87) (done everything [. . .] I've been an impresario in the 1960s and 1970s, assistant to all my directors, I've arranged texts, undertaken translations which I've never taken artistic or financial credit for; I've done everything). During the censorious years of the Franco regime she was to stage the work of some of Europe and the USA's most contentious dramatists – Genet, O'Neill, Sartre, Brecht. Described as a Mediterranean Helene Weigel by the critic Marcos Ordóñez (1998: 36), the success with García in *Las criadas* and *Yerma* converted her into 'la mejor embajadora de la escena española fuera de nuestro país' (Santa-Cruz 1989: 38) (the best ambassador of the Spanish theatre outside Spain). Referred to by *Diario de Barcelona* in 1976 as 'esa catalana universal' (Ruiz de Villalobos 1976: 2) (that universal Catalan) – a phrase also used, not uncoincidentally, to describe Xirgu – , both her Catalan accent and her activity as a successful company impresario served throughout the Franco years as a prominent signifier of the 'otherness' within the landscape of a centralised Spain. Within Catalonia, her refusal to associate herself with Pujol's CiU Generalitat has, arguably, led to her ostracism at a time when specifically Catalan-language theatre was being promoted. For novelist Terenci Moix her own evolution as a performer echoes that of the country: beginning as the actress of the *progres* (progressives), she justified nudity on stage both in *Yerma* and *Divinas palabras*. Going on to become an establishment figure in the 1980s she has repeatedly questioned the boundaries that define both the centre and the margins (1998: 31). She is arguably the most important performer of her generation. Indeed for Arrabal, in the 1970s Espert, along with Ellen Stewart, Ruth Escobar, Mira Trailovic and Ninon Tallon Karlweiss 'controlled an informal international theatre network powerful enough to get productions of their choice mounted anywhere in the world' (cited in Londré 1985: 2).

While she was to work with Espriu on *Una altra Fedra, si us plau*, unlike Xirgu, hers has not been a career vindicated on new Iberian dramaturgy. Indeed she was to recognise the paucity of contemporary Spanish dramatists as early as 1969. She had hoped to work with Buero Vallejo but he never provided her with a work for the company (cited in Primer Acto 1969b: 39) and her attempts to stage Arrabal in 1969 were frustrated by the censors. Her 'nomadic' company, rehearsing where it could, was able to attract a middle-class audience through productions like *Gigi* and *La idiota* (The Idiot) (1963), an adaptation of Marcel Achard's *L'Idiote*. This audience then remained loyal to her, watching her increasingly adventurous repertoire during the 1960s and 1970s (Compte 1975: 263). Working during a censorious climate that tried to ban her productions of *Las criadas*, *Yerma* and *Divinas palabras*, Espert has never been afraid to affiliate herself to contentious ventures. Her cinematic career may have been erratic but her association with such radical filmic projects as Arrabal's *Viva la muerte,* Bardem's *A las cinco de la tarde/At Five in the Afternoon* (1960) and Catalan director Vicenç Lluch's *El certificado/The Certificate* (1968) – another collaboration with Marsillach – and *Laia* (1970) served to position her as a dissident figure. Espert has acknowledged that all too rarely has she been offered challenging cinematic roles. Never attracted to the short rehearsals permitted by cinematic filming, she saw *Actrius*, her first filmic appearance for twenty-two years, as a swan song to cinema (cited in Rubio 1996: 45). Certainly her attraction to the project may have been in part due to the involvement of arguably the best-known Catalan-language dramatist of the Franco period, Benet i Jornet, as well as the chance to work with Ventura Pons whose roots lie in theatre.[37] Pons had invited Espert to work with him on *Twelfth Night* in 1968 but she had been contracted elsewhere and unable to take up the offer. Certainly those films she has appeared in have often been marked by their theatrical associations – *Viva la muerte*, written and directed by dramatist Arrabal, *Maria Rosa* (1964), directed by her husband Armando Moreno and based on Guimerà's play of the same title, and *Laia* based on the novel by Espriu.

If Espert has become a cultural spokesperson and mouthpiece for her genera-tion, it is partly because she had never been afraid to speak out both during the Franco era and afterwards, exposing social and cultural injustices and finding fault with the cultural policy of the PSOE when she felt its effects were threatening the development of theatre in Spain (Millas 1982: 7).[38] The fact that she secured Ninon Tallon Karlweiss, Peter Brook and Robert Wilson's US agent, to manage her inter-national career, gave her a high-profile exposure that her contemporaries could never really match. In the words of Antonina Rodrigo and Rosa Romà, 'més a més d'excel.lent actriu es un mite que ve a recordarnos el temps en què el teatre era un acte de resistència (catalana) i democràtica' (1989: 34) (as well as an excellent actress, she is a myth who reminds us of the time when the theatre was an act of [Catalan] and democratic resistance). Adoring the myth of Xirgu – she was to stage a homage to the actress on her death at the Poliorama where she was then playing in *Las criadas* and re-created a recital given by García Lorca and Xirgu in 1935 with Lluís Pasqual in *La oscura raíz* – she has herself gone on to become a mythical figure in contemporary Spain and beyond. Hers has been a career where, in her own words, 'me lo jugué todo en cada espectáculo' (cited in Monleón 1983b: 85) (I risked it all in each production). Her roles have recognised marginal existences, and, as such, at a time of political and economic change, have had profound social resonance. The self-sufficiency of her company, surviving without state subsidies in the Franco era, provided an image of female self-sufficiency and independence. Her extensive rehearsal periods with her company – on average two and a half months per work – have promoted a degree of professionalism and a standard of work equalled by few of her contemporaries. Indeed plans for a collaboration with Robert Lepage on a production of *La Celestina* for the twenty-first century are tes-tament to the international recognition she continues to enjoy as both performer and producer.

At the end of the 1960s Peter Brook invited her and García to join his inter-national theatre research centre, the Centre International de Recherche Théâtrale

---

37 Indeed, in her memoirs, she describes the film has having a 'espíritu teatral' (Espert and Ordóñez 2002: 321) (theatrical spirit).

38 In her memoirs, Espert cites how, in 1970, fearing police reprisals in the aftermath of the protests against the Burgos Trials, she left Spain for France where she remained for a number of months; see Espert and Ordóñez 2002: 134–6. She goes on to cite further incidents of receiving hate mail whenever there was a march against the regime, attacks in her dressing room following a remark made about the military (81) and death threats following the death of Carrero Blanco in 1973 (157).

(CIRT), in Paris. She declined the offer. Soon after Giscard d'Estaing proposed she create a centre for cultural investigation in Bordeaux that she initially refused. The venture, which would have seen Brook working in northern France, Grotowski in the west and Espert in the south, may well have created an artistic infrastructure unrivalled in Western Europe.[39] Her decision to remain in Spain has had far-reaching consequences for the country's theatrical evolution; her collaboration with García provided a mould for director's theatre taken up in the late 1970s and 1980s by such figures as Lluís Pasqual and more recently by a younger generation like Calixto Bieito and Àlex Rigola. In the words of dramatist José Luis Alonso de Santos, she remains a powerful model for the Spanish theatre across almost five decades, and has demonstrated that theatre can follow paths that go beyond routine and established conventions (1986: 104).

39 For Espert's views on this, see Rodrigo and Romà 1989: 29.

5
The age of the director: Lluís Pasqual

Alguien dijo que Cataluña – y probablemente la sentencia es extensible, dice Pasqual, a España – es un país que siente rabia por los que se van y desprecio por los que se quedan. (José Luis Vicente Mosquete 1986: 16)

(Someone said that Catalonia – and probably the opinion is extendable, Pasqual states, to Spain – is a country which feels resentment towards those who go and contempt for those who stay.)

Pasqual is coming home! Thus was news of Pasqual's return to Barcelona in 1997 after six years in Paris euphorically greeted in the Spanish press. After sampling the attractions of the international directing circuit, Pasqual was back to open the newly renovated and refurbished Bartrina theatre in his home town of Reus and to formally announce with Mayor of Barcelona designate Joan Clos that he would be taking charge of a project which he then described as 'un parque temático en el que se ofrecerá teatro, danza y música; en el que se podrá cenar y obtener información sobre espectáculos; en el que habrá una emisora de radio ceñida a los espectadores, y también un movimiento continuo de alumnos de teatro, etcétera' (cited in Pérez de Olaguer 1997a: 56) (a theme park which will offer theatre, dance, music; where you will be able have dinner and obtain information on productions; where there will be a radio station for the spectators and also a continuous stream of theatre students, etc.).

Throughout the month of May, even before the appointment was officially announced on the 23rd, a plethora of features, editorials and reviews offered comments on the subject. Perversely these touched only briefly on his plans for the ambitiously named 'Ciutat del Teatre' (City of Theatre) and his search for a new home in Barcelona, the city where he established his reputation with the theatre he helped to found – the Lliure. Rather it was the controversy surrounding his appointment, with Joan Font and Albert Boadella, high-profile directors of Els Comediants and Els Joglars respectively, both openly outlining their displeasure at an appointment they claimed was made in a secretive and undemocratic manner after a meeting held on 14 January in which it was agreed that Antoni Dalmau, President of the Fundació del Teatre Lliure, was to take charge of the project. Whatever their claims and misgivings, speculation that Pasqual had been offered the directorship of the project had been rife for some time with conversations between the then Mayor of Barcelona, Pasqual Maragall and Lluís Pasqual taking place regularly over the past ten years and *El Mundo* reporting that Maragall had repeatedly offered him a role as co-ordinator of the ambitious and as yet incomplete performance complex in Montjuïc as early as 1990 (Anon. 1997b: 4). Whatever headlines such as 'Días de polémica' (Baget Herms 1997: 8) (Polemical days), 'La Cuidad del Teatro pone en pie de guerra a los divos de la escena catalana' (Tena 1997: 110) (The City of Theatre places the divas of the Catalan stage on war alert)', and 'Albert Boadella amenaza con una campaña de "terrorismo cultural"' (Pérez de Olaguer 1997b: 75) (Albert Boadella threatens a campaign of 'cultural terrorism') might suggest, *El País*' Joan de Sagarra was to argue that Maragall would not launch such an ambitious project without counting on the guidance of Pasqual, arguably Spain's most successful twentieth-century director (1997a: 2).

In many ways the reservations voiced about Pasqual's appointment seemed to revolve around the way in which he was appointed, rather than the appointment *per se*. A socialist affiliated to Maragall's Ajuntament (City Council) who has repeatedly expressed his misgivings about Catalan president Jordi Pujol's cultural politics, and a major player on the European theatre scene during the 1990s, he represented a logical choice to front a theatrical project which sought to provide a theatrical alternative to Pujol's Generalitat-funded Teatre Nacional de Catalunya (TNC). At one point in 1995 Pasqual was fundamentally involved with the running of four significant arts organisations: the Odéon-Théâtre de l'Europe, of which he was artistic director between 1990–96, the Centro Dramático Nacional, where he formed part of a three person programming team while Isabel Navarro was director (1995–96), the Venice Biennale (1995–96) and the Teatre Lliure, where he remained part of the artistic infrastructure until 2000. Pasqual's return to Barcelona in 1997 consolidated a commitment to re-establishing himself as part of a theatrical landscape which he had helped to shape during the 1970s and early 1980s, but controversy around the perceived political charge of the appointment continued. Pasqual's plans for a theatre 'city' which would group together El Mercat de les Flors, the new Lliure building at the former Palau de l'Agricultura, and the Institut del Teatre, however, failed to ignite support either from Barcelona's theatrical community or Maragall's successor as mayor, Joan Clos, raising questions about both the funding necessary to maintain such an ambitious venture and its viability in a city already coping with the grand expense of the TNC (Antón 1999b: 15). Certainly Pasqual's association as co-artistic director (with Guillem-Jordi Graells) of the Lliure between 1998 and 2000 served to bind the Ciutat del Teatre project rather too closely with the fate of the Lliure, again generating dissent from sectors of the Catalan theatre community. The delayed opening (until the autumn of 2001) of both the Institut del Teatre (with two theatre auditoria) and the new Lliure (with a main auditorium of 750 and smaller Espai Lliure of up to 172), as well as the curtailed opening programme of the Lliure, have served to ensure that the Ciutat del Teatre remains as polemical as the TNC (Aubach 2000: 14–15). Pasqual's resignation from the artistic directorship of the Lliure following protracted debates about its financial and artistic future waged with the Ajuntament – both in private and publicly through the extensive press interest generated by the case – has served to disassociate Pasqual somewhat from a Catalan theatre scene where he has enjoyed a dominant role since the late 1970s. While he still has a home in the city, a significant proportion of his directing ventures in the twenty-first century have been in Buenos Aires, where he has continued an association with Argentine actor Alfredo Alcón which began in 1983 with *La vida del Rey Eduardo II de Inglaterra* (*The Life of Edward II of England*).

It is too early to tell what the future of the Ciutat del Teatre might be, but Pasqual's importance within the Spanish contemporary theatre scene remains unquestionable. During the 1990s he formed part of a European superleague of directors which included such figures as Patrice Chéreau, Peter Stein, Luc Bondy, Stephane Braunschweig, Giorgio Strehler, Jonathan Miller, Jorge Lavelli, Deborah Warner, and the two adopted Americans Robert Wilson and Peter Sellars. These are figures equally in demand as opera producers but whose careers have largely flourished on revelatory productions of the classics. All work regularly in the subsidised venues and large-scale festivals, and all, bar Miller and Stein, have, at some time, gravitated towards Paris where they have either run a theatre – Pasqual and Strehler the Odéon, Chéreau Nanterre, Lavelli La Colline – or formed a regular component of a particular venue's repertoire: Sellars, Warner and Wilson at MC Bobigny 93, Warner at the Odéon. One talks of seeing Sellars' *Persians* at Edinburgh, Warner's *Coriolanus* at Salzburg, and Pasqual's *Roberto Zucco* in Venice as in the first half of the twentieth century one talked of seeing Xirgu's *Yerma* and Olivier's *Hamlet*. During the 1990s in Spain, as in many other European countries, audiences were drawn to the theatre as much for the person who directed the play as for the story, the author who wrote it or the actors who performed in it. Pasqual's period as artistic director of the Centro Dramático Nacional between 1983 and 1989 inaugurated the age of the director within Spain as a series of high-profile co-productions favoured a particular brand of theatrical creativity that proved exportable across the European theatre circuit. During these years Spanish dramatists conspicuously bemoaned the power wielded by Pasqual as *metteur en scène* and the fact that, more often than not, he chose to ignore the work of contemporary dramatists, deciding instead to stage and restage the plays of a select number of 'dead' playwrights – most conspicuously García Lorca and Valle-Inclán – with whom he redefined theatre during the 1980s. These texts, seen in France and Italy, were to become part of the dialogue as well as the market of theatre across nations. Eschewing realism in favour of a more conceptual aesthetic, they offered indications of a rich dramaturgical tradition which had suffered neglect or ignominy during the censorious years of the Franco regime. While it may be been primarily the dramatists of the new democratic Spain that have been analysed and promoted in print (Aznar Soler [ed.] 1996: Halsey and Zatlin [eds] 1999; O'Connor [ed.] 1996), it is the 'other' Pasqual who in the words of one anonymous critic, succeeded in placing Spain in Europe 'por la trampilla de un teatro' (Anon. 1985: 4) (through the hatchway of a theatre).

While Pasqual's career has been largely forged in the post-Franco years, he has spoken of the 'political education' gained 'living in a family that was basically

Republican but silent' and the challenges of beginning to work in theatre during the late 1960s and early 1970s. 'Not having a pesesta to put on theatre with, having to rehearse for six months for a three-day performance with the police in the theatre, gives you a civic training you never forget' (Pasqual 1996: 211). It is indeed this 'civic training' which has shaped his commitment to a vision of theatre as public service and a desire to shape an aesthetic which has prioritised the staging of a wide repertory of largely twentieth-century works within the climate of euphoric innovation which Pasqual attributes to the years between 1975 and 1987, when a newly democratic Spain was able to forge cultural discourses outside the parameters of censorship (Pasqual 1996: 212). While Pasqual claims that he has only ever sought to stage works in a 'normal' way (1996: 212), this 'normality' has manifested itself through a daring, revisionist approach which has presented plays which could not be easily staged during the Franco years, stripping them of past associations and presenting them anew to domestic audiences uncluttered by the memory of previous stage interpretations. Indeed, his ideal audience member has never been a complacent spectator, rather he has stated that all his work is staged with an imaginary spectator in mind who has something of a philosopher, his mother, a boy, a blind person, a deaf person and a foreigner. For Pasqual, each project needs to reach out to all of these (Huguet 2002: 25).

Any glance at the Lliure's programming since 1976, or his choice of repertoire while artistic director of the Centro Dramático Nacional or the Odéon-Théâtre de l'Europe, indicates a marked attraction on Pasqual's part to works which defy a linear logic and which concern themselves with duplicity, the split self, the relationship between differing registers of reality, conflicts between the rational and the passionate, and the very art of theatre which is grounded in illusionistic practices. He has thus been credited with bringing to the stage dramatic works that had previously been branded 'impossible' and lain dormant for decades.

Although perceived as a director who is most comfortable working within the classical repertory, his career has been shaped by eclectic directorial choices including devised work – like *La setmana tràgica* (The Tragic Week) (1975) and *Camí de nit, 1854* (Path of Night, 1854) (1976) – , contemporary writing, including Genet's *Le Balcon (The Balcony)* (presented as *El balcó*) (1980) and Salvador Espriu's *Una altra Fedra, si us plau* (Another Phaedra, Please) (1978), small cast adaptations of Brecht's reworking of Marlowe's *The Life of Edward II of England* (1994), Tom Kompinsky's commercial *Duet for One (Duet per a un sol violí)* with Rosa Maria Sardà's company (1982), and lush, elegant productions of operatic stalwarts like *La Traviata* (1995). This chapter will provide an introduction to the work of a director who has, since the mid-1970s, first at the Lliure, then at the Centro Dramático Nacional and the Odéon-Théâtre de l'Europe, shown himself to be a shrewd and imaginative programmer and a delicate orchestrator of stage action. Renowned for his detailed work with actors and his striking re-appropriation of conventional spaces, his painterly, emotionally-charged productions are undoubtedly amongst the most provocative and memorable of the contemporary Spanish theatre. Rather than provide a chronological account of Pasqual's trajectory, the chapter will examine his contribution to Spain's theatre in the post-Franco era primarily through the prisms of his stagings of twentieth-century non-naturalistic works, including *Le Balcon*, *The Life of Edward II of England*, Valle-Inclán's *Luces de bohemia (Bohemian Lights)* (1984), and the more oblique dramaturgy of Spain's best-known modern playwright, Federico García Lorca. While the 'other' texts that he promoted may have been subject to substantial academic attention, his own productions of them have never generated analogous academic interest. This chapter is an attempt to remedy that balance.

Fabià Puigserver and the Teatre Lliure

Born in Reus, Tarragona on 5 June 1951 to an Andalusian mother and a Catalan father, theatre fascinated Pasqual from an early age. As a child he was regularly taken to watch touring *zarzuelas* (Spanish operettas) and it was indeed his ability as a teenager to memorise the *zarzuelas* he listened to on the radio and on record that swayed his father into believing his son should be encouraged to pursue further study. As a teenager Pasqual had already worked with the independent group, La Tartana, where he had performed in a number of their productions and directed Arnold Wesker's *Roots (Les arrels)* (1968) and Salvador Espriu's *Antígona* (1969). An early indication of the selective nature of Pasqual's interests lies in the fact that, even before entering Barcelona's Universidad Autónoma in 1969, he had directed new writing (*Roots*), Catalan writing (*Antígona*), and a European classic (Eugène Labiche's *An Italian Straw Hat*) (*Un barret de palla d'Italia*) (1969), all in Catalan. These strands, which were to define the programming at the Lliure, were therefore visible seven years before the Lliure was even conceived.

Throughout the early 1970s, alongside his studies of Catalan Philology at the Autónoma, Pasqual took courses at the Estudis Nous de Teatre (where he met Els Joglars founder Albert Boadella), and worked with the Grup d'Estudis Teatrals d'Horta, then directed by Josep Montanyès, where he concentrated on developing his acting and technical skills. Although he had directed pieces, including *Reus, París, Londres* (1972), at his local Fortuny theatre in Reus, it was while teaching at Barcelona's Institut del Teatre, where he co-directed the Artaud and Grotowski inspired *Duplòpia* (1974) with Iago Pericot and Pere Planella, and at the Escola de Teatre de l'Orfeó de Sants, that his work first generated substantial critical attention. This was also, crucially, where key collaborations were forged. *La setmana tràgica* was his first project with the writer/dramaturg Guillem-Jordi Graells and the designer Fabià Puigserver, figures with whom he has worked regularly since and who, like Planella, came to form, through the Lliure, an intrinsic component of Barcelona's theatrical landscape. It is with Puigserver especially that Pasqual forged a unique working relationship lasting sixteen years and encompassing twenty-three productions, productions which Pasqual himself has described as children born of 'a deep love, from being in love with each other' (cited in Delgado 1998b: 100).

Any examination of Pasqual has to take into account his collaborative working methods and this is manifest most clearly in the relationship with Puigserver. Pasqual has spoken of learning 'a lot from Fabià, and I think Fabià did the same from me. Our relationship was a constant, living exchange' (cited in Delgado 1998b: 100). Pasqual offered Puigserver energy, dynamism and a facility for working with actors which Pasqual has claimed the designer lacked. Although Puigserver did work irregularly as a director he was far more comfortable with the materials of design:

To work with actors, you have to be a 'liar' in the artistic sense of the word. To drive someone, often despite themselves, to a meeting place with the character, with the writer's poetry, you have to be a 'liar'. You have to be a 'liar' to make the actor become that instrument that will explain the writer's poetry. And Fabià was a man with a direct line between his head, his heart, and his hands. He did a lot of work with his hands, he was a great craftsman [. . .] He learnt the basics of engineering so he would be able to make the sets for *Yerma* without being an engineer. Actors, however, are a much more unyielding material, much harder to work with than cardboard, leather, silk, or wood. Sometimes that material was beyond him, and he used to get enormously angry. (Pasqual, cited in Delgado 1998b: 101–2)

For a figure in his mid-twenties like Pasqual it is crucial to realise how, in the dying years of the Franco dictatorship as well as its immediate aftermath, Puigserver represented the possibilities offered by the world beyond the Pyrenees. Although Puigserver was born in Spain in 1938, his Communist family had fled Spain for France and then emigrated to Poland in the early 1950s. Puigserver had originally wanted to be an actor or a director, but he trained in theatre design at the School of Fine Arts in Warsaw, collaborating with Andrzej Sadowski at the Dramatyczny theatre before returning to Barcelona in 1959. He was soon affiliated with the alternative theatre movement, working in the early 1960s at the design studio of Andreu Vallvé and at Gràcia's Teatre del Cercle Catòlic and the Agrupació Dramàtica de Barcelona (ADB) before entering the Escola d'Art Dramàtic Adrià Gual (EADAG) ostensibly as a student, but soon practising as a stage designer and teacher of design. Although he returned briefly to Poland in 1967, it was in Barcelona that he chose to remain. Here his impact was profound. Reorganising the Design department of the Institut del Theatre, from 1970 he was, along with Iago Pericot, to train a generation of scenographers including Montse Amenós, Ramon Ivars, Joan-Josep Guillén, Josep Massagué, Andreu Rabal, Isidre Prunés, Antoni Belart, Pep Durán, Nina Pawlowsky, Llorenç Corbella, César Olivar and Antoni Bueso. As an art director he collaborated with the filmmakers Vicenç Lluch on *Laia* (1970) and Glauber Rocha on *Cabeças cortadas/Severed Heads* (1970). In 1974 he also created the Teatre de l'Escorpí at the Aliança del Poble Nou (1974). In many ways the ground work for the Lliure was prepared by Puigserver's association with such ventures as the Operació Off-Barcelona in 1967 at the Aliança de Poble Nou and the Teatre de l'Escorpí. Both these initiatives, as well as his earlier association with the ADB and EADAG, sought to forge alternative theatrical structures, promote a more radical alternative repertory and establish the means for modes of performance that embraced non-naturalistic theatrical vocabularies.

By the time Puigserver worked on *La setmana tràgica* he had collaborated with most of the major Spanish directors – Ricard Salvat, Albert Boadella, Francesc

Nel.lo, Mario Gas, Miguel Narros – and was already an internationally recognised designer, having produced the much-lauded canvas design for Víctor García's production of *Yerma* (1971). As Pasqual has stated: 'Peter Brook says that set design for the theatre is divided into "before the canvas set and after the canvas set". *Yerma* was a tremendous contribution to contemporary theatre' (cited in Delgado 1998b: 101). In Puigserver Pasqual found a designer who transcended the parameters of baroque design which had hitherto dominated the Spanish mainstream stage and who, importantly, had international experience. As John London has stated in his overview of twentieth-century Spanish stage design: 'It is difficult to overemphasise the professionalism of Puigserver's background in comparison to the general situation in post-War Spain' (1998: 50). Puigserver was a craftsman with a meticulous eye for detail, insistent on working on every aspect of his design's construction. He was also a minimalist, determined to strip the stage of superficial decor, and capable of providing a visual analogy for the dramatic tension in the text (London 1998: 52).

In the spring of 1976, as Spain was in the process of emerging from the shackles of the old regime under the transitional monarchic democracy being negotiated by Prime Minister Adolfo Suárez, Pasqual and Puigserver joined forces with director Pere Planella to co-found the Teatre Lliure Collective which they housed in a building in the Gràcia area of Barcelona renovated for the economical sum of nine million pesetas (£45,000). While they were the three directors, the company was a co-operative incorporating a range of professionals including experienced performers like Carlota Soldevila and untrained amateurs like the then nineteen-year old Lluís Homar, who eventually gave up his studies in Law to concentrate on his theatrical career. The building was an old workers' co-operative (La Lealtad), rather than an established proscenium-arch venue and Puigserver's design of the theatre provided a polyvalent performance space which could adapt to the requirements of each new project. The co-operative aimed to eschew the star system in fostering a Catalan-language theatre which both re-imagined the classics in bold, revisionist ways and presented international works which had rarely been seen in Spain. Puigserver was to describe the Lliure as an austere theatre (cited in Rovira 1986a: 15) with the collective taking responsibility for much of the physical development of the space in 1976 and subsequently for the running of the venue, with the director of each production assuming responsibility for casting, but with a system of equal pay in operation where performers might have a lead role in one production and a walk on role in another.[1]

Their inaugural production, written and directed by Pasqual and designed by Puigserver, *Camí de nit, 1854,* opened on 1 December 1976 and followed the documentary vein of *La setmana tràgica* in its dramatic reconstruction of the political struggles of the labour activist Josep Barceto and the Bienni Progressista of 1854–86 to establish better working conditions in the aftermath of Barcelona's industrial revolution. As with *La setmana tràgica*, which had challenged customary

---

1 For the 1976 manifesto of the Lliure, see Martí i Pol *et al.* 1987: 274–80.

actor–audience relationships through an orchestration of space whereby the actors encircled the audience subverting habitual framing boundaries, *Camí de nit, 1854* proved a thoroughly researched, inventive ensemble piece. Its epic sweep and prominent re-writing of history seemed an apt metaphor for a company whose manifesto appeared to be questioning established theatrical practices and presenting a less emphatic and overtly gestural performance style than that to which Spanish theatregoers were largely accustomed. The fact that Catalan *nova cançó* (New Song) singer Lluís Llach undertook responsibility for the music further underscored the radical implications of the production.[2]

Pasqual has acknowledged on numerous occasions the influence of Ariane Mnouchkine's *1789* (1970) and *1793* (1972) on his early productions with Puigserver (Cabal and Alonso de Santos 1985: 214). Mnouchkine offered a new carnivalesque and celebratory model for political theatre which was to inform both *La setmana tràgica* and *Camí de nit, 1854*. Paris had, until 1976, provided Pasqual's only real contact with international theatre. Largely uninterested in either the commercial or the independent strands of Spanish theatre, he looked abroad for inspiration and further training. Using Puigserver's contacts in the Polish theatre, he chose to spend some time at the National Theatre of Warsaw, where he assisted Adam Hanuszkiewicz on his 1976 production of Chekhov's *Platanov*. Here he claims he

learnt to watch and observe. Since I couldn't speak Polish, particularly at the beginning, it was amazing, since when you don't understand the language you pay much more attention to other things. That's why it's very difficult to perform in a foreign country, because you're more aware of the traps. You're more aware of performance, because you're solely dependent on that. I would say that what I most learned about in Poland was the freedom of actors on the stage, and in particular, musicality – not just of language, but of performance. Polish is a language that has a great many registers. It's a language which goes from the shrillest of the shrill to the gravest of the grave. It's something the Italians do in a very natural way, but that doesn't really happen in Spanish [. . .] That's what I learned about most: fluidity, freedom of interpretation, and what I call 'ping-pong'. 'Ping-pong' is the communication between one actor and another; the triangle that develops between the actors and the audience; this constant returning of the ball in a musical way. What I mean is, actors are not individuals. They're individuals at the service of other individuals. (cited in Delgado: 1998b: 91)

During the years following Pasqual's residencies at the National Theatre of Warsaw and Milan's Piccolo Teatro (1978), where he worked as Strehler's assistant, his collaborations with Puigserver demonstrated a fascination with working in the round and an extraordinary capacity to conjure magical stage moments from elemental ingredients. He credits his time in Poland as crucial in shaping his capacity to 'watch and observe' performers (cited in Delgado 1998b: 91–2). From Strehler he learned to 'set standards for quality, and to want more; never to be satisfied [. . .] a good training is not one that teaches you, but one that you can learn from' (cited

2 For an introduction to the *nova cançó*, see Boyle 1995.

in Delgado 1998b: 93).[3] He cites both Strehler and Brook as key formative influences on his work, acknowledging that from the former he discovered 'the idea of the illusionist, the magician, of making what doesn't exist appear, done in a majestic, artistic way' and from the latter 'simplicity, authenticity, purity, where earth is earth and wood is wood' (Pasqual 1996: 214). The impact of both directors is visible not only in the visual echoes of Brook's *Cherry Orchard* (1981) on his own production in 2000 but also in his staging of *The Tempest (La tempestad)* with veteran actor Alfredo Alcón in 2000 in an intimate black box where a silver six-metre curtain fell, allowing the performers to appear and disappear in a series of intricate light games.

Pasqual openly acknowledges that he has never tried to, nor does he believe anyone can, 'be original' (1996: 214). Originality he perceives as a dangerous nineteenth-century concept which constrains and imprisons. As such he has readily admitted key influences on his work. Theatre for Pasqual has always been what he himself terms 'a learning process'; a way of spending time with favourite plays, fine tuning them during long runs by listening to performances, allowing them to be 'adjusted to the audience', breathing with the audience, recognising that productions shift and change with every performance and every audience (1996: 215). He has always been attracted to more oblique dramatic works and never felt the need to pursue a realist aesthetic; 'Realism in the theatre bores me', he has insisted: 'In the theatre, I demand of myself and of others the capacity for metaphor, for [. . .] poetry [. . .] the capacity for a door to be many things, a door being the least of them' (1996: 218). If Pasqual and Puigserver were, despite the Lliure's early co-operative structure, to be seen as responsible for shaping the company's aesthetic, it was precisely because both their collaborative director–designer relationship and the latter's work as a director gravitated around writing the performance text within the confines of a particular space where the very process of observation and participation was inscribed into the event itself, challenging passive attitudes of expectation and customary practices of spectator reception.[4]

The Life of Edward II of England and *Le Balcon*: stagings and restagings

While Pasqual had been responsible for an intimist staging of Büchner's *Leonce and Lena*, opening on 18 June 1977 prior to his departure for Poland, the productions staged at the Lliure following 1978 showed the work of a more subtle director who favoured an intense rehearsal period where he could 'rework' favourite plays, getting to know them and battling with their intricacies and demons. One of the features of Pasqual's directorial work has been a return to certain works which haunt him. He first staged *As You Like It* at the Lliure in 1983 (*Al vostre gust*), going on to restage it in 1989 at the Comédie Française (*Comme il vous plaira*): the first Spaniard to direct at the venerated home of French classical drama in its three-hun-

---

3 For further comments on his period at the Piccolo, see Pasqual 1996: 214–15.
4 For Puigserver's own views on this, see Abellán 1993: 214.

dred year history.[5] The first production, eschewing realist vocabularies, was set in a mythical self-referential space dominated by a giant mirror suspended from the ceiling – a device to be used by Calixto Bieito for his 1998 English-language production of *La vida es sueño* as *Life is a Dream* at the Edinburgh International Festival – which provided a dazzling image of an elusive, uncontrollable world of which the audience were as much a part as the performers. Reflections of the characters trapped within worlds of their own making and finally contained within the heterosexual closures of the narrative served to accentuate both the metatheatrical thematics of the work and the playful gender reversals which ensue in the magical space of Arden. In Barcelona, the 1983 production was much admired (Benach 1983: 14–15), but in its Parisian staging, despite the positive endorsement of the Spanish critics and a substantial number of the French reviewers (Pérez Coterillo 1990: 6–9), doubts were raised about the supposed dislocation of costumes from the decor (Cournot 1989: 10). Pasqual has admitted an error in agreeing to restage it four years later in a different language and in a different climate where the timing and resonances failed, in his view, to ignite audiences or critics (1996: 208).

Pasqual has staged Brecht's reworking of Marlowe's *The Life of Edward II of England* four times, with each production staged as a vehicle for a particular performer or performers. The play's first outing in Catalan in 1978 (*La vida del Rei Eduard II d'Anglaterra*) was proposed by Josep Maria Flotats, who was at the time still living and working in France.[6] Although Flotats was not to base himself in Barcelona until 1984, the staging was to mark Flotats's symbolic return from self-imposed exile. In 1983 Pasqual's restaging in Castilian (cited in a translation by Jaime Gil de Biedma and Carlos Barral) bought together Argentine actor Alfredo Alcón as Edward and Juan Gea as Gaveston. During the 1988 revival the latter role was taken by Antonio Banderas who was gaining international attention following his appearances in Almodóvar's *Matador* (1986), *La ley del deseo/The Law of Desire* (1987) and *Mujeres al borde de un ataque de nervios/Women on the Verge of a Nervous Breakdown* (1988). In 1994, at the Odéon-Théâtre de l'Europe, Pasqual presented what he termed a pared-down fifty-minute 'bilingual English/French edition' of the play as 'a montage of memories' of a king now imprisoned within the Tower of London (cited in Taylor 1994: 22). Inaugurating the English writing season at the Odéon which ran during late 1994 and early 1995, Pasqual picked an eclectic group of actors including Linus Roache (tellingly a feminised Richard II in James Macdonald's production of the play for the Royal Exchange Theatre, Manchester in 1992) in the role of Edward, and Welsh actor Michael Sheen, whose mercurial presence as an elusive, playful Gaveston served in the words of critic Paul Taylor to brilliantly intimate

the paradox in the central power-relation: that Edward, in obstinately refusing to resign his crown and in prolonging civil war, holds in edgy thrall the man who guards him and

5 For further details, see Pérez Coterillo 1990.
6 For further details, see Badiou 1986: 36. Flotats had worked with the Renaud-Barrault company and the Théâtre National Populaire; in the early 1980s he was to go on to work with the Comédie Française.

the men he alights as favourites. He may be compelled to trot around tied to a rope but he's got the strained, nervy figure who is holding it on the end of a string, too. (1994: 22)

Whereas Taylor was less impressed by the French version, the presence of Franco-African performer Emile Abossolo M'bo in the role of Spencer-Gaveston further served to delineate the associations of Pasqual's reading of the work. Indeed for Pasqual the play remains a powerful parable on the mechanisms of power and desire and the regulations placed on deviations from the norm (cited in P. 1978: 62). Brecht's re-envisaging of the tale made the homosexual relationship between Edward and Gaveston the centre of the narrative and the unequivocal reason for the King's fall. Issues around the construction of self and nationhood were foregrounded by a circular, circus-like, sandy set where the boundaries between private and public spheres collapsed, creating a space where the masculine runs riot and Queen Anne can only ever be a marginalised, passive being. The rich, earthy sand was complemented by a colour scheme of costumes in autumnal shades with the demise of Edward foregrounded by his attire in mummified, decomposing, cream-coloured rags. In all four productions the role of Edward was taken by performers whose 'otherness' played into their characterisation of the King as outsider. In 1978 Flotats's forced enunciation in Catalan and rhetorical performance style offered an aggressive violence that *El Correo Catalán*'s Joan-Anton Benach felt appropriate to the piece (1978: 29). In 1983 and 1988 Alfredo Alcón envisaged Edward as a dissonant figure whose musical vocalisation and melodious intonation, betraying an Argentine accent, further accentuated his status as a 'foreigner' within the court. This was to be commented on by *ABC*'s Lorenzo López Sancho who felt that his dramatic register, bordering on melodrama, was ill-suited to the role (1983: 78; 1988b: 109). In the third revival, the presence of Banderas, an actor more suited to and with greater experience in film, with romantic good looks and a more subdued brand of masculinity, served further to position both men outside the coterie of the court's rigid heterosexual (and by association patriarchal) values. Interestingly, *Ya*'s Alberto de la Hera drew attention to the hushed tones of Banderas's Gaveston which were barely audible in the open, expansive set (1988b: 44), while *ABC*'s López Sancho saw the characterisation as less volatile than Gea's: less the indignant lover than a masterful athlete perfectly in control of his seduction of the wayward king (1988b: 109). In Paris the dismemberment of the play as *Spencer's Book/Le Livre de Spencer*, as well as the multiracial casting decisions within the French version and the non-homogenised English-language casting – an English Edward, a Welsh Gaveston and a Canadian Mortimer – reinforced Pasqual's revisionist approach.

Le Balcon, Genet's 1956 study of institutional hypocrisy and the dynamics around oppressor and oppressed, had first been presented by Pasqual at the Lliure in 1980. Genet's 'Balcony', a brothel which functions as a mirror reflecting power relations, was housed within a Puigserver-designed metallic frame (mischievously echoing the structure of a theatre's proscenium) adorned with mirrors, where the spectators looked directly into the space as if watching themselves reflected in a mirror's concave lens. The frame, providing dissonant acoustic accompaniment to the action, also served effectively to reinforce the sense of refuge/entrapment denoted by the brothel in its bunker-like associations. Positioned within the greater frame of the Lliure's architectural structure, it also intensified the metatheatrical thematics of the play. Genet's 'house of illusions' was here conjured as a playful space of vaudeville acrobatics where the boundaries between participants and spectators were consistently ruptured. Theatre was here a performance rite embedded in a culture of surveillance – a motif which was also to permeate Pasqual's reading of García Lorca's *El público* (*The Public*) (1986).

Certainly the metatheatrics of role play which inform the play were realised in Puigserver's rich ceremonial costumes. The theatricality of both the costumes and the self-conscious performance style served to underlie Genet's dictum that power is dependent on theatricality for its execution (1977: 14). Rosa Maria Sardà delivered a caustic Madame Irma whose team of whores assist the clients seeking escape from their mundane occupations – plumber, fireman, bank clerk. They assume the mantle of authority through the adoption of three key roles – a bishop, a general and a judge –, enacting a series of tableaux that demonstrate the hypocritical mechanisms of power. The resonance of these functions within the climate of a country recently emerged from the shackles of a dictatorship that relied on 'morality, religion and the military' for its ideological base has already been delineated by Phyllis Zatlin (1994: 133). Indeed the revolution raging outside the brothel is extinguished by the appearance of these symbols of power dressed in all their finery on the balcony accompanied by Madame Irma's regal queen – realised in Pasqual's staging by giant marionettes crafted by Glòria Cid. Pasqual himself has listed the Spanish references which inform the work – from the crucifix above the door in the opening scene, to the role of Carmen, which he has viewed as an almost García Lorca character, to the resemblance between the chief of police and Franco, to the conjuring of the Valley of the Fallen in the final scene as the site of Roger's castration (1980–81: 55–6).

The production premiered on 26 June 1980 as a pre-season taster, returning to open the new season in September of that year. Pasqual had secured Genet's approval for changes made including the prostitute in the first scene becoming a young boy dressed as a girl at her First Communion and the substitution of the wig sequence at the end of Scene Four for a violent encounter between a woman dressed as if for a Holy Week procession and a beggar who offers her a bunch of flowers.[7] While some critics may have displayed a pedantic obsession with the implications of Pasqual's changes in their responses to the work (Sagarra 1980: 52; Gabancho 1980: 31), others, like *El Correo Catalán*'s Josep Urdeix (1980: 31), recognised the impact of a production that is now recognised as 'next to the García-Espert *Las criadas* [*The Maids*], the most influential staging of Genet in Spain' (Zatlin 1994: 132). Genet was to distance himself from the work, not seeing it in

---

7 For a description and discussion of the changes, see Pasqual 1980–81: 56 and Abellán 1980: 64–5.

January 1981 while in Spain because he felt it a product of an earlier age that he could barely remember. Nevertheless Pasqual testifies to Genet's delight at the play's debut staging in Spain within alternative parameters – both in Barcelona and in Catalan (in Carme Serrallonga's translation). His endorsement of Pasqual's changes and ideas for the production was to result in Pasqual's honouring a promise to Genet that he would stage the piece in French. On 2 May 1991 *Le Balcon* opened at the Odéon-Théâtre de l'Europe – its premiere delayed by a three-week strike by technical staff. The screen and stage designer Gerardo Vera working with Bernard Michel converted the lavish red velvet decor of the Odéon theatre into a lush, opulent brothel, positioning the audience both on the stage and in the boxes. The stalls were re-configured to create a circular-shaped brothel described by *El País'* Sagarra as part-circus part-bullring – here perhaps once again accenting the Spanish associations of the piece (1991a: 36). While the French press may have voiced reservations about the fact that the play now looked dated (Godard 1991: 9), they too admired Pasqual's focus on the Spanish undertones of the play realised through a melange of imagery from Barcelona's transvestite scene to the Civil Guard and the *corrida* (Boué 1991: 20), and the international dimension lent to the production by a cast drawn from different corners of the globe (Dumur 1991: 155). While reservations may have been expressed by *Le Figaro*'s Pierre Marcabru (1991a: 22), he was one of few dissenting voices and the production served to consolidate Pasqual's reputation as a director who was willing to re-configure the Odéon's auditorium in theatrical endeavours which questioned audience assumptions about space, place and identity.

L'hort dels cirerers (2000): *The Cherry Orchard* as a farewell to the Lliure

Critics have often expressed surprise that a director like Pasqual, who seems most contented working within an anti-realist theatrical register, should be drawn to the work of Anton Chekhov (Cabal and Alonso de Santos 1985: 223). For Pasqual, however, Chekhov's dramaturgy transcends the prisms of realism (cited in Antón 2000a: 14). And indeed it was through the discourse of impressionism that his staging of *The Three Sisters* (*Les tres germanes*), opening on 29 June 1979 in a translation by Joan Oliver, was realised (Urdeix 1979: 29). A horizontal picture-frame stage served to generate the image of perusing an old photograph album where the characters animated a world realised in tones of muted sepia.[8] A cyclorama stretching across the back of the stage subtly delineated the climate and mood changes and further accentuated the impression of poring over a canvas. Interestingly critics drew attention to the fact that Pasqual's production aesthetic seemed rooted more in theatre and cinema than life (Abellán 1986b: 58; Vilà i Folch 1979: 26), further indicating the intertextual resonances that have served to ground his work within particular cultural iconographies and sign systems. Punctuated by resonant

---

8 The production premiered for two performances in June and was then seen in a longer run during the 1979/80 season opening on 24 October 1979. The set was also used for Pasqual's production of *Rosa i Maria* (1979), a solo show conceived for Rosa Maria Sardà.

silences, Pasqual's reading was structured like a musical symphony which, in the words of *El Periódico*'s Gonzalo Pérez de Olaguer, rendered Chekhov's particular atmosphere the true protagonist of the piece (1979b: 27; 1979c: 188). The crumbling of a particular social fabric was brilliantly rendered in a staging where the passing of time was evocatively realised through the endless pacing on the wooden floor, the opening and closing of doors and the ephemerality of a space where the characters sometimes appeared like shadows trapped in the pictorial box of another era.

It was to Chekhov that Pasqual was to return in staging a swan song to the company's Gràcia venue that opened on 17 February 2000. While the summer move to the new auditorium at the Palau de l'Agricultura (constructed for the 1929 Universal Exhibition and renovated by architect Manuel Núñez) beside the Mercat de les Flors in Montjuïc was postponed until autumn 2001, Pasqual's reading of *The Cherry Orchard* proved a suitably reflective staging of the play, which brilliantly exploited every crack and crevice of the familiar theatre in its imaginative retelling of Chekhov's tale of loss, change and the inescapable need to move on. This was a production marked by the presence of well-worn suitcases and trunks, detritus of an *ancien régime* that is no longer current. The characters' comings and goings dominated proceedings suggesting a mood of transience and journeying from the production's very opening. The theatre space was here prominently on display, its back doors into the dressing rooms and backstage area becoming part of the very fabric of Pasqual's landscape. Softly opened for Act Two they allowed the characters to weave their way through the open environment. Hung with lace curtains in Act Three, they suggested the fragility of the world celebrated at the dance. For the final act the doors, like the family, were prised apart, exposing the backstage area

15 Jordi Bosch (as Lopakhin), Anna Lizaran (as Liubov), Rosa Vila (as Vària), Santi Sans (as Firs), Fermí Reixach (as Gàiev), Francesc Garrido (as Trofimov), and Bea Segura (as Ània) in *L'hort dels cirerers* (2000)

through which the actors moved. It was in many ways the theatre itself that became the staging's protagonist.

Designed by Pasqual and lit in association with Xavi Clot, *L'hort dels cirerers* may have relied on costumes that evoked the play's turn-of-the-century setting but the production was realised within what Phyllis Zatlin termed 'a thoroughly theatricalised' register which is

set from the opening scene when the merchant Lopakhin (Jordi Bosch) and the housekeeper Dunaixa (Tilda Espluga) came running in from their respective locations on the ground and upper hallway levels. They addressed the audience about their not being ready; their consternation at first seemed to be that of actors unprepared for their performance rather than characters concerned about the immediate arrival of the train bearing Liubov and her daughter Ania. (2000: 111)

The fourth wall tumbled as the characters moved across to confide in the audience, sharing their fears, preoccupations and joys. An actor sitting amongst the spectators lighting up a cigar later provided the cue for Liubov to enquire as to who had been smoking in her home. The move to the Palau de l'Agricultura venue was openly commented on as a model of the new auditorium was revealed onstage in the first act as Lopakhin began to discuss the sale of the orchard. At the end of Act Three as news of the sale of the orchard reached the family, Liubov (significantly veteran Lliure performer Anna Lizaran) wept beside the upstage model of the Lliure. This was to be the orchard simultaneously mourned for and celebrated in this production as audience and performers openly shared the complicit resonances of Pasqual's reading. Rather than efface the imminent move, the production commented on it with suitcases displayed on the staircase leading from the foyer to the auditorium and carpets rolled up from act to act. As the family left the stage, the safety shutters crashed down and Firs (Santi Sans) remained alone to experience the desolation of abandonment. His acknowledgement of the self-referentiality of the moment was depicted through his location of a glass of champagne left over from the earlier party which he raised in what Zatlin has termed 'a symbolic toast to the theatrical company itself and its loyal patrons' (2000: 112).[9]

Lizaran, Natascha in the earlier *Les tres germanes,* and Queen Anne in the Catalan production of *The Life of Edward II of England,* evoked a series of past performances in her attractive Liubov: compassionate, playful, emotional. Rushing to the audience to share her excitement at arriving home, hers was an exuberant central figure (echoing her own role as perhaps the Lliure's most resonant female performer). Gliding across the stage with effortless grace, she proved a marked antidote to her brother, Fermí Reixach's stiff but rather dapper Gàiev. With his hand formally placed in his left pocket, this white-suited Gàiev appeared ill-equipped for the challenges facing him. He and Liubov giggled like errant children trapped within the nursery in which Chekhov sets the first act. As the play pro-

9 For a discussion of Flotats's 1997 staging of Chekhov's *The Seagull* which was equally read through the prisms of the immediate history of the venue in which it was being staged, see Chapter 4, 166–72.

gressed Lizaran's Liubov became an ever more ephemeral presence. In Act Two she appeared dressed in layers of lacy cream fabric held in place by a large pink bow fastened across her waist. Floating through the landscape like a ghost, she looked increasingly vulnerable – a point highlighted by Pasqual as the beggar aggressively grabbed Vària's shawl and a visibly shaken Liubov desperately handed him money in the hope that he would take it and disappear. A frail Gàiev, dressed in clothes that appeared too big for him, was wrapped by Firs in a long coat, as if keen to protect his childlike charge from the evening chill as the sun set before them.

Against this fragility, Pasqual painted a handsomely robust Lopakhin. Jordi Bosch's landowner was a lively, confident extrovert. Only when jokes flew around his relationship with Vària was his habitual exuberance tempered. Returning from the auction, he could barely control his excitement and danced, drunk with elation at the realisation that the cherry orchard was finally his. Sitting in a wicker chair as Gàiev left to seek solace in the billiard room, we were given a sense of him establishing his ascendancy across the new empire he now presided over. In the final act, dressed in sombre and respectable grey, he paced up and down waiting for the family to leave so that he could finally enjoy the glittering prize under whose shadow he had lived for so long. The final meeting with Vària had them both following each other and the luggage across the stage with painful awkwardness. As the embarrassed Lopakhin exited at the first available opportunity, Rosa Vila's heartbroken Vària was left contemplating what might have been.

If the production proved such a fitting closing production for the Gràcia venue, it was precisely because it was conceived as an ensemble piece where all class interests were given a voice. The family predicament was always framed within a larger social milieu of a community in flux. Tilda Espluga's flighty Dunaixa pursued Nacho Fresneda's sulky Iaixa with an urgency that betrayed the fear of rejection. Francesc Garrido's Trofímov, gaunt, impressionable, energetic and passionate in argument, was both a physical and temperamental antidote to the solid Lopakhin. Manel Dueso's Epikhòdov staggered drunkenly from act to act. As he tripped over a cherry branch in his first appearance we were given an indication of a man unable to control either what he says or what he does. Teresa Lozano realised a wizened, bony Carlota, observing the proceedings as she conjured tricks from the performing poodle who accompanied her. Hers was a figure more at home in a Weimar cabaret than a Russian dacha – the characterisation here perhaps commenting on the Lliure's tradition of subversive musical theatre/cabaret work like Brecht/Weill's *Ascenció y caiguda de la ciutat de Mahagonny* (*Rise and Fall of the City of Mahagonny*) (1977), and Hacks/Offenbach's *La bella Helena* (*La belle Hélène*) (1979). Carlota constantly bemoaned her lack of identity and it is perhaps significant here that Pasqual reinvented her with every appearance. From intrepid traveller in the second act to tuxedo-clad conjurer and ventriloquist at the dance, she erupted from the unknown and disappeared back into it in a range of fantastic costumes – a marked contrast to the hovering Vària aspiring towards spiritual wandering but grounded to the home by the set of keys that dangled loudly from the belt of her dark gowns. Against the pessimistic Vària, Bea Segura's Ània embodied the hopes of a bright new future for the Lliure in a new home whose largest auditorium takes the name of Fabià Puigserver. The latter's presence was echoed through the sense of absence that haunts the space (specifically the death of Liubov's son).

All the characters were conceived in some way or other as misfits and outcasts but all found a place in the magical space in which the production was grounded. As the audience surveyed the empty stage over which Gàiev and Liubov desperately embraced, weeping uncontrollably, their black travelling clothes grieve for the life they leave behind. Pasqual's reading, grounded in the specific situation of the Lliure's *adieu*, transcended that very specificity to embrace wider concerns about displacement and life-changing decisions which are thrust upon us by the necessity of the situations in which we find ourselves.

The use of Joan Oliver's translation – in a year celebrating the centenary of his birth – was not lost on critics whose glowing reviews located the production firmly within the prisms of an endangered world which the characters fear leaving (Ley 2000: 4; Benach 2000: 70; Pérez de Olaguer 2000: 48). Pasqual too was to articulate in a series of interviews his hopes and fears for the new move and the need to move on (Cuadrado 2000: 10; Santos 2000 65–7; Fondevila 2000a: 70). This was in effect what he was to do, resigning the artistic directorship of the Lliure he had shared with Guillem-Jordi Graells since 1998 and choosing to initiate projects largely in Argentina.[10]

Despite the recent well-documented problems encountered by the Lliure, its impact during the final quarter of the twentieth century has, arguably, been unmatched by any other Spanish theatre company.[11] Opening in the mid-1970s it became emblematic of a new spirit of change and renovation sweeping the country. For *La Vanguardia*'s Benach the opening of the Lliure is analogous in numerous ways to the inauguration of André Antoine's Théâtre Libre in March 1887 and a key moment in post-Franco theatre (1986: 12–13). On its tenth anniversary Maria Aurèlia Capmany was to cite it as responsible for fostering a new professionalism in Catalan theatre (1986: 10). It may have been vociferously criticised in print during the late 1970s for not undertaking the staging of Catalan drama (Pérez de Olaguer 1979a: 51), but the Lliure never aspired, unlike the Romea, to be a home to this writing. Its mandate was more in the vein of Strehler's Piccolo theatre of Milan, namely to undertake a civic purpose within a particular locality with a predominantly international repertoire. The presence of Miquel Martí i Pol's *Amb vidres a la sang* (With Glass in the Blood) (1978), Boadella's *Operació Ubú* (1981), Espriu's *Primera història d'Esther* (*The Story of Esther*) (1982), Rusiñol's *L'hèroe* (The Hero)

---

10 As a result of Argentina's economic collapse, *Edipo XXI*, a reconfiguration of Sophocles' *Oedipus Rex* and *Oedipus at Colonus* with extracts of texts from Aeschylus, Euripides and Genet, planned for early 2002, opened at Barcelona's Grec Festival on 16 July. The production positioned the tale within contemporary prisms of refugee displacement and exile with Alcón's Oedipus conceived as a nomad expelled from house and home. For further details, see Benach 2002, Delgado 2002c, Ley 2002, and Pérez de Olaguer 2002.

11 For further details on the Lliure's financial and artistic problems, see Antón 2000b, Antón 2000c and Fondevila 2001.

(1983), Joan Oliver's *El 30 d'abril* (1987) and *Cantonada Brossa* (Brossa Corner) (1999) – a homage to the playwright/poet/visual artist – however, suggests a commitment to exploring less obvious avenues of Catalan writing which critics might have too easily written off. In 1987 statistics compiled on the Lliure indicated that twenty-three per cent of the company's programming had consisted of Catalan writing (Castells Altirriba 1987: 110). Indeed Puigserver and Graells confirmed this commitment to Catalan work as early as 1979 when they spoke of wishing to inaugurate the venue with a Catalan piece which had direct relevance to the situation in Catalonia in the transition years (cited in Cabal 1989: 12–13).

The stream of performers, designers, musicians and dancers associated with the Lliure confirm its status as a remarkable creative enterprise. Its founder members included Anna Lizaran (b. 1944), training with Jacques Lecoq when Pasqual invited her to join the co-operative; Lluís Homar (b. 1957), who was to succeed Puigserver as the company's artistic director, joined at the age of nineteen, crediting it with teaching him all he knows about theatre (cited in Rovira 1986c: 19); Imma Colomer and Fermí Reixach (b. 1946), who began their careers with Els Comediants, and Carlota Soldevila, who was a founder member of Els Joglars. Domènec Reixach (b. 1948), now director of TNC, also began there as a performer in the mid-1970s. Lighting designer Xavier Clot (b. 1953) (now perhaps best known internationally for his work with Calixto Bieito) has been there since its inception. Invited performers have included Josep Maria Flotats (b. 1939) and Rosa Maria Sardà (b. 1941); the latter went on to work with Pasqual at the CDN on *Mother Courage and Her Children* (*Madre Coraje y sus hijos*) in 1986. Carles Santos (b. 1940) first collaborated with the Lliure on the musical direction of Puigserver's production of *The Rise and Fall of the City of Mahagonny* (*Ascensió i caiguda de la ciutat de Mahagonny*) in 1977. Josep Pons (b. 1957), now director of Granada's City Orchestra, was until 1997 music director of the Lliure's Chamber Orchestra, which he co-founded in 1985. Cesc Gelabert (b. 1953) and Lydia Azzopardi (b. 1949) founded a dance company at the Lliure that is now also resident at Berlin's Hebbel Theater. The Gelabert-Azzopardi company, exhaustingly exploring new dance-theatre vocabularies, have been at the forefront of European choreography for the past ten years. Gelabert's collaborations with Pasqual include the choreography for *El público* in 1986. A younger generation of directors like Calixto Bieito (b. 1963) and Pep Anton Gómez (b. 1966) have also made conspicuous debuts at the Lliure.

For Pasqual the Lliure has always been a private theatre with the vocation of a public theatre (cited in Rovira 1986b: 17). Since 1987–88, its co-operative structure has been replaced by a foundation (Fundació Teatre Lliure–Teatre Públic de Barcelona), which has negotiated the development of the new building. Never shying from controversy, the corrosive *Operació Ubú*, staged by Boadella as a critique of Pujol's style of government, was held responsible by Planella for the decision to award Flotats, rather than the Lliure staff, the directorship of the TNC project (cited in Abellán 1986a: 33). More recently Pasqual's uneasy relationships with both Pujol and the City Council's Cultural Counsellor Ferran Mascarell – disputes with the latter over the Lliure's funding led directly to Pasqual's resignation – have served to generate serious concerns around the Palau de l'Agricultura seeking to function as an 'alternative' national theatre to the TNC.[12] With the sudden death of Josep Montanyès, Pasqual's successor as artistic director at he Lliure, on 10 November 2002, there is speculation that Pasqual may return to a theatre that remains a member of the Union of Theatres of Europe. Whether he returns to the helm or not, his legacy remains significant.

The Centro Dramático Nacional (1983–89): promoting 'impossible' theatre

En el teatro te puedes inventar la vida, es una grande y maravillosa mentira. (Pasqual, cited in Rivière 1983: 10)

(In the theatre you can invent life, it's a large and marvellous lie.)

Pasqual had already made a mark at the CDN before being appointed artistic director in 1983. His staging of Büchner's *Leonce and Lena* (*Leonci i Lena*) was seen at the María Guerrero theatre in September 1979 as part of a Lliure visit to the CDN. In 1981 Pasqual directed arguably the centrepiece production of the Calderón stagings which marked the 300th anniversary of his death, a contentious reading of *La hija del aire* (*The Daughter of the Air*) which opened at Seville's Lope de Vega theatre on 25 April, touring across Spain before being seen at the María Guerrero with Ana Belén in the title role in the autumn of that same year.[13] While his years at the CDN were not marked by a commitment to nurturing new writers, he was to gain the company an international profile through directing nine productions that sought to introduce Spanish audiences to 'lost' classics (Haro Tecglen 1989a: 30). These included five high-profile stagings of the 'unknown' work of García Lorca, as well as Valle-Inclán's *Luces de bohemia* (1984). As with his programming with the Lliure, Shakespeare and Brecht were also to feature as directorial choices. In addition, Pasqual was to display a commitment to promoting a decentralised theatre culture by bringing to the CDN the work of dramatists and companies outside Madrid: Valencian dramatist Rodolf Sirera's *El veneno del teatro* (*The Audition*) opened on 10 November 1983; Els Comediants' *Dimonis* (*Devils*) opened at the Retiro Park on 8 October 1983; Els Joglars' *Teledeum* opened at the Sala Olimpia on 26 April 1984; two productions by the Centre Dramàtic de la Generalitat de Catalunya visited in the 1984–85 season; Els Comediants *Alé* (*Breath*) opened at the María Guerrero on 1 November 1985; the Lliure brought Puigserver's production of Pablo Neruda's *Fulgor y muerte de Joaquín Murieta* (*Splendor and Death of Joaquín Murieta*), presented in Catalan as *Fulgor i mort de Joaquín Murieta* in

12 For further details, see the daily discussions that were published in *La Vanguardia* between 21 and 28 July 2000 in which a range of directors and performers including Josep Montanyès, Joan Ollé, Joan Lluís Bozzo, Hermann Bonnin, Roger Bernat, Pepe Rubianes, Borja Sitjà and Carme Portaceli participated: Fondevila 2000, Sesé 2000a–g.
13 For further details on the production, see Pérez Coterillo 1982 and Pérez Sierra *et al.* 1981. Belén replaced Espert who was forced to pull out of the production because of her commitments to *Doña Rosita la soltera* (*Doña Rosita the Spinster*).

March 1986; Seville's Esperpento theatre was represented with a staging of Valle-Inclán's *La marquesa Rosalinda* (The Marquise Rosalind) in April 1987; the Centre Dramàtic de la Generalitat Valenciana visited the following season with the same play and Manfred Karge's *Max Gericke (Max Gericke: Un home d'urgència)* in September 1988.

Part of Pasqual's agenda in raising the international profile of the theatre involved both securing European dates for CDN productions and the hosting of international work: Yugoslav director Zlatko Bourek's *Hamlet* opened at the Sala Olimpia on 27 March 1984; Strehler's staging of Goldoni's *Arlecchino, the Servant of Two Masters (Arlecchino, Servitore di due padroni)* opened at the María Guerrero on 1 June 1984 – Strehler was to return with Pirandello's *As You Desire Me (Come tu mi vuoi)* in 1989; Jerôme Savary's *Bye, Bye Show Biz* opened at the María Guerrero on 20 June 1984; Buenos Aires' Muncipal General theatre San Martín brought Schiller's *Maria Stuart (María Estuardo)* in March 1986; the Théâtre National Populaire (TNP) and the Festival d'Avignon were featured with Klaus-Michael Grüber's production of Hermann Broch's *La Récit de la servante Zerline* (The Story of the Servant Zerlina) in June 1988; Lindsay Kemp followed up a visit in February 1984 with *Nijinsky* with *Alice* in December 1988. Pasqual's expansionist plans for the CDN also involved incorporating the Sala Olimpia as a second space for smaller-scale work and establishing the convention of a single nightly performance at 8.30 p.m.

Following *The Life of Edward II of England,* Pasqual's choice to direct Valle-Inclán's *Luces de bohemia* as a co-production with Giorgio Strehler's Odéon-Théâtre de l'Europe was part of a strategy devised to accord the CDN a distinct identity as a venue which sought to produce plays that other theatres dare not risk (artistically or financially). The play, first published in 1920, had never been produced in the dramatist's lifetime with its professional Spanish premiere only taking place on 1 October 1970, at Valencia's Principal theatre under the direction of José Tamayo. The play had already been seen in France in 1963 in Georges Wilson's TNP production, but its caustic reflection of Madrid's turbulent post-1918 social climate and episodic structure was evidently perceived as a poisoned chalice by directors who feared the mutilating cuts that would be imposed on the piece during the Franco regime.[14] Expounding Valle-Inclán's theory of the grotesque, the *esperpento*, the play poses veritable challenges to any prospective director: the detailed stage directions, the varied locations – dingy taverns, cemeteries at dusk, darkened attic rooms, glass-strewn streets, cave-like bookshops – , the specific allusions to streets, cafes, monuments and historical figures – politicians, writers and artists. The episodic form, as in Brecht's work, functions as a dramatic statement which, like James Joyce's *Ulysses,* charts the journey of an anti-hero through a capital city – 'un Madrid absurdo, brilliante y hambriento' (1961a: 8) (an absurd, brilliant and

---

14 *Primer Acto*'s publication of the play in 1961 was unable to include the dialogue between Max and the prostitute La Lunares in Scene 10. For further details of the censors' attempts to curb two performances of the play by the Seville-based company Esperpento, see Pérez Coterillo 1984a: 5–6.

hungry Madrid) – as much a product of the author's imagination as historical reality.

Pasqual's proposition of the play as the first co-production between the CDN and the Théâtre de l'Europe seemed to gravitate around a desire to provide 'una imagen que no esperaban de nosotros' (Pasqual, cited in Vicente Mosquete 1984: 10) (an image which they didn't expect from us), eschewing the more familiar Golden Age repertory or García Lorca's better-known work. It is not insignificant that initially Strehler rejected Pasqual's choice of play. For Pasqual the play should be staged by each generation through the prisms of the contemporary Spanish realities that serve to inform and ground any reading of the text (cited in Sagarra 1984: 36).

Pasqual chose to situate his staging in an environment that directly commented on the dramatist's theory of the *esperpento,* an aesthetic of synthetic deformation which perturbs and disturbs the viewer/reader but is, at the same time, beautiful in the mathematical precision of its distortion. The concave mirror which calls into question the sharp binaries of tragic/comic, bizarre/conventional, the real/unreal, fiction/history was here refracted through Puigserver's set: a floor of mirrored tiles which captured the desolation of ransacked streets. Shadowy lighting rendered what Pasqual termed a 'lumpen' Madrid, suggesting the courtyard of a prison and a black hole wrapped in spiders' webs, propounded through barricades that were raised and lowered to create the different locations of Valle-Inclán's city. Environment was evoked through suggestion. The design was self-consciously theatrical, marked, as with a number of the director's previous stagings, with a cyclorama which conjured the sunrise and sunset in a series of cubist colours, 'como un *Guernica* coloreado' (Pasqual, cited in Sagarra 1984: 36) (like a coloured *Guernica*). This theatricality was also played out in the performance register that juggled a variety of acting styles from the *sainete* to farce and Beckettian minimalism. While *ABC*'s Lorenzo López Sancho (1984: 68) and *Primer Acto*'s Domingo Ynduráin (1984: 45) judged this *melange* overly exaggerated, it served to root the production in a metonymic idiom where the audience's imagination was stimulated through the performers – all clad in costumes evocative of 1918 Madrid – and their manipulation of the design environment's evocative resonances.

The production premiered on 13 February 1984 with a cast of forty, headed by José María Rodero (who had taken the role in Tamayo's earlier production) as the blind poet-seer Max Estrella and Carlos Lucena as his wily sidekick Don Latino. The audience at the Odéon included the Spanish Minister of Culture and his French counterpart Jack Lang. French critics were captivated by the production (Vicente Mosquete 1984: 9–10), which went on to enjoy a lengthy tour across Spain and a number of Lisbon dates before opening at the María Guerrero theatre on 23 October of that year. Reviews applauded Pasqual's bold vision of the piece, the choreography of the ensemble cast and the elegant beauty of the production. Ynduráin, however, questioned Pasqual's 'fidelity' to Valle-Inclán's allusive stage directions (1984: 46–8) – a criticism which had also beset García's 1975 production of *Divinas palabras* (*Divine Words*) – , but the director's visualisation of the play served to displace doubts about around the text's theatrical potential (Álvaro 1985:

59–64). The production was revived in early 1987, playing at the Municipal theatre of Girona on 8 May 1987 before going on a tour incorporating Spanish, Mexican and Russian dates which concluded at the María Guerrero theatre in May and June 1987.

With his later productions at the CDN, *Madre Coraje y sus hijos* (premiering at the María Guerrero theatre on 5 February 1986), and *Julio César* (*Julius Caesar*) (premiering at the same venue on 15 March 1988), Pasqual also demonstrated an affiliation towards plays whose stage directions defy the logic of fourth-wall naturalism. Pasqual turned to Brecht's 1938 play, using Buero Vallejo's version of the text which had first been staged by José Tamayo in 1966, because he felt it particularly relevant to the pervasive climate of 'histeria, neurosis y amenaza' (cited in Reigosa 1986: 14) (hysteria, neurosis and threats) which was then gripping the country: this was a year of increased ETA activity, Spain's referendum on NATO membership, and the *Ley de Extranjería* which served to compromise the status of guest workers and to discriminate against the non-white populations of Ceuta and Melilla.[15]

As with *Luces de bohemia*, Pasqual consciously avoided the production being weighed down by the dramatist's theoretical writings. As such the songs were dispensed with – although Paul Dessau's music was used to delineate mood and change of scene – and the *Verfremdungseffekt* was rendered through the prisms of a demonstrative performance aesthetic that was heavily indebted to popular cabaret and circus. The rhetorical acting register did not entirely convince *El País'* Eduardo Haro Tecglen (1986a: 25) or *ABC*'s López Sancho (1986a: 71), but *Diario 16*'s José Monleón, one of the earliest advocates of Brecht's work in Spain, was to applaud it as an exemplary staging, in its re-imagining of Brecht's aesthetic within an appropriate stage environment (1986a: ix). Puigserver's design evoked a circus ring with search-like spot lights bearing down to illuminate the space. A giant fence served also to suggest the prison-like associations of the location and a revolve allowed Courage's cart to be dragged around in endless circles. A plethora of special effects, including falling snow, driving rain, and the sound of canon-fire, served to provide concrete signs that suggested both the ravages of time and the prolonged effects of war. For *Ya*'s Julia Arroyo, however, this served only to imbue the staging with a cold formal beauty which smothered the raw humanity of the play. Nevertheless Pasqual's decision to cast Catalan actress Rosa Maria Sardà as a young Courage was seen as one of the production's strengths by Arroyo (1986: 48). Sardà, best known as a television performer, was decisively cast against type as the war-hardened profiteer. Her 'outsider' status was doubly reinforced by the associations around her casting and her Catalan identity. While *El Público*'s Carlos Reigosa disapproved of the tension between Sardà and Courage being visible in the production (1986: 14), it is precisely this interplay between performer and role that rendered the reading so compelling.

15 Joan de Sagarra's review of the Barcelona outing of the play directly commented on the government's NATO campaigning that had formed the backdrop to the Madrid performances; see Sagarra 1986b.

When the production opened at Barcelona's Mercat de les Flors on 21 May 1986, Sagarra (1986b: 34) was to comment on the critical doubts that had been raised by his colleague at *El Páis*, Haro Tecglen (1986a: 25), as to the production's shrinkage of the play's epic qualities. And while he too recognised that Pasqual's reading of the play might not suit more orthodox Brechtians, he was quick to commend Sardà's vibrant Courage which he felt had been unjustly dismissed by the Madrid critics who were unable to contextualise the performance within a repertoire of her past theatrical roles, judging her only against her most recent television appearance in *Aquí te quiero ver* (I Want to See You Here). For representatives of the Catalan critical establishment, like Pérez de Olaguer, the resonances of casting Sardà in the role were clearly much richer (1986a: 56). Indeed Sagarra was to view Sardà's performance as standing alongside that of Antoine Vitez's 1973 Courage, Ecelyne Istria (1986b: 34). In addition, paradoxically, Sardà's television success may have secured the production a sell-out run in Madrid, serving to bring a different audience to the María Guerrero theatre.

Perhaps more so than *Mother Courage*, *Julius Caesar* was viewed by Pasqual and Puigserver through the prisms of contemporary Spain. Puigserver's original scenographic idea had involved reproducing the Cámara de Diputados (Chamber of Deputies) of the Spanish parliament – a concept partly appropriated by designer Alfons Flores for Calixto Bieito's production of Verdi's *Un ballo in maschera* set in late 1970s for the Liceu theatre in December 2000. But in the end he opted for an expansive, mausoleum-like semicircular wall of black textured marble that progressively imprisoned the characters with different spatial areas delineated through lighting. Manuel Vázquez Montalbán's translation undertook a process of what Pasqual termed 'cortar y coser' (cutting and pasting) to render a two-hour version with twenty-one as opposed to fifty-eight roles which he felt better suited the conventions of a late twentieth-century audience (cited in Galindo 1988a: 88). The action unfolding both on the stage and in the auditorium, where performers were planted amongst the audience, emphasised Pasqual's view of the play as a study of the political behaviour of human beings (cited in Muñoz 1988: 43). These staging decisions also served to stress its relevance to late 1980s Spain at a time of political uncertainty with the PSOE losing control of major cities in the 1987 local elections, heightened ETA activity following the death of ETA leader Txomin and the high profile arrests of police implicated in the GAL (Grupos Anti-Terroristas de Liberación) scandal. The presence of numerous political dignitaries (including the then Minister of Culture Javier Solana), on the opening night, significantly coinciding with the ides of March, served to further accentuate the contemporary political resonances of the play.

Once more Haro Tecglen, writing in the liberal newspaper *El País*, was a combative dissenter who resented Pasqual and Puigserver's digressive reading that he felt had been misguidedly foisted on the play (1988a: 38). The Madrid-based critics obsessively delineated Pasqual's cuts (Hera 1988a: 44; López Sancho 1988a: 111). Doubts as to the actors (which included Uruguayan Walter Vidarte as Cassius and Argentine Miguel Ángel Solá as Mark Antony) were raised by *Diario 16*'s José

Monleón, who located the problem in the absence of a performance tradition for Shakespeare in Spain (1988: v). Catalan critics who travelled to Madrid for the opening night displayed a greater tolerance of Pasqual and Puigserver's decision and failed to castigate the production for supplanting poetry as the undeniable dominant of Shakespeare's work (Pérez de Olaguer 1988: 39; Benach 1988: 37). It is now possible to recognise the importance of this production in opening up the CDN as a space for the Elizabethan playwright's work – contentious stagings of *Hamlet* and *The Merchant of Venice* translated by Vicente Molina Foix and directed by José Carlos Plaza were to follow in 1989 and 1992 respectively. The overt pruning of the play was to find echoes in Calixto Bieito's later pared-down dissections of Calderón's *La vida es sueño* (*Life is a Dream*) first seen in English in 1998 and restaged in Castilian for the 400th celebrations of Calderón's birth in 2000, and *Macbeth* in 2002. In addition, Pasqual and Puigserver's concept of the politicians as grey-suited businessmen with white togas resting over their attire – the togas substituted for scarlet capes during the civil war – pre-empted Peter Stein's 1993 visualisation of the politicians. Pasqual was to recognise the manner in which the audience's act of observing the performance could be articulated and made visible on the stage through the numerous references to oratory and interpretation, rendering a reading which visibly explored the cultivated nature of politics and the highly problematic relationship between character and performance. The male political arena in which the play unfolded was seen as a society defined by rhetoric where deception is all pervasive. In exploring what goes on behind the closed doors of politics, the macrocosm presented to the audience was that of a rotting corpse trapped inside a mausoleum. The plethora of references to sickness and decay, as well as to isolated body parts, served to present the political as a strongly physical, corrupt, dislocated and decaying dominion. If Pasqual was to view the exercise of staging the play as impossible for actors and director alike, it was precisely because there could be no definitive reading (1988: 31). *Julio César*, like all of Pasqual's collaborations with Puigserver, visibly negotiated the relationship between the era in which the text was first written, the era in which it is now being staged and the plethora (or otherwise) of performances that have filled these two points. While the production was not seen outside of Spain, the work on García Lorca's lesser-known plays was to reach international audiences, introducing both the plays and the director to the European theatre circuit.

Pasqual and García Lorca: from the Centro Dramático Nacional to the Odéon-Théâtre de l'Europe and beyond

It is perhaps not surprising that García Lorca, who enjoyed a chequered production history during the Franco regime, should have been chosen by Pasqual as a figure ripe for re-appropriation.[16] During the mid-1980s, as the fiftieth anniversary of his

---

16 For details on the reception of his poetry during the Franco era, see Wahnón 1995. For details on the ways in which censorship affected productions of the plays, see Abellán 1989.

death approached, it was the rural tragedies to which directors continued to turn. The fact that Spain's cultural construction has been irrevocably linked with the culture of flamenco for about two hundred years has allowed García Lorca's more obviously Andalusian work to be read and marketed through accessible clichés which could not be applied with the same ease to the work of his contemporaries or successors. As one of the first martyrs of the Civil War, García Lorca creates a romantic subject for exploitation, and his writings have been read as a mirror of his much-publicised life, as reflections of Andalusian life during the 1920s and 1930s, as elegies where his own death is anticipated, and as metaphors for his homosexuality, demonstrating how sexual and social deviancy leads to destruction.

Whilst I am not suggesting that the works can be reduced to the readings which we allocate and that may be dominant at any one time, oblique works, like *El público* and *Comedia sin título*, and the shorter plays, like *La doncella, el marinero y el estudiante* (*The Maiden, the Sailor and the Student*) and *Posada* (*Inn*), have come to question the accepted image of García Lorca as 'a colourful, castanet-clicking gypsy with a tragic social conscience' (London 1996: 7). The difference between Pasqual and his contemporaries José Luis Gómez, José Carlos Plaza and Nuria Espert lies in the fact that he has granted a central position to works hitherto regarded as peripheral. During 1986–87 he presented a major García Lorca season at the CDN where his own production of *El público* was framed within *Sonetos del amor oscuro* (*Sonnets of Dark Love*), a programme of recitals by Amancio Prada staged by Pasqual and first seen in the previous season, and *5 Lorcas 5*, a grouping of five short pieces directed by five different directors including José Luis Alonso, Joan Baixas and Lindsey Kemp. The choice clearly indicated a wish to allow one of Spain's major directors, Alonso, to tackle García Lorca for the first time. It provided Kemp (who in *Cruel Garden* had created a grand elegiac reading of the poet's life and work) with the opportunity to refashion *El paseo de Buster Keaton* (*Buster Keaton's Outing*) and gave Baixas – founder member of La Claca, whose legendary show *Mori el merma* (Death to the Monster), with puppets and masks designed by Joan Miró, had been one of the theatrical highlights of the transition years – the staging of *La doncella, el marinero y el estudiante*. Pasqual himself directed Antonio Banderas, then still predominantly recognised as a stage actor, in *Dialogo del Amargo* (*Dialogue of Amargo, the Bitter One*).

This season, presented on the fiftieth anniversary of his death, re-envisaged García Lorca. Both a process of re-appropriation and scholarship, *5 Lorcas 5* was made up of short, predominantly unfamiliar works which reject narrative logic in favour of a dramaturgical structure that defiantly challenges the reassuring tendencies of the realist play. Although *Dialogo del Amargo* and *La escena del Teniente Coronel de la Guardia Civil* (*Scene of the Lieutenant Colonel of the Civil Guard*) inhabit more familiar gypsy territory, their inclusion within a programme which included more dissident fragmented pieces like *El paseo de Buster Keaton* and *La doncella, el marinero y el estudiante*, occupying an uneasy space between film and performance script, served to juxtapose these different García Lorcas, thus destabilising any possibility of reading the dramatist through accredited values.

The 1987–88 season continued the García Lorca dissection with a production of *Los caminos de Federico* (Federico's Steps),[17] a spectacle conceived with Alfredo Alcón (b. 1930). Seen in Madrid just after the revival of Pasqual's production of *El público* in June 1988, it featured Alcón constructing a playful García Lorca confiding in and flirting with his audience. In contrast to the grand theatrics of *Cruel Garden*, the emphasis was on storytelling, colliding poems all layered and folded over and above each other. Rather than a structured whole, the spectacle emphasised an inscribed body upon whom conflicting discourses had been written. Here García Lorca was examined as a commodity, transformed into the many identities societies have accorded him: prophet, seer, artist, musician, son, lover, social rights crusader, surrealist, director – a displacing gaze where the performing body replays historically defined identities which recognise that culture enjoys an ideological role.

The fact that Pasqual presented the premiere of *El público* while artistic director of the CDN, an organisation receiving generous subsidy from the Ministry of Culture, suggests a recognition of the cultural value of the text. Dispensing with a reverential reading which might have presented this excavated playscript to a curious audience with a rigidly sacred precision, much like Ultz's 1988 production at Stratford East, Pasqual and his designer Fabià Puigserver chose a more playful approach which recognised and celebrated not only the complex interaction of differing linguistic and dramatic discourses in the play, but also the specific function of the eccentric stage directions. Rather than simply providing a mimetic reproduction of the directions presented in the text, Pasqual and Puigserver chose to radically reinterpret them. Rejecting the proscenium stage, although commenting on its trappings in a series of complex and striking ways, Pasqual and Puigserver created a performance space which was both fluid and idiomatic. Moving away from reverential fidelity, they used the opening stage directions' stipulations of 'Decorado azul' (García Lorca 1996b: 282) (Blue decor), to create a playing area which recognised the colliding temporal systems at work when an avant-garde play from 1930 is staged for the first time in 1986.

It had been Pasqual and Puigserver's intention to premiere the play in Granada in a purpose-built mobile theatre designed by Puigserver and Amat. Although the scheme received initial backing from the Ministry of Culture, problems emerged over running and maintenance costs and the building was never realised. The intricate designs produced for the interior of the theatre by Puigserver and the exterior by Amat, published in 1988 as *El Teatro Federico García Lorca*, demonstrate the need to re-envisage the performance space for plays like *El público* which gravitate around a fundamental questioning of established conventions of dramatic construction. Already at the Lliure and the CDN Pasqual's collaborations with Puigserver demonstrated a fascination with working in the round where the actors are especially exposed and unable to escape the presence of the audience,

---

17 This was a co-production with the Teatro Municipal General San Martín in Buenos Aires. The production was first seen in Buenos Aires in July 1987.

and an extraordinary capacity to conjure magical stage moments from elemental ingredients. Interestingly, Pasqual has often stated that, if when he reads a play he knows how to do it, then he won't stage it (1996: 208). He continually postponed producing *El público*, announcing it for his second season as artistic director of Madrid's Centro Dramático Nacional but not daring to stage it at the time because it scared him (cited in Delgado 1998b: 95).[18] When it was finally produced two years later, the production was regarded as part of an ongoing agenda of bringing to the stage incomplete or 'impossible' dramatic works.[19] As with his earlier production of *Luces de bohemia*, the staging provided an evanescent meditation on the text which recognised the existence of conflicting articulations and fragmentations and dispensed with psychological identity as the sole pivot on which interpretation of character turns. Critics who faulted Pasqual's work with the actors on characterisation, like *Diario 16*'s Ignacio Amestoy, clearly adhered to a reading of personality that falls within the limited criteria of psychological realism (1987: 39). *ABC*'s López Sancho, however, was quick to recognise that the conception of character visible in the play has more to do with Genet's cruel and violent mirror games than Pirandello's metatheatricality (1987: 73).

Relocating the playtext in a socio-cultural context that differs from that which engenders it always involves a process of reinvention. The Pasqual/Puigserver reading of *El público* posited a recognition of the production process which questions the playwright's status as privileged point of origin, at the pinnacle of a hierarchical power structure that recognises the director as a supposedly secondary figure.[20] Rather than simply seeing their task as the 'extraction' of meaning from García Lorca's text, in interviews published to promote the production Pasqual and Puigserver recognised their own engagement in a creative dialogue with the play (cited in Torres 1987: 9). Taking the direction of 'Las ventanas son radiografías' (1996b: 282) ('The windows are X-ray negatives') (Edwards 1994: 61) as a starting point, director and designer moved to create 'un teatro imaginario' (Pasqual 1987: 6) (an imaginary theatre) perhaps even a theatre beneath the sand. Upstage the fossilised trappings of the proscenium-arch stage and its reductive perspectivism created a glaring reminder of the theatre of the open air. Extracted from their habitual context the stiff, plush red, gold, white and blue curtains stood starkly as a constant reminder of an architectural structure which no longer seemed relevant to the products framed within it.

Jan Kott, author of the seminal *Shakespeare Our Contemporary*, writes of collisions taking place when a text meets with a 'new political and intellectual experience [...] and new theatrical techniques' (1968: 146). Recognising the

---

18 Pasqual was later to announce a production of Valle-Inclán's *Comedias bárbaras* (Savage Plays) for the 1988–89 season but he was not, in the end, to direct the trilogy which was only staged in the 1990–91 season by his successor at the CDN José Carlos Plaza.

19 For a far fuller description of the production, see Delgado and Edwards 1990 and Smith 1998a: 118–38.

20 A point made by Constantinidis (1993: 14).

traditions of theatrical interpretation in which they were working and the expectations national and international audiences may bring to a 'García Lorca' or Pasqual/Puigserver production, the staging highlighted the interpretative and significative layers that form part of any theatrical product. Every production witnessed is 'intertextual', set against a background of prior performances, interpretations and meanings. The beauty of *El público*, as conceived by Pasqual and Puigserver, was the overt theatrical articulation of this process. Its subject became as much the dominant artistic referents of the time in which it was written as the contemporary situation in which it was being staged and performance history between these two temporal axes. As such, stage directions that Puigserver regarded as products of the surrealist context in which García Lorca was immersed were radically reinterpreted.

Removing the stage and the orchestra stalls of the María Guerrero theatre provided an expansive, almost circular playing area of sparkling blue sand, a transformative space which simultaneously served to evoke the circus ring, a lunar landscape, a beach and a *corral*. Only a single row of stall seats remained, primarily for the actors, a dislocated reminder of a theatrical model that was inverted as the audience observed actors watching other actors, hence denying the stability of a single field of vision. Both Pasqual (1987: 6–9) and Puigserver (1987: 9–11) have repeatedly commented on the ever-shifting nature of theatrical meaning. Stage directions that may have seemed radical fifty years earlier are now read against a catalogue of artistic and technological innovations that has modified their impact. Pasqual and Puigserver's refusal to efface the disparities between the theatrical and social codes of 1930 and 1986[21] provided a vibrant *mise en scène* where a collage of dramatic, rhetorical, literary, medical, cinematic, Biblical, performative and sexual discourses all came into play. Indeed *Ya*'s Antonio Pelayo was to see echoes of Buñuel's early surrealist work in Pasqual's staging (1986a: 45). Narrative or thematic coherence was emphatically negated as Pasqual refused to endorse readings that would reduce the play to a single issue.[22]

Rather the emphasis was on polyphony. In *El público*, the cumulative acts of realist dramaturgy are replaced by a 'Drama en cuadros' (1996b: 117) (Play in frames). These 'frames' dispense with spatial or temporal coherence, offering an array of characters whose relation to each other is never concretely defined. Visually realised by differing acting styles – from the *Tanztheater* of the white horses to the operatic register of Julieta's anguished soliloquies, from the seductive writhings of the Figura de Pámpanos/Figure of Vine Leaves and Figura de Cascabeles/Figure of Bells to the awkward reciting of Juan Echanove's Pastor Bobo/Silly Shepherd and the clinical, measured debate between the Prestidigitador/Magician and Director in the final scene – , the choreographed movement resisted easy categorisation, recognising its own performative referents. Transitions of mood and tone are rapid

---

21 Although the production opened at the Piccolo Teatro, Milan on 12 December 1986, its run at Madrid's María Guerrero theatre did not begin until January 1987.
22 'Sería reductor decir que esta obra trata solamente de la homosexualidad de Lorca' (Pasqual 1987: 7) (It would be reductive to say that this play is solely about Lorca's homosexuality).

in García Lorca's language; here they were made visible thorough a dynamic physicalisation of action.

In the third scene of the play when the Hombre 1/First Man claims he has no mask, the Director reveals that there is nothing but masks. In Pasqual's production, gender, sexuality, social and political interaction were all presented as imitative performance, a game where the tension between visibility and invisibility found its most resonant manifestation through the character of the Prestidigitador/Magician whose function lies in conjuring illusions. The theatrical trickery accompanying his entry for the final minutes of the play, fan in hand silhouetted by a spot on a curtain some distance away, provided an alluring manifestation of the ephemeral intangibility of performance, becoming itself only through disappearance (see Figure 16).[23]

In *El público,* as staged by Pasqual, theatricality was the definitive idiom. Costumes alluded to the play's variant generic registers, and were not fixed to any definable period or tradition. In the case of the Pastor Bobo/Silly Shepherd – part clown, part fool – differing layers of costume superimposed military insignia, signs of domesticity (an apron), profession (a sheepskin wipe), femininity (earrings) and classical antecedents (a hose, a handkerchief tied around the head). Emphatic colour coding in a costume scheme dominated by red, white and black commented on the audience's expectations (Julieta/Juliet dressed in sculpted white, Elena/ Helen positioned on platform pedestal heels, the Emperador/Emperor in white toga and red cape). Signs of discontinuity soon appeared as Julieta was placed in an imagistic network dissonant from that in which the audience may have initially conceptualised her. Verbal and visual dislocation found their exquisite counterpoint as Julieta's encounters with the horses delineated a confrontation of performance styles, ideologies, icons and desires (see Figure 17). The physically masked and visibly disembodied entities populating the stage provided a carnivalesque antagonism of conflicting roles.[24] Connections were teased and traced by an audience whose attempts to locate 'intentional' meaning were continually frustrated.

It was the journey, the process of reading and interpretation, which was the crux of Pasqual's production. Positing the process as a journey with Puigserver where participants included painter Frederic Amat, who collaborated with Puigserver on the design, musician and composer Josep María Arrizabalaga and actor Alfredo Alcón, Pasqual acknowledged the ongoing capacity of texts to carry on meaning effectively forever (1987: 6). Interpretation can never be complete. The French philosopher Jacques Derrida writes of reading as 'transformational', denying 'a finished signified beneath a textual surface' (1981: 63). Like the superimposed masks paraded before us at a dizzying speed in Pasqual's *El público*, when surfaces are displaced they reveal other surfaces. When even gender and sexuality are presented as representation, the real is implicitly acknowledged as absent. Pleasure lies in the peeling away of the masks, the search for an elusive referent, a non-existent essence which can never be revealed. As Pasqual has affirmed, 'el

---

23 The point concerning performance is made by Phelan (1993: 146).
24 For a study of *commedia dell' arte* and the carnivalesque in García Lorca, see George 1995: 153–65. For a study of the carnivalesque in *El público*, see Ros 1996.

16 Prestidigitador/Magician (Walter Vidarte) fans himself as one of the back curtains is raised for the Director's final entry in the closing scene of *El público* (1986)

17 Primer caballo blanco/First White Horse (José Luis Reina) and Caballo negro/Black Horse (Manuel de Blas) do battle over Julieta (Maruchi León) in *El público* (1986)

amor, la felicidad sólo existen mientras los buscamos' (1987: 7) (Love and happiness only exist while we search for them).

An interplay of light and darkness – flickers and shadows, expansive spots which sought out the characters and into which the characters slid – divided and controlled the performance space creating multiple areas and contrasting perspectives. Intimate spaces, long corridors, and expansive arenas of decisive physical and ideological conflict all offered a malleability and fluidity of space which was physicalised through the encounters (physical, musical and visual) enacted across the space. The focus was on the performers interacting in a physical landscape where visibility was not necessarily desirable and where desire always exceeded the means by which it could be satisfied.

Superimposed performative masks seduced the audience into believing that beneath a role lies 'truth', but truth proved an elusive concept in Pasqual's staging. Absolutes were negated. Comparing the piece to a Mozart 'Sonata', Pasqual consistently recognised the particularity of the reading of the play presented through the production: the many surfaces, reflections and prisms always denying a definitive rendition (1987: 6). The circular setting served to implicate the audience in a relationship which renegotiated private and public spheres. Pasqual has admitted in interviews that when he first read the play in 1978 'no entendí nada de nada' (1987: 6) (I understood absolutely nothing). On the eve of the production's opening he spoke of areas of the play 'que se han ido aclarando, otras que permanecen en la oscuridad total' (1987: 7) (which have become clearer, others which remain in total darkness). Pasqual's production may have begun with white lights permeating the darkness of the playing area, seeking to make visible the opaque, but visibility, as Pasqual recognises, has its limitations.

The critic Peggy Phelan writes of visibility as a 'trap [. . .] it summons surveillance and the law; it possesses voyeurism, fetishism, the colonialist/imperial appetite for possession' (1993: 6). In Pasqual's production the interplay of visibility and invisibility was brutally enacted on the body of El Desnudo Rojo/The Red Nude. Punishment became performative, mapped out on a naked body crucified on a grid metal bed frame consequently framed by a white sheet and then reframed again by a gold curtain. It was a public ceremony enacted on the most private of locations to an audience confronting the unexpected. The visibility of his genitalia, the invisibility of the four partially lit students debating Romeo and Juliet as their shadows climbed along the curtains behind the nude figure, the women dressed in black fumbling in the dark to make their way through the dimmed auditorium, all functioned as metaphors for a production which operated around the praxis of revelation: the revelation of García Lorca's 'unknown' play never previously produced in Spain, the revelation of an 'unknown' García Lorca which refuses to re-confirm the populist associations of his best known works, the revelation of a different María Guerrero theatre far removed from its habitual proscenium frame.

It is no coincidence that Pasqual's staging was co-produced by Milan's Piccolo Teatro and the Théâtre de l'Europe, of which Giorgio Strehler was then also artistic director. Strehler's practice, based always on detailed research and a celebration of the transformative capacity of the stage, offered a model of theatre where the methodologies of performance and the fluidity of the historical and contemporary function of a playtext were of paramount importance. Premiering in Milan at the newly-constructed Piccolo Studio on 12 December 1986 before being seen in Paris after the María Guerrero run in April 1988, *El público* offered Italian and French audiences a production which deviated sharply from cultural precedents and questioned popular conceptions of García Lorca as a folkloric dramatist whose thematics were conveniently related to a Latin temperament. It was to be greeted by superlative responses in the Italian and French press (Pelayo 1986b: 44; Capdevila 1988: 44) and the prize for Best Foreign Language production by the Association of French critics (Galindo 1988b: 101). As with his later production of *Comedia sin título*, again seen in both Madrid and Paris, Pasqual promoted the Hispanic cultural heritage abroad without reducing it to a single hegemonic product. In examining the press reviews of the production's Paris and Milan performances, Paul Julian Smith has commented on the 'continuing unease' of critics about the play's homosexual theme and onstage nudity in teasing out the contradictory positions occupied by a staging which both celebrated the dramatist's 'universality' and accommodation of 'multiple interpretations', and demonstrated the necessity to police 'the limits of decency, both at home and elsewhere' (1998b: 77).

Within Spain, critics recognised the incomplete nature of the play and the difficulty of finding a stage register for a work that defied classification. While *Diario 16*'s Amestoy voiced doubts around Pasqual's ability to 'clarify' the play or identify with the dramatist's discourse (1987: 39), for *Ya*'s Hera Pasqual's staging succeeded precisely because it conceived a visual vocabulary for the eclectic literary discourses of the text (1987: 46). *El País*' Haro Tecglen too recognised Pasqual's skill in crafting a staging distinguished by excellent ensemble playing, which majestically brought together the different thematic strands and metaphoric images of a disjointed work (1987: 25). The staging was further revived in Madrid in June 1988 following a tour which encompassed dates in Girona, Paris, Seville, Valencia and Barcelona. Plans to visit New York and Berlin had to be cancelled because of problems locating an appropriate space for Puigserver's ambitious set.

While working on *El público*, Puigserver spoke of his desire to work with plays that veered away from the obvious, where the language was poetic and where the emphasis was on showing rather than telling (1987: 9–10). Opening on 23 June 1989, *Comedia sin título*, Pasqual's final production as artistic director of the CDN, took another of the 'impossible' incomplete plays, described by García Lorca as 'una obra en la que no puedo escribir nada, ni una línea, porque se han desatado y andan por los aires la verdad y la mentira, el hambre y la poesia' (cited in Monleón 1989: 22) (a play in which I cannot write anything, not even a line, because truth and lies, hunger and poetry have become untied and wander through the air) and reinhabited it to provide alternative spectator/performer configurations which disallowed complacent aestheticisation. As with his production of *El público*, the play was reinvented as a reflection on the politics and function of theatre. Hinging on the slight plot of a revolution breaking out outside a theatre where rehearsals for

A Midsummer Night's Dream are taking place, the play's narrative style provides a decisive commentary on the construction of theatre and self. The ornate splendour of the María Guerrero theatre was decisively placed on display, providing a frame for the rehearsals of Shakespeare's play (presented in Jaime Gil de Biedma's translation) which Pasqual included in his staging.

Critic Leonard Tennenhouse views *A Midsummer Night's Dream* as a study of 'authority grown archaic', where 'inversions – of gender, age, status, even of species – violate all the categories organising Elizabethan reality itself' (1994: 111). García Lorca's piece also constructs a space where chaos threatens the hermetic world enclosed within the proscenium frame. Imanol Arias, returning to the stage after a decade of working predominantly in film, presented an Autor/Author who struggled to remain in control, directing proceedings from a lit auditorium where he was tormented by actors planted in the audience who verbally assaulted those struggling onstage.[25] Disorder enveloped the auditorium as an explosion from outside ruptured a section of the stage (see Figure 18). As more of the stage collapsed, rubble and dust fell over the audience. Some spectators dashed out in haste, ignorant of the illusion conjured by Pasqual and Puigserver. Others waited for a curtain call that never came. Pasqual views the play as 'muy alegre y terrible a la vez [. . .] una declaración de amor y de guerra al teatro' (cited in Landaburu 1990: 125) (very bright and terrible at the same time . . . a declaration of love and war on theatre). Composed on the eve of the Civil War, it is for him both a denunciation of the evasive nature of the Spanish stage in the 1930s and, like *El público*, a manifesto for a theatrical practice which dispenses with the centrality of a single perception and reinvents the purposes and strategies of theatre in consistently disquieting ways.

As García Lorca's 'impossible' plays oblige us to expand the dramaturgical vocabulary at our disposal and acquire new reading codes, so Pasqual, in providing alternative theatrical configurations, undermined the spectators' sense of themselves as a cohesive group, destabilising the recognised boundaries of audience and performer.[26] The street outside, a rumbling symbol of the 'other' feared by the closed-in audience, threatened to invade their complacent and illusionist existence. Panic set in and the boundaries between the private space of the auditorium and the undefined public space of the world beyond collapsed. Violence erupted in the interior body of the theatre as the bombing impacted on their protected environment; order could no longer be staged and the structures which upheld that order fell apart.

25 His casting brought associations with the 'outsider' roles he had taken in films of the 1980s, perhaps most significantly the emotionally tortured terrorist in Uribe's *La muerte de Mikel/Mikel's Death* (1983) and the Robin Hood-like renegade of Vicente Aranda's *El Lute* and *El Lute II* (1987 and 1988). In all these films he provided forceful interpretations of elusive objects of desire on whom oppressed contingents projected their hopes and fantasies for the future.

26 Even those cast members like Juan Echanove and Walter Vidarte, who had also featured in *El público*, were here allocated roles which stood in stark contrast to those enjoyed in *El público*, thus defying the expectations of stratas of the audience who may have been expecting them to occupy more familiar character territory.

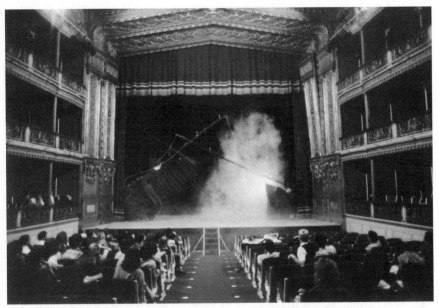

18 The collapse of the theatre in the final scene of *Comedia sin título* (1989)

In the opening moments of the play the Autor announces that 'ver la realidad es difícil. Y enseñarla, mucho más' (1996b: 769) (to see reality is difficult. And to show it even more so). Pasqual and Puigserver created a stage reality which they repeatedly foregrounded as representation, manipulating its vocabulary to reveal how 'the real is read through representation, and representation is read through the real' (Phelan 1993: 2). Reviewing the Madrid production Monleón argued that it articulated not merely a possibility for a new methodology of theatre but significantly a way of understanding its social function in times of political change (1989: 27). In its provocative and unnerving spirit and its reframing of Shakespeare's disembodied play, the production stood against the boundaries of accepted or sanitised taste, the 'cultura de plástico' (Pasqual and Muñoz 1995: 39) which Pasqual has repeatedly denounced for its corrupting and debilitating complacency (cited in Ytak 1993: 90–1).[27]

ABC's López Sancho (1989a: 103), *Diario 16*'s Amestoy (1989: 33) and *El País*' Rosana Torres (1989: 53) judged the production a fitting culmination to Pasqual's artistic directorship at the CDN: a masterful, audacious staging, majestically cast and choreographed. *El Público*'s Juanjo Guerenabarrena too applauded the production's adept invasion of the audience's space and the lead performances of Marisa Paredes (Titania/Actriz/Actress), Arias (Autor/Author) and Juan Echanove as the reactionary Espectador II/Second Spectator (1989a: 34–5). No

---

27 Smith (1998b: 78) has classified Pasqual's production of *El público* in similar terms 'as a challenge to the hegemony of a complacent Socialist government which has restored the parameters of "normality" supported by politicians of other parties'.

critic was to pick up Pasqual's subtle incorporation of references from the work of Chéreau, Brook, and Strehler (cited in Guerenabarrena 1989b: 36); rather post-opening night reports concentrated on the array of politicians and cultural figures who had attended the premiere (García Lorca's sister Isabel, his friend Rafael Alberti, the Minister of Culture Jorge Semprún and biographer Ian Gibson) and validated the production with their enthusiasm for Pasqual's vision of the play (C. 1989: 56; P. 1989: 35). *El País'* Haro Tecglen may have wondered at Pasqual's motives in 'destroying' the theatre whose artistic directorship he was about to give up but similarly admired the elegant beauty of the production (1989b: 32).

It is significant that Pasqual chose *Comedia sin título* both to close his tenure at the CDN and as his inaugural production as artistic director of the Odéon-Théâtre de l'Europe in 1990, a year after making his French-language debut with *As You Like It (Comme il vous plaira)* at the Comédie Française. His arrival was decisively announced with a production that heralded the physical collapse of the existing Odéon. Pasqual radically restructured the Odéon, which had been previously shared between the Théâtre de l'Europe and the Comédie Française, creating a second performance space and encouraging international co-productions. The increased funding he was to receive from France's Ministry of Culture was to convert it into the third largest state-subsidised theatre in France after the Comédie Française and the Théâtre National de Chaillot.

Pasqual was to stage *Comedia sin título* both in French as *Sans titre* and Castilian Spanish, significantly assuming the role of the Autor in the Castilian-language production. The French-language production of the play ran from 5 October to 18 November 1990 with Castilian-language performances between 13 and 17 October. The French critics were effectively polarised by this staging – a marked contrast both to their response to *El público* and with the Spanish critics' more favourable response. While *Le Quotidien de Paris'* Armelle Heliot thought the piece a beautifully staged venture which evoked memories of May 1968 and the scandal surrounding Genet's *Les Paravents (The Screens)* (1990: 25),[28] *Le Figaro's* Pierre Marcabru denounced the play as anachronistic and absurd, a misguided choice as an opening production for the new artistic director of a subsidised national theatre in that it denounces the reason of theatre itself (1990: 33). For Pasqual, however, the production decisively indicated a cultural strategy which sought to emphasise cultural specificity, here expressly enacted through a focus on the problems inherent in translating García Lorca into French and the different performance traditions of French and Spanish actors (1996: 207–8, 215–16). Rather than erase difference in search of some naive concept of cultural globalisation, Pasqual sought, both in the production and in his subsequent programming, to emphasise diversity and particularity.[29] Referring to himself as more Spanish in Paris than he is in Spain, Pasqual has strongly refuted the concept of 'international theatre' (1996:

---

28 For further details on the events of 1968 and *Les Paravents*, see Chapter 3, 107–10.
29 Strehler (1996: 268) uses 'diversity and particularity' to refer to his own ideals of what a European theatre could be.

216–18).

As with Strehler before him, Pasqual's directorial choices can be classified as part of a vision of theatre as public service where traditions are revisited, revised and transformed. As Pasqual, Puigserver and Planella had conceived a social role for the Lliure within the landscape of Gràcia, so with the Odéon-Théâtre de l'Europe Pasqual looked to create the possibilities for a European theatre that went beyond political institutions or bland standardisation. For Pasqual *Comedia sin título/Sans titre* inaugurated a theatrical strategy that could offer a means of interrogating what the oscillating discourses of a new Europe might be and how theatre might participate in the debates raging through the shifting boundaries of the continent (cited in Sagarra 1990b: 34). In addition, it announced Pasqual's intersecting identities: a Catalan who collaborated with a regular designer, whose interests lay in metatheatrical dramaturgy, engaging with the myths of his own theatrical culture but working within a landscape whose 'otherness' he acknowledged.[30]

His subsequent García Lorca project, *Haciendo Lorca* (Making Lorca) (1996), completed his five year tenure at the Odéon. Originally conceived as a reworking of *Bodas de sangre* (*Blood Wedding*), for a cast of two, it mutated during rehearsal into a meditation on the play beginning with and centring on the characters of Death and the Moon. Adapted, dismantled and reorganised for Alfredo Alcón and Nuria Espert, the piece emerged like Peter Brook's 1998 performed essay on *Hamlet, Qui est là?*, as a process of weaving together research, reflections, relocated sections of the play, and juxtaposed sections from other texts. The emphasis was on narrative discontinuity where bodies of inherited meaning came together to comment on the conflicts played out in the writings. Interestingly it was precisely this narrative discontinuity which disappointed critics, like *Primer Acto*'s Eduardo Pérez Rasilla, who searched for a linear cohesion in the piece (1996: 104–6).

The metaphor of a shifting, ephemeral García Lorca was brilliantly conjured by the core design metaphor of the crane provided by Frederic Amat (b. 1952), the painter/designer who worked with Puigserver on *El público* and with whom Pasqual has, since the death of Puigserver in 1991, forged a new collaboration.[31] Pasqual locates in Amat, 'the ability to sweep away all the incidental things and [. . .] reach the single word that suggests a whole world' (cited in Delgado 1998b: 103). The dark crane, operated by a team of four technicians, alluded to Puigserver's canvas membrane for García's *Yerma* both in its audacity, its concrete physicalisation of the dramatics of the piece, and its creation of a visual environment which emphatically rejected mimetic realism. Propelling Alcón across the stage while Espert hovered in

30 Franco-Argentine director Jorge Lavelli also opened his tenure as director of a French national theatre with one of García Lorca's 'impossible' plays. His 1988 production of *El público* (*Le Public*) at The Théâtre National de la Colline announced the theatre's agenda as the promotion of contemporary world writing rather than just that of France, but significantly writing which was transgressive and violent, which allowed the director a decisive role and which reflected Lavelli's artistic aspirations. For further details see Satgé 1996: 1–7.

31 Pasqual has also forged other significant scenographic partnerships with Ezio Frigerio and Luciano Damiani, Strehler's regular designers. For further details, see 222.

pools of light below, first keeping them apart and then bringing them together, it offered a vertical organisation of space which stressed the capacity of technology and stage machinery to magnify, distort, and augment.[32] The presence of both Alcón and Espert, renowned García Lorca performers whose readings of the writer's works as actors and more recently directors have been seen across Europe and Latin America, served to authenticate and endorse the production, but also significantly acknowledged the key role each performer had played in shaping Pasqual's conception of García Lorca as dramatic material as well as the texture and shape of the piece itself.[33]

La oscura raíz (The Dark Root), a two-hander performed intermittently since February 1998 by Pasqual and Nuria Espert, again emphasised the journey of discovering and 'making' Lorca, rendering visible the very process of configuration. Although the genesis for the production came from a meeting between García Lorca and Margarita Xirgu on the stage of the Teatro Goya in 1935, it moved beyond this encounter, with Espert reciting (and through that very act simultaneously recalling and implicitly acknowledging) sections of her most celebrated roles – Doña Rosita and Yerma, as well as the poems she recalls narrating in her youth.[34] In its juxtaposition of poems, lectures, letters, and fragments of recalled dialogue, Pasqual's performance created an ambiguous persona, at once director, performer, excavator and critic, recalling the García Lorca he created in Edgardo Cozarinsky's film La barraca (1994). In his contemporary attire and direct address of the audience, however, he implicitly rebutted simplistic identification – he was decisively not García Lorca incarnate – in favour of an interpretative position that recognised both the traces of past performances and the specificity of his own public and private identities.

Pasqual has identified the significant role that García Lorca's correspondence formed in his preparatory reading when planning to stage El público (cited in Delgado 1998b: 96). La oscura raíz also made concrete 'una línea de descubrir una y otra vez al poeta' (Pasqual, cited in Olivares 1998: xii) (a process of discovering the poet again and again). It was not, as the critic Juan Carlos Olivares acknowledged, about the construction of a character but rather a personal positioning before ideas

32 This is a point made by Canadian director Robert Lepage in Charest 1997: 111.
33 Pasqual has admitted seeing García's production of Yerma over forty times while it toured Spain in the early 1970s and found himself unable to even think about staging the play because he has always been unable to view it outside the prisms of García's staging; see Guerenabarrena 1989b: 36 and Delgado 1998b: 92. For further details on Espert's collaborations with Pasqual, see 156 and 180–1. Alcón, who performed with María Casares in Margarita Xirgu's 1963 production of Yerma, had spent time in Madrid during the 1960s where his roles included Orin (to Espert's Lavinia) in José Luis Alonso's staging of Mourning Becomes Electra (A Electra le sienta bien el luto) (1965), covered in Chapter 4, 137–8. His roles at the CDN under Pasqual's direction (King Edward in La vida del Rey Eduardo II de Inglaterra (1983), García Lorca in Los caminos de Federico (1988), and the agonised Director in El público) have been covered earlier in the chapter.
34 Espert discusses this in Barbotegi S.L., La oscura raíz, www.infoescena.es/Barbotegi/obras/1001.asp. For further details on Espert's roles in Yerma and Doña Rosita la soltera, see 146–51 and 156–9.

and emotions which may be as much Pasqual's as García Lorca's (1998: xii). It was a recognition of the impossibility of presenting a truthful or real García Lorca, an understanding of the blurred and ever-shifting boundaries between truth and lies which is the territory of theatre and an articulation of the complex ways in which the self is mapped within cultural, social, economic and political parameters.

If *La oscura raíz* concerned itself with the resonance of García Lorca's writings,[35] *Bengues* (Devils) (1998), a collaboration with Antonio Canales' dance company, was engendered from the destruction of *La casa de Bernarda Alba* (*The House of Bernarda Alba*), García Lorca's least lyrical play, and its reinvention through the violent idiom of flamenco (Pasqual, cited in Peinado 1997: 19). The dominant black colour scheme remained, but the visual staticism was displaced by the frenzied temperament of the spectacle. Unlike Rafael Aguilar's version for Antonio Gades in the 1970s, where the lone male figure of Bernarda functioned as an abhorrent outsider distanced from the feminine society in which she exists, here all the cast, excepting María la Coneja's María Josefa, were male. As such all the characters were implicated within the system of restrictive surveillance operating within the domestic space. Gender was posited as visibly imitative with selected signs of femininity (the turn of the century boots and earrings) worn by Canales' Bernarda serving to locate the feminine upon the male performing body. This holds with Pasqual's view that the feminine as created on the male is always more feminine precisely because it is performed through markings and defined through the masculine. As such it brutally articulated the manner in which the definition of woman is inscribed through its relation to the male (cited in Marinero 1997: 10).[36] Gender boundaries were constructed by a performance state that conspicuously juggled its own ambiguous insecurities. The subliminal artifice of theatre here de-fortified the rigid codification that informed all the identities presented before us. Flamenco, which Pasqual had always consciously avoided working with, was stripped of its showy folkloric adornments. The body as focal object of desire was contained, regimentalised and ultimately destroyed by the rules of a society whose more political facade found its counterpoint in *Guernica,* the dance tapestry based on Picasso's painting which was presented alongside *Bengues* and which served to implicate Bernarda within a larger regime which, according to Canales, orders and endorses the fascism enacted in Picasso's *Guernica* (cited in Marinero 1997: 12). The body here functioned as the text on which the intersecting discourses of political and cultural history are written. Each piece was a collage which, according to Canales, has no beginning or end, a reflection on the enduring significance of cultural products

35 Resonance here is understood through the definition posited by theatre director Robert Lepage as not just what the texts say but the way they say it, reflecting what is being told and the mood of the characters, the musicality which demands it be spoken in a non-natural way, almost sung; see Charest (1997: 127–8).

36 Phelan (1993: 17) theorises this marking of the feminine through a recourse to Lacan's writings on the phallic function which posit that 'the frame of the phallic mark' permits visibility 'of that which she is not [. . .] The image of the woman is made to submit to the phallic function and is re-marked and revised as that which belongs to him'.

which have been situated within the turbulent socio-political context which engendered them (cited in Marinero 1997: 12).[37]

Just as Pasqual had been at the forefront of celebrations for the fiftieth anniversary of the playwright's death, so he assumed a primary role in the events that marked the García Lorca centenary in 1998. These began as soon as the new year was celebrated with 'Una mirada a Lorca' (A Glance at Lorca), an event in Granada attended by the King and Queen, clearly offering their endorsement both of the poet-playwright denigrated by the Franco regime, and of the 'Año Lorca' celebrations which the event officially inaugurated. Although conceived by Jorge de Persia, the programme was directed by Pasqual to designs by Amat, with the Granada City Orchestra and the Chorus of Barcelona's Palau de la Música conducted by Josep Pons, founder of the Lliure's Chamber Orchestra. Held at the appropriately named Auditorio Manuel de Falla in Granada, it featured excerpts of pieces by the poet's friend de Falla, as well as other composers admired by García Lorca including Stravinsky, Debussy and Albéniz. Two piano pieces, 'Pensamiento poético' and 'Granada', composed by García Lorca in his youth, were played by Daniel Ligorio, and the young actor Juan Diego Botto recited a series of poems written by García Lorca between the ages of eighteen and twenty-two. Francisco Merino provided a rendition from *Don Cristóbal*, the puppets of Fernando Gómez and Pilar Gálvez offered the 'Nana del Galapaguito' (Lullaby of Galapaguito) performed to a recording by La Argentinita accompanied on the piano by García Lorca, and the presence of singers Enrique and Estrella Morente provided a kaleidoscopic collage where the emphasis was not on a singular writing subject but rather a mythical entity, both celebrated and interrogated through his writings, compositions, acknowledged musical influences and collaborations.[38] There was no attempt to define García Lorca, rather the eclectic programme sought to self-consciously construct a García Lorca where disparity was staged and where the elusive shifting persona of the playwright became part of the spectacle: a being constructed from the works, a series of masks where the point of origin is never located, a brilliant game of mirrors where reflections of truth and lies merge to present a series of events which never deliver a unified real.

In 1995 while speaking at the Edinburgh International Festival the American director Peter Sellars drew attention to the malleability of the classics as 'something that is larger than anybody's particular point of view, and yet they have a moral dimension that won't go away' (1995: 18). This 'moral dimension' allows these classic works to be appropriated, processed and reinvented for the demands of the social, political and cultural climate in which they are staged. Pasqual locates in such classical texts the capacity to ensure that an audience are shaken and confronted with alternative ways of seeing (cited in Cuadrado 1998: 5). For director

---

37 Pasqual has returned to flamenco for his most recent García Lorca venture: a version of *Mariana Pineda* with music by Manolo Sanlúcar for dancer Sara Baras which premiered on 16 September 2002 at Seville's Teatro de la Maestranza as part of the Flamenco Biennial.

38 For further details of the event, see Tarín 1998.

José Samano, discussing his 'Año Lorca' tribute *Un rato, un minuto, un segundo* (A Short While, a Minute, a Second), performed by Lola Herrera and Carmen Linares at Barcelona's Tívoli theatre in March 1998, the governing idea was to ensure the spectators left the theatre knowing exactly who García Lorca was (cited in Sesé 1998: 45). For Pasqual the proposition has always been more elusive; there is no essential García Lorca, no infallible ideological position, no universal truth to be plucked from his diverse body of work.

'¡Quién sabe como era Lorca!' (cited in Antón 1998: 36) (Who knows what Lorca was like!), Pasqual stated while rehearsing *Como canta una ciudad de noviembre a noviembre* (How a City Sings from November to November), a reconstruction of a lecture on the city of Granada, its music, smells, and taste, given in 1933 at Buenos Aires' Sociedad de Amigos del Arte and then later in 1935 at Barcelona's Casal del Metge by the Granadine dramatist. Presented at Barcelona's Teatre Lliure in May 1998, it featured Juan Echanove, collaborating with Pasqual on a García Lorca text for the third time, and offering an evocation of the poet which consciously rejected imitative strategies in favour of a measured contemplation of the musicality of a specific lecture, affirming the fascination of Granada's popular songs which the dramatist knew and re-created on the piano. Musically arranged by Josep María Arrizabalaga, another collaborator on *El público* and *Comedia sin título*, the interplay of sounds, vocal and musical, offered a texture where audience attempts to visually identify with the poet were eluded by the silhouetted Echanove.

Echanove has admitted that his conceptions of García Lorca have been inextricably shaped by those of Pasqual (cited in Antón 1998: 36). Pasqual too has endeavoured to place the project within a configuration where the marks of their earlier ventures are recognised (1998: n.pag.). Cultural domination, as the critic Jonathan Dollimore posits, 'is not a static unalterable thing; it is rather a process, one always being contested, always having to be renewed' (1994: 14). Pasqual's productions indicate the multiple García Lorcas that can be imagined, invented and dreamed when one is freed from a reductively 'intentionalist' approach. Each of his collaborations has demonstrated the capacity of these texts to offer modes of thinking about society which move beyond tame standardisation and cohesive consolidation towards a negotiation of those shifting parameters through which our lives are constantly redefined.

Aristocrat of the Catalan theatre

In recognising Pasqual as one of his theatrical grandchildren, the late Giorgio Strehler implicitly identified the degree to which Pasqual's theatre, for all its visual brilliance, has placed the actor in a central position (cited in Pistolesi 1986: 87). Pasqual himself has acknowledged the fact that his own work as a director

is very much like that of an actor performing it. I have to picture myself in a physical way, in a psychological way: 'What the hell was this writer thinking at that moment to write this?' 'Who was he angry with?' 'Who was he in love with?' 'Why was he desperate?' I need to know this just as an actor needs to know what's happening to his character, because that's the only way I can do my job. (1996: 212)

One of the reasons he believes that the collaboration with Puigserver was so fruitful is precisely because the latter allowed him the space to be able to realise this: 'he looked after things in a plastic way, I looked after the actors' (1996: 213). Indeed Pasqual's lengthy rehearsal periods and detailed work with actors were to provide models which carried further the practices promoted by Espert and García in the period between 1969 and 1976.

Pasqual has been discerning about his choice of projects. He refused the artistic directorship of the Mercat de les Flors in the early 1990s, preferring to retain his association with the Lliure (Fondevila 1993a: 2). At the Odéon-Théâtre de l'Europe his judicious programming sought to provide thematic strands that offered a taster of both known and unknown works and companies. Strengthening its reputation as a major producing venue, he explored the concept of a 'European' theatre, programming Hispanic, Russian and British seasons, as well as inviting to Paris and/or (co-)producing the work of major European directors – Luc Bondy, Klaus-Michael Grüber, Strehler, Braunschweig, Patrice Chéreau, Deborah Warner – and dramatists – Botho Strauss, Frank McGuinness, Bernard-Marie Koltès, Alexander Galin. His own productions at the Odéon included a staging of Lope de Vega's *El caballero de Olmedo* (*The Knight of Olmedo*), a project he had hoped to realise at the CDN, which had first premiered at the Avignon Festival that summer before opening at the Odéon's Grande Salle on 10 November 1992. This project was one of a number Pasqual was to realise with Strehler's regular designer Ezio Frigerio. Since the death of Puigserver Pasqual has turned to Frigerio and Luciano Damiani, another scenographic partner of Strehler's, when staging more established or conservative works. Both have provided Pasqual with far more ornate, baroque and vertical structures than Puigserver. As such he was to collaborate with Frigerio (and his wife, costume designer Franca Squarciapino) on the inaugural production of the Russian season, *Les Estivants* (*Summerfolk*) in January 1994. With Damiani he staged *La Traviata* at Salzburg in 1995, one of a number of opera productions he has worked on since making his operatic debut in 1982 at Madrid's Teatro de la Zarzuela with Camille Saint-Saëns's *Samson et Dalila*. The projects with Frigerio and Damiani, however, have often seemed engulfed by the architectural grandeur of the sets actualised by these two designers, for Pasqual's work with actors and singers appears most impressive when realised within the parameters of the less cluttered conceptual designs realised by Puigserver.

As part of the 1994 Russian season Pasqual was to travel to St. Petersburg to work with the renowned ensemble company, the Maly Dramatic Theatre. The first foreign director invited to work with the company, he staged Bernard-Marie Koltès's controversial final play, *Roberto Zucco*, a piece he had directed a year earlier for the Lliure in Catalan at the then undeveloped Palau de l'Agricultura. Following its performances at the Odéon between 23 and 27 March 1994, it visited St. Petersburg in the early months of 1995. Here it polarised the city's critics and audiences and was vociferously denounced by the Maly's artistic director Lev Dodin as 'an unfortunate piece of European debris which has somehow landed with a crash in his theatre' (O'Mahony 1995: 8). Amat's design, displaying a technological set of intrusive video monitors that exemplified a hostile visual world of uncompromising violence where surveillance functioned as the order of the day, grounded the piece in a post-modern aesthetic of startling contemporaneity. It was, however, Pasqual's work reining 'in the normally indulgent tendencies of the actors, coercing them into streamlined performances of brittle power', which most impressed the critics (O'Mahony 1995: 8).

It has perhaps been Pasqual's collaboration with Amat that has provided the most satisfying productions of the last ten years. For *Tirano Banderas* (*Banderas the Tyrant*) (1992), an inspired Spanish-language adaptation of Valle-Inclán's monumental novel on despotism in an unnamed Latin-American state, sponsored by Spain's Quincentennial Commission, Amat created a dazzling visual correlation for the unstable political situation in a spinning merry-go-round set. More recently for *Waiting for Godot* (*Tot esperant Godot*) which opened at the Lliure on 10 February 1999, before being seen on the festival circuit in Lisbon, Strasbourg, Sarajevo and Madrid, Amat offered a horizontal set of cinematic dimensions. Pasqual proffered a bold metatheatrical reading of the play where Vladimir and Estragon were thrown onto a stage on which harsh spotlights mercilessly picked them out and illuminated them before an audience for whom they performed their vaudeville rituals of endless waiting. Against a white wall resembling a blank film screen, a solitary and twisted iron tree stood out from a set of abandoned chairs and other discarded detritus encrusted into a mound of rock. This was the end of the world, the rubbish heap of society where veteran Lliure actress Lizaran's animated Vladimir and Eduard Fernández's deftly passive Estragon sought release from their boredom. When it arrived in the form of Francesc Orella's despotic ringmaster Pozzo and Roger Coma's wildly pathetic Lucky, performance and all its physical trappings became the production's defining metaphor. *La Vanguardia*'s Benach summed up the importance of the production in a review significantly entitled 'Un Godot para la historia' (1999: 46) (A Godot for posterity), an importance echoed by *El País*' Pablo Ley, who saw in the staging an indication of what the quality of the new Lliure might be, 'la aristocracia del teatro catalán' (1999a: 39) (the aristocracy of Catalan theatre).

Alongside Pasqual's accomplishments at the Lliure, delineated earlier in this chapter, it is worth reiterating his achievements at the CDN, where his six-year period as artistic director has not yet been matched by the current incumbent, Juan Carlos Pérez de la Fuente. At the CDN he attempted to convert a theatre that he considered afflicted with the structure of a Francoist national theatre into a democratic European institution, which was in effect recognised by the company's incorporation into the Union of Theatres of Europe under his tenureship (Sagarra 1989b: 44). His groundbreaking productions as artistic director included two stagings: 'para la historia del espectáculo los estrenos mundiales de los dos Lorcas más arriesgados' (Guerenabarrena 1989b: 36) (for theatrical history the world premieres of Lorca's two most hazardous plays). Even when he has handled better-known works like *La casa de Bernarda Alba* and *Bodas de sangre*, these have mutated into unfamiliar textual entities that have defied spectator expectations. There has certainly been a process of identification with the dramatist's more unusual work – which Pasqual locates in a shared birthday (5 June) and the fact that he has staged both *El público* and *Comedia sin título* at around the same time in his life that the dramatist wrote them. The dramatist's sister Isabel García Lorca has judged Pasqual 'el director que mejor le entiende [a García Lorca]' (cited in Torres 1989: 53) (the director who best understands him). While Pasqual may no longer enjoy the status conferred on him by *El Público*'s editor Moisés Pérez Coterillo in 1990, 'Lluís I de Francia [. . .] el más internacional de nuestros directores de escena' (1990: 6, 9) (Lluís I of France [. . .] the most international of our stage directors), the collaborative work with Fabià Puigserver especially – described by Espert as 'un tandem irrepetible' (Espert and Ordóñez 2002: 179) (a one-off tandem) – has rendered him a seminal figure within post-Franco theatre. His presence, rehearsing a scene from *Haciendo Lorca* – reworked for Marisa Paredes – at the end of *Todo sobre mi madre/All About My Mother* (1999), serves both as an indication of his iconic status within the country's theatre scene and a sly nod on the part of Almodóvar to a figure equally responsible for shaping Banderas's early trajectory. Pasqual may not be as well known in the English-speaking world as his former assistant, Bieito, but he has paved the way for those, like Bieito, who have subsequently dazzled (and polarised) foreign audiences with their conceptual productions of Spanish classics.

6
Contrived performances: La Cubana

Every performance is a contrivance by its nature. (W. S. Gilbert, cited in Hoberman 1999)

Cada catalán tiene un actor dentro. (Jordi Milán, cited in Montero 1989: 8)

(Each Catalan has an actor inside.)

The Catalan performance group La Cubana emerged in 1980, at a time of great social change in Spain. The death of Franco in 1975 had initiated a process of transition towards democracy that was to see Juan Carlos crowned king on 22 November of that year, and a wealth of political and social legislation which was to restore democracy to Spain. Censorship was abolished in 1977; adultery, homosexuality and the sale of contraception decriminalised in 1978; divorce legalised in 1981 and abortion in 1984. Democratic elections were held in June 1977, initiating a process of parliamentary debate that was to see the approval of a new constitution in 1978. This constitution was to see a move away from the centralisation policies pursued by the Franco regime and the implementation of a policy of political autonomy which was to secure home rule for the Basque country and Catalonia in January 1980 and the election of Jordi Pujol as Catalan president in March of that year.[1]

For Catalonia especially this marked a break away from centralism, which had brutally repressed a Catalan language and culture in the need to establish and then maintain a sense of homogenous Spanish national unity. Francoism prohibited the speaking of Catalan in public, outlawed the Catalan-language press, and refashioned the nationalist landscape of the Catalan capital Barcelona by renaming prominent Catalan streets and squares (like Plaça Catalunya which became Plaza del Ejército Español, La Gran Via de les Corts Catalanes which became Avenida de José Antonio, and the Paral.lel which was named after the Marqués del Duero). If Francoism sought to diffuse and fracture Catalan, Galician and Basque identities, increasingly from the 1950s onwards, resistance to the centralising regime came in a double-pronged attack. As Eugène van Erven points out in his study, *Radical People's Theatre*, 'apart from ETA's spectacular actions and the often brutally dispersed student demonstrations, the most consistent anti-Franco resistance developed in the cultural field' (1988: 146) where an alternative theatre movement, labelled *teatro independiente* (TI) (independent theatre) sought to pioneer a shift in

1 For further details, see Hooper 1995: 13–50 and Carr 1980: 173–88.

theatrical vocabulary towards non-textual dramaturgies which questioned the primacy of the written play.

While TI was a country-wide movement which sought to revitalise Spain's theatrical culture by eschewing the 'official' theatre of the Franco regime, its resonances in Catalonia, where it articulated a protest against the political and linguistic impositions of the Franco regime, proved particularly strong. The first generation of TI groups, which included Els Joglars (The Jesters) (formed in 1962) and Els Comediants (The Actors) (formed in 1971), promoted a climate of artistic interdisciplinarity, re-envisaging theatrical languages with their corrosive political and social satires and exuberant indoor and outdoor spectacles. Both these companies, active during an era that had effectively prohibited the speaking of Catalan in public, chose not to perform in the 'coloniser's' Castilian language and developed new physical vocabularies of performance. Two of the founder members of Els Joglars – Anton Font and Albert Boadella – had spent formative periods in Paris. Boadella had studied mime with Pierre Saragoussi, a former pupil of Étienne Decroux, and taken part in workshops run by Jacques Lecoq. Joan Font, too, who remains the director of Els Comediants, trained with Lecoq.

This kinetic training as well as the continued presence of censorship in Spanish theatre until 1977 led both companies towards the forging of a non-textual dramaturgy which could not easily fall prey to the censor's controlling gaze. Appropriating elements from popular culture and *fiestas* while merging the discourses of mime, circus, choreography, caricature, satire, parody and imagistic theatre, they constructed a performance language which moved away from literary and psychological trends in theatre, crafting an oppositional cultural practice which saw their productions avoid traditional performance spaces like the proscenium-arch stage associated with 'official' theatre in favour of appropriated non-conventional venues. Performing on streets, in garages and squares, they used the techniques of improvisation to cultivate a different performer/audience relationship which questioned existing hierarchies in its direct address of the audience or its infiltration of the audience's space, and encouraged participation and provocation both in the private and the public spheres. Els Joglars collaborated with innovative designers like Iago Pericot on *Mary d'ous* (Egg Mary) (1972) and Fabià Puigserver on *Àlias Serrallonga* (1974) and *M-7 Catalònia* (1978), initiating bold new models of scenography which promoted a visual style of sparse economy and multiple spectator viewpoints. An emphasis on the musical, physical and visual provided an assertive strategy that challenged mainstream theatre practice. Alternative models of company organisation that owed much to French post-1968 practices of *création collective* sought to distance the TI groups from a theatrical prototype that privileged economic profit. Instead co-operative organisational structures encouraged participation from performers who, in turn, worked as technicians, and came from a range of disciplines. This stressed a creative process that undermined fixed roles and where even figures like Boadella and Font, who have long been viewed as the companies' *de facto* directors, assumed multiple roles within the ensemble's infrastructure.[2]

2 For further details on *teatro independiente*, see Fernández Torres 1987.

While performers like Joan Manuel Serrat and Lluís Llach too provided strategies of resistance to the regime in its dying days, it is these performance groups which have come to represent in David George and John London's words 'Catalan theatre beyond Catalonia' (1996: 15) or what Albert Boadella sees as a Catalan national theatre (cited in Ragué-Arias 1991: 30). The transformations in theatrical vocabularies witnessed in the 1960s permeated Catalan culture in the 1970s and 1980s as the ideological framework of Francoism was progressively dismantled. While Els Joglars have continued along a theatrical journey which explores the political and social climate of Catalonia, negotiating the sometimes fractuous transition from dictatorship to democracy, and Els Comediants' theatricality has continued to probe Mediterranean festive popular cultures, a new generation of theatrical troupes emerged in the late 1970s and early 1980s, like La Fura dels Baus, La Cubana and El Tricicle, which followed the interdisciplinary leads established by the earlier companies. Highlighting theatricality, their practice juggled mime, music, theatre, dance, acrobatics and circus to consolidate interdisciplinarity as the dominant artistic aesthetic of post-Francoist Catalonia. The hybrid spectacles of La Fura dels Baus and La Cubana merged the conventions of popular street *fiestas* with the language of cinema, vaudeville and rock concerts, offering both the recuperation of past cultural traditions and the reforging of new artistic discourses.

La Fura dels Baus's acrobatic pyrotechnics, aggressive sensorial performance style and multimedia aesthetic, as well as a non-reliance on verbal vocabularies of theatre, has seen them evolve into a state-funded business, undertaking lucrative advertising contracts, cinematic ventures, large-scale operatic projects and promotional campaigns (as their choreographing of the dazzling opening ceremony of the 1992 Barcelona Olympics displayed). Like Els Comediants, who were responsible for the closing ceremony of the 1992 Olympics, La Fura have gained substantial international acclaim. However, La Cubana have, arguably, been the most successful ensemble within Spain, clocking up a record-breaking 426,178 spectators during their run at Barcelona's Tívoli theatre with *Cegada de amor* (*Blinded by Love*) between 28 January 1994 and 25 June 1995. Nevertheless, their international touring has been infrequent. While the company visited Havana with *Cómeme el coco, negro* (Soft-soap Me, Black Man) in 1991 and Buenos Aires with *Cegada de amor* in 1998, outside the Spanish-speaking world they have made only brief forays to the London International Festival of Theatre in 1987, a select number of French festivals with *La tempestad* (*The Tempest*) in 1987, Lyon's Dance Biennial with *Cubanadas a la carta* (Slices of Cubana à la Carte) in 1992, and the Edinburgh International Festival with *Cegada de amor* in 1997. As such their trajectory may not have been subject to the same degree of critical or academic attention outside Spain that marks La Fura dels Baus's body of work. This chapter seeks to argue, nevertheless, that La Cubana's importance within post-Franco Spain has been substantial. Encompassing street performances, television series, corporate ventures with their subsidiary company 'Mamá mulata', as well as large-scale productions within more conventional proscenium-arch venues, La Cubana have served to further validate van Erven's view that the TI was 'instrumental in creating ever larger spaces of freedom in Spain, during the final decade of the Franco dictatorship and immediately following it, in the crucial transition period from November 1975 until 1982' (1988: 147).

Public participation: the reworking of street theatre in *Cubana Delikatessen* (1983) and *Cubanadas a la carta* (1988)

[. . .] era after era, the most vital theatrical experiences occur outside the legitimate places constructed for the purpose. (Brook 1972: 74)

El teatro que hacemos es como la vida misma, pero dándole la vuelta. Nos interesa que el espectador no sepa muy bien dónde está la verdad y dónde la mentira. La calle es el escenario más grande del mundo. Las tiendas, los escaparates o una obra de construcción se convierten en espectáculos. Hay que estar allí para vivirlos. (Milán, cited in Montero 1989: 8)

(The theatre we do is like life itself, but turned around. We are interested in spectators not really knowing what is true and what is a lie. The street is the largest stage in the world. Shops, window displays or a construction work are converted into shows. You have to be there to experience them.)

La Cubana were formed in Sitges in 1980 by Jordi Milán (b. 1951) and Vicky Plana (b. 1951). Milán and Plana had been members of El Gall Groc, a group based in the city's Casino Prado Suburense, which had staged a range of works in Catalan during the mid- to late 1970s, including Ionesco's *La Cantatrice chauve* (*The Bald Prima Donna*) and Arrabal's *Guernika*. When the group folded, Milán and Plana went on to form La Cubana, joined by four other members of the earlier troupe. As with La Fura dels Baus, very few of the early group members who were involved in early productions, like *Cubana Delikatessen,* had formal theatre training. Both Milán and Plana had studied interior design at Barcelona's IADE.

The company's name originated from Milán's view that theatre is an adventure. Coastal towns in Spain were the first points of contact with Spanish America, the point of departure for immigrants seeking their fortune in the new world. If they returned they were known as *cubanos*, the name thus becoming synonymous with adventure (cited in Rotger 1985: 37; López 1991: 43). In Sitges, if someone has a great imagination, they are often referred to as having landed in Havana (Montero 1989: 8). The associations of La Cubana for the Sitges-based company suggested risk, playfulness and exoticism.

Sitges has long enjoyed an 'alternative' status as firstly a vibrant modernist centre, home of Picasso associate Santiago Rusiñol (1861–1931) and more recently the gay capital of Catalonia, host to an annual carnival held in February/March marked by extravagant masked balls and outrageous parades, and an international theatre festival held since 1969. Carnival has always had a strong presence in the town, even during the Franco regime. María-José Ragué-Arias argues that this was certainly in part due to Minister of Information and Tourism Manuel Fraga Iribarne's awareness in the 1960s that Sitges was a lucrative tourist resort which could exploit the festive associations of carnival to attract international visitors (1991: 29).[3] For Mikhail Bakhtin carnival has always allowed for the celebration of 'temporary liberation from the prevailing truth and the established order; it marked the suspension of all hierarchical rank, privileges, norms and prohibitions [. . .] hostile to all that was immortalised and completed' (1968: 10). Fraga Iribarne may have judged carnival a folkloric attraction but, as Baz Kershaw has indicated, its allure lies precisely in its counter-cultural potential:

carnival undermines the distinction between observer and participant; it takes place outside existing social and cultural institutions, occupying real space-time in streets and open spaces; it is pluralistic, able to absorb contradictory practices within a single expressive domain; it delights in the body and in all the pleasures of the body, sexual, gustatory, scopophilic; it is accessible and it is excessive, enjoying spectacle and grotesque exaggerations of the norm. Above all, carnival inverts the everyday, workaday world of rules, regulations and laws, challenging the hierarchies of normality in a counterhegemonic, satirical, and sartorial parody of power [. . .] carnival *appears* to be totally anti-structural, opposed to all order, anarchic and liberating in its wilful refusal of systematic governance. (my emphasis) (1992: 72–3)

Such a definition could, as I will come to indicate throughout this chapter, summarise La Cubana's trajectory that has relied, especially in its first three productions, almost on 'accidental' spectators who stumble across the performance, rather than those who make a conscious decision to go to the theatre. For Plana the decision to create street theatre came out of necessity. Not having a space to call their own, they appropriated public spaces (cited in Colomer 1984: 5). The company's first production, *Dels Vicis Capitals* (Of the Capital Vices), clocking up over sixty performances, was based on two Mallorcan *entremeses* (interludes) by Llorenç Moyá Gilbert de la Portella, and a third adapted by José María Perea from an anonymous *entremés* from the sixteenth century. Presented at the 1981 Sitges Festival, it was conceived as a production for a proscenium arch but staged in a square in the town framed by the Cau Ferrat museum – the home of modernist writer and artist Santiago Rusiñol – and the Maricel de Mar museum. Here already the company could be seen to utilise the urban landscape as a creative backdrop, emphasising the distinctive qualities of the performance context. In addition, the decision to present eighteenth-century popular Catalan works which sprung from religious pageants firmly established the company's Catalan credentials, affiliating them to groups like Els Joglars and Els Comediants who had pioneered a theatrical language which established a field of resistance to the Castilianisation imposed by the Francoist state.

Their subsequent production, *Agua al siete* (Water to Room Seven) (1982), a 50–minute café-theatre piece written by Perea (who was to collaborate with Milán and Plana on the script of *La tempestad*), again relied on the existing materials of the performance space, the Jazz Drac's pub in Sitges. Within the pub's seedy surroundings, the keeper of a brothel explained details of the establishment's clientele to an enraptured public. The twelve roles were played by a cast of four setting up a

---

3 For further details of Sitges' theatrical culture, see Fàbregas 1984.

convention of inventive doubling and multiple role-play which has marked all the company's work. Indeed the production was to provide the prototype for a model of theatre which 're-appropriated' non-theatrical spaces, prioritised role over character, and stressed the theatricality of the everyday. A populist impulse has governed the company's aesthetic from the very beginning and is evident not merely in the carnivalesque influences but also from the inspiration that the company acknowledge from the *prensa rosa* (gossip magazines) whose protagonists form a particular frame of reference for a powerful demographic group of the population (Milán, cited in Navarro 1990: 7–8).

The company's first major success, *Cubana Delikatessen* (1983), evidently played out a number of these features. The twelve actions that made up the event, performed by eighteen actors, took place in public places where people going about their daily business could participate, albeit unknowingly, in the evolving performances. First presented at the Sitges Festival in 1983 to superlative reviews, the piece marked the company's transition from amateur to professional as the initial performances generated bookings that led to a two-year tour across Spain.

An analysis of the production in its Barcelona dates between 25 and 29 January 1984, as part of the Teatre Obert programme of the Centre Dramàtic de la Generalitat, provides some indication of how the actions, or 'happenings' as they were sometimes referred to, were situated in precise geographical locations at a variety of times which broke away from the established timetable of evening theatrical events. Not all the actions were performed in all cities; rather the company constructed a programme for each stage of the tour that sought to ensure that the vignettes emanated from the available public sites. In Barcelona this produced four visual actions that were seen through shop windows where ambiguity resulted from that fact that audiences could see what was going on but were unable to hear what was being said, the effect thus being of looking into a fish task. 'Autómatas' (Automation), performed on the second floor of a shop on the Portal de l'Àngel in the old town, had five actors as mannequins performing as if part of a music box that had been temporarily wound up at twenty-minute intervals. 'Ventana de arte' (Art Window) also took place in the Portal de l'Àngel in the window of upmarket clothes store Cortefiel. Here a prostitute, reclining languorously on satin pillows, sought self-gratification through the consumption of grapes, dried fruits, and cigarettes (see Figure 19). Fanning herself lethargically and indulging in phone conversations about which an audience could only speculate, the heavily made-up figure appeared to parody both the flimsily-clad women in the peepshows which litter Amsterdam's red-light district and Goya's *majas*. By masking the performer's body behind a saucy seaside cut-out, the power relations of the voyeuristic gaze were consciously subverted. There was an intended disjunction between the evocative gestures of the performer and the cartoonesque attire in which she was dressed, thus indicating how the marks of femininity are not ontological but rather performed, so that sexuality is clearly viewed as social construction.

'Voyeurs: voyez-vous', another interrogation of voyeurism and the politics of the gaze, again took place in the window of Cortefiel. Here a two-way mirror gave

19 'Ventana de arte' (Art Window) an 'action' from *Cubana Delikatessen* (1983)

the passers-by a view into adjacent changing rooms where they could watch the clients trying on different outfits assisted by store attendants. Publicity slogans repeated on a tape provided the only soundtrack. While the spectators may have seen the lip movements that gave some clue as to what was occurring, the fissure between the visual and the aural served again to frustrate traditional ways of seeing. This split between the visual and the aural was also a feature of 'Teatro por teléfono' (Theatre by Telephone), another action that allowed audiences to listen in on a phone conversation between two prostitutes where references to a range of visual activities served as a constant reminder of the fact that this dimension was inaccessible. 'La cena' (The Supper) played on the distance separating performers and spectators, as a lavish banquet where two families attired in ghostly white partook of a dinner where *foie gras* was served from a severed human head. Again here, the spectators' inability to hear what was being said served to ensure that the mystery of the diners' identities and their relation to the severed head remained undisclosed. Resolutions were, as such, never provided.

This was not the case with the vignettes that evolved in spaces where spectators were clearly implicated in the action. 'Una trampa para Teresa' (A Trap for Teresa), which took place in Carrer del Hospital, by the Romea theatre, revolved around a woman inadvertently trapped behind the shutters of a shop by the employee locking up. Attracting passers-by who inevitably speculated on how such a calamity might have happened, a veritable commotion sprang up outside the store as observers interacted with Teresa's friends who all sought to find a way of releasing her. Xavier Fàbregas reported a passer-by purchasing a cup of lime tea from a local bar and passing it to Teresa through the shutters (1984: 29). Finally a locksmith and a fireman arrived, the latter freeing her with a spectacular explosion. While Teresa, her friends, the employee who locked her in, the locksmith and fireman were played by company members, this was not immediately evident to the other spectators, as performers in La Cubana's work often take the role of onlookers.

In 'Adoquinado macrobiótico' (Macrobiotic Paving), a market stall selling curative stones was set up in the famous Boqueria market off the Ramblas. The traders sought to sell stones that they claimed cured a range of illnesses and complaints. Actors planted in the audience asked provocative questions as the traders sought to sell the magical stones. Over a space of some five hours up to 700 spectators may have passed through, stopping to listen to the narratives spun by Vicky Plana (Fondevila 1986: 29). If 'Adoquinado macrobiótico' could last up to five hours, 'Su sexo' (Her Sex) lasted a mere minute and a half. Evolving over two balconies, it featured a lover being caught red-handed by a husband returning early from work and being forced to flee through a balcony window in his underpants. If balconies once evoked the romantic pinings of Romeo and Juliet, here La Cubana showed them in a somewhat less Byronic vein: as the escape route for clandestine encounters based on deception. 'Mesa petitoria' (Begging Table) set up a table in Plaça Catalunya just opposite the Banco de España where distinguished ladies dressed in *peineta* (ornamental comb), sought to generate funds for a worthy cause – unsubsidised actors.

While Tours La Cubana may have been the event where spectators were most aware that they were entering into a game, it too played with the politics of disruption in its deconstruction of the discourse of organised tours. Tours La Cubana, coming at a time when the city was beginning to reinvent itself as an attractive and modern metropolis in its bid to host the 1992 Olympic Games, offered an ironic tourist trip around a city where company members played both earnest guides and eccentric members of a tourist party. The Barcelona presented to those who signed up (including the planted actors playing a pious Italian tourist and a Catalan nun) was not that of Gaudí and striking modernist architecture, but rather remnants of a ninth-century mosque, a fictional spa, a peasant farmer, and a florist from the Ramblas who climbed onto the bus distributing artichokes and ears of corn to all the women passengers. The passengers, all encouraged to wear their sun caps and glasses handed out in plastic bags by guides who strongly recommended holding onto the bags in case of travel sickness, were treated to a tour of the mundane – a tax payer leaving the Delegación de Hacienda (Finance building) on the Via Laetana – and the marvellous – two aristocrats dressed in ornate evening-wear having tea in period drawing room on a *parterre* in the midst of the traffic.[4] Theirs was an absurdist 'other' Barcelona that cheerfully sent up the expectations around a city tour. As with their other 'happenings', Tours La Cubana sought to examine how all social action and interaction is performative. Playfulness infiltrated a field that was once rigidly bound by form. With surroundings clearly integrated into the performance, theatre was demystified. In *Cubana Delikatessen* the mere act of gazing served to render an event performance, inferring it as an object to be scrutinised.

---

4 For further details on the realisation of the different scenarios of *Cubana Delikatessen* around Barcelona, see Badiou 1984.

La Cubana were to exploit the success of these actions in staging *saraos* for private companies throughout the mid- to late-1980s. These served as the prototype for their affiliated company, Mamá mulata (Mulatto Mother) (formed in 1998), which tailors their theatrical tricks to the demands of a corporate event or party. Like La Fura dels Baus, who have also branched out lucratively into advertising and promotion work, this arm of La Cubana's work has allowed them to survive financially in a climate which has claimed as casualties other performance groups of their generation like Zotal and Curial Teatre. La Cubana's organisation of the Sitges carnival opening and closing ceremonies in 1985, and the inauguration of the Fira de Teatre de Tàrrega (Street theatre fair of Tàrrega) in 1986, again used parody as an effective tool, integrating real personalities with fictional celebrities, in a send-up of the protocol and conventions of such ceremonies.

In 1988 La Cubana adopted a similar formula in *Cubanadas a la carta*, a selection of sequences described by critic María-José Ragué-Arias as a restaurant menu comprised of twelve dishes (1991: 29). Once more the emphasis was on presenting these actions in unexpected environments and once more, as with *Cubana Delikatessen*, the police were sometimes called in by passers-by to mediate, leading, in the case of one sequence at Calle Montera in the heart of Madrid's red-light district where a group of prostitutes were locked in a porch, to actors, prostitutes and a representative of the Ministry of Culture which had funded the event, being herded off to the local police station.[5]

These vignettes were of a participatory model. 'Vivo cantando' (I Live to Sing), for example, featured two women wandering around shops who only communicate to each other through song. 'Ya somos ricos' (Now We're Rich) had a group of ex-beggars who had won the lottery returning to their past haunts to return money to the public that had given generously while they were struggling to survive (see Figure 20). 'Solo ante el peligro' (Alone in the Face of Danger) had a series of brides turning up at the doors of a locked church. Waiting for the grooms to arrive they discussed whether the church could accommodate all the weddings. Swapping photos of their grooms they realised that the grooms are actually a single man who finally turned up to face the wrath of the brides. Protesting that there had been a terrible mistake, he was attacked by both the brides and the audience who had gathered around to see what all the commotion was about. 'Tostados a la plancha' (Roasted on the Beach), first staged at Tàrrega, created a beach on pavements where actors warned passers-by of the dangers that prolonged exposure to the sun might bring. 'Los limpias' (The Cleaners) had a series of actors in formal evening dress polishing car windscreens while 'Récord mundial' (World Record) brought together hundreds of spectators in an attempt to shatter previous records of mass balloon blowing.

Cubanadas a la carta was conceived as part of a trilogy made up also of *Cómeme el coco, negro*, and *Cubana Marathon Dancing* (1992) which summarised the three principal facets of the company's work: street theatre, metatheatre and participa-

---

5 For further details, see Montero 1989.

20 'Ya somos ricos' (Now We're Rich), an 'action' from *Cubanadas a la carta* (1988)

tory theatre. *Cubanadas a la carta* often toured with *La tempestad* and the later *Cómeme el coco, negro* in the late 1980s. Indeed sequences both from *Cubanadas a la carta* and *Cubana Delikatessen* were to play alongside *La tempestad* in London as part of LIFT 1987. 'Solo ante el peligro' was performed outside Westminster Cathedral, 'Adoquinado macrobiótico' at Rupert Street Market and 'La cena' in Reiss on Long Acre in Covent Garden.[6]

Deconstructing established theatre: *La tempestad* (1986)

As I have delineated earlier in this chapter, La Cubana followed the ruptures established by Els Joglars and Els Comediants who had earlier pioneered the use of alternative performance spaces and fractured established audience/actor configurations. Els Joglars's *Àlias Serrallonga* (1974) had seen the action evolve on three stages, which facilitated a more physical audience involvement as spectators, shepherded from stage to stage, interacted with the audience. In *M-7 Catalònia* (1978) the audience were led to believe that they were attending a conference rather than a play and were woven into the very fabric of the event. Participation in the public sphere that had so long been discouraged within Spain was here visibly encouraged, thus breaking down the respectful conventions which governed theatrical spectatorship throughout the twentieth century. Spanish critics have tended to ignore possible associations with Els Joglars, instead tracing La Cubana's pen-

6 For further details, see Culshaw 1987.

chant for site specific performance to the avant-garde 'happenings' pioneered by Allan Kaprow in 1959, which sought to present disjointed events in non-theatrical spaces for an audience's consumption. While the events were meticulously scripted and rehearsed, the impression given was that of spontaneity. Improvisation was encouraged, prising apart the boundaries of art and life as audiences moved the action forward in often unexpected ways. Milán clearly situates audiences as the protagonists in La Cubana's shows, recognising the ways in which participation can and does affect the shape of the piece (cited in Barrado 1992: 12). With *La tempestad*, the company applied the techniques acquired in *Cubana Delikatessen* to a venture that ostensibly took place within the confines of a traditional proscenium-arch theatre.

Crafted by Milán, Plana and Perea, the piece has been judged by Catalan critic Mercè Saumell to be part of a re-theatricalisation of traditional spaces that was to increasingly mark the company's work since the mid-1980s with the text, in effect, becoming 'a pretext for decodifying a series of theatrical situations inside a conventional theatre' (1996: 125). The show began innocuously enough with a staging of Shakespeare's *The Tempest* in José María Valverde's Castilian translation performed within a slightly raked traditional proscenium-arch stage. The photographs in the programme of the performers striking actorly poses in period dress complete with false biographies lulled the audience into a false sense of security. The leaden, emphatic acting style clearly sought to suggest an approach of reverent importance towards the work, reinforcing associations of the Bard as a symbol of 'high art' to be worshipped by spectators who pay for the privilege of listening to his inspired theatre. Members of the company disguised as paying punters sought to deflate this pretentious aspiration towards a definitive aesthetic by arriving late and removing their wet outer garments in the aisle, burping, coughing, snoring and noisily devouring sweets.

Following Prospero's expository explanation to Miranda, as the latter lies sleeping by his side, the audience became aware that the tempest conjured by Prospero (significantly played by the production's director Milán) to shipwreck his brother Antonio's ship, had actually engulfed the theatre. A heavy storm supposedly raging outside the building was causing rain to drip from the roof and, as darkness enveloped the auditorium, the audience were told that the performance was to be cancelled because of severe weather conditions. Forced to don colour-coded plastic macs tied to their seats, the audience were warned that the raging tempest was not merely afflicting the theatre but all of the surrounding areas and that they would be obliged to undertake emergency survival procedures until the theatre could be evacuated. A simulated tempest was taking place in and around the theatre with power cuts, rolls of thunder, 'backcloths collapsing, scuffles in the aisles and, in the best touch of the evening, a befrocked figure seen clinging on to the dress-circle rail while suspended over the stalls' (Billington 1987: 28). Emergency lights came on and theatre staff – ushers, ticket sellers, toilet attendants – were called in to assist the audience. The emergency drill was co-ordinated by a brusquely efficient representative of a Red-Cross-like organisation. Cast members, like Ariel, indicated where the lavatories could be found and provided blow-up dolls to provide some kind of comfort to distressed audience members.

The audience was split into groups that could engage in any number of activities organised to bolster moral. A Festival Folclórico del Diluvio (Folkloric Rain Festival) allowed for the singalong of relevant numbers, and television screens transmitted reports of the ravages of the tempest in the area – in Catalonia this featured a well-known TV presenter Florencio Solchaga further serving to authenticate the company narrative of a destructive tempest wreaking havoc on the surrounding environment. Swimming lessons were offered. Mattresses were brought in for the audience to spend the night on. A confessional was provided for those who feared the end might be nigh, with a priest available for those who wanted to arrange a wedding while there was still time. A Red Cross emergency hospital dispensed medical assistance while a tombola provided entertainment for those determined to have a good time despite the appalling meteorological conditions.

All these events took place in the inner recesses of the theatre, a space habitually inaccessible to the audience. At the end of the evening a large, yellow submarine dangled down from the ceiling as part of a rescue operation. As the audience left the theatre to the sound of The Beatles' 'Yellow Submarine', they were greeted by the wind machines that were conjuring the tempest. Jordi Milán, both Prospero and the director of the production, here had his status as all-powerful stage manager doubly reinforced by his dual roles. This was an irreverent deconstruction both of the conventions that govern Shakespeare production and of a theatre-going process that allows the audience to seek security in the darkened anonymity of their seats. Resituating the frame of theatre, the audience clearly became the base around which the action revolved. They may have attended the performance as voyeurs but the inversion of habitual theatrical rules ensured that it was they who were participating in the creation of the theatrical event.

The production, opening at the Retiro theatre as part of the Sitges Festival in April 1986, went on to play at Barcelona's Romea theatre and Madrid's Sala Olimpia later that year before embarking on a tour of other Spanish cities. Spanish critics were to judge the show risky but rewarding (Pérez de Olaguer 1986b: 56), recognising that the pleasure experienced depended to a large extent on the degree of audience participation (Monleón 1986b: vii). El País' Eduardo Haro Tecglen, while citing the influence of happenings on the venture, was admiring of the company's technique (1986b: 38). ABC's Lorenzo López Sancho, reviewing the show during its Madrid performances at the Sala Olimpia's Centro Nacional de Nuevas Tendencias Escénicas (National Centre of New Scenic Tendencies), however, argued that this was hackneyed material seen all too often before in 1960s happenings and inappropriate for a venue which purported to be staging cutting-edge work (1986c: 87). British critics, commenting on the piece during its controversial run at Sadler's Wells theatre for LIFT 1987, were on the whole dismissingly disparaging about the staging. The Guardian's Michael Billington referred to it suspiciously as 'Catalonian camp' (1987: 28), while Anthony Looch in the Daily

Telegraph described it in unequivocal terms as the worst theatrical experience of his life (1987: 10). For many reviewers the production was inseparable from the scandal that followed the first night performance on 13 July when complaints from local residents to Islington council resulted in the council ordering the company to cut the final minutes of the show (where the audience spilled out onto the pavement outside the theatre to face the simulated tempest, to the sound of raging police sirens and a suspected fire). The cars along Rosebery Avenue, reported *El Público*'s Nicolás Sola, stopping to see what the commotion was all about, were accused of causing extensive traffic jams (1987: 56–7). Such a traffic build-up, along with the commotion that resulted from the audience rushing out from the theatre, was judged to be a public nuisance by the Council. When a compromise couldn't be reached, Sadler's Wells was obliged to close the production rather than face losing its licence.[7] The cancellation served further to bind La Cubana to a Catalan tradition of anarchic performance that had met problems with a censorious British bureaucracy in earlier years – both La Fura dels Baus and Els Comediants had suffered a similar fate during previous London outings.

Cómeme el coco, negro: Backstage music-hall

Jordi Milán, director de La Cubana, sostiene que cualquier teatrero ha deseado algún día ponerse una mochila de plumas y actuar en el escenario al ritmo de una música de 'swing'. (Pérez de Olaguer 1989: 41)

(Jordi Milán, the director of La Cubana, argues that any theatre maker has wanted at some point to place a plume headdress on and perform on a stage to the rhythm of a swing tune.)

The company's next full length production, *Cómeme el coco, negro* opened in a specially constructed marquee at Barcelona's Mercat de les Flors on 3 June 1989, following a company restructuring which was to see Plana leave the company and Milán emerge as *de facto* artistic director. Originally conceived as a portrait of the internal dynamics of La Cubana, the show soon evolved into a homage to the music-hall revues of companies like el Teatro Chino de Manolita Chen's (Manolita Chen's Chinese Theatre) and Teatro Argentina, as well as the popular theatres of Barcelona's Paral.lel, El Molino and El Arnau or Zaragoza's Oasis.[8] Interestingly El Molino performer Xus Estruch was Milán's assistant director on the piece and Juan de la Prada, for many years the musical director of El Molino, crafted six of the production's musical numbers. Joan-Anton Benach's review of *Cómeme el coco, negro* mentioned the visit of the Teatro Chino de Manolita Chen in Barcelona during December 1973, replete with a *melange* of oriental ballets and bastardised flamenco

---

7   For further details, see Anon. 1987a and Attwood and Kartal 1987. The Spanish newspapers also covered the controversy but were rather partisan in their evaluation of the English critics in arguing that the one London performance had been an unequivocal critical and commercial success; see, for example, Anon. 1987b.

8   For further details, see Montero 1989.

dance (1989: 41). *ABC*'s Lorenzo López Sancho evoked the celebrated acts of El Molino – Mirko, Pepita Blanco, Carmen Cuenca and Bella Dorita – in locating prototypes for La Cubana's revue (1989b: 115). The companies and venues recalled by Benach and López Sancho juxtaposed magic acts with tangos, *cuplés*, antiphonal comedy sketches, interrupted monologues, jugglers, ventriloquists, and well-known numbers from *zarzuelas* (Spanish operettas). Flourishing during the Franco regime, which tended to focus its censorious gaze around the amount of cleavage revealed by the women's costumes, their generic formula allowed for a firm degree of audience participation whilst simultaneously evoking the seedy decaying landscape of a post-Civil War Spain ideologically trapped in the past.[9] As early as 1970, Tábano Teatro had employed the format of el Teatro Chino de Manolita Chen as the framework for their *Castañuela 70* (Castanet 70), which used an episodic revue structure to satirise the conservatism of Spanish society.[10] La Cubana's revisiting of the genre may have been in less politically contentious times, but it effectively probed both the dynamics of the genre and its problematic associations with regard to race and gender which had escaped Tábano's treatment.

Using variety as a framing device, La Cubana were re-conceived as Teatro Cubano de Revista (The Cubana Vaudeville Theatre), a musical review company now past their prime. The exterior of the Mercat de les Flors was redecorated as a fairground booth with flashing lights, and tired, gaudy posters that greeted the audience on their arrival. The audience arrived for what they believed was a 10.00 p.m. start only to be told by an increasingly irritated company manager (Jordi Milán) that that the show had actually begun at 9.00 p.m. and that the venue had given the wrong timetable to the press resulting in a misprint on the tickets. Diffusing audience discontent and shepherding them into the auditorium he led them to believe that there was only half an hour of the show left to run. On a tawdry set that had seen better days, the vaudeville show was seen to be in full swing, parading a diverse assortment of variety acts. The cast of twelve presented over forty characters. From the torch song singer belting out a number on strategies for survival and strength in a world where the path of love rarely runs smoothly, to a folkloric singer, Nieves Blanco, in a stiff crinoline wired black dress decorated with large red flowers, matching *peineta* and fan rendering a theatrical version of 'María de las Mercedes' as she slid across the stage like a hefty barge, this was a stage world of swaying painted backdrops, well-worn red curtains, and formulaic routines. The aptly named Martín España, evoking Antonio Molina, sang 'Soy minero' (I'm a Miner) with grand gestures in a lurid sky-blue sparkling shirt; a trio of buxom blondes decked in platinum wigs danced around the stage; a Brazilian carnival routine led by Paulina São Paulo and her troupe of skimpily dressed male dancers clad in orange and black sambaed across the front of the stage.

This was a company where each performer had their allocated role: a comic *vedette* (starlet), an exotic *vedette*, the super *vedette* who now trades on her glory

---

9 For further details on this type of music-hall work, see García Pintado 1980.
10 For further details, see Tábano/Las madres del cordero 1970.

years, the male and female chorus. A short sketch led by the comic *vedette* Mari Merche Otero presented a bickering family who have invited their daughter's Kenyan boyfriend to dinner. Arriving in blackface, the latter's rampant sexuality wreaked havoc on the evening's plans, confirming Mari Merche's worst unarticulated fears. Mother and boyfriend danced a frenzied Charleston before the daughter arrived to say that she now has a new Valencian boyfriend. The super *vedette* Lidia Clavel led the grand finale, an extravaganza of sequined bejewelled costumes, glittering tiaras, and ostentatious plumes which filled the tiny ramshackle stage with exuberant verve.

The programme further reinforced the metatheatrics of the piece. Cast biographies were dispensed with in favour of a pictorial programme with photographs of the fictional company stars complete with their stage names and demarcated roles. As such when the 'revue' ended, the audience were left unsure as to what their next move should be. Initially, the actors peeped through the curtains to see if the audience were still there. Gradually they appeared on stage announcing that they had to perform in Santiago tomorrow so the set would have to be dismantled whether the audience were still there or not. Consequently, the second part of the production effectively began with the stripping of the theatrical facade. Curtains were pulled down and folded with the audience's assistance (see Figure 21). The internal politics of the company were revealed as the ageing star Lidia Clavel resented Nieves making her fold curtains when it was the chorus's responsibility to do so. Lidia, keen to maintain her position at the hierarchical pinnacle of the company, played up to the audience, singing while the stage was pulled down around her. Nieves accused a male company member of stealing her false eyelashes. Discord reigned when individual company members placed their own interests above those of the task in hand: the packing up of the show.

21 The departing music-hall company folds up curtains with the audience's help in *Cómeme el coco, negro* (1989)

A chain of audience members was assembled to help load the props and stage machinery into the van waiting outside the theatre. The romance of life on the road was visibly deflated as the characters recounted tales of hurried get-outs and get-ins. Gossip effused from the troupe as they confided in the audience about the stinginess of Mari Merche – confirmed as the latter comes on stage asking the audience for a twenty-five peseta piece to make a call – Lidia's refusal to grow old gracefully and the male genitalia of Lidia's dog Gunilla. Sandwiches were ordered and shared amongst the audience, the two wardrobe mistresses donned plumes as they pontificated on the allure of stage feathers. The daughter of one of the wardrobe mistresses arrived with Gunilla, shyly revealing how she babysat the dog. Aspiring to be an artiste, she gave a slow-motion demonstration of one of the numbers which had been effortlessly performed during the show. The crafting of the illusion was therefore rendered before our eyes. Members of the audience were draped in plumes and brought onto what remained of the stage to participate in a choral number. As with the backstage musical, the emphasis was on a theatrical community coming together, only here it was not to put on a show but rather to dismantle it. And indeed, as the stage was pulled apart, the artifice of theatre was visibly deconstructed.

The metatheatrics allowed both entry for the audience into a backstage world whose glamour and fame were effectively dissected and, where they themselves, in the words of one reviewer, were made to feel that they play a part in the survival of theatre (Avilés 1990: 32). Generic conventions were prised apart. The work undertaken by the troupe was effectively deglamourised as the company was shown to be a social and economic institution. The wardrobe mistresses revealed how they put the costumes together, justifying the pervasive number of yellow plumes in terms of their reduced cost – the colour is superstitiously regarded within the Catalan theatrical world as bad luck.[11] Rampant individualism was frowned on as the theatrical body was shown to be more effective when working as a team. In *Cómeme el coco, negro*, el Teatro Cubano de Revista demonstrated the ways in which both pre- and post-production preparations form part of the theatrical event.

Baz Kershaw has indicated how blackface minstrelsy – 'the spectacle of a white person blacking-up his (or her) face and pretending to be a person of colour' – can appear 'inevitably racist, an expression of white supremacy: an unambiguously oppressive misuse of cultural power' (1999: 140–1). Kershaw has located blackface minstrelsy as 'part of the wider histories of Empire, colonialism, and slavery' (141) and indeed La Cubana's fictional biography of el Teatro Cubano de Revista presented the company as the product of a coloniser who returned to Spain having made his fortune in Cuba, forming a company with performers he brought back with him. As the performers aged and the impresario died, so a new generation of Spanish performers took their place. Blackface thus coincided with the loss of Empire symbolised by 1898. The actor in blackface (playing the Kenyan boyfriend) functioned as a com-

11 It is also used significantly in *Cegada de amor*, see 251. For further details on yellow as an unlucky colour within the Catalan stage, see Villar de Queiroz 2000: 209.

ment on the politics of Empire that provided caricatured portrayals of black artistes unproblematically accepted during the era of these itinerant companies.

The performance of blackface in *Cómeme el coco, negro* was also, to use Kershaw's terminology, about the '"inversion" of inversion' in that 'the lowly performers – white common people – symbolically lower their status – partly identifying with black common people – to produce a vulnerability that participated in the marginality of both and simultaneously promoted their combined strengths' (1999: 143).[12] The blackface sequence in *Cómeme el coco, negro* both challenged and unsettled liberal assumptions about the institutional racism prevalent in Spain, linking it to colonial expansion in Spanish America (where these companies both originated and peddled their wares). Actor Santi Millán offered a distorted figure, exaggeratedly made up with a wild wig, huge red lips and poorly applied black make-up. A bold checked shirt, green blazer and trousers that were clearly too short for him provided the concept of a constructed image: the white man's projection of a black man. Hackneyed stereotypes around black men's unrestrained sexuality were interrogated as La Cubana, following the dramatic strategy of The Wooster Group, appropriated the convention to provide a critique of racism: 'the blackface does not designate a real black persona but indicates that a theatrical convention is being deployed, a performance style which frees the performer to revel not in social reality, but in its unreality' (Savran 1988: 31). If colonialism is ultimately about control and submission, the Spanish family were unable to constrain the black mask. La Cubana made no attempt to efface the problematic gender and racial politics of such vaudeville routines. Racism and sexism are profoundly inscribed within Spanish culture. Their symbols cannot easily be erased; rather they are there to be mediated, interpreted and challenged by audiences. In addition, the emphasis throughout the production on disguise – the *vedettes* negotiated high-coiffured wigs which delineated their status as exotic other (Paulina São Paulo) and company sex symbol (Lidia Clavel), the male performers sported a range of manicured wigs – served to break down the binary categories around which so many social and cultural definitions are structured. The black mask worn by Santi Millán was displayed as a mask demonstrating how an interplay of theatrical surfaces can question notions of colour and race. The multiple doubling that took place – some actors played up to four roles encompassing different age ranges and character types – frustrated any attempts to 'bond' with an individual character as protagonist. The doubling executed by blackface minstrelsy is, according to theatre historian Joseph Roach, about hybrid performance, one actor wearing 'two distinct masks – the mask of blackness on the surface and the mask of whiteness underneath' (1995: 54). La Cubana have consistently provided a theatre of masks that performs the absence of a fixed identity. In *Cómeme el coco, negro* the persona of the actors was never disclosed as the performance ended with company members either departing for Santiago de Compostela or handing out *churros* (Spanish doughnuts) and hot chocolate to the audience on the latter's departure from the theatre.

12 Kershaw takes his argument from Cockrell 1997: 141.

Press reviews judged *Cómeme el coco, negro* an ingenious and witty dissection of the music-hall formula and the finest Cubana production to date (Pérez de Olaguer 1989: 40–3; Sagarra 1989a: 46). The initial sold-out dates at the Mercat de les Flors were followed by a longer run in early 1990 at the Victòria theatre – sandwiched rather appropriately on the Paral.lel between the Apolo and El Molino – , and a later transfer in April of that year to the old Capitol cinema, where it proved the city's most commercially successful production of the year seen by 99,596 spectators (Pérez de Olaguer 1991a: 54). Arriving for a run at Madrid's Nuevo Apolo theatre in November 1989, the company announced their entrance in the city by embarking on a publicity stunt in the midst of the city's main thoroughfare, Paseo de la Castellana, offering the bemused drivers a range of musical numbers.[13] If *Ya*'s Alberto de la Hera was slightly less exuberant in his praise of the production than his Catalan contemporaries, judging the variety routines rather passé, he still recognised the venture as a theatrical tour de force (1989: 60). An extensive Spanish tour in 1991 often had the company arriving in a city to great fanfare and dismounting from a bus or a series of cars in full costume to undertake press conferences as the Teatro Cubano de Revista.[14] The production returned to Barcelona from 18 July to 31 August 1991, undergoing a number of transformations during its run at the gardens of the Gran Casino, including ex Joglar Jesús Agelet appearing as a formally-attired compere, and the revelation of a 'hidden' set of different stages which appeared at the end of the show presenting some of the ideas refined in the company's next piece, *Cubana Marathon Dancing*. While the period Eivissa orchestra (where half of the musicians proved to be mannequins) perched on one stage provided the music, dance classes, the possibility of renting a dance partner, and an array of 1960s style singers resplendent in outrageous outfits kept the party swinging well into the night.[15] In September of that year the production closed at the Havana Theatre Festival, the show's only dates outside Spain.[16] Seen by 484,500 spectators in Spain in its 535 performances, with a CD of its songs released on the PD1 label in June 1990, its imaginative use of the rhetorical conventions of revue performance secured it both critical appreciation and sell-out runs across Spain over a two year period. Unlike a number of their contemporaries in the independent theatre, La Cubana had succeeded in utilising popular genres to populist participatory ends.

1992 and all that: *Cubana Marathon Dancing* (1992)

Un baile similar a *Danzad, danzad, malditos*, pero a la catalana. (Milán, cited in Luengo 1990: 7)

(A dance similar to *They Shoot Horses, Don't They?* [dir. Sydney Pollack, 1969], but Catalan style.)

13 For further details, see P. 1989 and Montero 1989.
14 For further details, see Pavón 1991 and Villamandos 1990.
15 For further details of all the changes, see Fondevila 1991.
16 For further details of the company's visit to Cuba, see Durán 1991.

La Cubana's next production, *Cubana Marathon Dancing*, was conceived for the three large cultural events of 1992, the Olympic Arts Festival (Olimpiada Cultural) in Barcelona, Madrid's programme as European City of Culture and Seville's Expo (Molina 1991: 56). While the latter two events eventually declined to participate as co-producers, the piece was prepared for the Festival de les Arts directed by Mario Gas as part of Barcelona's Olympic celebrations. Written by Milán, Santi Millán and José Corbacho, it opened at the Mercat de les Flors on 2 July 1992, running for twenty-two performances with a cast of over eighty musicians, dancers and performers.

In *Cubana Marathon Dancing* La Cubana were once more re-imagined as a mutated entity, but, as fitting with the thrusting commercial ethos of 1992, as a North American multinational, Cubana Incorporated, about to establish an office in Barcelona, whose diverse interests ranged from condoms to construction. Rather than recruiting personnel through more established means, they chose to hold a twelve-hour dance marathon that sought to weed out those who lacked the stamina, drive and ambition to survive in the corporate climate personified by Cubana Incorporated. Cubana Incorporated staff dressed in sanitised 1940s-style white uniforms accessorised with red trim, and marked by outlandish 'twinset and pearl' type jet-black wigs and horn-rimmed glasses, described by *ABC*'s Núria Cuadrado as occupying a style somewhere between futurism and Almodovaresque (1992: xv), patrolled the premises both physically and virtually, from giant video screens which provided potted histories of the organisation.

On entering the Mercat, the participants – numbering up to 1,000 a night – were classified numerically. Handed a giant number to drape over their heads and across their chests and backs and a plastic bag which contained ammunition for the evening ahead in the form of a glucose lollypop, their watches were taped up so that they could no longer slavishly adhere to 'individual' time but rather be governed by the 'communal' time represented by two giant clocks positioned in the central performance space. The materialist benefits of working for Cubana Incorporated were lavishly laid out for the participants in a window display of ostentatious excess that evoked television quiz shows. The circular venue had a central dance arena where the participants were herded in anticipation of the commencement of the dance marathon, and elevated platforms mysteriously covered by white curtains that opened to reveal to the discerning dancer a range of services in partitioned booths. Health checks were offered in the form of supervised balloon blowing to measure lung capacity; a massage parlour saw the purveying of brutal pummelling on unsuspecting members of the public and imaginative advice on diet and how it affects the feet; a foot clinic provided advice on whether the shoes being worn would withstand a long dance marathon, with the possibility of being fitted for new shoes; for those arriving alone twenty-five pesetas could secure temporary rental of a dance partner from an array of different sized models; a smoking room allowed those who needed a nicotine fix to inhale away while continuing to dance without contaminating the other participants; a colourful bar, stocked high with bottles, and serviced by flamboyantly attired staff, administered a range of water cocktails, further reinforcing the multinational's slavishly held belief that all artificial stimulants were prohibited in the unblemished culture of Cubana Incorporated. A supple dance teacher shared the secrets of his craft with willing participants who were given the chance to brush up on rusty routines. Videos projected on giant screens told of the rewards granted to those working for Cubana Incorporated while staff from the organisation marching on the platform stage to the tune of jaunty anthems gave the participants practical advice on how to withstand the rigours of a lengthy dance marathon with simple exercise routines designed to increase stamina. Fights breaking out amongst the participants and mishaps suffered by over-enthusiastic dancers who had to be carried from the venue on stretchers were all orchestrated and stage-managed by Cubana actors planted among the spectator-participants.

As the dance marathon commenced, the Eivissa orchestra, made up both of human musicians and mannequins, kicked off a journey through popular dance music accompanied by a range of eccentrically-clad guest singers who made their way through a repertoire of well-known numbers. Mambo singers with expansive gestures and ill-fitting wigs, *pasodoble* Latin artistes with ominously hairy chests performing an amusing variation on the *cha, cha, cha*, a suave crooner who emerged from a giant, gliding birthday cake offered a veritable contrast to the gangly male singer dressed in a striped boating jacket and sporting an improbably retro hairstyle. Representing the different regions of Spain, Luisita González del Moral gave a flavour of Catalan song while Miguelito de Altequera, dressed in a gold-sequined take on the Andalusian *señorito*, rendered a flamboyant version of 'Mi Jaca' (My Horse) and the appropriately named Manolita de Córdoba, smothered in pink and black ruffles, provided a suitably anguished rendition of the popular folkloric number 'No te vayas de Navarra' (Don't Leave Navarre). In a year where, as John Hooper has astutely observed, Spain was seeking to make a 'spectacular re-entry' into the international arena 'after the isolation of the Franco years' (1995: 69), these regional singers served to interrogate how the 'performance' of Spain remained attached to outdated clichés of fiery *señoritas* and macho Latin crooners. In a token nod to Spain's position within Europe, a *coloratura* soprano, a male tenor's operatic waltz and a German drinking song offered further musico-cultural dimensions of European high and popular art to challenge and divert the audience.

As the dance marathon was in full flow, the Los Angeles-based president of Cubana Incorporated, Mr Matthew, appeared to the sound of an upbeat company anthem espousing the virtues of a commercialist ethos where the participants were encouraged to sing along (the lyrics graphically projected onto a large video screen). Balloons dropped from the ceiling and flags flew about the dance arena as Matthew and his suitably glamorous consort made their way across the dance floor throwing money to the participants and urging them to pledge their support to the organisation. The moment served as the culmination to a production that had satirised a shallow 'one size fits all' global culture where any slogan fits any cause. Appropriating and re-contextualising the language of sanitised advertising, the festive event articulated veritable doubts about both the PSOE's avid encouragement of international monetarist investment in Spain whatever the local cost and the preparations for the Olympics which had seen hundreds of prostitutes and transvestites herded out of town in the hope of 'cleaning' up the centre of the city.[17]

At the press conference for the production, held appropriately at the Hotel Havana a week before *Cubana Marathon Dancing* opened, Jordi Milán addressed journalists on three television screens with regard to La Cubana's takeover by Cubana Incorporated. He was then interrupted by a member of the latter company watching over the proceedings who warned the journalists that they ought to be careful about what they reported for they might find themselves owned by Cubana Incorporated and out of a job if their reports failed to find favour with the corporation (Cuadrado 1992: xv). This was a multinational whose aims and aspirations remained opaque. Resembling shop mannequins, their regimentalised staff spouted jargonistic sound-bites for participants fluent in the discourses of a commercial buy-and-sell culture. During *Cubana Marathon Dancing* the culture of ominous surveillance represented by Cubana Incorporated saw dismembered voices emanating from the giant loudspeakers, urging the participants to continue dancing. This culture was unwittingly exposed by Manolita de Córdoba when she asked the organisation who had just presented her with a giant birthday cake how they knew it was her birthday. The ominous reply made clear that it was Cubana Incorporated's business to know everything about her. Her protests were drowned out by a company voice making clear that whether it is her birthday or not is immaterial, they have designated the date her birthday and she is expected to follow the celebrations prepared by Cubana Incorporated.

The circular arena in which the dance marathon took place shares characteristics of Michel Foucault's panopticon, the prison structure whereby power is exercised both through surveillance and the self-regulation that this generates. The theatrical cells in which Foucault's subjects are trapped were here realised through the carceral culture of vigilant observation that the mysterious Cubana Incorporated enact.[18] *Cubana Marathon Dancing* became an object lesson in how all social action is performed. All the participants were confined to an imprisoning culture of visibility where constant observation left them subject to a disciplinary ethos. The giant video screen that greeted participants on arrival into the dance hall documented the rise of Cubana Incorporated into a multinational with a 15,000 workforce worldwide. Employees described the misery of their existences pre-Cubana Incorporated and extolled the virtues of working for this sharing, caring organisation. Loudspeakers echoed big brother messages of the benefits of adherence to the corporation's ethos. Along a giant catwalk pristine dancers offered slick demonstrations of perfectly co-ordinated, almost mechanised movements to which the participants below in their crowded quarters could only aspire. At a time when Spain was seeking acceptance within the structures of the European Union, attempting to bolster her credentials through 1992's Olympics, Expo and European Capital of Culture showcases, *Cubana Marathon Dancing* warned of the

---

17 For further details on the clean-up operation for the Olympics, see Bruce 1992.
18 For further details on the panopticon, see Foucault 1985: 170–228.

dangers of seeking to embrace a sanitised global culture where the local traditions were sacrificed, prostituted or reworked to fit the demands of the larger organisational body. 1992 marked the beginnings of a recession that the Socialist government, hoping to capitalise on the high economic growth which had followed Spain's entry into the European Union, had been seeking to camouflage.[19]

Cubana Incorporated may have promised the dance marathon participants a future of material comforts and emotional satisfaction within the confines of its extended family, but the production's ending served to question a culture of absolutes where the excesses of power (like greed and corruption) are decisively masked. The *deus ex machina* finale, where a giant explosion, evocative of an earthquake, caused the lights to dramatically go out, may have recalled the company's earlier *La tempestad* but this was to prove no tempest. Rather it was a kitsch re-imagining of the end of the world with cardboard painted clouds holding singing angels and cherubs announcing that the participants could now choose a life in the heavens or in hell opening up at the other side of the dance hall. In the style of Els Comediants' *Dimonis* (*Devils*) (1982), devils and angels playfully led a conga that divided the audience into opposing halves of the hall. A parody of evangelical broadcasts which promise life everlasting in spectacular fashion, here the afterlife turned out to be a camp musical extravaganza where the icons of hell proved as alluring as those of the heavens.

Cubana Marathon Dancing is, in many ways, La Cubana's most political show to date, in that it questioned the politics of international investment that marked the boom years of the late 1980s by envisaging an ominous multi-corporation spreading its evangelistic tentacles into Catalonia. During the Olympic euphoria, as multinationals were pouring into Barcelona, La Cubana questioned the long-term wisdom of an unquestioning embrace of foreign interests. In addition, Cubana Incorporated's crusading zeal, as noted by *ABC*'s Pablo Ley (1992: ix), owes much to the US-style religious television broadcasts which feature across the cable channel network. In the immediate aftermath of the introduction of privately owned channels to a Spanish television network which had, until 1989, been controlled by the state, La Cubana may have been both commenting on TVE (Televisión Española), established as a state monopoly and mouthpiece in 1956, and warning of the insidious programme content of privately-owned channels embroiled in the necessary commercial battle for ratings.[20]

The production had initially been scheduled to run at the Mercat de les Flors from 18 June to 9 August. The Festival de les Arts had originally agreed to fund it to the tune of twenty-five million of the forty-one million peseta production budget. As the Mercat quibbled over the originally agreed company get-in date of 1 June, and a compromise space at the old Born market could not be used because of double bookings, La Cubana, fearing substantial financial losses which could not be made up during a short run, withdrew their participation, making clear their

---

19 On the recession, see Hooper 1995: 68–81.
20 For further details on Spanish television during this time, see Hooper 1995: 306–21.

dismay at a festival which was tottering amidst disagreements between the Olimpiada Cultural and the Ajuntament (City Council).[21] An arrangement was finally reached with the Grec Festival which agreed to come on board as a further co-producer. The budgetary constraints that had threatened the project may have played a part in La Cubana's decision to use the piece to articulate questions around the possible dismantling of official funding sources for oppositional artistic practices. While the show was technically admired by El Periódico's Gonzalo Pérez de Olaguer (1992: 66), El País' Sagarra judged the script inferior to that of Cómeme el coco, negro (1992a: 30). Perhaps critical reservations may, in part, have been due to the production's refusal to endorse the jubilant spirit that officials expected from artistic bodies associated with the 1992 celebrations. The production, nevertheless, proved a spectacular commercial success, attracting around a thousand spectator-participants per performance with a televised version screened on Canal 33 on 10 October of the same year. La Fura dels Baus and Els Comediants may have grabbed the international headlines with a 3.5 billion audience for their choreographed performances within the opening and closing ceremonies of the Olympics on 25 July and 9 August, but it was La Cubana who dissected the problematic implications of 'belonging' to cultural and political global infrastructures in the democratic era.[22]

Neither truth nor lie: *Cegada de amor* (1994)

Motifs around identity were also to dominate La Cubana's next production, *Cegada de amor*. Conceived and rehearsed during 1993, the show involved the recruitment of new performers as Milán had lost three key collaborators since *Cubana Marathon Dancing*: the actress Carme Montornés who had died in September of that year and Mont Plans and Mercè Comas who were then working with other companies (Pérez de Olaguer 1993: 53). Preparations were shrouded in secrecy with select press releases offering indications of a further mutation of the company from the Cubana Incorporated of *Cubana Marathon Dancing* to Cubana Films. The information 'leaked' to the press in late 1993 referred to renowned Spanish filmmaker Fernando Colomo directing a film titled *Cegada de amor* alongside Milán and another screen director titled Antonio Valdivieso with a fictional cast including Pepa Castro and Rosita Alfaro. With a screenplay by Joaquim Oristrell, Milán and Cubana performer José Corbacho, the film was supposedly to be shot in December 1993 at Poblenou's Gala Studios, a month before the scheduled premiere of the film at the Tívoli theatre. A carefully managed press conference three days prior to the production's opening presented an elaborate biography of the thirty-nine year old Valdivieso with a filmography of cinematic works including *Crucigrama de amores/Crossword of Love*, *Torero Cha-cha-cha/Bullfighter Cha-cha-cha*, *La Virgen travesti/The Transvestite Virgin* and *El nudo/The Knot*. The titles of these films and

21 For further details, see Fondevila 1992, Antón 1992 and Pons 1994.
22 For further information on La Fura dels Baus' and Els Comediants' participation within the Olympic Games, see Saumell 2001: 305–21.

claims made about Valdivieso's international profile served, alongside the director's flamboyant personality, to firmly position him as an Almodóvar clone.

The production's Barcelona opening on 28 January proved a glitzy event bringing together the great and good of the overlapping worlds of Catalan theatre and film, including Joan Font of Els Comediants, El Tricicle, La Fura dels Baus, actress Teresa Gimpera and filmmaker Ventura Pons. Avidly reported in the press as 'el Tívoli a lo Hollywood' (Pérez de Olaguer 1994b: 57) (Tívoli Hollywood style), it served both to indicate the kudos that the Cubana now enjoyed and to construct the illusion of a high-profile film premiere. Fictional performer résumés in the programme further reinforced the illusion of a backstage film drama populated by performers, the director, producer, their next of kin, and the extended family – the behind-the-scenes crew who ensure that, whatever calamities ensue, the show goes on.

Audience members were escorted into the auditorium by dutiful ushers, disguised members of the company handing out 3–D heart-shaped glasses in pink and green. Those who arrived asking when the show would begin were firmly informed that this was a cinema screening. Indeed *Cegada de amor* began as a film replete with opulent kitsch opening credits laying out the production's baroque aesthetic redolent of 1950s Hollywood movies' day-glo palette of colours. The film told the tale of Estrellita, a 'young' girl from La Mancha, who meets the goofy Jean-François, a French medical student, while on holiday in Barcelona. Their romance leads Estrellita to Paris where Jean-François throws a birthday party for her at his groovy Paris apartment, designed in geometric shapes that lend it the air of an animated chessboard. When her lavish three-tier birthday cake is brought in, a freak accident occurs as droppings from the dove hidden in the top tier of the cake blind her. It is following this incident, as the ageing Estrellita storms off the set at the indignity of being blinded by birdshit, that the audience realised that it had been watching the shooting of a musical romance. The backstage action reveals Estrellita to be a tantrum-throwing actress pushing fifty who has been bought out of retirement by flamboyant director Antonio Valdivieso who is himself romantically involved with Jaime Blanchard, the Franco-Spanish actor who plays Estrellita's love interest, Jean-François. Valdivieso, accompanied on set by his opinionated mother, Doña Trinidad Cordillo, replete in twin set and horn-rimmed glasses, tries to placate the outraged Estrellita but she remains closeted in her dressing room with her entourage (antiquated nanny Lolita, dishevelled make-up-artist Glòria and ageing camp hairdresser Jesús). Doña Trinidad pays her a timely visit but her efforts to flatter the star fail to soothe the hysterical Estrellita. With Estrellita's personal groomers, Valdivieso and Antònia, the head cleaner, loitering outside Estrellita's dressing room in search of novel gossip, the arrival of Estrellita's manager and lover, producer Andrew Marçal, throws a new spanner into the works. He brings with him the results of Estrellita's pregnancy test. Their conversation makes clear that this is not her first pregnancy but now Estrellita wants to keep the baby. As Marçal is wedded, to the much evoked but ever absent Eulàlia Casademunt, marriage to Estrellita is not an option. Marçal's solution involves marrying off Estrellita to his clownish son Jorgito Luis. At the official engagement photograph Estrellita clandestinely slips Jaime a note, informing him that he is the father of her unborn child and hoping that, once their work on the film is over, they can elope together. The 'backstage' on-screen antics were progressively mirrored by 'offstage' antics in the cinema. As the production team prepared to resume shooting, audience commotion in the auditorium of the Tívoli escalated. A middle-aged spectator armed with a protective handbag, Juanita Rigombei, who had earlier been re-seated by the weary ushers because she had been molested by the man next to her, noisily launched a fresh complaint. An elderly usher and the theatre cleaner, Rosario, attempted to find a solution. Two football hooligans who had been lewdly offering asides on the intrigues of the narrative, sending up any artistic pretensions the film might aspire to, also decided to get involved. An indignant spectator, Paquito, who had been complaining when the film switched from Castilian to Catalan, was not soothed by the subtitles that had appeared on-screen to placate his accusations, and switched his complaints to Rosario and the usher who were frenetically attempting to re-seat the agitated Juanita. The increasingly irritated actors and crew on-screen peered into the auditorium to try and quell the commotion so that shooting could resume. Paquito stood in disgust as Marçal addressed the spectators in Catalan and was not placated by Marçal's comments in Castilian that Spain is a state made up of different nations. Calls to silence come to nothing and finally in desperation the director's domineering mother, the formidable Doña Trinidad, burst through the screen and onto the stage. Dragging the disruptive Juanita into the film with her where she could be seated among the privileged few watching the shoot, Trinidad initiated the two-way process of stage-screen interaction which continued for the duration of the shoot. This involved both on-screen figures escaping into the auditorium (as seen in Figure 22) and audience members being lured on-screen, as when a Valencian psychiatrist, Amparo, was invited to treat the hysterical Estrellita and a selection of audience members were dressed as Holy Week penitents or Nazarenes, marching from the stage to the screen, all witnesses to the kitsch miracle of Estrellita's sight being restored following a pioneering operation performed by Jean-François, who had completed his medical studies in record-breaking time and qualified as an ophthalmologist.

Cegada de amor proved an entertaining and imaginative variation on the backstage musical. Temporary hitches disrupted the shooting schedule but gradually, despite the many entertaining distractions (including a pained confession by Jaime to Antonio of what might have happened at a dinner between him and Estrellita), the filming resumed, culminating in the lavish Holy Week procession where Estrellita's protective blindfold was removed. Seeing Jean-François below her, she fittingly burst into song, gleefully celebrating the restoration of her sight. Beginning with the gentle heckling from the on-screen actors and production team as the Cubana actors planted in the audience (Juanita, Paquito and the two hooligans, Josele and Sebastián) caused pandemonium in the auditorium, the pretence was pursued that the completion of the film depended on the audience's collaboration. When Estrellita's breakdown jeopardised the shoot, she was flamboyantly treated

22 La Cubana's *Cegada de amor* (1994). Theatre actress Rosita Alfaro (Cati Solivellas) storms off-screen in disgust while actor Jaime Blanchard (Santi Millán) and director Antonio Valdivieso (José Corbacho) look on from the stage and Valdivieso's formidable mother, Doña Trinidad Gordillo (Sílvia Aleacar) frowns from on-screen

by a psychiatrist in the audience. To boost her ego, Valdivieso brought Estrellita to the front of the stage to answer audience questions on her illustrious career, questions he hopes will cheer her and ensure she realises how well loved she remains despite her crippling insecurities.

The action evolved simultaneously in the theatre where the film was being screened and the studio where the film was being shot. This allowed for some glorious *coups de théâtre,* most tellingly when Marçal collapsed to the floor with a suspected heart attack in gruesome close-up and his hand fell through the celluloid onto the floor of the stage. The proscenium was playfully discarded as performers leapt through the screen to share secrets with the audience. It was this seamless bouncing between celluloid screen and the stage, referred to by Milán as 'film – in three dimensions' (La Cubana 1997: n.pag), which was to most astound the critics. The simultaneous screen and stage action, as Paul Julian Smith has astutely noted, ruptured both cinematic and theatrical frames of representation, destabilising 'the relation between the authenticating presence (the live voice and body) and alienating absence (the technically mediated image): as the Broadway-style show tune of the finale reminds us, this unclassifiable spectacle is "neither truth nor lie"' (2000: 61).

Marketed as a film and appropriately opening at a theatre that had functioned as a cinema for much of the century, the production was conceived by Milán as both as a 'culebrón' (soap opera) and a game between cinema and theatre (cited in Muntané 1994: 19): 'We have merged the "magic" of cinema with the "presence" of theatre, creating a very precise and technical Molotov cocktail that might be described as a three-dimensional show' (Mazorra and Burnet 1997: 30). While Milán may have veered towards labelling the production as theatre – 'el cine lo utilizamos, pero es un espectáculo de teatro' (García-Garzón 1996: 4) (we use cinema but it's a theatre production), El Mundo's María-José Ragué-Arias read the production as a vindication of the 'truth' of theatre versus the 'lie' of cinema (1994a: 75).[23] For Scottish critic Tom Shields, seeing the production at the Edinburgh International Festival in 1997, this was no fusion between theatre and cinema but rather a 'thumping head-on collision between the two forms' (1997: 17). La Cubana actor José Corbacho, whose five roles in the show included Valdivieso and the hooligan Sebastián Flores, saw the message of the show as 'que el cine es desde el punto de vista de la audiencia más fácil que el teatro, pero que no hay que conformarse tan sólo con él (cited in Ramos 1997: 26) (cinema is, from the audience's point of view, easier than the theatre, but you shouldn't be content just with that).

Indeed, as with Cómeme el coco, negro, the show ruptured established theatrical conventions. El País' Joan de Sagarra noted that both productions began with the audience settling to watch a particular spectacle (a variety revue in the former, a film in the latter), which was then interrupted, mutating into a backstage drama (1994: 34). For ABC's Juan Carlos Olivares, the production's achievement lay not only in taking cinema to the theatre, providing thrilling three-dimensional action, but in granting the spectator the amazing experience that Woody Allen was to reserve solely for Mia Farrow in The Purple Rose of Cairo (1985) (1994: xi). El Periódico's Pérez de Olaguer, admiring the production as further indication of the company's ability to surprise, also chose to dwell on the symbiosis of theatre and cinema that Milán successfully orchestrated (1994c: 57). La Vanguardia's Benach may have located theatrical multimedia antecedents for the show in the work of Holland's Mickery Theater (1994: 62), but what he failed to acknowledge was the scale of Cegada de amor, which bore little relation to the small-scale work staged at the more compact Dutch venue. Indeed the monumental success of the production, which I will delineate later in this chapter, seems to be more in line with film than theatre. Drawing on populist forms like the Latin American soap operas or culebrones which have saturated Spanish television over the past fifteen years, the company crafted a production which, while refusing to be pinned down to a precise temporal setting, effectively deconstructed particular icons of ethnic identity, like Estrellita and Valdivieso, with strong temporal associations (Marisol and Almodóvar).

23 The show was filled with telling references to the differences between both disciplines with fictional actress Rosita Alfaro storming off-screen in disgust at the poor treatment theatrical performers receive when they work on film. Estrellita was knowingly clad in yellow for much of the film. For observations on the use of yellow in Cómeme el coco, negro, see 240.

While Milán did not wish *Cegada de amor* to be interpreted as a parody of figures such as Almodóvar and Marisol (cited in Muntané 1994: 18), preferring to classify it as 'una versión muy a La Cubana de Pedro Almodóvar' (cited in Gaforot 1994: 24) (a Cubana-style version of Pedro Almodóvar), both were repeatedly evoked in reviews of the production. While *ABC*'s Juan Carlos Olivares (1994: xi), *El País*' Sagarra (1994: 34) and *La Vanguardia*'s Santiago Fondevila (1993b: 43) were to recognise the parody of Almodóvar, Spain's most internationally known contemporary filmmaker, in *Cegada de amor*, Olivares felt it misguided to reduce the production to the status of a homage to the Manchegan director. Indeed, for Olivares, John Waters and Jacques Demy were equally present as intertextual resonances. He located echoes of *Cry Baby* (1990) in the bold colour scheme of the *mise en scène*, and traces of *Hairspray* (1988) in the wild backcombed pseudo-beehive blonde wig and coiffured quiff cut sported by Estrellita and Jean-François respectively, while the patterned choreography of the early musical numbers found a precedent in Demy's 1967 film *Les Demoiselles de Rochefort/The Young Ladies of Rochefort* (1994: xi). Estrellita may have aspired to be the elegant innocent blonde personified by Catherine Deneuve in her collaborations with Demy, but her characterisation rather evoked Julieta Serrano's deranged wife Lucía, trapped in a similarly late 1950s early 1960s retro look in Almodóvar's hugely successful *Mujeres al borde de un ataque de nervios/Women on the Verge of a Nervous Breakdown* (1988). *Cegada de amor*'s melodramatic plot, film-within-a-film stratagem and production design of lurid colours was also a point of contact with Almodóvar's later *¡Átame!/Tie Me Up! Tie Me Down!* (1990). Moreover, the casting of Almodóvar's own mother, Francisca Caballero, as Marina's mother in the latter feature again suggested parallels with Valdivieso's larger-than-life mother, the conniving matriarch Trinidad Gordillo. In addition, the colourful backstage crew of Valdivieso's film included script girl Rossy Crespo, who bore more than a passing resemblance to Almodóvar regular Rossy de Palma (see Figure 23). The descriptions of further members of the film's technical team who found their way into cinema through unconventional routes likewise suggested analogies with Almodóvar collaborators.

Olivares drew attention to the production's intertextual references to a series of populist Spanish films from the 1960s, including *Rocío de La Mancha/Rocío from La Mancha* (1962) and *La reina de Chantecler/The Queen of Chantecler* (1962) (1994: xi). The former featured the child prodigy Rocío Dúrcal (the pseudonym of Ángeles de las Heras b. 1945), whose own journey into cinema was also marked by the guidance of a male producer Luis Sanz, the latter Ana Mariscal (the pseudonym of Ana María Arroyo b. 1925), another child prodigy who was to enjoy a prolific cinematic career. While Estrellita Verdiales' name suggested points of contact with Estrellita Castro, a popular singer who maintained the same distinctive hairstyle of her youth well into her seventies, perhaps the most conspicuous model for Estrellita Verdiales was Marisol (pseudonym of Josefa Flores González b. 1948), another figure shepherded into cinema by a male producer, Manuel J. Goyanes. Like Marisol, Estrellita Verdiales is a pseudonym devised for performer María Soledad Benavente – a nod here perhaps to the Nobel Prize-winning playwright Jacinto

23 Harmony on set in La Cubana's *Cegada de amor* (1994). Estrellita Verdiales (Anna Barrachina) and Jaime Blanchard (Santi Millán) in the role of Jean-François enact domestic bliss watched over by script girl Rossy Crespo (María José Pérez)

Benavente who was often accused of 'selling out' during the Franco regime. Estrellita's peroxide wig with its prominent turn-ups also recalls Marisol's Aryan hair colour and distinctive styling. From her debut with *Un rayo de luz/A Ray of Light* in 1960, Marisol – her name tellingly evoking both sea and sun – functioned as the Spanish Shirley Temple. Marisol's marriage to Goyanes' son Carlos also has parallels in Estrellita's sham engagement to Jorgito Luis. The fictional biographies in the programme informed the spectator that Estrellita Verdiales, a child star moulded by producer Andreu Marçal, made her cinematic debut in 1956, subsequently starring in over eighty films including *La niña del convento/The Convent Girl*, *Estrellita en el campo/Estrellita in the Countryside*, *Estrellita en la ciudad/Estrellita in the City* and *Pan, amor y Estrellita/Bread, Love and Estrellita*. Their very titles evoke films made by Marisol in the 1960s including *Marisol, rumbo a Río/Marisol bound for Rio* (1963) and *Las cuatro bodas de Marisol/The Four Weddings of Marisol* (1967). This latter film has, significantly, narrative parallels with *Cegada de amor*, as Marisol is wooed by a Frenchman who proposes to her on a film set.

In an interview granted before *Cegada de amor*'s opening, Estrellita was to position herself alongside Marisol, Rocío and Joselito (Fondevila 1994: 35). Whereas Marisol's retirement from the screen saw her reinvention as Pepa Flores and an association with radical film ventures like Bardem's *La corrupción de Chris Miller/The Corruption of Chris Miller* (1972) which marked a firm disassociation with the perky teenage Marisol of the 1960s, La Cubana's Estrellita was coaxed back on-screen by Valdivieso, eleven years after her retirement, to star aged forty-seven in a variation of her former role. Estrellita's removal of her intricately styled wig behind the closed doors of her dressing room further served to comment on the manufacturing of stars for public consumption. Whereas traditional programmes feature biographies of the actors, here it was the roles that were subject to that attention. Through the role of Estrellita, *Cegada de amor* was able to interrogate the myth of femininity fashioned to adhere to a particular ideal. Estrellita functioned as a personification of contemporary obsessions with the cultivation of eternal youth. Such youth, as the removal of Estrellita's wig to reveal a dishevelled crop of grey hair indicated, was as artificial as the environment in which her adolescent romance was played out. As the camera pulled back following the blinding of Estrellita, the fuchsia-coloured walls adorned with gold trimming were shown to be part of an elaborately constructed set. As with Estrellita's cheerful on-screen personality, refusing to acknowledge social discontent or inequality and embodied in her sugary number 'El mundo es maravilloso' (The World is Wonderful), these emblems were exposed as fabrications. Spontaneous identity was seen to be carefully orchestrated and rehearsed. The illusion of Estrellita's adolescence had been maintained through a refusal on Marçal's part to allow her to take the contraceptive pill, the binding of her breasts, pasty make-up and an anachronistic hairstyle. Marisol too suffered moulding. Her brown hair was dyed blonde and her nose shaped by plastic surgery. If, as Peter Evans has indicated, 'Marisol refracted in her all singing all dancing all talking vivacity the hectic expression of a nation's sham illusion of Utopian festivity' (forthcoming), then La Cubana's production exposed the fraudulence of this iconography. *Cegada de amor* articulated the dangers of myth propagated as truth. Estrellita may be *manchega*, a distinction she shares with Almodóvar, and the two icons of her trashy song 'Mancheguita', Don Quixote and Manchegan cheese, but her clearest antecedent was the Andalusian Marisol: an image of the 'new' Spain promoted by Franco in the interests of nurturing the burgeoning tourist trade.

The symbolism of child stars maintained 'forever young' through a range of dubious means is a telling indictment of an ideology which feared the consequences of allowing them to mature into adulthood. Like Marisol, Estrellita has remained a precocious teenager. The camera focused on her by Colomo, however, was unforgiving of the ravages of age and a veritable anachronism emerged in the contrast between her pastel girlish attire and low-healed shoes and her well-worn features. Whereas Marisol's films are in many ways recognisable products of the 1960s, Paul Julian Smith has also noted the 'confused' chronology of *Cegada de amor* (2000: 63–5). The Marisol referent clearly alludes to the 1960s, and, while the production aesthetic owes more to the 1950s, the Almodóvar references and fashion-styling of the film's production team suggest the late 1980s. The pleasure in the confusion of boundaries played out here was further reinforced in the hybrid nature of the spectacle, which included the quasi-cakewalk Broadway pastiche of the final song, the Euro-pop/rock beat of 'Estrellita mon cherie' [*sic*], the saccharine-coated love angst of the opening credits number, 'Cegada de amor', the reggae meets 1960s lounge instrumental during Estrellita's party, 'Madison dans la maison' (Madison in the House), the jaunty singalong of 'La canción del Nazareno' (the Nazarene Song) and the *saeta* which accompanied the Holy Week procession making its way under

Estrellita's balcony. Joan Vives' pastiche music and lyrics parodied a range of musical forms. As such the production juggled references from the Hollywood backstage musical – exposing the process of 'making' art and rendering it as entertainment as opposed to industrial product – with on-screen partnerships spilling out into the off-screen arena.[24] Whereas the narrative of the film being shot by Valdivieso provided a clean, closed finale where the coming together of the couple and the film functioned as a synonym for stability and social order, the glitzy premiere enacted on-screen presented 'alternative' romantic configurations, with Estrellita's baby handled by Amparo, whose psychobabble Estrellita now quotes unquestioningly. Jaime meanwhile could be seen shyly taking the hand of Jorgito Luis. These homosexual liaisons clearly remodelled the closure associated with the feel-good final chorus number, 'Ni verdad ni mentira' (Neither Truth nor Lies), a song whose very lyrics reiterated the unclassifiable nature of this hybrid postmodern spectacle.

Paul Julian Smith's valuable assessment of the piece within the discourses of postmodernism astutely notes references from child prodigies in the imaginary film titles of Estrellita's screen career. *Pan, amor y Estrellita* is a direct reference to Ladislao Vajda's *Marcelino, pan, y vino/Marcelino, Bread, and Wine* (1954) 'the first and most famous of the orphan melodrama cycle [. . .] in which a boy lodges in a priest's household' (2000: 63). Echoes with Joselito's career can also be traced. Estrellita makes reference to the fact that she allowed herself to be sunk in the way he was, and her chronology of films begins in the year that he too made his cinematic debut, 1956. Indeed Smith appraises La Cubana's use of anachronism in the piece as faithfulness 'to the originals they parody [. . .] the child stars were anachronistic in their own time out of sync with changing times even as they enjoyed their greatest success' (2000: 63).[25]

El Mundo's Rague-Arias was to see points of contact between the film and 1950s cinema (1994a: 75) but the production's cinematic references go far beyond that of Iberian films of the period. There are echoes of François Truffaut's *La Nuit Américaine/Day for Night* (1973) in the storyline of a filmshoot inhabited by trivial celebrities with an overblown sense of their own importance. The film's narrative also owes much to Douglas Sirk's *Magnificent Obsession* (1954), where Rock Hudson plays the decadent playboy who returns to medicine after recognising his responsibility in causing the death of a doctor and the blindness of his widow. The idea of actors entering the screen was pioneered as early as 1924 by Buster Keaton in *Sherlock Junior*, the tale of a projectionist who pushes his way into the film he is projecting, struggling to keep up with the predicaments occurring frantically around him. The use of particular notable theme tunes from bygone melodramatic blockbusters – Lara's theme from *Doctor Zhivago* (1965) and Tara's theme from

---

24 For further details on the characteristics of the Hollywood musical, see Feuer 1993.

25 Smith (2000: 64) cites film historian Carlos F. Heredero (1993: 230–4), who observes that Joselito's settings suggested the claustrophobic, clerical world of the 1940s, and while Marisol many have personified the materialist desires of the 1960s, her ever-absent parents harked back to the immediate post-War years.

Gone with the Wind (1939) – also served to root the production within a context of dramatic excess. Argentine critic Susana Freire, reviewing the production for Argentine daily *La Nación*, was one of the few critics to pick up on the rich array of filmic references (1998: 3). *El País'* Haro Tecglen (1996: 33) and *ABC*'s Julio Martínez Velasco (1997: 99) were more indicative of a critical establishment that dwelled almost exclusively on the Marisol and Almodóvar connections and the narrative echoes of *The Purple Rose of Cairo* (1985).

The film component of *Cegada de amor* had been shot at Barcelona's Gala studios during the show's year long preparation period and involved a cast and crew of a almost a hundred. Performed live by a cast of ten taking thirty-nine roles, the perfectly synchronised performances reliant on rapid costume changes without the benefit of dressers were much admired by critics who reviewed the Barcelona opening (Pérez 1994: 45; Ragué-Arias 1994a: 75). Superlative reviews served to generate interest in the show and the company were able to fill the Tívoli with its 1,040 capacity to eighty-four per cent during the first year of *Cegada de amor*'s run with a total of 302,893 spectators. Attracting an audience who, in Milán's view, had never previously been to the theatre, *Cegada de amor* became the most commercially successful production of 1994 (cited in Pérez de Olaguer 1995a: 54).[26] Its first anniversary was marked by a special post-performance celebration where the audience were handed special Estrellita Verdiales masks and yellow pom-poms which they waved frenetically as Estrellita lapped up their applause and the celebrations spilled out into the car park along the street, Carrer de Casp, where a giant party took place.[27] Indeed the seventeen months of the Barcelona run generated over half a million spectators, breaking all previous theatre-going records in the city. Reworked almost entirely into Castilian during mid-1995, it then toured across Spain until 1998, eventually seen by over a million spectators. Dates in Palma de Mallorca in October 1995 involved transforming Poble Espanyol's Sala Magna into a local cinema. In Madrid, during an eleven-month run at the Lope de Vega theatre beginning on 25 January 1996, the company staged a number of promotional photo events across city landmarks including sunbathing outside the Kio towers and paddling in the Plaza de España during the traditionally sleepy month of August and a glitzy farewell parade through the Gran Vía in January 1997.[28] *El País'* Haro Tecglen (1996: 33) and *Ya*'s Hera (1996: 59) were in agreement with their Catalan contemporaries, praising the technical skills, meticulous timing and theatricalised register of the performers. *ABC*'s López Sancho may have wearied of what he felt excessive repetition of certain key tricks but acknowledged the mastery of the company and the boldness of the production's central premise (1996: 77).

26 With the Liceu in the process of being rebuilt after the fire which razed it to the ground on 31 January 1994, the Tívoli was to end up as the most successful Barcelona theatre of 1994 with audience figures of 283,366, double that of its nearest rival, the Victòria, with 132,398. For further details, see Redacción 1995.
27 For further details, see Antón 1995.
28 For further details, see Fernández 1996 and Anon. 1997a.

Indeed the Spanish tour, playing to record-breaking audience numbers, generated extraordinary reviews in a range of regional newspapers across the country.[29] The particular interaction between the stage characters and their screen incarnations rendered understudies an impossibility. Actor José Corbacho, however, felt that, despite what may have appeared a gruelling schedule, the company's policy of coming together after each performance to discuss the dynamic of the show ensured that the production remained fresh and vigorous (cited in Herrero 1997: 55). It is perhaps worth considering that *Cegada de amor*'s commercial success came despite the fact that it touched on a range of issues usually regarded as box-office poison: the Church, homosexuality, nationalism, and democracy. Even Franco, a sacred figure for many right-wingers almost twenty years after his death, was alluded to. The indignant middle-aged 'fascist' who heckled the screen protesting at the Catalan language dialogue was significantly named Paquito, the diminutive of Francisco, a nod perhaps to a dictator who was similarly obsessed with the eradication of regional languages and likewise sported a thin moustache.

The first Cubana show to tour internationally since *La tempestad, Cegada de amor* was 're-conceived' for its foreign dates at the Edinburgh International Festival in August 1997 and Buenos Aires' Avenida theatre between March and June 1998. When the run ended on 14 June after 1,308 performances, the production had been seen by a total of 1,042,418 spectators. For its foreign dates the production was framed within a pre-show exhibition in the foyer of the performance space that asked key questions about the cultural referents of the production – What is a child prodigy? What is Catalonia? What is Valencia? What is Holy Week? – with answers supplied through a video, posters and other graphic and written materials overseen by company members dressed as ushers. The programmes also included an insert with a glossary of terms with definitions of terms such as Valencia's *falla fiesta*, Nazarenes,[30] and *Mancheguita*, the diminutive term for a girl from La Mancha.

Both the Argentine and the British critical establishment followed their Iberian contemporaries in applauding the production's imaginative energy.[31] For the Edinburgh run, a subtitling of the film, the translation of the script into Spanglish and the incorporation of local references to Sean Connery and Cherie Blair further served to tailor the production to the demands of a non-Hispanic audience. Described as 'the gaudiest, most dashing and most buoyant show' of that year's festival (Clapp 1997: 8), 'Hollywood meets Euro-trash' (Lockerbie 1997: 13) and a 'roguish satire on the follies and pretensions of showbiz people' (Burnet 1997: 49), British reviewers admired the 'breathtaking virtuosity' with which the 'technical mixing of the realms' of theatre and film were handled (Gross 1997: 9), placing it

---

29 For a selection of the excellent reviews that the production received during this period, see Gil 1995, Martínez Velasco 1997 and Almeida 1995.

30 Even when the show played in Catalonia, as Valdivieso rehearses the Nazarenes, Jaime questioned whether the local audience would know what the Nazarenes of Andalusia's Holy Week processions are.

31 For an assessment of the British press response, see Sanz 1997. For two indicative Argentine reviews, see Cuestas 1998 and Freire 1998.

as a 'mad mix of Pirandello and the Crazy Gang' (Billington 1997: 6). 'The manic disruptiveness disguises enormous discipline', taking on 'the whole subject of what-is-truth, what-is-reality with an anarchic zest that jumbles up Fifties advertising, soap opera, panto and Pirandello' (Butler 1997: 11). Only a few dissenting voices like the *Sunday Times'* John Peter felt the joke ran out of steam after twenty minutes (1997: 14). Following its sell-out success at the Edinburgh Festival, plans for a West End production, 'Braille for Love', are still underway although Milán has no plans to direct this Anglicised version.

Filmed for television and broadcast in January 2001, *Cegada de amor* has acquired a legendary status. A decorative plaque at the Tívoli celebrates the show's record-breaking run in the theatre. Further, in 1997, Estrellita Verdiales was immortalised in wax, taking her position alongside her Manchegan ancestors Don Quixote and Sancho Panza and theatrical forefathers Lope de Vega, Molière and Shakespeare at Barcelona's Wax Museum (Redacción 1997: 33). *Cegada de amor* pointed to contemporary anxieties around the role of theatre in a media-dominated culture. This was theatre as event, prioritising interaction rather than re-enactment within a localised context. The comical 3–D glasses that the audience were told to put on at the beginning of the film never held the key to *Cegada de amor*. Rather they functioned as a mocking joke on spectator gullibility. As Smith observes: 'such tacky gimmicks will not be needed to see live actors on the stage, and indeed, planted amongst the audience itself' (2000: 63). In *Cegada de amor*, La Cubana showed themselves to be tricksters of the modern world. Guardians of the liminal realm,[32] they willingly deceived the audience, leading them into a space where they were playfully confronted with the confusion of once delineated boundaries. *Cegada de amor* consolidated the company's reputation as emblems of duality who operated within the space of misrule.

A different way of viewing an exhibition: *Equipatge per al 2000. Més de pressa, més de pressa* (2000)

La Cubana's productions often evolve over many years and it is not unusual for the company to be touring a production whilst working on the genesis of a new project. *Equipatge per al 2000. Més de pressa, més de pressa* (2000: What Should We Take? Faster and Faster), running from 14 December 1999 to 12 March 2000, was conceived for Barcelona's Centre de Cultura Contemporània – one of the city's more recent artistic endeavours, opening in 1994 and housed in the conversion of the nineteenth-century Casa de Caritat hospice. Although the venue seeks to position itself as an urban space which promotes discussion and experimentation around municipal environments, it has occasionally been perceived as a less focused companion to its neighbour along Carrer Montalegre, the Museu d'Art Contemporani (MACBA) and has hitherto struggled to find a place within the city's abundant museum culture.

---

32 A phrase I have appropriated from Wright (2000: 6), who uses it to describe the trickster.

The need to continue experimenting with a genre which demands renewal was cited by CCCB's director, Josep Ramoneda, as a determining reason for the commission of La Cubana but there was also a recognition of the directions installation art is taking in its redrawing the boundaries around art and theatre (1999: 4–5). As with Deborah Warner's Tower Project at London's Euston Tower in June 1999 as part of the London International Festival of Theatre (LIFT), which incorporated performers into its narrative environment, *Equipatge per al 2000* refashioned the relationship between art and theatre. Temporal ephemerality rather than permanent exposure suggests that installation art has been performative from its very inception, enticing viewers into an encounter where they function as part of the action but which endures only as a memory. Site-specific worlds are entered by an audience who function as activators placed on the spot, so to speak, and forced to respond to the demands of the situation. In this sense, *Equipatge per al 2000* developed strategies pioneered in the company's street theatre as well as *La tempestad* and *Cegada de amor* where theatre is taken beyond the parameters of display towards carefully orchestrated situations where the curiosity of the spectator meets with the company's pre-prepared bag of tricks.

Més de pressa, més de pressa – both the subtitle and the theme of the exhibition – refers, as Ramoneda documented in a programme note, to the general sense, at least in the developed world, of time accelerating (1999: 4–5). Here, however, the concept of speed and control was handled with veritable irony and parody as the audience's sense of time and place was called into question by a staged journey where narrative was discarded in favour of scenarios that gelled together within a larger kaleidoscopic structure. Billed on the poster and programme cover as 'una manera diferent de veure una exposició' (a different way of viewing an exhibition), the company provided a bold, fascinating and witty interface of theatre and museum culture which defied easy categorisation and where 2,000 square metres of exhibition space – divided into seven diverse spaces (Fondevila 1999: 49, 53) – was re-imagined to create a landscape of interconnecting rooms in which twentieth-century gadgets now viewed as indispensable were examined in a context which capitalised on La Cubana's habitual love of rupture with the norms governing theatrical construction.

In a guided tour of around ninety minutes, which was repeated up to five times each evening and performed by two casts of twenty actors and ten extras planted amongst the audience – the second beginning as the first was an hour into the show – a group of up to fifty spectators/participants were invited to embark on a theatrical journey which began in the ticket foyer where an exhibition of select items invited the audience to identify what they considered to be the most influential invention of the twentieth century.[33] An eclectic list incorporating the aspirin, the

33 The programme divided the show into three acts made up of seven sequences: a first act structured around inventions of the twentieth century; the second act dealing with (a) the notion of gaining time through the universe of domestic tasks; (b) time is money through a journey to the world of work; (c) losing time? Or how we pass the time; (d) holding on to time through images of immortality; the third act concentrated on suffering time, on 'not being able to stop' and on future time; the conclusion asked 'what is time'?

fridge, the telephone, television, radio, the zip, the credit card, biro pens, Tupperware, the pill, the computer, the aeroplane and the washing machine, was laid out with accompanying documentation testifying to their impact in our age. These were shared reference points, part of a collective history for the largely Catalan audience who were invited to peruse visual and written commentaries which situated them within international, national and regional histories.

Encouraged by hovering guides armed with pens and advice to choose their 'key' innovation, the spectators huddled around a mass of discarded suitcases assembled in the central aisle – a metaphor both for the journey to be undertaken and the baggage which is carried from one century to another. The guides, flamboyantly dressed in fluorescent green suits at once indicative of and parodying the standardisation which is a hallmark of the leisure industry with its emphasis on logo and recognisable emblems, hurried the audience through to another room whilst removing their completed selection forms. Here, however, the brightly coloured wigs and larger than life uniforms served to defiantly remind us of the contrived nature of contemporary consumer culture where corporate identity subsumes individual aspirations.

Steered into a room shaped like a black box, the guides used the choices made by audience members to begin a contemplation of a century's obsession with time, its elusive manifestations and its stubborn refusal to facilitate its control. Issued with a small bright blue zip-up suitcase complete with outside pocket in which a number of key objects relevant to the odyssey were placed, the audience were then rushed across corridors and escalators before being reassembled in a larger-than-life kitchen with masked monitors. As with Els Comediants' 1997 production *Tempus* (Time), produced at the Teatre Nacional de Catalunya, and their December 1999 daily performances on and around the facade of La Pedrera, Gaudí's art nouveau apartment building along Passeig de Gràcia, time and its discontents functioned as the central peg on which the production's various narrative traits were hung. Els Comediants used the rippling luminous facade of one of Barcelona's most celebrated landmarks as the environment for a daily ritualistic enactment of the passing of time – a giant calendar had a redundant page ripped from it by a performer who appeared half-man, half-bird and encouraged the audience to believe he had defied gravity by stepping down the building to an accompanying soundtrack performed by a metallic figure in a colourful box which seemed to resemble the intestines of a working clock. Whereas Els Comediants negotiated the wrought metal and undulating masonry of the wave-like exterior creating a performance space from Barcelona's architectural surfaces, La Cubana collaborated with architect Dani Freixes to rework the exhibition space allocated by Ramoneda into a set of interconnecting rooms each designed to comment on some facet of our obsession with gadgets which provides the illusion of rendering us better able to mould and discipline our time.[34]

34 Interestingly La Fura dels Baus also contributed to the millennium festivities with a performance structured around virtual authorship at Barcelona's Plaça Catalunya entitled *L'Home del Mil.lenni* (Millennium Man) and based around the construction of a giant metallic skeletal structure. For further details, see Antón 1999a; see also Chapter 4, 133.

The mobile phone and suitcase given to the audience to carry also served as a reminder of performance as a display of consumer culture. The array of gadgets, inventions and artefacts manifest in the production pointed to the materiality of culture in the contemporary age, a materiality that manifests itself through objects guarded and handed down from one generation to another. We cannot free ourselves from the fragmented detritus of our modern age, the ghostly simulacra that haunts our media-saturated society. Here it functioned as the audience's accompaniment. In contrast to this lies the ephemerality of moments not captured within reproductive images or material objects, the gaps between the photographs of a life displayed in a corridor, the reflections around what has been seen and what has been done, the improvised moments of performers responding to the demands of a particular audience. *Equipatge per al 2000* questioned a vision of art as commodity offering a commentary on the growth of consumerism in theatre witnessed in the 1980s and 1990s with the sale of show merchandise and the prominent foyer display of buyable goods. Commodity fetishism became the target of a piece which positioned the audience as discerning shoppers suspended within a contemporary world where the real becomes unknowable, the calamity of a society where representation is all-pervasive.

The company's habitual practice of planting members of the troupe dressed as outlandish versions of the public in the audience was here used not only to stimulate discussion and encourage particular debates but also to remind that audience of the nature of the museum environment. The female actors dressed as eccentric middle-aged housewives enjoying an exhibition stopover en route to the supermarket performed part of a daily ritual whose intricacies were on show in the domestic surroundings created by Freixes with interior designer Oriol Pibernat (part of the now-dissolved design consultancy Grupo Berenguer which included Norberto Chaves, Jorge Pensi and Alberto Liévore). In the wacky, cartoonesque kitchen three generations of women from a single family discussed the changing nature of the domestic sphere. A career driven twenty-something single woman remained in thrall to her mobile phone, gliding across the kitchen in a chic designer trouser suit as her mother and grandmother conversed about the domestic appliances which have revolutionised their lives. Advertisements from earlier decades, which appeared at select moments from obscured monitors, indicated the surreptitious modes of indoctrination which, to use Louis Althusser's phrase, 'interpellate' individuals through the social practices in which they engage into an ideology that they actively, if unwittingly, promote (1971: 153–6). Television functioned in the scenario as a metaphor for the consumerist subject who is the focus of the domestic narrative enacted before us. The advertisements that bombard the women may have provided a unified subject but the bickering women served to supersede the image decentring each other as they vied to enforce their viewpoint.

According to *El País'* Pablo Ley, a corrosive dissection of the phenomena of time and space and its potential representation was in many ways the pivot of *Equipatge per al 2000* (1999b: 51). From the outset, the audience were ushered with some urgency by campily dressed security guards through a maze of ticking clocks and watches. The poster and programme cover presented a smiling 1950s house-wife sautéing a clock as it speeds towards 12.00. The shape of the clock at once recalls Salvador Dalí's melting clocks in his 1931 painting *The Persistence of Memory*. This powerful icon of an earlier modernist era was utilised to spectacular effect by La Cubana's Catalan contemporaries, Els Joglars, as the culmination of a tableau on the impact of World War II in *DAAALÍ* (1999), their visual exploration of the myth of Dalí as perhaps Spain's most significant twentieth-century cultural icon. Dalí's reworking of European romantic landscape painting[35] into a deserted plain adorned only with dripping clocks was re-imagined again here as the blurred soft clock is tossed up high by a new icon who looks out at her readers with a blank-ness projected onto the anonymous checks of her computer-generated attire. Here her glossy image, to quote the postmodern critic Fredric Jameson, ratified 'the tri-umph of all values of contemporary consumer society, of late capitalist consump-tion' (1993: 85).

In *Equipatge per al 2000* the passing of time was shown to be all pervasive, at one stage quite literally so, when the audience were instructed to open the outside pocket of the case in which a mobile phone requested them to take their seats on an aircraft which then whisked them away on a journey through the last hundred years. A team of identically clad hostesses in tightly tailored yellow suits and defi-antly permed black wigs processed through the cabin with a series of objects from the twentieth century – most conspicuously credit cards, computers and mobile phones – paraded before us in protective glass cases which testify to their cherished value in contemporary culture. These, like the aeroplane, functioned as metaphors for working environments where time is measured digitally and where speed is all. But the sense of losing and gaining time was shown to be an illusion, created to give a fallacy of control over a phenomenon which resists it.

Once again here, the primly attired airhostesses – male performers in drag – commented on ideas articulated in some form or other in all La Cubana's recent work that all gender is drag, because imitation is at the very centre of gender play.

In imitating gender, drag implicitly reveals the imitative nature of gender itself – as well as its contingency. Indeed, part of the pleasure, the giddiness of the performance is in the recognition of a radical contingency in the relation between sex and gender in the face of cultural configurations of causal unities that are regularly assumed to be natural and necessary. (Butler 1990: 137–8)

As in the company's 1992 television series *Teresina S.A.* and *Cegada de amor*, drag did not function here as a secondary imitation because there was no fixed gender or origin to be impersonated. Our attention as spectators was constantly drawn to the fact that gender binarisms are performative. La Cubana's cultural texts negoti-ate the impossibility of an erasure of self and image. The performance articulated the impossibility of reading the 'real' in a world where all has been marketed and commodified for consumption. In repackaging the discourses of consumption, *Equipatge per al 2000* interrogated an appropriating capitalism where everything –

35 A characteristic of the painting located by Wilson (1980: 16).

as the penultimate scene in the meditation lounge indicates – can be bought or sold if the price is right.

Equipatge per al 2000 also commented on the politics of voyeurism and its role in crafting a culture of material consumption. This was achieved through the very clever conversion of one of the galleries into what looked and felt like an enormous underground car park where each wall was mirrored to magnify the effect of about twelve or so Seat cars, in which solitary figures engage in private rituals (sunbathing, embroidery, watching television, a *siesta*, drinking, gambling). In many ways it was the most disturbing scene of the show in that interaction was defiantly refused as the actors ignored the spectators peering into their intricately constructed worlds. The anonymous car park, a threatening subterranean space, was here presented as the ultimate metaphor for the regimentalised compartmentalisation of contemporary existence and a bewildering enclosure marked by surveillance (carried out by piercing headlights) and brutal regimentation (witnessed in the rigid positioning of the cars). The car-saturated society that Spain has now become – catalogued in the opening exhibit – was here exposed as a lonely urban wasteland where the spectators became disorientated shadows. The motorised culture may offer protection for those encased within its protective frame but for those outside the glazed metal coffins abandoned in the car park created by La Cubana the space was a vast necropolis, a commercial spectacle of peepshows where spectators sought reflections of their own ceremonies.

An engagement with issues around national and regional identity, which has marked their previous presentations, surfaced also in *Equipatge per al 2000* as the commentaries accompanying the automobile exhibits informed the audience that *fiesta* and *siesta* are the most recognisable words in the Spanish language. Performed in Catalan, the production negotatiated the Catalan-Castilian axis in its strategically placed security guards who performed their surveillance with a self-conscious urgency gained from North American police dramas. Their dialogues as the audience were taken to an exhibition room to observe a neon question mark and invited to reflect upon its meaning at once sent up the earnestness of much museum culture – this solemnity was also satirised through the guides' luminous uniforms whose cut had its referent in the uniforms of those employed in museums across the Western world. The guards' digressive conversations around football and leisure activities served as a reminder of what Emma Dent Coad views as art's public image: 'an item of consumption, a highbrow, elitist activity where connoisseurs, intellectuals and patrons mingle' (1995: 375). The Andalusian accent of one of the two flamboyant guards positioned them within a particular class structure of economic immigrants now residing in Catalonia. Functioning as an indicator of social acceptance amongst the region's upper and middle classes, Catalan became the 'official' language of the exhibition and, by association, the cultural power base. The guards' intransient refusal to speak the language of the production located them as social and cultural outsiders, and further reflected the corrosive political vein that had proved such a feature of the company's earlier dramatic ventures. Here stereotypes are moulded into the terrain of ironic self-contemplation as the two guards, in the manner of the gravediggers at Ophelia's grave, deflated the pretensions of the situation in which they were placed. La Cubana's satire, targeted at institutional ostentation, escaped political straightjackets while defiantly recognising that 'in the postmodernist world complicity and subversion are inextricably intertwined' (Carlson 1996: 173).

As with previous Cubana presentations, film, media technology and sleight of hand played a key role, as for example in the gallery where the audience were asked to pose for a group commemorative photograph which was then immediately projected on to the screen opposite: a blurred graphic of an instant captured in time.[36] The photographer's attempts to philosophise around the nature of his craft were constantly deflated by his chatty assistant whose mundane anecdotes provided a healthy antidote to his rambling logic. Patriarchal authority was constantly called into question within the performance as institutionalised masculinity[37] was held up to ridicule by the opinionated housewives planted in the audience. Here they, like so many of the other women characters in La Cubana's work, introduced 'into the playing of the role a subversive and parodic self-consciousness' (Carlson 1996: 175), a mimicry which dispensed with mimesis in favour of the re-envisaging of life as spectacle which is such a distinctive feature of theatricality.

In the penultimate room of the exhibition Doctor Sentis' seductive tones asked the audience to relax and meditate. Asked 'What is time?', they were told that the answer lay inside the suitcases. When unzipped, however, the suitcases were shown to hold only an empty Perspex box. Like performance, time similarly evades containment and qualification. Doctor Sentis' totalising discourses failed to provide adequate answers to the questions the performance posed. Instructed to leave the suitcase behind in an airport-style baggage depositor, the audience then moved out into a foyer area to enjoy a glass of cava, courtesy of Freixenet, one of the project's principal sponsors: the Dionysian moment of a communal raising of glasses to the new year in a shared celebration contrasted with the disposability of the suitcase and mobile phone. Habitually, at exhibitions, it is only the select few invited to the opening reception who partake of the celebratory drink. Here all were included in the game. The emphasis on play explored the very boundaries of theatrical representation, playing out some of the questions about theatre and performance that have been pervasive in critical thinking over the past two decades. While Milán refused to categorise the production as either theatre or installation art (cited in Ginart 1999: 13), *Equipatge per al 2000*'s reliance on the idioms of both media served as with *Cegada de amor* and the company's most recent production, *Una nit d'Òpera*, to refute conventional framing signifiers in favour of a theatrical discourse which inhabits the very boundaries of differing art forms.

36 Interestingly this scene was immediately followed by the audience's entry into a corridor of photographs where they were shown the life of a woman captured in frozen, catalogued images.

37 This was personified not only by the male characters like the photographer but also by the woman doctor, Sentis, associated with institutionalism.

The news that La Cubana had turned their attention to opera may have generated some surprise but opera had already enjoyed a discreet presence in *Cubana Delikatessen*. 'Tours la Cubana' ended its journey at the rehearsal of singer Montserrat Batallé (a thinly disguised referent for Montserrat Caballé) with the compact Sala Mozart standing in for the Gran Teatre del Liceu. With *Una nit d'Òpera* it was the Tívoli that was to be re-envisaged as an opera house to rival the Liceu. The Gran Teatre de l'Òpera was to house a production whose title, recalling the Marx Brothers' 1935 film *A Night at the Opera*, provided a telling forewarning of the pranks and routines that were to ensue. For *Una nit d'Òpera* offered an unusual telling of Verdi's *Aida* in the year of the centenary of Verdi's death. Following hot on the heels of the Liceu's revival of the 1945 *Aida* designed by Josep Mestres Cabanes (1898–1990) with 120 grand painted backdrops evoking the splendours of ancient Egypt, La Cubana provided a fictitious company's rendition of *Aida*. El Gran Teatre de l'Òpera were presented as an eminent Catalan company with an illustrious past represented by the signed photographs and posters which littered the backstage corridors the audience were led through as they made their way to Òpera a l'Abast's (Opera at Your Fingertips) educational introduction to opera. The list of illustrious past productions juxtaposed the great and the good of the opera world (José Carreras, Joan Sutherland and a host of other singing stars) with the fictitious divas who were to feature in that evening's performance of *Aida*: the sexually rapacious Italian soprano Renata Pampanini, the larger-than-life Catalan mezzo Violeta Santesmases, the drunken tenor Richard MacMaster and the vain Australian baritone John Spencer.

The audience, walking through the stage area where final preparations for that evening's *Aida* were being made, were led into a specially constructed backstage space where they were guided to their seats by Òpera a l'Abast's diligent staff. With a dedication bordering on the evangelical, the staff escorted the bemused audience through to listen to one of their group dressed in pristine pastel pink giving a talk on the virtues and history of *Aida*.[38] Òpera a l'Abast, set up in 1992 by Daniel Matabosch (a hybrid perhaps of Daniel Martínez, the charismatic head of Focus production company and Joan Matabosch, the current artistic director of the Liceu), was established to take opera to the people, supposedly opening up that most elitist of art forms to 'ordinary' folks. As members of the company 'planted' in the audience voiced concern as to whether *Aida* would be shown in all its glory giving spectators a full frontal view of the stage, the members of Òpera a l'Abast wondered what the audience could expect having only paid 3,900 pesetas (£15) for tickets. Though it can be seen as an operatic version of *Noises Off*, the production also served as a corrosive dissection of the conventions and prejudices of an art form which has thrived on its social exclusion. From the moment when the audience

---

38 Although I describe the costume worn when I first saw the production on 29 July 2001, in the performance I saw a year later on 13 July 2002 the character was dressed in an equally gaudy burgundy sequined dress. Further changes included a pruning of the interplay between the chorus-like backstage staff and the substitution of two much larger screens.

entered the theatre, the segregation that separates the wealthy from those who pop-ulate the gods was enforced as the illusion was given that the foyer entrance was forbidden to the spectators. Mannequins posing in all their finery in the Tívoli foyer, to which the audience were barred access, indicated how opera has always been a place to be seen as much as to see, a point reinforced by the subscriber who made his way backstage indicating how his box may not offer a great view of the stage action but that 'being seen' at the opera is a significant social statement.

As the audience made their way into the theatre through the stage area, they were unaware of how those already seated were able to watch them making their precarious way through the ornately painted fabric columns and statues through to their seats. As in past productions, the audience were as much performers as the 'official' company members and this was reinforced by a number of participatory moments in the production where unsuspecting audience members were picked out to substitute for injured singers or to supplement a dwindled chorus as tri-umphant soldier extras returning from the wars. A giant mirror placed in front of the audience at such moments served to further reinforce the dynamic around seeing/being seen, commenting on the fundamental narcissism that lies at the heart of all theatre watching.

The design by Castells Planas de Cardedeu and Jordi Bulbena provided an open backstage area dominated by doors to dressing rooms downstage left and right and a table downstage left adorned with wig-stands and headdresses. Two large screens suspended above the dressing rooms offered the means through

24 La Cubana's backstage look at *Aida, Una nit d'Òpera* (2001). An image from the staging of the opera showing Italian soprano Renata Pampanini as Aida in the extreme left of the photo, with mezzo Violeta Santesmases as Amneris to her immediate right

which an educational film on opera, its history and legacy was presented by a cartoon Verdi look-alike for whom, ultimately, opera is merely a grander version of theatre: the stage is bigger, the singers are larger and the works are longer. In addition, once the 'official' production of *Aida* began, this was where the audience were given a front-stage projection of Gran Teatre de l'Òpera's lavish production, prepared with the assistance of Moscow's State Philharmonic Orchestra and the chorus of Òpera Helikon. The Gran Teatre de l'Òpera's staging, however, soon became incidental to the main action that focused on the backstage crew who offered their comments, asides and observations on the ensuing onstage and off-stage action. These were the protagonists of *Una nit d'Òpera*: the two firemen on duty during the performance who explained how opera has brought out the sensitive sides in their nature and occasionally got carried away with the action, singing along rather too loudly for comfort; the elderly technicians, Señor Toribio and Pepitu, who kept the show rolling despite the mishaps that inevitably ensued; the efficient prim stage manager, Antonieta; and the large hairdresser, Esperança, with her high hair, pink jacket and precarious black stilettos and her two sidekicks: Consol, the bubbly blonde make-up artist adorned in kitsch jewellery, and the middle-aged wardrobe mistress, Lolita, who functioned as an alternative chorus on the action, presenting it at as a soap opera of intriguing love triangles and necessary sacrifices to the greater glory of opera.

Into this world crashed the dysfunctional divas who slammed in and out of their dressing rooms preparing to go onstage. Renata Pampanini, a grand Italian

25 The audience's view of the scene from the specially constructed 'backstage' area shows the valiant off-stage efforts to ensure that there are no onstage mishaps during the performance of *Aida*

soprano accompanied by her immaculately attired mother, Lucía, refused point black to be made up as an Ethiopian princess, emerging instead in a series of extravagant outfits which defied her status as a captured prisoner. Renata was presented as the deadly rival of local mezzo-soprano Violeta Santesmases, a rather wooden performer who only has two grand gestures and who resents Pampanini's clout and upstaging of Princess Amneris. The tensions between them became more ominous as Pampanini seduced Santesmases' husband, Roberto, leading to a deadly onstage duet where offstage tensions resulted in Santesmases slapping Pampanini so hard that her contact lenses fell out, rendering the soprano virtually blind. La Cubana orchestrated a number of gloriously wicked set pieces around the mishaps that ensued during the production. These included the manic search for the missing contact lenses, the visually impaired Pampanini being guided on stage by the backstage staff who coach her through the final act, Santesmases losing her voice and having to be replaced by her countertenor husband, tenor Richard MacMaster tumbling on- and offstage in a drunken stupor, and improvisations as the ladder to allow Amneris to glide into her bath in Act Two failed to materialise and the backstage crew were obliged to step in and save Santesmases from a nasty accident.

As in *Cegada de amor* the audience delighted in the stage trickery exposed before them: the ripples of the Nile created by a backstage hand, the swimmer who feigned swimming across the river, the maid who poured water into a bowl as she fabricated the creation of a sumptuous bath for Amneris, the illusion of an army on the move created by audience extras who marched in a loop across the back of the stage, the fabric columns which swung precariously when knocked by Santesmases. In its display of the mechanics of production, this process simultaneously exposed the spontaneity of 'creation' as a fallacy. Jordi Milán has always demonstrated a love of the artifice of theatre and his deconstruction of the world of opera was as much a homage to the nineteenth-century world of flying backdrops and opulent effects as it was a dissection of the operatic formula. Again, as in La Cubana's previous work, imaginative doubling and rapid costume changes allowed the cast of fourteen (only two of which – Jaume Baucis and David Ramírez – had been with the company for *Cegada de amor*) to play over forty differing characters. Some made only cameo appearances, like the snobby musical director Gerard de la Font who swanned through the backstage area without a word for anybody and Ramon Pujol (the keen-to-please President of Pampanini's fan club, pompously named the Associació de Pampanistas). Others reappeared at regular intervals, like the flamboyant Argentine director of the show Mario Pascual (an amalgamation perhaps of Mario Gas and Lluís Pasqual, two of Barcelona's best known directors). Gas was similarly known for his mane of grey hair and Pasqual for frequently dressing in black. In the naming of the baritone Richard MacMaster there may also be an affectionate nod to Brian McMaster, director of the Edinburgh International Festival who brought *Cegada de amor* to Edinburgh in 1997.

As with *Cegada de amor*, this was in many ways a homage to the aesthetics of the backstage musical, as the final chorus number on the magic of opera delightfully showed. The reliance on the concept of community – the operatic company as a family of sorts which must come together and work as a team to ensure the show goes on – firmly situated *Una nit d'Òpera*, like La Cubana's earlier *Cómeme el coco, negro*, within the formula of the Hollywood backstage musical. The final number on the magic of opera accompanied by busily flying columns, a view of the Gran Teatre de l'Òpera's cupola uncannily resembling that of the Liceu and the backstage staff re-clad in the costumes of the stars, suggested a popular re-appropriation or taming of opera – not unlike that featured in *A Night at the Opera* and other musicals where the elitist and outdated traditions conventions of opera are challenged or reworked. The number was marked by the same quality of ostentatiousness and joyous excess that proved such a trait of *Cegada de amor*. As in their earlier reworking of Shakespeare's *The Tempest* as an exercise in surviving the excesses of a storm, opera as high or classical art was here juxtaposed with a more populist vaudeville tradition embodied in the show's final number. The boundaries between high and popular art were clearly shown to be no longer as fixed or as mutually exclusive as past critics may have believed. Belying their roots in street theatre, La Cubana brazenly showed that the whole world is a stage. Alternative stages abounded in *Una nit d'Òpera* with multiple areas of action vying for the audience's attention. The mononarrative of a nineteenth-century artefact, *Aida,* was replaced by a plethora of micronarratives that highlighted the work that goes into producing art. All the backstage crew were consistently busy: the seamstress accompanied by her sewing box, the make-up artist with an assortment of brushes strapped to her waist; the hairdresser touching up the wigs whenever possible. Perhaps more so than *Cómeme el coco, negro* and *Cegada de amor, Una nit d'Òpera* presented a homage to the efforts of those who toil industriously behind the scenes in the name of art.

As with the earlier shows, audience participation was moulded to form part of the very shape of the piece. A cut-out Egyptian headdress was included in the programme for each audience member to sport during the popular Grand March when, in truly kitsch fashion, the triumphant Egyptian army returned from the wars with Ethiopia. A mirror tilted towards the auditorium allowed the audience to narcissistically watch themselves giving glory to Radamès as a dozen of their number were randomly picked out and attired as chorus members enacting the return of a victorious army parading in a loop along the back of the stage, itself a satire on the more conventional interpretations of this scene. With company performers playing outraged spectators and the disgruntled student tenor who erects protest banners in the dress circle, no audience member could be sure of remaining protected within the anonymity of their seat. As La Cubana have shown in all their artistic ventures, any spectator may be drawn into the narrative intrigues that ensue when the audience/actor boundaries are pulled down.

In an age, where, as Jeremy Tambling indicates, 'opera performed live has lost its innocence, since for most opera-goers now their primary awareness of the music is not through performance but through reproduction' (1994: 11), *Una nit d'Òpera* served as a reminder of the unpredictability and ephemerality of performance. Whereas opera may have traditionally been seen to have more in common with a visit to the elitist museum than the populist movies, La Cubana turned these associations on their head. As with the Marx Brothers' *A Night at the Opera*, which similarly dismembers another Verdi opera, *Il trovatore*, *Una nit d'Òpera* proved 'strangely affectionate towards what it demolishes' (Kramer 1994: 257). The tone of the piece was certainly more in line with the elegiac pitch of *Cómeme el coco, negro* than the acerbic sarcasm of *Cegada de amor*. Indeed *Aida*'s tragic ending was here defiantly displaced by a comic romance where communal energy won out over individual egotism. As with *Cegada de amor*, however, actors planted amongst the audience provided unexpected narrative interruptions as with the student tenor who accosted audience members while they were queuing to enter the theatre demanding the right to sing. After popping up in the upper circle to mount his protest at his exclusion from the company, he was later given his chance. Coming on for Richard MacMaster who collapsed on stage in the final act, his duet with Pampanini provided a feel-good finale where the guy gets both the girl and instant fame, saving the day so that, in the tradition of the backstage musical, the show continues. While the flying up and down of the paper columns in the show's final show-stopping number provided glimpses of a theatrical environment which evoked the architectural particularities of the Liceu, and Milán has acknowledged that the idea for *Una nit d'Òpera* came to him while watching a woman sob uncontrollably as the renowned opera house went up in flames in 1994, lamenting that she had never seen the inside of the theatre (cited in Rubio 2001: 6), the show rested firmly within the territory of the backstage musical: what Milán has described as 'vodevil tierno, poético' (cited in Rodríguez 2001: 48) (tender, poetic vaudeville).

While *ABC*'s Iolanda Madariaga's appreciative review situated the piece within the company's trajectory of 'darle vuelta a todo' (2001) (turning everything on its head), *El Periódico*'s Pérez de Olaguer felt that La Cubana's habitual bag of tricks here failed to cohere (2001). *La Vanguardia*'s Benach shared some of Pérez de Olaguer's reservations as to the overrunning of certain scenes, but was nevertheless ultimately won over by the ebullient energy of the performers and Milán's piquant script (2001: 45). As with *Cegada de amor*, *Una nit d'Òpera* enjoyed a prolific run at the Tívoli closing in September 2002 after a fifteen-month season. There are no plans, at present, to tour the show but, with a new production already envisaged, the company's zany, playfully subversive brand of theatre looks set to return to Barcelona's stages in the not so distant future.

Dislocation and provocation

It is perhaps ironic that La Cubana who have, within Spain, enjoyed the most resonant commercial successes of any of their contemporaries, nevertheless have failed to garner the same degree of international academic critical attention. While Eugène van Erven's *Radical People's Theatre* and Bim Mason's *Street Theatre and Other Outdoor Performance*, published in 1988 and 1992 respectively, have familiarised theatre studies academics and readers with the practices of Els Joglars and

Els Comediants, and La Fura dels Baus have been cited in key performance studies' texts like Alan Read's *Theatre and Everyday Life* (1993), RoseLee Goldberg's *Performance: Live Art Since 1960* (1998), and Michael Rush's *New Media in Late 20th Century Art* (1999), La Cubana have languished in the realms of international academic anonymity.[39] This may perhaps have to do with the fact that, despite emerging from the TI, theirs has always been a wordier theatre than that of La Fura dels Baus or Els Comediants and as such perhaps perceived to 'tour' less effectively beyond the domestic Iberian market. As early as 1986, *El País'* Barcelona theatre critic Joan de Sagarra was to speculate as to why the Ministry of Culture had not chosen the company as part of the Spanish theatre season put together to visit Italy the following year (1986a: 31). La Cubana's international profile may certainly have been less pronounced than that of their contemporaries La Fura dels Baus and Els Comediants precisely because they have only toured internationally intermittently. Indeed Milán has cited the bureaucratic furore around the *La tempestad*'s London dates as responsible for making him wary of trying to promote the company abroad (Pons 1994: 73). Lying between the text-driven theatre of the national theatre companies and the physical interdisciplinary vocabularies of Els Comediants and La Fura dels Baus, La Cubana have proved more awkward to classify. While Milán has posited that all these performance groups share with La Cubana the ideal of a theatre which is not actor-centred but rather character-centred (cited in Pérez de Olaguer 1995a: 54), the company have in some way stood apart from La Fura and Els Joglars. As early as 1989, the critic Marcos Ordóñez judged La Cubana's work more difficult to categorise than that of Els Joglars and La Fura dels Baus and, as such, concluded that the company occupied a more ambivalent position within the Catalan performance scene (1989: 110).

La Cubana have, however, been at the cutting edge of performance practices in Catalonia since the early 1980s. While La Fura moved into cinema in 1999 with a ten-minute sequence in Carlos Saura's film *Goya en Burdeos/Goya in Bordeaux* (1999), choreographed by Jürgen Müller and Pep Gatell, Fernando Colomo had already pioneered La Cubana's entry into film with *Cegada de amor* five years earlier. La Fura dels Baus first engaged with Shakespeare only in 1997 with *Work in Progress/Macbeth*, devised (and directed) by Pep Gatell and Jürgen Müller. La Cubana, however, had already dismantled *The Tempest* as early as 1986. Like La Fura they have been astute in seeking private finance to fund their theatrical experiments. In 1989 Milán asserted that the company had received only seven million pesetas to date (cited in Montero 1989: 8). Indeed Catalonia's Generalitat initially refused any degree of subsidy for *La tempestad*, which was produced by Madrid's Punto y Raya company at an initial cost of nine million pesetas. *Cegada de amor* received some funding from the Ministry of Culture and the Generalitat de Catalunya but relied on private sponsorship from Freixenet and Vichy, two recognisable Catalan brands of cava and water. Freixenet continued this relationship

---

39 The work of La Fura dels Baus is also commented on in numerous articles by non-
    Hispanists; see, for example, Birringer 1996 and Fischer-Lichte 1997.

with *Equipatge per al 2000* and *Una nit d'Òpera*. The latter piece's expensive production costs have necessitated the recruitment of further sponsors including the
conservative Catalan daily, *La Vanguardia*, Catalunya Ràdio and TV3. Indeed the
glossy programme for *Una nit d'Òpera* is a far cry from the meagre handbills that
are usually handed out in Spanish theatres. Here lavish advertisements for San
Miguel beer, American Express cards and La Caixa's theatre tickets service point
to the kudos that an association with La Cubana now brings. Commercialism may
have been sent up in the 'Cubana Incorporated Hymn' of *Cubana Marathon Dancing*, but the company's new offices and storage space in L'Hospitalet de Llobregat,
promotional work, and an association with the Balaña theatre group, owners of the
Tívoli theatre, point to a hardened pragmatism which has ensured their survival in
an increasingly competitive climate.

La Cubana's move into television offered Milán the chance to build up new
audiences who would then follow the company into the theatre (cited in Pérez de
Olaguer 1994a: 29). His initial television ideas included a *Dallas*-like TV series,[40]
but their TV debut on Catalan-language TV3 was a New Year special, *Per cap d'any
TV3 no fa res* (TV3 Isn't Doing a New Year Programme This Year) (1990), where
TV3's decision not to show an end-of-year show motivated the employees to create
their own improvised entertainment in the studio. This was followed in 1991 by *Els
Grau*, a series for the same channel where three generations of a Catalan family
offered five minute snippets of television criticism on forthcoming broadcast offerings. Their next excursion onto the small screen came in 1992 with *Teresina S.A.*,
another Catalan-language offering for TV3. Revolving around a family of three
unmarried sisters, all named after a different Saint Teresa, living and working in
their flat in Barcelona's Gràcia district, *Teresina S.A.* ruptured the conventional
sitcom formula in its use of parody, its overt self-reflexivity, its direct engagement
with social rituals and traditions, its collapse of the private/public boundaries and
its hyperbolic performance style.[41] La Cubana moved to TVE (Televisión Española)
in 1994 for a Christmas Eve special that aimed to re-create a typical festive dinner
at the home of a Spanish family chosen by chance. Described by *La Vanguardia*'s J.
M. Baget Herms as a television happening (1994: 6), it developed the mannered,
rhetorical screen-performance style pioneered in their earlier theatrical and television work. Their most recent television work, in 1999, was a series for Telecinco,
Me lo dijo Pérez (Pérez Told Me), which further flipped stereotypes into the terrain
of ironic self contemplation, reclaiming and rewiring ludicrous but pervasive myths
which have shaped the perception of Spanish and Catalan identities.

While Milán is often seen as the creative force and primary figurehead of the
company, the works are formed and structured through a process of collective
improvisation and the company have functioned as a co-operative since turning
professional in 1984, with a wage structure that has no room for celebrity fees.[42] For
Cegada de amor all the company members were equal shareholders in the produc-

---

40 For further details, see Luengo 1990.
41 For an excellent discussion of *Teresina S.A.*, see Fernàndez 1998.
42 For further details, see Muntané 1994: 19 and Pérez de Olaguer 1994a.

tion's success; an investment that ensured none felt tempted to leave a show where replacements were an impossibility (Christopher 1997: 8). Indeed Milán has never aspired to work as a director outside the framework of the company, despite offers to direct at the Liceu and the TNC.[43]

Although Josep Palou has referred to 'desconcertar y provocar' (dislocate and provoke) as the two axes around which La Cubana's work revolves (1994: 12), for Milán it has never been about provoking an audience but rather a reciprocal process of game play, which can be observed in any classroom, on any market stall, or at any wedding. All social rituals are for Milán profoundly theatrical and when viewed by a non-participant the absurdity of the rules that govern those conventions become almost illogical (cited in Arco 1991: 62). Theatre is for him 'imaginación al máximo. Para nosotros el teatro y la vida son casi una misma cosa. A las escenas cotidianas se les pone un poco de aceite cultural y se llevan al teatro (cited in Arco 1991: 62) (utmost imagination. For us theatre and life are almost the same thing. You add a little cultural oil to ordinary scenes and take them to the theatre). This is achieved through what he terms beginning a story that is then turned on its head (cited in Pérez de Olaguer 1994a: 29). Eschewing performance methodologies, the company have sought to provide bilingual works which reflect the bilingual culture of Catalonia. And their stages have questioned and debated key issues around nationalism, identity and the differing community structures in which individuals now function. Theirs is a theatre rooted in popular vaudeville traditions, something the company acknowledged with a tongue-in-cheek reference to popular singer and actor Antonio Molina as an influence on their methodology in *Cómeme el coco, negro* (cited in García-Garzón 1996: 5). While *Cómeme el coco, negro* and *Cegada de amor* both satirised the cult of celebrity, the company has always moved against the star system by featuring largely unknown performers. Theirs is a theatre where actor personality cannot impose itself over characterisation and this has seen new performers come in at regular intervals with Milán remaining as the creative force of the company, thus maintaining a sense of continuity. While Milán acknowledges that each show emerges from the company's previous production (cited in Pérez de Olaguer 1994a: 29), every new project has, in the view of critic Juan Carlos Olivares, served to define anew the theatrical experience (1994: xi).

All the company's productions are organised and executed with precise efficiency, often necessitating long gestation and rehearsal periods.[44] While it is possible to argue (as Kershaw has done with respect to British theatre) that within such methodically-constructed structures participation may be little more than a tokenistic gesture towards self-determination (1992: 237), it is precisely the unknown and unpredictable nature of an audience's involvement that provides the show's motor. And indeed La Cubana have consistently exploited their audiences' 'mixed and

---

43 For further details, see Pérez de Olaguer 1995a.
44 With *Una nit d'Òpera*, for example, while the piece was rehearsed for nine months beginning in September 2000, preparatory work on the set design, costumes and dramaturgical imput was begun in mid-1999.

contradictory demands for voyeuristic distanciation and exhibitionistic participation' (Smith 2000: 63). For Milán theatre should never be about repetitively performing a particular show but rather should involve daily risk-taking: 'es aventura más que otra cosa' (cited in García-Garzón 1996: 5) (adventure more than anything else). Certainly the company have always been dependent on the collusion of an inclined audience. A performance of *Cómeme el coco, negro* for the over sixties sponsored by a prominent building society abruptly ended when the audience politely exited the theatre on being told by the company that the revue was over (Benach 1990a: 35). In their questioning of the cultural frames with which we read theatre, La Cubana have established more pliable audience-actor interactions. Emerging during the early years of democracy in Spain, their participatory practices have helped promote a vision of culture which stresses involvement (as opposed to detached observation) and provocation (as opposed to complacency), underlining the theatricality of theatre and its role in responding to the political and social debates of the age.

Conclusion

David Thatcher Gies warns of the dangers that beset any attempt to write a nation's theatrical history over the course of a century. 'To chart it with any degree of accuracy forces us into a series of decisions – choices . . . ' (Gies 1994: 349). My decisions have involved beginning from the peripheries in documenting the work of certain performers and directors who have impacted upon, and indeed reshaped, public understandings of theatre and its role in society. This is not to imply, however, that others have not similarly influenced the theatrical landscape in which they have worked. Lluís Pasqual's observations, cited as the epigraph to the book, acknowledge the phenomenally-gifted actors Spain has produced. Alongside Espert he lists José Bódalo (1916–85) and José María Rodero (1922–91). And indeed, although both enjoyed extensive trajectories, neither has, to the best of my knowledge, been subject to the degree of biographical or critical attention bestowed on film actors.[1] Although Josep Maria Flotats is not cited by Pasqual, he too has been a palpable presence on the contemporary Spanish stage since returning from France in the mid-1980s. As director of the hugely influential Companyia Josep Maria Flotats at the Poliorama theatre he has, like Pasqual at the Lliure, gone

---

1 Bódalo was a regular associate of José Luis Alonso, working with him on a significant number of the latter's productions as artistic director of the Teatro Nacional María Guerrero between 1960 and 1975. In the first four years of Alonso's tenure alone these included Chekhov's *The Cherry Orchard* (*El jardín de los cerezos*) (1960), the premiere of Ionesco's *Rhinocéros* (*Rinoceronte*) (1961), Jardiel Poncela's *Eloisa está debajo de un almendro* (*Eloise is Under an Almond Tree*) (1961) and Carlos Arniches' *Los caciques* (The Local Rulers) (1963). Rodero too had a great range, appearing in premiere productions of Buero Vallejo's symbolic realist works like *En la ardiente oscuridad* (*In the Burning Darkness*) and *El tragaluz* (*The Basement Window*) (1967), and contemporary plays like Antonio Gala's *Los verdes campos del Edén* (*The Green Fields of Eden*) (1964). Perhaps his greatest legacy lies in providing a performance register for Valle-Inclán's work. He was to perform the role of the blind poet-seer Max Estrella of *Luces de bohemia* (*Bohemian Lights*) in both José Tamayo's 1971 staging and Pasqual's 1984 reading: the latter production is covered in Chapter 5, 200–3. He also appeared as Montenegro in Alonso's production of *Romance de lobos* (*Wolves! Wolves!*) in 1970. For an appreciation of Rodero that credits him with erasing from the Spanish stage the shocking memory of the war, see Alonso de Santos 1987. For an appreciation of Bódalo, see Alonso 1985. For an example of the kind of astute critical analysis of film stars that has yet to be applied to theatre stars, see Perriam 2003 and Evans forthcoming.

on to play a seminal role in reshaping the Catalan theatrical scene since 1985. Indeed Flotats's diffusion of a professionalism and training acquired in France has assisted in building up Barcelona's status as Spain's *de facto* theatrical capital. Straddling both acting and directing, he has proved a public mouthpiece for Catalan theatre with considerable resonance in the Parisian landscape where he performed for much of the 1960s, 1970s and early 1980s. His decision to initiate the programming at the Teatre Nacional de Catalunya (TNC) with Tony Kushner's *Angels in America*, was greeted with considerable outrage by Catalan dramatists like Josep Maria Benet i Jornet who felt it inappropriate to 'open' a Catalan national theatre with a North American play (Alonso, *et al.* 1996: 13–14). However unpopular his programming decisions, as I briefly delineate in Chapter 4, 166–72, Flotats was to repeatedly stimulate debate about what a national theatre should do and how it should function within Catalonia.

While Bódalo, Rodero and Flotats straddle the second half of the century, a number of the directors I refer to in the introduction, also virtually unknown in the English-speaking world, pioneered the conceptual and practical co-ordination of stage elements into a coherent whole which is commonly understood as 'directing'. As a dramatist, director and teacher at Barcelona's Teatre Íntim which he founded in 1898, Adrià Gual pioneered ensemble models of performing, the fusion of different art forms which might appeal to the senses, and a symbolist concept of decor which dispensed with three-dimensional scenery in favour of more abstract models. An early mentor of Xirgu, his technical innovations, used by future generations, included the dimming of lights during a performance (George 2002: 23). Indeed the Escola Catalana d'Art Dramàtic (ECAD) (the Catalan School of Dramatic Art) which he founded in 1913 has long been admired both as a model for rigorous performance training and 'an attempt to form the basis of the Catalan National Theatre' (George 2002: 23).

Recent Catalan reappraisals of Gual's work reveal an impact matching that of Paul Fort's Théâtre d'Art and the Moscow Art Theatre which has sadly remained unrecognised beyond Catalonia (Batlle i Jordà *et al.* 1992). Indeed, as early as 1925, Manuel Pedroso cited Gual as the exception in a theatrical culture which saw the director as a secondary figure, largely responsible for handing out roles and watching rehearsals (1925: 5). Cipriano de Rivas Cherif, himself responsible for staging the first productions of *Divinas palabras* in 1933 and *Yerma* in 1934 and a key collaborator of Xirgu's during the 1930s, judged Gual a revolutionary figure producing work of a quality akin to that of Edward Gordon Craig, Jacques Copeau and Lugné-Poë (1923: 331). If he was absent from Guillermo Heras's list of pioneering directors in the period 1875 to 1930, this may have more to do with his decision to remain in Catalonia where he wrote and worked predominantly in Catalan than the particulars of his stage practice. Heras (b. 1952), director between 1984 and 1993 of the Centro Nacional de Nuevas Tendencias Escénicas – a state-subsidised theatre for the promotion of more experimental dramaturgy and non-texual performance – presents Rivas Cherif, alongside Emilio Mario, Gregorio Martínez Sierra (1881–1947) and García Lorca as the veritable pioneers of directorial practice in

Spain (1992: 141). Mario (the pseudonym of Mario Emilio López Chaves), working in the last decades of the nineteenth century, was familiar with the most recent
developments in Parisian theatre, and sought to bring some of the spirit of André
Antoine and his Théâtre Libre to Madrid's Teatro de la Comedia in the years after
1875 in his staging of more unconventional works like Benito Pérez Galdós's *La
loca de la casa* (The Madwoman in the House) in 1893 and Joaquín Dicenta's *Juan
José* in 1895.[2]

Gregorio Martínez Sierra, perhaps best known in the English-speaking world
as the director responsible for García Lorca's poorly received theatrical debut, *El
maleficio de la mariposa* (*The Butterfly's Evil Spell*), presented at the Eslava theatre
in 1920, like Gual evolved a directorial aesthetic based on a repudiation of naturalism's pervasive language in favour of more spectacular interdisciplinary productions. His Teatro de Arte (Art Theatre) at the Eslava theatre, mentioned in Chapter
1, is often berated for giving a platform to his own dramas and those of mainstream
contemporary playwrights like Carlos Arniches (1866–1943), Pedro Muñoz Seca
and Eduardo Marquina. Nevertheless, he premiered Miguel de Falla's ballets *El
amor brujo* (A Love Bewitched) in 1915 (at the Lara theatre) and *El sombrero de tres
picos* (The Three-Cornered Hat) two years later, as well as stagings of Jacinto
Grau's *El hijo pródigo* (The Prodigal Son) (1918) and García Lorca's debut play
with professional designs constructed in the company's workshop. These moved
defiantly away from the painted backcloth, indicating a commitment to the scenic
elements of production which was to effectively launch the careers of three of the
century's most important designers: Siegfried Burmann (1890–1980), Manuel
Fontanals (1893–1972) and Rafael Pérez Barradas (1890–1929).[3]

While my own interest in the work of directors and actors has determined the
choice of practitioners focused on in this study, their working collaborations with
key designers is pivotal to any understanding of their artistic journeys. The
German-born Burmann, a disciple of Max Reinhardt who had worked with Reinhardt's designer Ernest Stern, spent time in Paris before moving to Spain in 1914
where he was to exert a considerable impact on scenography until the 1950s. 'A
master at using lighting to create multiple perspectives', he introduced 'the location
of actors at varying heights so that dialogue or interaction could take place with
characters on different levels' (London: 1998: 34). Burmann's extensive trajectory
was to see him forge productive relationships with different generations of directors from Martínez Sierra and Rivas Cherif through to José Luis Alonso. The acqui-
sition of his archive by Barcelona's Institut del Teatre in the mid-1990s should pave
the way for future research into his prolific design work spanning over four decades.

While dramatist-designer Francisco Nieva may, as John London has also
observed, bemoan the mediocrity of Spanish stage design (Nieva 1986: 12; London
1998: 25), the contribution of visionaries such as Iago Pericot (b. 1929), Fabià
Puigserver (1938–91) Marià Andreu (1888–1976) and Antoni Clavé (b. 1913) both

2   For further details, see Sobejano 1974.
3   For further details, see Reyero Hermosilla 1980.

within Spain and abroad – Andreu and Clavé worked in England, France, Italy and the United States – should not be underestimated. Whilst I have documented the international responses to Puigserver's design of *Yerma* (1971) and García Lorca's 'impossible' plays in the late 1980s, this is a small component of a remarkably prolific output. Both Puigserver and Pericot's functionally conceptual design work with Els Joglars, building on models from the 1930s like those of La Barraca (London 1998: 47) provided strong prototypes for the spatial environments of the later generation of independent theatre makers like Els Comediants, La Fura dels Baus and La Cubana.[4]

The theatrical design work of Spanish painters has received scant attention but 'Picasso's sets for Diaghilev's productions of *Parade* and *Le Tricorne* (The Three-Cornered Hat), like Dalí's work with [García] Lorca and Adrià Gual and some of Joan Miró's set designs are in the mainstream of European experimentalism' (London 1998: 35).[5] The Uruguayan Pérez Barradas, Fontanals and Néstor were three further painters of the 1920s who turned to theatre design. Dalí (1904–89) was also to collaborate with Luis Escobar and Huberto Pérez de la Ossa, providing a contentious surrealist decor for José Zorrilla's *Don Juan Tenorio* in 1949. Antoni Tàpies (b. 1923) worked with Joan Brossa on the set of *Or i sal* (Gold and Salt) in 1961. More recently, as Chapter 5 has shown, Frederic Amat (b. 1952) has turned to scenography, providing aggressive, deconstructive sets that build both on the work of his scenographic mentor Puigserver and on his own multi-textured, expressionistic art.

Indeed the roots of much post-War theatre lie in the fertile years between 1906 and 1936 which Xirgu so dominated. David George has recently documented the Madrid-based productions of actor Enric Borràs in the pre-War years (2002: 55–81) but the legacy of the acting models laid out by these two practitioners on future generations of performers remains to be scrutinised. The trajectories of Casares, Espert and Pasqual have all engaged with Xirgu's theatrical and pedagogical practice. Even the directors and designers who have often been associated with the supposedly retrograde 'endorsed' theatre of the Franco era, like Cayetano Luca de Tena and Luis Escobar, followed Xirgu's example in considering practices outside Spain in their promotion of more advanced vocabularies of theatre.[6] As I mention in Chapter 3, Casares is known to have admired Escobar's work, which she saw in Paris in 1958 (105). In his preparations for his English-language staging of Valle-Inclán's *Comedias barbaras*, presented as *Barbaric Comedies* at the 2000 Edinburgh festival, director Calixto Bieito drew on the notebooks of Alonso's 1970 production of *Romance de lobos* (*Wolves! Wolves!*). As well as Bieito, Alonso's disciples included two of his successors as artistic directors of the Centro Dramático Nacional, José

4 For a comprehensive study of Catalan stage design, see Bravo 1986.
5 For further details on Miró's work, see Fernando 1994; on Picasso, see Ocaña 1996; on Dalí, see Gibson 1998.
6 Luca de Tena visited the Third Reich's Chamber of Culture to observe German theatre in 1942 and his admiration of the technical facilities of Berlin's Schiller theatre are known to have impressed him; see London 1998: 43.

Carlos Plaza and Juan Carlos Pérez de la Fuente. Miguel Narros, Francisco Nieva and Lluís Pasqual have also recognised his pervasive influence over the contemporary Spanish theatre (Nieva 1990; Redacción 1990). Espert refers to him as the best director of actors that Spain has produced. Indeed she categorises her favourite directors – Pasqual, Lavelli, Mario Gas and Jorge Lavelli – as Alonso's 'hijos' (sons) when describing their ability to tread the stage with the performer, using gesture, movement and inflexion to mark out the internal dynamics of character (Espert and Ordóñez 2002: 79–80, 178–9). The 'other' theatres of such practitioners live on in the work of those who saw their productions, read their articles espousing a renovation and renewal of the Spanish stage or worked with them.

Too often much of twentieth-century Spanish theatre has been 'forgotten' by those composing the larger histories of international theatre. Xirgu's omission from the pantheon of major European actresses has already been mentioned (22, 56–66) but even the treatment accorded to Casares conveniently overlooks her Castilian-language work in appraising her contribution to the French stage. Too regularly she is cited as a supporting player in Jean Vilar's TNP or the stage journeys of Albert Camus's existentialist dramas, but the scope of her theatrical activities demonstrates wider implications for the categorisation and documentation of Spanish theatre. The internationalism of Lluís Pasqual, like that of Xirgu and Enrique Rambal before him, has nourished 'other' theatrical cultures beyond the Iberian peninsula. La Cubana, like Els Joglars, have pushed theatre away from the proscenium arch into public spaces where their ludic theatricality has undermined the usual physical separation that frames the theatrical performance. There is no need for me to use the conclusion to reiterate the achievements of these practitioners delineated over the course of the book. Rather my concentration on highlighting the work of some of their 'forgotten' contemporaries (and here I refer to institutions as well as individuals) suggests areas for future investigation in advocating an approach which prises apart established assumptions of how theatrical importance is attributed.

Spain has been harshly judged throughout the century as isolated from innovatory currents in stage practice, but even a cursory glance at the figure who is often credited as the country's first stage director, Emilio Mario, points to a familiarity with prevailing French and German theatrical trends which was, in all probability, in no way reciprocated by his French and German contemporaries. In the early 1920s *The Times*' critic Henry Leach made a reference to the richness of a Spanish theatre which boasted Pérez Galdós, María Guerrero and Enric Borràs (1921: 7–15). Nevertheless, Jesús Rubio Jiménez's assertion that 'el teatro sigue ocupando un lugar secundario en el estudio de la cultura del cambio de siglo' (1999b: 16) (theatre continues to occupy a secondary role in the study of *fin de siècle* culture) could be applied to the way in which Spanish theatre has been viewed throughout the century by the English-speaking world. In its dissection of the trajectories of six representative practitioners this book questions assumptions about the remnants that haunt the past century's theatrical psyche.

Xirgu, Rambal, Casares, Espert, Pasqual and La Cubana have all played a seminal role in constructing what is understood to be twentieth-century Spanish theatre. Whilst positivism has alerted us all to the problems inherent in 'passing off contested events as historical facts' (Roach 1992: 294), attempted partial reconstructions of the past productions of these practitioners serve to provide some indication as to what these performances might have looked like and why many have remained undocumented by previous generations of theatre historians. Certainly the construction of narratives is itself shaped by the priorities and desires of the historical moment. At a certain social instance it may have been necessary to construct a theatrical narrative which posited Antonio Buero Vallejo and Alfonso Sastre as the pinnacles of post-Civil War theatre, but my exploration of the work of these six practitioners' theatrical ventures serves to expand the parameters of collective memory, arguing not for a more 'truthful' version of theatrical criticism but rather probing alternative readings which dislodge the primacy of the text. The privileging of the literary over the theatrical which focuses on the written text, in evidence since Aristotle noted the production of stage effects had more to do with machinery than poetry (Aristotle, Horace, Longinus 1983: 41), may have done a disservice both to 'intertheatrical' texts, like those of Rambal and La Cubana, which privilege the non-verbal and work within populist or feminised genres like melodrama, and to the work of directors and performers. Joseph Roach's assertion that 'on the margins of literacy and orality, performance events (or the anecdotes through which they most often survive in memory) may enter into the reconstruction of historic cultural configurations with no less authority than other texts' (1992: 295) presents a challenge for us to move beyond the received dramatic canon towards interactions between artists and audiences which justly recognise the place of the *doing* of performance in shaping theatrical and social landscapes.

Bibliography

A., L. de (1953), 'Anoche estreno de la compañía de Rambal, en el Teatro Lope de Vega la obra titulada *¡Arsénico!', ABC* (24 January): 31.

A., R. (1946), untitled, *Escenario*, n.pag. (Located at the Fundación Juan March's Biblioteca de Teatro Español Contemporáneo.)

Abellán, Joan (1980), 'Conversación con Lluís Pasqual. El Lliure/Genet/*El balcó*', *Pipirijaina*, 16 (September–October): 59–68.

—(1986a), 'Pere Planella: Sublime decisión', in Cuadernos *El Público*, 10: 31–3.

—(1986b), 'Imágenes de un espectador fiel', in Cuadernos *El Público*, 10: 49–69

—(1993), 'Fabià Puigserver, escenógrafo', in Graells and Hormigón (eds): 195–225.

Abellán, Manuel L. (1989), La censura teatral del franquismo', *Estreno*, 15/1 (Autumn): 20–3.

ADE Teatro (1999), *Teatro de la España del siglo XX, 1: 1900–1939*, special number of *ADE Teatro*, 77.

Agate, May (1969), *Madame Sarah [Bernhardt]*. New York: Blom.

Aguilar, Carlos and Jaume Genover (1996), *Las estrellas de nuestro cine: 500 biofilmografías de intérpretes españoles*. Madrid: Alianza Editorial.

Aguilera Sastre, Juan and Manuel Aznar Soler (1999), *Cipriano de Rivas Cherif y el teatro español de su época (1891–1967)*, Teoría y Práctica del Teatro, 16. Madrid: Publicaciones de la Asociación de Directores de Escena de España.

Agustí, Ignasi (1935), 'La darrera obra de García Lorca. *Doña Rosita la soltera o El lenguaje de las flores* al Principal', *L'Instant* (16 December): 6.

Albee, Edward (1965), *Who's Afraid of Virginia Woolf?* Harmondsworth: Penguin.

Alberti, Rafael (1977), *El adefesio*. Barcelona: Aymá S.A. Editora.

—(1987), *La arboleda perdida, libros III y IV de memorias*. Barcelona: Seix Barral.

Alier, Roger (1990), 'Una Marton "espertizada" triunfó en *Elektra*', *La Vanguardia* (29 January): 29.

—(1993), 'Five-o'clock-tea-*Carmen*', *La Vanguardia* (19 March): 52.

Almeida, Manuel (1995), 'Rueda de prensa en tres actos', *La Gaceta de Las Palmas* (8 December): 17.

Alonso, Ángel (1976), '*Divinas palabras*', *Pipirijaina*, 2 (November): 51–2.

Alonso, Eduardo, Josep Maria Benet i Jornet, Hermann Bonnin, Joan Carles Dauder, José Manuel García Iglesias, José Alfonso Gil Albors, Joan Francesc Marco, Adolfo Marsillach, Joan de Sagarra, Rodolf Sirera, Domènec Reixach, Antoni Tordera (1996), 'Puntos de vista: ¿Qué teatro público?', *Escena*, 34 (November): 12–21.

Alonso, José Luis (1965), 'Mi versión de *A Electra le sienta bien el luto*', *Primer Acto*, 70: 23–6.

—(1985), 'José Bódalo, final de partida', *El Público*, 24 (September): 3.

—(1991), *Teatro de cada día: Escritos sobre teatro*, (ed.) Juan Antonio Hormigón, Teoría y Práctica del Teatro, 4. Madrid: Publicaciones de la Asociación de Directores de Escena de España.

Alonso de Santos, José Luis (1986), 'Yo vi la *Yerma* de Nuria Espert', *Primer Acto*, 212 (January–February): 104–5.

—(1987), 'José María Rodero', *Primer Acto*, 217 (January–February): 32–3.

Althusser, Louis (1971), *Lenin and Philosophy*, trans. Ben Brewster. London: New Left Books.

Álvarez Barrientos, Joaquín (1987), 'Desarrollo del teatro popular a finales del siglo XVIII', in Álvarez Barrientos and Cea Bermudez (eds): 215–26.

—(1991), 'Enrique Rambal (1889–1956)', in Ermanno Caldera (ed.), *Teatro di Magia 2*. Rome: Bulzoni Editore: 91–114.

Álvarez Barrientos, Joaquín and Antonio Cea Bermudez (eds) (1987), *Actas de las jornadas sobre teatro popular en España*. Madrid: Consejo Superior de Investigaciones Científicas.

Álvarez Juno, José (1999), 'History, politics and culture, 1875–1936', in Gies (ed.): 67–103.

Álvaro, Francisco (1966), *El espectador y la crítica (El teatro en España en 1965)*. Valladolid: Edición del autor.

—(1968), *El espectador y la crítica (El teatro en España en 1967)*. Valladolid: Edición del autor.

—(1970), *El espectador y la crítica (El teatro en España en 1969)*. Valladolid: Edición del autor.

—(1972), *El espectador y la crítica (El teatro en España en 1971)*. Madrid: Editorial Prensa Española.

—(1977), *El espectador y la crítica (El teatro en España en 1976)*. Madrid: Editorial Prensa Española.

—(1978), *El espectador y la crítica (El teatro en España en 1977)*. Valladolid: Edición del autor.

—(1981), *El espectador y la crítica (El teatro en España en 1980)*. Valladolid: Edición del autor.

—(1984), *El espectador y la crítica (El teatro en España en 1983)*. Valladolid: Edición del autor.

—(1985), *El espectador y la crítica (El teatro en España en 1984)*. Valladolid: Edición del autor.

Amat, Frederic (1988), *El Teatro Federico García Lorca*. Granada: Diputación Provisional de Granada.

Amestoy, Ignacio (1987), 'La inmadurez de *El público*', *Diario 16* (18 January): 39.

—(1989), 'Cum Laude', *Diario 16* (24 June): 33.

—(1997), 'Josep Maria Flotats: *La gaviota* es el grito del censurado', *El Mundo* [Catalunya] (11 October), 'La Esfera' supplement: 4–5.

—(1999), 'Margarita Xirgu, maestra', in ADE Teatro: 240–3.

Amich i Bert, Josep 'Amichatis' (1914), 'Los Teatros. Novedades. Debut de la actriz Margarita Xirgu', *El Día Gráfico* (31 May): 8–9.

Amorós, Andrés (1999a), 'El teatro popular: Enrique Rambal' (unpublished): 1–8.

—(1999b), 'Teatro Popular', in Amorós and Díez Borque (eds): 135–45.

Amorós, Andrés and José María Díez Borque (eds) (1999), *Historia de los espectáculos en España*. Madrid: Editorial Castalia.

Andrews, Nigel (1999), 'So that's what all the fuss is about', *Financial Times* (15 April): 28.

Anon. (1935a), 'Teló enlaire', *L'Esquella de la Torratxa* (13 September): 1481.

—(1935b), 'En el Barcelona se estrenó *Yerma* de García Lorca con un éxito inolvidable', *La Vanguardia* (18 September): 27.

—(1946), *Escenario* (Uncredited press cutting located at the Fundación Juan March's Biblioteca de Teatro Español Contemporáneo).

—(1953a), 'El porqué del éxito de la gran película *El prisionero de Parma*, presentada por Hispano-Mexicana-Films', *Primer Plano*, 13/669 (9 August): n.pag.

—(1953b), 'Hoy, estreno en el Palacio de la Música *Orfeo* de Jean Cocteau', *Ya* (10 November): 6.

—(1964a), '*Divinas palabras*', *Leoplan* (16 September).

—(1964b), 'Palabras no tan divinas', *Atlántida* (21 October).

—(1967a), 'Bilingual production is slated at college', *Daily Hampshire Gazette* (28 April).

—(1967b), 'Spanish and English play by Lorca is planned', *Springfield Mass., Daily News* (26 April).

—(1967c), '*Médéa* un grand spectacle', *Le Méridional* (19 July): 10.

—(1967d), 'Impasses', *Les Lettres Françaises* (11 October): 19.

—(1967e), 'Le premier ministre a retrouvé Sénèque' (uncredited press clipping, Archives Nationales, Paris).

—(1967f), 'Entrevista con Nuria Espert', *Primer Acto*, 84: 16–22.

—(1969a), 'Falleció Margarita Xirgu', *Diario de Barcelona* (26 April): 3–4.

—(1969b), 'Ha muerto Margarita Xirgu', *El Correo Catalán* (26 April): 3.

—(1969c), 'Última hora Montevideo. Ha fallecido Margarita Xirgu', *La Vanguardia Española* (26 April): 5.

—(1969d), 'Muere Margarita Xirgu, una catalana universal', *Diario de Barcelona* (27 April): 2.

—(1969e), 'Margarita Xirgu. Una catalana de talla universal. Sesenta años de teatro se hallan representados en la actriz desaparecida', *El Correo Catalán* (27 April): 36.

—(1969f), 'Tributo en memoria de la gran Margarita Xirgu. Evocación de la actriz a sus ochenta años', *La Vanguardia Española* (27 April): 24.

—(1973), 'Un acontecimiento *Yerma* esta noche, en el Coliseum', *La Vanguardia Española* (14 February): 53.

—(1982a), 'Homenaje a Margarita Xirgu', *Primer Acto*, 192 (January–February): 106.

—(1982b), 'Muere en París el director teatral argentino Víctor García', *El País* (30 August): 1, 32.

—(1983a), 'Núria Espert, elogio de la pasión viva', *El País* (27 August), 'Artes' supplement: 5.

—(1983b), 'Elogios para Nuria Espert en el Festival de Edimburgo', *El País* (2 September): 19.

—(1985), 'Lluís Pasqual, Caballero frances', *El Público*, 20 (May): 4.

—(1986), 'Tiempo de homenajes. Nuria Espert: una altra *Yerma*, si us plau', *El Público*, 30 (March): 36–7.

—(1987a), 'Damper on *The Tempest*'s torrent', *Evening Standard* (16 July): 3.

—(1987b), 'El grupo español La Cubana, obligado a suspender sus actuaciones en Londres', *Ideal* (18 July): 22.

—(1987c), '*Yerma* en Berlín', *Primer Acto*, 221 (November–December): 132.

—(1988), 'El centenario de la Xirgu', *Primer Acto*, 226 (November–December): 149.

—(1990), 'Núria Espert: "Me excita pensar que me puedo partir la cabeza en este estreno"', *ABC* (24 May): 103.

—(1997a), 'La Cubana se despide de Madrid', *ABC* (10 January): 112.

—(1997b), 'Pasqual acepta diseñar la Ciutat del Teatre', *El Mundo* [Catalunya] (13 May), 'Barcelona' supplement: 4.

Antón, Jacinto (1992), 'La Cubana renuncia a actuar en el Festival de las Artes y aduce falta de apoyo institucional', *El País* (1 May): 35.

—(1995), 'La apoteosis de Estrellita Verdiales, huerfanita', *El País* [Edición Barcelona] (1 February), 'Cataluña' supplement: 8.

—(1998), 'Lluís Pasqual: "¡Quién sabe cómo era Lorca!"', *El País* (12 May): 36.

—(1999a), 'La Fura dels Baus crea la gran ceremonia de fin de año en Barcelona', *El País* [Edición Cataluña] (2 December), 'Cataluña' supplement: 9.

—(1999b), 'El sector teatral expresa su descontento con el proyecto de Pasqual para la Ciutat del Teatre', *El País* [Edición Cataluña] (3 December), 'Cataluña' supplement: 15.

—(2000a), 'Lluís Pasqual: *L'hort dels cirerers* es una historia de personas, personas, y personas', *El País* [Edición Cataluña] (16 February), 'Cataluña' supplement: 14.

—(2000b), 'Pasqual decide no liderar el cambio del Teatre Lliure', *El País* [Edición Cataluña] (19 July): 'Cataluña' supplement: 1, 6.

—(2000c), 'El Lliure y los idus de marzo', *El País* [Edición Cataluña] (22 July), 'Cataluña' supplement: 3.

Antón, Jacinto and Agustí Fancelli (1997), 'Sense Flotats, el TNC serà un museu', *El País* [Edición Cataluña] (6 November), 'Quadern' supplement: 1–2.

Aranda, Quim (1997), 'Flotats triunfa ante su verdugo con *La gavina*', *El Mundo* (Catalunya), (15 October), 'Barcelona' supplement: 4.

Araujo-Costa, Luis (1933), 'Veladas teatrales. Español. Estreno de la tragicomedia en tres jornadas divididas en quince cuadros, de don Ramón del Valle-Inclán *Divinas palabras*', *La Época* (17 November): 1.

Arce, Juan Carlos (1983), 'A medio siglo de *Divinas palabras*', *El Público*, 2 (November): 6.

Arco, Antonio (1991), 'Jordi Milán: "Nuestros espectáculos están copiados de la vida, por eso son cachondos"', *La Verdad* (18 May): 62.

Arco, Miguel Ángel del (2000), 'Cincuenta intelectuales y artistas escogen a los maestros españoles de la cultura', *Tiempo*, 922 (3 January): 14–22.

Aristotle, Horace, Longinus (1983), *Classical Literary Criticism*, trans. T. S. Dorsch. Harmondsworth: Penguin.

Arroyo, Julia (1986), 'Madre Coraje y sus hijos. Sólo belleza formal', *Ya* (8 February): 48.

Artis, Andreu A. (1935a), 'Teatre. La més gran actualitat. Els teatres castellà i català, a través de l'interès i de la passió de Margarida Xirgu', *La Rambla de Catalunya* (16 September): 5.

—(1935b), 'Principal Palace. *Bodas de sangre* per Margarida Xirgu', *La Rambla de Catalunya* (25 November): 11.

Aslan, Odette (1975), 'L'interprétation des *Bonnes*', in Bablet and Jacquot (eds): 173–200.

—(1988), *Roger Blin,* trans. Ruby Cohn. Cambridge: Cambridge University Press.

Attwood, Brian and Yasmine Kartal (1987), 'LIFT dealt a double blow', *The Stage and Television Today* (23 July): 2.

Aubach, Jordi (2000), 'Proyecto Ciudad del Teatro. Una metrópolis para la escena', *Escena*, 61 (2000): 14–15.

Audouard, Yvan (1966), 'Un auteur dans le vent ou pet en Algérie', *Paris Presse* (27 April): 7.

Avilés, Juan Carlos (1990), '*Cómeme el coco, negro*', *Guía Madrid*, 83 (10–16 November): 32.

Ayén, Xavi (1999), 'Los intelectuales quieren mandar', *La Vanguardia* (17 September): 48.

Aznar Navarro, F. (1920), 'Informaciones teatrales. *El maleficio de la mariposa*', *La Correspondencia de España* (23 March): 4.

Aznar Soler, Manuel (1996), *Veinte años de teatro y democracia en España* (1975–1995). Barcelona: C.I.T.E.C.

Bablet, Denis (1975), 'Tentative et conclusion', in Bablet and Jacquot (eds): 305–10.

Bablet, Denis and Jean Jacquot (eds) (1975), *Les Voies de la création théâtrale, Vol. 4*. Paris: Centre National de la Recherche Scientifique.

Badiou, Maryse (1984), 'Las locas aventuras de La Cubana', *El Público*, 6 (March): 24–6.

—(1986), 'Josep Maria Flotats: La puerta de entrada', in Cuadernos *El Público*, 10: 36–8.

—(1988), 'Molins del Rei recuerda a Margarita Xirgu', *El Público*, 61 (October): 34–5.

Baget Herms, J. M. (1994), 'Opinión. Una Nochebuena sin secretos', *La Vanguardia* (27 December), 'Revista' supplement: 6.

—(1997), 'Días de polémica', *La Vanguardia* (14 May), 'Revista' supplement: 8.

Bakhtin, Mikhail (1968), *Rabelais and His World*, trans. Hélène Iswolsky. Cambridge: Massachusetts Institute of Technology Press.

Banham, Martin (ed.) (1988), *The Cambridge Companion to Theatre*. Cambridge: Cambridge University Press.

Barber, John (1977), 'Primitive romp from play about words', *Daily Telegraph* (15 June): 15.

—(1986), 'Hunger gives way to despair', *Daily Telegraph* (20 August): 8.

Barber, Stephen (1993), *Antonin Artaud: Blows and Bombs*. London and Boston: Faber & Faber.

Baring, Maurice (1934), *Sarah Bernhardt.* New York: D. Appleton Century Company.

Barjaval, René (1948), '*L'État de siège*', *Carrefour* (3 November): 11.

Barrado, Mercedes (1992), 'La Cubana: Así somos si así nos parece', *Hoy* (14 November): 12.

Barthes, Roland (1975), *The Pleasure of the Text*, trans. Richard Miller. New York: Hill & Wang.

—(1993), 'Une tragédienne sans public', in *Oeuvres complètes. Vol. 1*. Paris: Seuil: 410–12.

Bassnett, Susan (1996), 'Adelaide Ristori', in Booth *et al.*: 117–69.

Batlle i Jordà, Carles, Isidre Bravo, and Jordi Coca (1992), *Adrià Gual: Mitja vida de modernisme*. Barcelona: Diputació de Barcelona.

Bayón, Miguel (1988), 'Entrevista María Casares: "En España se malgasta mucha energía"', *Cambio 16*, 873 (22 August): 45.

Beauvoir, Simone de (1965), *The Prime of Life*, trans. Peter Green. Harmondsworth: Penguin Books.

Beckmesser (1997), 'El Teatro Real: una crisis interminable', *ABC* (17 February): 90.

Belasko, Ana (1999), 'Adolfo Marsillach y Nuria Espert se reencuentran en los escenarios', *El Mundo* (7 May), consulted online (www.el-mundo.es).

Bellveser, Ricardo (1987), *Teatro de la encrucijada*. Valencia: Ayuntamiento de Valencia.

Benach, Joan-Anton (1969), '*Las criadas*: entre el servilismo y la rebeldia', *El Correo Catalán* (23 February): 26.

—(1973), 'Yerma: Lorca sobre la lona', El Correo Catalán (16 February): 34.

—(1977), 'Teatro Barcelona. El adefesio, plástico y monumental', El Correo Catalán (6 March): 31

—(1978), 'Eduard II de Marlowe-Bercht, gran espectáculo de actores', El Correo Catalán (12 May): 29.

—(1983), 'El Teatre Lliure en el misterio de Shakespeare', El Público, 3 (December): 14–15.

—(1986), 'Diez años de Teatre Lliure: Muchas horas de placer', in Cuadernos El Público, 10: 11–14.

—(1988), 'Shakespeare y la banda de los catalanes', La Vanguardia (17 March): 37.

—(1989), 'La Cubana estrena Cómeme el coco, negro. Las tripas del "music-hall"', La Vanguardia (5 June): 41.

—(1990a), 'Aquellas generosas variedades', La Vanguardia (30 January): 35.

—(1990b), 'Núria Espert en Maquillaje: la generosa confesión de una diva', La Vanguardia (26 May): 45.

—(1991a), 'Aviñón se resiste al Valle-Inclán de Lavelli', La Vanguardia (11 July): 37.

—(1991b), '¿La "grandeur" cultural en peligro?', La Vanguardia (11 July): 37.

—(1991c), 'Seis horas con Valle-Inclán', La Vanguardia (6 October): 79.

—(1994), 'La Cubana y el reflote de Banesto', La Vanguardia (30 January): 62.

—(1995), 'Tragicomedia sobre el final de la utopía', La Vanguardia (8 May): 44.

—(1996), 'Una perenne y apasionada virginidad', La Vanguardia (23 November): 43.

—(1997), 'Brillante Gavina con perdigones incluidos', La Vanguardia (16 October): 53.

—(1999), 'Un Godot para la historia', La Vanguardia (15 February): 46.

—(2000), 'Aires de cambio para un gran Chejov', La Vanguardia (20 February): 70.

—(2001), 'Alocada tramoya del bel canto', La Vanguardia (14 June): 45.

—(2002), 'La cara y cruz de una gran tragedia', La Vanguardia (18 July): 40.

Benavente, Jacinto (1922), Teatro 1, 5th edn. Madrid: Librería de los Suc. de Hernando.

Bernat y Durán (1935), 'En el Principal Palace. Bodas de sangre. De Federico García Lorca, interpretada por Margarita Xirgu', El Noticiero Universal (28 November): 10.

Billington, Michael (1983), 'Dona [sic] Rosita', Guardian (31 August): 9.

—(1986), 'Women in chains', Guardian (10 September): 9.

—(1987), 'La tempestad', Guardian (15 July): 28.

—(1997), 'Enter Catalans at the charge. Blinded by Love', Guardian (16 August): 6.

Birringer, Johannes (1996), 'This is the theatre that was expected and foreseen', Performance Research, 1/1: 32–45.

Blyth, Alan (1989), 'Butterfly for all seasons', Daily Telegraph (25 January): 14.

Bonavía, Salvador (1913), 'Una conversa amb l'Enric Borràs', El Teatre Català (17 May): 317–18.

Bonnín Valls, Ignacio (1998), El teatro español desde 1940 a 1980. Estudio histórico-crítico de tendencias y autores. Barcelona: Ediciones Octaedro, S.L.

Booth, Michael R., John Stokes, Susan Bassnett (1996), Three Tragic Actresses: Siddons, Rachel, Ristori. Cambridge: Cambridge University Press.

Borrás, Tomás and Valentín de Pedro (1930), Fabiola o Los mártires cristianos. Madrid: La Farsa.

Boué, Michel (1991), 'Dans les miroirs du bordel', L'Humanité (22 May): 20.

Boyle, Catherine (1992), Chilean Theater, 1973–1985: Marginality, Power, Selfhood. London and Toronto: Associated University Presses.

—(1995), 'The politics of popular music: On the dynamics of new song', in Graham and Labanyi (eds): 291–4.

Bradby, David (1984), Modern French Drama: 1940–1980. Cambridge: Cambridge University Press.

—(1994), 'Genet, the theatre and the Algerian war', Theatre Research International, 19/3: 226–37.

Bradby, David and Maria M. Delgado (2002), 'Introduction: Piecing together the Paris jigsaw', in Bradby and Delgado (eds): 1–33.

—(eds) (2002), The Paris Jigsaw: Internationalism and the City's Stages. Manchester: Manchester University Press.

Bradshaw, Nick (1999), 'Actresses', Time Out (14–21 April): 78.

Bratton, Jacky (2000), 'Reading the intertheatrical; or, the mysterious disappearance of Susanna

Centlivre', in Maggie B. Gale and Viv Gardner (eds), *Women and Performance: New Histories, New Historiographies*. Manchester: Manchester University Press: 7–24.

Bravo, Isidre (1986), *L'escenografia catalana*. Barcelona: Diputació de Barcelona.

Bravo, Julio (1998), 'Nuria Espert, en nombre de María Callas', *ABC* (16 March): 104–5.

Brennan, Mary (1983), '*Dona [sic] Rosita*', *Glasgow Herald* (31 August): 4.

Bronfen, Elisabeth (1992), *Over Her Dead Body: Death, Femininity and the Aesthetic*. Manchester: Manchester University Press.

Brook, Peter (1972), *The Empty Space*. Harmondsworth: Penguin.

Brown G. G. (1972), *A Literary History of Spain: The Twentieth Century*. London and New York: Ernest Benn and Barnes & Noble.

Bruce, Peter (1992), 'Catalan socialists and nationalists play games with the Games', *Financial Times* (24 July): 2.

Brunstein, Robert (1973), 'Tragedy on a trampoline', *Observer* (8 April): 34.

Buero Vallejo, Antonio (1985), *Historia de una escalera. Las meninas*. Madrid: Espasa-Calpe.

Burgos, Carmen de 'Colombine' (n.d.), *Confidencias de artistas*. Madrid: Sociedad Española de Librería.

Burgueño, María Esther and Roger Mirza (1988), 'Margarita en América, una pasión inextinguible', in Cuadernos *El Público*, 36: 21–7.

Burguet i Ardiaca, Francesc (1985), 'María Casares: "El teatro es todo lo contrario de un debate"', *El País* [Edición Cataluña] (6 August): 21.

—(1991), 'Sis hores de teatre poden arribar a cansar', *El Diari de Barcelona* (6 October): 37.

Burnet, Andrew (1997), '*Cegada de amor (Blinded by Love)*', *The List* (22–28 August): 49.

Butler, Judith (1990), *Gender Trouble*. London: Routledge.

Butler, Robert (1997), 'Love in a time of interactive kitschness', *Independent on Sunday* (17 August), 'The Critics' supplement: 11.

C., A. (1933), 'Informaciones teatrales. En Madrid. Español: *Divinas palabras*', *ABC* (17 November): 37.

C., S. (1989), 'El público de Lorca', *Diario 16* (24 June): 56.

Cabal, Fermín (1989), 'Tras la temporada de Madrid, repaso a tres años de trabajo. Teatre Lliure "Un teatro de arte para todos"', *Primer Acto*, 182 (December): 7–26.

Cabal, Fermín and José Luis Alonso de Santos (1985), *Teatro español de los 80*. Madrid: Editorial Fundamentos.

Caballero, Óscar (1991), 'María Casares deslumbra París con sus francesas *Comedias bárbaras*', *La Vanguardia* (5 June): 62.

—(1996), 'María Casares, el gran mito del teatro francés, fallece a los 74 años', *La Vanguardia* (23 November): 43.

—(2000), 'La residencia de María Casares será un modélico centro de creación', *La Vanguardia* (13 May): 61.

Camp, André (1985), 'Illusions comiques et dramatiques', *L'Avant-Scène Théâtre*, 763 (1 February): 49–51.

Camus, Albert (1948), *L'État de siège*. Paris: Éditions Gallimard.

—(1950), *Les Justes*. Paris: Éditions Gallimard.

—(1958), *Caligula suivi de Le Malentendu*. Paris: Éditions Gallimard.

Canning, Hugh (1991),'Tragic waste of *Carmen*'s magic', *Sunday Times* (5 May): 5.

Cantieri Mora, Giovanni (1960), 'Ovaciones y protestas para el *Hamlet* de Nuria Espert', *Primer Acto*, 15 (July–August): 60.

Cañizares Bundorf, Nathalie (1999), 'María Guerrero: La buena estrella', in ADE Teatro 1999: 234–6.

—(2000), *Memoria de un escenario: Teatro María Guerrero, 1885–2000*. Madrid: Ministerio de Educación y Cultura, Instituto Nacional de las Artes Escénicas y de la Música.

Capdevilla, Lluís (1935), 'Interpretació, direcció i "mise en scène" de *Doña Rosita la soltera o El lenguaje de las flores*', *L'Humanitat* (17 September): 2.

Capdevila, Montse (1988), 'París aplaude la versión de *El público* de Pasqual', *El Periódico* (8 April): 44.

Capmany, Maria Aurèlia (1986), 'La fe más oportunista', in Cuadernos *El Público*, 10: 10.

Carlson, Marvin (1996), *Performance: A Critical Introduction*. London and New York: Routledge.

Caro Baroja, Julio (1974), *Teatro popular y de magia*. Madrid: Biblioteca de Ciencias Històrics, Revista de Occidente.

Carr, Raymond (1980), *Modern Spain 1875–1980*. Oxford, New York, Toronto, Melbourne: Oxford University Press.

Carretero, José María 'El Caballero Audaz' (n.d.), *Lo que sé por mí. Confesiones del siglo (Segunda serie)*. Madrid: Viuda e Hijos de Sanz Calleja.

—(1943) *Galería. Más de cien vidas extraordinarias contadas por sus protagonistas y comentadas por El Caballero Audaz*. Madrid: Ediciones Caballero Audaz.

Carrion, Ambrosi (1916), 'El moment actual del teatre català. Conceptes', *El Teatre Català* (22 January): 54.

Casacuberta, Margarida (1997), *Santiago Rusiñol: Vida, literatura i mite*. Barcelona: Curial/Publicacions de l'Abadia de Montserrat.

Casarès, Maria (1980), *Résidente privilégiée*. Paris: Librairie Arthème Fayard.

—(1981), *Residente privilegiada*, trans. Fabián García-Prieto Buendía and Enrique Sordo. Barcelona: Editorial Argos Vergara, S.A.

—(1990a), 'Les confins au centre du monde', *Alternatives Théâtrales*, 35–6 (June): 25–8.

—(1990b), 'Comédiens, entretiens-portraits – 7', *Théâtre/Public*, 96 (November–December): 12–16.

—(1991), 'Don Ramon', in Philippe Bourrut Lacouture (ed.), *Comédies barbares*. Paris: Éditions Archimbaud-Mentha: 1–2.

—(1997), 'Une résidente privilégiée', *Theatre/Public*, 135 (May–June): 8–13.

Castellón, Antonio (1975), 'Proyectos de reforma del teatro español 1920/1939', *Primer Acto*, 176 (January): 4–13.

Castells, Joan (1976), 'Valle-Inclán, según la fuerza de Nuria Espert y la imaginación creadora de Víctor García', *Diario de Barcelona* (7 October): 24.

Castells, Manuel (1997), *The Information Age. Economy, Society and Culture. Vol. 1: The Power of Identity*. Oxford: Blackwell.

Castells Altirriba, Joan (1987), 'El "Lliure" hacia un nuevo modelo de teatro. Aspira a una sede en las Arenas', *Primer Acto*, 218 (March–April): 108–12.

Castro, Antonio (1979), 'Entrevista con Carlos Saura', *Dirigido Por,* 69: 44–51.

Cendrós, Teresa (1997), 'Núria Espert y Rosa Maria Sardà encarnan en *Actrius* a personajes inspirados en ellas mismas', *El País* [Edición Cataluña] (15 January), 'Cataluña' supplement: 8.

Centeno, Enrique (1994), '*El cerco de Leningrado*, dos mujeres en la utopía', *Diario 16* (14 October): 32.

Centro de Investigaciones Literarias Españolas y Hispanoamericanas (1990), *Quién es quién en el teatro y el cine español e hispanoamericano*. Barcelona: C.I.L.E.H.

Centro Dramático Nacional (ed.) (1984), *Luces de bohemia*. Madrid: Ministerio de Cultura, Instituto Nacional de las Artes Escénicas y de la Música.

—(ed.) (1986a), *Madre Coraje y sus hijos*. Madrid: Ministerio de Cultura, Instituto Nacional de las Artes Escénicas y de la Música.

—(ed.) (1986b), *5 Lorcas 5*. Madrid: Ministerio de Cultura, Instituto Nacional de las Artes Escénicas y de la Música.

—(ed.) (1987), *El público*. Madrid: Ministerio de Cultura, Instituto Nacional de las Artes Escénicas y de la Música.

—(ed.) (1988), *La vida del Rey Eduardo II de Inglaterra*. Madrid: Ministerio de Cultura, Instituto Nacional de las Artes Escénicas y de la Música.

—(ed.) (1989), *Comedia sin título*. Madrid: Ministerio de Cultura, Instituto Nacional de las Artes Escénicas y de la Música.

Cester, Xavier (1999), 'Per fi!', *Avui* (9 October): 55.

Chabás, Juan (1933), 'Se estrena en el Español *Divinas palabras*, de Valle-Inclán', *Luz* (17 November): 6.

Chaillet, Ned (1977), '*Divinas palabras*', *Plays and Players* (August): 26–7.

Charensol, Georges (1947), 'Dos películas francesas, *Le Mariage de Ramuntcho* y *La séptima puerta*', *Cinema* (15 July): n.pag.

Charest, Rémy (1997), *Robert Lepage: Connecting Flights*. London: Methuen Drama.

Chekhov, Anton (1997), *La gavina*, trans. Raquel Ribó. Barcelona: Edicions del Teatre Nacional.

Christopher, James (1997), 'This Spanish director doesn't care for plots. He prefers pigeons', *Observer* (17 August), 'Review' supplement: 8.

Clapp, Susanna (1997), 'Catalonia dreamin'', *Observer* (17 August), 'Review' supplement: 8.

Claver, José María (1971), 'Rampas y focos para *Yerma* en un montaje quizá contradictorio', *Ya* (1 December): 43.

Clements, Andrew (1989), '*La Traviata*', *Financial Times* (27 April): 27.

Coad, Emma Dent (1995), 'Artistic patronage and enterprise culture', in Graham and Labanyi (eds): 373–6.

Cobb, C. H. (n.d.), 'Recuperation: an aspect of the cultural policy of the Francoist regime' (unpublished): 1–14.

Cockrell, Dale (1997), *Demons of Disorder: Early Blackface Minstrels and Their World*. Cambridge: Cambridge University Press.

Cohn, Ruby (1998), *From Desire to Godot: Pocket Theater of Post War Paris*. London and New York: Calder Publications/Riverrun Press.

Colomer, Víctor (1984), 'Vicky Plana, La Cubana', *Diario de Sabadell* (2 March): 5.

Cominges, Jorge de (1997), 'Actrices', *Fotogramas* (January): 10.

Comisión Nacional del Centenario García Lorca (1998), *Federico García Lorca (1898–1936)*. Madrid: tf. Editores.

Compte, Carmen (1975), '*Les Bonnes* dans la réalisation espagnole de Victor Garcia', in Bablet and Jacquot (eds): 257–78.

Constantinidis, Stratos E. (1993), *Theatre Under Deconstruction? A Question of Approach*. New York and London: Garland Press.

Coppermann, Annie (1986), '*Quai Ouest*', *Les Échos* (5 May): 30.

Corbalán, Pablo (1971), 'La popularidad de García Lorca (A propósito de *Yerma*)', *El Noticiero Universal* (13 December): 7.

Corberó, Salvador (1973), 'Triunfo de Nuria Espert con la *Yerma* de García Lorca – García – Puigserver', *Diario de Barcelona* (16 February): 19.

Cornago Bernal, Óscar (1999), *La vanguardia teatral en España (1965–1975): Del ritual al juego*. Madrid: Visor.

—(2001), *Discurso teórico y puesta en escena en los años sesenta: La encrucijada de los 'realismos'*. Madrid: Consejo Superior de Investigaciones Científicas, Instituto de la Lengua Española.

Costa, Jordi (1997), 'Made in heaven', *Avui* (20 January): 37.

Costaz, Gilles (1991), 'Une fresque baroque', *Les Échos* (15 July): 26.

Cournot, Michel (1989), 'La comédie de libertés', *Le Monde* (23 December): 10.

—(1991), 'Roses de sang', *Le Monde* (12 July): 11.

Coveney, Michael (1977), '*Divinas palabras*', *Financial Times* (15 June): 3.

Cowan, David F. (1983), '*Dona [sic] Rosita*', *The Stage* (15 September): 23.

Craig, Sandy (1983), 'Lorca's elegy to youth', *Sunday Times* (21 August), 'Magazine' supplement: 36.

Crisp, Colin (1993), *The Classic French Cinema, 1930–1960*. Bloomington and Indianapolis: Indiana University Press.

Cruz, Juan (1982), 'Muere en París el director teatral Víctor García' *El País* (30 August): 32.

Cruz Hernández, María (1969), 'Editorial', *Yorick*, 34 (May): 4.

Cruz Salido (1935), 'En Barcelona. Margarita Xirgu. Estreno de una obra de García Lorca', *Política* (15 December): 2.

Cuadernos *El Público*, 10 (1986), *El Lliure cumple diez años*, (ed.) Joan Abellán. Madrid: Centro de Documentación Teatral.

—, 36 (1988), *Margarita Xirgu: Crónica de una pasión*. Madrid: Centro de Documentación Teatral.

Cuadrado, Núria (1992), '*Cubana Marathon Dancing*, o cómo bailar hasta morir', *ABC* (26 June),

'Cataluña' supplement: xv.

—(1998), 'El inflejo de una luz especial', *El Mundo* [Catalunya], (16 May) 'La Esfera' supplement: 5.

—(2000), 'Lluís Pasqual/Director del Teatre Lliure. "Defenderé el Teatre Lliure pero no me disfrazaré de Juana de Arco"', *El Mundo* [Catalunya] (13 February), 'Catalunya' supplement: 10.

Cuestas, Amalia (1998), *'Blinded by Love*: Hilarious imagination', *Buenos Aires Herald* (18 March): 9.

Cueva, Jorge de la (1933), 'Español. *Divinas palabras*', *El Debate* (17 November): 6.

Cueva, José de la (1931), 'Correo de teatros. En el Español. *Fermín Galán*', *Informaciones* (2 June): 6.

—(1933), 'Correo de teatros. En el Español, *Divinas palabras*', *Informaciones* (17 November): 7.

Cuevas, Ángel (1976), 'Tívoli. *Divinas palabras*', *La Prensa* (8 October): 25.

Culshaw, Peter (1987), untitled preview of *La tempestad, City Limits* (9–16 July): 66.

Davies, Lisa E. (1973), 'Oscar Wilde in Spain', *Comparative Literature*, 25: 136–52.

Delgado, Maria M. (1998a), 'Enrique Rambal (1889–1956): The forgotten auteur of Spanish popular theatre', in *Spanish Theatre 1920–1995: Strategies in Protest and Imagination* (2), *Contemporary Theatre Review*, 7/3: 67–92.

—(1998b), 'Redefining Spanish theatre: Lluís Pasqual on directing, Fabià Puigserver, and the Lliure', in *Spanish Theatre 1920–1995: Strategies in Protest and Imagination* (3), *Contemporary Theatre Review*, 7/4: 81–109.

—(1999), 'Lluís Pasqual's unknown Lorcas', in Sebastian Doggart and Michael Thompson (eds), *Fire, Blood and the Alphabet: One Hundred Years of Lorca*. Durham: Durham Modern Languages Series, University of Durham: 81–106.

—(2000), 'Federico García Lorca: An icon for every age', in Caridad Svich (ed.), *Federico García Lorca, Impossible Theater*. Hanover, New Hampshire: Smith & Kraus: viii–xiv.

—(2001a), 'Inscribing the invisible: Enrique Rambal and twentieth-century Spanish theatre' in *Morality and Justice: The Challenge of European Theatre*, a special issue of *European Studies*, 17: 191–207.

—(2001b), *Inscription and Erasure on the Twentieth-Century Spanish Stage: The Popular Theatre of Enrique Rambal*, Papers in Spanish and Latin American Theatre History, 8. London: Department of Hispanic Studies, Queen Mary, University of London.

—(2001c), 'Barcelona', *Plays International*, 16/12 (September–October): 28–32.

—(2002a), 'An Argentine in Paris: An interview with Jorge Lavelli', in Bradby and Delgado (eds): 218–31.

—(2002b), '"Paris as a kind of meeting point": An email interview with Lluís Pasqual', in Bradby and Delgado (eds): 211–17.

—(2002c), 'Barcelona', *Plays International*, 17/12 (September–October): 26–9.

Delgado, Maria M. and Gwynne Edwards (1990), 'From Madrid to Stratford East: *The Public* in performance', *Estreno*, 16/2 (Autumn): 11–18, 6.

Delgado, Maria M. and Paul Heritage (eds) (1996), *In Contact with the Gods? Directors Talk Theatre*. Manchester: Manchester University Press.

Derrida, Jacques (1978), *Writing and Difference*, trans. Alan Bass. London: Routledge.

—(1981), *Positions*, trans. Alan Bass. London: Athlone Press.

Diamond, Elin (1996), *Performance and Cultural Politics*. London: Routledge.

Díez-Canedo, Enrique (1931), 'Información teatral. *Fermín Galán*', *El Sol* (2 June): 1.

—(1934), 'Información teatral. *Yerma*, el poema trágico de Federico García Lorca, obtuvo un extraordinario éxito en el Español', *La Voz* (31 December): 3.

—(1935), 'Notas del domingo. Margarita Xirgu terminó su temporada con *El villano en su rincón*', *La Voz* (24 June): 5.

—(1968), *Artículos de crítica teatral: El teatro español de 1914 a 1936, 1. Elementos de renovación*. Mexico: Joaquín Mortiz.

Díez Crespo, M. (1971), '*Yerma,* en versión de Víctor García', *El Alcázar* (1 December): 16.

—(1980), '*Doña Rosita la soltera* de García Lorca', *El Alcázar* (14 September): 35.

Dollimore, Jonathan (1994), 'Introduction: Shakespeare, cultural materialism and the new historicism', in Dollimore and Sinfield (eds): 2–17.

Dollimore, Jonathan and Alan Sinfield (eds) (1994), *Political Shakespeare: Essays in Cultural Materialism,* 2nd edn. Manchester: Manchester University Press.

Doménech, Ricardo (1965), '*A Electra le sienta bien el luto*', *Primer Acto,* 70 (1965): 27–9.

—(1968), 'Cinco estrenos para la historia del teatro español', *Primer Acto,* 100 (December): 18–34.

Donald (1953), 'Ayer se estrenó *Orfeo* en el Palacio de la Música', *ABC* (11 November): 39.

Dougherty, Dru (1999), 'Theater and culture, 1868–1936', in Gies (ed.): 211–21.

—(2000), '"Es un asco el teatro"; Eduardo Marquina y el estreno de *Mariana Pineda* en Barcelona (1927)', in Monegal and Micó (eds): 17–31.

Dougherty, Dru and María Francisca Vilches de Frutos (1990), *La escena madrileña entre 1918 y 1926: Análisis y documentación.* Madrid: Editorial Fundamentos.

—(1993), 'Valle-Inclán y el teatro de su época: La recepción en Madrid de *La cabeza del bautista*', in Schiavo (ed.): 61–70.

—(eds) (1992), *El teatro en España entre la tradición y la vanguardia (1918–39).* Madrid: Consejo Superior de Investigaciones Científicas/Fundación Federico García Lorca/Tabacalera, S.A.

Dumur, Guy (1966), 'Le pire est toujours sûr', *Le Nouvel Observateur* (27 April): 38.

—(1973), 'A pleins poumons', *Le Nouvel Observateur* (8 October): 62.

—(1976), 'Démons et fantômes', *Le Nouvel Observateur* (1 March): 85.

—(1983), 'Le défi de Patrice Chéreau', *Le Nouvel Observateur* (17 June): 95.

—(1991), 'La fête du verbe. Bordel de luxe', *Le Nouvel Observateur* (16 May): 155.

Duponchelle, Valérie (1991), 'L'Espagne réhabilite Valle-Inclán', *Le Figaro* (undated press cutting from the Maison Jean Vilar, Avignon).

Durán, Silvia (1991), 'La Cubana se despide de *Cómeme el coco, negro* en La Habana', *La Vanguardia* (29 August): 27.

Dussane, Beatrice (1953), *Maria Casarès.* Paris: Calmann-Lévy.

Eaude, Michael (2001), 'A life in writing', *Guardian* (10 February), 'Saturday Review' supplement: 11.

Eder, Richard (1971), 'Madrid: Triumph of Lorca's *Yerma*', *New York Times* (27 December): 36.

Edwards, Gwynne (1985), *Dramatists in Perspective: Spanish Theatre in the Twentieth Century.* Cardiff: University of Wales Press.

—(1999), '*Yerma* on Stage', *Anales de la Literatura Española Contemporánea,* 24/3: 433–51.

—(2000), 'Productions of *La casa de Bernarda Alba*', *Anales de la Literatura Española Contemporánea,* 25: 671–700.

—(ed.) (1994), *Lorca Plays: Three.* London: Methuen Drama.

Eichelbaum, Samuel (1946), '*El adefesio*', *Sur,* 14/117 (July): 100–2.

Ellman, Richard (ed.) (1969), *The Artist as Critic: Critical Writings of Oscar Wilde.* New York: Random House.

Elorza, Antonio (1995), 'Some perspectives on the nation-state and autonomies in Spain', in Graham and Labanyi (eds): 332–6.

Elsaesser, Thomas (1985), 'Tales of sound and fury: Observations on the family melodrama', in Bill Nichols (ed.), *Movies and Methods II.* Los Angeles and London: University of California Press: 165–89.

Elsom, John (1977), 'Organ-grinders', *The Listener* (23 June): 827–8.

Erven, Eugène van (1988), *Radical People's Theatre.* Bloomington and Indianapolis: Indiana University Press.

Espert, Nuria (1982), 'Carta apasionada a un amigo de Víctor García', *El País* (31 Agosto): 20.

—(1986), 'Una Bernarda de carne y de sangre', *Primer Acto,* 215 (September–October), 8–13.

—(1990), 'Hacer, no hablar', *El Público,* 81 (November–December): 86–9.

Espert, Nuria and Marcos Ordóñez (2002), *De aire y fuego. Memorias.* Madrid: Aguilar.

Espinosa Domínguez, Carlos (1988), '*Retrato de una pasión inextinguible*', *El Público,* 63 (December): 67.

Evans, Peter (forthcoming), 'Marisol: the Spanish Cinderella', in Antonio Lázaro-Reboll and Andy Willis (eds), *Spanish Popular Cinema*. Manchester: Manchester University Press.

Fàbregas, Xavier (1971), *Àngel Guimerà: Les dimensions d'un mite*, Llibres a l'Abast, 91. Barcelona: Edicions 62.

—(1978), *Història del teatre català*. Barcelona: Milla.

—(1983), 'Ambición grande, con realización mediana', *La Vanguardia* (22 May): 63.

—(1984), 'Recetas para cazar espectadores', *El Público*, 6 (March): 27–9.

—(1985a), 'María Casares en el Grec, con una divertida comedia de Copi. Un memorable *Madame Lucienne*', *La Vanguardia* (8 August): 23.

—(1985b), 'Oscar Wilde, la diva y el cuclillo', *La Vanguardia* (14 August): 19.

Falquez-Certain, Miguel (2000), '"What is your substance, whereof are you made?": An interview with Virginia Rambal', *Ollantay*, 6/11: 96–112.

Fancelli, Agustí (1990), 'Un triunfo de los que no se olvidan', *El País* [Edición Barcelona] (29 January): 30.

—(1992), 'Por la puerta grande', *El País* (26 April): 35.

—(1999), 'La ópera regresa al Liceu', *El País* [Edición Cataluña] (8 October): 46.

Farreras, Martí (1983), 'Fantasía dentro de la fantasía', *El País* [Edición Barcelona] (22 May): 35.

Feldman, Sharon (1998), 'National Theater/National identity: Els Joglars and the question of cultural politics in Catalonia', *Gestos*, 25: 35–50.

Fernán-Gómez, Fernando (1990), *El tiempo amarillo: Memorias Vol 1 – 1921–1943*. Madrid: Editorial Debate.

Fernàndez, Josep-Anton (1995), 'Becoming normal: Cultural production and cultural policy in Catalonia', in Graham and Labanyi (eds): 342–6.

—(1998), 'Sex, lies and traditions: La Cubana's *Teresina S.A.*', *Journal of the Institute of Romance Studies*, 6: 265–76.

Fernández, Juan (1996), 'Madrid veranea "a la Cubana"', *El Periódico* (13 August), 'El Periódico del Verano' supplement: 3.

Fernández, Mónica (1999), 'Nuria Espert: "La obra tiene muchos ingredientes para ser especial"', *La Vanguardia* (16 October), consulted online (www.lavanguardia.es).

Fernández Almagro, Melchor (1933), 'El teatro. Español. Estreno de la tragicomedia en tres jornadas, original de D. Ramón del Valle-Inclán, *Divinas palabras*', *El Sol* (17 November): 8.

—(1934), 'Las novedades teatrales. Español. Estreno de *Yerma*, poema trágico en tres actos, original de F. G. L.', *El Sol* (30 December): 8.

Fernández Cifuentes, Luis (1988), 'La verdad de la vida: Gibson versus Lorca', *Boletín de la Fundación Federico García Lorca*, 4: 87–101.

Fernández Santos, Ángel (1969), '*Las criadas* de Jean Genet en el Teatro Fígaro de Madrid', *Insula*, 275–6 (October–November): 30.

Fernández Torres, Alberto (1987), *Documentos sobre el Teatro Independiente español*. Madrid: Ministerio de Cultura.

Fernando, Jordi (ed.) (1994), *Miró en escena*. Barcelona: Fundació Joan Miró/Ajuntament de Barcelona.

Ferran y Mayoral, J. (1910), '*Salomé* al Principal', *Teatralia*, 3/58 (12 February): 257–8.

Feuer, Jane (1993), *The Hollywood Musical*. Basingstoke: Macmillan.

Finch, Hilary (1987), 'Sweeping away the clichés', *The Times* (30 April): 23.

Fischer-Lichte, Erica (1997), 'Performance art and ritual: Bodies in performance', *Theatre Research International*, 22/1: 22–37.

Fondevila, Santiago (1986), 'Anecdotario de una vendedora de "piedras medicinales"', *La Vanguardia* (26 April): 29.

—(1991), 'La Cubana, nada nuevo y nada viejo, sigue sorprendiendo', *La Vanguardia* (21 July): 49.

—(1992), 'El Festival Olímpic de les Arts pierde el estreno del último espectáculo de La Cubana', *La Vanguardia* (1 May): 29.

—(1993a), 'El arte necesita cosas tangibles', *La Vanguardia* (9 September), 'Revista' supplement: 2–3.

—(1993b), 'La Cubana funde cine y teatro en el espectáculo *Cegada de amor*', *La Vanguardia* (15 December): 43.

—(1994), 'La Cubana descubrirá el viernes cómo se mezcla cine y teatro en *Cegada de amor*', *La Vanguardia* (25 January): 35.

—(1999), 'La Cubana propone en el CCCB un viaje por la percepción del tiempo', *La Vanguardia* (17 December): 49, 53.

—(2000a), 'Entrevista a Lluís Pasqual, director del Teatre Lliure. "No podemos ir románticamente a Montjuïc"', *La Vanguardia* (20 February): 70.

—(2000b), 'Debate sobre el futuro del Teatre Lliure. Josep Montanyès, actor, director y miembro de la junta de gobierno del teatro. "El Lliure es una casa de mucha gente y precisa incorporar nuevos creadores"', *La Vanguardia* (21 July): 39.

—(2001), 'Seis actores para un drama', *La Vanguardia* (5 April): 44.

Forbes, Jill (1997), *Les Enfants du paradis*, BFI Film Classics. London: British Film Institute.

Foucault, Michel (1985), *Discipline and Punish: The Birth of the Prison*, trans. Alan Sheridan. Harmondsworth: Penguin.

Freeman, Edward (1971), *The Theatre of Albert Camus*. London: Methuen & Co. Ltd.

Freire, Susana (1998), 'El humor sale a La Cubana', *La Nación* (15 March): 3.

Gabancho, Patricia (1980), '*El balcó* de Genet, crítica mordaz y gran espectáculo', *El Noticiero Universal* (28 June): 31.

—(1983), '*La tempestat*, de Shakespeare, sometida a los recursos técnicos', *El Noticiero Universal* (21 May): 30.

Gabriel y Galán, J. A. (1976), '*El adefesio*, un adefesio de alto nivel', *Fotogramas*, 31/1459 (8 October): 34–5.

Gaforot, Xavier (1994), '*Cegada de amor*, una version "muy a La Cubana de Pedro Almodóvar"', *Diario 16* (11 March): 24.

Galey, Matthieu (1967), 'Le messe et le cirque – *Médéa* de Sénèque', *Nouvelles Littéraires* (12 October): 13.

—(1976), '*Divinas palabras*. Loin de nous . . .', *Le Quotidien de Paris* (24 February): 11.

Galindo, Carlos (1988a), 'El CDN ante un nuevo Rubicón: Lluís Pasqual se enfrenta a *Julio César*', *ABC* (14 March): 88.

—(1988b), '*El público*, premiado por la crítica especializada de París', *ABC* (8 June): 101.

Gallén, Enric (1985), *El teatre a la ciutat de Barcelona durant el règim franquista (1939–1954)*, Monografies de Teatre, 19. Barcelona: Institut del Teatre.

—(1988), 'Margarita y Cataluña: La forja de una primera actriz', in Cuadernos *El Público*, 36: 6–13.

García de Candamo, Bernardo (1914), 'Del cartel de anoche. Princesa. *Salomé*', *El Mundo* (21 May): 1.

García del Busto, José Luis (1999), 'Una magnifica producción de *Turandot*, a la altura de la reapertura del Liceo de Barcelona', *ABC* (9 October): 44.

García-Garzón, Juan Ignacio (1986), 'Lorca en Londres', *ABC* (30 August), 'Sábado Cultural' supplement: v–viii.

—(1996), 'Amor a La Cubana', *ABC* (25 January), 'ABC del Ocio' supplement: 4–7.

García Lorca, Federico (1996a), *Obras Completas. 1 Poesía*, (ed.) Miguel García-Posada. Barcelona: Galaxia Gutenberg/Círculo de Lectores.

—(1996b), *Obras Completas. 2 Teatro*, (ed.) Miguel García-Posada. Barcelona: Galaxia Gutenberg/Círculo de Lectores.

—(1996c), *Obras Completas. 3 Prosa*, (ed.) Miguel García-Posada. Barcelona: Galaxia Gutenberg/Círculo de Lectores.

—(1996d), *Obras Completas. 4 Primeros escritos*, (ed.) Miguel García-Posada. Barcelona: Galaxia Gutenberg/Círculo de Lectores.

García Lorenzo, Luciano (ed.) (2000), *Estado actual de los estudios calderonianos*. Almagro and Kassel: Edition Reichenberger.

García Osuna, Carlos (1980), '*Doña Rosita la soltera o El lenguaje de las flores*', *El Imparcial* (17 September): 23.

García Pintado, Ángel (1980), 'El grotesco viste de seda', *Pipirijaina*, 17 (November–December), 4–7.

—(1988), 'El compromiso', in Cuadernos *El Público*, 36: 15–19.

García Plata, Valentina (1996), 'Primeras teorías españolas de la puesta en escena: Adrià Gual', *Anales de la Literatura Española Contemporánea*, 21/3 (1996): 291–312.

García-Posada, Miguel (1982), 'García Lorca en Uruguay', *Triunfo*, 21–2 (July–August): 82–8.

García Rico, Eduardo (1976), '*El adefesio*, de Rafael Alberti (La convivencia es posible)', *Pueblo* (27 September): 13.

García Ruiz, Víctor (1999), *Continuidad y ruptura en el teatro español de la posguerra*. Pamplona: Ediciones Universidad de Navarra, S.A.

García Templado, José (1980), *El teatro anterior a 1939*. Madrid: Editorial Cincel.

Gasch, Sebastià (1934), 'Margarida Xirgu', *Mirador*, 285 (19 July): 5.

Gautier, Jean-Jacques (1948), 'Au Théâtre Marigny *L'État de siège* d'Albert Camus', *Le Figaro* (29 October): 4.

—(1966), 'A l'Odéon *Les Paravents* de Jean Genet', *Le Figaro* (23 April): 18.

—(1967), 'A l'Odéon, *Médéa* de Sénèque', *Le Figaro* (7 October): 24.

Genet, Jean (1963), 'Texto de *Las criadas*', trans. Manuel Herrero and Armando Moreno, *Primer Acto* 113 (October): 47–63.

—(1968), *Les Bonnes*. Paris: Éditions Gallimard.

—(1979), *Le Balcon*. Paris: Éditions Gallimard.

—(1977), 'Jean Genet talks to Hubert Fichte', *The New Review*, 37: 9–21.

—(1981), *Les Paravents*. Paris: Éditions Gallimard.

George, David (1995), *The History of the Commedia dell' arte in Modern Hispanic Literature With Special Attention to the Work of García Lorca*. Lewiston/Queenston/Lampeter: The Edwin Mellen Press.

—(2000), '"Le 'Mythe fin-de-siècle' par excellence": Catalan and Spanish versions of Oscar Wilde's *Salomé*', *Romance Studies*, 18/2 (December): 113–24.

—(2002), *The Theatre in Madrid and Barcelona, 1892–1936: Rivals or Collaborators?* Cardiff: University of Wales Press.

George, David and John London (1996), 'Introduction', in George and London (eds): 11–18.

—(eds) (1996), *Contemporary Catalan Theatre: An Introduction*. Sheffield: The Anglo-Catalan Society.

Gibson, Ian (1984), 'Las derechas ante el estreno de *Yerma*', *El Público*, 15 (December), 10–12.

—(1989), *Federico García Lorca: A Life*. New York: Pantheon Books.

—(1998), *The Shameful Life of Salvador Dalí*. London: Faber & Faber.

Gies, David Thatcher (1988), *Theatre and Politics in Nineteenth-Century Spain: Juan Grimaldi as Impresario and Government Agent*. Cambridge: Cambridge University Press.

—(1994), *The Theatre in Nineteenth-Century Spain*. Cambridge: Cambridge University Press.

—(ed.) (1999), *The Cambridge Companion to Modern Spanish Culture*. Cambridge: Cambridge University Press.

Gil, Carlos (1995), 'Espectáculo cegador', *Egin* (18 August): 11.

Gil, Iñaki (1996), 'El teatro se queda sin la voz rota de María Casares', *El Mundo* (23 November): 45.

Gilbey, Ryan (1999), '*Actresses*', *Express* (16 April): 50.

Ginart, Belén (1999), 'La Cubana saluda al 2000', *El País* [Edición Cataluña] (17 December), 'Cataluña' supplement: 13.

Gisbert, Joan Manuel (1978), '*Una altra Fedra, si us plau*', *Pipirijaina*, 7 (June): 66–8.

Godard, Colette (1976), '*Divines paroles* à Chaillot', *Le Monde* (20–21 February): 20.

—(1983), 'Absurd heroes in a crazy saga', *Guardian* (10 July): 13.

—(1986), '*Quai Ouest* à Nanterre. L'épopée de l'amour', *Le Monde* (29 April): 18.

—(1991), 'Les milles miroirs de l'illusion', *Le Monde* (6 May): 9.

Goldberg, RoseLee (1998), *Performance: Live Art Since the 60s*. New York and London: Thames and Hudson.

Gómez, Juan J. (2000), 'Nuria Espert echa en falta en el teatro una generación intermedia de actores', *El País* [Edición Cataluña], (2 September): 32.

Gómez Tello (1953), 'El prisionero de Parma', Primer Plano, 13/670 (16 August): n.pag.

González Ruano, César (1949), '¡Ya se salvó el teatro! Parece que vuelve Margarita Xirgu', La Vanguardia Española (26 August): 2.

Gortari, Carlos (1976), 'El adefesio de Rafael Alberti', Pipirijaina, 2 (November): 49–50.

Gousseland, Jack (1976), 'Le grand sorcier de l'angoisse', Le Point, 179 (23 February): 98–9.

Graells, G. J. and J. A. Hormigón (eds), Fabià Puigserver: Hombre de teatro, Teoría y práctica del teatro, 6. Madrid: Publicaciones de la Asociación del Directores de Escena de España.

Graham, Helen and Jo Labanyi (1995) (eds), Spanish Cultural Studies: An Introduction. Oxford: Oxford University Press.

Grimaldi, Juan de (1986), La pata de cabra, (ed.) David T. Gies. Rome: Bulone Editore.

Gross, John (1997), 'Grotesque Eurokitsch delights', Sunday Telegraph (17 August), 'Sunday Review' supplement: 9.

Gual, Adrià (1960), Mitja vida de teatre. Memòries. Barcelona: Editorial Aedos.

Guansé, Domènec (1988), 'Toda una vida', in Cuadernos El Público, 36: 29–63.

Gubern, Román (1981), La censura: Función política y ordenamiento jurídico bajo el franquismo (1936–1975). Barcelona: Peninsula.

Guerenabarrena, Juanjo (1989a), 'Contar mentiras para contar verdades', El Público, 70–1 (July–August): 34–5.

—(1989b), 'Lluís Pasqual: Para ser coherente, esta obra no se debe hacer', El Público, 70–1 (July–August): 36–9.

Guerrero Martín, José (1990), 'Núria Espert dirige su primera ópera en España', La Vanguardia (21 January), 'Segundo Cuaderno' supplement: 1–7.

Guzmán, Antonio (1934), 'Monumental. El desparecido', Cinegramas, 13 (9 December): n.pag.

Halsey, Martha T. (1973), Antonio Buero Vallejo. New York: Twayne.

Halsey, Martha T. and Phyllis Zatlin (eds) (1988), The Contemporary Spanish Theater: A Collection of Critical Essays. Lanham, MD: University Press of America.

—(eds) (1999), Entre Actos: Diálogos sobre teatro español entre siglos. University Park, PA: Estreno.

Haro, Eduardo (1935), 'Margarita Xirgu en Barcelona, Doña Rosita la soltera o El lenguaje de las flores, comedia en tres actos, de Federico García Lorca', La Libertad (19 December): 1–2.

Haro Tecglen, Eduardo (1980), 'Perenne García Lorca', El País (14 September): 28.

—(1982), 'El genio roto', El País (30 August): 32.

—(1984), 'Lecciones de un acontecimiento', El País (11 November): 39.

—(1986a), 'Teatro. Madre Coraje y sus hijos. Un relato sin emoción', El País (8 February): 25.

—(1986b), 'Teatro. La tempestad. Una fiesta parateatral', El País (13 October): 38.

—(1987), 'Teatro. El público. La tragedia del amor imposible', El País (18 January): 25.

—(1988a), 'Suma de varios errores', El País (17 March): 38.

—(1988b), 'Nuria Espert, en el Covent Garden', El País (10 December): 37.

—(1989a), 'Lo que deja atrás', El País (1 March): 30.

—(1989b), 'El orden reina en Madrid', El País (25 June): 32.

—(1994), 'Epitafio borroso', El País (15 October), 'Babelia. Revista de Cultura' supplement: 8.

—(1996), 'Sobre todo, ingenio', El País (27 January): 33.

Harris, Thomas (1991), 'The building of popular images: Grace Kelly and Marilyn Monroe', in Christine Gledhill (ed.), Stardom: Industry of Desire. London: Routledge: 40–4.

Harrison, Joseph and Alan Hoyle (eds) (2000), Spain's 1898 Crisis: Regeneration, Modernism, Postcolonialism. Manchester: Manchester University Press.

Hartnoll, Phyllis (1967), The Oxford Companion to the Theatre, 3rd edn. London: Oxford University Press.

Hayes, Malcolm (1987), 'Westernised weepie', Sunday Telegraph (3 May): 19.

Heliot, Armelle (1986), 'Soleil de Nuit', Le Quotidien de Paris (30 April): 26.

—(1990), 'Sans titre. Un coup de poing', Le Quotidien de Paris (8 October): 25.

Hera, Alberto de la (1987), 'El público, de Federico García Lorca', Ya (18 January): 46.

—(1988a), 'Julio César de William Shakespeare. La frescura y belleza de Shakespeare', Ya (22 March): 44.

—(1988b), 'La vida del Rey Eduardo II de Inglaterra, de Marlowe y Brecht. Un espectáculo excelente y fresco', Ya (8 November): 44.

—(1989), 'Cómeme el coco, negro de Jordi Milán. Divertido juguete cómico', Ya (13 November): 60.

—(1994), 'Aplausos para dos actrices', Ya (20 October): 35.

—(1996), 'Trabajo excepcional', Ya (27 January): 59.

Heras, Guillermo (1992), 'Ausensias y carencias en el discurso de la puesta en escena española de los años 20 y 30', in Dougherty and Vilches de Frutos (eds) (1992): 139–46.

Hermoso, Borja (1991) 'Valle-Inclán no es francés', El Mundo (11 July), 'UVE' supplement: 1–2.

—(1997), 'Luces y sombras del Teatro Real', El Mundo [Catalunya] (19 December): 7.

—(1998), 'Soy menos desesperada y más feliz que Maria Callas', El Mundo [Catalunya] (15 March): 59.

Hernández, Mario (1979), 'Cronologia y estreno de Yerma, poema trágico de García Lorca', Revista de Archivos, Bibliotecas y Museos, 82/2 (April–June): 289–315.

Heredero, Carlos F. (1993), Las huellas del tiempo: Cine español 1951–61. Madrid: Filmoteca.

Herrero, Roberto (1997), 'La Cubana triunfa en Donostia con 22.000 espectadores en un mes', El Diario Vasco (26 July): 55.

Higgins, John (1988), 'Butterfly in a corrugated iron cage', The Times (2 November): 20.

Higuera, Felipe (1993), 'El teatro nacional María Guerrero (1940–1952)', in Peláez (ed.): 80–105.

Higuera Rojas, Eulalia Dolores de la (1980), Mujeres en la vida de García Lorca. Granada: Diputación de Granada y Editora Nacional.

Hoberman, J. (1999), 'Your shows', Village Voice (15–21 December), consulted online (www.villagevoice.com).

Holt, Marion Peter (1975), The Contemporary Spanish Theatre (1949–1972). Boston: Twayne.

—(1999), 'Buero Vallejo's fifty years on stage: The neglected performance history', Estreno, 25/1 (Spring): 42–9, 63.

—(2001), 'Spain: A legacy to explore and a nascent Eurotheatre', Western European Stages, 13/1 (Winter): 143–8.

Hooper, John (1995), The New Spaniards. London: Penguin.

Hormigón, Juan Antonio (1999), 'Los teatros íntimos y experimentales en Barcelona y Madrid (1900–1936)', in ADE Teatro: 117–26.

Huguet, Estel (2002), 'Los clásicos no son aburridos. Entrevista a Lluís Pasqual, director de escena', La Vanguardia (14 July), 'Magazine' supplement: 24–5.

Iglesias Feijóo, Luis (1993), 'La recepción crítica de Divinas palabras', Anales de la Literatura Española Contemporánea, 18/3: 639–91.

Jameson, Fredric (1993), Signatures of the Visible. London: Routledge.

Jones, Anny Brooksbank (1997), Women in Contemporary Spain. Manchester: Manchester University Press.

Jongh, Nicholas de (1986), 'Fresco of frustration', Guardian (20 August): 9.

Jordà, J. M. (1910), 'Teatro Principal. Salomé de Oscar Wilde', La Publicidad (6 February): 5.

Josselin, Jean-François (1991), 'Le bonheurs de Maria Casarès', Le Nouvel Observateur (11–17 July): 74–5.

Jouve, Nicole Ward (1994), 'A woman in black and white', Sight and Sound, 4/7 (July): 29.

Joven, Antonio (1982), 'Con José R. Morales', Primer Acto, 192 (January–February): 108–10.

Joya, Juan Manuel (1999), 'El actor y la primera mitad del siglo XX', in ADE Teatro: 220–33.

Junyent, José María (1962), 'Talía. El deseo bajo los olmos', El Correo Catalán (10 May): 11.

Keating, Michael (1996), Nations against the State: The New Politics of Nationalism in Quebec, Catalonia and Scotland. New York: St. Martin's Press.

Kelley, Erna Berndt (1967), 'Margarita Xirgu at Smith', Smith Alumnae Quarterly (August): 32–3.

Kennedy, Michael (1991), 'Animal magic and gypsy tricks', Sunday Telegraph (5 May), 'Review' supplement: xv.

Kenyon, Nicholas (1989), 'Exaggerated Espertise', Observer (30 April): 45.

Kershaw, Baz (1992), The Politics of Performance: Radical Theatre as Cultural Intervention. London and New York: Routledge.

—(1999), *The Radical in Performance: Between Brecht and Baudrillard*. London and New York: Routledge.

Kingston, Jeremy (1987), 'Fortress of family tyranny', *The Times* (17 January): 16.

Kirkpatrick, Susan (2000), 'The "feminine" element: *Fin-de-siècle* Spain, modernity and the woman writer', in Harrison and Hoyle (eds): 146–55.

Kirkup, James (1996), 'Maria Casarès: Free spirit of the French stage', *Guardian* (26 November): 16.

Koltès, Bernard-Marie (1985), *Quai Ouest*. Paris: Les Éditions de Minuit.

—(1999), *Une part de ma vie. Entretiens (1983–1989)*. Paris. Les Éditions de Minuit.

Kott, Jan (1968), 'I can't get no satisfaction', *The Drama Review*, 48 (Autumn): 143–9.

Kramer, Lawrence (1994), 'The Singing salami: Unsystematic reflections of the Marx Brothers' *A Night at the Opera*', in Tambling (ed.): 253–65.

La Bardonnie, Mathilde (1991), 'Rires barbares de Valle-Inclán', *Libération* (12 July): 25–7.

La Cubana (1997), 'Why this show?', in the Edinburgh International Festival programme of *Cegada de amor/Blinded by Love* (12–23 August): n.pag.

Labanyi, Jo (1997), 'Race, gender and disavowal in Spanish cinema of the early Franco period: The missionary film and the folkloric musical', *Screen* 38/3 (Autumn): 215–31.

Ladra, David (1990), 'Una conversación con Nuria Espert', *Primer Acto*, 232 (January–February): 49–53.

Lafargue, André (1991), 'Maria Casarès: La dame en son palais', *Le Parisien* (9 July): 34.

Laín Entralgo, Pedro (1972a), 'Resurrección de *Yerma*', *La Gaceta Ilustrada*, 17/798 (23 January): 3.

—(1972b), 'El drama de *Yerma*', *La Gaceta Ilustrada*, 17/799 (30 January): 3.

Landaburu, Ander (1990), 'Lluís Pasqual y Lorca son una fiesta en Paris', *Cambio 16*, 990 (12 November): 125–8.

Laubreaux, Raymond and Pierre-Bernard Marquet (1983), '*Les Paravents*', *L'Éducation Hebdo* (16 June): 6–7.

Lavelli, Jorge (1997), 'Hommage à l'amie', *Théâtre/Public*, 135 (May–June): 5–6.

Le Galliene, Eva (1966), *The Mystic in the Theatre of Eleonora Duse*. New York: Farrar, Straus & Giroux.

Leach, Henry (1921), 'Las cosas que un español audaz ha oído', in José María Carretero 'El Caballero Audaz', *Lo que sé por mí. Confesiones del siglo (Décima y última serie)*. Madrid: Editorial 'Mundo Latino'.

Léonardini, Jean-Pierre (1991), 'Remission impossible?, *L'Humanité* (12 July): 20.

Lewis, Ward B. (1983), 'Exile drama: The example of Argentina', in Moeller (ed.): 233–43.

Ley, Pablo (1992), 'El decepcionante *Marathon* de La Cubana', *ABC* (6 July), 'Cataluña' supplement: ix.

—(1999a), '¡Enormes!', *El País* [Edición Cataluña] (15 February): 39.

—(1999b), 'Transitar el tiempo, tejerlo, multiplicarlo', *El País* [Edición Cataluña] (22 December): 51.

—(2000), '*L'hort dels cirerers*. El fin del mundo', *El País* [Edición Cataluña] (20 February), 'Cataluña' supplement: 4.

—(2001), 'Una versión de *Medea* que mira hacia otro lado', *El País* [Edición Cataluña] (3 August): 33.

—(2002),'Teatro. *Edipo XX1*. Obra enigmática', *El País* [Edición Cataluña] (18 July): 41.

Llovet, Enrique (1965), 'Estreno de *A Electra le sienta bien el luto*', *ABC* (30 October): 17.

Lockerbie, Catherine (1997), 'La Cubana', *The Scotsman* (March), 'Festival Preview' supplement: 13.

London, John (1996), 'Introduction', in *The Unknown Federico García Lorca*. London: Atlas: 7–22.

—(1997), *Reception and Renewal in Modern Spanish Theatre: 1939–1963*. London: Modern Humanities Research Association.

—(1998), 'Twentieth-century Spanish set design', in *Spanish Theatre 1920–1995: Strategies in*

Protest and Imagination (2), *Contemporary Theatre Review*, 7/3: 25–56.

Londré, Felicia Hardison (1985), 'Bringing Arrabal home: The theatre of Nuria Espert', Unpublished paper delivered at the American Theatre Association Convention Toronto (4–7 August): 1–21.

Looch, Anthony (1987), 'Audience in a tempest', *Daily Telegraph* (15 July): 10.

López, José Antonio (1991), 'Jordi Milán: La Cubana ofrece hechos cotidianos', *Diario de Cádiz* (29 April): 43.

López Pinillos, J. 'Pármeno' (1920), *Cómo se conquista la notoriedad*. Madrid: Pueyo.

López Sancho, Lorenzo (1976), '*El adefesio*, un acto teatral pleno de significados', *ABC* (26 September): 62.

—(1983), '*La vida de Eduardo II de Inglaterra*, un Marlowe exacerbado', *ABC* (1 December): 78.

—(1984), '*Luces de bohemia*, al aguafuerte por el Centro Dramático Nacional', *ABC* (31 October): 68.

—(1986a), '*Madre Coraje* gira en el escenario del María Guerrero', *ABC* (8 February): 71.

—(1986b), '"La *Yerma*" de Víctor García conmemora la muerte de García Lorca', *ABC* (9 February): 78.

—(1986c), '*La tempestad, happening* de La Cubana, en la Olimpia', *ABC* (12 October): 87.

—(1987), '*El público*, el provocador y escandaloso poema lorquiano, se presentó ayer en Madrid', *ABC* (17 January): 73.

—(1988a), '"Digest" del *Julio César* en el Centro Dramático Nacional', *ABC* (17 March): 111.

—(1988b), 'El *Eduardo II*, Marlowe y embrocación en el María Guerrero', *ABC* (20 October): 109.

—(1989a), '*Comedia sin título* o cómo hacer gran espectáculo con muy poco texto', *ABC* (24 June): 103.

—(1989b), 'Cubanerías de "music hall" en el Nuevo Apolo', *ABC* (12 November): 115.

—(1994), '*El cerco de Leningrado*, nostalgia y dos grandes actrices en el María Guerrero', *ABC* (14 October): 100.

—(1996), '*Cegada de amor*, aventura cineteatral', *ABC* (27 January): 77.

Loppert, Max (1988), 'Rare Verdian statement is made with *Rigoletto*', *Financial Times* (10 December), 'Weekend FT' supplement: xix.

Lottman, Herbert R. (1981), *Camus: A Biography*. London: Pan Books.

Luca de Tena, Cayetano (1953), 'Ensayo general (notas, experiencias y fracasos de un director de escena', *Teatro*, 5 (March): 28–32.

Luengo, Pilar (1990), 'Jordi Millán [*sic*]: "Los mercados son las catedrales del teatro"', *El Sol* (12 August): 7.

Luján, Néstor (1969), 'La muerte de Margarita Xirgu', *Destino* 1648 (3 May): 66.

M. P., E. (1986), '"A pesar de este éxito no me siento directora, sino una actriz que dirige", declara Núria Espert', *La Vanguardia* (10 Septiembre): 30.

McCarthy, Jim (1999), *Political Theatre During the Spanish Civil War*. Cardiff: University of Wales Press.

McKendrick, Melveena (1994), *The Revealing Image: Stage Portraits in the Theatre of the Golden Age*, Papers in Spanish Theatre History 2. London: Department of Hispanic Studies, Queen Mary & Westfield College.

Machado, Manuel (1920), '*El maleficio de la mariposa*', *La Libertad* (19 March): 2.

—(1933), 'Español. *Divinas palabras*, de Valle-Inclán', *La Libertad* (17 November): 4.

Madariaga, Iolanda G. (2001), 'Teatro. *Una nit d'Òpera*', *El Mundo* (15 June): consulted online (www.el-mundo.es).

Manegat, Julio (1960), 'Con la muerte de Camus se pierde uno de los más importantes valores de la literatura contemporánea', *El Noticiero Universal* (5 January): 5, 11.

—(1969), 'Ha muerto Margarita Xirgu: Al caer el gran telón ante una gran actriz', *El Noticiero Universal* (26 April): 24.

—(1976), 'En el Tívoli. Divinas, acaso lejanas palabras . . . ', *El Noticiero Universal* (7 October): 30.

—(1977), 'Alberti, *El adefesio*, y María Casares', *El Noticiero Universal* (7 March): 33.

Marcabru, Pierre (1966), 'Le Claudel de l'innommable', *Candide* (25 April): 38.

—(1967), 'Casarès sait souffrir', *Candide* (16 October): 43.

—(1976), '*Divinas palabras* pour l'œil', *France-Soir* (21 February): 13.

—(1990), 'Gadget culturel', *Le Figaro* (9 October): 33.

—(1991a), 'Théâtre. *Le Balcon* de Jean Genet. L'opacité de l'ennui', *Le Figaro* (4 May): 22.

—(1991b), 'Un monstre bizarre et obscur', *Le Figaro* (11 July): 22 .

—(1991c), 'Plus théâtral et moins rébarbatif', *Le Figaro* (12 July): 21.

Marcel, Gabriel (1948), '*L'État de siège*', *Les Nouvelles Littéraires* (11 November): 8.

—(1966), 'Le Procès de Jean Genet', *Les Nouvelles Littéraires* (21 April): 1–13.

Marín Alcalde, Alberto (1933), 'Estreno de *Divinas palabras* en el Español', *Ahora* (17 November); 22.

Marinero, Cristina (1997), 'La Señora Canales', *El Mundo* (16 November), 'La Revista' supplement: 8–13.

Mariñas, Jesús (1976), 'En secreto en 2 columnas', *La Prensa* (7 October): 25.

Marks, Laurence (1986), 'The stars bring Lorca to London', *Observer* (10 August), 'Weekend' supplement: 44.

Marqueríe, Alfredo (1944), 'Calderón. Estreno de *Rebeca*, comedia dramática de gran espectáculo, en 27 cuadros', *ABC* (11 June): 34.

—(1950), 'Informaciones y noticias teatrales y cinematográficas, *ABC* (22 March): 21.

—(1962), 'Informaciones teatrales y cinematográficas. Estreno en el Reina Victoria de *El deseo bajo los olmos*', *ABC* (15 September): 73.

—(1969), *El teatro que yo he visto*. Barcelona: Editorial Bruguera.

—(1971), 'Estreno de *Yerma*', *Pueblo* (30 November): 48.

Marsillach, Adolfo (1998), *Tan lejos, tan cerca. Mi vida*. Barcelona: Tusquets Editores.

—(1999), 'Borrás y unas fotos', in ADE Teatro: 237–9.

Martí, Octavi (1996), 'Muere María Casares, gran trágica del teatro', *El País* (23 November): 27.

Martí i Pol, Miquel, Emili Teixidor, Lluís Pasqual, Fabià Puigserver, Francesc Burguet i Ardiaca (1987), *Teatre Lliure 1976–1987*. Barcelona: Institut del Teatre.

Martín, José (1969), 'En el Poliorama. Estreno de *Las criadas*', *El Noticiero Universal* (21 February): 30.

Martínez, Raimundo (1977), '*El adefesio*, de Alberti, en Barcelona. María Casares: "El teatro debe exorcizar a los tabús españoles"', *El Noticiero Universal* (5 March): 21.

Martínez Ortiz, José (1989), *Rambal: Mago de la escena española, valenciano ilustre, hijo de Utiel*. Utiel: Gráficas Llogodi.

Martínez Roger, Ángel (1997), 'Paseo por la escenografía teatral española', *Primer Acto*, 269 (May–July): 34–44.

Martínez Tomás, A. (1962), 'Talía. Estreno del drama de Eugenio O'Neill *El deseo bajo los olmos* por la Compañía de Nuria Espert', *La Vanguardia Española* (11 May): 27.

—(1969), 'Poliorama, *Las criadas* (*Les Bonnes*) de Jean Genet', *La Vanguardia Española* (22 February): 44.

—(1973), 'Coliseum. *Yerma* en versión escenográfica de Víctor García y presentación de Nuria Espert', *La Vanguardia Española* (16 February): 56.

—(1976), 'Tívoli. *Divinas palabras* de Valle-Inclán, en nueva versión de Víctor García', *La Vanguardia Española* (7 October): 62.

—(1977), '*El adefesio*, de Rafael Alberti, y presentación de María Casares', *La Vanguardia Española* (6 March): 51.

Martínez Velasco, Julio (1997), '*Cegada de amor*, otro demencial desmadre de La Cubana', *ABC* (27 April): 99.

Martori, Joan (1995), *La projecció d'Àngel Guimerà a Madrid (1891–1924)*, Textos i Estudis de Cultura Catalana, 46. Barcelona: Curial Edicions Catalanes/Publicacions de l'Abadia de Montserrat.

—(1996), 'Guimerà en Madrid', *Anales de la Literatura Española Contemporánea*, 21/3: 313–27.

Mas Ferrer, Jaime (1978), *Vida y mito de Joaquín Dicenta*. Alicante: Instituto de Estudios Alicantinos.

Maso, Ángeles (1977), 'María Casares: Ha venido a trabajar y a observar: "Pero veo que es la gente la que me pregunta a mí'", *La Vanguardia Española* (5 March): 37.

Mason, Bim (1992), *Street Theatre and Other Outdoor Performance*. London: Routledge.

Matabosch, Joan (1988), 'Nuria Espert: La ópera es una fascinante y frágil cristalería', *ABC* (30 November), 'Cataluña' supplement: viii–ix.

—(1989), 'Nuria Espert: El arte político ya no existe', in *ABC* (1 October), 'Blanco y Negro' *ABC dominical* supplement, 76–9.

—(1990), 'El público liceísta aplaudió, en pie, la histórica *Elektra* de Núria Espert', *ABC* (29 January), 'Cataluña' supplement: xiii.

—(1993), 'Abusar es mal usar', *ABC* (19 March), 'Cataluña' supplement: xiii.

Maté, Luis (1978), *Del teatro anterior a la democracia*. Valladolid: Talleres Gráficos CERES, S.A.

Maycock, Robert (1991), 'A close-up on the real world', *Independent* (29 April): 14.

Mazorra, Javier and Andrew Burnet (1997), 'Script tease', *The List* (8 August): 30.

Medina, Roberto (1963), '*Yerma*', *Historium* (31 July): n.pag.

Melendres, Jaume (1976), 'De las formas de aplaudir', *Tele/eXpres* (31 August): 20.

Menéndez Ayuso, Emilio (1973), 'El teatro español, hoy. Un público en busca de autor', *Triunfo*, 541 (10 February): 32–5.

Millas, Jaime (1982), 'Nuria Espert, entre Lorca, Genet y Shakespeare', *El País* (31 December), 'Artes' supplement: 7.

Milne, Rodney (1989), '*Rigoletto*', *Opera* (February): 226–31.

—(1991), 'Sliding scale', *Evening Standard* (29 April): 41.

Miquís, Alejandro (1914), 'Novedades teatrales. En la Princesa, *Salomé*', *Diario Universal* (21 May): 1.

Moeller, Hans-Bernhard (1983a), 'Introduction: Exile literature and the role of comparative literary scholarship', in Moeller (ed.): 7–22.

—(1983b), 'Historical background and patterns of the exodus of European exile writers', in Moeller (ed.): 49–67.

—(ed.) (1983), *Latin America and the Literature of Exile: A Comparative View of the 20th-Century European Refugee Writers in the New World*. Heidelberg: Carl Winter Universitätsverlag.

Moix, Terenci (1998), 'Grandeza de Nuria Espert', *La Vanguardia* (29 March): 31.

Molina, Margot (1991), 'La Cubana prepara su nuevo espectáculo, *Marathon dancing*, para 1992', *El País* [Edición Barcelona] (27 May): 56.

Molinero, Lola (1985), 'Uno de los ases de la direccíon teatral llega al Teatre Grec con el tándem Casares-Copi. Jorge Lavelli: "Cualquier estilo escénico debe estar alimentado por la verdad para ser creíble"', *La Vanguardia* (6 August): 25.

Monegal, Antonio and José María Micó (eds) (2000), *Federico García Lorca i Catalunya*. Barcelona: Universitat Pompeu Fabra.

Monegal, Ferrán (1976), 'Carta a Nuria Espert: Festivales que algo queda', *Tele/eXpres* (31 August): 20.

Monelle, Raymond (1989), 'Lasting passion', *Independent* (27 April): 18.

Monleón, Ángela (1988), 'Con Nuria Espert. Desde la interpretación, la ópera', *Primer Acto*, 223 (March–May): 42–5.

—(1994), '*El cerco de Leningrado*: Nuria Espert', *Primer Acto*, 253 (March–April): 87–90.

Monleón, José (1962a), '*El deseo bajo los olmos* de O'Neill', *Primer Acto*, 34 (May), 49–50.

—(1962b), '*El deseo bajo los olmos* de Eugenio O'Neill', *Primer Acto*, 36 (October): 38–9.

—(1970), 'Del *Marat-Sade* a *Las criadas*', *Primer Acto*, 116 (January): 10–13.

—(1971a), 'Ensayos de *Yerma*', *Primer Acto*, 137 (October): 10–13.

—(1971b), 'Con Víctor García y Nuria Espert', *Primer Acto*, 137 (October): 14–21.

—(1977a), 'Introducción a *El adefesio*', in Alberti (1977): 6–23.

—(1977b), 'Entrevista con Rafael Alberti', in Alberti (1977): 25–33.

—(1982), 'Teatro Principal de Valencia', *Primer Acto*, 196 (November–December): 44–5.

—(1983a), '*Las criadas*: Testimonio de una reconstruccion', *Diario 16* (23 January): viii–ix.

—(1983b), 'Con Nuria Espert, en dos tiempos', *Primer Acto*, 20 (November): 85–7.

—(1986a), 'Un Brecht riguroso y académico', *Diario 16* (8 February) 'Guia 16' supplement: ix.

—(1986b), '*La tempestad*', *Diario 16* (18 October), 'Guia 16' supplement: vii.

—(1988), '*Julio César*', *Diario 16* (18 March), 'Vivir en Madrid' supplement: v.

—(1989), 'Relevo en el CDN. El último Pasqual. *Comedia sin título*', *Primer Acto*, 230 (September–October): 21–7.

—(1990), *Tiempo y teatro de Rafael Alberti*. Madrid: Primer Acto/Fundación Rafael Alberti.

—(1997), 'La ausencia de María Casares', *Primer Acto*, 267 (January–February): 102–5.

Montero Alonso, José (1969), 'Historia gráfica de Margarita Xirgu', *Semana* (May): 5–8, 52–3.

Montero, Manuel (1989), 'La Cubana. "El teatro que hacemos es como la vida misma, pero dándole la vuelta"', *El Periódico* (12 November), 'La Gente' supplement: 8.

Morales, María Luz (1935a), 'Teatro Barcelona. Un sensacional estreno. *Yerma*, poema trágico en tres actos, de Federico García Lorca', *La Vanguardia* (19 September): 10.

—(1935b), 'Teatro Principal. Presentación de la Compañía de Margarita Xirgu, con *Bodas de sangre* de García Lorca', *La Vanguardia* (24 November): 11.

—(1962), 'Escenarios y pantallas. Teatro Talía', *Diario de Barcelona* (11 May): 40.

—(1969) 'Teatro Poliorama: La Compañía de Nuria Espert presenta *Las criadas* de Jean Genet, en traducción de Manuel Herrero', *Diario de Barcelona* (22 February): 25.

Moreno Monzón, Eduardo and Baerlam (1944), *Jonathan! El monstruo invisible – intriga de miedo y de misterio en cuatro actos*. Madrid: Talía.

Mori, Arturo (1933), 'Anoche en el Español. *Divinas palabras* de D. Ramón del Valle-Inclán', *El Liberal* (17 November): 6.

Morla Lynch, Carlos (1958), *En España con Federico García Lorca (Páginas de un diario íntimo, 1928–1936)*. Madrid: Aguilar.

Morris, C. Brian (1989), 'Voices in void: Speech in *La casa de Bernarda Alba*', *Hispania*, 72/3, (September): 498–509.

Mortimer, John (1972), 'Tricks on the trampoline', *Observer* (23 April): 31.

Muntané, Sílvia (1994), 'La Cubana. Juguem a disfrassar-nos', *Regal Insurance* (Summer): 17–19.

Muñoz, Diego (1988), 'Quiero ser fiel a Shakespeare y al tiempo que vivimos', *La Vanguardia* (11 March): 43.

Navarro, Núria (1990), 'La Cubana. Sexo, disfraces y "rock and roll"', *El Periódico* (25 February), 'La Gente' supplement: 7–8.

Nerson, Jacques (1986), '*Quai Ouest*: Deuxième édition', *Le Figaro* (5 July), 'Magazine' supplement: 22.

Nicholas, Robert L. (1972), *The Tragic Stages of Antonio Buero Vallejo*. Valencia: Estudios de Hispanófila.

Nieva, Francisco (1986), 'La no historia de la escenografía teatral en España', in Cuadernos El Público, 14, *Paisaje intermitente de la escenografía española*, (ed.) Moises Pérez Coterillo. Madrid: Centro de Documentación Teatral: 4–15.

—(1990), 'José Luis Alonso, el director que sabía demasiado', *ABC* (9 October): 101.

Noguero, Joaquim (1997), 'Fer de mals, virtuts', *Avui* (16 October): 42.

Northcott, Bayen (1988), 'Composer's revenge', *Independent* (10 December), 'Weekend' supplement: 31.

Nourry, Philippe (1976), '*Divines paroles*. Une ténébreuse magie', *Le Figaro* (23 February): 21.

Nussac, Sylvie de (ed.) (1990), *Nanterre Amandiers: Les Années Chéreau 1982–1990*. Paris: Imprimerie Nationale Éditions.

Obregón, Antonio de (1935), 'Un estreno en el Principal Palace de Barcelona', *Diario de Madrid* (14 December): 2.

O'Connor, Patricia W. (1966), 'Government censorship in the contemporary Spanish theatre', *Educational Theater Journal*, 18: 443–9.

—(1984), 'Post-Franco theater: From limitation to liberty to license', *Hispanic Journal*, 4/3: 55–73.

—(1988a), *Dramaturgas españolas de hoy: una introducción*. Madrid: Editorial Fundamentos.

—(1988b), 'Guideposts to twentieth-century Spanish plays in English', *Estreno*, 14/2 (Autumn): 43–8.

—(1996), *Antonio Buero Vallejo en sus espejos*. Madrid: Editorial Fundamentos.

—(ed.) (1996) *Plays of the New Democratic Spain (1976–1990)*. Lanham, New York and London:

University Press of America.

Ocaña, María Teresa (ed.) (1996), *Picasso y el teatro*. Barcelona: Museu Picasso/Ajuntament de Barcelona/Àmbit Serveis Editorials.

Ochoa, Carmelo (1976), '*Divinas palabras*', *El Noticiero Universal* (26 August): 23.

Oliva (1973), 'Teatro-Cine. Coliseum. *Yerma*', *Solidaridad Nacional* (16 February): 15.

Oliva, César (1989), *El teatro desde 1936*. Madrid, Alhambra.

Olivares, Juan Carlos (1994), 'Más bonita que ninguna', *ABC* (30 January), 'Cataluña' supplement: xi.

—(1997), 'Chéjov salva *La gaviota* de Flotats', *ABC* (16 October): 95.

—(1998), 'El pellizco de Lorca', *ABC* (12 February), 'Cataluña' supplement: xii.

Olivier, Jean-Jacques (1970),' Paris', *Plays and Players*, 17/11 (August): 52–3.

Olmo, Lauro (1970), *La camisa. El cuerpo. El cuarto poder*. Madrid: Taurus.

Oltra, Roberto (1988), 'María Casares, primera película en España: "Sartre y Camus me seducían de modo muy diferente"', *Tiempo* (22 August): 94–6.

O'Mahony, John (1995), 'Abroad Canvas', *Observer* (19 March): 8.

Ordóñez, Marcos (1989), 'Abróchase los cinturones: Llega La Cubana', *ABC* (7 November): 110.

—(1997), 'Notes sobre *La gavina*', *Avui* (27 October): 39.

—(1998), 'Els problemes del llistó', *Avui* (2 March): 36.

—(2002), *Comedia con fantasmas*. Barcelona: Plaza & Janés.

Oro, César (1997), 'María Casares', *Hispania*, 80/3 (September): 585.

Ortega, Francisco (1997), 'En la muerte de María Casares', *Primer Acto*, 267 (January–February): 106–16.

Ortega y Gasset, José (1963), 'Meditación del marco', in *Obras Completas. 2 El espectador (1916–34)*. Madrid: Revista del Occidente: 307–13.

—(1982), *Ideas sobre el teatro y la novela*. Madrid: Revista del Occidente/Alianza Editorial.

P., B. (1989), 'Conmoción en el estreno de *Comedia sin título*', *Diario 16* (24 June): 35.

P., C. (1976), 'Estreno de *Divinas palabras*, según el montaje de Víctor García – Nuria Espert', *La Vanguardia Española* (26 August): 32.

—(1978) 'El séptimo espectáculo en dos años. *Eduard II* de Marlowe, en el Teatre Lliure', *La Vanguardia* (9 May): 62.

P., J. (1953), 'Teatro ¡*Arsénico!*', *El Alcázar* (24 January): 2.

P., T. (1989), *Cómeme el coco, negro*, un paseo por el music-hall', *Ya* (10 November): 48.

Paget, Jean (1966), '*Les Paravents* de Jean Genet. Sublime!', *Combat* (23 April): 8.

—(1967), '*Médéa* de Sénèque', *Combat* (7 October): 12.

Palau Fabre, Josep (1935), 'D'una conversa amb García Lorca', *La Humanitat* (4 October): 2.

Palou, Josep (1994), 'Un hatajo de mentirosos', *El País* (21 January), 'El País de las Tentaciones' supplement: 12–14.

Paredes, Félix (1933), 'En el Español. *Divinas palabras* de D. Ramón del Valle-Inclán', *La Terra* (17 November): 2.

Pasqual, Lluís (1980–81), 'Notas de lectura y montaje', *Primer Acto*, 187 (December–January): 55–6.

—(1987), 'La verdad del amor y del teatro', *El Público*, 40 (January): 6–9.

—(1988), 'La palabra es el actor', *El País* (13 March): 31.

—(1996), 'In conversation with Maria M. Delgado and Paul Taylor at the Royal Exchange Theatre, Manchester', in Delgado and Heritage (eds): 206–19.

—(1998), Press release for *Como canta una ciudad de noviembre a noviembre* (May): n.pag.

Pasqual, Lluís and Diego Muñoz (1995), 'No me encuentro bien bajo la cultura catalana que representa Jordi Pujol', *La Vanguardia* (8 May): 39.

Pavón, Juan Luis (1991), 'La Cubana pretende poner a revienta caldera el Lope de Vega con *Cómeme el coco, negro*', *ABC* (22 May): 87.

Pedret Muntañola, J. (1966), 'Teatre Romea. *La bona persona de Sezuan* de Bertolt Brecht', *La Vanguardia Española* (24 December): 54.

Pedroso, Manuel (1925), 'Nuestras campañas. Hacia un teatro nuevo. La liga Pro Drama', *Her-*

aldo de Madrid (8 August): 5.

Peinado, Pablo (1997), 'Antonio Canales + Lluís Pasqual', *Zero Quincenal* (November): 18–19.

Peláez, Andres (ed.) (1993), *Historia de los teatros nacionales: (Volumen primero) 1939–1962*. Madrid: Centro de Documentación Teatral, Ministerio de Cultura, Instituto Nacional de las Artes Escénicas y de la Música.

—(1995), *Historia de los teatros nacionales: (Volumen segundo) 1960–1985*. Madrid: Centro de Documentación Teatral, Ministerio de Cultura, Instituto Nacional de las Artes Escénicas y de la Música.

Pelayo, Antonio (1986a), '*El público*, de García Lorca, ovacionado durante ocho minutos en Milán', *Ya* (14 December): 45.

—(1986b), 'Críticas muy favorables a *El público* en los más destacados diarios italianos', *Ya* (15 December): 44.

Pereda, Rosa María (1976), 'Lo que en Francia me hacía sonreír, en España me emociona', *El País* (25 July): 31.

Pérez, Xavier (1994), 'Tots els Oscars del món', *Avui* (30 January): 45.

Pérez Coterillo, Moisés (1982), '*La hija del aire*. Vuelo rasante', *Pipirijaina*, 21 (March): 8–9.

—(1983), 'Mérida recuerda a Margarita Xirgu', *El Público*, 0 (Summer): 16–19.

—(1984a), 'Valle-Inclán viaja a París', *El Público*, 5 (February): 4–6.

—(1984b), 'Nuria Espert: "Víctor García mereció la palabra genio"', *El Público*, 14 (November): 9–11.

—(1990), 'Lluís I de Francia. Un catalán en la Comédie', *El Público*, 76 (January-February): 6–9.

Pérez de Olaguer, Gonzalo (1973), '*Yerma* de Lorca', *Yorick*, 57–8 (January–March): 103–5.

—(1979a), 'Temporada teatral en Catalunya: Crisis, pero menos', *Pipirijaina*, 10 (September–October): 49–54.

—(1979b), '*Les tres germanes*', *El Periódico* (6 November): 27.

—(1979c), 'Chejov en el Lliure', *Primer Acto*, 182 (December): 188.

—(1983), 'Núria Espert recibe una lluvia de aplausos por *La tempestat*', *El Periódico* (21 May): 35.

—(1985a), 'Copi, autor, actor, dibujante y escritor', *El Periódico* (6 August): 22.

—(1985b), 'María Casares actúa en España por segunda vez en su carrera', *El Periódico* (6 August): 22.

—(1985c), '*La nuit de Madame Lucienne*', *El Periódico* (8 August): 27.

—(1986a), 'Un desequilibrado hermoso espectáculo', *El Periódico* (24 May): 56.

—(1986b), 'El colosal "show" de La Cubana', *El Periódico* (30 September): 56.

—(1988), 'El *Julio César* de Lluís Pasqual sorprende y desconcierta', *El Periódico* (17 March): 39.

—(1989), 'La Cubana. Triunfo del boca a boca en *Cómeme el coco, negro*', *El Público*, 70–1 (July–August): 40–3.

—(1991a), 'Barcelona vive el "boom" del musical', *El Periódico* (16 January): 54.

—(1991b), 'Me fascina hacer este Valle-Inclán', *El Periódico* (7 July): 53.

—(1991c), 'El director introducirá cambios en el montaje en Barcelona', *El Periódico* (11 July): 51.

—(1991d), 'Valle-Inclán desata la polémica', *El Periódico* (11 July): 51.

—(1991e), 'Bravos y ovaciones tras más de seis horas de *Comédies barbares*', *El Periódico* (6 October): 62.

—(1992), 'Danzad, danzad, malditos', *El Periódico* (5 July): 66.

—(1993), 'La Cubana realiza un montaje de cine', *El Periódico* (15 December): 53.

—(1994a), '*Cegada de amor* es La Cubana 100%', *El Periódico* (24 January): 28–9.

—(1994b), 'La noche de La Cubana', *El Periódico* (30 January): 57.

—(1994c), 'Arriesgada simbiosis entre cine y teatro', *El Periódico* (30 January): 57.

—(1995a), 'Milán: "Esperábamos durar tres meses"', *El Periódico* (29 January): 54.

—(1995b), 'Metáfora sobre las utopías', *El Periódico* (4 May): 58.

—(1997a), 'Pasqual: "La Ciutat del Teatre será un parquetemático"', *El Periódico* (24 May): 56.

—(1997b), '"Albert Boadella amenaza con una campaña de "terrorismo cultural"', *El Periódico* (30 May): 75.

—(1997c), 'Un vuelo intermitente', *El Periódico* (16 October): 60.

—(2000), 'Un adiós y una gran noche teatral', *El Periódico* (27 February): 48.

—(2001), 'Una mirada irónica de La Cubana al "bel canto"', *El Periódico* (14 June): consulted online (www.elperiodico.es).

—(2002), 'Teatro. *Edipo XXI*, un personaje visto con ojos de hoy', *El Periódico* (18 July): 66.

Pérez Rasilla, Eduardo (1996), '*Haciendo Lorca*', *Primer Acto*, 264 (June–August), 104–6.

Pérez Sierra, Rafael, Lluís Pasqual, Francisco Ruiz Ramón, José Luis Aranguren, Eduardo Haro Tecglen, Francisco Rico and José Monleón, '*La hija del aire*. Analisis y polémica' (1981), *Primer Acto*, 190–1 (November–December): 27–60.

Perriam, Chris (2003), *Stars and Masculinities in Spanish Cinema: From Banderas to Bardem*. Oxford: Oxford University Press.

Peter, John (1997), 'Pitfalls amid the excitement', *Sunday Times* (17 August), 'Culture' supplement: 14.

Phelan, Peggy (1993), *Unmarked: The Politics of Performance*. London and New York: Routledge.

—(1997), *Mourning Sex: Performing Public Memories*. London and New York: Routledge.

—(1998), 'Introduction: The ends of performance', in Peggy Phelan and Jill Lane (eds), *The Ends of Performance*. London and New York: New York University Press: 1–19.

Pistolesi, Alejandro (1986), 'Milán, gran escenario del estreno mundial de *El público*, de Federico García Lorca', *ABC* (12 December): 87.

Poirot-Delpech, B. (1966), '*Les Paravents*', *Le Monde* (23 April): 14.

—(1967), '*Médéa*, de Sénèque', *Le Monde* (7 October): 14.

Pons, Pere (1994), 'La cuarta dimensión del teatro. La Cubana', *Ajoblanco*, 65 (July–August): 72–3.

Pontiero, Giovanni (1982), *Duse on Tour: Guido Noccioli's Diaries 1906–7*. Manchester: Manchester University Press.

Porcel, Baltasar (1980), '*Doña Rosita*, el desencanto político', *La Vanguardia* (17 October): 5.

Prego, Adolfo (1971), '*Yerma* de Víctor García en la Comedia', *ABC* (1 December): 81.

Preston, Paul (1996), *A Concise History of the Spanish Civil War*. London: Fontana.

—(1999), *¡Comrades!: Portraits from The Spanish Civil War*. London: HarperCollins.

Primer Acto (1968), '*Las criadas* por sus tres ínterpretes', *Primer Acto*, 115 (December): 20–7.

—(1969a), 'La muerte de Margarita Xirgu', *Primer Acto*, 108 (May): 8–9.

—(1969b), 'Con Nuria Espert', *Primer Acto,* 113 (October): 36–44.

Puigserver, Fabià (1987), 'Lo importante es el viaje', *El Público*, 40 (January): 9–11.

Pujol, Xavier (1993), 'No lo vuelvan a hacer', *El País* [Edición Barcelona] (19 March): 29.

Quiñonero, Juan Pedro (1989), 'La escena francesa aprovecha los premios Molière para castigar la gestión de Jack Lang', *ABC* (9 May): 89.

—(1996), 'La tragedia pierde su voz más desgarrada, María Casares', *ABC* (23 November): 103.

R. C., M. (1927), '*Mariana de Pineda* [*sic*]', *La Vanguardia* (26 June): 15.

Radigales, Montse (1988), 'Núria Espert sorprende en Londres con un nuevo *Rigoletto*', *El Periódico* (10 December): 65.

Ragué-Arias, María-José (1991), 'La Cubana, el gran éxito del teatro catalán en 1989', *Estreno,* 17/1 (Spring): 26–30.

—(1993), 'Women and the women's movement in contemporary Spanish theatre', *New Theatre Quarterly*, 9/35: 203–10.

—(1994a), 'La Cubana, *Cegada de amor*', *El Mundo* [Catalunya] (30 January): 75.

—(1994b), 'Dos actrices, un autor, un texto', *El Mundo* [Catalunya] (31 May): 54.

—(1996), *El teatro de fin de milenio en España (De 1975 hasta hoy)*. Barcelona: Editorial Ariel.

—(1997) 'Un gran espectáculo', *El Mundo* [Catalunya] (16 October): 55.

Rambal, Enrique, Manuel Soriano Torres and José Javier Perez Bultó (1944a), *Drácula. Adaptación libre de la fantástica novela del mismo título, de Bram Stoker, hecha en un prólogo y dos partes, dividida en veinticinco cuadros.* Madrid: Talía.

—(1944b), *Rebeca. Comedia dramático de gran espectáculo, en un prólogo y dos jornadas, divididas en veitisiete* [*sic*] *cuadros, adaptación de la novela del mismo título de Daphne du Maurier. Ilus-*

traciones musicales del maestro Arquellades. Madrid: Talía.

Ramoneda, Josep (1999), 'Un gènere singular/Un género singular', in the programme to *Equipatge per al 2000. Més de pressa, més de pressa*, Centre de Cultura Contemporània de Barcelona: 4–5.

Ramos, Rafael (1997), 'La Cubana triunfa en el Festival de Edimburgo con *Cegada de amor*', *La Vanguardia* (15 August): 26.

Ratcliffe, Michael (1986a), 'Lust in a woman's shoe', *Observer* (24 August): 17.

—(1986b), 'Adela and her sisters', *Observer* (14 September): 23.

Read, Alan (1993), *Theatre & Everyday Life: An Ethics of Performance*. London and New York: Routledge.

Redacción (1995), 'La asistencia al teatro en Barcelona registró un sustancial aumento en 1994', *La Vanguardia* (19 January): 35.

—(1997), '*Cegada de amor* llega al millón de espectadores y se va a hacer las Américas', *La Vanguardia* (26 November): 33.

Redacción/agencias (1990), 'Suicidio del director teatral José Luis Alonso', *La Vanguardia* (9 October): 43, 49.

Regás, Xavier (1972), 'En busca del tiempo perdido. Una merienda . . . de negros, a oscuras', *Tele/eXpres* (18 March): 8.

Reigosa, Carlos G. (1986), '*Madre Coraje*, un Brecht neutral y necesario', *El Público*, 30 (March): 14–15.

Rela, Walter (1980), *Historia del teatro uruguayo, 1807–1979*. Montevideo: Ediciones de la Alianza.

Rey Faraldos, Gloria (1986), 'Notas sobre teatro ruso en España', *Segismundo*, 20: 265–88.

Reyero Hermosilla, Carlos (1980), *Gregorio Martínez Sierra y su Teatro de Arte*. Madrid: Fundación Juan March.

Reynolds, Margaret (2000), 'Performing Medea: or, why is Medea a woman?', in Edith Hall, Fiona Macintosh and Oliver Taplin (eds), *Medea in Performance 1500–2000*. Oxford: Legenda, European Humanities Research Centre, University of Oxford: 119–43.

Rivas Cherif, Cipriano de (1922), 'Teatros', *La Pluma* (28 September): 222–4.

—(1923), Un crítico incipiente', *La Pluma*, 35 (April): 328–31.

Rivière, Margarita (1983), 'Lluís Pasqual, director del Centro Dramático Nacional. "La gente ya no necesita que el teatro exista"', *El Periódico* (17 August): 10.

Rivollet, André (1966), 'Pas de bataille des *Paravents*', *Aux Écoutes* (21 April): 40.

Roach, Joseph R. (1989), 'Theatre history and the ideology of the aesthetic', *Theatre Journal*, 14/2 (May): 155–68.

—(1992), 'Introduction: Theatre history and historiography', in Janelle G. Renelt and Joseph R. Roach (eds), *Critical Theory and Performance*. Ann Arbor: University of Michigan Press: 293–8.

—(1995), 'Culture and performance in the circum-Atlantic world', in Andrew Parker and Eve Kosofsky Sedgwick (eds), *Performativity and Performance*. London: Routledge: 45–63.

Roberts, Peter (1969), 'Belgrade International Theatre Festival', *Plays and Players*, 17/2 (November): 54–8.

Rodrigo, Antonina (1974), *Margarita Xirgu y su teatro*. Barcelona: Editorial Planeta.

—(1984a), *Xirgu*, Gent Nostra 32. Badalona: Edicions de Nou Art Thor.

—(1984b), *García Lorca: El amigo de Catalunya*. Barcelona: Edhasa.

—(1988), 'Cronologia', in Cuadernos *El Público*, 36: 65–71.

—(2000), 'Federico García Lorca y Margarita Xirgu. Teatro y compromiso', in Monegal and Micó (eds): 33–48.

Rodrigo, Antonina and Rosa Romà (1989), *Núria Espert*, Gent Nostra 75. Barcelona: Edicions de Nou Art Thor.

Rodríguez, Delfina P. (1997), '*Salomé*': La influencia de Oscar Wilde en las literaturas hispánicas*, Colección Alternativas. Oviedo: Universidad de Oviedo.

Rodríguez, Mariano (2001), 'La Cubana propone en *Una nit d'Òpera* su *Aida* vista entre bastidores', *La Vanguardia* (12 June): 48.

Rodríguez de León, A. (1956), 'Enrique Rambal, Creador de Grandes Espectáculos', n.pub. n.pag. (Uncredited press clipping located at the Fundación Juan March's Biblioteca de Teatro Español Contemporáneo).

Rodríguez Méndez, José María (1974), *La incultura teatral en España*. Barcelona: Editorial Laia.

Romero, Enrique (1972), '*Yerma*: forma y contenido', *Triunfo* (5 February): 42.

Ros, Xon de (1996), 'Lorca's *El público*: An invitation to the carnival of film', in Derek Harris (ed.), *Changing Times in Hispanic Culture*. Aberdeen: Centre for the Study of the Hispanic Avant-Garde, University of Aberdeen: 110–21.

Rossell, Marina, Victòria Camps, Rosa Regàs, Montserrat Minobis, Núria Ribó, Magda Puyo, Núria Espert (1999), '*LHome del Mil.lenni*', *La Vanguardia* (31 December): 24.

Rotger, Francisco (1985), 'Aviso a los navegantes: La Cubana anda suelta por Palma', *El Día de Baleares* (17 January): 37.

Roumel, Pierre (1967), 'Médéa ou le cas Casarès', *Le Provençal* (19 July): 5.

Rovira, Bru (1986a), 'Fabià Puigserver: Un teatro austero', in Cuadernos *El Público*, 10: 14–16.

—(1986b), 'Lluís Pasqual: Perspectiva interior desde fuera', in *Cuadernos El Público*, 10: 16–17.

—(1986c), 'Lluís Homar: La alquimia del Lliure', in *Cuadernos El Público*, 10: 19–20.

Rubio, Teresa (1996), 'Espert regresa al cine con *Actrius*', *El Periódico* (16 July): 45.

—(2001), 'La Cubana muestra su visión de la ópera en un nuevo montaje', *El Periódico* (4 May): 6.

Rubio Jiménez, Jesús (1993), 'Una actriz apasionada para un texto apasionante: Mimí Aguglia y Valle-Inclán', in Schiavo (ed.): 71–85.

—(1998), 'La renovación teatral en el cambio de siglo: 1880–1914', in Miguel Medina (ed.), *Teatro y pensamiento en la regeneración del 98*. Madrid: Resad: 207–41.

—(1999a), 'Espectáculos teatrales, Siglo XX', in Amorós and Díez Borque (eds): 105–35.

—(1999b), 'Los nuevos horizontes de la literatura dramática de 1900 a 1920', in ADE Teatro: 16–26.

—(2000) 'Margarita Xirgu (1888–1969): Una actriz comprometida', in Luciano García Lorenzo (ed.), *Autoras y actrices en la historia del teatro español*. Murcia: Universidad de Murcia, Servicio de Publicaciones: 179–200.

Rudder, Robert S. (1975), *The Literature of Spain in English Translation. A Bibliography*. New York: Frederick Ungar Publishing Co.

Ruiz de Villalobos (1976), 'Durante un mes Nuria Espert, con *Divinas palabras*, hace que el Tívoli vuelva a ser teatro', *Diario de Barcelona* (5 October): 2.

Ruiz Mantilla, Jesús (2000), 'La resaca del Real', *El País* (16 January): 38.

Ruiz Ramón, Francisco (1984), *Historia del teatro español: Siglo XX*, 6th edn. Madrid: Ediciones Cátedra.

Rush, Michael (1999), *New Media in Late 20th-Century Art*. London: Thames and Hudson.

S. (1935), 'Al Teatre Barcelona *Yerma* de Federico García Lorca', *La Veu de Catalunya* (19 September): 9.

Sagarra, Joan de (1966), '*La bona persona de Sezuan* de Bertolt Brecht', *El Correo Catalán* (23 December): 30.

—(1976), 'Estrenos, Teatro Griego, *Divinas palabras*', *Mundo Diario* (26 August): 21.

—(1980), '*El balcó*, en el Lliure. Genet y la nomenclatura', *La Vanguardia* (25 September): 52.

—(1984), 'La consagración internacional de Lluís Pasqual', *El País* [Edición Barcelona] (12 February): 36.

—(1985a), 'Se agradece el fresco', *El País* [Edición Barcelona] (6 August): 21.

—(1985b), 'La frustrada aparición de María Casares', *El País* [Edición Barcelona] (8 August): 21.

—(1985c), 'Un regalo desaprovechado', *El País* [Edición Barcelona] (14 August): 21.

—(1986a), 'El grupo catalán de teatro La Cubana estrenará en Madrid su nuevo espectáculo', *El País* [Edición Barcelona] (10 April): 31.

—(1986b), 'Teatro. *Madre Coraje y sus hijos*. No apto para brechtianos', *El País* [Edición Barcelona] (23 May): 34.

—(1989a), 'Tonto el que se la pierda', *El País* [Edición Barcelona] (7 June): 46.

—(1989b), '¡Viva la revolución!', *El País* [Edición Barcelona] (10 June): 44.

—(1990a), 'La Nuria de siempre', *El País* [Edición Barcelona] (25 May): 48.

—(1990b), 'Un Teatro del Estado no puede ser rentable', *El País* [Edición Barcelona] (6 October): 34.

—(1990c), 'El retorno del monstruo sagrado', *El País* [Edición Barcelona] (17 November): 49.

—(1991a), 'Teatro. *Le Balcon*', *El País* [Edición Barcelona] (15 May): 36.

—(1991b), 'Jorge Lavelli: "En el teatro de Valle-Inclán no hay respuestas, sino interrogantes"', *El País* [Edición Barcelona] (9 July): 34.

—(1991c), 'El público de Aviñón deserta en el estreno de la *Comedias bárbaras* de Jorge Lavelli', *El País* [Edición Barcelona] (11 July): 33.

—(1991d), 'La crítica francesa aviva la polémica por las *Comedias bárbaras* de Valle-Inclán', *El País* [Edición Barcelona] (13 July): 29.

—(1991e), 'Valle-Inclán, en frances', *El Páis* [Edición Barcelona] (6 October): 26.

—(1992a), 'Danzad, danzad, benditos', *El País* [Edición Barcelona] (5 July): 30.

—(1992b), 'Sólo para mitómanos', *El País* [Edición Barcelona] (30 July): 27.

—(1994), 'Teatro. *Cegada de amor*. Un híbrido agradecidísimo', *El País* [Edición Barcelona] (31 January): 34.

—(1997a), 'La Ciutat del Teatre (primer asalto)', *El País* [Edición Cataluña] (10 May), 'Cataluña' supplement: 2.

—(1997b), '¿Quién le paga el mármol?', *El País* [Edición Cataluña] (13 September): 31.

—(1997c), 'Ni fu ni fa', *El País* [Edición Cataluña] (16 October): 43.

Said, Edward W. (1995), *Orientalism: Western Conceptions of the Orient*. London: Penguin.

Saintova, Tania (1967), 'Jorge Lavelli, le plus original et le moins connu des jeunes metteurs en scène', *Combat* (14 August): 8.

Salaün, Serge (1996), 'El paralelo barcelonés (1894–1936)', *Anales de la Literatura Española Contemporánea*, 21/3: 329–49.

Salvat, Ricard (1967), 'De *La bona persona de Sezuan* a *La persona buena de Sezuán*: Notas a mi puesta en escena', *Primer Acto*, 84: 11–15.

—(1974), 'Prólogo. Antonina Rodrigo interpreta a Margarita Xirgu', in Rodrigo (1974): 11–17.

—(1975), 'De *El adefesio* a *Noche de guerra en el Museo del Prado*', *Primer Acto*, 178 (March): 13–17.

—(1988), 'Revisió necessària de les grans aportacions de Margarita Xirgu', in Andrés Peláez (ed.), *Margarita Xirgu, 1888–1969*. Madrid: Ministerio de Cultura: 9–29.

Sánchez, José Antonio (1998), '"The impossible theatre": The Spanish stage in the time of the avant-garde', in *Spanish Theatre 1920–1995: Strategies in Protest and Imagination (1)*, *Contemporary Theatre Review*, 7/2: 7–30.

Sánchez Boxa, G. (1935), 'Principal Palace: *Doña Rosita la soltera o El lenguaje de las flores*, de Federico García Lorca', *El Día Gráfico* (14 December): 15.

Sánchez Mellado, Luz (2000), 'Hijas de su madre', *El País* (30 April), 'Semanal' supplement: 55–65.

Sandier, Gilles (1966), 'Genet, un exorciste de génie', *Arts* (3 May): 57.

Sandoval, Antoni F. (1999), 'Adolfo Marsillach: Con esta obra he redescubierto el interés por el teatro', *La Vanguardia* (15 October): 62.

Santa-Cruz, Lola (1989), 'Núria Espert: El poder arrastrado por las sirenas', *El Público*, 64 (January): 36–8.

Santero, F. Javier (1997), 'La Intervención General del Estado detecta irregularidades en las obras del Teatro Real', *El Mundo* [Catalunya] (19 December): 6–7.

Santos, Care (2000), 'Adiós al viejo Lliure', *El Mundo* [Catalunya] (13 February), 'El Cultural' supplement: 65–7.

Sanz, Felipe (1997), 'Catalonia según La Cubana', *El Periódico* (20 August): 35.

Sarmiento, Miguel (1917), 'Margarita Xirgu', *La Publicidad* (8 April): 3.

Sastre, Alfonso (1959), 'Brindis por *Anna Christie*', *Primer Acto*, 9 (1959): 7–9.

—(1986), *Escuadra hacia la muerte. La mordaza*, (ed.) Farris Anderson, 5th edn. Madrid: Editorial Castalia.

Satgé, Alain (1996), *Jorge Lavelli, Des années soixante aux années Colline: Un parcours en liberté*. Paris: Presses Universitaires de France.

Saumell, Mercè (1996), 'Performance groups in Catalonia', in George and London (eds): 103–28.

—(2001), *Teatre contemporani de dramatúrgia visual a Catalunya (1960–1992). Aportacions formals. Connexions amb el panorama internacional. Els Joglars, Els Comediants i La Fura dels Baus*, Ph.D. thesis, 2001, University of Barcelona.

Savran, David (1988), *Breaking the Rules. The Wooster Group*. New York: Theatre Communications Group.

Schiavo, Leda (ed.), *Valle-Inclán hoy. Estudios críticos y bibliográficos*. Alcalá de Henares: Servio de Publicaciones de la Universidad de Alcalá de Henares.

Schroeder, Juan Germán (1971), 'Miscelánea teatral 1945–1960', *Yorick*, 49–50 (October–December): 18–24.

Sellars, Peter (1995), 'In conversation with Ruth Mackenzie at the Edinburgh International Festival' (14 August) (transcript): 1–19.

Sesé, Teresa (1991), 'Valle-Inclán no es un autor de digestiones dominicales', *La Vanguardia* (4 October): 46–7.

—(1998), 'Lola Herrera y Carmen Linares evocan la figura de Lorca en el Tívoli', *La Vanguardia* (17 March): 45.

—(2000a), 'Debate sobre el futuro del Teatre Lliure/2. Joan Ollé, director teatral. "El Lliure ha pecado de miopía"', *La Vanguardia* (22 July): 42.

—(2000b), 'Debate sobre el futuro del Teatre Lliure/3. Joan Lluís Bozzo, director de Dagoll Dagom. "El Lliure tiene que volver a ilusionar al entorno teatral"', *La Vanguardia* (23 July): 47.

—(2000c), 'Debate sobre el futuro del Teatre Lliure/4. Hermann Bonnin, actor y director. "Falta madurez en los gestores culturales"', *La Vanguardia* (24 July): 42.

—(2000d), 'Debate sobre el futuro del Teatre Lliure/5. Roger Bernat, fundador de la compañía General Elèctrica. "El Lliure no tiene proyecto artístico"', *La Vanguardia* (25 July): 45.

—(2000e), 'Debate sobre el futuro del Teatre Lliure/6. Pepe Rubianes, actor. "¿Por qué tienen que regalar un teatro?"', *La Vanguardia* (26 July): 39.

—(2000f), 'Debate sobre el futuro del Teatre Lliure/7. Borja Sitjà, director del festival Grec. "El Lliure es el patrimonio de todos"', *La Vanguardia* (27 July): 37.

—(2000g), 'Debate sobre el futuro del Teatre Lliure/8. Carme Portaceli, directora teatral. "Aquí, cualquier proyecto suscita recelos"', *La Vanguardia* (28 July): 41.

Shields, Tom (1997), 'Camera, lights, and chaos', *Herald* (6 August): 17.

Shorter, Eric (1987), 'Lorca's dark domestic world', *Daily Telegraph* (19 January): 9.

Sirera, Rodolf (1989), 'Prologo. Rambal y la historia del teatro español contemporáneo', in Martínez Ortiz: 9–14.

Skinner, Cornellia Otis (1966), *Madame Sarah*. Boston: Houghton.

Smith, Paul Julian (1998a), *The Theatre of García Lorca: Text, Performance, Psychoanalysis*. Cambridge and New York: Cambridge University Press.

—(1998b), 'The Lorca cult: Theatre, cinema, and print media in 1980s Spain', *Spanish Theatre 1920–1995: Strategies in Protest and Imagination (3), Contemporary Theatre Review*, 7/4: 65–80.

—(2000), *The Moderns: Time, Space and Subjectivity in Contemporary Spanish Culture*. Oxford: Oxford University Press.

Sobejano, Gonzalo (1974), 'Efectos de *Realidad*', *Estudios Escénicos*, 8: 41–61.

Sola, Nicolás (1986), 'Nuria Espert: He buscado una verdad nueva', *El Público*, 37 (October): 6–8.

—(1987), 'LIFT 87: Teatro del mundo entero en Londres', *El Público*, 48 (September): 56–7.

Soria, Josep. M. (1971), 'Nuria Espert, en Barcelona con otro triunfo', *Tele/eXpres* (26 May): 33.

Soriano, Jacinto (1988), 'María Casares: Teatro en carne viva', *El Público*, 58–9 (July–August): 60–2.

Soriano Torres, Manuel and Enrique Rambal (1945), *Venganza oriental: Comedia exótica dramática,* adapted from the play by Matheson Lang and Marian Osmond. Madrid: Talía.

Spalek, John M. (1983), 'The varieties of exile experience: German, Polish, and Spanish writers', in Moeller (ed.): 71–90.

Staif, Kive (1965), '*Divinas palabras* y *Los cuernos de Don Friolera*', *Primer Acto*, 63: 60–2.

Stainton, Leslie (1999), *Lorca: A Dream of Life.* New York: Farrar, Straus & Giroux.

Steegmuller, Francis (1970), *Cocteau: A Biography.* London and Basingstoke: Macmillan.

Stokes, John (1996), 'Rachel Félix', in Booth *et al.*: 66–116.

Strehler, Giorgio (1996), 'In response to questions put to him by the editors and Eli Malka, 4 October 1995', in Delgado and Heritage (eds): 264–76.

Szuchman, Mark D. (1983), 'Aliens in Latin America: Functions, cycles and reactions', in Moeller (ed.) (1983): 25–47.

T. (1928), 'Informaciones de espectáculos, teatros, conciertos, circos', *ABC* (25 February): 39.

Tábano/Las madres del cordero (1970), 'Historia de un repiqueteo', *Primer Acto,* 125 (October): 36–40.

Tamayo, José (1953), 'El teatro español visto por un director', *Teatro*, 5 (March): 33–8.

Tambling, Jeremy (1994), 'Introduction: Opera in the distraction culture', in Tambling (ed.): 1–23.

—(ed.) (1994), *A Night in at the Opera: Media Representations of Opera.* London: John Libbet & Company.

Tarín, Carlos (1998), 'La música abre en Granada el Año Lorca', *El Correo de Andalucia* (16 January): 6.

Taylor, Paul (1994), 'Agincourt revisited', *Independent* (14 November): 22.

Tena, Carmelo (1997), 'La Ciudad del Teatro pone en pie de guerra a los divos de la escena catalana', *Tiempo de Hoy* (2 June): 110–11.

Tennenhouse, Leonard (1994), 'Strategies of state and political plays: *A Midsummer Night's Dream, Henry IV, Henry V, Henry VIII*', in Dollimore and Sinfield (eds): 109–28.

Terry, Arthur (1972), *A Literary History of Spain: Catalan Literature.* London and New York: Ernest Benn and Barnes & Noble.

Thébaud, Marion (1991), 'Hurlements de loups dans la cour d'honneur', *Le Figaro* (9 July): 22.

Thody, Philip (1996), 'Maria Casarès', in David Pickering (ed.), *International Directory of Theatre. 3 Actors, Directors and Designers.* New York and London: St. James Press: 154–5.

Thomas, Hugh (1990), *The Spanish Civil War.* London: Penguin.

Todd, Olivier (1998), *Albert Camus: A Life,* trans. Benjamin Ivry. London: Vintage, Random House.

Torre, Amelia de la, Manuel Dicenta, Nuria Espert, Fernando F. Gómez, María Paz Ballesteros, Julián Mateos (1965), 'Encuesta. ¿Cual es su método de interpretación?', *Primer Acto*, 69: 18–24.

Torrente Ballester, Gonzalo (1957), *Teatro español contemporáneo.* Madrid: Editorial Guadarrama.

Torres, Rosana (1986), 'La crítica elogia el montaje de Núria Espert', *El País* (10 September): 22.

—(1987), 'El desfile de los dramas del espectador', *El País* (16 January): 9.

—(1989), 'Lluís Pasqual destroza el escenario en *Comedia sin título*', *El País* (24 June): 53.

—(1999), 'Marsillach y Nuria Espert ya no tienen miedo a Virginia Woolf', *El País* (10 May): 44.

Trancón, Santiago (1988), 'Nuria Espert: "He procurado adaptarme al espíritu de las óperas, y no ellas a mí"', *ABC* (17 April): 113.

Trenas, Julio (1976), '*El adefesio*, de Rafael Alberti. Valoracion: 9', *Arriba* (26 September): 26–7.

Tristán (1914), 'De teatros. Princesa, *Salomé*', *El Liberal* (21 May): 3.

Tydeman, William and Steven Price (1996), *Wilde. Salome.* Cambridge, New York and Melbourne: Cambridge University Press.

Urdeix, Josep (1979), 'La tenaz esperanza de vivir. *Les tres germanes*', *El Correo Catalán* (6 Noviembre): 29.

—(1980), '*El balcó.* Desnuda contemplación de nuestra frágil imagen', *El Correo Catalán* (1 October): 31.

Ureña, Luis (1942), *Rambal (Veinticinco años de actor y empresario).* San Sebastian: Imprenta

V. Echeverría.

Uriarte, Luis (n.d), *El retablo de Talía*. Madrid: Imprenta Española.

Valle-Inclán, Ramón del (1961a), *Luces de bohemia. Esperpento*. Madrid: Espasa-Calpe.

—(1961b), *Retablo de la avaricia, la lujuria y la muerte (Ligazón, La rosa de papel, El embrujado, La cabeza del Bautista, Sacrilegio)*. Madrid: Espasa Calpe.

Vàzquez, Anna (1989), 'Estrenes de teatre català', in Enric Gallén (ed.), *Romea, 125 anys*. Barcelona: Generalitat de Catalunya, Departament de Cultura: 121–50.

Vicente Mosquete, José Luis (1984), 'Valle-Inclán vuelve a casa', *El Público*, 13 (October): 9–10.

—(1986), 'Lluís Pasqual: Perspectiva interior desde fuera', in Cuadernos *El Público*, 10: 16–17.

Vidal, Buenaventura L. (1933), 'La vida teatral. Estrenos. Español. *Divinas palabras*, adaptación, en tres actos, de la obra de D. Ramón del Valle-Inclán', *La Nación* (17 November): 9.

Vilà i Folch, Joaquim (1979), 'Anar a veure *Les tres germanes*', *Avui* (29 November): 26.

Vilar, Jean (1991), *Jean Vilar par lui-méme*. Avignon: Maison Jean Vilar.

Vilaró i Guillemí, R. (1914), 'A propòsit del retorn de na Marguerida Xirgu', *El Teatre Català*, 3/118 (30 May): 357–8.

Vilches de Frutos, María Francisca (1998), 'Directors of the twentieth-century Spanish stage', in *Spanish Theatre 1920–1995: Strategies in Protest and Imagination* (2), *Contemporary Theatre Review*, 7/3: 1–23.

Vilches de Frutos, María Francisca and Dru Dougherty (1992a), *Los estrenos teatrales de Federico García Lorca (1920–1945)*. Madrid: Tabapress.

—(1992b), 'Federico García Lorca como director de escena', in Dougherty and Vilches de Frutos (eds) 1992: 241–51,

—(1997), *La escena madrileña entre 1926 y 1931. Un lustro de transición*. Madrid: Editorial Fundamentos.

Villamandos, Itziar (1990), '"La Cubana", un alarde de imaginación, sorpresas y buen teatro', *Deia* (17 October): 58.

Villan, Javier (1994), 'Esencia de teatro', *El Mundo* (14 October): 91.

—(1999), 'Crepúsculo y dinamita', *El Mundo* (9 May), consulted online (www.el-mundo.es).

Villar de Queiroz, Fernando A. Pinheiro (2000), 'Artistic interdisciplinarity and La Fura dels Baus (1979–1989)', Ph.D. thesis, Queen Mary, University of London.

Vincendeau, Ginette (2000), *Stars and Stardom in French Cinema*. London and New York: Continuum.

—(ed.) (1995), *Encyclopedia of European Cinema*. London: Cassell/British Film Institute.

Vizcaíno Casas, Fernando (1981), *La España de la posguerra (1939–1953)*. Barcelona: Planeta.

—(1984), *Personajes de entonces . . .* Barcelona: Planeta.

Wahnón, Sultana (1995), 'La recepción de García Lorca en la España de la posguerra', *Nueva Revista de Filologia Hispánica*, 93: 409–31.

Wardle, Irving (1977), 'Experiment in an alien classic', *The Times* (15 June): 11.

—(1986), 'Maternal tyrant's rule', *The Times* (9 September): 11.

Wehle, Philippa (1984), '*The Screens*', *Performing Arts Journal*, 8/1: 72–4.

Wellwarth, George E. (1970), *The New Wave Spanish Theater*. New York and London: New York University Press.

Werson, Gerard (1988), 'For singers and players', *The Stage* (1 December): 12.

Wesker, Arnold (1986), 'Nuria Espert abre para Lorca las puertas de la escena británica', *El Público*, 37 (October): 3.

White, Edmund (1993), *Genet*. London: Chatto & Windus.

Whitton, David (1987), *Stage Directors in Modern France*. Manchester: Manchester University Press.

Williams, Raymond (1981), *Culture*. London: Fontana.

Wilson, Simon (1980), *Salvador Dalí*. London: Tate Gallery.

Wonenburger, César (2000), 'Pero, ¿qué es lo que pasa con el Real', *Diario 16* (16 January), 'Domingo Express' supplement: 8–9.

Woodward, Christopher (1992), *The Buildings of Europe, Barcelona*. Manchester: Manchester University Press.

Wright, Sarah (2000), *The Trickster-Function in the Theatre of García Lorca*. London: Tamesis.

Ynduráin, Domingo (1984), '*Luces de bohemia*', *Primer Acto*, 205 (September–October): 44–9.

Yorick (1914), 'La Xirgu, esperança nostra', *L'Esquella de la Torratxa* (5 June): 370–1.

Ytak (1993), *Lluís Pasqual: Camí de teatre*. Barcelona: Alter Pirene.

Zatlin, Phyllis (1990), 'Brecht in Spain', *Theatre History Studies*, 10: 57–66.

—(1994), *Cross Cultural Approaches to Theatre: The Spanish-French Connection*. Metuchen, N.J. and London: The Scarecrow Press, Inc.

—(1999), 'Theater and culture, 1936–1996', in Gies (ed.): 222–36.

—(2000), 'The Lliure's farewell performance of *The Cherry Orchard*', *Western European Stages*, 12/3 (Autumn): 111–12.

General index

Page numbers in *italic* refer to illustrations; 'n.' after a page reference indicates the number of a footnote on that page.

Title index

Theatrical or dramatic works are listed in the original Castilian-Spanish (S), Catalan (C) or French (F) with accompanying translations into English or translations when the piece has been staged in numerous languages; some pieces presented in Italian may also be listed with the original Italian (I) title. As with the main manuscript a translation in italics signals that the piece is available in English translation, or in the case of performance texts, that they have been seen in the English-speaking world. Film works are listed in their original language with an English translation if necessary and date. As a rule, no translations are provided for operatic works. Dance pieces are accompanied by a translation if known through a translated title in the English-speaking world. Where different pieces share the same title, a guide to authorship is shown. Entries are given in strict word-by-word alphabetical order according to the first letter of the title.